SUPPLEMENTAR
International

Chartered Institute of Arbitrators

AuthorHouse™ UK
1663 Liberty Drive
Bloomington, IN 47403 USA
www.authorhouse.co.uk
Phone: 0800.197.4150

Supplementary Material: International Arbitration
Compiled by Elina Zlatanska

ISBN: 978-1-5049-3658-3 (sc)
ISBN: 978-1-5049-3657-6 (hc)

Published by AuthorHouse 02/06/2015

SUPPLEMENTARY MATERIAL
International Arbitration

Compiled by Elina Zlatanska

The law is stated as at 02 January 2015

PREFACE

International Commercial Arbitration is the fastest growing dispute settlement discipline. The complexities surrounding its regulatory framework combined with an ever-increasing — and constantly evolving — set of acts, rules, guidelines, protocols, regulations, national legislation, international treaties, and so on may appear daunting at first glance.

The relevant legislation is so vast that it would be impossible to include it in a single volume. This "collection of documents" or "supplementary material" is designed to provide the required reading for all those who are eager to pursue a career in arbitration through the Chartered Institute of Arbitrators' pathways programme.

Therefore, utility rather than completeness has been the main objective of this publication. Other sources of information can be found at the end of the book in order to help you gain a better and broader understanding of the subject matter.

I would like to encourage students to read beyond the pages of this book and that is why I have suggested further reading at the beginning of each document. I hope that you will find the additional list of commentaries and website links useful. I also hope that this compilation of documents will continue to be a handy companion throughout your arbitration career.

The documents have been printed in alphabetical order and, as far as possible, the information contained in this book is accurate at the time of going to press. The format of the original version of each document has been altered in order to suit the Chartered Institute of Arbitrators' publishing guidelines.

Finally, I am really grateful to Julio César Betancourt, the Institute's Head of Research and Academic Affairs, for his invaluable suggestions for inclusion, formatting, and other improvements relating to this publication. I would also like to thank Anita Phillips, Education and Training Manager, and Karen Cheel, Education Officer, for their support and advice. I would also like to take the opportunity to thank all the relevant institutions for permission to reproduce the material listed in the table of contents.

Elina Zlatanska
Visiting Research Fellow

TABLE OF CONTENTS

SUPPLEMENTARY MATERIAL
International Arbitration

AAA/ICDR INTERNATIONAL ARBITRATION RULES *

Article 1 — Scope of These Rules

1. Where parties have agreed to arbitrate disputes under these International Arbitration Rules ("Rules"), or have provided for arbitration of an international dispute by the International Centre for Dispute Resolution (ICDR) or the American Arbitration Association (AAA) without designating particular rules, the arbitration shall take place in accordance with these Rules as in effect at the date of commencement of the arbitration, subject to modifications that the parties may adopt in writing. The ICDR is the Administrator of these Rules.
2. These Rules govern the arbitration, except that, where any such rule is in conflict with any provision of the law applicable to the arbitration from which the parties cannot derogate, that provision shall prevail.
3. When parties agree to arbitrate under these Rules, or when they provide for arbitration of an international dispute by the ICDR or the AAA without designating particular rules, they thereby authorize the ICDR to administer the arbitration. These Rules specify the duties and responsibilities of the ICDR, a division of the AAA, as the Administrator. The Administrator may provide services through any of the ICDR's case management offices or through the facilities of the AAA or arbitral institutions with which the ICDR or the AAA has agreements of cooperation. Arbitrations administered under these Rules shall be administered only by the ICDR or by an individual or organization authorized by the ICDR to do so.
4. Unless the parties agree or the Administrator determines otherwise, the International Expedited Procedures shall apply in any case in which no disclosed claim or counterclaim exceeds USD $250,000 exclusive of interest and the costs of arbitration. The parties may also agree to use the International Expedited Procedures in other cases. The International Expedited Procedures shall be applied as described in Articles E-1 through E-10 of these Rules, in addition to any other portion of these Rules that is not in conflict with the Expedited Procedures. Where no party's claim or counterclaim exceeds USD $100,000 exclusive of interest, attorneys' fees, and other arbitration costs, the dispute shall be resolved by written submissions only unless the arbitrator determines that an oral hearing is necessary.

Commencing the Arbitration

Article 2 — Notice of Arbitration

1. The party initiating arbitration ("Claimant") shall, in compliance with Article 10, give written Notice of Arbitration to the Administrator and at the same time to the party against whom a claim is being made ("Respondent").

* For a commentary on the AAA/ICDR International Arbitration Rules, see Martin F. Gusy, James M. Hosking and Franz T. Schwarz, *A Guide to the ICDR International Arbitration Rules* (2nd ed., Oxford University Press, June 2015) (forthcoming).

The Claimant may also initiate the arbitration through the Administrator's online filing system located at www.icdr.org.

2. The arbitration shall be deemed to commence on the date on which the Administrator receives the Notice of Arbitration.

3. The Notice of Arbitration shall contain the following information:

a. a demand that the dispute be referred to arbitration;

b. the names, addresses, telephone numbers, fax numbers, and email addresses of the parties and, if known, of their representatives;

c. a copy of the entire arbitration clause or agreement being invoked, and, where claims are made under more than one arbitration agreement, a copy of the arbitration agreement under which each claim is made;

d. a reference to any contract out of or in relation to which the dispute arises;

e. a description of the claim and of the facts supporting it;

f. the relief or remedy sought and any amount claimed; and

g. optionally, proposals, consistent with any prior agreement between or among the parties, as to the means of designating the arbitrators, the number of arbitrators, the place of arbitration, the language(s) of the arbitration, and any interest in mediating the dispute.

4. The Notice of Arbitration shall be accompanied by the appropriate filing fee.

5. Upon receipt of the Notice of Arbitration, the Administrator shall communicate with all parties with respect to the arbitration and shall acknowledge the commencement of the arbitration.

Article 3 — Answer and Counterclaim

1. Within 30 days after the commencement of the arbitration, Respondent shall submit to Claimant, to any other parties, and to the Administrator a written Answer to the Notice of Arbitration.

2. At the time Respondent submits its Answer, Respondent may make any counterclaims covered by the agreement to arbitrate or assert any setoffs and Claimant shall within 30 days submit to Respondent, to any other parties, and to the Administrator a written Answer to the counterclaim or setoffs.

3. A counterclaim or setoff shall contain the same information required of a Notice of Arbitration under Article 2(3) and shall be accompanied by the appropriate filing fee.

4. Respondent shall within 30 days after the commencement of the arbitration submit to Claimant, to any other parties, and to the Administrator a response to any proposals by Claimant not previously agreed upon, or

submit its own proposals, consistent with any prior agreement between or among the parties, as to the means of designating the arbitrators, the number of arbitrators, the place of the arbitration, the language(s) of the arbitration, and any interest in mediating the dispute.
5. The arbitral tribunal, or the Administrator if the tribunal has not yet been constituted, may extend any of the time limits established in this Article if it considers such an extension justified.
6. Failure of Respondent to submit an Answer shall not preclude the arbitration from proceeding.
7. In arbitrations with multiple parties, Respondent may make claims or assert setoffs against another Respondent and Claimant may make claims or assert setoffs against another Claimant in accordance with the provisions of this Article 3.

Article 4 — Administrative Conference

The Administrator may conduct an administrative conference before the arbitral tribunal is constituted to facilitate party discussion and agreement on issues such as arbitrator selection, mediating the dispute, process efficiencies, and any other administrative matters.

Article 5 — Mediation

Following the time for submission of an Answer, the Administrator may invite the parties to mediate in accordance with the ICDR's International Mediation Rules. At any stage of the proceedings, the parties may agree to mediate in accordance with the ICDR's International Mediation Rules. Unless the parties agree otherwise, the mediation shall proceed concurrently with arbitration and the mediator shall not be an arbitrator appointed to the case.

Article 6 — Emergency Measures of Protection

1. A party may apply for emergency relief before the constitution of the arbitral tribunal by submitting a written notice to the Administrator and to all other parties setting forth the nature of the relief sought, the reasons why such relief is required on an emergency basis, and the reasons why the party is entitled to such relief. The notice shall be submitted concurrent with or following the submission of a Notice of Arbitration. Such notice may be given by email, or as otherwise permitted by Article 10, and must include a statement certifying that all parties have been notified or an explanation of the steps taken in good faith to notify all parties.
2. Within one business day of receipt of the notice as provided in Article 6 (1), the Administrator shall appoint a single emergency arbitrator. Prior to accepting appointment, a prospective emergency arbitrator shall, in

accordance with Article 13, disclose to the Administrator any circumstances that may give rise to justifiable doubts as to the arbitrator's impartiality or independence. Any challenge to the appointment of the emergency arbitrator must be made within one business day of the communication by the Administrator to the parties of the appointment of the emergency arbitrator and the circumstances disclosed.

3. The emergency arbitrator shall as soon as possible, and in any event within two business days of appointment, establish a schedule for consideration of the application for emergency relief. Such schedule shall provide a reasonable opportunity to all parties to be heard and may provide for proceedings by telephone, video, written submissions, or other suitable means, as alternatives to an in-person hearing. The emergency arbitrator shall have the authority vested in the arbitral tribunal under Article 19, including the authority to rule on her/his own jurisdiction, and shall resolve any disputes over the applicability of this Article.

4. The emergency arbitrator shall have the power to order or award any interim or conservancy measures that the emergency arbitrator deems necessary, including injunctive relief and measures for the protection or conservation of property. Any such measures may take the form of an interim award or of an order. The emergency arbitrator shall give reasons in either case. The emergency arbitrator may modify or vacate the interim award or order. Any interim award or order shall have the same effect as an interim measure made pursuant to Article 24 and shall be binding on the parties when rendered. The parties shall undertake to comply with such an interim award or order without delay.

5. The emergency arbitrator shall have no further power to act after the arbitral tribunal is constituted. Once the tribunal has been constituted, the tribunal may reconsider, modify, or vacate the interim award or order of emergency relief issued by the emergency arbitrator. The emergency arbitrator may not serve as a member of the tribunal unless the parties agree otherwise.

6. Any interim award or order of emergency relief may be conditioned on provision of appropriate security by the party seeking such relief.

7. A request for interim measures addressed by a party to a judicial authority shall not be deemed incompatible with this Article 6 or with the agreement to arbitrate or a waiver of the right to arbitrate.

8. The costs associated with applications for emergency relief shall be addressed by the emergency arbitrator, subject to the power of the arbitral tribunal to determine finally the allocation of such costs.

Article 7 — Joinder

1. A party wishing to join an additional party to the arbitration shall submit to the Administrator a Notice of Arbitration against the additional party. No additional party may be joined after the appointment of any arbitrator, unless all parties, including the additional party, otherwise agree. The party wishing to join the additional party shall, at that same time, submit the Notice of Arbitration to the additional party and all other parties. The date on which such Notice of Arbitration is received by the Administrator shall be deemed to be the date of the commencement of arbitration against the additional party. Any joinder shall be subject to the provisions of Articles 12 and 19.

2. The request for joinder shall contain the same information required of a Notice of Arbitration under Article 2(3) and shall be accompanied by the appropriate filing fee.

3. The additional party shall submit an Answer in accordance with the provisions of Article 3.

4. The additional party may make claims, counterclaims, or assert setoffs against any other party in accordance with the provisions of Article 3.

Article 8 — Consolidation

1. At the request of a party, the Administrator may appoint a consolidation arbitrator, who will have the power to consolidate two or more arbitrations pending under these Rules, or these and other arbitration rules administered by the AAA or ICDR, into a single arbitration where:

a. the parties have expressly agreed to consolidation; or

b. all of the claims and counterclaims in the arbitrations are made under the same arbitration agreement; or

c. the claims, counterclaims, or setoffs in the arbitrations are made under more than one arbitration agreement; the arbitrations involve the same parties; the disputes in the arbitrations arise in connection with the same legal relationship; and the consolidation arbitrator finds the arbitration agreements to be compatible.

2. A consolidation arbitrator shall be appointed as follows:

a. The Administrator shall notify the parties in writing of its intention to appoint a consolidation arbitrator and invite the parties to agree upon a procedure for the appointment of a consolidation arbitrator.

b. If the parties have not within 15 days of such notice agreed upon a procedure for appointment of a consolidation arbitrator, the Administrator shall appoint the consolidation arbitrator.

c. Absent the agreement of all parties, the consolidation arbitrator shall not

be an arbitrator who is appointed to any pending arbitration subject to potential consolidation under this Article.
d. The provisions of Articles 13-15 of these Rules shall apply to the appointment of the consolidation arbitrator.
3. In deciding whether to consolidate, the consolidation arbitrator shall consult the parties and may consult the arbitral tribunal(s) and may take into account all relevant circumstances, including:
a. applicable law;
b. whether one or more arbitrators have been appointed in more than one of the arbitrations and, if so, whether the same or different persons have been appointed;
c. the progress already made in the arbitrations;
d. whether the arbitrations raise common issues of law and/or facts; and
e. whether the consolidation of the arbitrations would serve the interests of justice and efficiency.
4. The consolidation arbitrator may order that any or all arbitrations subject to potential consolidation be stayed pending a ruling on a request for consolidation.
5. When arbitrations are consolidated, they shall be consolidated into the arbitration that commenced first, unless otherwise agreed by all parties or the consolidation arbitrator finds otherwise.
6. Where the consolidation arbitrator decides to consolidate an arbitration with one or more other arbitrations, each party in those arbitrations shall be deemed to have waived its right to appoint an arbitrator. The consolidation arbitrator may revoke the appointment of any arbitrators and may select one of the previously-appointed tribunals to serve in the consolidated proceeding. The Administrator shall, as necessary, complete the appointment of the tribunal in the consolidated proceeding. Absent the agreement of all parties, the consolidation arbitrator shall not be appointed in the consolidated proceeding.
7. The decision as to consolidation, which need not include a statement of reasons, shall be rendered within 15 days of the date for final submissions on consolidation.

Article 9 — Amendment or Supplement of Claim, Counterclaim, or Defense

Any party may amend or supplement its claim, counterclaim, setoff, or defense unless the arbitral tribunal considers it inappropriate to allow such amendment or supplement because of the party's delay in making it, prejudice to the other parties, or any other circumstances. A party may not amend or supplement a claim or counterclaim if the amendment or supplement would fall outside the scope of the agreement to arbitrate. The tribunal may permit an amendment or supplement subject to an award of costs and/or the payment of filing fees as determined by the Administrator.

Article 10 — Notices

1. Unless otherwise agreed by the parties or ordered by the arbitral tribunal, all notices and written communications may be transmitted by any means of communication that allows for a record of its transmission including mail, courier, fax, or other written forms of electronic communication addressed to the party or its representative at its last-known address, or by personal service.

2. For the purpose of calculating a period of time under these Rules, such period shall begin to run on the day following the day when a notice is made. If the last day of such period is an official holiday at the place received, the period is extended until the first business day that follows. Official holidays occurring during the running of the period of time are included in calculating the period.

The Tribunal

Article 11 — Number of Arbitrators

If the parties have not agreed on the number of arbitrators, one arbitrator shall be appointed unless the Administrator determines in its discretion that three arbitrators are appropriate because of the size, complexity, or other circumstances of the case.

Article 12 — Appointment of Arbitrators

1. The parties may agree upon any procedure for appointing arbitrators and shall inform the Administrator as to such procedure. In the absence of party agreement as to the method of appointment, the Administrator may use the ICDR list method as provided in Article 12(6).

2. The parties may agree to select arbitrators, with or without the assistance of the Administrator. When such selections are made, the parties shall take into account the arbitrators' availability to serve and shall notify the Administrator so that a Notice of Appointment can be communicated to the arbitrators, together with a copy of these Rules.

3. If within 45 days after the commencement of the arbitration, all parties have not agreed on a procedure for appointing the arbitrator(s) or have not agreed on the selection of the arbitrator(s), the Administrator shall, at the written request of any party, appoint the arbitrator(s). Where the parties have agreed upon a procedure for selecting the arbitrator(s), but all appointments have not been made within the time limits provided by that

procedure, the Administrator shall, at the written request of any party, perform all functions provided for in that procedure that remain to be performed.

4. In making appointments, the Administrator shall, after inviting consultation with the parties, endeavor to appoint suitable arbitrators, taking into account their availability to serve. At the request of any party or on its own initiative, the Administrator may appoint nationals of a country other than that of any of the parties.

5. If there are more than two parties to the arbitration, the Administrator may appoint all arbitrators unless the parties have agreed otherwise no later than 45 days after the commencement of the arbitration.

6. If the parties have not selected an arbitrator(s) and have not agreed upon any other method of appointment, the Administrator, at its discretion, may appoint the arbitrator(s) in the following manner using the ICDR list method. The Administrator shall send simultaneously to each party an identical list of names of persons for consideration as arbitrator(s). The parties are encouraged to agree to an arbitrator(s) from the submitted list and shall advise the Administrator of their agreement. If, after receipt of the list, the parties are unable to agree upon an arbitrator(s), each party shall have 15 days from the transmittal date in which to strike names objected to, number the remaining names in order of preference, and return the list to the Administrator. The parties are not required to exchange selection lists. If a party does not return the list within the time specified, all persons named therein shall be deemed acceptable. From among the persons who have been approved on the parties' lists, and in accordance with the designated order of mutual preference, the Administrator shall invite an arbitrator(s) to serve. If the parties fail to agree on any of the persons listed, or if acceptable arbitrators are unable or unavailable to act, or if for any other reason the appointment cannot be made from the submitted lists, the Administrator shall have the power to make the appointment without the submission of additional lists. The Administrator shall, if necessary, designate the presiding arbitrator in consultation with the tribunal.

7. The appointment of an arbitrator is effective upon receipt by the Administrator of the Administrator's Notice of Appointment completed and signed by the arbitrator.

Article 13 — Impartiality and Independence of Arbitrator

1. Arbitrators acting under these Rules shall be impartial and independent and shall act in accordance with the terms of the Notice of Appointment provided by the Administrator.

2. Upon accepting appointment, an arbitrator shall sign the Notice of Appointment provided by the Administrator affirming that the arbitrator is available to serve and is independent and impartial. The arbitrator shall disclose any circumstances that may give rise to justifiable doubts as to the arbitrator's impartiality or independence and any other relevant facts the arbitrator wishes to bring to the attention of the parties.
3. If, at any stage during the arbitration, circumstances arise that may give rise to such doubts, an arbitrator or party shall promptly disclose such information to all parties and to the Administrator. Upon receipt of such information from an arbitrator or a party, the Administrator shall communicate it to all parties and to the tribunal.
4. Disclosure by an arbitrator or party does not necessarily indicate belief by the arbitrator or party that the disclosed information gives rise to justifiable doubts as to the arbitrator's impartiality or independence.
5. Failure of a party to disclose any circumstances that may give rise to justifiable doubts as to an arbitrator's impartiality or independence within a reasonable period after the party becomes aware of such information constitutes a waiver of the right to challenge an arbitrator based on those circumstances.
6. No party or anyone acting on its behalf shall have any *ex parte* communication relating to the case with any arbitrator, or with any candidate for party-appointed arbitrator, except to advise the candidate of the general nature of the controversy and of the anticipated proceedings and to discuss the candidate's qualifications, availability, or impartiality and independence in relation to the parties, or to discuss the suitability of candidates for selection as a presiding arbitrator where the parties or party-appointed arbitrators are to participate in that selection. No party or anyone acting on its behalf shall have any ex parte communication relating to the case with any candidate for presiding arbitrator.

Article 14 — Challenge of an Arbitrator

1. A party may challenge an arbitrator whenever circumstances exist that give rise to justifiable doubts as to the arbitrator's impartiality or independence. A party shall send a written notice of the challenge to the Administrator within 15 days after being notified of the appointment of the arbitrator or within 15 days after the circumstances giving rise to the challenge become known to that party. The challenge shall state in writing the reasons for the challenge. The party shall not send this notice to any member of the arbitral tribunal.
2. Upon receipt of such a challenge, the Administrator shall notify the other

party of the challenge and give such party an opportunity to respond. The Administrator shall not send the notice of challenge to any member of the tribunal but shall notify the tribunal that a challenge has been received, without identifying the party challenging. The Administrator may advise the challenged arbitrator of the challenge and request information from the challenged arbitrator relating to the challenge. When an arbitrator has been challenged by a party, the other party may agree to the acceptance of the challenge and, if there is agreement, the arbitrator shall withdraw. The challenged arbitrator, after consultation with the Administrator, also may withdraw in the absence of such agreement. In neither case does withdrawal imply acceptance of the validity of the grounds for the challenge.

3. If the other party does not agree to the challenge or the challenged arbitrator does not withdraw, the Administrator in its sole discretion shall make the decision on the challenge.

4. The Administrator, on its own initiative, may remove an arbitrator for failing to perform his or her duties.

Article 15 — Replacement of an Arbitrator

1. If an arbitrator resigns, is incapable of performing the duties of an arbitrator, or is removed for any reason and the office becomes vacant, a substitute arbitrator shall be appointed pursuant to the provisions of Article 12, unless the parties otherwise agree.

2. If a substitute arbitrator is appointed under this Article, unless the parties otherwise agree the arbitral tribunal shall determine at its sole discretion whether all or part of the case shall be repeated.

3. If an arbitrator on a three-person arbitral tribunal fails to participate in the arbitration for reasons other than those identified in Article 15(1), the two other arbitrators shall have the power in their sole discretion to continue the arbitration and to make any decision, ruling, order, or award, notwithstanding the failure of the third arbitrator to participate. In determining whether to continue the arbitration or to render any decision, ruling, order, or award without the participation of an arbitrator, the two other arbitrators shall take into account the stage of the arbitration, the reason, if any, expressed by the third arbitrator for such non-participation and such other matters as they consider appropriate in the circumstances of the case. In the event that the two other arbitrators determine not to continue the arbitration without the participation of the third arbitrator, the Administrator on proof satisfactory to it shall declare the office vacant, and a substitute arbitrator shall be appointed pursuant to the provisions of Article 12, unless the parties otherwise agree.

General Conditions

Article 16 — Party Representation

Any party may be represented in the arbitration. The names, addresses, telephone numbers, fax numbers, and email addresses of representatives shall be communicated in writing to the other party and to the Administrator. Unless instructed otherwise by the Administrator, once the arbitral tribunal has been established, the parties or their representatives may communicate in writing directly with the tribunal with simultaneous copies to the other party and, unless otherwise instructed by the Administrator, to the Administrator. The conduct of party representatives shall be in accordance with such guidelines as the ICDR may issue on the subject.

Article 17 — Place of Arbitration

1. If the parties do not agree on the place of arbitration by a date established by the Administrator, the Administrator may initially determine the place of arbitration, subject to the power of the arbitral tribunal to determine finally the place of arbitration within 45 days after its constitution.
2. The tribunal may meet at any place it deems appropriate for any purpose, including to conduct hearings, hold conferences, hear witnesses, inspect property or documents, or deliberate, and, if done elsewhere than the place of arbitration, the arbitration shall be deemed conducted at the place of arbitration and any award shall be deemed made at the place of arbitration.

Article 18 — Language of Arbitration

If the parties have not agreed otherwise, the language(s) of the arbitration shall be the language(s) of the documents containing the arbitration agreement, subject to the power of the arbitral tribunal to determine otherwise. The tribunal may order that any documents delivered in another language shall be accompanied by a translation into the language(s) of the arbitration.

Article 19 — Arbitral Jurisdiction

1. The arbitral tribunal shall have the power to rule on its own jurisdiction, including any objections with respect to the existence, scope, or validity of the arbitration agreement(s), or with respect to whether all of the claims, counterclaims, and setoffs made in the arbitration may be determined in a single arbitration.
2. The tribunal shall have the power to determine the existence or validity of a contract of which an arbitration clause forms a part. Such an arbitration clause shall be treated as an agreement independent of the other terms of the contract. A decision by the tribunal that the contract is null and void shall

not for that reason alone render invalid the arbitration clause.
3. A party must object to the jurisdiction of the tribunal or to arbitral jurisdiction respecting the admissibility of a claim, counterclaim, or setoff no later than the filing of the Answer, as provided in Article 3, to the claim, counterclaim, or setoff that gives rise to the objection. The tribunal may extend such time limit and may rule on any objection under this Article as a preliminary matter or as part of the final award.
4. Issues regarding arbitral jurisdiction raised prior to the constitution of the tribunal shall not preclude the Administrator from proceeding with administration and shall be referred to the tribunal for determination once constituted.

Article 20 — Conduct of Proceedings

1. Subject to these Rules, the arbitral tribunal may conduct the arbitration in whatever manner it considers appropriate, provided that the parties are treated with equality and that each party has the right to be heard and is given a fair opportunity to present its case.
2. The tribunal shall conduct the proceedings with a view to expediting the resolution of the dispute. The tribunal may, promptly after being constituted, conduct a preparatory conference with the parties for the purpose of organizing, scheduling, and agreeing to procedures, including the setting of deadlines for any submissions by the parties. In establishing procedures for the case, the tribunal and the parties may consider how technology, including electronic communications, could be used to increase the efficiency and economy of the proceedings.
3. The tribunal may decide preliminary issues, bifurcate proceedings, direct the order of proof, exclude cumulative or irrelevant testimony or other evidence, and direct the parties to focus their presentations on issues whose resolution could dispose of all or part of the case.
4. At any time during the proceedings, the tribunal may order the parties to produce documents, exhibits, or other evidence it deems necessary or appropriate. Unless the parties agree otherwise in writing, the tribunal shall apply Article 21.
5. Documents or information submitted to the tribunal by one party shall at the same time be transmitted by that party to all parties and, unless instructed otherwise by the Administrator, to the Administrator.
6. The tribunal shall determine the admissibility, relevance, materiality, and weight of the evidence.
7. The parties shall make every effort to avoid unnecessary delay and expense in the arbitration. The arbitral tribunal may allocate costs, draw

adverse inferences, and take such additional steps as are necessary to protect the efficiency and integrity of the arbitration.

Article 21 — Exchange of Information

1. The arbitral tribunal shall manage the exchange of information between the parties with a view to maintaining efficiency and economy. The tribunal and the parties should endeavor to avoid unnecessary delay and expense while at the same time avoiding surprise, assuring equality of treatment, and safeguarding each party's opportunity to present its claims and defenses fairly.
2. The parties may provide the tribunal with their views on the appropriate level of information exchange for each case, but the tribunal retains final authority. To the extent that the parties wish to depart from this Article, they may do so only by written agreement and in consultation with the tribunal.
3. The parties shall exchange all documents upon which each intends to rely on a schedule set by the tribunal.
4. The tribunal may, upon application, require a party to make available to another party documents in that party's possession not otherwise available to the party seeking the documents, that are reasonably believed to exist and to be relevant and material to the outcome of the case. Requests for documents shall contain a description of specific documents or classes of documents, along with an explanation of their relevance and materiality to the outcome of the case.
5. The tribunal may condition any exchange of information subject to claims of commercial or technical confidentiality on appropriate measures to protect such confidentiality.
6. When documents to be exchanged are maintained in electronic form, the party in possession of such documents may make them available in the form (which may be paper copies) most convenient and economical for it, unless the tribunal determines, on application, that there is a compelling need for access to the documents in a different form. Requests for documents maintained in electronic form should be narrowly focused and structured to make searching for them as economical as possible. The tribunal may direct testing or other means of focusing and limiting any search.
7. The tribunal may, on application, require a party to permit inspection on reasonable notice of relevant premises or objects.
8. In resolving any dispute about pre-hearing exchanges of information, the tribunal shall require a requesting party to justify the time and expense that its request may involve and may condition granting such a request on the payment of part or all of the cost by the party seeking the information. The

tribunal may also allocate the costs of providing information among the parties, either in an interim order or in an award.
9. In the event a party fails to comply with an order for information exchange, the tribunal may draw adverse inferences and may take such failure into account in allocating costs.
10. Depositions, interrogatories, and requests to admit as developed for use in U.S. court procedures generally are not appropriate procedures for obtaining information in an arbitration under these Rules.

Article 22 — Privilege

The arbitral tribunal shall take into account applicable principles of privilege, such as those involving the confidentiality of communications between a lawyer and client. When the parties, their counsel, or their documents would be subject under applicable law to different rules, the tribunal should, to the extent possible, apply the same rule to all parties, giving preference to the rule that provides the highest level of protection.

Article 23 — Hearing

1. The arbitral tribunal shall give the parties reasonable notice of the date, time, and place of any oral hearing.
2. At least 15 days before the hearings, each party shall give the tribunal and the other parties the names and addresses of any witnesses it intends to present, the subject of their testimony, and the languages in which such witnesses will give their testimony.
3. The tribunal shall determine the manner in which witnesses are examined and who shall be present during witness examination.
4. Unless otherwise agreed by the parties or directed by the tribunal, evidence of witnesses may be presented in the form of written statements signed by them. In accordance with a schedule set by the tribunal, each party shall notify the tribunal and the other parties of the names of any witnesses who have presented a witness statement whom it requests to examine. The tribunal may require any witness to appear at a hearing. If a witness whose appearance has been requested fails to appear without valid excuse as determined by the tribunal, the tribunal may disregard any written statement by that witness.
5. The tribunal may direct that witnesses be examined through means that do not require their physical presence.
6. Hearings are private unless the parties agree otherwise or the law provides to the contrary.

Article 24 — Interim Measures

1. At the request of any party, the arbitral tribunal may order or award any

interim or conservatory measures it deems necessary, including injunctive relief and measures for the protection or conservation of property.
2. Such interim measures may take the form of an interim order or award, and the tribunal may require security for the costs of such measures.
3. A request for interim measures addressed by a party to a judicial authority shall not be deemed incompatible with the agreement to arbitrate or a waiver of the right to arbitrate.
4. The arbitral tribunal may in its discretion allocate costs associated with applications for interim relief in any interim order or award or in the final award.
5. An application for emergency relief prior to the constitution of the arbitral tribunal may be made as provided for in Article 6.

Article 25 — Tribunal-Appointed Expert

1. The arbitral tribunal, after consultation with the parties, may appoint one or more independent experts to report to it, in writing, on issues designated by the tribunal and communicated to the parties.
2. The parties shall provide such an expert with any relevant information or produce for inspection any relevant documents or goods that the expert may require. Any dispute between a party and the expert as to the relevance of the requested information or goods shall be referred to the tribunal for decision.
3. Upon receipt of an expert's report, the tribunal shall send a copy of the report to all parties and shall give the parties an opportunity to express, in writing, their opinion of the report. A party may examine any document on which the expert has relied in such a report.
4. At the request of any party, the tribunal shall give the parties an opportunity to question the expert at a hearing. At this hearing, parties may present expert witnesses to testify on the points at issue.

Article 26 — Default

1. If a party fails to submit an Answer in accordance with Article 3, the arbitral tribunal may proceed with the arbitration.
2. If a party, duly notified under these Rules, fails to appear at a hearing without showing sufficient cause for such failure, the tribunal may proceed with the hearing.
3. If a party, duly invited to produce evidence or take any other steps in the proceedings, fails to do so within the time established by the tribunal without showing sufficient cause for such failure, the tribunal may make the award on the evidence before it.

Article 27 — Closure of Hearing
1. The arbitral tribunal may ask the parties if they have any further submissions and upon receiving negative replies or if satisfied that the record is complete, the tribunal may declare the arbitral hearing closed.
2. The tribunal in its discretion, on its own motion, or upon application of a party, may reopen the arbitral hearing at any time before the award is made.
Article 28 — Waiver
A party who knows of any non-compliance with any provision or requirement of the Rules or the arbitration agreement, and proceeds with the arbitration without promptly stating an objection in writing, waives the right to object.
Article 29 — Awards, Orders, Decisions and Rulings
1. In addition to making a final award, the arbitral tribunal may make interim, interlocutory, or partial awards, orders, decisions, and rulings.
2. When there is more than one arbitrator, any award, order, decision, or ruling of the tribunal shall be made by a majority of the arbitrators.
3. When the parties or the tribunal so authorize, the presiding arbitrator may make orders, decisions, or rulings on questions of procedure, including exchanges of information, subject to revision by the tribunal.
Article 30 — Time, Form, and Effect of Award
1. Awards shall be made in writing by the arbitral tribunal and shall be final and binding on the parties. The tribunal shall make every effort to deliberate and prepare the award as quickly as possible after the hearing. Unless otherwise agreed by the parties, specified by law, or determined by the Administrator, the final award shall be made no later than 60 days from the date of the closing of the hearing. The parties shall carry out any such award without delay and, absent agreement otherwise, waive irrevocably their right to any form of appeal, review, or recourse to any court or other judicial authority, insofar as such waiver can validly be made. The tribunal shall state the reasons upon which an award is based, unless the parties have agreed that no reasons need be given.
2. An award shall be signed by the arbitrator(s) and shall state the date on which the award was made and the place of arbitration pursuant to Article 17. Where there is more than one arbitrator and any of them fails to sign an award, the award shall include or be accompanied by a statement of the reason for the absence of such signature.
3. An award may be made public only with the consent of all parties or as required by law, except that the Administrator may publish or otherwise make publicly available selected awards, orders, decisions, and rulings that

have become public in the course of enforcement or otherwise and, unless otherwise agreed by the parties, may publish selected awards, orders, decisions, and rulings that have been edited to conceal the names of the parties and other identifying details.

4. The award shall be transmitted in draft form by the tribunal to the Administrator. The award shall be communicated to the parties by the Administrator.

5. If applicable law requires an award to be filed or registered, the tribunal shall cause such requirement to be satisfied. It is the responsibility of the parties to bring such requirements or any other procedural requirements of the place of arbitration to the attention of the tribunal.

Article 31 — Applicable Laws and Remedies

1. The arbitral tribunal shall apply the substantive law(s) or rules of law agreed by the parties as applicable to the dispute. Failing such an agreement by the parties, the tribunal shall apply such law(s) or rules of law as it determines to be appropriate.

2. In arbitrations involving the application of contracts, the tribunal shall decide in accordance with the terms of the contract and shall take into account usages of the trade applicable to the contract.

3. The tribunal shall not decide as *amiable compositeur* or *ex aequo et bono* unless the parties have expressly authorized it to do so.

4. A monetary award shall be in the currency or currencies of the contract unless the tribunal considers another currency more appropriate, and the tribunal may award such pre-award and post-award interest, simple or compound, as it considers appropriate, taking into consideration the contract and applicable law(s).

5. Unless the parties agree otherwise, the parties expressly waive and forego any right to punitive, exemplary, or similar damages unless any applicable law(s) requires that compensatory damages be increased in a specified manner. This provision shall not apply to an award of arbitration costs to a party to compensate for misconduct in the arbitration.

Article 32 — Settlement or Other Reasons for Termination

1. If the parties settle the dispute before a final award is made, the arbitral tribunal shall terminate the arbitration and, if requested by all parties, may record the settlement in the form of a consent award on agreed terms. The tribunal is not obliged to give reasons for such an award.

2. If continuation of the arbitration becomes unnecessary or impossible due to the non-payment of deposits required by the Administrator, the arbitration may be suspended or terminated as provided in Article 36(3).

3. If continuation of the arbitration becomes unnecessary or impossible for any reason other than as stated in Sections 1 and 2 of this Article, the tribunal shall inform the parties of its intention to terminate the arbitration. The tribunal shall thereafter issue an order terminating the arbitration, unless a party raises justifiable grounds for objection.

Article 33 — Interpretation and Correction of Award

1. Within 30 days after the receipt of an award, any party, with notice to the other party, may request the arbitral tribunal to interpret the award or correct any clerical, typographical, or computational errors or make an additional award as to claims, counterclaims, or setoffs presented but omitted from the award.

2. If the tribunal considers such a request justified after considering the contentions of the parties, it shall comply with such a request within 30 days after receipt of the parties' last submissions respecting the requested interpretation, correction, or additional award. Any interpretation, correction, or additional award made by the tribunal shall contain reasoning and shall form part of the award.

3. The tribunal on its own initiative may, within 30 days of the date of the award, correct any clerical, typographical, or computational errors or make an additional award as to claims presented but omitted from the award.

4. The parties shall be responsible for all costs associated with any request for interpretation, correction, or an additional award, and the tribunal may allocate such costs.

Article 34 — Costs of Arbitration

The arbitral tribunal shall fix the costs of arbitration in its award(s). The tribunal may allocate such costs among the parties if it determines that allocation is reasonable, taking into account the circumstances of the case.

Such costs may include:

a. the fees and expenses of the arbitrators;

b. the costs of assistance required by the tribunal, including its experts;

c. the fees and expenses of the Administrator;

d. the reasonable legal and other costs incurred by the parties;

e. any costs incurred in connection with a notice for interim or emergency relief pursuant to Articles 6 or 24;

f. any costs incurred in connection with a request for consolidation pursuant to Article 8; and

g. any costs associated with information exchange pursuant to Article 21.

Article 35 — Fees and Expenses of Arbitral Tribunal

1. The fees and expenses of the arbitrators shall be reasonable in amount,

taking into account the time spent by the arbitrators, the size and complexity of the case, and any other relevant circumstances.
2. As soon as practicable after the commencement of the arbitration, the Administrator shall designate an appropriate daily or hourly rate of compensation in consultation with the parties and all arbitrators, taking into account the arbitrators' stated rate of compensation and the size and complexity of the case.
3. Any dispute regarding the fees and expenses of the arbitrators shall be determined by the Administrator.

Article 36 — Deposits

1. The Administrator may request that the parties deposit appropriate amounts as an advance for the costs referred to in Article 34.
2. During the course of the arbitration, the Administrator may request supplementary deposits from the parties.
3. If the deposits requested are not paid promptly and in full, the Administrator shall so inform the parties in order that one or more of them may make the required payment. If such payment is not made, the arbitral tribunal may order the suspension or termination of the proceedings. If the tribunal has not yet been appointed, the Administrator may suspend or terminate the proceedings.
4. Failure of a party asserting a claim or counterclaim to pay the required deposits shall be deemed a withdrawal of the claim or counterclaim.
5. After the final award has been made, the Administrator shall render an accounting to the parties of the deposits received and return any unexpended balance to the parties.

Article 37 — Confidentiality

1. Confidential information disclosed during the arbitration by the parties or by witnesses shall not be divulged by an arbitrator or by the Administrator. Except as provided in Article 30, unless otherwise agreed by the parties or required by applicable law, the members of the arbitral tribunal and the Administrator shall keep confidential all matters relating to the arbitration or the award.
2. Unless the parties agree otherwise, the tribunal may make orders concerning the confidentiality of the arbitration or any matters in connection with the arbitration and may take measures for protecting trade secrets and confidential information.

Article 38 — Exclusion of Liability

The members of the arbitral tribunal, any emergency arbitrator appointed under Article 6, any consolidation arbitrator appointed under Article 8, and the Administrator shall not be liable to any party for any act or omission in connection with any arbitration under these Rules, except to the extent that such a limitation of liability is prohibited by applicable law. The parties agree that no arbitrator, emergency arbitrator, or consolidation arbitrator, nor the Administrator shall be under any obligation to make any statement about the arbitration, and no party shall seek to make any of these persons a party or witness in any judicial or other proceedings relating to the arbitration.

Article 39 — Interpretation of Rules

The arbitral tribunal, any emergency arbitrator appointed under Article 6, and any consolidation arbitrator appointed under Article 8, shall interpret and apply these Rules insofar as they relate to their powers and duties. The Administrator shall interpret and apply all other Rules.

International Expedited Procedures

Article E-1 — Scope of Expedited Procedures

These Expedited Procedures supplement the International Arbitration Rules as provided in Article 1(4).

Article E-2 — Detailed Submissions

Parties are to present detailed submissions on the facts, claims, counterclaims, setoffs and defenses, together with all of the evidence then available on which such party intends to rely, in the Notice of Arbitration and the Answer. The arbitrator, in consultation with the parties, shall establish a procedural order, including a timetable, for completion of any written submissions.

Article E-3 — Administrative Conference

The Administrator may conduct an administrative conference with the parties and their representatives to discuss the application of these procedures, arbitrator selection, mediating the dispute, and any other administrative matters.

Article E-4 — Objection to the Applicability of the Expedited Procedures

If an objection is submitted before the arbitrator is appointed, the Administrator may initially determine the applicability of these Expedited Procedures, subject to the power of the arbitrator to make a final determination. The arbitrator shall take into account the amount in dispute and any other relevant circumstances.

Article E-5 — Changes of Claim or Counterclaim

If, after filing of the initial claims and counterclaims, a party amends its claim or counterclaim to exceed USD $250,000.00 exclusive of interest and the costs of arbitration, the case will continue to be administered pursuant to these Expedited Procedures unless the parties agree otherwise, or the Administrator or the arbitrator determines otherwise. After the arbitrator is appointed, no new or different claim, counterclaim or setoff and no change in amount may be submitted except with the arbitrator's consent.

Article E-6 — Appointment and Qualifications of the Arbitrator

A sole arbitrator shall be appointed as follows. The Administrator shall simultaneously submit to each party an identical list of five proposed arbitrators. The parties may agree to an arbitrator from this list and shall so advise the Administrator. If the parties are unable to agree upon an arbitrator, each party may strike two names from the list and return it to the Administrator within 10 days from the transmittal date of the list to the parties. The parties are not required to exchange selection lists. If the parties fail to agree on any of the arbitrators or if acceptable arbitrators are unable or unavailable to act, or if for any other reason the appointment cannot be made from the submitted lists, the Administrator may make the appointment without the circulation of additional lists. The parties will be given notice by the Administrator of the appointment of the arbitrator, together with any disclosures.

Article E-7 — Procedural Conference and Order

After the arbitrator's appointment, the arbitrator may schedule a procedural conference call with the parties, their representatives, and the Administrator to discuss the procedure and schedule for the case. Within 14 days of appointment, the arbitrator shall issue a procedural order.

Article E-8 — Proceedings by Written Submissions

In expedited proceedings based on written submissions, all submissions are due within 60 days of the date of the procedural order, unless the arbitrator determines otherwise. The arbitrator may require an oral hearing if deemed necessary.

Article E-9 — Proceedings with an Oral Hearing

In expedited proceedings in which an oral hearing is to be held, the arbitrator shall set the date, time, and location of the hearing. The oral hearing shall take place within 60 days of the date of the procedural order unless the arbitrator deems it necessary to extend that period. Hearings may take place in person or via video conference or other suitable means, at the discretion of the arbitrator. Generally, there will be no transcript or stenographic record. Any party desiring a stenographic record may arrange for one. The oral hearing shall not exceed one day unless the arbitrator determines otherwise. The Administrator will notify the parties in advance of the hearing date.

Article E-10 — The Award

Awards shall be made in writing and shall be final and binding on the parties. Unless otherwise agreed by the parties, specified by law, or determined by the Administrator, the award shall be made not later than 30 days from the date of the closing of the hearing or from the time established for final written submissions.

Administrative Fees

Administrative Fee Schedules (Standard and Flexible Fee)

The ICDR has two administrative fee options for parties filing claims or counterclaims: the Standard Fee Schedule and the Flexible Fee Schedule. The Standard Fee Schedule has a two-payment schedule, and the Flexible Fee Schedule has a three-payment schedule that offers lower initial filing fees but potentially higher total administrative fees of approximately 12% to 19% for cases that proceed to a hearing. The administrative fees of the ICDR are based on the amount of the claim or counterclaim. Arbitrator compensation is not included in this schedule. Unless the parties agree otherwise, arbitrator compensation and administrative fees are subject to allocation by the arbitrator in the award.

Fees for Incomplete or Deficient Filings

Where the applicable arbitration agreement does not reference the ICDR or the AAA, the ICDR will attempt to obtain the agreement of the other parties to the dispute to have the arbitration administered by the ICDR. However, where the ICDR is unable to obtain the agreement of the parties to have the ICDR administer the arbitration, the ICDR will administratively close the case and will not proceed with the administration of the arbitration. In these cases, the ICDR will return the filing fees to the filing party, less the amount specified in the fee schedule below for deficient filings.

Parties that file demands for arbitration that are incomplete or otherwise do not meet the filing requirements contained in these Rules shall also be charged the amount specified below for deficient filings if they fail or are unable to respond to the ICDR's request to correct the deficiency.

Fees for Additional Services

The ICDR reserves the right to assess additional administrative fees for services performed by the ICDR beyond those provided for in these Rules, which may be required by the parties' agreement or stipulation.

Suspension for Non-payment

If arbitrator compensation or administrative charges have not been paid in full, the administrator may so inform the parties in order that one of them may advance the required payment. If such payment is not made, the tribunal may order the suspension or termination of the proceedings. If no arbitrator has yet been appointed, the ICDR may suspend or terminate the proceedings.

Standard Fee Schedule

An Initial Filing Fee is payable in full by a filing party when a claim, counterclaim, setoff or additional claim, counterclaim, or setoff is filed. A Final Fee will be incurred for all cases that proceed to their first hearing. This fee will be payable in advance at the time that the first hearing is scheduled. This fee will be refunded at the conclusion of the case if no hearings have occurred. However, if the Administrator is not notified at least 24 hours before the time of the scheduled hearing, the Final Fee will remain due and will not be refunded.

These fees will be billed in accordance with the Schedule 1 (see page 26).

Fees are subject to increase if the amount of a claim or counterclaim is modified after the initial filing date. Fees are subject to decrease if the amount of a claim or counterclaim is modified before the first hearing.

The minimum fees for any case having three or more arbitrators are $2,800 for the filing fee, plus a $1,250 Case Service Fee.

Each party on cases filed under either the Flexible Fee Schedule or the Standard Fee Schedule that are held in abeyance for one year will be assessed an annual abeyance fee of $300. If a party refuses to pay the assessed fee, the other party or parties may pay the entire fee on behalf of all parties, failing which the matter will be administratively closed.

For more information, please contact the ICDR at +1.212.484.4181.

Refund Schedule for Standard Fee Schedule

The ICDR offers a refund schedule on filing fees connected with the Standard Fee Schedule. For cases with claims up to $75,000, a minimum filing fee of $350 will not be refunded. For all other cases, a minimum fee of $600 will not be refunded. Subject to the minimum fee requirements, refunds will be calculated as follows:

- 100% of the filing fee, above the minimum fee, will be refunded if the case is settled or withdrawn within five calendar days of filing.
- 50% of the filing fee will be refunded if the case is settled or withdrawn between six and 30 calendar days of filing.
- 25% of the filing fee will be refunded if the case is settled or withdrawn between 31 and 60 calendar days of filing.

No refund will be made once an arbitrator has been appointed (this includes one arbitrator on a three-arbitrator panel). No refunds will be granted on awarded cases.

Note: The date of receipt of the demand for arbitration with the ICDR will be used to calculate refunds of filing fees for both claims and counterclaims.

Flexible Fee Schedule

A non-refundable Initial Filing Fee is payable in full by a filing party when a claim, counterclaim, or additional claim is filed. Upon receipt of the Demand for Arbitration, the ICDR will promptly initiate the case and notify all parties as well as establish the due date for filing of an Answer, which may include a Counterclaim. In order to proceed with the further administration of the arbitration and appointment of the arbitrator(s), the appropriate, non-refundable Proceed Fee outlined below must be paid.

If a Proceed Fee is not submitted within 90 days of the filing of the Claimant's Demand for Arbitration, the ICDR will administratively close the file and notify all parties.

No refunds or refund schedule will apply to the Filing or Proceed Fees once received.

The Flexible Fee Schedule below also may be utilized for the filing of counterclaims. However, as with the Claimant's claim, the counterclaim will not be presented to the arbitrator until the Proceed Fee is paid.

A Final Fee will be incurred for all claims and/or counterclaims that proceed to their first hearing. This fee will be payable in advance when the first hearing is scheduled but will be refunded at the conclusion of the case if no hearings have occurred. However, if the administrator is not notified of a cancellation at least 24 hours before the time of the scheduled hearing, the Final Fee will remain due and will not be refunded.

All fees will be billed in accordance with Schedule 2 (see page 27).

All fees are subject to increase if the amount of a claim or counterclaim is modified after the initial filing date. Fees are subject to decrease if the amount of a claim or counterclaim is modified before the first hearing.

The minimum fees for any case having three or more arbitrators are $1,000 for the Initial Filing Fee; $2,125 for the Proceed Fee; and $1,250 for the Final Fee.

Under the Flexible Fee Schedule, a party's obligation to pay the Proceed Fee shall remain in effect regardless of any agreement of the parties to stay, postpone, or otherwise modify the arbitration proceedings. Parties that, through mutual agreement, have held their case in abeyance for one year will be assessed an annual abeyance fee of $300. If a party refuses to pay the assessed fee, the other party or parties may pay the entire fee on behalf

of all parties, otherwise the matter will be administratively closed.
Note: The date of receipt by the ICDR of the demand/notice for arbitration will be used to calculate the 90-day time limit for payment of the Proceed Fee.

For more information, please contact the ICDR at +1.212.484.4181.

There is no Refund Schedule in the Flexible Fee Schedule.

Expedited Procedures — Fees and Compensation

There are no additional administrative fees beyond the Fees outlined above to initiate a case under the Expedited Procedures. The compensation of the arbitrator will be determined by the Administrator, in consultation with the arbitrator, and in consideration of the specific nature of the case and the amount in dispute. There is no refund schedule for cases managed under the Expedited Procedures.

Hearing Room Rental

The fees described above do not cover the cost of hearing rooms, which are available on a rental basis. Check with the ICDR for availability and rates.

Schedule 1

Amount of Claim	Initial Filing Fee	Final Fee
Above $0 to $10,000	$775	$200
Above $10,000 to $75,000	$975	$300
Above $75,000 to $150,000	$1,850	$750
Above $150,000 to $300,000	$2,800	$1,250
Above $300,000 to $500,000	$4,350	$1,750
Above $500,000 to $1,000,000	$6,200	$2,500
Above $1,000,000 to $5,000,000	$8,200	$3,250
Above $5,000,000 to $10,000,000	$10,200	$4,000
Above $10,000,000	Base fee of $12,800 plus .01% of the amount of claim above $10,000,000 Fee Capped at $65,000	$6,000
Nonmonetary Claims[1]	$3,350	$1,250
Deficient Claim Filing[2]	$350	
Additional Services[3]		

[1] This fee is applicable when a claim or counterclaim is not for a monetary amount. Where a monetary claim amount is not known, parties will be required to state a range of claims or be subject to a filing fee of $10,200.

[2] The Deficient Claim Filing Fee shall not be charged in cases filed by a consumer in an arbitration governed by the Supplementary Procedures for the Resolution of Consumer-Related Disputes or in cases filed by an Employee who is submitting a dispute to arbitration pursuant to an employer-promulgated plan.

[3] The ICDR may assess additional fees where procedures or services outside the Rules sections are required under the parties' agreement or by stipulation.

Schedule 2

Amount of Claim	Initial Filing Fee	Proceed Fee	Final Fee
Above $0 to $10,000	$400	$475	$200
Above $10,000 to $75,000	$625	$500	$300
Above $75,000 to $150,000	$850	$1,250	$750
Above $150,000 to $300,000	$1,000	$2,125	$1,250
Above $300,000 to $500,000	$1,500	$3,400	$1,750
Above $500,000 to $1,000,000	$2,500	$4,500	$2,500
Above $1,000,000 to $5,000,000	$2,500	$6,700	$3,250
Above $5,000,000 to $10,000,000	$3,500	$8,200	$4,000
Above $10,000,000	$4,500	$10,300 plus 0,1% of claim amount over $10,000,000 up to $65,000	$6,000
Nonmonetary Claims[1]	$2,000	$2,000	$1,250
Deficient Claim Filing	$350		
Additional Services[2]			

[1] This fee is applicable when a claim or counterclaim is not for a monetary amount. Where a monetary claim amount is not known, parties will be required to state a range of claims or be subject to a filing fee of $3,500 and a proceed fee of $8,200.

[2] The ICDR reserves the right to assess additional administrative fees for services performed by the ICDR beyond those provided for in these Rules and which may be required by the parties' agreement or stipulation.

ARBITRATION ACT 1996 (CHAPTER 23) *

An Act to restate and improve the law relating to arbitration pursuant to an arbitration agreement; to make other provision relating to arbitration and arbitration awards; and for connected purposes. [17th June 1996]
Be it enacted by the Queen's most Excellent Majesty, by and with the advice and consent of the Lords Spiritual and Temporal, and Commons, in this present Parliament assembled, and by the authority of the same, as follows:

Part I
Arbitration Pursuant to an Arbitration Agreement
Introductory

1 — General Principles
The provisions of this Part are founded on the following principles, and shall be construed accordingly
(a) the object of arbitration is to obtain the fair resolution of disputes by an impartial tribunal without unnecessary delay or expense;
(b) the parties should be free to agree how their disputes are resolved, subject only to such safeguards as are necessary in the public interest;
(c) in matters governed by this Part the court should not intervene except as provided by this Part.

2 — Scope of Application of Provisions
(1) The provisions of this Part apply where the seat of the arbitration is in England and Wales or Northern Ireland.
(2) The following sections apply even if the seat of the arbitration is outside England and Wales or Northern Ireland or no seat has been designated or determined
(a) sections 9 to 11 (stay of legal proceedings, etc.), and
(b) section 66 (enforcement of arbitral awards).
(3) The powers conferred by the following sections apply even if the seat of the arbitration is outside England and Wales or Northern Ireland or no seat has been designated or determined
(a) section 43 (securing the attendance of witnesses), and
(b) section 44 (court powers exercisable in support of arbitral proceedings);
but the court may refuse to exercise any such power if, in the opinion of the court, the fact that the seat of the arbitration is outside England and Wales or Northern Ireland, or that when designated or determined the seat is likely to be outside England and Wales or Northern Ireland, makes it inappropriate to do so.
(4) The court may exercise a power conferred by any provision of this Part not mentioned in subsection (2) or (3) for the purpose of supporting the

---

* For a commentary on the Arbitration Act 1996, see Robert Merkin and Louis Flannery, *Arbitration Act 1996* (5th edn, Informa, 2014) and Bruce Harris, Rowan Planterose and Jonathan Tecks, *Arbitration Act 1996: Commentary* (5th edn, Wiley Blackwell, 2014).

arbitral process where
(a) no seat of the arbitration has been designated or determined, and
(b) by reason of a connection with England and Wales or Northern Ireland the court is satisfied that it is appropriate to do so.
(5) Section 7 (separability of arbitration agreement) and section 8 (death of a party) apply where the law applicable to the arbitration agreement is the law of England and Wales or Northern Ireland even if the seat of the arbitration is outside England and Wales or Northern Ireland or has not been designated or determined.

3 — The Seat of the Arbitration

In this Part "the seat of the arbitration" means the juridical seat of the arbitration designated
(a) by the parties to the arbitration agreement, or
(b) by any arbitral or other institution or person vested by the parties with powers in that regard, or
(c) by the arbitral tribunal if so authorised by the parties,
or determined, in the absence of any such designation, having regard to the parties' agreement and all the relevant circumstances.

4 — Mandatory and Non-mandatory Provisions

(1) The mandatory provisions of this Part are listed in Schedule 1 and have effect notwithstanding any agreement to the contrary.
(2) The other provisions of this Part (the "non-mandatory provisions") allow the parties to make their own arrangements by agreement but provide rules which apply in the absence of such agreement.
(3) The parties may make such arrangements by agreeing to the application of institutional rules or providing any other means by which a matter may be decided.
(4) It is immaterial whether or not the law applicable to the parties' agreement is the law of England and Wales or, as the case may be, Northern Ireland.
(5) The choice of a law other than the law of England and Wales or Northern Ireland as the applicable law in respect of a matter provided for by a non-mandatory provision of this Part is equivalent to an agreement making provision about that matter.
For this purpose an applicable law determined in accordance with the parties' agreement, or which is objectively determined in the absence of any express or implied choice, shall be treated as chosen by the parties.

5 — Agreements to be in Writing

(1) The provisions of this Part apply only where the arbitration agreement is

in writing, and any other agreement between the parties as to any matter is effective for the purposes of this Part only if in writing.
The expressions "agreement", "agree" and "agreed" shall be construed accordingly.
(2) There is an agreement in writing
(a) if the agreement is made in writing (whether or not it is signed by the parties),
(b) if the agreement is made by exchange of communications in writing, or
(c) if the agreement is evidenced in writing.
(3) Where parties agree otherwise than in writing by reference to terms which are in writing, they make an agreement in writing.
(4) An agreement is evidenced in writing if an agreement made otherwise than in writing is recorded by one of the parties, or by a third party, with the authority of the parties to the agreement.
(5) An exchange of written submissions in arbitral or legal proceedings in which the existence of an agreement otherwise than in writing is alleged by one party against another party and not denied by the other party in his response constitutes as between those parties an agreement in writing to the effect alleged.
(6) References in this Part to anything being written or in writing include its being recorded by any means.

The Arbitration Agreement

6 — Definition of Arbitration Agreement

(1) In this Part an "arbitration agreement" means an agreement to submit to arbitration present or future disputes (whether they are contractual or not).
(2) The reference in an agreement to a written form of arbitration clause or to a document containing an arbitration clause constitutes an arbitration agreement if the reference is such as to make that clause part of the agreement.

7 — Separability of Arbitration Agreement

Unless otherwise agreed by the parties, an arbitration agreement which forms or was intended to form part of another agreement (whether or not in writing) shall not be regarded as invalid, non-existent or ineffective because that other agreement is invalid, or did not come into existence or has become ineffective, and it shall for that purpose be treated as a distinct agreement.

8 — Whether Agreement Discharged by Death of a Party

(1) Unless otherwise agreed by the parties, an arbitration agreement is not discharged by the death of a party and may be enforced by or against the

personal representatives of that party.
(2) Subsection (1) does not affect the operation of any enactment or rule of law by virtue of which a substantive right or obligation is extinguished by death.

Stay of Legal Proceedings

9 — Stay of Legal Proceedings

(1) A party to an arbitration agreement against whom legal proceedings are brought (whether by way of claim or counterclaim) in respect of a matter which under the agreement is to be referred to arbitration may (upon notice to the other parties to the proceedings) apply to the court in which the proceedings have been brought to stay the proceedings so far as they concern that matter.
(2) An application may be made notwithstanding that the matter is to be referred to arbitration only after the exhaustion of other dispute resolution procedures.
(3) An application may not be made by a person before taking the appropriate procedural step (if any) to acknowledge the legal proceedings against him or after he has taken any step in those proceedings to answer the substantive claim.
(4) On an application under this section the court shall grant a stay unless satisfied that the arbitration agreement is null and void, inoperative, or incapable of being performed.
(5) If the court refuses to stay the legal proceedings, any provision that an award is a condition precedent to the bringing of legal proceedings in respect of any matter is of no effect in relation to those proceedings.

10 — Reference of Interpleader Issue to Arbitration

(1) Where in legal proceedings relief by way of interpleader is granted and any issue between the claimants is one in respect of which there is an arbitration agreement between them, the court granting the relief shall direct that the issue be determined in accordance with the agreement unless the circumstances are such that proceedings brought by a claimant in respect of the matter would not be stayed.
(2) Where subsection (1) applies but the court does not direct that the issue be determined in accordance with the arbitration agreement, any provision that an award is a condition precedent to the bringing of legal proceedings in respect of any matter shall not affect the determination of that issue by the court.

11 — Retention of Security Where Admiralty Proceedings Stayed

(1) Where Admiralty proceedings are stayed on the ground that the dispute

in question should be submitted to arbitration, the court granting the stay may, if in those proceedings property has been arrested or bail or other security has been given to prevent or obtain release from arrest

(a) order that the property arrested be retained as security for the satisfaction of any award given in the arbitration in respect of that dispute, or

(b) order that the stay of those proceedings be conditional on the provision of equivalent security for the satisfaction of any such award.

(2) Subject to any provision made by rules of court and to any necessary modifications, the same law and practice shall apply in relation to property retained in pursuance of an order as would apply if it were held for the purposes of proceedings in the court making the order.

Commencement of Arbitral Proceedings

12 — Power of Court to Extend Time for Beginning Arbitral Proceedings, etc.

(1) Where an arbitration agreement to refer future disputes to arbitration provides that a claim shall be barred, or the claimant's right extinguished, unless the claimant takes within a time fixed by the agreement some step

(a) to begin arbitral proceedings, or

(b) to begin other dispute resolution procedures which must be exhausted before arbitral proceedings can be begun,

the court may by order extend the time for taking that step.

(2) Any party to the arbitration agreement may apply for such an order (upon notice to the other parties), but only after a claim has arisen and after exhausting any available arbitral process for obtaining an extension of time.

(3) The court shall make an order only if satisfied

(a) that the circumstances are such as were outside the reasonable contemplation of the parties when they agreed the provision in question, and that it would be just to extend the time, or

(b) that the conduct of one party makes it unjust to hold the other party to the strict terms of the provision in question.

(4) The court may extend the time for such period and on such terms as it thinks fit, and may do so whether or not the time previously fixed (by agreement or by a previous order) has expired.

(5) An order under this section does not affect the operation of the Limitation Acts (see section 13).

(6) The leave of the court is required for any appeal from a decision of the court under this section.

13 — Application of Limitation Acts

(1) The Limitation Acts apply to arbitral proceedings as they apply to legal

proceedings.
(2) The court may order that in computing the time prescribed by the Limitation Acts for the commencement of proceedings (including arbitral proceedings) in respect of a dispute which was the subject matter
(a) of an award which the court orders to be set aside or declares to be of no effect, or
(b) of the affected part of an award which the court orders to be set aside in part, or declares to be in part of no effect,
the period between the commencement of the arbitration and the date of the order referred to in paragraph (a) or (b) shall be excluded.
(3) In determining for the purposes of the Limitation Acts when a cause of action accrued, any provision that an award is a condition precedent to the bringing of legal proceedings in respect of a matter to which an arbitration agreement applies shall be disregarded.
(4) In this Part "the Limitation Acts" means
(a) in England and Wales, the Limitation Act 1980, the Foreign Limitation Periods Act 1984 and any other enactment (whenever passed) relating to the limitation of actions;
(b) in Northern Ireland, the Limitation (Northern Ireland) Order 1989, the Foreign Limitation Periods (Northern Ireland) Order 1985 and any other enactment (whenever passed) relating to the limitation of actions.

14 — Commencement of Arbitral Proceedings

(1) The parties are free to agree when arbitral proceedings are to be regarded as commenced for the purposes of this Part and for the purposes of the Limitation Acts.
(2) If there is no such agreement the following provisions apply.
(3) Where the arbitrator is named or designated in the arbitration agreement, arbitral proceedings are commenced in respect of a matter when one party serves on the other party or parties a notice in writing requiring him or them to submit that matter to the person so named or designated.
(4) Where the arbitrator or arbitrators are to be appointed by the parties, arbitral proceedings are commenced in respect of a matter when one party serves on the other party or parties notice in writing requiring him or them to appoint an arbitrator or to agree to the appointment of an arbitrator in respect of that matter.
(5) Where the arbitrator or arbitrators are to be appointed by a person other than a party to the proceedings, arbitral proceedings are commenced in respect of a matter when one party gives notice in writing to that person requesting him to make the appointment in respect of that matter.

The Arbitral Tribunal

15 — The Arbitral Tribunal

(1) The parties are free to agree on the number of arbitrators to form the tribunal and whether there is to be a chairman or umpire.

(2) Unless otherwise agreed by the parties, an agreement that the number of arbitrators shall be two or any other even number shall be understood as requiring the appointment of an additional arbitrator as chairman of the tribunal.

(3) If there is no agreement as to the number of arbitrators, the tribunal shall consist of a sole arbitrator.

16 — Procedure for Appointment of Arbitrators

(1) The parties are free to agree on the procedure for appointing the arbitrator or arbitrators, including the procedure for appointing any chairman or umpire.

(2) If or to the extent that there is no such agreement, the following provisions apply.

(3) If the tribunal is to consist of a sole arbitrator, the parties shall jointly appoint the arbitrator not later than 28 days after service of a request in writing by either party to do so.

(4) If the tribunal is to consist of two arbitrators, each party shall appoint one arbitrator not later than 14 days after service of a request in writing by either party to do so.

(5) If the tribunal is to consist of three arbitrators

(a) each party shall appoint one arbitrator not later than 14 days after service of a request in writing by either party to do so, and

(b) the two so appointed shall forthwith appoint a third arbitrator as the chairman of the tribunal.

(6) If the tribunal is to consist of two arbitrators and an umpire

(a) each party shall appoint one arbitrator not later than 14 days after service of a request in writing by either party to do so, and

(b) the two so appointed may appoint an umpire at any time after they themselves are appointed and shall do so before any substantive hearing or forthwith if they cannot agree on a matter relating to the arbitration.

(7) In any other case (in particular, if there are more than two parties) section 18 applies as in the case of a failure of the agreed appointment procedure.

17 — Power in Case of Default to Appoint Sole Arbitrator

(1) Unless the parties otherwise agree, where each of two parties to an arbitration agreement is to appoint an arbitrator and one party ("the party in

default") refuses to do so, or fails to do so within the time specified, the other party, having duly appointed his arbitrator, may give notice in writing to the party in default that he proposes to appoint his arbitrator to act as sole arbitrator.

(2) If the party in default does not within 7 clear days of that notice being given

(a) make the required appointment, and

(b) notify the other party that he has done so,

the other party may appoint his arbitrator as sole arbitrator whose award shall be binding on both parties as if he had been so appointed by agreement.

(3) Where a sole arbitrator has been appointed under subsection (2), the party in default may (upon notice to the appointing party) apply to the court which may set aside the appointment.

(4) The leave of the court is required for any appeal from a decision of the court under this section.

18 — Failure of Appointment Procedure

(1) The parties are free to agree what is to happen in the event of a failure of the procedure for the appointment of the arbitral tribunal.

There is no failure if an appointment is duly made under section 17 (power in case of default to appoint sole arbitrator), unless that appointment is set aside.

(2) If or to the extent that there is no such agreement any party to the arbitration agreement may (upon notice to the other parties) apply to the court to exercise its powers under this section.

(3) Those powers are

(a) to give directions as to the making of any necessary appointments;

(b) to direct that the tribunal shall be constituted by such appointments (or any one or more of them) as have been made;

(c) to revoke any appointments already made;

(d) to make any necessary appointments itself.

(4) An appointment made by the court under this section has effect as if made with the agreement of the parties.

(5) The leave of the court is required for any appeal from a decision of the court under this section.

19 — Court to Have Regard to Agreed Qualifications

In deciding whether to exercise, and in considering how to exercise, any of its powers under section 16 (procedure for appointment of arbitrators) or section 18 (failure of appointment procedure), the court shall have due regard to any agreement of the parties as to the qualifications required of the arbitrators.

20 — Chairman

(1) Where the parties have agreed that there is to be a chairman, they are free to agree what the functions of the chairman are to be in relation to the making of decisions, orders and awards.

(2) If or to the extent that there is no such agreement, the following provisions apply.

(3) Decisions, orders and awards shall be made by all or a majority of the arbitrators (including the chairman).

(4) The view of the chairman shall prevail in relation to a decision, order or award in respect of which there is neither unanimity nor a majority under subsection (3).

21 — Umpire

(1) Where the parties have agreed that there is to be an umpire, they are free to agree what the functions of the umpire are to be, and in particular

(a) whether he is to attend the proceedings, and

(b) when he is to replace the other arbitrators as the tribunal with power to make decisions, orders and awards.

(2) If or to the extent that there is no such agreement, the following provisions apply.

(3) The umpire shall attend the proceedings and be supplied with the same documents and other materials as are supplied to the other arbitrators.

(4) Decisions, orders and awards shall be made by the other arbitrators unless and until they cannot agree on a matter relating to the arbitration.

In that event they shall forthwith give notice in writing to the parties and the umpire, whereupon the umpire shall replace them as the tribunal with power to make decisions, orders and awards as if he were sole arbitrator.

(5) If the arbitrators cannot agree but fail to give notice of that fact, or if any of them fails to join in the giving of notice, any party to the arbitral proceedings may (upon notice to the other parties and to the tribunal) apply to the court which may order that the umpire shall replace the other arbitrators as the tribunal with power to make decisions, orders and awards as if he were sole arbitrator.

(6) The leave of the court is required for any appeal from a decision of the court under this section.

22 — Decision-making Where No Chairman or Umpire

(1) Where the parties agree that there shall be two or more arbitrators with no chairman or umpire, the parties are free to agree how the tribunal is to

make decisions, orders and awards.
(2) If there is no such agreement, decisions, orders and awards shall be made by all or a majority of the arbitrators.

23 — Revocation of Arbitrator's Authority

(1) The parties are free to agree in what circumstances the authority of an arbitrator may be revoked.
(2) If or to the extent that there is no such agreement the following provisions apply.
(3) The authority of an arbitrator may not be revoked except
(a) by the parties acting jointly, or
(b) by an arbitral or other institution or person vested by the parties with powers in that regard.
(4) Revocation of the authority of an arbitrator by the parties acting jointly must be agreed in writing unless the parties also agree (whether or not in writing) to terminate the arbitration agreement.
(5) Nothing in this section affects the power of the court
(a) to revoke an appointment under section 18 (powers exercisable in case of failure of appointment procedure), or
(b) to remove an arbitrator on the grounds specified in section 24.

24 — Power of Court to Remove Arbitrator

(1) A party to arbitral proceedings may (upon notice to the other parties, to the arbitrator concerned and to any other arbitrator) apply to the court to remove an arbitrator on any of the following grounds
(a) that circumstances exist that give rise to justifiable doubts as to his impartiality;
(b) that he does not possess the qualifications required by the arbitration agreement;
(c) that he is physically or mentally incapable of conducting the proceedings or there are justifiable doubts as to his capacity to do so;
(d) that he has refused or failed
(i) properly to conduct the proceedings, or
(ii) to use all reasonable despatch in conducting the proceedings or making an award,
and that substantial injustice has been or will be caused to the applicant.
(2) If there is an arbitral or other institution or person vested by the parties with power to remove an arbitrator, the court shall not exercise its power of removal unless satisfied that the applicant has first exhausted any available recourse to that institution or person.
(3) The arbitral tribunal may continue the arbitral proceedings and make an

award while an application to the court under this section is pending.
(4) Where the court removes an arbitrator, it may make such order as it thinks fit with respect to his entitlement (if any) to fees or expenses, or the repayment of any fees or expenses already paid.
(5) The arbitrator concerned is entitled to appear and be heard by the court before it makes any order under this section.
(6) The leave of the court is required for any appeal from a decision of the court under this section.

25 — Resignation of Arbitrator

(1) The parties are free to agree with an arbitrator as to the consequences of his resignation as regards
(a) his entitlement (if any) to fees or expenses, and
(b) any liability thereby incurred by him.
(2) If or to the extent that there is no such agreement the following provisions apply.
(3) An arbitrator who resigns his appointment may (upon notice to the parties) apply to the court
(a) to grant him relief from any liability thereby incurred by him, and
(b) to make such order as it thinks fit with respect to his entitlement (if any) to fees or expenses or the repayment of any fees or expenses already paid.
(4) If the court is satisfied that in all the circumstances it was reasonable for the arbitrator to resign, it may grant such relief as is mentioned in subsection (3)(a) on such terms as it thinks fit.
(5) The leave of the court is required for any appeal from a decision of the court under this section.

26 — Death of Arbitrator or Person Appointing Him

(1) The authority of an arbitrator is personal and ceases on his death.
(2) Unless otherwise agreed by the parties, the death of the person by whom an arbitrator was appointed does not revoke the arbitrator's authority.

27 — Filling of Vacancy, etc.

(1) Where an arbitrator ceases to hold office, the parties are free to agree
(a) whether and if so how the vacancy is to be filled,
(b) whether and if so to what extent the previous proceedings should stand, and
(c) what effect (if any) his ceasing to hold office has on any appointment made by him (alone or jointly).
(2) If or to the extent that there is no such agreement, the following provisions apply.
(3) The provisions of sections 16 (procedure for appointment of arbitrators)

and 18 (failure of appointment procedure) apply in relation to the filling of the vacancy as in relation to an original appointment.

(4) The tribunal (when reconstituted) shall determine whether and if so to what extent the previous proceedings should stand.

This does not affect any right of a party to challenge those proceedings on any ground which had arisen before the arbitrator ceased to hold office.

(5) His ceasing to hold office does not affect any appointment by him (alone or jointly) of another arbitrator, in particular any appointment of a chairman or umpire.

28 — Joint and Several Liability of Parties to Arbitrators for Fees and Expenses

(1) The parties are jointly and severally liable to pay to the arbitrators such reasonable fees and expenses (if any) as are appropriate in the circumstances.

(2) Any party may apply to the court (upon notice to the other parties and to the arbitrators) which may order that the amount of the arbitrators' fees and expenses shall be considered and adjusted by such means and upon such terms as it may direct.

(3) If the application is made after any amount has been paid to the arbitrators by way of fees or expenses, the court may order the repayment of such amount (if any) as is shown to be excessive, but shall not do so unless it is shown that it is reasonable in the circumstances to order repayment.

(4) The above provisions have effect subject to any order of the court under section 24(4) or 25(3)(b) (order as to entitlement to fees or expenses in case of removal or resignation of arbitrator).

(5) Nothing in this section affects any liability of a party to any other party to pay all or any of the costs of the arbitration (see sections 59 to 65) or any contractual right of an arbitrator to payment of his fees and expenses.

(6) In this section references to arbitrators include an arbitrator who has ceased to act and an umpire who has not replaced the other arbitrators.

29 — Immunity of Arbitrator

(1) An arbitrator is not liable for anything done or omitted in the discharge or purported discharge of his functions as arbitrator unless the act or omission is shown to have been in bad faith.

(2) Subsection (1) applies to an employee or agent of an arbitrator as it applies to the arbitrator himself.

(3) This section does not affect any liability incurred by an arbitrator by reason of his resigning (but see section 25).

Jurisdiction of the Arbitral Tribunal

30 — Competence of Tribunal to Rule on Its Own Jurisdiction

(1) Unless otherwise agreed by the parties, the arbitral tribunal may rule on its own substantive jurisdiction, that is, as to

(a) whether there is a valid arbitration agreement,

(b) whether the tribunal is properly constituted, and

(c) what matters have been submitted to arbitration in accordance with the arbitration agreement.

(2) Any such ruling may be challenged by any available arbitral process of appeal or review or in accordance with the provisions of this Part.

31 — Objection to Substantive Jurisdiction of Tribunal

(1) An objection that the arbitral tribunal lacks substantive jurisdiction at the outset of the proceedings must be raised by a party not later than the time he takes the first step in the proceedings to contest the merits of any matter in relation to which he challenges the tribunal's jurisdiction.

A party is not precluded from raising such an objection by the fact that he has appointed or participated in the appointment of an arbitrator.

(2) Any objection during the course of the arbitral proceedings that the arbitral tribunal is exceeding its substantive jurisdiction must be made as soon as possible after the matter alleged to be beyond its jurisdiction is raised.

(3) The arbitral tribunal may admit an objection later than the time specified in subsection (1) or (2) if it considers the delay justified.

(4) Where an objection is duly taken to the tribunal's substantive jurisdiction and the tribunal has power to rule on its own jurisdiction, it may

(a) rule on the matter in an award as to jurisdiction, or

(b) deal with the objection in its award on the merits.

If the parties agree which of these courses the tribunal should take, the tribunal shall proceed accordingly.

(5) The tribunal may in any case, and shall if the parties so agree, stay proceedings whilst an application is made to the court under section 32 (determination of preliminary point of jurisdiction).

32 — Determination of Preliminary Point of Jurisdiction

(1) The court may, on the application of a party to arbitral proceedings (upon notice to the other parties), determine any question as to the substantive jurisdiction of the tribunal.

A party may lose the right to object (see section 73).

(2) An application under this section shall not be considered unless

(a) it is made with the agreement in writing of all the other parties to the

proceedings, or
(b) it is made with the permission of the tribunal and the court is satisfied
(i) that the determination of the question is likely to produce substantial savings in costs,
(ii) that the application was made without delay, and
(iii) that there is good reason why the matter should be decided by the court.
(3) An application under this section, unless made with the agreement of all the other parties to the proceedings, shall state the grounds on which it is said that the matter should be decided by the court.
(4) Unless otherwise agreed by the parties, the arbitral tribunal may continue the arbitral proceedings and make an award while an application to the court under this section is pending.
(5) Unless the court gives leave, no appeal lies from a decision of the court whether the conditions specified in subsection (2) are met.
(6) The decision of the court on the question of jurisdiction shall be treated as a judgment of the court for the purposes of an appeal.
But no appeal lies without the leave of the court which shall not be given unless the court considers that the question involves a point of law which is one of general importance or is one which for some other special reason should be considered by the Court of Appeal.

The Arbitral Proceedings

33 — General Duty of the Tribunal

(1) The tribunal shall
(a) act fairly and impartially as between the parties, giving each party a reasonable opportunity of putting his case and dealing with that of his opponent, and
(b) adopt procedures suitable to the circumstances of the particular case, avoiding unnecessary delay or expense, so as to provide a fair means for the resolution of the matters falling to be determined.
(2) The tribunal shall comply with that general duty in conducting the arbitral proceedings, in its decisions on matters of procedure and evidence and in the exercise of all other powers conferred on it.

34 — Procedural and Evidential Matters

(1) It shall be for the tribunal to decide all procedural and evidential matters subject to the right of the parties to agree any matter.
(2) Procedural and evidential matters include
(a) when and where any part of the proceedings is to be held;
(b) the language or languages to be used in the proceedings and whether translations of any relevant documents are to be supplied;

(c) whether any and if so what form of written statements of claim and defence are to be used, when these should be supplied and the extent to which such statements can be later amended;
(d) whether any and if so which documents or classes of documents should be disclosed between and produced by the parties and at what stage;
(e) whether any and if so what questions should be put to and answered by the respective parties and when and in what form this should be done;
(f) whether to apply strict rules of evidence (or any other rules) as to the admissibility, relevance or weight of any material (oral, written or other) sought to be tendered on any matters of fact or opinion, and the time, manner and form in which such material should be exchanged and presented;
(g) whether and to what extent the tribunal should itself take the initiative in ascertaining the facts and the law;
(h) whether and to what extent there should be oral or written evidence or submissions.
(3) The tribunal may fix the time within which any directions given by it are to be complied with, and may if it thinks fit extend the time so fixed (whether or not it has expired).

35 — Consolidation of Proceedings and Concurrent Hearings

(1) The parties are free to agree
(a) that the arbitral proceedings shall be consolidated with other arbitral proceedings, or
(b) that concurrent hearings shall be held,
on such terms as may be agreed.
(2) Unless the parties agree to confer such power on the tribunal, the tribunal has no power to order consolidation of proceedings or concurrent hearings.

36 — Legal or Other Representation

Unless otherwise agreed by the parties, a party to arbitral proceedings may be represented in the proceedings by a lawyer or other person chosen by him.

37 — Power to Appoint Experts, Legal Advisers or Assessors

(1) Unless otherwise agreed by the parties
(a) the tribunal may
(i) appoint experts or legal advisers to report to it and the parties, or
(ii) appoint assessors to assist it on technical matters,
and may allow any such expert, legal adviser or assessor to attend the proceedings; and

(b) the parties shall be given a reasonable opportunity to comment on any information, opinion or advice offered by any such person.

(2) The fees and expenses of an expert, legal adviser or assessor appointed by the tribunal for which the arbitrators are liable are expenses of the arbitrators for the purposes of this Part.

38 — General Powers Exercisable by the Tribunal

(1) The parties are free to agree on the powers exercisable by the arbitral tribunal for the purposes of and in relation to the proceedings.

(2) Unless otherwise agreed by the parties the tribunal has the following powers.

(3) The tribunal may order a claimant to provide security for the costs of the arbitration.

This power shall not be exercised on the ground that the claimant is

(a) an individual ordinarily resident outside the United Kingdom, or

(b) a corporation or association incorporated or formed under the law of a country outside the United Kingdom, or whose central management and control is exercised outside the United Kingdom.

(4) The tribunal may give directions in relation to any property which is the subject of the proceedings or as to which any question arises in the proceedings, and which is owned by or is in the possession of a party to the proceedings

(a) for the inspection, photographing, preservation, custody or detention of the property by the tribunal, an expert or a party, or

(b) ordering that samples be taken from, or any observation be made of or experiment conducted upon, the property.

(5) The tribunal may direct that a party or witness shall be examined on oath or affirmation, and may for that purpose administer any necessary oath or take any necessary affirmation.

(6) The tribunal may give directions to a party for the preservation for the purposes of the proceedings of any evidence in his custody or control.

39 — Power to Make Provisional Awards

(1) The parties are free to agree that the tribunal shall have power to order on a provisional basis any relief which it would have power to grant in a final award.

(2) This includes, for instance, making

(a) a provisional order for the payment of money or the disposition of property as between the parties, or

(b) an order to make an interim payment on account of the costs of the arbitration.

(3) Any such order shall be subject to the tribunal's final adjudication; and the tribunal's final award, on the merits or as to costs, shall take account of any such order.

(4) Unless the parties agree to confer such power on the tribunal, the tribunal has no such power.

This does not affect its powers under section 47 (awards on different issues, etc.).

40 — General Duty of Parties

(1) The parties shall do all things necessary for the proper and expeditious conduct of the arbitral proceedings.

(2) This includes

(a) complying without delay with any determination of the tribunal as to procedural or evidential matters, or with any order or directions of the tribunal, and

(b) where appropriate, taking without delay any necessary steps to obtain a decision of the court on a preliminary question of jurisdiction or law (see sections 32 and 45).

41 — Powers of Tribunal in Case of Party's Default

(1) The parties are free to agree on the powers of the tribunal in case of a party's failure to do something necessary for the proper and expeditious conduct of the arbitration.

(2) Unless otherwise agreed by the parties, the following provisions apply.

(3) If the tribunal is satisfied that there has been inordinate and inexcusable delay on the part of the claimant in pursuing his claim and that the delay

(a) gives rise, or is likely to give rise, to a substantial risk that it is not possible to have a fair resolution of the issues in that claim, or

(b) has caused, or is likely to cause, serious prejudice to the respondent,

the tribunal may make an award dismissing the claim.

(4) If without showing sufficient cause a party

(a) fails to attend or be represented at an oral hearing of which due notice was given, or

(b) where matters are to be dealt with in writing, fails after due notice to submit written evidence or make written submissions,

the tribunal may continue the proceedings in the absence of that party or, as the case may be, without any written evidence or submissions on his behalf, and may make an award on the basis of the evidence before it.

(5) If without showing sufficient cause a party fails to comply with any order or directions of the tribunal, the tribunal may make a peremptory order to the same effect, prescribing such time for compliance with it as the

tribunal considers appropriate.
(6) If a claimant fails to comply with a peremptory order of the tribunal to provide security for costs, the tribunal may make an award dismissing his claim.
(7) If a party fails to comply with any other kind of peremptory order, then, without prejudice to section 42 (enforcement by court of tribunal's peremptory orders), the tribunal may do any of the following
(a) direct that the party in default shall not be entitled to rely upon any allegation or material which was the subject matter of the order;
(b) draw such adverse inferences from the act of non-compliance as the circumstances justify;
(c) proceed to an award on the basis of such materials as have been properly provided to it;
(d) make such order as it thinks fit as to the payment of costs of the arbitration incurred in consequence of the non-compliance.

Powers of Court in Relation to Arbitral Proceedings

42 — Enforcement of Peremptory Orders of Tribunal

(1) Unless otherwise agreed by the parties, the court may make an order requiring a party to comply with a peremptory order made by the tribunal.
(2) An application for an order under this section may be made
(a) by the tribunal (upon notice to the parties),
(b) by a party to the arbitral proceedings with the permission of the tribunal (and upon notice to the other parties), or
(c) where the parties have agreed that the powers of the court under this section shall be available.
(3) The court shall not act unless it is satisfied that the applicant has exhausted any available arbitral process in respect of failure to comply with the tribunal's order.
(4) No order shall be made under this section unless the court is satisfied that the person to whom the tribunal's order was directed has failed to comply with it within the time prescribed in the order or, if no time was prescribed, within a reasonable time.
(5) The leave of the court is required for any appeal from a decision of the court under this section.

43 — Securing the Attendance of Witnesses

(1) A party to arbitral proceedings may use the same court procedures as are available in relation to legal proceedings to secure the attendance before the tribunal of a witness in order to give oral testimony or to produce documents or other material evidence.

(2) This may only be done with the permission of the tribunal or the agreement of the other parties.
(3) The court procedures may only be used if
(a) the witness is in the United Kingdom, and
(b) the arbitral proceedings are being conducted in England and Wales or as the case may be, Northern Ireland.
(4) A person shall not be compelled by virtue of this section to produce any document or other material evidence which he could not be compelled to produce in legal proceedings.

44 — Court Powers Exercisable in Support of Arbitral Proceedings

(1) Unless otherwise agreed by the parties, the court has for the purposes of and in relation to arbitral proceedings the same power of making orders about the matters listed below as it has for the purposes of and in relation to legal proceedings.
(2) Those matters are
(a) the taking of the evidence of witnesses;
(b) the preservation of evidence;
(c) making orders relating to property which is the subject of the proceedings or as to which any question arises in the proceedings
(i) for the inspection, photographing, preservation, custody or detention of the property, or
(ii) ordering that samples be taken from, or any observation be made of or experiment conducted upon, the property;
and for that purpose authorising any person to enter any premises in the possession or control of a party to the arbitration;
(d) the sale of any goods the subject of the proceedings;
(e) the granting of an interim injunction or the appointment of a receiver.
(3) If the case is one of urgency, the court may, on the application of a party or proposed party to the arbitral proceedings, make such orders as it thinks necessary for the purpose of preserving evidence or assets.
(4) If the case is not one of urgency, the court shall act only on the application of a party to the arbitral proceedings (upon notice to the other parties and to the tribunal) made with the permission of the tribunal or the agreement in writing of the other parties.
(5) In any case the court shall act only if or to the extent that the arbitral tribunal, and any arbitral or other institution or person vested by the parties with power in that regard, has no power or is unable for the time being to act effectively.
(6) If the court so orders, an order made by it under this section shall cease

to have effect in whole or in part on the order of the tribunal or of any such arbitral or other institution or person having power to act in relation to the subject matter of the order.

(7) The leave of the court is required for any appeal from a decision of the court under this section.

45 — Determination of Preliminary Point of Law

(1) Unless otherwise agreed by the parties, the court may on the application of a party to arbitral proceedings (upon notice to the other parties) determine any question of law arising in the course of the proceedings which the court is satisfied substantially affects the rights of one or more of the parties.

An agreement to dispense with reasons for the tribunal's award shall be considered an agreement to exclude the court's jurisdiction under this section.

(2) An application under this section shall not be considered unless

(a) it is made with the agreement of all the other parties to the proceedings, or

(b) it is made with the permission of the tribunal and the court is satisfied

(i) that the determination of the question is likely to produce substantial savings in costs, and

(ii) that the application was made without delay.

(3) The application shall identify the question of law to be determined and, unless made with the agreement of all the other parties to the proceedings, shall state the grounds on which it is said that the question should be decided by the court.

(4) Unless otherwise agreed by the parties, the arbitral tribunal may continue the arbitral proceedings and make an award while an application to the court under this section is pending.

(5) Unless the court gives leave, no appeal lies from a decision of the court whether the conditions specified in subsection (2) are met.

(6) The decision of the court on the question of law shall be treated as a judgment of the court for the purposes of an appeal.

But no appeal lies without the leave of the court which shall not be given unless the court considers that the question is one of general importance, or is one which for some other special reason should be considered by the Court of Appeal.

The Award

46 — Rules Applicable to Substance of Dispute

(1) The arbitral tribunal shall decide the dispute

(a) in accordance with the law chosen by the parties as applicable to the substance of the dispute, or
(b) if the parties so agree, in accordance with such other considerations as are agreed by them or determined by the tribunal.
(2) For this purpose the choice of the laws of a country shall be understood to refer to the substantive laws of that country and not its conflict of laws rules.
(3) If or to the extent that there is no such choice or agreement, the tribunal shall apply the law determined by the conflict of laws rules which it considers applicable.

47 — Awards on Different Issues, etc.

(1) Unless otherwise agreed by the parties, the tribunal may make more than one award at different times on different aspects of the matters to be determined.
(2) The tribunal may, in particular, make an award relating
(a) to an issue affecting the whole claim, or
(b) to a part only of the claims or cross-claims submitted to it for decision.
(3) If the tribunal does so, it shall specify in its award the issue, or the claim or part of a claim, which is the subject matter of the award.

48 — Remedies

(1) The parties are free to agree on the powers exercisable by the arbitral tribunal as regards remedies.
(2) Unless otherwise agreed by the parties, the tribunal has the following powers.
(3) The tribunal may make a declaration as to any matter to be determined in the proceedings.
(4) The tribunal may order the payment of a sum of money, in any currency.
(5) The tribunal has the same powers as the court
(a) to order a party to do or refrain from doing anything;
(b) to order specific performance of a contract (other than a contract relating to land);
(c) to order the rectification, setting aside or cancellation of a deed or other document.

49 — Interest

(1) The parties are free to agree on the powers of the tribunal as regards the award of interest.
(2) Unless otherwise agreed by the parties the following provisions apply.
(3) The tribunal may award simple or compound interest from such dates, at such rates and with such rests as it considers meets the justice of the case

(a) on the whole or part of any amount awarded by the tribunal, in respect of any period up to the date of the award;
(b) on the whole or part of any amount claimed in the arbitration and outstanding at the commencement of the arbitral proceedings but paid before the award was made, in respect of any period up to the date of payment.
(4) The tribunal may award simple or compound interest from the date of the award (or any later date) until payment, at such rates and with such rests as it considers meets the justice of the case, on the outstanding amount of any award (including any award of interest under subsection (3) and any award as to costs).
(5) References in this section to an amount awarded by the tribunal include an amount payable in consequence of a declaratory award by the tribunal.
(6) The above provisions do not affect any other power of the tribunal to award interest.

50 — Extension of Time for Making Award

(1) Where the time for making an award is limited by or in pursuance of the arbitration agreement, then, unless otherwise agreed by the parties, the court may in accordance with the following provisions by order extend that time.
(2) An application for an order under this section may be made
(a) by the tribunal (upon notice to the parties), or
(b) by any party to the proceedings (upon notice to the tribunal and the other parties),
but only after exhausting any available arbitral process for obtaining an extension of time.
(3) The court shall only make an order if satisfied that a substantial injustice would otherwise be done.
(4) The court may extend the time for such period and on such terms as it thinks fit, and may do so whether or not the time previously fixed (by or under the agreement or by a previous order) has expired.
(5) The leave of the court is required for any appeal from a decision of the court under this section.

51 — Settlement

(1) If during arbitral proceedings the parties settle the dispute, the following provisions apply unless otherwise agreed by the parties.
(2) The tribunal shall terminate the substantive proceedings and, if so requested by the parties and not objected to by the tribunal, shall record the settlement in the form of an agreed award.
(3) An agreed award shall state that it is an award of the tribunal and shall

have the same status and effect as any other award on the merits of the case.
(4) The following provisions of this Part relating to awards (sections 52 to 58) apply to an agreed award.
(5) Unless the parties have also settled the matter of the payment of the costs of the arbitration, the provisions of this Part relating to costs (sections 59 to 65) continue to apply.

52 — Form of Award

(1) The parties are free to agree on the form of an award.
(2) If or to the extent that there is no such agreement, the following provisions apply.
(3) The award shall be in writing signed by all the arbitrators or all those assenting to the award.
(4) The award shall contain the reasons for the award unless it is an agreed award or the parties have agreed to dispense with reasons.
(5) The award shall state the seat of the arbitration and the date when the award is made.

53 — Place Where Award Treated as Made

Unless otherwise agreed by the parties, where the seat of the arbitration is in England and Wales or Northern Ireland, any award in the proceedings shall be treated as made there, regardless of where it was signed, dispatched or delivered to any of the parties.

54 — Date of Award

(1) Unless otherwise agreed by the parties, the tribunal may decide what is to be taken to be the date on which the award was made.
(2) In the absence of any such decision, the date of the award shall be taken to be the date on which it is signed by the arbitrator or, where more than one arbitrator signs the award, by the last of them.

55 — Notification of Award

(1) The parties are free to agree on the requirements as to notification of the award to the parties.
(2) If there is no such agreement, the award shall be notified to the parties by service on them of copies of the award, which shall be done without delay after the award is made.
(3) Nothing in this section affects section 56 (power to withhold award in case of non-payment).

56 — Power to Withhold Award in Case of Non-payment

(1) The tribunal may refuse to deliver an award to the parties except upon full payment of the fees and expenses of the arbitrators.
(2) If the tribunal refuses on that ground to deliver an award, a party to the

arbitral proceedings may (upon notice to the other parties and the tribunal) apply to the court, which may order that
(a) the tribunal shall deliver the award on the payment into court by the applicant of the fees and expenses demanded, or such lesser amount as the court may specify,
(b) the amount of the fees and expenses properly payable shall be determined by such means and upon such terms as the court may direct, and
(c) out of the money paid into court there shall be paid out such fees and expenses as may be found to be properly payable and the balance of the money (if any) shall be paid out to the applicant.
(3) For this purpose the amount of fees and expenses properly payable is the amount the applicant is liable to pay under section 28 or any agreement relating to the payment of the arbitrators.
(4) No application to the court may be made where there is any available arbitral process for appeal or review of the amount of the fees or expenses demanded.
(5) References in this section to arbitrators include an arbitrator who has ceased to act and an umpire who has not replaced the other arbitrators.
(6) The above provisions of this section also apply in relation to any arbitral or other institution or person vested by the parties with powers in relation to the delivery of the tribunal's award.
As they so apply, the references to the fees and expenses of the arbitrators shall be construed as including the fees and expenses of that institution or person.
(7) The leave of the court is required for any appeal from a decision of the court under this section.
(8) Nothing in this section shall be construed as excluding an application under section 28 where payment has been made to the arbitrators in order to obtain the award.

57 — Correction of Award or Additional Award

(1) The parties are free to agree on the powers of the tribunal to correct an award or make an additional award.
(2) If or to the extent there is no such agreement, the following provisions apply.
(3) The tribunal may on its own initiative or on the application of a party
(a) correct an award so as to remove any clerical mistake or error arising from an accidental slip or omission or clarify or remove any ambiguity in the award, or
(b) make an additional award in respect of any claim (including a claim for

interest or costs) which was presented to the tribunal but was not dealt with in the award.

These powers shall not be exercised without first affording the other parties a reasonable opportunity to make representations to the tribunal.

(4) Any application for the exercise of those powers must be made within 28 days of the date of the award or such longer period as the parties may agree.

(5) Any correction of an award shall be made within 28 days of the date the application was received by the tribunal or, where the correction is made by the tribunal on its own initiative, within 28 days of the date of the award or, in either case, such longer period as the parties may agree.

(6) Any additional award shall be made within 56 days of the date of the original award or such longer period as the parties may agree.

(7) Any correction of an award shall form part of the award.

58 — Effect of Award

(1) Unless otherwise agreed by the parties, an award made by the tribunal pursuant to an arbitration agreement is final and binding both on the parties and on any persons claiming through or under them.

(2) This does not affect the right of a person to challenge the award by any available arbitral process of appeal or review or in accordance with the provisions of this Part.

Costs of the Arbitration

59 — Costs of the Arbitration

(1) References in this Part to the costs of the arbitration are to

(a) the arbitrators' fees and expenses,

(b) the fees and expenses of any arbitral institution concerned, and

(c) the legal or other costs of the parties.

(2) Any such reference includes the costs of or incidental to any proceedings to determine the amount of the recoverable costs of the arbitration (see section 63).

60 — Agreement to Pay Costs in Any Event

An agreement which has the effect that a party is to pay the whole or part of the costs of the arbitration in any event is only valid if made after the dispute in question has arisen.

61 — Award of Costs

(1) The tribunal may make an award allocating the costs of the arbitration as between the parties, subject to any agreement of the parties.

(2) Unless the parties otherwise agree, the tribunal shall award costs on the general principle that costs should follow the event except where it appears

to the tribunal that in the circumstances this is not appropriate in relation to the whole or part of the costs.

62 — Effect of Agreement or Award About Costs

Unless the parties otherwise agree, any obligation under an agreement between them as to how the costs of the arbitration are to be borne, or under an award allocating the costs of the arbitration, extends only to such costs as are recoverable.

63 — The Recoverable Costs of the Arbitration

(1) The parties are free to agree what costs of the arbitration are recoverable.

(2) If or to the extent there is no such agreement, the following provisions apply.

(3) The tribunal may determine by award the recoverable costs of the arbitration on such basis as it thinks fit.

If it does so, it shall specify

(a) the basis on which it has acted, and

(b) the items of recoverable costs and the amount referable to each.

(4) If the tribunal does not determine the recoverable costs of the arbitration, any party to the arbitral proceedings may apply to the court (upon notice to the other parties) which may

(a) determine the recoverable costs of the arbitration on such basis as it thinks fit, or

(b) order that they shall be determined by such means and upon such terms as it may specify.

(5) Unless the tribunal or the court determines otherwise

(a) the recoverable costs of the arbitration shall be determined on the basis that there shall be allowed a reasonable amount in respect of all costs reasonably incurred, and

(b) any doubt as to whether costs were reasonably incurred or were reasonable in amount shall be resolved in favour of the paying party.

(6) The above provisions have effect subject to section 64 (recoverable fees and expenses of arbitrators).

(7) Nothing in this section affects any right of the arbitrators, any expert, legal adviser or assessor appointed by the tribunal, or any arbitral institution, to payment of their fees and expenses.

64 — Recoverable Fees and Expenses of Arbitrators

(1) Unless otherwise agreed by the parties, the recoverable costs of the arbitration shall include in respect of the fees and expenses of the arbitrators only such reasonable fees and expenses as are appropriate in the

circumstances.

(2) If there is any question as to what reasonable fees and expenses are appropriate in the circumstances, and the matter is not already before the court on an application under section 63(4), the court may on the application of any party (upon notice to the other parties)

(a) determine the matter, or

(b) order that it be determined by such means and upon such terms as the court may specify.

(3) Subsection (1) has effect subject to any order of the court under section 24(4) or 25(3)(b) (order as to entitlement to fees or expenses in case of removal or resignation of arbitrator).

(4) Nothing in this section affects any right of the arbitrator to payment of his fees and expenses.

65 — Power to Limit Recoverable Costs

(1) Unless otherwise agreed by the parties, the tribunal may direct that the recoverable costs of the arbitration, or of any part of the arbitral proceedings, shall be limited to a specified amount.

(2) Any direction may be made or varied at any stage, but this must be done sufficiently in advance of the incurring of costs to which it relates, or the taking of any steps in the proceedings which may be affected by it, for the limit to be taken into account.

Powers of the Court in Relation to Award

66 — Enforcement of the Award

(1) An award made by the tribunal pursuant to an arbitration agreement may, by leave of the court, be enforced in the same manner as a judgment or order of the court to the same effect.

(2) Where leave is so given, judgment may be entered in terms of the award.

(3) Leave to enforce an award shall not be given where, or to the extent that, the person against whom it is sought to be enforced shows that the tribunal lacked substantive jurisdiction to make the award.

The right to raise such an objection may have been lost (see section 73).

(4) Nothing in this section affects the recognition or enforcement of an award under any other enactment or rule of law, in particular under Part II of the Arbitration Act 1950 (enforcement of awards under Geneva Convention) or the provisions of Part III of this Act relating to the recognition and enforcement of awards under the New York Convention or by an action on the award.

67 — Challenging the Award: Substantive Jurisdiction

(1) A party to arbitral proceedings may (upon notice to the other parties and

to the tribunal) apply to the court
(a) challenging any award of the arbitral tribunal as to its substantive jurisdiction; or
(b) for an order declaring an award made by the tribunal on the merits to be of no effect, in whole or in part, because the tribunal did not have substantive jurisdiction.
A party may lose the right to object (see section 73) and the right to apply is subject to the restrictions in section 70(2) and (3).
(2) The arbitral tribunal may continue the arbitral proceedings and make a further award while an application to the court under this section is pending in relation to an award as to jurisdiction.
(3) On an application under this section challenging an award of the arbitral tribunal as to its substantive jurisdiction, the court may by order
(a) confirm the award,
(b) vary the award, or
(c) set aside the award in whole or in part.
(4) The leave of the court is required for any appeal from a decision of the court under this section.

68 — Challenging the Award: Serious Irregularity

(1) A party to arbitral proceedings may (upon notice to the other parties and to the tribunal) apply to the court challenging an award in the proceedings on the ground of serious irregularity affecting the tribunal, the proceedings or the award.
A party may lose the right to object (see section 73) and the right to apply is subject to the restrictions in section 70(2) and (3).
(2) Serious irregularity means an irregularity of one or more of the following kinds which the court considers has caused or will cause substantial injustice to the applicant
(a) failure by the tribunal to comply with section 33 (general duty of tribunal);
(b) the tribunal exceeding its powers (otherwise than by exceeding its substantive jurisdiction: see section 67);
(c) failure by the tribunal to conduct the proceedings in accordance with the procedure agreed by the parties;
(d) failure by the tribunal to deal with all the issues that were put to it;
(e) any arbitral or other institution or person vested by the parties with powers in relation to the proceedings or the award exceeding its powers;
(f) uncertainty or ambiguity as to the effect of the award;
(g) the award being obtained by fraud or the award or the way in which it

was procured being contrary to public policy;
(h) failure to comply with the requirements as to the form of the award; or
(i) any irregularity in the conduct of the proceedings or in the award which is admitted by the tribunal or by any arbitral or other institution or person vested by the parties with powers in relation to the proceedings or the award.
(3) If there is shown to be serious irregularity affecting the tribunal, the proceedings or the award, the court may
(a) remit the award to the tribunal, in whole or in part, for reconsideration,
(b) set the award aside in whole or in part, or
(c) declare the award to be of no effect, in whole or in part.
The court shall not exercise its power to set aside or to declare an award to be of no effect, in whole or in part, unless it is satisfied that it would be inappropriate to remit the matters in question to the tribunal for reconsideration.
(4) The leave of the court is required for any appeal from a decision of the court under this section.

69 — Appeal on Point of Law

(1) Unless otherwise agreed by the parties, a party to arbitral proceedings may (upon notice to the other parties and to the tribunal) appeal to the court on a question of law arising out of an award made in the proceedings.
An agreement to dispense with reasons for the tribunal's award shall be considered an agreement to exclude the court's jurisdiction under this section.
(2) An appeal shall not be brought under this section except
(a) with the agreement of all the other parties to the proceedings, or
(b) with the leave of the court.
The right to appeal is also subject to the restrictions in section 70(2) and (3).
(3) Leave to appeal shall be given only if the court is satisfied
(a) that the determination of the question will substantially affect the rights of one or more of the parties,
(b) that the question is one which the tribunal was asked to determine,
(c) that, on the basis of the findings of fact in the award
(i) the decision of the tribunal on the question is obviously wrong, or
(ii) the question is one of general public importance and the decision of the tribunal is at least open to serious doubt, and
(d) that, despite the agreement of the parties to resolve the matter by arbitration, it is just and proper in all the circumstances for the court to determine the question.

(4) An application for leave to appeal under this section shall identify the question of law to be determined and state the grounds on which it is alleged that leave to appeal should be granted.
(5) The court shall determine an application for leave to appeal under this section without a hearing unless it appears to the court that a hearing is required.
(6) The leave of the court is required for any appeal from a decision of the court under this section to grant or refuse leave to appeal.
(7) On an appeal under this section the court may be order
(a) confirm the award,
(b) vary the award,
(c) remit the award to the tribunal, in whole or in part, for reconsideration in the light of the court's determination, or
(d) set aside the award in whole or in part.
The court shall not exercise its power to set aside an award, in whole or in part, unless it is satisfied that it would be inappropriate to remit the matters in question to the tribunal for reconsideration.
(8) The decision of the court on an appeal under this section shall be treated as a judgment of the court for the purposes of a further appeal.
But no such appeal lies without the leave of the court which shall not be given unless the court considers that the question is one of general importance or is one which for some other special reason should be considered by the Court of Appeal.

70 — Challenge or Appeal: Supplementary Provisions

(1) The following provisions apply to an application or appeal under section 67, 68 or 69.
(2) An application or appeal may not be brought if the applicant or appellant has not first exhausted
(a) any available arbitral process of appeal or review, and
(b) any available recourse under section 57 (correction of award or additional award).
(3) Any application or appeal must be brought within 28 days of the date of the award or, if there has been any arbitral process of appeal or review, of the date when the applicant or appellant was notified of the result of that process.
(4) If on an application or appeal it appears to the court that the award
(a) does not contain the tribunal's reasons, or
(b) does not set out the tribunal's reasons in sufficient detail to enable the court properly to consider the application or appeal, the court may order the

tribunal to state the reasons for its award in sufficient detail for that purpose.
(5) Where the court makes an order under subsection (4), it may make such further order as it thinks fit with respect to any additional costs of the arbitration resulting from its order.
(6) The court may order the applicant or appellant to provide security for the costs of the application or appeal, and may direct that the application or appeal be dismissed if the order is not complied with.
The power to order security for costs shall not be exercised on the ground that the applicant or appellant is
(a) an individual ordinarily resident outside the United Kingdom, or
(b) a corporation or association incorporated or formed under the law of a country outside the United Kingdom, or whose central management and control is exercised outside the United Kingdom.
(7) The court may order that any money payable under the award shall be brought into court or otherwise secured pending the determination of the application or appeal, and may direct that the application or appeal be dismissed if the order is not complied with.
(8) The court may grant leave to appeal subject to conditions to the same or similar effect as an order under subsection (6) or (7).
This does not affect the general discretion of the court to grant leave subject to conditions.

71 — Challenge or Appeal: Effect of Order of Court

(1) The following provisions have effect where the court makes an order under section 67, 68 or 69 with respect to an award.
(2) Where the award is varied, the variation has effect as part of the tribunal's award.
(3) Where the award is remitted to the tribunal, in whole or in part, for reconsideration, the tribunal shall make a fresh award in respect of the matters remitted within three months of the date of the order for remission or such longer or shorter period as the court may direct.
(4) Where the award is set aside or declared to be of no effect, in whole or in part, the court may also order that any provision that an award is a condition precedent to the bringing of legal proceedings in respect of a matter to which the arbitration agreement applies, is of no effect as regards the subject matter of the award or, as the case may be, the relevant part of the award.

Miscellaneous

72 — Saving for Rights of Person Who Takes No Part in Proceedings

(1) A person alleged to be a party to arbitral proceedings but who takes no

part in the proceedings may question
(a) whether there is a valid arbitration agreement,
(b) whether the tribunal is properly constituted, or
(c) what matters have been submitted to arbitration in accordance with the arbitration agreement,
by proceedings in the court for a declaration or injunction or other appropriate relief.
(2) He also has the same right as a party to the arbitral proceedings to challenge an award
(a) by an application under section 67 on the ground of lack of substantive jurisdiction in relation to him, or
(b) by an application under section 68 on the ground of serious irregularity (within the meaning of that section) affecting him;
and section 70(2) (duty to exhaust arbitral procedures) does not apply in his case.

73 — Loss of Right to Object

(1) If a party to arbitral proceedings takes part, or continues to take part, in the proceedings without making, either forthwith or within such time as is allowed by the arbitration agreement or the tribunal or by any provision of this Part, any objection
(a) that the tribunal lacks substantive jurisdiction,
(b) that the proceedings have been improperly conducted,
(c) that there has been a failure to comply with the arbitration agreement or with any provision of this Part, or
(d) that there has been any other irregularity affecting the tribunal or the proceedings,
he may not raise that objection later, before the tribunal or the court, unless he shows that, at the time he took part or continued to take part in the proceedings, he did not know and could not with reasonable diligence have discovered the grounds for the objection.
(2) Where the arbitral tribunal rules that it has substantive jurisdiction and a party to arbitral proceedings who could have questioned that ruling
(a) by any available arbitral process of appeal or review, or
(b) by challenging the award,
does not do so, or does not do so within the time allowed by the arbitration agreement or any provision of this Part, he may not object later to the tribunal's substantive jurisdiction on any ground which was the subject of that ruling.

74 — Immunity of Arbitral Institutions, etc.

(1) An arbitral or other institution or person designated or requested by the parties to appoint or nominate an arbitrator is not liable for anything done or omitted in the discharge or purported discharge of that function unless the act or omission is shown to have been in bad faith.

(2) An arbitral or other institution or person by whom an arbitrator is appointed or nominated is not liable, by reason of having appointed or nominated him, for anything done or omitted by the arbitrator (or his employees or agents) in the discharge or purported discharge of his functions as arbitrator.

(3) The above provisions apply to an employee or agent of an arbitral or other institution or person as they apply to the institution or person himself.

75 — Charge to Secure Payment of Solicitors' Costs

The powers of the court to make declarations and orders under section 73 of the Solicitors Act 1974 or Article 71H of the Solicitors (Northern Ireland) Order 1976 (power to charge property recovered in the proceedings with the payment of solicitors' costs) may be exercised in relation to arbitral proceedings as if those proceedings were proceedings in the court.

Supplementary

76 — Service of Notices, etc.

(1) The parties are free to agree on the manner of service of any notice or other document required or authorised to be given or served in pursuance of the arbitration agreement or for the purposes of the arbitral proceedings.

(2) If or to the extent that there is no such agreement the following provisions apply.

(3) A notice or other document may be served on a person by any effective means.

(4) If a notice or other document is addressed, pre-paid and delivered by post

(a) to the addressee's last known principal residence or, if he is or has been carrying on a trade, profession or business, his last known principal business address, or

(b) where the addressee is a body corporate, to the body's registered or principal office, it shall be treated as effectively served.

(5) This section does not apply to the service of documents for the purposes of legal proceedings, for which provision is made by rules of court.

(6) References in this Part to a notice or other document include any form of communication in writing and references to giving or serving a notice or other document shall be construed accordingly.

77 — Powers of Court in Relation to Service of Documents

(1) This section applies where service of a document on a person in the manner agreed by the parties, or in accordance with provisions of section 76 having effect in default of agreement, is not reasonably practicable.

(2) Unless otherwise agreed by the parties, the court may make such order as it thinks fit

(a) for service in such manner as the court may direct, or

(b) dispensing with service of the document.

(3) Any party to the arbitration agreement may apply for an order, but only after exhausting any available arbitral process for resolving the matter.

(4) The leave of the court is required for any appeal from a decision of the court under this section.

78 — Reckoning Periods of Time

(1) The parties are free to agree on the method of reckoning periods of time for the purposes of any provision agreed by them or any provision of this Part having effect in default of such agreement.

(2) If or to the extent there is no such agreement, periods of time shall be reckoned in accordance with the following provisions.

(3) Where the act is required to be done within a specified period after or from a specified date, the period begins immediately after that date.

(4) Where the act is required to be done a specified number of clear days after a specified date, at least that number of days must intervene between the day on which the act is done and that date.

(5) Where the period is a period of seven days or less which would include a Saturday, Sunday or a public holiday in the place where anything which has to be done within the period falls to be done, that day shall be excluded. In relation to England and Wales or Northern Ireland, a "public holiday" means Christmas Day, Good Friday or a day which under the Banking and Financial Dealings Act 1971 is a bank holiday.

79 — Power of Court to Extend Time Limits Relating to Arbitral Proceedings

(1) Unless the parties otherwise agree, the court may by order extend any time limit agreed by them in relation to any matter relating to the arbitral proceedings or specified in any provision of this Part having effect in default of such agreement.

This section does not apply to a time limit to which section 12 applies (power of court to extend time for beginning arbitral proceedings, etc.).

(2) An application for an order may be made

(a) by any party to the arbitral proceedings (upon notice to the other parties and to the tribunal), or

(b) by the arbitral tribunal (upon notice to the parties).

(3) The court shall not exercise its power to extend a time limit unless it is satisfied

(a) that any available recourse to the tribunal, or to any arbitral or other institution or person vested by the parties with power in that regard, has first been exhausted, and

(b) that a substantial injustice would otherwise be done.

(4) The court's power under this section may be exercised whether or not the time has already expired.

(5) An order under this section may be made on such terms as the court thinks fit.

(6) The leave of the court is required for any appeal from a decision of the court under this section.

80 — Notice and Other Requirements in Connection with Legal Proceedings

(1) References in this Part to an application, appeal or other step in relation to legal proceedings being taken "upon notice" to the other parties to the arbitral proceedings, or to the tribunal, are to such notice of the originating process as is required by rules of court and do not impose any separate requirement.

(2) Rules of court shall be made

(a) requiring such notice to be given as indicated by any provision of this Part, and

(b) as to the manner, form and content of any such notice.

(3) Subject to any provision made by rules of court, a requirement to give notice to the tribunal of legal proceedings shall be construed

(a) if there is more than one arbitrator, as a requirement to give notice to each of them; and

(b) if the tribunal is not fully constituted, as a requirement to give notice to any arbitrator who has been appointed.

(4) References in this Part to making an application or appeal to the court within a specified period are to the issue within that period of the appropriate originating process in accordance with rules of court.

(5) Where any provision of this Part requires an application or appeal to he made to the court within a specified time, the rules of court relating to the reckoning of periods, the extending or abridging of periods, and the consequences of not taking a step within the period prescribed by the rules, apply in relation to that requirement.

(6) Provision may be made by rules of court amending the provisions of this Part

(a) with respect to the time within which any application or appeal to the court must be made,

(b) so as to keep any provision made by this Part in relation to arbitral proceedings in step with the corresponding provision of rules of court applying in relation to proceedings in the court, or

(c) so as to keep any provision made by this Part in relation to legal proceedings in step with the corresponding provision of rules of court applying generally in relation to proceedings in the court.

(7) Nothing in this section affects the generality of the power to make rules of court.

81 — Saving for Certain Matters Governed by Common Law

(1) Nothing in this Part shall be construed as excluding the operation of any rule of law consistent with the provisions of this Part, in particular, any rule of law as to

(a) matters which are not capable of settlement by arbitration;

(b) the effect of an oral arbitration agreement; or

(c) the refusal of recognition or enforcement of an arbitral award on grounds of public policy.

(2) Nothing in this Act shall be construed as reviving any jurisdiction of the court to set aside or remit an award on the ground of errors of fact or law on the face of the award.

82 — Minor Definitions

(1) In this Part

"arbitrator", unless the context otherwise requires, includes an umpire;

"available arbitral process", in relation to any matter, includes any process of appeal to or review by an arbitral or other institution or person vested by the parties with powers in relation to that matter;

"claimant", unless the context otherwise requires, includes a counterclaimant, and related expressions shall be construed accordingly;

"dispute" includes any difference;

"enactment" includes an enactment contained in Northern Ireland legislation;

"legal proceedings" means civil proceedings in the High Court or a county court;

"peremptory order" means an order made under section 41(5) or made in exercise of any corresponding power conferred by the parties;

"premises" includes land, buildings, moveable structures, vehicles, vessels,

aircraft and hovercraft;
"question of law" means
(a) for a court in England and Wales, a question of the law of England and Wales, and
(b) for a court in Northern Ireland, a question of the law of Northern Ireland; "substantive jurisdiction", in relation to an arbitral tribunal, refers to the matters specified in section 30(1)(a) to (c), and references to the tribunal exceeding its substantive jurisdiction shall be construed accordingly.
(2) References in this Part to a party to an arbitration agreement include any person claiming under or through a party to the agreement.

83 — Index of Defined Expressions: Part I

In this Part the expressions listed below are defined or otherwise explained by the provisions indicated

agreement, agree and agreed: section 5(1)
agreement in writing: section 5(2) to (5)
arbitration agreement: sections 6 and 5(1)
arbitrator: section 82(1)
available arbitral process: section 82(1)
claimant: section 82(1)
commencement (in relation to arbitral proceedings): section 14
costs of the arbitration: section 59
the court: section 105
dispute: section 82(1)
enactment: section 82(1)
legal proceedings: section 82(1)
Limitation Acts: section 13(4)
notice (or other document) section 76(6)
party:
— in relation to an arbitration agreement: section 82(2)
— where section 106(2) or (3) applies: section 106(4)
peremptory order: section 82(1) (and see section 41(5))
premises: section 82(1)
question of law: section 82(1)
recoverable costs: sections 63 and 64
seat of the arbitration: section 3
serve and service (of notice or other document): section 76(6)
substantive jurisdiction (in relation to an arbitral tribunal): section 82(1) (and see section 30(1)(a) to (c))

upon notice (to the parties or the tribunal): section 80
written and in writing: section 5(6)

84 — Transitional Provisions

(1) The provisions of this Part do not apply to arbitral proceedings commenced before the date on which this Part comes into force.

(2) They apply to arbitral proceedings commenced on or after that date under an arbitration agreement whenever made.

(3) The above provisions have effect subject to any transitional provision made by an order under section 109(2) (power to include transitional provisions in commencement order).

Part II

Other Provisions Relating to Arbitration

Domestic Arbitration Agreements

85 — Modification of Part I in Relation to Domestic Arbitration Agreement

(1) In the case of a domestic arbitration agreement the provisions of Part I are modified in accordance with the following sections.

(2) For this purpose a "domestic arbitration agreement" means an arbitration agreement to which none of the parties is

(a) an individual who is a national of, or habitually resident in, a state other than the United Kingdom, or

(b) a body corporate which is incorporated in, or whose central control and management is exercised in, a state other than the United Kingdom, and under which the seat of the arbitration (if the seat has been designated or determined) is in the United Kingdom.

(3) In subsection (2) "arbitration agreement" and "seat of the arbitration" have the same meaning as in Part I (see sections 3, 5(1) and 6).

86 — Staying of Legal Proceedings

(1) In section 9 (stay of legal proceedings), subsection (4) (stay unless the arbitration agreement is null and void, inoperative, or incapable of being performed) does not apply to a domestic arbitration agreement.

(2) On an application under that section in relation to a domestic arbitration agreement the court shall grant a stay unless satisfied

(a) that the arbitration agreement is null and void, inoperative, or incapable of being performed, or

(b) that there are other sufficient grounds for not requiring the parties to abide by the arbitration agreement.

(3) The court may treat as a sufficient ground under subsection (2)(b) the fact that the applicant is or was at any material time not ready and willing to

do all things necessary for the proper conduct of the arbitration or of any other dispute resolution procedures required to be exhausted before resorting to arbitration.

(4) For the purposes of this section the question whether an arbitration agreement is a domestic arbitration agreement shall be determined by reference to the facts at the time the legal proceedings are commenced.

87 — Effectiveness of Agreement to Exclude Court's Jurisdiction

(1) In the case of a domestic arbitration agreement any agreement to exclude the jurisdiction of the court under

(a) section 45 (determination of preliminary point of law), or

(b) section 69 (challenging the award: appeal on point of law),

is not effective unless entered into after the commencement of the arbitral proceedings in which the question arises or the award is made.

(2) For this purpose the commencement of the arbitral proceedings has the same meaning as in Part I (see section 14).

(3) For the purposes of this section the question whether an arbitration agreement is a domestic arbitration agreement shall be determined by reference to the facts at the time the agreement is entered into.

88 — Power to Repeal or Amend Sections 85 to 87

(1) The Secretary of State may by order repeal or amend the provisions of sections 85 to 87.

(2) An order under this section may contain such supplementary, incidental and transitional provisions as appear to the Secretary of State to be appropriate.

(3) An order under this section shall be made by statutory instrument and no such order shall be made unless a draft of it has been laid before and approved by a resolution of each House of Parliament.

Consumer Arbitration Agreements

89 — Application of Unfair Terms Regulations to Consumer Arbitration Agreements

(1) The following sections extend the application of the Unfair Terms in Consumer Contracts Regulations 1994 in relation to a term which constitutes an arbitration agreement.

For this purpose "arbitration agreement" means an agreement to submit to arbitration present or future disputes or differences (whether or not contractual).

(2) In those sections "the Regulations" means these regulations and includes any regulations amending or replacing those regulations.

(3) Those sections apply whatever the law applicable to the arbitration

agreement.

90 — Regulations Apply Where Consumer is a Legal Person

The Regulations apply where the consumer is a legal person as they apply where the consumer is a natural person.

91 — Arbitration Agreement Unfair Where Modest Amount Sought

(1) A term which constitutes an arbitration agreement is unfair for the purposes of the Regulations so far as it relates to a claim for a pecuniary remedy which does not exceed the amount specified by order for the purposes of this section.

(2) Orders under this section may make different provision for different cases and for different purposes.

(3) The power to make orders under this section is exercisable

(a) for England and Wales, by the Secretary of State with the concurrence of the Lord Chancellor,

(b) for Scotland, by the Secretary of State with the concurrence of the Lord Advocate, and

(c) for Northern Ireland, by the Department of Economic Development for Northern Ireland with the concurrence of the Lord Chancellor.

(4) Any such order for England and Wales or Scotland shall be made by statutory instrument which shall be subject to annulment in pursuance of a resolution of either House of Parliament.

(5) Any such order for Northern Ireland shall be a statutory rule for the purposes of the Statutory Rules (Northern Ireland) Order 1979 and shall be subject to negative resolution, within the meaning of section 41(6) of the Interpretation Act (Northern Ireland) 1954.

Small Claims Arbitration in the County Court

92 — Exclusion of Part I in Relation to Small Claims Arbitration in the County Court

Nothing in Part I of this Act applies to arbitration under section 64 of the County Courts Act 1984.

Appointment of Judges as Arbitrators

93 — Appointment of Judges as Arbitrators

(1) A judge of the Commercial Court or an official referee may, if in all the circumstances he thinks fit, accept appointment as a sole arbitrator or as umpire by or by virtue of an arbitration agreement.

(2) A judge of the Commercial Court shall not do so unless the Lord Chief Justice has informed him that, having regard to the state of business in the High Court and the Crown Court, he can be made available.

(3) An official referee shall not do so unless the Lord Chief Justice has

informed him that, having regard to the state of official referees' business, he can be made available.
(4) The fees payable for the services of a judge of the Commercial Court or official referee as arbitrator or umpire shall be taken in the High Court.
(5) In this section
"arbitration agreement" has the same meaning as in Part I; and
"official referee" means a person nominated under section 68(1)(a) of the Supreme Court Act 1981 to deal with official referees' business.
(6) The provisions of Part I of this Act apply to arbitration before a person appointed under this section with the modifications specified in Schedule 2.

Statutory Arbitrations

94 — Application of Part I to Statutory Arbitrations

(1) The provisions of Part I apply to every arbitration under an enactment (a "statutory arbitration"), whether the enactment was passed or made before or after the commencement of this Act, subject to the adaptations and exclusions specified in sections 95 to 98.
(2) The provisions of Part I do not apply to a statutory arbitration if or to the extent that their application
(a) is inconsistent with the provisions of the enactment concerned, with any rules or procedure authorised or recognised by it, or;
(b) is excluded by any other enactment.
(3) In this section and the following provisions of this Part "enactment"
(a) in England and Wales, includes an enactment contained in subordinate legislation within the meaning of the Interpretation Act 1978;
(b) in Northern Ireland, means a statutory provision within the meaning of section 1(f) of the Interpretation Act (Northern Ireland) 1954.

95 — General Adaptation of Provisions in Relation to Statutory Arbitrations

(1) The provisions of Part I apply to a statutory arbitration
(a) as if the arbitration were pursuant to an arbitration agreement and as if the enactment were that agreement, and
(b) as if the persons by and against whom a claim subject to arbitration in pursuance of the enactment may be or has been made were parties to that agreement.
(2) Every statutory arbitration shall be taken to have its seat in England and Wales or, as the case may be, in Northern Ireland.

96 — Specific Adaptations of Provisions in Relation to Statutory Arbitrations

(1) The following provisions of Part I apply to a statutory arbitration with

the following adaptations.
(2) In section 30(1) (competence of tribunal to rule on its own jurisdiction), the reference in paragraph (a) to whether there is a valid arbitration agreement shall be construed as a reference to whether the enactment applies to the dispute or difference in question.
(3) Section 35 (consolidation of proceedings and concurrent hearings) applies only so as to authorise the consolidation of proceedings, or concurrent hearings in proceedings, under the same enactment.
(4) Section 46 (rules applicable to substance of dispute) applies with the omission of subsection (1)(b) (determination in accordance with considerations agreed by parties).

97 — Provisions Excluded from Applying to Statutory Arbitrations

The following provisions of Part I do not apply in relation to a statutory arbitration
(a) section 8 (whether agreement discharged by death of a party);
(b) section 12 (power of court to extend agreed time limits);
(c) sections 9(5), 10(2) and 71(4) (restrictions on effect of provision that award condition precedent to right to bring legal proceedings).

98 — Power to Make Further Provision by Regulations

(1) The Secretary of State may make provision by regulations for adapting or excluding any provision of Part I in relation to statutory arbitrations in general or statutory arbitrations of any particular description.
(2) The power is exercisable whether the enactment concerned is passed or made before or after the commencement of this Act.
(3) Regulations under this section shall be made by statutory instrument which shall be subject to annulment in pursuance of a resolution of either House of Parliament.

Part III
Recognition and Enforcement of Certain Foreign Awards
Enforcement of Geneva Convention Awards

99 — Continuation of Part II of the Arbitration Act 1950

Part II of the Arbitration Act 1950 (enforcement of certain foreign awards) continues to apply in relation to foreign awards within the meaning of that Part which are not also New York Convention awards.

Recognition and Enforcement of New York Convention Awards

100 — New York Convention Awards

(1) In this Part a "New York Convention award" means an award made, in pursuance of an arbitration agreement, in the territory of a state (other than the United Kingdom) which is a party to the New York Convention.

(2) For the purposes of subsection (1) and of the provisions of this Part relating to such awards
(a) "arbitration agreement" means an arbitration agreement in writing, and
(b) an award shall be treated as made at the seat of the arbitration, regardless of where it was signed, dispatched or delivered to any of the parties.
In this subsection "agreement in writing" and "seat of the arbitration" have the same meaning as in Part I.
(3) If Her Majesty by Order in Council declares that a state specified in the Order is a party to the New York Convention, or is a party in respect of any territory so specified, the Order shall, while in force, be conclusive evidence of that fact.
(4) In this section "the New York Convention" means the Convention on the Recognition and Enforcement of Foreign Arbitral Awards adopted by the United Nations Conference on International Commercial Arbitration on 10th June 1958.

101 — Recognition and Enforcement of Awards

(1) A New York Convention award shall be recognised as binding on the persons as between whom it was made, and may accordingly be relied on by those persons by way of defence, set-off or otherwise in any legal proceedings in England and Wales or Northern Ireland.
(2) A New York Convention award may, by leave of the court, be enforced in the same manner as a judgment or order of the court to the same effect.
As to the meaning of "the court" see section 105.
(3) Where leave is so given, judgment may be entered in terms of the award.

102 — Evidence to be Produced by Party Seeking Recognition or Enforcement

(1) A party seeking the recognition or enforcement of a New York Convention award must produce
(a) the duly authenticated original award or a duly certified copy of it, and
(b) the original arbitration agreement or a duly certified copy of it.
(2) If the award or agreement is in a foreign language, the party must also produce a translation of it certified by an official or sworn translator or by a diplomatic or consular agent.

103 — Refusal of Recognition or Enforcement

(1) Recognition or enforcement of a New York Convention award shall not be refused except in the following cases.
(2) Recognition or enforcement of the award may be refused if the person against whom it is invoked proves

(a) that a party to the arbitration agreement was (under the law applicable to him) under some incapacity;
(b) that the arbitration agreement was not valid under the law to which the parties subjected it or, failing any indication thereon, under the law of the country where the award was made;
(c) that he was not given proper notice of the appointment of the arbitrator or of the arbitration proceedings or was otherwise unable to present his case;
(d) that the award deals with a difference not contemplated by or not falling within the terms of the submission to arbitration or contains decisions on matters beyond the scope of the submission to arbitration (but see subsection (4));
(e) that the composition of the arbitral tribunal or the arbitral procedure was not in accordance with the agreement of the parties or, failing such agreement, with the law of the country in which the arbitration took place;
(f) that the award has not yet become binding on the parties, or has been set aside or suspended by a competent authority of the country in which, or under the law of which, it was made.
(3) Recognition or enforcement of the award may also be refused if the award is in respect of a matter which is not capable of settlement by arbitration, or if it would be contrary to public policy to recognise or enforce the award.
(4) An award which contains decisions on matters not submitted to arbitration may be recognised or enforced to the extent that it contains decisions on matters submitted to arbitration which can be separated from those on matters not so submitted.
(5) Where an application for the setting aside or suspension of the award has been made to such a competent authority as is mentioned in subsection (2)(f), the court before which the award is sought to be relied upon may, if it considers it proper, adjourn the decision on the recognition or enforcement of the award.
It may also on the application of the party claiming recognition or enforcement of the award order the other party to give suitable security.

104 — Saving for Other Bases of Recognition or Enforcement

Nothing in the preceding provisions of this Part affects any right to rely upon or enforce a New York Convention award at common law or under section 66.

Part IV
General Provisions

105 — Meaning of "the court": Jurisdiction of High Court and County Court

(1) In this Act "the court" means the High Court or a county court, subject to the following provisions.

(2) The Lord Chancellor may by order make provision

(a) allocating proceedings under this Act to the High Court or to county courts; or

(b) specifying proceedings under this Act which may be commenced or taken only in the High Court or in a county court.

(3) The Lord Chancellor may by order make provision requiring proceedings of any specified description under this Act in relation to which a county court has jurisdiction to be commenced or taken in one or more specified county courts.

Any jurisdiction so exercisable by a specified county court is exercisable throughout England and Wales or, as the case may be, Northern Ireland.

(4) An order under this section

(a) may differentiate between categories of proceedings by reference to such criteria as the Lord Chancellor sees fit to specify, and

(b) may make such incidental or transitional provision as the Lord Chancellor considers necessary or expedient.

(5) An order under this section for England and Wales shall be made by statutory instrument which shall be subject to annulment in pursuance of a resolution of either House of Parliament.

(6) An order under this section for Northern Ireland shall be a statutory rule for the purposes of the Statutory Rules (Northern Ireland) Order 1979 which shall be subject to negative resolution (within the meaning of section 41(6) of the Interpretation Act (Northern Ireland) 1954.

106 — Crown Application

(1) Part I of this Act applies to any arbitration agreement to which Her Majesty, either in right of the Crown or of the Duchy of Lancaster or otherwise, or the Duke of Cornwall, is a party.

(2) Where Her Majesty is party to an arbitration agreement otherwise than in right of the Crown, Her Majesty shall be represented for the purposes of any arbitral proceedings

(a) where the agreement was entered into by Her Majesty in right of the Duchy of Lancaster, by the Chancellor of the Duchy or such person as he may appoint, and

(b) in any other case, by such person as Her Majesty may appoint in writing under the Royal Sign Manual.

(3) Where the Duke of Cornwall is party to an arbitration agreement, he shall be represented for the purposes of any arbitral proceedings by such person as he may appoint.

(4) References in Part I to a party or the parties to the arbitration agreement or to arbitral proceedings shall be construed, where subsection (2) or (3) applies, as references to the person representing Her Majesty or the Duke of Cornwall.

107 — Consequential Amendments and Repeals

(1) The enactments specified in Schedule 3 are amended in accordance with that Schedule, the amendments being consequential on the provisions of this Act.

(2) The enactments specified in Schedule 4 are repealed to the extent specified.

108 — Extent

(1) The provisions of this Act extend to England and Wales and, except as mentioned below, to Northern Ireland.

(2) The following provisions of Part II do not extend to Northern Ireland- section 92 (exclusion of Part I in relation to small claims arbitration in the county court), and section 93 and Schedule 2 (appointment of judges as arbitrators).

(3) Sections 89, 90 and 91 (consumer arbitration agreements) extend to Scotland and the provisions of Schedules 3 and 4 (consequential amendments and repeals) extend to Scotland so far as they relate to enactments which so extend, subject as follows.

(4) The repeal of the Arbitration Act 1975 extends only to England and Wales and Northern Ireland.

109 — Commencement

(1) The provisions of this Act come into force on such day as the Secretary of State may appoint by order made by statutory instrument, and different days may be appointed for different purposes.

(2) An order under subsection (1) may contain such transitional provisions as appear to the Secretary of State to be appropriate.

110 — Short title

This Act may be cited as the Arbitration Act 1996.

SCHEDULES

Schedule 1 (Section 4(1))

Mandatory Provisions of Part I

sections 9 to 11 (stay of legal proceedings);
section 12 (power of court to extend agreed time limits);
section 13 (application of Limitation Acts);
section 24 (power of court to remove arbitrator);
section 26(1) (effect of death of arbitrator);
section 28 (liability of parties for fees and expenses of arbitrators);
section 29 (immunity of arbitrator);
section 31 (objection to substantive jurisdiction of tribunal);
section 32 (determination of preliminary point of jurisdiction);
section 33 (general duty of tribunal);
section 37(2) (items to be treated as expenses of arbitrators);
section 40 (general duty of parties);
section 43 (securing the attendance of witnesses);
section 56 (power to withhold award in case of non-payment);
section 60 (effectiveness of agreement for payment of costs in any event);
section 66 (enforcement of award);
sections 67 and 68 (challenging the award: substantive jurisdiction and serious irregularity), and sections 70 and 71 (supplementary provisions; effect of order of court) so far as relating to those sections;
section 72 (saving for rights of person who takes no part in proceedings);
section 73 (loss of right to object);
section 74 (immunity of arbitral institutions, etc.);
section 75 (charge to secure payment of solicitors' costs).

Schedule 2 (Section 93(6))

Modifications of Part I in Relation to Judge-arbitrators

1 — Introductory

In this Schedule "Judge-arbitrator" means a judge of the Commercial Court or official referee appointed as arbitrator or umpire under section 93.

2 — General

(1) Subject to the following provisions of this Schedule, references in Part I to the court shall be construed in relation to a judge-arbitrator, or in relation to the appointment of a judge-arbitrator, as references to the Court of Appeal.

(2) The references in sections 32(6), 45(6) and 69(8) to the Court of Appeal shall in such a case be construed as references to the Supreme Court.

3 — Arbitrator's Fees

(1) The power of the court in section 28(2) to order consideration and adjustment of the liability of a party for the fees of an arbitrator may be exercised by a judge-arbitrator.

(2) Any such exercise of the power is subject to the powers of the Court of Appeal under sections 24(4) and 25(3)(b) (directions as to entitlement to fees or expenses in case of removal or resignation).

4 — Exercise of Court Powers in Support of Arbitration

(1) Where the arbitral tribunal consists of or includes a judge-arbitrator the powers of the court under sections 42 to 44 (enforcement of peremptory orders, summoning witnesses, and other court powers) are exercisable by the High Court and also by the judge-arbitrator himself.

(2) Anything done by a judge-arbitrator in the exercise of those powers shall be regarded as done by him in his capacity as judge of the High Court and have effect as if done by that court.

Nothing in this sub-paragraph prejudices any power vested in him as arbitrator or umpire.

5 — Extension of Time for Making Award

(1) The power conferred by section 50 (extension of time for making award) is exercisable by the judge-arbitrator himself.

(2) Any appeal from a decision of a judge-arbitrator under that section lies to the Court of Appeal with the leave of that court.

6 — Withholding Award in Case of Non-payment

(1) The provisions of paragraph 7 apply in place of the provisions of section 56 (power to withhold award in the case of non-payment) in relation to the withholding of an award for non-payment of the fees and expenses of a judge-arbitrator.

(2) This does not affect the application of section 56 in relation to the delivery of such an award by an arbitral or other institution or person vested by the parties with powers in relation to the delivery of the award.

7 — Withholding Award in Case of Non-payment

(1) A judge-arbitrator may refuse to deliver an award except upon payment of the fees and expenses mentioned in section 56(1).

(2) The judge-arbitrator may, on an application by a party to the arbitral proceedings, order that if he pays into the High Court the fees and expenses demanded, or such lesser amount as the judge-arbitrator may specify

(a) the award shall be delivered,

(b) the amount of the fees and expenses properly payable shall be determined by such means and upon such terms as he may direct, and

(c) out of the money paid into court there shall be paid out such fees and expenses as may be found to be properly payable and the balance of the money (if any) shall be paid out to the applicant.
(3) For this purpose the amount of fees and expenses properly payable is the amount the applicant is liable to pay under section 28 or any agreement relating to the payment of the arbitrator.
(4) No application to the judge-arbitrator under this paragraph may be made where there is any available arbitral process for appeal or review of the amount of the fees or expenses demanded.
(5) Any appeal from a decision of a judge-arbitrator under this paragraph lies to the Court of Appeal with the leave of that court.
(6) Where a party to arbitral proceedings appeals under sub-paragraph (5), an arbitrator is entitled to appear and be heard.

8 — Correction of Award or Additional Award

Subsections (4) to (6) of section 57 (correction of award or additional award: time limit for application or exercise of power) do not apply to a judge-arbitrator.

9 — Costs

Where the arbitral tribunal consists of or includes a judge-arbitrator the powers of the court under section 63(4) (determination of recoverable costs) shall be exercised by the High Court.

10 — Costs

(1) The power of the court under section 64 to determine an arbitrator's reasonable fees and expenses may be exercised by a judge-arbitrator.
(2) Any such exercise of the power is subject to the powers of the Court of Appeal under sections 24(4) and 25(3)(b) (directions as to entitlement to fees or expenses in case of removal or resignation).

11 — Enforcement of Award

The leave of the court required by section 66 (enforcement of award) may in the case of an award of a judge-arbitrator be given by the judge-arbitrator himself.

12 — Solicitors' Costs

The powers of the court to make declarations and orders under the provisions applied by section 75 (power to charge property recovered in arbitral proceedings with the payment of solicitors' costs) may be exercised by the judge-arbitrator.

13 — Powers of Court in Relation to Service of Documents

(1) The power of the court under section 77(2) (powers of court in relation to service of documents) is exercisable by the judge-arbitrator.

(2) Any appeal from a decision of a judge-arbitrator under that section lies to the Court of Appeal with the leave of that court.

14 — Powers of Court to Extend Time Limits Relating to Arbitral Proceedings

(1) The power conferred by section 79 (power of court to extend time limits relating to arbitral proceedings) is exercisable by the judge-arbitrator himself.

(2) Any appeal from a decision of a judge-arbitrator under that section lies to the Court of Appeal with the leave of that court.

Schedule 3 (Section 107(1))

Consequential Amendments

Merchant Shipping Act 1894 (c.60)

1 — In section 496 of the Merchant Shipping Act 1894 (provisions as to deposits by owners of goods), after subsection (4) insert "(5) In subsection (3) the expression "legal proceedings" includes arbitral proceedings and as respects England and Wales and Northern Ireland the provisions of section 14 of the Arbitration Act 1996 apply to determine when such proceedings are commenced.".

Stannaries Court (Abolition) Act 1896 (c.45)

2 — In section 4(1) of the Stannaries Court (Abolition) Act 1896 (references of certain disputes to arbitration), for the words from "tried before" to "any such reference" substitute "referred to arbitration before himself or before an arbitrator agreed on by the parties or an officer of the court".

Tithe Act 1936 (c.43)

3 — Sch. 3 para. 3 repealed (22.7.2004) by Statute Law (Repeals) Act 2004 (c. 14), s. 1(1), {Sch. 1 Pt. 6Group 3}

Education Act 1944 (c.31)

4 — Sch. 3 para. 4 repealed (1.11.1996) by 1996 c. 56, ss. 582(2)(3), 583 (2), Sch. 38 Pt. I, Sch. 39 (with s. 1(4))

Commonwealth Telegraphs Act 1949 (c.39)

5 — In section 8(2) of the Commonwealth Telegraphs Act 1949 (proceedings of referees under the Act) for "the Arbitration Acts 1889 to 1934, or the Arbitration Act (Northern Ireland) 1937," substitute "Part I of the Arbitration Act 1996".

Lands Tribunal Act 1949 (c.42)

6 — Sch. 3 para. 6 repealed (1.6.2009) by The Transfer of Tribunal Functions (Lands Tribunal and Miscellaneous Amendments) Order 2009 (S.I. 2009/1307), art. 5(5), Sch. 4 (with Sch. 5)

Wireless Telegraphy Act 1949 (c.54)

7 — Sch. 3 para. 7 repealed (25.7.2003) by Communications Act 2003 (c. 21), ss. 406, 411(2)(3), Sch. 19(1)(with Schs. 18, 19(1) Note 1); S.I. 2003/1900, art. 2(1), Sch. 1 (with arts. 3-6)

Patents Act 1949 (c.87)

8 — In section 67 of the Patents Act 1949 (proceedings as to infringement of pre-1978patents referred to comptroller), for "The Arbitration Acts 1889 to 1934" substitute "Part I of the Arbitration Act 1996".

National Health Service (Amendment) Act 1949 (c.93)

9 — In section 7(8) of the M19National Health Service (Amendment) Act 1949 (arbitration in relation to hardship arising from the National Health Service Act1946 or the Act), for "the Arbitration Acts 1889 to 1934" substitute "Part I of the Arbitration Act 1996" and for "the said Acts" substitute "Part I of that Act".

Arbitration Act 1950 (c.27)

10 — In section 36(1) of the Arbitration Act 1950 (effect of foreign awards enforceable under Part II of that Act) for "section 26 of this Act" substitute "section 66 of the Arbitration Act 1996".

Interpretation Act (Northern Ireland) 1954 (c.33 (N.I.))

11 — In section 46(2) of the Interpretation Act (Northern Ireland) 1954 (miscellaneous definitions), for the definition of "arbitrator" substitute ""arbitrator" has the same meaning as in Part I of the Arbitration Act 1996;".

Agricultural Marketing Act 1958 (c.47)

12 — In section 12(1) of the Agricultural Marketing Act 1958 (application of provisions of Arbitration Act 1950)

(a) for the words from the beginning to "shall apply" substitute "Sections 45 and 69 of the Arbitration Act 1996 (which relate to the determination by the court of questions of law) and section 66 of that Act (enforcement of awards) apply"; and

(b) for "an arbitration" substitute "arbitral proceedings".

Carriage by Air Act 1961 (c.27)

13 — (1) The Carriage by Air Act 1961 is amended as follows.

(2) In section 5(3) (time for bringing proceedings)

(a) for "an arbitration" in the first place where it occurs substitute "arbitral proceedings"; and

(b) for the words from "and subsections (3) and (4)" to the end substitute "and the provisions of section 14 of the Arbitration Act 1996 apply to determine when such proceedings are commenced.".

(3) In section 11(c) (application of section 5 to Scotland)
(a) for "subsections (3) and (4)" substitute "the provisions of section 14 of the Arbitration Act 1996"; and
(b) for "an arbitration" substitute "arbitral proceedings".

Factories Act 1961 (c.34)

14 — In the Factories Act 1961, for section 171 (application of Arbitration Act 1950), substitute
"171 Application of the Arbitration Act 1996.
Part I of the Arbitration Act 1996 does not apply to proceedings under this Act except in so far as it may be applied by regulations made under this Act.".

Clergy Pensions Measure 1961 (No. 3)

15 — In the Clergy Pensions Measure 1961, section 38(4) (determination of questions), for the words "The Arbitration Act 1950" substitute "Part I of the Arbitration Act 1996".

Transport Act 1962 (c.46)

16 — (1) The Transport Act 1962 is amended as follows.
(2) In section 74(6)(f) (proceedings before referees in pension disputes), for the words "the Arbitration Act 1950" substitute "Part I of the Arbitration Act 1996".
(3) In section 81(7) (proceedings before referees in compensation disputes), for the words "the Arbitration Act 1950" substitute "Part I of the Arbitration Act 1996".
(4) In Schedule 7, Part IV (pensions), in paragraph 17(5) for the words "the Arbitration Act 1950" substitute "Part I of the Arbitration Act 1996".

Corn Rents Act 1963 (c.14)

17 — In the Corn Rents Act 1963, section 1(5) (schemes for apportioning corn rents, etc.), for the words "the Arbitration Act 1950" substitute "Part I of the Arbitration Act 1996".

Plant Varieties and Seeds Act 1964 (c.14)

18 — Sch. 3 para. 18 repealed (8.5.1998) by 1997 c. 66, s. 52, Sch. 4; S.I. 1998/1028, art. 2

Lands Tribunal and Compensation Act (Northern Ireland) 1964 (c.29 (N.I.))

19 — In section 9 of the Lands Tribunal and Compensation Act (Northern Ireland) 1964 (proceedings of Lands Tribunal), in subsection (3) (where Tribunal acts as arbitrator) for "the Arbitration Act (Northern Ireland) 1937" substitute "Part I of the Arbitration Act 1996".

Industrial and Provident Societies Act 1965 (c.12)

20 — (1) Section 60 of the Industrial and Provident Societies Act 1965 is amended as follows.

(2) In subsection (8) (procedure for hearing disputes between society and member, etc.)

(a) in paragraph (a) for "the Arbitration Act 1950" substitute "Part I of the Arbitration Act 1996"; and

(b) in paragraph (b) omit "by virtue of section 12 of the said Act of 1950".

(3) For subsection (9) substitute

"(9) The court or registrar to whom any dispute is referred under subsections (2) to (7) may at the request of either party state a case on any question of law arising in the dispute for the opinion of the High Court or, as the case maybe, the Court of Session.".

Carriage of Goods by Road Act 1965 (c.37)

21 — In section 7(2) of the Carriage of Goods by Road Act 1965 (arbitrations: time at which deemed to commence), for paragraphs (a) and (b) substitute "(a) as respects England and Wales and Northern Ireland, the provisions of section 14(3) to (5) of the Arbitration Act 1996 (which determine the time at which an arbitration is commenced) apply;".

Factories Act (Northern Ireland) 1965 (c.20 (N.I.))

22 — In section 171 of the Factories Act (Northern Ireland) 1965 (application of Arbitration Act), for "The Arbitration Act (Northern Ireland) 1937" substitute "Part I of the Arbitration Act 1996".

Commonwealth Secretariat Act 1966 (c.10)

23 — Sch. 3 para. 23 omitted (7.6.2005) by virtue of International Organisations Act 2005 (c. 20), ss. 1(2),11(with s. 1(3)); S.I. 2005/1870, art. 2 and said provision repealed (prosp.) by International Organisations Act 2005 (c. 20), s. 9, Sch.

Arbitration (International Investment Disputes) Act 1966 (c.41)

24 — In the Arbitration (International Investment Disputes) Act 1966, for section 3 (application of Arbitration Act 1950 and other enactments) substitute

"3 Application of provisions of Arbitration Act 1996.

(1) The Lord Chancellor may by order direct that any of the provisions contained in sections 36 and 38 to 44 of the Arbitration Act 1996 (provisions concerning the conduct of arbitral proceedings, etc.) shall apply to such proceedings pursuant to the Convention as are specified in the order with or without any modifications or exceptions specified in the order.

(2) Subject to subsection (1), the Arbitration Act 1996 shall not apply to

proceedings pursuant to the Convention, but this subsection shall not be taken as affecting section 9 of that Act (stay of legal proceedings in respect of matter subject to arbitration).

(3) An order made under this section

(a) may be varied or revoked by a subsequent order so made, and

(b) shall be contained in a statutory instrument.".

Poultry Improvement Act (Northern Ireland) 1968 (c.12 (N.I.))

25 — In paragraph 10(4) of the Schedule to the Poultry Improvement Act (Northern Ireland) 1968 (reference of disputes), for "The Arbitration Act (Northern Ireland) 1937" substitute "Part I of the Arbitration Act 1996".

Industrial and Provident Societies Act (Northern Ireland) 1969 (c.24 (N.I.))

26 — (1) Section 69 of the Industrial and Provident Societies Act (Northern Ireland) 1969(decision of disputes) is amended as follows.

(2) In subsection (7) (decision of disputes)

(a) in the opening words, omit the words from "and without prejudice" to"1937";

(b) at the beginning of paragraph (a) insert "without prejudice to any powers exercisable by virtue of Part I of the Arbitration Act 1996,"; and

(c) in paragraph (b) omit "the registrar or" and "registrar or" and for the words from "as might have been granted by the High Court" to the end substitute" as might be granted by the registrar".

(3) For subsection (8) substitute

"(8) The court or registrar to whom any dispute is referred under subsections (2) to (6) may at the request of either party state a case on any question of law arising in the dispute for the opinion of the High Court.".

Health and Personal Social Services (Northern Ireland) Order 1972 (N.I.14)

27 — In Article 105(6) of the Health and Personal Social Services (Northern Ireland) Order 1972 (arbitrations under the Order), for "the Arbitration Act (Northern Ireland) 1937" substitute "Part I of the Arbitration Act 1996".

Consumer Credit Act (c.39)

28 — (1) Section 146 of the Consumer Credit Act 1974 is amended as follows.

(2) In subsection (2) (solicitor engaged in contentious business), for "section 86(1) of the Solicitors Act 1957" substitute "section 87(1) of the Solicitors Act 1974".

(3) In subsection (4) (solicitor in Northern Ireland engaged in contentious

business), for the words from "business done" to "Administration of Estates (Northern Ireland) Order 1979" substitute "contentious business (as defined in Article 3(2) of the Solicitors (Northern Ireland) Order 1976.".

Friendly Societies Act 1974 (c.46)

29 — (1) The Friendly Societies Act 1974 is amended as follows.

(2) For section 78(1) (statement of case) substitute

"(1) Any arbitrator, arbiter or umpire to whom a dispute falling within section 76above is referred under the rules of a registered society or branch may at the request of either party state a case on any question of law arising in the dispute for the opinion of the High Court or, as the case may be, the Court of Session.".

(3) In section 83(3) (procedure on objections to amalgamations etc. of friendly societies), for "the Arbitration Act 1950 or, in Northern Ireland, the Arbitration Act (Northern Ireland) 1937" substitute "Part I of the Arbitration Act 1996".

Industry Act 1975 (c.68)

30 — In Schedule 3 to the Industry Act (arbitration of disputes relating to vesting and compensation orders), in paragraph 14 (application of certain provisions of Arbitration Acts)

(a) for "the Arbitration Act 1950 or, in Northern Ireland, the Arbitration Act (Northern Ireland) 1937" substitute "Part I of the Arbitration Act 1996", and

(b) for "that Act" substitute "that Part".

Industrial Relations (Northern Ireland) Order 1976 (N.I.16)

31 — Sch. 3 para. 31 repealed (24.9.1996) by S.I. 1996/1921 (N.I. 18), art. 28, Sch. 3

Aircraft and Shipbuilding Industries Act 1977 (c.3)

32 — In Schedule 7 to the Aircraft and Shipbuilding Industries Act 1977 (procedure of Arbitration Tribunal), in paragraph 2

(a) for "the Arbitration Act 1950 or, in Northern Ireland, the Arbitration Act (Northern Ireland) 1937" substitute "Part I of the Arbitration Act 1996",and

(b) for "that Act" substitute "that Part".

Patents Act 1977 (c.37)

33 — In section 130 of the Patents Act 1977 (interpretation), in subsection (8) (exclusion of Arbitration Act) for "The Arbitration Act 1950" substitute "Part I of the Arbitration Act 1996".

Judicature (Northern Ireland) Act 1978 (c.23)

34 — (1) The Judicature (Northern Ireland) Act 1978 is amended as follows.

(2) In section 35(2) (restrictions on appeals to the Court of Appeal), after

paragraph (f) insert
"(fa) except as provided by Part I of the Arbitration Act 1996, from any decision of the High Court under that Part;".
(3) In section 55(2) (rules of court) after paragraph (c) insert "(cc) providing for any prescribed part of the jurisdiction of the High Court in relation to the trial of any action involving matters of account to be exercised in the prescribed manner by a person agreed by the parties and for the remuneration of any such person;".

Health and Safety at Work (Northern Ireland) Order 1978 (N.I.9)

35 — In Schedule 4 to the Health and Safety at Work (Northern Ireland) Order 1978(licensing provisions), in paragraph 3, for "The Arbitration Act (Northern Ireland) 1937" substitute "Part I of the Arbitration Act 1996".

County Courts (Northern Ireland) Order 1980 (N.I.3)

36 — (1) The County Courts (Northern Ireland) Order 1980 is amended as follows.
(2) In Article 30 (civil jurisdiction exercisable by district judge)
(a) for paragraph (2) substitute
"(2) Any order, decision or determination made by a district judge under this Article (other than one made in dealing with a claim by way of arbitration under paragraph (3)) shall be embodied in a decree which for all purposes (including the right of appeal under Part VI) shall have the like effect as a decree pronounced by a county court judge.";
(b) for paragraphs (4) and (5) substitute
"(4) Where in any action to which paragraph (1) applies the claim is dealt with by way of arbitration under paragraph (3)
(a) any award made by the district judge in dealing with the claim shall be embodied in a decree which for all purposes (except the right of appeal under Part VI) shall have the like effect as a decree pronounced by a county court judge;
(b) the district judge may, and shall if so required by the High Court, state for the determination of the High Court any question of law arising out of an award so made;
(c) except as provided by sub-paragraph (b), any award so made shall be final; and
(d) except as otherwise provided by county court rules, no costs shall be awarded in connection with the action.
(5) Subject to paragraph (4), county court rules may
(a) apply any of the provisions of Part I of the Arbitration Act 1996 to arbitrations under paragraph (3) with such modifications as may be

prescribed;
(b) prescribe the rules of evidence to be followed on any arbitration under paragraph (3) and, in particular, make provision with respect to the manner of taking and questioning evidence.
(5A) Except as provided by virtue of paragraph (5)(a), Part I of the Arbitration Act 1996 shall not apply to an arbitration under paragraph (3).".
(3) After Article 61 insert
"Appeals from decisions under Part I of Arbitration Act 1996
61A (1) Article 61 does not apply to a decision of a county court judge made in the exercise of the jurisdiction conferred by Part I of the Arbitration Act 1996.
(2) Any party dissatisfied with a decision of the county court made in the exercise of the jurisdiction conferred by any of the following provisions of Part I of the Arbitration Act 1996, namely
(a) section 32 (question as to substantive jurisdiction of arbitral tribunal);
(b) section 45 (question of law arising in course of arbitral proceedings);
(c) section 67 (challenging award of arbitral tribunal: substantive jurisdiction);
(d) section 68 (challenging award of arbitral tribunal: serious irregularity);
(e) section 69 (appeal on point of law), may, subject to the provisions of that Part, appeal from that decision to the Court of Appeal.
(3) Any party dissatisfied with any decision of a county court made in the exercise of the jurisdiction conferred by any other provision of Part I of the Arbitration Act 1996 may, subject to the provisions of that Part, appeal from that decision to the High Court.
(4) The decision of the Court of Appeal on an appeal under paragraph (2) shall be final.".

Supreme Court Act 1981 (c.54)

37 — (1) The Supreme Court Act 1981 is amended as follows.
(2) In section 18(1) (restrictions on appeals to the Court of Appeal), for paragraph (g) substitute
"(g) except as provided by Part I of the Arbitration Act 1996, from any decision of the High Court under that Part;".
(3) In section 151 (interpretation, etc.), in the definition of "arbitration agreement", for "the Arbitration Act 1950 by virtue of section 32 of that Act;" substitute "Part I of the Arbitration Act 1996;".

Merchant Shipping (Liner Conferences) Act 1982 (c.37)

38 — In section 7(5) of the Merchant Shipping (Liner Conferences) Act 1982 (stay of legal proceedings), for the words from "section 4(1)" to the

end substitute "section 9 of the Arbitration Act 1996 (which also provides for the staying of legal proceedings).".

Agricultural Marketing (Northern Ireland) Order 1982 (N.I.12)

39 — In Article 14 of the Agricultural Marketing (Northern Ireland) Order 1982(application of provisions of Arbitration Act (Northern Ireland) 1937)

(a) for the words from the beginning to "shall apply" substitute "Section 45and 69 of the Arbitration Act 1996 (which relate to the determination by the court of questions of law) and section 66 of that Act (enforcement of awards)" apply; and

(b) for "an arbitration" substitute "arbitral proceedings".

Mental Health Act 1983 (c.20)

40 — In section 78 of the Mental Health Act 1983 (procedure of Mental Health Review Tribunals), in subsection (9) for "The Arbitration Act 1950" substitute "Part I of the Arbitration Act 1996".

Registered Homes Act 1984 (c.23)

41 — Sch. 3 para. 41 repealed (1.4.2002 for E.W.) by 2000 c. 14, ss. 117 (2), 122, Sch. 6; S.I. 2001/4150, art.3(3)(c)(xi) (subject to art. 4 and to S.I. 2002/1493, art. 4) (as amended by S.I. 2002/1493, art. 6); S.I.2002/920, art. 3(3)(g)(ix) (subject to art. 3(4)(5), Schs. 1-3 and with art. 3(6)-(10))

In section 43 of the Registered Homes Act 1984 (procedure of Registered Homes Tribunals), in subsection (3) for "The Arbitration Act 1950" substitute "Part I of the Arbitration Act 1996".

Housing Act 1985 (c.68)

42 — In section 47(3) of the Housing Act 1985 (agreement as to determination of matters relating to service charges) for "section 32 of the Arbitration Act 1950" substitute "Part I of the Arbitration Act 1996".

Landlord and Tenant Act 1985 (c.70)

43 — Sch. 3 para. 43 repealed (1.9.1997) by 1996 c. 52, s. 227, Sch. 19, Pt. III; S.I. 1997/1851, art. 1, 2

Credit Unions (Northern Ireland) Order 1985 (N.I.12)

44 — (1) Article 72 of the Credit Unions (Northern Ireland) Order 1985 (decision of disputes) is amended as follows.

(2) In paragraph (7)

(a) in the opening words, omit the words from "and without prejudice" to "1937";

(b) at the beginning of sub-paragraph (a) insert "without prejudice to any powers exercisable by virtue of Part I of the Arbitration Act 1996,"; and

(c) in sub-paragraph (b) omit "the registrar or" and "registrar or" and for the words from "as might have been granted by the High Court" to the end

substitute "as might be granted by the registrar".
(3) For paragraph (8) substitute
"(8) The court or registrar to whom any dispute is referred under paragraphs (2) to (6) may at the request of either party state a case on any question of law arising in the dispute for the opinion of the High Court.".

Agricultural Holdings Act 1986 (c.5)

45 — Sch. 3 para. 45 repealed (19.10.2006) by The Regulatory Reform (Agricultural Tenancies) (England and Wales) Order 2006 (S.I. 2006/2805), arts. 1(1), 18, Sch. 2 (with art. 10)

Insolvency Act 1986 (c.45)

46 — In the Insolvency Act 1986, after section 349 insert
"349A Arbitration agreements to which bankrupt is party.
(1) This section applies where a bankrupt had become party to a contract containing an arbitration agreement before the commencement of his bankruptcy.
(2) If the trustee in bankruptcy adopts the contract, the arbitration agreement is enforceable by or against the trustee in relation to matters arising from or connected with the contract.
(3) If the trustee in bankruptcy does not adopt the contract and a matter to which the arbitration agreement applies requires to be determined in connection with or for the purposes of the bankruptcy proceedings
(a) the trustee with the consent of the creditors' committee, or
(b) any other party to the agreement, may apply to the court which may, if it thinks fit in all the circumstances of the case, order that the matter be referred to arbitration in accordance with the arbitration agreement.
(4) In this section
"arbitration agreement" has the same meaning as in Part I of the Arbitration Act 1996; and
"the court" means the court which has jurisdiction in the bankruptcy proceedings.".

Building Societies Act 1986 (c.53)

47 — In Part II of Schedule 14 to the Building Societies Act 1986 (settlement of disputes: arbitration), in paragraph 5(6) for "the Arbitration Act 1950 and the Arbitration Act1979 or, in Northern Ireland, the Arbitration Act (Northern Ireland) 1937" substitute "Part I of the Arbitration Act 1996".

Mental Health (Northern Ireland) Order 1986 (N.I.4)

48 — In Article 83 of the Mental Health (Northern Ireland) Order 1986 (procedure of Mental Health Review Tribunal), in paragraph (8) for "The

Arbitration Act (Northern Ireland) 1937" substitute "Part I of the Arbitration Act 1996".

Multilateral Investment Guarantee Agency Act 1988 (c.8)

49 — For section 6 of the Multilateral Investment Guarantee Agency Act 1988 (application of Arbitration Act) substitute

"6 Application of Arbitration Act.

(1) The Lord Chancellor may by order made by statutory instrument direct that any of the provisions of sections 36 and 38 to 44 of the Arbitration Act1996 (provisions in relation to the conduct of the arbitral proceedings, etc.) apply, with such modifications or exceptions as are specified in the order, to such arbitration proceedings pursuant to Annex II to the Convention as are specified in the order.

(2) Except as provided by an order under subsection (1) above, no provision of Part I of the Arbitration Act 1996 other than section 9 (stay of legal proceedings) applies to any such proceedings.".

Copyright, Designs and Patents Act 1988 (c.48)

50 — In section 150 of the Copyright, Designs and Patents Act 1988 (Lord Chancellor's power to make rules for Copyright Tribunal), for subsection (2) substitute

"(2) The rules may apply in relation to the Tribunal, as respects proceedings in England and Wales or Northern Ireland, any of the provisions of Part I of the Arbitration Act 1996.".

Fair Employment (Northern Ireland) Act 1989 (c.32)

51 — Sch. 3 para. 51 repealed (1.3.1999) by S.I. 1998/3162, art. 105(4), Sch. 5; S.R. 1999/81, art. 3

Limitation (Northern Ireland) Order 1989 (N.I.11)

52 — In Article 2(2) of the Limitation (Northern Ireland) Order 1989 (interpretation), in the definition of "arbitration agreement", for "the Arbitration Act (Northern Ireland) 1937" substitute "Part I of the Arbitration Act 1996".

Insolvency (Northern Ireland) Order 1989 (N.I.19)

53 — In the Insolvency (Northern Ireland) Order 1989, after Article 320 insert

"Arbitration agreements to which bankrupt is party.

320A (1) This Article applies where a bankrupt had become party to a contract containing an arbitration agreement before the commencement of his bankruptcy.

(2) If the trustee in bankruptcy adopts the contract, the arbitration agreement is enforceable by or against the trustee in relation to matters arising from or

connected with the contract.

(3) If the trustee in bankruptcy does not adopt the contract and a matter to which the arbitration agreement applies requires to be determined in connection with or for the purposes of the bankruptcy proceedings

(a) the trustee with the consent of the creditors' committee, or

(b) any other party to the agreement, may apply to the court which may, if it thinks fit in all the circumstances of the case, order that the matter be referred to arbitration in accordance with the arbitration agreement.

(4) In this Article

"arbitration agreement" has the same meaning as in Part I of the Arbitration Act 1996; and

"the court" means the court which has jurisdiction in the bankruptcy proceedings.".

Social Security Administration Act 1992 (c.5)

54 — In section 59 of the Social Security Administration Act 1992 (procedure for inquiries, etc.), in subsection (7), for "The Arbitration Act 1950" substitute "Part I of the Arbitration Act 1996".

Social Security Administration (Northern Ireland) Act 1992 (c.8)

55 — Sch. 3 para. 55 repealed (29.11.1999) by S.I. 1998/1506, art. 78(2), Sch. 7; S.R. 1999/472, art. 2(2)(1)(a), Sch. I

Trade Union and Labour Relations (Consolidation) Act 1992 (c.52)

56 — In sections 212(5) and 263(6) of the Trade Union and Labour Relations (Consolidation) Act 1992 (application of Arbitration Act) for "the Arbitration Act1950" substitute "Part I of the Arbitration Act 1996".

Industrial Relations (Northern Ireland) Order 1992 (N.I.5)

57 — In Articles 84(9) and 92(5) of the Industrial Relations (Northern Ireland) Order1992 (application of Arbitration Act) for "The Arbitration Act (Northern Ireland) 1937" substitute "Part I of the Arbitration Act 1996".

Registered Homes (Northern Ireland) Order 1992 (N.I.20)

58 — In Article 33(3) of the Registered Homes (Northern Ireland) Order 1992 (procedure of Registered Homes Tribunal) for "The Arbitration Act (Northern Ireland) 1937" substitute "Part I of the Arbitration Act 1996".

Education Act 1993 (c.35)

59 — Sch. 3 para. 59 repealed (1.11.1996) by 1996 c. 56, ss. 582(2)(3), 583 (2), Sch. 38 Pt. I, Sch. 39 (withs. 1(4))

Roads (Northern Ireland) Order 1993 (N.I.15)

60 — (1) The Roads (Northern Ireland) Order 1993 is amended as follows.

(2) In Article 131 (application of Arbitration Act) for "the Arbitration Act (Northern Ireland) 1937" substitute "Part I of the Arbitration Act 1996".

(3) In Schedule 4 (disputes), in paragraph 3(2) for "the Arbitration Act (Northern Ireland) 1937" substitute "Part I of the Arbitration Act 1996".

Merchant Shipping Act 1995 (c.21)

61 — In Part II of Schedule 6 to the Merchant Shipping Act 1995 (provisions having effect in connection with Convention Relating to the Carriage of Passengers and Their Luggage by Sea), for paragraph 7 substitute

"7 Article 16 shall apply to arbitral proceedings as it applies to an action; and, as respects England and Wales and Northern Ireland, the provisions of section 14 of the Arbitration Act 1996 apply to determine for the purposes of that Article when an arbitration is commenced.".

Employment Tribunals Act 1996 (c.17)

62 — In section 6(2) of the Employment Tribunals Act 1996 (procedure of employment tribunals), for "The Arbitration Act 1950" substitute "Part I of the Arbitration Act 1996".

Schedule 4 (Section 107(2))
Repeals

Chapter	Short Title	Extent of Repeal
1892 c. 43.	Military Lands Act 1892.	In section 21(b), the words "under the Arbitration Act 1889".
1922 c. 51.	Allotments Act 1922.	In section 21(3), the words "under the Arbitration Act 1889".
1937 c. 8 (N.I.).	Arbitration Act (Northern Ireland) 1937.	The whole Act.
1949 c. 54.	Wireless Telegraphy Act 1949.	In Schedule 2, paragraph 3(3).
1949 c. 97.	National Parks and Access to the Countryside Act 1949.	In section 18(4), the words from "Without prejudice" to "England or Wales".
1950 c. 27.	Arbitration Act 1950.	Part I. Section 42(3).
1958 c. 47.	Agricultural Marketing Act 1958.	Section 53(8).
1962 c. 46.	Transport Act 1962.	In Schedule 11, Part II, paragraph 7.
1964 c. 14.	Plant Varieties and Seeds Act 1964.	In Section 10(4) the words from "or in section 9" to "three arbitrators". Section 39(3)(i)(c).
1964 c. 29 (N.I.).	Lands Tribunal and Compensation Act (Northern Ireland) 1964.	In section 9(3) the words from "so, however, that" to the end.
1965 c. 12.	Industrial and Provident Societies Act 1965.	In section 60(8)(b), the words "by virtue of section 12 of the said Act of 1950".
1965 c. 37.	Carriage of Goods by Road Act 1965.	Section 7(2)(b).
1965 c. 13 (N.I.).	New Towns Act (Northern Ireland) 1965.	In section 27(2), the words from "under and in accordance with" to the end.
1969 c. 24 (N.I.).	Industrial and Provident Societies Act (Northern Ireland) 1969.	In Section 69(7)—(a) in the opening words, the words from "and without prejudice" to "1937"; (b) in paragraph (b), the words "the registrar or" and "registrar or".

1970 c. 31.	Administration of Justice Act 1970.	Section 4. Schedule 3.
1973 c. 41.	Fair Trading Act 1973.	Section 33(2)(d).
1973 N.I. 1.	Drainage (Northern Ireland) Order 1973.	In Article 15(4), the words from "under and in accordance" to the end. Article 40(4). In Schedule 7, in paragraph 9 (2), the words "under and in accordance" to the end.
1974 c. 47.	Solicitors Act 1974.	In section 87(1), in the definition of "contentious business", the words "appointed under the Arbitration Act 1950".
1975 c. 3.	Arbitration Act 1975.	The whole Act.
1975 c. 74.	Petroleum and Submarine Pipe-Lines Act 1975.	In Part II of Schedule 2—(a) in model clause 40(2) the words "in accordance with the Arbitration Act 1950"; (b) in model clause 40(2B), the words "in accordance with the Arbitration Act (Northern Ireland) 1937". In Part II of Schedule 3, in model clause 38(2), the words "in accordance with the Arbitration Act 1950".
1976 N.I. 12.	Solicitors (Northern Ireland) Order 1976.	In Article 3(2), in the entry "contentious business", the words "appointed under the Arbitration Act (Northern Ireland) 1937". Article 71H(3).
1977 c. 37.	Patents Act 1977.	In section 52(4), the words "section 21 of the Arbitration Act 1950, or as the case may be, section 22 of the Arbitration Act (Northern Ireland) 1937 (statement of cases by arbitrators); but". Section 131(e).
1977 c. 38	Administration of Justice Act 1977.	Section 17(2).

1978 c. 23.	Judicature (Northern Ireland) Act 1978.	In section 35(2), paragraph (g)(v). In Schedule 5, the amendment to the Arbitration Act 1950.
1979 c. 42.	Arbitration Act 1979.	The whole Act.
1980 c. 58.	Limitation Act 1980.	Section 34.
1980 N.I. 3.	County Courts (Northern Ireland) Order 1980.	Article 31(3).
1981 c. 54.	Supreme Court act 1981.	Section 148.
1982 c. 27.	Civil Jurisdiction and Judgments Act 1982.	Section 25(3)(c) and (5). In Section 26—(a) in subsection (1) the words "to arbitration or", (b) in subsection 1(a)(i) the words "arbitration or"; (c) in subsection (2) the words "arbitration or".
1982 c. 53.	Administration of Justice Act 1982.	Section 15(6). In Schedule 1, Part IV.
1984 c. 5	Merchant Shipping Act 1984.	Section 4(8).
1984 c. 12.	Telecommunications Act 1984.	Schedule 2, paragraph 13(8).
1984 c. 16.	Foreign Limitation Periods Act 1984.	Section 5.
1984 c. 28.	County Courts Act 1984.	In Schedule 2, paragraph 70.
1985 c. 61.	Administration of Justice Act 1985.	Section 58. In Schedule 9, paragraph 15.
1985 c. 68.	Housing Act 1985.	In Schedule 18, in paragraph 6 (2) the words from "and the Arbitration Act 1950" to the end.
1985 N.I. 12.	Credit Unions (Northern Ireland) Order 1985.	In Article 72(7)—(a) in the opening words, the words from "and without prejudice" to "1937"; (b) the words "the registrar or" and "registrar or".
1986 c. 45.	Insolvency Act 1986.	In Schedule 14, the entry relating to the Arbitration act 1950.
1988 c. 8.	Multilateral Investment Guarantee Agency Act 1988.	Section 8(3).

1988 c. 21.	Consumer Arbitration Agreements Act 1988.	The whole Act.
1989 N.I. 11.	Limitation (Northern Ireland) Order 1989.	Article 72. In schedule 3, paragraph 1.
1989 N.I. 19.	.Insolvency (Northern Ireland) Order 1989.	In Part II of Schedule 9, paragraph 66.
1990 c. 41.	Courts and Legal Services Act 1990.	Sections 99 and 101 to 103.
1991 N.I. 7.	Food Safety (Northern Ireland) Order 1991.	In Articles 8(8) and 11(10), the words from "and the provisions" to the end.
1992 c. 40.	Friendly Societies Act 1992.	In Schedule 16, paragraph 30 (1).
1995 c. 8.	Agricultural Tenancies Act 1995.	Section 28(4).
1995 c. 21.	Merchant Shipping Act 1995.	Section 96(10). Section 264(9).
1995 c. 42.	Private International Law (Miscellaneous Provisions) Act 1995.	Section 3.

An act to further and better facilitate resolution of disputes by arbitration; to give the force of law to the UNCITRAL Model Law on International Commercial Arbitration (as amended by the united nations commission on international trade law on 7 July 2006) in respect of both international arbitration and other arbitration; to give the force of law to the protocol on arbitration clauses opened at Geneva on the 24th day of September 1923, the convention on the execution of foreign arbitral awards done at Geneva on the 26th day of September 1927, the convention on the recognition and enforcement of foreign arbitral awards done at New York on 10 June 1958 and to the convention on the settlement of investment disputes between states and nationals of other states opened for signature in Washington on 18 march 1965; to repeal the arbitration acts 1954 to 1998; and to provide for related matters.

[8th March, 2010]

Be it enacted by the Oireachtas as follows:

Part 1

Preliminary and General

1 — Short Title and Commencement

(1) This Act may be cited as the Arbitration Act 2010.

(2) This Act shall come into operation 3 months after its passing.

2 — Interpretation

(1) In this Act:

arbitration	means (a) an international commercial arbitration, or (b) an arbitration which is not an international commercial arbitration;
arbitration agreement	shall be construed in accordance with Option 1 of Article 7; "award" includes a partial award;
consumer	means a natural person, whether in the State or not, who is acting for purposes outside the person's trade, business or profession;
Geneva Convention	means the Convention on the Execution of Foreign Arbitral Awards done at Geneva on the 26th day of September, 1927, the text of which is set out in Schedule 4;
Geneva Protocol	means the Protocol on Arbitration Clauses opened at Geneva on the 24th day of September, 1923, the text of which is set out in Schedule 5;
Minister	means the Minister for Justice, Equality and Law Reform;

* For a commentary on the Arbitration Act 2010, see Barry Mansfield, *Arbitration Act 2010 and Model Law: A Commentary* (Clarus Press, 2012). See also, Explanatory Memorandum to the Arbitration Act 2010, available at: <http://www.irishstatutebook.ie/pdf/2010/en.act.2010.0001.pdf>.

Model Law	means the UNCITRAL Model Law on International Commercial Arbitration (as adopted by the United Nations Commission on International Trade Law on 21 June 1985, with amendments as adopted by that Commission at its thirty-ninth session on 7 July 2006), the text of which is set out in Schedule 1;
New York Convention	means the Convention on the Recognition and Enforcement of Foreign Arbitral Awards, done at New York on 10 June 1958, the text of which is set out in Schedule 2;
State authority	means (a) a Minister of the Government, (b) the Commissioners of Public Works in Ireland, (c) the Irish Land Commission, (d) the Revenue Commissioners, (e) a body established by or under any enactment, and financed wholly or partly, whether directly or indirectly, by moneys provided, or loans made or guaranteed, by a Minister of the Government or the issue of shares held by or on behalf of any Minister of the Government;
Washington Convention	means the Convention on the Settlement of Investment Disputes between States and Nationals of Other States opened for signature in Washington on 18 March 1965, the text of which is set out in Schedule 3;

(2) In this Act

(a) a word or expression that is used in this Act and that is also used in the Model Law has, unless the context otherwise requires, the same meaning in this Act as it has in the Model Law, and

(b) a reference to an Article is a reference to an Article of the Model Law.

3 — Application of Act

(1) This Act shall not apply to an arbitration under an arbitration agreement concerning an arbitration which has commenced before the operative date but shall apply to an arbitration commenced on or after the operative date.

(2) In this section, "operative date" means the date on which this Act comes into operation pursuant to section 1.

4 — Repeals and Effect of Repeals

(1) Subject to subsection (2), the Arbitration Acts 1954 to 1998 are

repealed.
(2) Subject to section 3, the repeal of the Acts referred to in subsection (1) shall not prejudice or affect any proceedings, whether or not pending at the time of the repeal, in respect of any right, privilege, obligation or liability and any proceedings taken under those Acts in respect of any such right, privilege, obligation or liability acquired, accrued or incurred under the Acts may be instituted, continued or enforced as if the Acts concerned had not been repealed.
(3) In this section "proceedings" includes arbitral proceedings and civil or criminal proceedings.

5 — Expenses

The expenses incurred by the Minister in the administration of this Act shall, to such extent as may be sanctioned by the Minister for Finance, be paid out of moneys provided by the Oireachtas.

Part 2
Arbitration

6 — Adoption of Model Law

Subject to this Act, the Model Law shall have the force of law in the State and shall apply to arbitrations under arbitration agreements concerning
(a) international commercial arbitrations, or
(b) arbitrations which are not international commercial arbitrations.

7 — Commencement of Arbitral Proceedings

(1) For the purposes of this Act and for the purposes of section 496 of the Merchant Shipping Act 1894 (as amended by section 29) arbitral proceedings shall be deemed to be commenced on
(a) the date on which the parties to an arbitration agreement so provide as being the commencement date for the purposes of the commencement of arbitral proceedings under the agreement, or
(b) where no provision has been made by the parties as to commencement of proceedings as referred to in paragraph (a), the date on which a written communication containing a request for the dispute to be referred to arbitration is received by the respondent.
(2) The Statute of Limitations 1957 is amended by substituting the following section for section 74:
74(1) For the purposes of this Act and for the purposes of any other limitation enactment, arbitral proceedings shall be deemed to be commenced on
(a) the date on which the parties to an arbitration agreement so provide as being the commencement date for the purposes of the commencement of

arbitral proceedings under the agreement, or
(b) where no provision has been made by the parties as to commencement as referred to in paragraph (a), the date on which a written communication containing a request for the dispute to be referred to arbitration is received by the respondent.
(2) For the purposes of subsection (1)(b), unless the parties otherwise agree a written communication is deemed to have been received if it is served or given to the respondent in one or more of the following ways:
(a) by delivering it to the respondent personally;
(b) by delivering it to the respondent's place of business, habitual residence or postal address;
(c) where none of the addresses referred to in paragraph (b) can be found after making reasonable inquiry, by sending it by pre-paid registered post or by any other form of recorded delivery service addressed to the respondent at his or her last known place of business, habitual residence or postal address.
(3) Unless the parties otherwise agree, where a written communication under this section has been delivered to a respondent in accordance with subsection (2), the communication is deemed to have been received on the day it was so delivered.
(4) For the purposes of subsection (2), a company registered under the Companies Acts shall be deemed to be habitually resident at its registered office in the State and every other body corporate (wherever it is incorporated) and every unincorporated body (wherever it carries out its activities) shall be deemed to be habitually resident at its principal office or place of business.

8 — Construction of Model Law and Construction of Arbitration Clauses

(1) Judicial notice shall be taken of the *travaux préparatoires* of the United Nations Commission on International Trade Law and its working group relating to the preparation of the Model Law.
(2) The *travaux préparatoires* referred to in subsection (1) may be considered when interpreting the meaning of any provision of the Model Law and shall be given such weight as is appropriate in the circumstances.
(3) Where parties agree that disputes under a contract or agreement or disputes arising out of a contract or agreement shall be submitted to arbitration, this shall include disputes as to the existence or validity of the contract or agreement.

9 — Functions of High Court

(1) The High Court is

(a) specified for the purposes of Article 6,

(b) the relevant court for the purposes of Article 9, and

(c) the court of competent jurisdiction for the purposes of Articles 17H, 17I, 17J, 27, 35 and 36.

(2) The functions of the High Court

(a) under an Article referred to in subsection (1), or

(b) under sections 10, 23 or 25,

shall be performed by the President or by such other judge of the High Court as may be nominated by the President subject to any rules of court made in that behalf.

(3) An application may be made in summary manner to the President or to such other judge of the High Court as may be nominated by the President under subsection (2).

(4) In this section "President" means the President of the High Court.

10 — Court Powers Exercisable in Support of Arbitral Proceedings

(1) Subject to subsection (2), the High Court shall have the same powers in relation to Articles 9 and 27 as it has in any other action or matter before the Court.

(2) When exercising any powers in relation to Articles 9 or 27, the High Court shall not, unless otherwise agreed by the parties, make any order relating to security for costs of the arbitration or make any order for discovery of documents.

11 — Determination of Court to be Final

There shall be no appeal from

(a) any court determination of a stay application, pursuant to Article 8(1) of the Model Law or Article II(3) of the New York Convention,

(b) any determination by the High Court

(i) of an application for setting aside an award under Article 34 of the Model Law, or

(ii) of an application under Chapter VIII of the Model Law for the recognition and enforcement of an award made in an international commercial arbitration, or

(c) any determination by the High Court in relation to an application to recognise or enforce an arbitral award pursant to the Geneva Convention, New York Convention or Washington Convention.

12 — Time Limits for Setting Aside Awards on Grounds of Public Policy

Notwithstanding Article 34(3), an application to the High Court to set aside an award on the grounds that the award is in conflict with the public policy of the State shall be made within a period of 56 days from the date on which the circumstances giving rise to the application became known or ought reasonably to have become known to the party concerned.

13 — Default Number of Arbitrators

Unless otherwise agreed by the parties, the arbitral tribunal shall consist of one arbitrator only.

14 — Examination of Witnesses

Unless otherwise agreed by the parties, the arbitral tribunal may for the purposes of the arbitral proceedings concerned

(a) direct that a party to an arbitration agreement or a witness who gives evidence in proceedings before the arbitral tribunal be examined on oath or on affirmation, and

(b) administer oaths or affirmations for the purposes of the examination.

15 — Taking Evidence in State in Aid of Foreign Arbitration

The reference in Article 27 to an arbitral tribunal includes a reference to an arbitral tribunal conducting arbitral proceedings in a place other than the State.

16 — Consolidation of and Concurrent Arbitrations

(1) Where the parties to an arbitration agreement so agree

(a) arbitral proceedings shall be consolidated with other arbitral proceedings, including arbitral proceedings involving a different party or parties with the agreement of that party or parties,

(b) concurrent hearings shall be held,

on such terms as may be agreed between the parties concerned.

(2) The arbitral tribunal shall not order the consolidation of proceedings or concurrent hearings unless the parties agree to the making of such an order.

17 — Reference of Interpleader to Arbitration

(1) Subject to subsection (2), where in legal proceedings relief by way of interpleader is granted by a court and it appears to the court that the issue between the claimants is one in respect of which there is an arbitration agreement between the claimants, the court shall direct that the issue between the claimants be determined in accordance with the agreement.

(2) A court shall not direct that the issue between the claimants referred to in subsection (1) be determined in accordance with the arbitration agreement concerned where the court finds that the arbitration agreement is

null and void, inoperative or incapable of being performed.
(3) Where subsection (1) applies but the court does not direct that the issue be determined in accordance with the arbitration agreement, any provision that an award is a condition precedent to the bringing of legal proceedings in respect of any matter shall not affect the determination of that issue by the court.

18 — Interest

(1) The parties to an arbitration agreement may agree on the arbitral tribunal's powers regarding the award of interest.
(2) Unless otherwise agreed by the parties, the arbitral tribunal may award simple or compound interest from the dates, at the rates and with the rests that it considers fair and reasonable
(a) on all or part of any amount awarded by the arbitral tribunal, in respect of any period up to the date of the award, or
(b) on all or part of any amount claimed in the arbitration and outstanding at the commencement of the arbitration but paid before the award was made, in respect of any period up to the date of payment.
(3) Unless otherwise agreed by the parties, the arbitral tribunal may award simple or compound interest from the date of the award (or any later date) until payment, at the rates and with the rests that it considers fair and reasonable, on the outstanding amount of any award (including any award of interest under subsection (2) and any award of costs).
(4) References in this section to an amount awarded by the arbitral tribunal include an amount payable in consequence of a declaratory award by the arbitral tribunal.
(5) This section is without prejudice to any other power of the arbitral tribunal to award interest.

19 — Security for Costs

(1) Without prejudice to the generality of Article 19, the arbitral tribunal may, unless otherwise agreed by the parties, order a party to provide security for the costs of the arbitration.
(2) A party shall not be ordered by an arbitral tribunal to provide security for the costs of the arbitration solely on the ground that the party is
(a) an individual who is domiciled, habitually resident, or carrying on business outside the State, or
(b) a body corporate established under a law of a place other than the State or whose central management and control is situated outside the State.

20 — Specific Performance

Without prejudice to the generality of the Model Law, an arbitral tribunal shall, unless otherwise agreed by the parties, have the power to make an award requiring specific performance of a contract (other than a contract for the sale of land).

21 — Recoverability of Costs, Fees and Expenses of Tribunal

(1) The parties to an arbitration agreement may make such provision as to the costs of the arbitration as they see fit.

(2) An agreement of the parties to arbitrate subject to the rules of an arbitral institution shall be deemed to be an agreement to abide by the rules of that institution as to the costs of the arbitration.

(3) Where no provision for costs is made as referred to in subsection (1) or where a consumer is not bound by an agreement as to costs pursuant to subsection (6), the arbitral tribunal shall, subject to subsection (4), determine by award those costs as it sees fit.

(4) In the case of an arbitration (other than an international commercial arbitration) the arbitral tribunal shall, on the request of any of the parties to the proceedings made not later than 21 working days after the determination by the tribunal in relation to costs, make an order for the taxation of costs of the arbitration by a Taxing Master of the High Court, or as the case may be, the County Registrar; and the Taxing Master, or as the case may be, the County Registrar, shall in relation to any such taxation, have (with any necessary modifications) all the functions for the time being conferred on him or her under any enactment or in any rules of court in relation to the taxation of costs to be paid by one party to another in proceedings before a court.

(5) Where the arbitral tribunal makes a determination under subsection (3), it shall specify

(a) the grounds on which it acted,

(b) the items of recoverable costs, fees or expenses, as appropriate, and the amount referable to each, and

(c) by and to whom they shall be paid.

(6) Without prejudice to the generality of the European Communities (Unfair Terms in Consumer Contracts) Regulations 1995 and 2000, an arbitration agreement

(a) to which one of the parties to the agreement is a consumer, and

(b) a term of which provides that each party shall bear his or her own costs,

shall be deemed to be an unfair term for the purposes of those Regulations.

(7) Section 3 of the Legal Practitioners (Ireland) Act 1876 shall apply as if an arbitration were a proceeding in the High Court and the Court may make declarations and orders accordingly.

(8) In this section references to
"costs" include costs as between the parties and the fees and expenses of the arbitral tribunal;
"fees and expenses of the arbitral tribunal" include the fees and expenses of any expert appointed by the tribunal.

22 — Restriction on Liability of Arbitrators, etc.

(1) An arbitrator shall not be liable in any proceedings for anything done or omitted in the discharge or purported discharge of his or her functions.

(2) Subsection (1) shall apply to an employee, agent or advisor of an arbitrator and to an expert appointed under Article 26, as it applies to the arbitrator.

(3) An arbitral or other institution or person designated or requested by the parties to appoint or nominate an arbitrator shall not be liable for anything done or omitted in the discharge or purported discharge of that function.

(4) An arbitral or other institution or person by whom an arbitrator is appointed or nominated shall not be liable for anything done or omitted by the arbitrator (or his or her employees or agents) in the discharge or purported discharge of his or her functions as arbitrator.

(5) Subsections (3) and (4) shall apply to an employee or agent of an arbitral or other institution or person as they apply to that arbitral or other institution or that person mentioned in those subsections.

23 — Effect of Award

(1) An award (other than an award within the meaning of section 25) made by an arbitral tribunal under an arbitration agreement shall be enforceable in the State either by action or, by leave of the High Court, in the same manner as a judgment or order of that Court with the same effect and where leave is given, judgment may be entered in terms of the award.

(2) An award that is referred to in subsection (1) shall, unless otherwise agreed by the parties, be treated as binding for all purposes on the parties between whom it was made, and may accordingly be relied on by any of those parties by way of defence, set-off or otherwise in any legal proceedings in the State.

(3) Nothing in this section shall be construed as affecting the recognition or enforcement of an award under the Geneva Convention, the New York Convention or the Washington Convention.

(4) Articles 35 and 36 shall not apply in respect of an award in arbitral proceedings which took place in the State.

24 — New York Convention, Geneva Convention and Geneva Protocol

(1) Subject to this Act

(a) the New York Convention,
(b) the Geneva Convention, and
(c) the Geneva Protocol,
shall have the force of law in the State.
(2) Subject to this Act, Article II(2) and Article VII(1) of the New York Convention shall be interpreted in accordance with the recommendation adopted by the United Nations Commission on International Trade Law on 7 July 2006 at its thirty-ninth session concerning the interpretation of those Articles.
(3) Subject to this Act, Article II(3) of the New York Convention shall be construed in accordance with Article 8 of the Model Law.
(4) The Minister for Foreign Affairs may by order declare that any state specified in the order is a party to the New York Convention and, while such order is in force, the order shall be evidence that such state is a party to the Convention.

25 — Non-application of Provisions of Act to Washington Convention, save in Certain Circumstances

(1) This Act other than
(a) sections 11, 14 and 15, and
(b) section 6, in so far as it gives the force of law to Article 8(1) of the Model Law,
shall not apply to proceedings pursuant to the Washington Convention.
(2) In this section, “award” means an award rendered pursuant to the Washington Convention and includes any decision made
(a) pursuant to Article 49(2) of that Convention in relation to any question which the Tribunal referred to in that Article had omitted to decide in the award, or in relation to the rectification of any clerical, arithmetical or similar error in the award,
(b) pursuant to Articles 50, 51 and 52 of that Convention, interpreting, revising or annulling the award, and
(c) pursuant to Article 61(2) of that Convention in relation to costs.
(3) Subject to this Act, the Washington Convention shall have the force of law in the State.
(4) The Minister for Finance may discharge any obligations of the Government arising under Article 17 of the Washington Convention and any sums required for this purpose; and any administrative expenses incurred by the Minister for Finance as a result of acceptance by the State of the Washington Convention shall be paid out of moneys provided by the Oireachtas.

(5) The pecuniary obligations imposed by an award shall, by leave of the High Court, be enforceable in the same manner as a judgment or order of the High Court to the same effect and, where leave is so given, judgment may be entered for the amount due or, as the case may be, the balance outstanding under the award.

(6) Any person who applies to the High Court under subsection (5) for leave to enforce the pecuniary obligations imposed by an award shall lodge with his or her application a copy of the award certified in accordance with Article 54(2) of the Washington Convention.

(7) Where an application is made to the High Court pursuant to subsection (5), the High Court shall, in any case where enforcement of an award has been stayed, whether provisionally or otherwise, in accordance with Articles 50, 51 or 52 of the Washington Convention, stay enforcement of the pecuniary obligations imposed by the award and may, in any case where an application has been made in accordance with any of those Articles which, if granted, might result in a stay on the enforcement of the award, stay enforcement of the pecuniary obligations imposed by the award.

26 — Survival of Agreement and Authority of Arbitral Tribunal in Event of Death

(1) An arbitration agreement shall not be discharged by the death of any party thereto, either as respects the deceased or any other party, but shall in such an event be enforceable by or against the personal representatives of the deceased.

(2) The authority of an arbitral tribunal shall not be revoked by the death of any party by whom he or she was appointed.

(3) Nothing in this section shall affect the operation of any enactment or rule of law by virtue of which any right of action is extinguished by the death of a person.

27 — Provisions in Event of Bankruptcy

(1) Where an arbitration agreement forms part of a contract to which a bankrupt is a party, the agreement shall, if the assignee or trustee in bankruptcy does not disclaim the contract, be enforceable by or against him or her insofar as it relates to any dispute arising out of, or in connection with, such a contract.

(2) Where

(a) a person who has been adjudicated bankrupt had, before the commencement of the bankruptcy, become a party to an arbitration agreement, and

(b) any matter to which the agreement applies requires to be determined in

connection with or for the purposes of the bankruptcy proceedings, and
(c) the case is one to which subsection (1) does not apply,
then, any other party to the agreement or the assignee or, with the consent of the committee of inspection, the trustee in bankruptcy, may apply to the court having jurisdiction in the bankruptcy proceedings for an order directing that the matter in question shall be referred to arbitration in accordance with the agreement and that court may, if it is of the opinion that having regard to all the circumstances of the case, the matter ought to be determined by arbitration, make an order accordingly.
(3) In this section "assignee" means the Official Assignee in Bankruptcy.

28 — Full Applicability to State Parties

This Act shall apply to an arbitration under an arbitration agreement to which a State authority is a party.

29 — Application of Act to Arbitrations under Other Acts

(1) This Act, other than the excluded provisions, shall apply to every arbitration under any other Act as if the arbitration were pursuant to an arbitration agreement and as if that other Act were an arbitration agreement, except in so far as this Act is inconsistent with that other Act or with any rules or procedure authorised or recognised under that other Act.
(2) The enactments specified in column (2) of Schedule 6 are amended to the extent specified in that Schedule.
(3) In subsection (3) of section 496 of the Merchant Shipping Act 1894, the reference to legal proceedings shall be construed as including a reference to arbitration.
(4) In this section, "excluded provisions" means subsections (2) and (3), subsection (3) of section 8, sections 17, 26, 27, 30 and 31 and Articles 12 and 13.

30 — Exclusion of Certain Arbitrations

(1) This Act shall not apply to
(a) an arbitration under an arbitration agreement providing for the reference to, or the settlement by, arbitration of any question relating to the terms or conditions of employment or the remuneration of any employees, including persons employed by or under the State or local authorities, or
(b) an arbitration under section 70 of the Industrial Relations Act 1946.
(2) Section 18 shall not apply to an arbitration conducted by a property arbitrator appointed under section 2 of the Property Values (Arbitration and Appeals) Act 1960.

31 — Arbitration Agreements and Small Claims, etc.

(1) Subject to subsection (2), a party to an arbitration agreement who is a

consumer shall not be bound (unless he or she otherwise agrees at any time after the dispute has arisen) by an arbitration agreement where

(a) the agreement between the parties contains a term which has not been individually negotiated concerning the requirement to submit to arbitration disputes which may arise, and

(b) the dispute which has arisen between the parties to the agreement involves a claim for an amount not exceeding €5,000.

(2) For the avoidance of doubt, a reference in this section to a consumer shall not include an amateur sportsperson who, in his or her capacity as such, is a party to an arbitration agreement that contains a term concerning the requirement to submit to arbitration.

Part 3

Reference to Arbitration where Proceedings Pending before Court

32 — Power of High Court and Circuit Court to Adjourn Proceedings to Facilitate Arbitration

(1) Without prejudice to any provision of any other enactment or rule of law, the High Court or the Circuit Court may at any time whether before or during the trial of any civil proceedings before it

(a) if it thinks it appropriate to do so, and

(b) the parties to the proceedings so consent,

by order adjourn the proceedings to enable the parties to consider whether any or all of the matters in dispute might be determined by arbitration.

(2) Where a court makes an order under subsection (1), the adjournment shall be for such period as the court thinks fit.

(3) The parties to the proceedings shall, on or before the expiry of the period referred to in subsection (2), inform the court hearing the civil proceedings concerned whether or not agreement has been reached between the parties that any or all of the matters in dispute should be dealt with by arbitration.

(4) Where such agreement has been reached, the agreement shall be treated as an arbitration agreement for the purposes of this Act.

(5) The court, in respect of an agreement referred to in subsection (4)

(a) where the agreement relates to all of the matters in dispute, shall by order provide for the discontinuance of the proceedings and may make such order as to the costs of the proceedings as it thinks fit, or

(b) where the agreement relates to part but not all of the matters in dispute, may make such order as to the discontinuance of the proceedings as it thinks fit.

(6) Where no agreement has been reached the court may make such order as

it thinks fit in relation to the continuance of the proceedings.
(7) This section is in addition to and not in substitution for any power of a court to adjourn civil proceedings before it.

SCHEDULES

Schedule 1 contains the text of the Model Law.[1]

Schedule 2 contains the text of the New York Convention.[2]

Schedule 3 contains the text of the Washington Convention.[3]

Schedule 4 contains the text of the Geneva Convention.[4]

Schedule 5 contains the text of the Geneva Protocol.[5]

Schedule 6 contains details of the enactments amended by this Act.[6]

[1] See UNCITRAL Model Law on International Commercial Arbitration, pp. 643-659.
[2] See New York Convention, pp. 256-260.
[3] The Washington Convention is not reproduced here.
[4] The Geneva Convention is not reproduced here.
[5] The Geneva Protocol is not reproduced here.
[6] Schedule 6 is not reproduced here.

ARBITRATION (SCOTLAND) ACT 2010 *

The Bill for this Act of the Scottish Parliament was passed by the Parliament on 18th November 2009 and received Royal Assent on 5th January 2010

An Act of the Scottish Parliament to make provision about arbitration.

Introductory

1 — Founding Principles

The founding principles of this Act are

(a) that the object of arbitration is to resolve disputes fairly, impartially and without unnecessary delay or expense,

(b) that parties should be free to agree how to resolve disputes subject only to such safeguards as are necessary in the public interest,

(c) that the court should not intervene in an arbitration except as provided by this Act.

Anyone construing this Act must have regard to the founding principles when doing so.

2 — Key Terms

In this Act, unless the contrary intention appears "arbitration" includes

(a) domestic arbitration,

(b) arbitration between parties residing, or carrying on business, anywhere in the United Kingdom, and

(c) international arbitration,

"arbitrator" means a sole arbitrator or a member of a tribunal,

"dispute" includes

(a) any refusal to accept a claim, and

(b) any other difference (whether contractual or not),

"party" means a party to an arbitration,

"rules" means the Scottish Arbitration Rules (see section 7), and

"tribunal" means a sole arbitrator or panel of arbitrators.

(2) References in this Act to "an arbitration", "the arbitration" or "arbitrations" are references to a particular arbitration process or, as the case may be, to particular arbitration processes.

(3) References in this Act to a tribunal conducting an arbitration are references to the tribunal doing anything in relation to the arbitration, including

(a) making a decision about procedure or evidence, and

(b) making an award.

3 — Seat of Arbitration

(1) An arbitration is "seated in Scotland" if

(a) Scotland is designated as the juridical seat of the arbitration

---

* For a commentary on the Arbitration (Scotland) Act 2010, see Fraser Davidson, Hew Dundas and David Bartos, *Arbitration (Scotland) Act 2010* (2nd edn, W. Green, 2014). See also, Hew Dundas, 'Chapter 27: Arbitration in Scotland' in Julian D. M. Lew and others (eds), *Arbitration in England,*

(i) by the parties,
(ii) by any third party to whom the parties give power to so designate, or
(iii) where the parties fail to designate or so authorise a third party, by the tribunal, or
(b) in the absence of any such designation, the court determines that Scotland is to be the juridical seat of the arbitration.
(2) The fact that an arbitration is seated in Scotland does not affect the substantive law to be used to decide the dispute.

Arbitration Agreements

4 — Arbitration Agreement

An "arbitration agreement" is an agreement to submit a present or future dispute to arbitration (including any agreement which provides for arbitration in accordance with arbitration provisions contained in a separate document).

5 — Separability

(1) An arbitration agreement which forms (or was intended to form) part only of an agreement is to be treated as a distinct agreement.
(2) An arbitration agreement is not void, voidable or otherwise unenforceable only because the agreement of which it forms part is void, voidable or otherwise unenforceable.
(3) A dispute about the validity of an agreement which includes an arbitration agreement may be arbitrated in accordance with that arbitration agreement.

6 — Law Governing Arbitration Agreement

Where
(a) the parties to an arbitration agreement agree that an arbitration under that agreement is to be seated in Scotland, but
(b) the arbitration agreement does not specify the law which is to govern it, then, unless the parties otherwise agree, the arbitration agreement is to be governed by Scots law.

Scottish Arbitration Rules

7 — Scottish Arbitration Rules

The Scottish Arbitration Rules set out in schedule 1 are to govern every arbitration seated in Scotland (unless, in the case of a default rule, the parties otherwise agree).

8 — Mandatory Rules

The following rules, called "mandatory rules", cannot be modified or disapplied (by an arbitration agreement, by any other agreement between the parties or by any other means) in relation to any arbitration seated in

with Chapters on Scotland and Ireland (Kluwer Law International, 2013), pp. 595-626.

Scotland
rule 3 (arbitrator to be an individual)
rule 4 (eligibility to act as an arbitrator)
rule 7 (failure of appointment procedure)
rule 8 (duty to disclose any conflict of interests)
rules 12 to 16 (removal or resignation of arbitrator or dismissal of tribunal)
rules 19 to 21 and 23 (jurisdiction of tribunal)
rules 24 and 25 (general duties of tribunal and parties)
rule 42 (point of law referral: procedure etc.)
rule 44 (time limit variation: procedure etc.)
rule 45 (securing attendance of witnesses and disclosure of evidence)
rule 48 (power to award payment and damages)
rule 50 (interest)
rule 54 (part awards)
rule 56 (power to withhold award if fees or expenses not paid)
rule 60 (arbitrators' fees and expenses)
rule 63 (ban on pre-dispute agreements about liability for arbitration expenses)
rules 67, 68, 70, 71 and 72 (challenging awards)
rules 73 to 75 (immunity)
rule 76 (loss of right to object)
rule 77 (independence of arbitrator)
rule 79 (death of arbitrator)
rule 82 (rules applicable to umpires)

9 — Default Rules

(1) The non-mandatory rules are called the "default rules".

(2) A default rule applies in relation to an arbitration seated in Scotland only in so far as the parties have not agreed to modify or disapply that rule (or any part of it) in relation to that arbitration.

(3) Parties may so agree

(a) in the arbitration agreement, or

(b) by any other means at any time before or after the arbitration begins.

(4) Parties are to be treated as having agreed to modify or disapply a default rule

(a) if or to the extent that the rule is inconsistent with or disapplied by

(i) the arbitration agreement,

(ii) any arbitration rules or other document (for example, the UNCITRAL Model Law, the UNCITRAL Arbitration Rules or other institutional rules) which the parties agree are to govern the arbitration, or

(iii) anything done with the agreement of the parties, or
(b) if they choose a law other than Scots law as the applicable law in respect of the rule's subject matter.
This subsection does not affect the generality of subsections (2) and (3).

Suspension of Legal Proceedings

10 — Suspension of Legal Proceedings

(1) The court must, on an application by a party to legal proceedings concerning any matter under dispute, sist those proceedings in so far as they concern that matter if
(a) an arbitration agreement provides that a dispute on the matter is to be resolved by arbitration (immediately or after the exhaustion of other dispute resolution procedures),
(b) the applicant is a party to the arbitration agreement (or is claiming through or under such a party),
(c) notice of the application has been given to the other parties to the legal proceedings,
(d) the applicant has not
(i) taken any step in the legal proceedings to answer any substantive claim against the applicant, or
(ii) otherwise acted since bringing the legal proceedings in a manner indicating a desire to have the dispute resolved by the legal proceedings rather than by arbitration, and
(e) nothing has caused the court to be satisfied that the arbitration agreement concerned is void, inoperative or incapable of being performed.
(2) Any provision in an arbitration agreement which prevents the bringing of the legal proceedings is void in relation to any proceedings which the court refuses to sist.
This subsection does not apply to statutory arbitrations.
(3) This section applies regardless of whether the arbitration concerned is to be seated in Scotland.

Enforcing and Challenging Arbitral Awards etc.

11 — Arbitral Award to be Final and Binding on Parties

(1) A tribunal's award is final and binding on the parties and any person claiming through or under them (but does not of itself bind any third party).
(2) In particular, an award ordering the rectification or reduction of a deed or other document is of no effect in so far as it would adversely affect the interests of any third party acting in good faith.
(3) This section does not affect the right of any person to challenge the award

(a) under Part 8 of the Scottish Arbitration Rules, or
(b) by any available arbitral process of appeal or review.
(4) This section does not apply in relation to a provisional award (see rule 53), such an award not being final and being binding only
(a) to the extent specified in the award, or
(b) until it is superseded by a subsequent award.

12 — Enforcement of Arbitral Awards

(1) The court may, on an application by any party, order that a tribunal's award may been forced as if it were an extract registered decree bearing a warrant for execution granted by the court.
(2) No such order may be made if the court is satisfied that the award is the subject of
(a) an appeal under Part 8 of the Scottish Arbitration Rules,
(b) an arbitral process of appeal or review, or
(c) a process of correction under rule 58 of the Scottish Arbitration Rules, which has not been finally determined.
(3) No such order may be made if the court is satisfied that the tribunal which made the award did not have jurisdiction to do so (and the court may restrict the extent of its order if satisfied that the tribunal did not have jurisdiction to make a part of the award).
(4) But a party may not object on the ground that the tribunal did not have jurisdiction if the party has lost the right to raise that objection by virtue of the Scottish Arbitration Rules (see rule 76).
(5) Unless the parties otherwise agree, a tribunal's award may be registered for execution in the Books of Council and Session or in the sheriff court books (provided that the arbitration agreement is itself so registered).
(6) This section applies regardless of whether the arbitration concerned was seated in Scotland.
(7) Nothing in this section or in section 13 affects any other right to rely on or enforce an award in pursuance of
(a) sections 19 to 21, or
(b) any other enactment or rule of law.
(8) In this section, "court" means the sheriff or the Court of Session.

13 — Court Intervention in Arbitrations

(1) Legal proceedings are competent in respect of
(a) a tribunal's award, or
(b) any other act or omission by a tribunal when conducting an arbitration, only as provided for in the Scottish Arbitration Rules (in so far as they apply to that arbitration) or in any other provision of this Act.

(2) In particular, a tribunal's award is not subject to review or appeal in any legal proceedings except as provided for in Part 8 of the Scottish Arbitration Rules.

(3) It is not competent for a party to raise the question of a tribunal's jurisdiction with the court except

(a) where objecting to an order being made under section 12, or

(b) as provided for in the Scottish Arbitration Rules (see rules 21, 22 and 67).

(4) Where the parties agree that the UNCITRAL Model Law is to apply to an arbitration, articles 6 and 11(2) to (5) of that Law are to have the force of law in Scotland in relation to that arbitration (as if article 6 specified the Court of Session and any sheriff court having jurisdiction).

14 — Persons Who Take No Part in Arbitral Proceedings

(1) A person alleged to be a party to an arbitration but who takes no part in the arbitration may, by court proceedings, question

(a) whether there is a valid arbitration agreement (or, in the case of a statutory arbitration, whether the enactment providing for arbitration applies to the dispute),

(b) whether the tribunal is properly constituted, or

(c) what matters have been submitted to arbitration in accordance with the arbitration agreement,

and the court may determine such a question by making such declaration, or by granting such interdict or other remedy, as it thinks appropriate.

(2) Such a person has the same right as a party who participates in the arbitration to appeal against any award made in the arbitration under rule 67 or 68 (jurisdictional and serious irregularity appeals) and rule 71(2) does not apply to such an appeal.

15 — Anonymity in Legal Proceedings

(1) A party to any civil proceedings relating to an arbitration (other than proceedings under section 12) may apply to the court for an order prohibiting the disclosure of the identity of a party to the arbitration in any report of the proceedings.

(2) On such an application, the court must grant the order unless satisfied that disclosure

(a) is required

(i) for the proper performance of the discloser's public functions, or

(ii) in order to enable any public body or office-holder to perform public functions properly,

(b) can reasonably be considered as being needed to protect a party's lawful

interests,
(c) would be in the public interest, or
(d) would be necessary in the interests of justice.
(3) The court's determination of an application for an order is final.

Statutory Arbitration

16 — Statutory Arbitration: Special Provisions

(1) "Statutory arbitration" is arbitration pursuant to an enactment which provides for a dispute to be submitted to arbitration.
(2) References in the Scottish Arbitration Rules (or in any other provision of this Act) to an arbitration agreement are, in the case of a statutory arbitration, references to the enactment which provides for a dispute to be resolved by arbitration.
(3) None of the Scottish Arbitration Rules (or other provisions of this Act) apply to a statutory arbitration if or to the extent that they are excluded by, or are inconsistent with, any provision made by virtue of any other enactment relating to the arbitration.
(4) Every statutory arbitration is to be taken to be seated in Scotland.
(5) The following rules do not apply in relation to statutory arbitration
rule 43 (extension of time limits)
rule 71(9) (power to declare provision of arbitration agreement void)
rule 80 (death of party)
(6) Despite rule 40, parties to a statutory arbitration may not agree to
(a) consolidate the arbitration with another arbitration,
(b) hold concurrent hearings, or
(c) authorise the tribunal to order such consolidation or the holding of concurrent hearings,
unless the arbitrations or hearings are to be conducted under the same enactment.

17 — Power to Adapt Enactments Providing for Statutory Arbitration

Ministers may by order
(a) modify any of the Scottish Arbitration Rules, or any other provisions of this Act, in so far as they apply to statutory arbitrations (or to particular statutory arbitrations),
(b) make such modifications of enactments which provide for disputes to be submitted to arbitration as they consider appropriate in consequence of, or in order to give full effect to, any of the Scottish Arbitration Rules or any other provisions of this Act.

Recognition and Enforcement of New York Convention Awards

18 — New York Convention Awards

(1) A "Convention award" is an award made in pursuance of a written arbitration agreement in the territory of a state (other than the United Kingdom) which is a party to the New York Convention.

(2) An award is to be treated for the purposes of this section as having been made at the seat of the arbitration.

(3) A declaration by Her Majesty by Order in Council that a state is a party to the Convention (or is a party in respect of any territory) is conclusive evidence of that fact.

19 — Recognition and Enforcement of New York Convention Awards

(1) A Convention award is to be recognised as binding on the persons as between whom it was made (and may accordingly be relied on by those persons in any legal proceedings in Scotland).

(2) The court may order that a Convention award may be enforced as if it were an extract registered decree bearing a warrant for execution granted by the court.

20 — Refusal of Recognition or Enforcement

(1) Recognition or enforcement of a Convention award may be refused only in accordance with this section.

(2) Recognition or enforcement of a Convention award may be refused if the person against whom it is invoked proves

(a) that a party was under some incapacity under the law applicable to the party,

(b) that the arbitration agreement was invalid under the law which the parties agree should govern it (or, failing any indication of that law, under the law of the country where the award was made),

(c) that the person

(i) was not given proper notice of the arbitral process or of the appointment of the tribunal, or

(ii) was otherwise unable to present the person's case,

(d) that the tribunal was constituted, or the arbitration was conducted, otherwise than in accordance with

(i) the agreement of the parties, or

(ii) failing such agreement, the law of the country where the arbitration took place.

(3) Recognition or enforcement of a Convention award may also be refused if the person against whom it is invoked proves that the award

(a) deals with a dispute not contemplated by or not falling within the

submission
to arbitration,
(b) contains decisions on matters beyond the scope of that submission,
(c) is not yet binding on the person, or
(d) has been set aside or suspended by a competent authority.
(4) Recognition or enforcement of a Convention award may also be refused if
(a) the award relates to a matter which is not capable of being settled by arbitration, or
(b) to do so would be contrary to public policy.
(5) A Convention award containing decisions on matters not submitted to arbitration may be recognised or enforced to the extent that it contains decisions on matters which were so submitted which are separable from decisions on matters not so submitted.
(6) The court before which a Convention award is sought to be relied on may, if an application for the setting aside or suspension of the award is made to a competent authority
(a) sist the decision on recognition or enforcement of the award,
(b) on the application of the party claiming recognition or enforcement, order the other party to give suitable security.
(7) In this section "competent authority" means a person who has authority to set aside or suspend the Convention award concerned in the country in which (or under the law of which) the Convention award concerned was made.

21 — Evidence to be Produced when Seeking Recognition or Enforcement

(1) A person seeking recognition or enforcement of a Convention award must produce
(a) the duly authenticated original award (or a duly certified copy of it), and
(b) the original arbitration agreement (or a duly certified copy of it).
(2) Such a person must also produce a translation of any award or agreement which is in a language other than English (certified by an official or sworn translator or by a diplomatic or consular agent).

22 — Saving for Other Bases of Recognition or Enforcement

Nothing in sections 19 to 21 affects any other right to rely on or enforce a Convention award in pursuance of any other enactment or rule of law.

Supplementary

23 — Prescription and Limitation

(1) The Prescription and Limitation (Scotland) Act 1973 (c. 52) is amended

as follows.
(2) In section 4 (positive prescription: interruption)
(a) in subsection (2)(b), after "Scotland" insert " in respect of which an arbitrator (or panel of arbitrators) has been appointed",
(b) in subsection (3)(a), for the words from "and" to "served" substitute "the date when the arbitration begins",
(c) for subsection (4) substitute
"(4) An arbitration begins for the purposes of this section
(a) when the parties to the arbitration agree that it begins, or
(b) in the absence of such agreement, in accordance with rule 1 of the Scottish Arbitration Rules (see section 7 of, and schedule 1 to, the Arbitration (Scotland) Act 2010 (asp 1)).".
(3) In section 9 (negative prescription: interruption)
(a) in subsection (3), for the words from "and" to "served" substitute "the date when the arbitration begins",
(b) in subsection (4), for "preliminary notice" substitute "the date when the arbitration begins".
(4) After section 19C, insert
"19CA Interruption of limitation period: arbitration
(1) Any period during which an arbitration is ongoing in relation to a matter is to be disregarded in any computation of the period specified in section 17 (2), 18(2), 18A(1) or 18B(2) of this Act in relation to that matter.
(2) In this section, "arbitration" means
(a) any arbitration in Scotland,
(b) any arbitration in a country other than Scotland, being an arbitration an award in which would be enforceable in Scotland.".
(5) In section 22A(4), for the words from "and" to "served" substitute "the date when the arbitration begins (within the meaning of section 4(4) of this Act)".
(6) After section 22C, insert
"22CA Interruption of limitation period for 1987 Act actions: arbitration
(1) Any period during which an arbitration is ongoing in relation to a matter is to be disregarded in any computation of the period specified in section 22B(2) or 22C(2) of this Act in relation to that matter.
(2) In this section, "arbitration" means
(a) any arbitration in Scotland,
(b) any arbitration in a country other than Scotland, being an arbitration an award in which would be enforceable in Scotland.".

24 — Arbitral Appointments Referee

(1) Ministers may, by order, authorise persons or types of person who may act as an arbitral appointments referee for the purposes of the Scottish Arbitration Rules.

(2) Ministers must, when making such an order, have regard to the desirability of ensuring that arbitral appointments referees

(a) have experience relevant to making arbitral appointments, and

(b) are able to provide training, and to operate disciplinary procedures, designed to ensure that arbitrators conduct themselves appropriately.

(3) Despite subsection (2)(b), an arbitral appointments referee is not obliged to appoint arbitrators in respect of whom the referee provides training or operates disciplinary procedures.

25 — Power of Judge to Act as Arbitrator or Umpire

(1) A judge may act as an arbitrator or umpire only where

(a) the dispute being arbitrated appears to the judge to be of commercial character,

and

(b) the Lord President, having considered the state of Court of Session business, has authorised the judge to so act.

(2) A fee of such amount as Ministers may by order prescribe is payable in the Court of Session for the services of a judge acting as an arbitrator or umpire.

(3) Any jurisdiction exercisable by the Outer House under the Scottish Arbitration Rules (or any other provision of this Act) in relation to

(a) a judge acting as a sole arbitrator or umpire, or

(b) a tribunal which the judge forms part of,

is to be exercisable instead by the Inner House (and the Inner House's decision on any matter is final).

(4) In this section

"judge" means a judge of the Court of Session, and

"Lord President" means the Lord President of the Court of Session.

26 — Amendments to UNCITRAL Model Law or Rules or New York Convention

(1) Ministers may by order modify

(a) the Scottish Arbitration Rules,

(b) any other provision of this Act, or

(c) any enactment which provides for disputes to be resolved by arbitration,

in such manner as they consider appropriate in consequence of any amendment made to the UNCITRAL Model Law, the UNCITRAL

Arbitration Rules or the New York Convention.
(2) Before making such an order, Ministers must consult such persons appearing to them to have an interest in the law of arbitration as they think fit.

27 — Amendment of Conveyancing (Scotland) Act 1924 (c. 27)

In section 46 of the Conveyancing (Scotland) Act 1924
(a) in subsection (2), for "This section" substitute "Subsection (1)", and
(b) after subsection (2) insert
"(3) Where
(a) an arbitral award orders the reduction of a deed or other document recorded in the Register of Sasines (or forming a midcouple or link of title in a title recorded in that Register), and
(b) the court orders that the award may be enforced in accordance with section 12 of the Arbitration (Scotland) Act 2010 (asp 1),
subsection (1) applies to the arbitral award as it applies to a decree of reduction of a deed recorded in the Register of Sasines.".

28 — Articles of Regulation 1695

The 25th Act of the Articles of Regulation 1695 does not apply in relation to arbitration.

29 — Repeals

The repeals of the enactments specified in column 1 of schedule 2 have effect to the extent specified in column 2.

30 — Arbitrability of Disputes

Nothing in this Act makes any dispute capable of being arbitrated if, because of its subject-matter, it would not otherwise be capable of being arbitrated.

Final Provisions

31 — Interpretation

(1) In this Act, unless the contrary intention appears

arbitral appointments referee	means a person authorised under section 24,
arbitration	has the meaning given by section 2,
arbitration agreement	has the meaning given by section 4,
arbitrator	has the meaning given by section 2,
claim	includes counterclaim,
Convention award	has the meaning given by section 18,
court	means the Outer House or the sheriff (except in sections 1, 3, 10, 13 and 15, where it means any court),

default rule	has the meaning given by section 9(1),
dispute	has the meaning given by section 2,
Inner House	means the Inner House of the Court of Session,
mandatory rule	has the meaning given by section 8,
Ministers	means the Scottish Ministers,
New York Convention	means the Convention on the Recognition and Enforcement of Foreign Arbitral Awards adopted by the United Nations Conference on International Commercial Arbitration on 10 June 1958,
Outer House	means the Outer House of the Court of Session,
party	is to be construed in accordance with section 2 and subsection (2) below,
rule	means one of the Scottish Arbitration Rules,
Scottish Arbitration Rules	means the rules set out in schedule 1,
seated in Scotland	has the meaning given by section 3,
statutory arbitration	has the meaning given by section 16(1),
Tribunal	has the meaning given by section 2,
UNCITRAL Arbitration Rules	means the arbitration rules adopted by UNCITRAL on 28 April 1976, and
UNCITRAL Model Law	means the UNCITRAL Model Law on International Commercial Arbitration as adopted by the United Nations Commission on International Trade Law on 21 June 1985 (as amended in 2006).

(2) This Act applies in relation to arbitrations and disputes between three or more parties as it applies in relation to arbitrations and disputes between two parties (with references to both parties being read in such cases as references to all the parties).

32 — Ancillary Provision

(1) Ministers may by order make any supplementary, incidental, consequential, transitional, transitory or saving provision which they consider appropriate for the purposes of, or in connection with, or for the purposes of giving full effect to, any provision of this Act.

(2) Such an order may modify any enactment, instrument or document.

33 — Orders

(1) Any power of Ministers to make orders under this Act

(a) is exercisable by statutory instrument, and

(b) includes power to make

(i) any supplementary, incidental, consequential, transitional, transitory or saving provision which Ministers consider appropriate,

(ii) different provision for different purposes.

(2) A statutory instrument containing such an order (or an Order in Council made under section 18) is subject to annulment in pursuance of a resolution of the Scottish Parliament.

This subsection does not apply

(a) to orders made under section 35(2) (commencement orders), or

(b) where subsection (3) makes contrary provision.

(3) An order

(a) under section 17 or 32 which adds to, replaces or omits any text in this or any other Act,

(b) under section 26, or

(c) under section 36(4),

may be made only if a draft of the statutory instrument containing the order has been laid before, and approved by resolution of, the Scottish Parliament.

34 — Crown Application

(1) This Act binds the Crown.

(2) Her Majesty may be represented in any arbitration to which she is a party otherwise than in right of the Crown by such person as she may appoint in writing under the Royal Sign Manual.

(3) The Prince and Steward of Scotland may be represented in any arbitration to which he is a party by such person as he may appoint.

(4) References in this Act to a party to an arbitration are, where subsection (2) or (3) applies, to be read as references to the appointed representative.

35 — Commencement

(1) The following provisions come into force on Royal Assent

section 2

sections 31 to 34

this section

section 37

(2) Other provisions come into force on the day Ministers by order appoint.

36 — Transitional Provisions

(1) This Act does not apply to an arbitration begun before commencement.

(2) This Act otherwise applies to an arbitration agreement whether made on, before or after commencement.
(3) Despite subsection (2), this Act does not apply to an arbitration arising under an arbitration agreement (other than an enactment) made before commencement if the parties agree that this Act is not to apply to that arbitration.
(4) Ministers may by order specify any day falling at least 5 years after commencement as the day on which subsection (3) is to cease to have effect.
(5) Before making such an order, Ministers must consult such persons appearing to them to have an interest in the law of arbitration as they think fit.
(6) Any reference to an arbiter in an arbitration agreement made before commencement is to be treated as being a reference to an arbitrator.
(7) Any reference in an enactment to a decree arbitral is to be treated for the purposes of section 12 as being a reference to a tribunal's award.
(8) An express provision in an arbitration agreement made before commencement which disapplies section 3 of the Administration of Justice (Scotland) Act 1972 (c. 59) in relation to an arbitration arising under that agreement is, unless the parties otherwise agree, to be treated as being an agreement to disapply rules 41 and 69 in relation to such an arbitration.
(9) In this section, "commencement" means the day on which this section comes into force.

37 — Short title

This Act is called the Arbitration (Scotland) Act 2010.

SCHEDULES

Schedule 1 (Introduced by Section 7)

Scottish Arbitration Rules

Mandatory rules are marked "M".
Default rules are marked "D".

Part 1

Commencement and Constitution of Tribunal etc.

Rule 1 — Commencement of Arbitration D

1 An arbitration begins when a party to an arbitration agreement (or any person claiming through or under such a party) gives the other party notice submitting a dispute to arbitration in accordance with the agreement.

Rule 2 — Appointment of Tribunal D

2 An arbitration agreement need not appoint (or provide for appointment of) the tribunal, but if it does so provide it may

(a) specify who is to form the tribunal,
(b) require the parties to appoint the tribunal,
(c) permit another person to appoint the tribunal, or
(d) provide for the tribunal to be appointed in any other way.

Rule 3 — Arbitrator to be an Individual M

3 Only an individual may act as an arbitrator.

Rule 4 — Eligibility to Act as Arbitrator M

4 An individual is ineligible to act as an arbitrator if the individual is

(a) aged under 16, or
(b) an incapable adult (within the meaning of section 1(6) of the Adults with Incapacity (Scotland) Act 2000 (asp 4)).

Rule 5 — Number of Arbitrators D

5 Where there is no agreement as to the number of arbitrators, the tribunal is to consist of a sole arbitrator.

Rule 6 — Method of Appointment D

6 The tribunal is to be appointed as follows

(a) where there is to be a sole arbitrator, the parties must appoint an eligible individual jointly (and must do so within 28 days of either party requesting the other to do so),
(b) where there is to be a tribunal consisting of two or more arbitrators
(i) each party must appoint an eligible individual as an arbitrator (and must do so within 28 days of the other party requesting it to do so), and
(ii) where more arbitrators are to be appointed, the arbitrators appointed by the parties must appoint eligible individuals as the remaining arbitrators.

Rule 7 — Failure of Appointment Procedure M

7 (1) This rule applies where a tribunal (or any arbitrator who is to form part of a tribunal) is not, or cannot be, appointed in accordance with

(a) any appointment procedure set out in the arbitration agreement (or otherwise agreed between the parties), or

(b) rule 6.

(2) Unless the parties otherwise agree, either party may refer the matter to an arbitral appointments referee.

(3) The referring party must give notice of the reference to the other party.

(4) That other party may object to the reference within 7 days of notice of reference being given by making an objection to

(a) the referring party, and

(b) the arbitral appointments referee.

(5) If

(a) no such objection is made within that 7 day period, or

(b) the other party waives the right to object before the end of that period, the arbitral appointments referee may make the necessary appointment.

(6) Where

(a) a party objects to the arbitral appointments referee making an appointment,

(b) an arbitral appointments referee fails to make an appointment within 21 days of the matter being referred, or

(c) the parties agree not to refer the matter to an arbitral appointments referee, the court may, on an application by any party, make the necessary appointment.

(7) The court's decision on whom to appoint is final.

(8) Before making an appointment under this rule, the arbitral appointments referee or, as the case may be, the court must have regard to

(a) the nature and subject-matter of the dispute,

(b) the terms of the arbitration agreement (including, in particular, any terms relating to appointment of arbitrators), and

(c) the skills, qualifications, knowledge and experience which would make an individual suitable to determine the dispute.

(9) Where an arbitral appointments referee or the court makes an appointment under this rule, the arbitration agreement has effect as if it required that appointment.

Rule 8 — Duty to Disclose any Conflict of Interests M

8 (1) This rule applies to

(a) arbitrators, and

(b) individuals who have been asked to be an arbitrator but who have not yet been appointed.

(2) An individual to whom this rule applies must, without delay disclose

(a) to the parties, and

(b) in the case of an individual not yet appointed as an arbitrator, to any arbitral appointments referee, other third party or court considering whether to appoint the individual as an arbitrator,

any circumstances known to the individual (or which become known to the individual before the arbitration ends) which might reasonably be considered relevant when considering whether the individual is impartial and independent.

Rule 9 — Arbitrator's Tenure D

9 An arbitrator's tenure ends if

(a) the arbitrator becomes ineligible to act as an arbitrator (see rule 4),

(b) the tribunal revokes the arbitrator's appointment (see rule 10),

(c) the arbitrator is removed by the parties, a third party or the Outer House (see rules 11 and 12),

(d) the Outer House dismisses the tribunal of which the arbitrator forms part (see rule 13), or

(e) the arbitrator resigns (see rule 15) or dies (see rule 79).

Rule 10 — Challenge to Appointment of Arbitrator D

10 (1) A party may object to the tribunal about the appointment of an arbitrator.

(2) An objection is competent only if

(a) it is made on the ground that the arbitrator

(i) is not impartial and independent,

(ii) has not treated the parties fairly, or

(iii) does not have a qualification which the parties agreed (before the arbitrator's appointment) that the arbitrator must have,

(b) it states the facts on which it is based,

(c) it is made within 14 days of the objector becoming aware of those facts, and

(d) notice of it is given to the other party.

(3) The tribunal may deal with an objection by confirming or revoking the appointment.

(4) If the tribunal fails to make a decision within 14 days of a competent objection being made, the appointment is revoked.

Rule 11 — Removal of Arbitrator by Parties D

11 (1) An arbitrator may be removed

(a) by the parties acting jointly, or
(b) by any third party to whom the parties give power to remove an arbitrator.
(2) A removal is effected by notifying the arbitrator.

Rule 12 — Removal of Arbitrator by Court M

12 The Outer House may remove an arbitrator if satisfied on the application by any party
(a) that the arbitrator is not impartial and independent,
(b) that the arbitrator has not treated the parties fairly,
(c) that the arbitrator is incapable of acting as an arbitrator in the arbitration (or that there are justifiable doubts about the arbitrator's ability to so act),
(d) that the arbitrator does not have a qualification which the parties agreed (before the arbitrator's appointment) that the arbitrator must have,
(e) that substantial injustice has been or will be caused to that party because the arbitrator has failed to conduct the arbitration in accordance with
(i) the arbitration agreement,
(ii) these rules (in so far as they apply), or
(iii) any other agreement by the parties relating to conduct of the arbitration.

Rule 13 — Dismissal of Tribunal by Court M

13 The Outer House may dismiss the tribunal if satisfied on the application by a party that substantial injustice has been or will be caused to that party because the tribunal has failed to conduct the arbitration in accordance with
(a) the arbitration agreement,
(b) these rules (in so far as they apply), or
(c) any other agreement by the parties relating to conduct of the arbitration.

Rule 14 — Removal and Dismissal by Court: Supplementary M

14 (1) The Outer House may remove an arbitrator, or dismiss the tribunal, only if
(a) the arbitrator or, as the case may be, tribunal has been
(i) notified of the application for removal or dismissal, and
(ii) given the opportunity to make representations, and
(b) the Outer House is satisfied
(i) that any recourse available under rule 10 has been exhausted, and
(ii) that any available recourse to a third party who the parties have agreed is to have power to remove an arbitrator (or dismiss the tribunal) has been exhausted.
(2) A decision of the Outer House under rule 12 or 13 is final.
(3) The tribunal may continue with the arbitration pending the Outer House's decision under rule 12 or 13.

Rule 15 — Resignation of Arbitrator M

15 (1) An arbitrator may resign (by giving notice of resignation to the parties and any other arbitrators) if

(a) the parties consent to the resignation,

(b) the arbitrator has a contractual right to resign in the circumstances,

(c) the arbitrator's appointment is challenged under rule 10 or 12,

(d) the parties disapply or modify rule 34(1) (expert opinions) after the arbitrator is appointed, or

(e) the Outer House has authorised the resignation.

(2) The Outer House may authorise a resignation only if satisfied, on an application by the arbitrator, that it is reasonable for the arbitrator to resign.

(3) The Outer House's determination of an application for resignation is final.

Rule 16 — Liability etc. of Arbitrator When Tenure Ends M

16 (1) Where an arbitrator's tenure ends, the Outer House may, on an application by any party or the arbitrator concerned, make such order as it thinks fit

(a) about the arbitrator's entitlement (if any) to fees and expenses,

(b) about the repaying of fees or expenses already paid to the arbitrator,

(c) where the arbitrator has resigned, about the arbitrator's liability in respect of acting as an arbitrator.

(2) The Outer House must, when considering whether to make an order in relation to an arbitrator who has resigned, have particular regard to whether the resignation was made in accordance with rule 15.

(3) The Outer House's determination of an application for an order is final.

Rule 17 — Reconstitution of Tribunal D

17 (1) Where an arbitrator's tenure ends, the tribunal must be reconstituted

(a) in accordance with the procedure used to constitute the original tribunal, or

(b) where that procedure fails, in accordance with rules 6 and 7.

(2) It is for the reconstituted tribunal to decide the extent, if any, to which previous proceedings (including any award made, appointment by or other act done by the previous tribunal) should stand.

(3) The reconstituted tribunal's decision does not affect a party's right to object or appeal on any ground which arose before the tribunal made its decision.

Rule 18 — Arbitrators Nominated in Arbitration Agreements D

18 Any provision in an arbitration agreement which specifies who is to be an arbitrator ceases to have effect in relation to an arbitration when the

specified individual's tenure as an arbitrator for that arbitration ends.

Part 2

Jurisdiction of Tribunal

Rule 19 — Power of Tribunal to Rule on own Jurisdiction M

19 The tribunal may rule on

(a) whether there is a valid arbitration agreement (or, in the case of a statutory arbitration, whether the enactment providing for arbitration applies to the dispute),

(b) whether the tribunal is properly constituted, and

(c) what matters have been submitted to arbitration in accordance with the arbitration agreement.

Rule 20 — Objections to Tribunal's Jurisdiction M

20 (1) Any party may object to the tribunal on the ground that the tribunal does not have, or has exceeded, its jurisdiction in relation to any matter.

(2) An objection must be made

(a) before, or as soon as is reasonably practicable after, the matter to which the objection relates is first raised in the arbitration, or

(b) where the tribunal considers that circumstances justify a later objection, by such later time as it may allow,

but, in any case, an objection may not be made after the tribunal makes its last award.

(3) If the tribunal upholds an objection it must

(a) end the arbitration in so far as it relates to a matter over which the tribunal has ruled it does not have jurisdiction, and

(b) set aside any provisional or part award already made in so far as the award relates to such a matter.

(4) The tribunal may

(a) rule on an objection independently from dealing with the subject-matter of the dispute, or

(b) delay ruling on an objection until it makes its award on the merits of the dispute (and include its ruling in that award),

but, where the parties agree which of these courses the tribunal should take, the tribunal must proceed accordingly.

Rule 21 — Appeal Against Tribunal's Ruling on Jurisdictional Objection M

21 (1) A party may, no later than 14 days after the tribunal's decision on an objection under rule 20, appeal to the Outer House against the decision.

(2) The tribunal may continue with the arbitration pending determination of the appeal.

(3) The Outer House's decision on the appeal is final.

Rule 22 — Referral of Point of Jurisdiction D

22 The Outer House may, on an application by any party, determine any question as to the tribunal's jurisdiction.

Rule 23 — Jurisdiction Referral: Procedure etc. M

23 (1) This rule applies only where an application is made under rule 22.

(2) Such an application is valid only if

(a) the parties have agreed that it may be made, or

(b) the tribunal has consented to it being made and the court is satisfied

(i) that determining the question is likely to produce substantial savings in expenses,

(ii) that the application was made without delay, and

(iii) that there is a good reason why the question should be determined by the court.

(3) The tribunal may continue with the arbitration pending determination of an application.

(4) The Outer House's determination of the question is final (as is any decision by the Outer House as to whether an application is valid).

Part 3
General Duties

Rule 24 — General Duty of the Tribunal M

24 (1) The tribunal must

(a) be impartial and independent,

(b) treat the parties fairly, and

(c) conduct the arbitration

(i) without unnecessary delay, and

(ii) without incurring unnecessary expense.

(2) Treating the parties fairly includes giving each party a reasonable opportunity to put its case and to deal with the other party's case.

Rule 25 — General Duty of the Parties M

25 The parties must ensure that the arbitration is conducted

(a) without unnecessary delay, and

(b) without incurring unnecessary expense.

Rule 26 — Confidentiality D

26 (1) Disclosure by the tribunal, any arbitrator or a party of confidential information relating to the arbitration is to be actionable as a breach of an obligation of confidence unless the disclosure.

(a) is authorised, expressly or impliedly, by the parties (or can reasonably be considered as having been so authorised),

(b) is required by the tribunal or is otherwise made to assist or enable the tribunal to conduct the arbitration,
(c) is required
(i) in order to comply with any enactment or rule of law,
(ii) for the proper performance of the discloser's public functions, or
(iii) in order to enable any public body or office-holder to perform public functions properly,
(d) can reasonably be considered as being needed to protect a party's lawful interests,
(e) is in the public interest,
(f) is necessary in the interests of justice, or
(g) is made in circumstances in which the discloser would have absolute privilege had the disclosed information been defamatory.
(2) The tribunal and the parties must take reasonable steps to prevent unauthorised disclosure of confidential information by any third party involved in the conduct of the arbitration.
(3) The tribunal must, at the outset of the arbitration, inform the parties of the obligations which this rule imposes on them.
(4) "Confidential information", in relation to an arbitration, means any information relating to
(a) the dispute,
(b) the arbitral proceedings,
(c) the award, or
(d) any civil proceedings relating to the arbitration in respect of which an order has been granted under section 15 of this Act,
which is not, and has never been, in the public domain.

Rule 27 — Tribunal Deliberations D

27 (1) The tribunal's deliberations may be undertaken in private and accordingly need not be disclosed to the parties.
(2) But, where an arbitrator fails to participate in any of the tribunal's deliberations, the tribunal must disclose that fact (and the extent of the failure) to the parties.

Part 4
Arbitral Proceedings

Rule 28 — Procedure and Evidence D

28 (1) It is for the tribunal to determine
(a) the procedure to be followed in the arbitration, and
(b) the admissibility, relevance, materiality and weight of any evidence.
(2) In particular, the tribunal may determine

(a) when and where the arbitration is to be conducted,
(b) whether parties are to submit claims or defences and, if so, when they should do so and the extent to which claims or defences may be amended,
(c) whether any documents or other evidence should be disclosed by or to any party and, if so, when such disclosures are to be made and to whom copies of disclosed documents and information are to be given,
(d) whether any and, if so, what questions are to be put to and answered by the parties,
(e) whether and, if so, to what extent the tribunal should take the initiative in ascertaining the facts and the law,
(f) the extent to which the arbitration is to proceed by way of
(i) hearings for the questioning of parties,
(ii) written or oral argument,
(iii) presentation or inspection of documents or other evidence, or
(iv) submission of documents or other evidence,
(g) the language to be used in the arbitration (and whether a party is to supply translations of any document or other evidence),
(h) whether to apply rules of evidence used in legal proceedings or any other rules of evidence.

Rule 29 — Place of Arbitration D

29 The tribunal may meet, and otherwise conduct the arbitration, anywhere it chooses (in or outwith Scotland).

Rule 30 — Tribunal Decisions D

30 (1) Where the tribunal is unable to make a decision unanimously (including any decision on an award), a decision made by the majority of the arbitrators is sufficient.

(2) Where there is neither unanimity nor a majority in favour of or opposed to making any decision
(a) the decision is to be made by the arbitrator nominated to chair the tribunal, or
(b) where no person has been so nominated, the decision is to be made
(i) where the tribunal consists of 3 or more arbitrators, by the last arbitrator to be appointed, or
(ii) where the tribunal consists of 2 arbitrators, by an umpire appointed by the tribunal or, where the tribunal fails to make an appointment within 14 days of being requested to do so by either party or any arbitrator, by an arbitral appointments referee (at the request of a party or an arbitrator).

Rule 31 — Tribunal Directions D

31 (1) The tribunal may give such directions to the parties as it considers

appropriate for the purposes of conducting the arbitration.

(2) A party must comply with such a direction by such time as the tribunal specifies.

Rule 32 — Power to Appoint Clerk, Agents or Employees etc. D

32 (1) The tribunal may appoint a clerk (and such other agents, employees or other persons as it thinks fit) to assist it in conducting the arbitration.

(2) But the parties' consent is required for any appointment in respect of which significant expenses are likely to arise.

Rule 33 — Party Representatives D

33 (1) A party may be represented in the arbitration by a lawyer or any other person.

(2) But the party must, before representation begins, give notice of the representative

(a) to the tribunal, and

(b) to the other party.

Rule 34 — Experts D

34 (1) The tribunal may obtain an expert opinion on any matter arising in the arbitration.

(2) The parties must be given a reasonable opportunity

(a) to make representations about any written expert opinion, and

(b) to hear any oral expert opinion and to ask questions of the expert giving it.

Rule 35 — Powers Relating to Property D

35 The tribunal may direct a party

(a) to allow the tribunal, an expert or another party

(i) to inspect, photograph, preserve or take custody of any property which that party owns or possesses which is the subject of the arbitration (or as to which any question arises in the arbitration), or

(ii) to take samples from, or conduct an experiment on, any such property, or

(b) to preserve any document or other evidence which the party possesses or controls.

Rule 36 — Oaths or Affirmations D

36 The tribunal may

(a) direct that a party or witness is to be examined on oath or affirmation, and

(b) administer an oath or affirmation for that purpose.

Rule 37 — Failure to Submit Claim or Defence Timeously D

37 (1) Where

(a) a party unnecessarily delays in submitting or in otherwise pursuing a claim,
(b) the tribunal considers that there is no good reason for the delay, and
(c) the tribunal is satisfied that the delay
(i) gives, or is likely to give, rise to a substantial risk that it will not be possible to resolve the issues in that claim fairly, or
(ii) has caused, or is likely to cause, serious prejudice to the other party, the tribunal must end the arbitration in so far as it relates to the subject-matter of the claim and may make such award (including an award on expenses) as it considers appropriate in consequence of the claim.
(2) Where
(a) a party unnecessarily delays in submitting a defence to the tribunal, and
(b) the tribunal considers that there is no good reason for the delay, the tribunal must proceed with the arbitration (but the delay is not, in itself, to be treated as an admission of anything).

Rule 38 — Failure to Attend Hearing or Provide Evidence D

38 Where
(a) a party fails
(i) to attend a hearing which the tribunal requested the party to attend a reasonable period in advance of the hearing, or
(ii) to produce any document or other evidence requested by the tribunal, and
(b) the tribunal considers that there is no good reason for the failure, the tribunal may proceed with the arbitration, and make its award, on the basis of the evidence (if any) before it.

Rule 39 — Failure to Comply with Tribunal Direction or Arbitration Agreement D

39 (1) Where a party fails to comply with
(a) any direction made by the tribunal, or
(b) any obligation imposed by
(i) the arbitration agreement,
(ii) these rules (in so far as they apply), or
(iii) any other agreement by the parties relating to conduct of the arbitration, the tribunal may order the party to so comply.
(2) Where a party fails to comply with an order made under this rule, the tribunal may do any of the following
(a) direct that the party is not entitled to rely on any allegation or material which was the subject-matter of the order,
(b) draw adverse inferences from the non-compliance,

(c) proceed with the arbitration and make its award,
(d) make such provisional award (including an award on expenses) as it considers appropriate in consequence of the non-compliance.

Rule 40 — Consolidation of Proceedings D

40 (1) Parties may agree
(a) to consolidate the arbitration with another arbitration, or
(b) to hold concurrent hearings.
(2) But the tribunal may not order such consolidation, or the holding of concurrent hearings, on its own initiative.

Part 5
Powers of Court in Relation to Arbitral Proceedings

Rule 41 — Referral of Point of Law D

41 The Outer House may, on an application by any party, determine any point of Scots law arising in the arbitration.

Rule 42 — Point of Law Referral: Procedure etc. M

42 (1) This rule applies only where an application is made under rule 41.
(2) Such an application is valid only if
(a) the parties have agreed that it may be made, or
(b) the tribunal has consented to it being made and the court is satisfied
(i) that determining the question is likely to produce substantial savings in expenses,
(ii) that the application was made without delay, and
(iii) that there is a good reason why the question should be determined by the court.
(3) The tribunal may continue with the arbitration pending determination of the application.
(4) The Outer House's determination of the question is final (as is any decision by the Outer House as to whether an application is valid).

Rule 43 — Variation of Time Limits Set by Parties D

43 The court may, on an application by the tribunal or any party, vary any time limit relating to the arbitration which is imposed
(a) in the arbitration agreement, or
(b) by virtue of any other agreement between the parties.

Rule 44 — Time Limit Variation: Procedure etc. M

44 (1) This rule applies only where an application for variation of time limit is made under rule 43.
(2) Such a variation may be made only if the court is satisfied
(a) that no arbitral process for varying the time limit is available, and
(b) that someone would suffer a substantial injustice if no variation was

made.
(3) It is for the court to determine the extent of any variation.
(4) The tribunal may continue with the arbitration pending determination of an application.
(5) The court's decision on whether to make a variation (and, if so, on the extent of the variation) is final.

Rule 45 — Court's Power to Order Attendance of Witnesses and Disclosure of Evidence M

45 (1) The court may, on an application by the tribunal or any party, order any person
(a) to attend a hearing for the purposes of giving evidence to the tribunal, or
(b) to disclose documents or other material evidence to the tribunal.
(2) But the court may not order a person to give any evidence, or to disclose anything, which the person would be entitled to refuse to give or disclose in civil proceedings.
(3) The tribunal may continue with the arbitration pending determination of an application.
(4) The court's decision on whether to make an order is final.

Rule 46 — Court's Other Powers in relation to Arbitration D

46 (1) The court has the same power in an arbitration as it has in civil proceedings
(a) to appoint a person to safeguard the interests of any party lacking capacity,
(b) to order the sale of any property in dispute in the arbitration,
(c) to make an order securing any amount in dispute in the arbitration,
(d) to make an order under section 1 of the Administration of Justice (Scotland) Act 1972 (c. 59),
(e) to grant warrant for arrestment or inhibition,
(f) to grant interdict (or interim interdict), or
(g) to grant any other interim or permanent order.
(2) But the court may take such action only
(a) on an application by any party, and
(b) if the arbitration has begun
(i) with the consent of the tribunal, or
(ii) where the court is satisfied that the case is one of urgency.
(3) The tribunal may continue with the arbitration pending determination of the application.
(4) This rule applies
(a) to arbitrations which have begun,

(b) where the court is satisfied
(i) that a dispute has arisen or might arise, and
(ii) that an arbitration agreement provides that such a dispute is to be resolved by arbitration.
(5) This rule does not affect
(a) any other powers which the court has under any enactment or rule of law in relation to arbitrations, or
(b) the tribunal's powers.

Part 6
Awards

Rule 47 — Rules Applicable to the Substance of the Dispute D

47 (1) The tribunal must decide the dispute in accordance with
(a) the law chosen by the parties as applicable to the substance of the dispute, or
(b) if no such choice is made (or where a purported choice is unlawful), the law determined by the conflict of law rules which the tribunal considers applicable.
(2) Accordingly, the tribunal must not decide the dispute on the basis of general considerations of justice, fairness or equity unless
(a) they form part of the law concerned, or
(b) the parties otherwise agree.
(3) When deciding the dispute, the tribunal must have regard to
(a) the provisions of any contract relating to the substance of the dispute,
(b) the normal commercial or trade usage of any undefined terms in the provisions of any such contract,
(c) any established commercial or trade customs or practices relevant to the substance of the dispute, and
(d) any other matter which the parties agree is relevant in the circumstances.

Rule 48 — Power to Award Payment and Damages M

48 (1) The tribunal's award may order the payment of a sum of money (including a sum in respect of damages).
(2) Such a sum must be specified
(a) in any currency agreed by the parties, or
(b) the absence of such agreement, in such currency as the tribunal considers appropriate.

Rule 49 — Other Remedies Available to Tribunal D

49 The tribunal's award may
(a) be of a declaratory nature,
(b) order a party to do or refrain from doing something (including ordering

the performance of a contractual obligation), or
(c) order the rectification or reduction of any deed or other document (other than a decree of court) to the extent permitted by the law governing the deed or document.

Rule 50 — Interest M

50 (1) The tribunal's award may order that interest is to be paid on
(a) the whole or part of any amount which the award orders to be paid (or which is payable in consequence of a declaratory award),
in respect of any period up to the date of the award,
(b) the whole or part of any amount which is
(i) claimed in the arbitration and outstanding when the arbitration began, but
(ii) paid before the tribunal made its award, in respect of any period up to the date of payment,
(c) the outstanding amount of any amounts awarded (including any award of arbitration expenses or pre-award interest under paragraph (a) or (b) in respect of any period from the date of the award up to the date of payment.
(2) An award ordering payment of interest may, in particular, specify
(a) the interest rate,
(b) the period for which interest is payable (including any rests which the tribunal considers appropriate).
(3) An award may make different interest provision in respect of different amounts.
(4) Interest is to be calculated
(a) in the manner agreed by the parties, or
(b) failing such agreement, in such manner as the tribunal determines.
(5) This rule does not affect any other power of the tribunal to award interest.

Rule 51 — Form of Award D

51 (1) The tribunal's award must be signed by all arbitrators or all those assenting to the award.
(2) The tribunal's award must state
(a) the seat of the arbitration,
(b) when the award is made and when it takes effect,
(c) the tribunal's reasons for the award, and
(d) whether any previous provisional or part award has been made (and the extent to which any previous provisional award is superseded or confirmed).
(3) The tribunal's award is made by delivering it to each of the parties in accordance with rule 83.

Rule 52 — Award Treated as Made in Scotland D

52 An award is to be treated as having been made in Scotland even if it is signed at, or delivered to or from, a place outwith Scotland.

Rule 53 — Provisional Awards D

53 The tribunal may make a provisional award granting any relief on a provisional basis which it has the power to grant permanently.

Rule 54 — Part Awards M

54 (1) The tribunal may make more than one award at different times on different aspects of the matters to be determined.

(2) A "part award" is an award which decides some (but not all) of the matters which the tribunal is to decide in the arbitration.

(3) A part award must specify the matters to which it relates.

Rule 55 — Draft Awards D

55 Before making an award, the tribunal

(a) may send a draft of its proposed award to the parties, and

(b) if it does so, must consider any representations from the parties about the draft which the tribunal receives by such time as it specifies.

Rule 56 — Power to Withhold Award on Non-payment of Fees or Expenses M

56 (1) The tribunal may refuse to deliver or send its award to the parties if any fees and expenses for which they are liable under rule 60 have not been paid in full.

(2) Where the tribunal so refuses, the court may (on an application by any party) order

(a) that the tribunal must deliver the award on the applicant paying into the court an amount equal to the fees and expenses demanded (or such lesser amount as may be specified in the order),

(b) that the amount paid into the court is to be used to pay the fees and expenses which the court determines as being properly payable, and

(c) that the balance (if any) of the amount paid into the court is to be repaid to the applicant.

(3) The court may make such an order only if the applicant has exhausted any available arbitral process of appeal or review of the amount of the fees and expenses demanded.

(4) The court's decision on an application under this rule is final.

Rule 57 — Arbitration to End on last Award or Early Settlement D

57 (1) An arbitration ends when the last award to be made in the arbitration is made (and no claim, including any claim for expenses or interest, is outstanding).

(2) But this does not prevent the tribunal from ending the arbitration before then under rule 20(3) or 37(1).
(3) The parties may end the arbitration at any time by notifying the tribunal that they have settled the dispute.
(4) On the request of the parties, the tribunal may make an award reflecting the terms of the settlement and these rules (except for rule 51(2)(c) and Part 8) apply to such an award as they apply to any other award.
(5) The fact that the arbitration has ended does not affect the operation of these rules (in so far as they apply) in relation to matters connected with the arbitration.

Rule 58 — Correcting an Award D

58 (1) The tribunal may correct an award so as to
(a) correct a clerical, typographical or other error in the award arising by virtue of accident or omission, or
(b) clarify or remove any ambiguity in the award.
(2) The tribunal may make such a correction
(a) on its own initiative, or
(b) on an application by any party.
(3) A party making an application under this rule must send a copy of the application to the other party at the same time as the application is made.
(4) Such an application is valid only if made
(a) within 28 days of the award concerned, or
(b) by such later date as the Outer House or the sheriff may, on an application by the party, specify (with any determination by the Outer House or the sheriff being final).
(5) The tribunal must, before deciding whether to correct an award, give
(a) where the tribunal proposed the correction, each of the parties,
(b) where a party application is made, the other party, a reasonable opportunity to make representations about the proposed correction.
(6) A correction may be made under this rule only
(a) where the tribunal proposed the correction, within 28 days of the award concerned being made, or
(b) where a party application is made, within 28 days of the application being made.
(7) Where a correction affects
(a) another part of the corrected award, or
(b) any other award made by the tribunal (relating to the substance of the dispute, expenses, interest or any other matter),
the tribunal may make such consequential correction of that other part or

award as it considers appropriate.
(8) A corrected award is to be treated as if it was made in its corrected form on the day the award was made.

Part 7
Arbitration Expenses

Rule 59 — Arbitration Expenses D

59 "Arbitration expenses" means
(a) the arbitrators' fees and expenses for which the parties are liable under rule 60,
(b) any expenses incurred by the tribunal when conducting the arbitration for which the parties are liable under rule 60,
(c) the parties' legal and other expenses, and
(d) the fees and expenses of
(i) any arbitral appointments referee, and
(ii) any other third party to whom the parties give powers in relation to the arbitration,
for which the parties are liable under rule 60.

Rule 60 — Arbitrators' Fees and Expenses M

60 (1) The parties are severally liable to pay to the arbitrators
(a) the arbitrators' fees and expenses, including
(i) the arbitrators' fees for conducting the arbitration,
(ii) expenses incurred personally by the arbitrators when conducting the arbitration, and
(b) expenses incurred by the tribunal when conducting the arbitration, including
(i) the fees and expenses of any clerk, agent, employee or other person appointed by the tribunal to assist it in conducting the arbitration,
(ii) the fees and expenses of any expert from whom the tribunal obtains an opinion,
(iii) any expenses in respect of meeting and hearing facilities, and
(iv) any expenses incurred in determining recoverable arbitration expenses.
(2) The parties are also severally liable to pay the fees and expenses of
(a) any arbitral appointments referee, and
(b) any other third party to whom the parties give powers in relation to the arbitration.
(3) The amount of fees and expenses payable under this rule and the payment terms are
(a) to be agreed by the parties and the arbitrators or, as the case may be, the arbitral appointments referee or other third party, or

(b) failing such agreement, to be determined by the Auditor of the Court of Session.

(4) Unless the Auditor of the Court of Session decides otherwise

(a) the amount of any fee is to be determined by the Auditor on the basis of a reasonable commercial rate of charge, and

(b) the amount of any expenses is to be determined by the Auditor on the basis that a reasonable amount is to be allowed in respect of all reasonably incurred expenses.

(5) The Auditor of the Court of Session may, when determining the amount of fees and expenses, order the repayment of any fees or expenses already paid which the Auditor considers excessive (and such an order has effect as if it was made by the court).

(6) This rule does not affect

(a) the parties' liability as between themselves for fees and expenses covered by this rule (see rules 62 and 65), or

(b) the Outer House's power to make an order under rule 16 (order relating to expenses in cases of arbitrator's resignation or removal).

Rule 61 — Recoverable Arbitration Expenses D

61 (1) The following arbitration expenses are recoverable

(a) the arbitrators' fees and expenses for which the parties are liable under rule 60,

(b) any expenses incurred by the tribunal when conducting the arbitration for which the parties are liable under rule 60, and

(c) the fees and expenses of any arbitral appointments referee (or any other third party to whom the parties give powers in relation to the arbitration) for which the parties are liable under rule 60.

(2) It is for the tribunal to

(a) determine the amount of the other arbitration expenses which are recoverable, or

(b) arrange for the Auditor of the Court of Session to determine that amount.

(3) Unless the tribunal or, as the case may be, the Auditor decides otherwise

(a) the amount of the other arbitration expenses which are recoverable must be determined on the basis that a reasonable amount is to be allowed in respect of all reasonably incurred expenses, and

(b) any doubt as to whether expenses were reasonably incurred or are reasonable in amount is to be resolved in favour of the person liable to pay the expenses.

Rule 62 — Liability for Recoverable Arbitration Expenses D

62 (1) The tribunal may make an award allocating the parties' liability between themselves for the recoverable arbitration expenses (or any part of those expenses).

(2) When making an award under this rule, the tribunal must have regard to the principle that expenses should follow a decision made in favour of a party except where this would be inappropriate in the circumstances.

(3) Until such an award is made (or where the tribunal chooses not to make such an award) in respect of recoverable arbitration expenses (or any part of them), the parties are, as between themselves, each liable

(a) for an equal share of any such expenses for which the parties are liable under rule 60, and

(b) for their own legal and other expenses.

(4) This rule does not affect

(a) the parties' several liability for fees and expenses under rule 60, or

(b) the liability of any party to any other third party.

Rule 63 — Ban on Pre-dispute Agreements about Liability for Arbitration Expenses M

63 Any agreement allocating the parties' liability between themselves for any or all of the arbitration expenses has no effect if entered into before the dispute being arbitrated has arisen.

Rule 64 — Security for Expenses D

64 (1) The tribunal may

(a) order a party making a claim to provide security for the recoverable arbitration expenses or any part of them, and

(b) if that order is not complied with, make an award dismissing any claim made by that party.

(2) But such an order may not be made only on the ground that the party

(a) is an individual who ordinarily resides outwith the United Kingdom, or

(b) is a body which is

(i) incorporated or formed under the law of a country outwith the United Kingdom, or

(ii) managed or controlled from outwith the United Kingdom.

Rule 65 — Limitation of Recoverable Arbitration Expenses D

65 (1) A provisional or part award may cap a party's liability for the recoverable arbitration expenses at an amount specified in the award.

(2) But an award imposing such a cap must be made sufficiently in advance of the expenses to which the cap relates being incurred, or the taking of any steps in the arbitration which may be affected by the cap, for the parties to

take account of it.

Rule 66 — Awards on Recoverable Arbitration Expenses D

66 An expenses award (under rule 62 or 65) may be made together with or separately from an award on the substance of the dispute (and these rules apply in relation to an expenses award as they apply to an award on the substance of the dispute).

Part 8
Challenging Awards

Rule 67 — Challenging an Award: Substantive Jurisdiction M

67 (1) A party may appeal to the Outer House against the tribunal's award on the ground that the tribunal did not have jurisdiction to make the award (a "jurisdictional appeal").

(2) The Outer House may decide a jurisdictional appeal by

(a) confirming the award,

(b) varying the award (or part of it), or

(c) setting aside the award (or part of it).

(3) Any variation by the Outer House has effect as part of the tribunal's award.

(4) An appeal may be made to the Inner House against the Outer House's decision on a jurisdictional appeal (but only with the leave of the Outer House).

(5) Leave may be given by the Outer House only where it considers

(a) that the proposed appeal would raise an important point of principle or practice, or

(b) that there is another compelling reason for the Inner House to consider the appeal.

(6) The Outer House's decision on whether to grant such leave is final.

(7) The Inner House's decision on such an appeal is final.

Rule 68 — Challenging an Award: Serious Irregularity M

68 (1) A party may appeal to the Outer House against the tribunal's award on the ground of serious irregularity (a "serious irregularity appeal").

(2) "Serious irregularity" means an irregularity of any of the following kinds which has caused, or will cause, substantial injustice to the appellant

(a) the tribunal failing to conduct the arbitration in accordance with

(i) the arbitration agreement,

(ii) these rules (in so far as they apply), or

(iii) any other agreement by the parties relating to conduct of the arbitration,

(b) the tribunal acting outwith its powers (other than by exceeding its jurisdiction),

(c) the tribunal failing to deal with all the issues that were put to it,
(d) any arbitral appointments referee or other third party to whom the parties give powers in relation to the arbitration acting outwith powers,
(e) uncertainty or ambiguity as to the award's effect,
(f) the award being
(i) contrary to public policy, or
(ii) obtained by fraud or in a way which is contrary to public policy,
(g) an arbitrator having not been impartial and independent,
(h) an arbitrator having not treated the parties fairly,
(i) an arbitrator having been incapable of acting as an arbitrator in the arbitration (or there being justifiable doubts about an arbitrator's ability to so act),
(j) an arbitrator not having a qualification which the parties agreed (before the arbitrator's appointment) that the arbitrator must have, or
(k) any other irregularity in the conduct of the arbitration or in the award which is admitted by
(i) the tribunal, or
(ii) any arbitral appointments referee or other third party to whom the parties give powers in relation to the arbitration.
(3) The Outer House may decide a serious irregularity appeal by
(a) confirming the award,
(b) ordering the tribunal to reconsider the award (or part of it), or
(c) if it considers reconsideration inappropriate, setting aside the award (or part of it).
(4) Where the Outer House decides a serious irregularity appeal (otherwise than by confirming the award) on the ground
(a) that the tribunal failed to conduct the arbitration in accordance with
(i) the arbitration agreement,
(ii) these rules (in so far as they apply), or
(iii) any other agreement by the parties relating to conduct of the arbitration,
(b) that an arbitrator has not been impartial and independent, or
(c) that an arbitrator has not treated the parties fairly,
it may also make such order as it thinks fit about any arbitrator's entitlement (if any) to fees and expenses (and such an order may provide for the repayment of fees or expenses already paid to the arbitrator).
(5) An appeal may be made to the Inner House against the Outer House's decision on a serious irregularity appeal (but only with the leave of the Outer House).
(6) Leave may be given by the Outer House only where it considers

(a) that the proposed appeal would raise an important point of principle or practice, or
(b) that there is another compelling reason for the Inner House to consider the appeal.
(7) The Outer House's decision on whether to grant such leave is final.
(8) The Inner House's decision on such an appeal is final.

Rule 69 — Challenging an Award: Legal Error D

69 (1) A party may appeal to the Outer House against the tribunal's award on the ground that the tribunal erred on a point of Scots law (a "legal error appeal").
(2) An agreement between the parties to disapply rule 51(2)(c) by dispensing with the tribunal's duty to state its reasons for its award is to be treated as an agreement to exclude the court's jurisdiction to consider a legal error appeal.

Rule 70 — Legal Error Appeals: Procedure etc. M

70 (1) This rule applies only where rule 69 applies.
(2) A legal error appeal may be made only
(a) with the agreement of the parties, or
(b) with the leave of the Outer House.
(3) Leave to make a legal error appeal may be given only if the Outer House is satisfied
(a) that deciding the point will substantially affect a party's rights,
(b) that the tribunal was asked to decide the point, and
(c) that, on the basis of the findings of fact in the award (including any facts which the tribunal treated as established for the purpose of deciding the point), the tribunal's decision on the point
(i) was obviously wrong, or
(ii) where the court considers the point to be of general importance, is open to serious doubt.
(4) An application for leave is valid only if it
(a) identifies the point of law concerned, and
(b) states why the applicant considers that leave should be granted.
(5) The Outer House must determine an application for leave without a hearing (unless satisfied that a hearing is required).
(6) The Outer House's determination of an application for leave is final.
(7) Any leave to appeal expires 7 days after it is granted (and so any legal error appeal made after then is accordingly invalid unless made with the agreement of the parties).
(8) The Outer House may decide a legal error appeal by

(a) confirming the award,
(b) ordering the tribunal to reconsider the award (or part of it), or
(c) if it considers reconsideration inappropriate, setting aside the award (or part of it).
(9) An appeal may be made to the Inner House against the Outer House's decision on a legal error appeal (but only with the leave of the Outer House).
(10) Leave may be given by the Outer House only where it considers
(a) that the proposed appeal would raise an important point of principle or practice, or
(b) that there is another compelling reason for the Inner House to consider the appeal.
(11) The Outer House's decision on whether to grant such leave is final.
(12) The Inner House's decision on such an appeal is final.

Rule 71 — Challenging an Award: Supplementary M

71 (1) This rule applies to
(a) jurisdictional appeals,
(b) serious irregularity appeals, and
(c) where rule 69 applies to the arbitration, legal error appeals, and references to "appeal" are to be construed accordingly.
(2) An appeal is competent only if the appellant has exhausted any available arbitral process of appeal or review (including any recourse available under rule 58).
(3) No appeal may be made against a provisional award.
(4) An appeal must be made no later than 28 days after the later of the following dates
(a) the date on which the award being appealed against is made,
(b) if the award is subject to a process of correction under rule 58, the date on which the tribunal decides whether to correct the award, or
(c) if there has been an arbitral process of appeal or review, the date on which the appellant was notified of the result of that process.
A legal error appeal is to be treated as having being made for the purposes of this rule if an application for leave is made.
(5) An application for leave to appeal against the Outer House's decision on an appeal must be made no later than 28 days after the date on which the decision is made (and any such leave expires 7 days after it is granted).
(6) An appellant must give notice of an appeal to the other party and the tribunal.
(7) The tribunal may continue with the arbitration pending determination of

an appeal against a part award.
(8) The Outer House (or the Inner House in the case of an appeal against the Outer House's decision) may
(a) order the tribunal to state its reasons for the award being appealed insufficient detail to enable the Outer House (or Inner House) to deal with the appeal properly, and
(b) make any other order it thinks fit with respect to any additional expenses arising from that order.
(9) Where the Outer House (or the Inner House in the case of an appeal against the Outer House's decision) decides an appeal by setting aside the award (or any part of it), it may also order that any provision in an arbitration agreement which prevents the bringing of legal proceedings in relation to the subject-matter of the award (or that part of it) is void.
(10) The Outer House (or the Inner House in the case of an appeal against the Outer House's decision) may
(a) order an appellant (or an applicant for leave to appeal) to provide security for the expenses of the appeal (or application), and
(b) dismiss the appeal (or application) if the order is not complied with.
(11) But such an order may not be made only on the ground that the appellant (or applicant)
(a) is an individual who ordinarily resides outwith the United Kingdom, or
(b) is a body which is
(i) incorporated or formed under the law of a country outwith the United Kingdom, or
(ii) managed or controlled from outwith the United Kingdom.
(12) The Outer House (or the Inner House in the case of an appeal against the Outer House's decision) may
(a) order that any amount due under an award being appealed (or any associated provisional award) must be paid into court or otherwise secured pending its decision on the appeal (or the application for leave to appeal), and
(b) dismiss the appeal (or application) if the order is not complied with.
(13) An appeal to the Inner House against any decision of the Outer House under this rule may be made only with the leave of the Outer House.
(14) An application for leave to appeal against such a decision must be made no later than 28 days after the date on which the decision is made (and any such leave expires 7 days after it is granted).
(15) Leave may be given by the Outer House only where it considers
(a) that the proposed appeal would raise an important point of principle or

practice, or
(b) that there is another compelling reason for the Inner House to consider the appeal.
(16) The Outer House's decision on whether to grant such leave is final.
(17) A decision of the Inner House under this rule (including any decision on an appeal against a decision by the Outer House) is final.

Rule 72 — Reconsideration by Tribunal M

72 (1) Where the Outer House or, as the case may be, the Inner House decides a serious irregularity appeal or a legal error appeal by ordering the tribunal to reconsider its award (or any part of it), the tribunal must make a new award in respect of the matter concerned (or confirm its original award) by no later than
(a) in the case of a decision by the Outer House
(i) where the decision is appealed, the day falling 3 months after the appeal (or, as the case may be, the application for leave to appeal)is dismissed or abandoned,
(ii) where the decision is not appealed, the day falling 3 months after the decision is made, or
(iii) such other day as the Outer House may specify,
(b) in the case of a decision by the Inner House
(i) the day falling 3 months after the decision is made, or
(ii) such other day as the Inner House may specify.
(2) These rules apply in relation to the new award as they apply in relation to the appealed award.

Part 9
Miscellaneous

Rule 73 — Immunity of Tribunal etc. M

73 (1) Neither the tribunal nor any arbitrator is liable for anything done or omitted in the performance, or purported performance, of the tribunal's functions.
(2) This rule does not apply
(a) if the act or omission is shown to have been in bad faith, or
(b) to any liability arising from an arbitrator's resignation (but see rule 16(1)(c)).
(3) This rule applies to any clerk, agent, employee or other person assisting the tribunal to perform its functions as it applies to the tribunal.

Rule 74 — Immunity of Appointing Arbitral Institution etc. M

74 (1) An arbitral appointments referee, or other third party who the parties ask to appoint or nominate an arbitrator, is not liable

(a) for anything done or omitted in the performance, or purported performance, of that function (unless the act or omission is shown to have been in bad faith), or
(b) for the acts or omissions of
(i) any arbitrator whom it nominates or appoints, or
(ii) the tribunal of which such an arbitrator forms part (or any clerk, agent or employee of that tribunal).
(2) This rule applies to an arbitral appointments referee's, or other third party's, agents and employees as it applies to the referee or other third party.

Rule 75 — Immunity of Experts, Witnesses and Legal Representatives M

75 Every person who participates in an arbitration as an expert, witness or legal representative has the same immunity in respect of acts or omissions as the person would have if the arbitration were civil proceedings.

Rule 76 — Loss of Right to Object M

76 (1) A party who participates in an arbitration without making a timeous objection on the ground
(a) that an arbitrator is ineligible to act as an arbitrator,
(b) that an arbitrator is not impartial and independent,
(c) that an arbitrator has not treated the parties fairly,
(d) that the tribunal does not have jurisdiction,
(e) that the arbitration has not been conducted in accordance with
(i) the arbitration agreement,
(ii) these rules (in so far as they apply), or
(iii) any other agreement by the parties relating to conduct of the arbitration,
(f) that the arbitration has been affected by any other serious irregularity, may not raise the objection later before the tribunal or the court.
(2) An objection is timeous if it is made
(a) as soon as reasonably practicable after the circumstances giving rise to the ground for objection first arose,
(b) by such later date as may be allowed by
(i) the arbitration agreement,
(ii) these rules (in so far as they apply),
(iii) the other party, or
(c) where the tribunal considers that circumstances justify a later objection, by such later date as it may allow.
(3) This rule does not apply where the party shows that it did not object timeously because it

(a) did not know of the ground for objection, and
(b) could not with reasonable diligence have discovered that ground.
(4) This rule does not allow a party to raise an objection which it is barred from raising for any reason other than failure to object timeously.

Rule 77 — Independence of Arbitrator M

77 For the purposes of these rules, an arbitrator is not independent in relation to an arbitration if
(a) the arbitrator's relationship with any party,
(b) the arbitrator's financial or other commercial interests, or
(c) anything else,
gives rise to justifiable doubts as to the arbitrator's impartiality.

Rule 78 — Consideration Where Arbitrator Judged not to be Impartial and Independent D

78 (1) This rule applies where
(a) an arbitrator is removed by the Outer House under rule 12 on the ground that the arbitrator is not impartial and independent,
(b) the tribunal is dismissed by the Outer House under rule 13 on the ground that it has failed to comply with its duty to be impartial and independent, or
(c) the tribunal's award (or any part of it) is returned to the tribunal for reconsideration, or is set aside, on either of those grounds (see rule 68).
(2) Where this rule applies, the Outer House must have particular regard to whether an arbitrator has complied with rule 8 when it is considering whether to make an order under rule 16(1) or 68(4) about
(a) the arbitrator's entitlement (if any) to fees or expenses,
(b) repaying fees or expenses already paid to the arbitrator.

Rule 79 — Death of Arbitrator M

79 An arbitrator's authority is personal and ceases on death.

Rule 80 — Death of Party D

80 (1) An arbitration agreement is not discharged by the death of a party and may been forced by or against the executor or other representative of that party.
(2) This rule does not affect the operation of any law by virtue of which a substantive right or obligation is extinguished by death.

Rule 81 — Unfair Treatment D

81 A tribunal (or arbitrator) who treats any party unfairly is, for the purposes of these rules, to be deemed not to have treated the parties fairly.

Rule 82 — Rules Applicable to Umpires M

82 (1) The following rules apply in relation to an umpire appointed under rule 30 (or otherwise with the agreement of the parties) as they apply in

relation to an arbitrator or, as the case may be, the tribunal
rule 4
rule 8
rules 10 to 14
rule 24
rule 26
rules 59, 60 and 61(1)
rule 68
rule 73
rules 76 to 79
(2) But the parties are, in so far as those rules are not mandatory rules, free to modify or disapply the way in which those rules would otherwise apply to an umpire.
Rule 83 — Formal Communications D
83 (1) A "formal communication" means any application, award, consent, direction, notice, objection, order, reference, request, requirement or waiver made or given or any document served
(a) in pursuance of an arbitration agreement,
(b) for the purposes of these rules (in so far as they apply), or
(c) otherwise in relation to an arbitration.
(2) A formal communication must be in writing.
(3) A formal communication is made, given or served if it is
(a) hand delivered to the person concerned,
(b) sent to the person concerned by first class post in a properly addressed envelope or package
(i) in the case of an individual, to the individual's principal place of business or usual or last known abode,
(ii) in the case of a body corporate, to the body's registered or principal office, or
(iii) in either case, to any postal address designated for the purpose by the intended recipient (such designation to be made by giving notice to the person giving or serving the formal communication), or
(c) sent to the person concerned in some other way (including by email, fax or other electronic means) which the sender reasonably considers likely to cause it to be delivered on the same or next day.
(4) A formal communication which is sent by email, fax or other electronic means is to be treated as being in writing only if it is legible and capable of being used for subsequent reference.
(5) A formal communication is, unless the contrary is proved, to be treated

as having been made, given or served
(a) where hand delivered, on the day of delivery,
(b) where posted, on the day on which it would be delivered in the ordinary course of post, or
(c) where sent in any other way described above, on the day after it is sent.
(6) The tribunal may determine that a formal communication
(a) is to be delivered in such other manner as it may direct, or
(b) need not be delivered,
but it may do so only if satisfied that it is not reasonably practicable for the formal communication to be made, given or served in accordance with this rule (or, as the case may be, with any contrary agreement between the parties).
(7) This rule does not apply in relation to any application, order, notice, document or other thing which is made, given or served in or for the purposes of legal proceedings.

Rule 84 — Periods of Time D

84 Periods of time are to be calculated for the purposes of an arbitration as follows
(a) where any act requires to be done within a specified period after or from a specified date or event, the period begins immediately after that date or, as the case may be, the date of that event, and
(b) where the period is a period of 7 days or less, the following days are to be ignored
(i) Saturdays and Sundays, and
(ii) any public holidays in the place where the act concerned is to be done.

Index

The words and other expressions listed in the following index are defined or otherwise explained for the purposes of these rules by the provisions indicated in the index.

Expression	Interpretation provision
arbitral appointments referee	section 24
arbitration	section 2
arbitration agreement	section 4
arbitration expenses	rule 59
arbitrator	section 2
claim	section 31(1)
court	section 31(1)
default rule	section 9(1)
dispute	section 2
independent	rule 77
Inner House	section 31(1)
mandatory rule	section 8
Outer House	section 31(1)
part award	rule 54
party	sections 2 and 31(2)
provisional award	rule 53
recoverable arbitration expenses	rule 61
rule	section 2
statutory arbitration	section 16(1)
tribunal	section 2

Schedule 2
(Introduced by Section 29)
Repeals

Enactment	Extent of Repeal
Arbitration (Scotland) Act 1894 (c. 13)	The whole Act
Arbitration Act 1950 (c. 27)	The whole Act
Administration of Justice (Scotland) Act 1972 (c. 59)	Section 3
Arbitration Act 1975 (c. 3)	The whole Act
Law Reform (Miscellaneous Provisions) (Scotland) Act 1980 (c. 55)	Section 17
Law Reform (Miscellaneous Provisions) (Scotland) Act	Section 66 Schedule 7

ARBITRATION RULES OF THE ARBITRATION INSTITUTE OF THE STOCKHOLM CHAMBER OF COMMERCE *

1 — About the SCC

The Arbitration Institute of the Stockholm Chamber of Commerce (the "SCC") is the body responsible for the administration of disputes in accordance with the "SCC Rules"; the Arbitration Rules of the Arbitration Institute of the Stockholm Chamber of Commerce (the "Arbitration Rules") and the Rules for Expedited Arbitrations of the Stockholm Chamber of Commerce (the "Rules for Expedited Arbitrations"), and other procedures or rules agreed upon by the parties. The SCC is com posed of a board of directors (the "Board") and a secretariat (the "Secretariat"). Detailed provisions regarding the organisation of the SCC are set out in Appendix I.

Commencement of Proceedings

Article 2 — Request for Arbitration

A Request for Arbitration shall include:

(i) a statement of the names, addresses, telephone and facsimile numbers and e-mail addresses of the parties and their counsel;

(ii) a summary of the dispute;

(iii) a preliminary statement of the relief sought by the Claimant;

(iv) a copy or description of the arbitration agreement or clause under which the dispute is to be settled;

(v) comments on the number of arbitrators and the seat of arbitration; and

(vi) if applicable, the name, address, telephone number, facsimile number and e-mail address of the arbitrator appointed by the Claimant.

Article 3 — Registration Fee

(1) Upon filing the Request for Arbitration, the Claimant shall pay a Registration Fee. The amount of the Registration Fee shall be determined in accordance with the Schedule of Costs (Appendix III) in force on the date when the Request for Arbitration is filed.

(2) If the Registration Fee is not paid upon filing the Request for Arbitration, the Secretariat shall set a time period within which the Claimant shall pay the Registration Fee. If the Registration Fee is not paid within this time period, the Secretariat shall dismiss the Request for Arbitration.

Article 4 — Commencement of Arbitration

Arbitration is commenced on the date when the SCC receives the Request for Arbitration.

Article 5 — Answer

(1) The Secretariat shall send a copy of the Request for Arbitration and the documents attached thereto to the Respondent. The Secretariat shall set a time period within which the Respondent shall submit an Answer to the SCC. The Answer shall include:

---

* For a commentary on the SCC Arbitration Rules, see Pierre Karrer, 'Swiss Rules of International Arbitration of the Swiss Chambers' Arbitration Institution in Institutional Arbitration – Commentary' in Rolf A. Schütze (ed), *Institutional Arbitration* (Beck/Hart, 2013). See also Jakob Ragnwaldh and

(i) any objections concerning the existence, validity or applicability of the arbitration agreement; however, failure to raise any objections shall not preclude the Respondent from subsequently raising such objections at any time up to and including the submission of the Statement of Defence;
(ii) an admission or denial of the relief sought in the Request for Arbitration;
(iii) a preliminary statement of any counterclaims or set-offs;
(iv) comments on the number of arbitrators and the seat of arbitration; and
(v) if applicable, the name, address, telephone number, facsimile number and e-mail address of the arbitrator appointed by the Respondent.
(2) The Secretariat shall send a copy of the Answer to the Claimant. The Claimant shall be given an opportunity to submit comments on the Answer.
(3) Failure by the Respondent to submit an Answer shall not prevent the arbitration from proceeding.

Article 6 — Request for Further Details

The Board may request further details from either party regarding any of their written submissions to the SCC. If the Claimant fails to comply with a request for further details, the Board may dismiss the case. If the Respondent fails to comply with a request for further details regarding its counterclaim or set-off, the Board may dismiss the counterclaim or set-off. Failure by the Respondent to otherwise comply with a request for further details shall not prevent the arbitration from proceeding.

Article 7 — Time Periods

The Board may, on application by either party or on its own motion, extend any time period which has been set for a party to comply with a particular direction.

Article 8 — Notices

(1) Any notice or other communication from the Secretariat or the Board shall be delivered to the last known address of the addressee.
(2) Any notice or other communication shall be delivered by courier or registered mail, facsimile transmission, e-mail or any other means of communication that provides a record of the sending thereof.
(3) A notice or communication sent in accordance with paragraph (2) shall be deemed to have been received by the addressee on the date it would normally have been received given the chosen means of communication.

Article 9 — Decisions by the Board

When necessary the Board shall:
(i) decide whether the SCC manifestly lacks jurisdiction over the dispute pursuant to Article 10 (i);

Fredrik Andersson, *A Guide to the SCC Arbitration Rules* (Kluwer Law International, August 2015) (forthcoming).

(ii) decide whether to consolidate cases pursuant to Article 11;
(iii) decide the number of arbitrators pursuant to Article 12;
(iv) make any appointment of arbitrators pursuant to Article 13;
(v) decide the seat of arbitration pursuant to Article 20; and
(vi) determine the Advance on Costs pursuant to Article 45.

Article 10 — Dismissal

The Board shall dismiss a case, in whole or in part, if:
(i) the SCC manifestly lacks jurisdiction over the dispute; or
(ii) the Advance on Costs is not paid pursuant to Article 45.

Article 11 — Consolidation

If arbitration is commenced concerning a legal relationship in respect of which an arbitration between the same parties is already pending under these Rules, the Board may, at the request of a party, decide to consolidate the new claims with the pending proceedings. Such decision may only be made after consulting the parties and the Arbitral Tribunal.

Composition of the Arbitral Tribunal

Article 12 — Number of Arbitrators

The parties may agree on the number of arbitrators. Where the parties have not agreed on the number of arbitrators, the Arbitral Tribunal shall consist of three arbitrators, unless the Board, taking into account the complexity of the case, the amount in dispute or other circumstances, decides that the dispute is to be decided by a sole arbitrator.

Article 13 — Appointment of Arbitrators

(1) The parties may agree on a different procedure for appointment of the Arbitral Tribunal than as provided under this Article. In such cases, if the Arbitral Tribunal has not been appointed within the time period agreed by the parties or, where the parties have not agreed on a time period, within the time period set by the Board, the appointment shall be made pursuant to paragraphs (2)-(6).

(2) Where the Arbitral Tribunal is to consist of a sole arbitrator, the parties shall be given 10 days within which to jointly appoint the arbitrator. If the parties fail to make the appointment within this time period, the arbitrator shall be appointed by the Board.

(3) Where the Arbitral Tribunal is to consist of more than one arbitrator, each party shall appoint an equal number of arbitrators and the Chairperson shall be appointed by the Board. Where a party fails to appoint arbitrator(s) within the stipulated time period, the Board shall make the appointment.

(4) Where there are multiple Claimants or Respondents and the Arbitral Tribunal is to consist of more than one arbitrator, the multiple Claimants,

jointly, and the multiple Respondents, jointly, shall appoint an equal number of arbitrators. If either side fails to make such joint appointment, the Board shall appoint the entire Arbitral Tribunal.

(5) If the parties are of different nationalities, the sole arbitrator or the Chairperson of the Arbitral Tribunal shall be of a different nationality than the parties, unless the parties have agreed otherwise or unless otherwise deemed appropriate by the Board.

(6) When appointing arbitrators, the Board shall consider the nature and circumstances of the dispute, the applicable law, the seat and language of the arbitration and the nationality of the parties.

Article 14 — Impartiality and Independence

(1) Every arbitrator must be impartial and independent.

(2) Before being appointed as arbitrator, a person shall disclose any circumstances which may give rise to justifiable doubts as to his/her impartiality or independence. If the person is appointed as arbitrator, he/she shall submit to the Secretariat a signed statement of impartiality and independence disclosing any circumstances which may give rise to justifiable doubts as to that person's impartiality or independence. The Secretariat shall send a copy of the statement of impartiality and independence to the parties and the other arbitrators.

(3) An arbitrator shall immediately inform the parties and the other arbitrators in writing where any circumstances referred to in paragraph (2) arise during the course of the arbitration.

Article 15 — Challenge to Arbitrators

(1) A party may challenge any arbitrator if circumstances exist which give rise to justifiable doubts as to the arbitrator's impartiality or independence or if he/she does not possess qualifications agreed by the parties. A party may challenge an arbitrator whom it has appointed or in whose appointment it has participated, only for reasons of which it becomes aware after the appointment was made.

(2) A challenge to an arbitrator shall be made by submitting a written statement to the Secretariat setting forth the reasons for the challenge within 15 days from when the circumstances giving rise to the challenge became known to the party. Failure by a party to challenge an arbitrator within the stipulated time period constitutes a waiver of the right to make the challenge.

(3) The Secretariat shall notify the parties and the arbitrators of the challenge and give them an opportunity to submit comments on the challenge.

(4) If the other party agrees to the challenge, the arbitrator shall resign. In all other cases, the Board shall make the final decision on the challenge.

Article 16 — Release from Appointment

(1) The Board shall release an arbitrator from appointment where:

(i) the Board accepts the resignation of an arbitrator;

(ii) a challenge to the arbitrator under Article 15 is sustained; or

(iii) the arbitrator is otherwise prevented from fulfilling his/her duties or fails to perform his/her functions in an adequate manner.

(2) Before the Board releases an arbitrator, the Secretariat may give the parties and the arbitrators an opportunity to submit comments.

Article 17 — Replacement of Arbitrators

(1) The Board shall appoint a new arbitrator where an arbitrator has been released from his/her appointment pursuant to Article 16, or where an arbitrator has died. If the arbitrator being replaced was appointed by a party, that party shall appoint the new arbitrator, unless otherwise deemed appropriate by the Board.

(2) Where the Arbitral Tribunal consists of three or more arbitrators, the Board may decide that the remaining arbitrators shall proceed with the arbitration. In making its decision, the Board shall take into account the stage of the arbitration and other relevant circumstances. Before making such decision, the parties and the arbitrators shall be given an opportunity to submit comments.

(3) Where an arbitrator has been replaced, the newly composed Arbitral Tribunal shall decide whether and to what extent the proceedings are to be repeated.

The Proceedings before the Arbitral Tribunal

Article 18 — Referral to the Arbitral Tribunal

When the Arbitral Tribunal has been appointed and the Advance on Costs has been paid, the Secretariat shall refer the case to the Arbitral Tribunal.

Article 19 — Conduct of the Arbitration

(1) Subject to these Rules and any agreement between the parties, the Arbitral Tribunal may conduct the arbitration in such manner as it considers appropriate.

(2) In all cases, the Arbitral Tribunal shall conduct the arbitration in an impartial, practical and expeditious manner, giving each party an equal and reasonable opportunity to present its case.

Article 20 — Seat of Arbitration

(1) Unless agreed upon by the parties, the Board shall decide the seat of arbitration.

(2) The Arbitral Tribunal may, after consultation with the parties, conduct hearings at any place which it considers appropriate. The Arbitral Tribunal may meet and deliberate at any place which it considers appropriate. If any hearing, meeting, or deliberation is held elsewhere than at the seat of arbitration, the arbitration shall be deemed to have taken place at the seat of arbitration.

(3) The award shall be deemed to have been made at the seat of arbitration.

Article 21 — Language

(1) Unless agreed upon by the parties, the Arbitral Tribunal shall determine the language(s) of the arbitration. In so determining, the Arbitral Tribunal shall have due regard to all relevant circumstances and shall give the parties an opportunity to submit comments.

(2) The Arbitral Tribunal may request that any documents submitted in languages other than the language(s) of the arbitration be accompanied by a translation into the language(s) of the arbitration.

Article 22 — Applicable Law

(1) The Arbitral Tribunal shall decide the merits of the dispute on the basis of the law(s) or rules of law agreed upon by the parties. In the absence of such agreement, the Arbitral Tribunal shall apply the law or rules of law which it considers to be most appropriate.

(2) Any designation made by the parties of the law of a given state shall be deemed to refer to the substantive law of that state and not to its conflict of laws rules.

(3) The Arbitral Tribunal shall decide the dispute *ex aequo et bono* or as *amiable compositeur* only if the parties have expressly authorised it to do so.

Article 23 — Provisional Timetable

After the referral of the case to the Arbitral Tribunal, the Arbitral Tribunal shall promptly consult with the parties with a view to establishing a provisional timetable for the conduct of the arbitration. The Arbitral Tribunal shall send a copy of the provisional timetable to the parties and to the Secretariat.

Article 24 — Written Submissions

(1) The Claimant shall, within the period of time determined by the Arbitral Tribunal, submit a Statement of Claim which shall include, unless previously submitted:

(i) the specific relief sought;

(ii) the material circumstances on which the Claimant relies; and

(iii) the documents on which the Claimant relies.

(2) The Respondent shall, within the period of time determined by the Arbitral Tribunal, submit a Statement of Defence which shall include, unless previously submitted:
(i) any objections concerning the existence, validity or applicability of the arbitration agreement;
(ii) a statement whether, and to what extent, the Respondent admits or denies the relief sought by the Claimant;
(iii) the material circumstances on which the Respondent relies;
(iv) any counterclaim or set-off and the grounds on which it is based; and
(v) the documents on which the Respondent relies.
(3) The Arbitral Tribunal may order the parties to submit additional written submissions.

Article 25 — Amendments

At any time prior to the close of proceedings pursuant to Article 34, a party may amend or supplement its claim, counterclaim, defence or set-off provided its case, as amended or supplemented, is still comprised by the arbitration agreement, unless the Arbitral Tribunal considers it inappropriate to allow such amendment or supplement having regard to the delay in making it, the prejudice to the other party or any other circumstances.

Article 26 — Evidence

(1) The admissibility, relevance, materiality and weight of evidence shall be for the Arbitral Tribunal to determine.
(2) The Arbitral Tribunal may order a party to identify the documentary evidence it intends to rely on and specify the circumstances intended to be proved by such evidence.
(3) At the request of a party, the Arbitral Tribunal may order a party to produce any documents or other evidence which may be relevant to the outcome of the case.

Article 27 — Hearings

(1) A hearing shall be held if requested by a party, or if deemed appropriate by the Arbitral Tribunal.
(2) The Arbitral Tribunal shall, in consultation with the parties, determine the date, time and location of any hearing and shall provide the parties with reasonable notice thereof.
(3) Unless otherwise agreed by the parties, hearings will be held in private.

Article 28 — Witnesses

(1) In advance of any hearing, the Arbitral Tribunal may order the parties to identify each witness or expert they intend to call and specify the circumstances intended to be proved by each testimony.

(2) The testimony of witnesses or party-appointed experts may be submitted in the form of signed statements.
(3) Any witness or expert, on whose testimony a party seeks to rely, shall attend a hearing for examination, unless otherwise agreed by the parties.

Article 29 — Experts Appointed by the Arbitral Tribunal

(1) After consultation with the parties, the Arbitral Tribunal may appoint one or more experts to report to it on specific issues set out by the Arbitral Tribunal in writing.
(2) Upon receipt of a report from an expert appointed by the Arbitral Tribunal, the Arbitral Tribunal shall send a copy of the report to the parties and shall give the parties an opportunity to submit written comments on the report.
(3) Upon the request of a party, the parties shall be given an opportunity to examine any expert appointed by the Arbitral Tribunal at a hearing.

Article 30 — Default

(1) If the Claimant, without showing good cause, fails to submit a Statement of Claim in accordance with Article 24, the Arbitral Tribunal shall terminate the proceedings provided the Respondent has not filed a counterclaim.
(2) If a party, without showing good cause, fails to submit a Statement of Defence or other written statement in accordance with Article 24, or fails to appear at a hearing, or otherwise fails to avail itself of the opportunity to present its case, the Arbitral Tribunal may proceed with the arbitration and make an award.
(3) If a party without good cause fails to comply with any provision of, or requirement under, these Rules or any procedural order given by the Arbitral Tribunal, the Arbitral Tribunal may draw such inferences as it considers appropriate.

Article 31 — Waiver

A party, who during the arbitration fails to object without delay to any failure to comply with the arbitration agreement, these Rules or other rules applicable to the proceedings, shall be deemed to have waived the right to object to such failure.

Article 32 — Interim Measures

(1) The Arbitral Tribunal may, at the request of a party, grant any interim measures it deems appropriate.
(2) The Arbitral Tribunal may order the party requesting an interim measure to provide appropriate security in connection with the measure.
(3) An interim measure shall take the form of an order or an award.
(4) Provisions with respect to interim measures requested before arbitration

has been commenced or a case has been referred to an Arbitral Tribunal are set out in Appendix II.

(5) A request for interim measures made by a party to a judicial authority is not incompatible with the arbitration agreement or with these Rules.

Article 33 — Communications from the Arbitral Tribunal

Article 8 shall apply to communications from the Arbitral Tribunal.

Article 34 — Close of Proceedings

The Arbitral Tribunal shall declare the proceedings closed when it is satisfied that the parties have had a reasonable opportunity to present their cases. In exceptional circumstances, prior to the making of the final award, the Arbitral Tribunal may reopen the proceedings on its own motion, or upon the application of a party.

Awards and Decisions

Article 35 — Awards and Decisions

(1) When the Arbitral Tribunal consists of more than one arbitrator, any award or other decision of the Arbitral Tribunal shall be made by a majority of the arbitrators or, failing a majority, by the Chairperson.

(2) The Arbitral Tribunal may decide that the Chairperson alone may make procedural rulings.

Article 36 — Making of Awards

(1) The Arbitral Tribunal shall make its award in writing, and, unless otherwise agreed by the parties, shall state the reasons upon which the award is based.

(2) An award shall include the date of the award and the seat of arbitration in accordance with Article 20.

(3) An award shall be signed by the arbitrators. If an arbitrator fails to sign an award, the signatures of the majority of the arbitrators or, failing a majority, of the Chairperson shall be sufficient, provided that the reason for the omission of the signature is stated in the award.

(4) The Arbitral Tribunal shall deliver a copy of the award to each of the parties and to the SCC without delay.

(5) If any arbitrator fails without valid cause to participate in the deliberations of the Arbitral Tribunal on an issue, such failure will not preclude a decision being made by the other arbitrators.

Article 37 — Time Limit for Final Award

The final award shall be made not later than six months from the date upon which the arbitration was referred to the Arbitral Tribunal pursuant to Article 18. The Board may extend this time limit upon a reasoned request from the Arbitral Tribunal or if otherwise deemed necessary.

Article 38 — Separate Award

The Arbitral Tribunal may decide a separate issue or part of the dispute in a separate award.

Article 39 — Settlement or Other Grounds for Termination of the Arbitration

(1) If the parties reach a settlement before the final award is made, the Arbitral Tribunal may, upon the request of both parties, record the settlement in the form of a consent award.

(2) If the arbitration for any other reason is terminated before the final award is made, the Arbitral Tribunal shall issue an award recording the termination.

Article 40 — Effect of an Award

An award shall be final and binding on the parties when rendered. By agreeing to arbitration under these Rules, the parties undertake to carry out any award without delay.

Article 41 — Correction and Interpretation of an Award

(1) Within 30 days of receiving an award, a party may, upon notice to the other party, request that the Arbitral Tribunal correct any clerical typographical or computational errors in the award, or provide an interpretation of a specific point or part of the award. If the Arbitral Tribunal considers the request justified, it shall make the correction or provide the interpretation within 30 days of receiving the request.

(2) The Arbitral Tribunal may correct any error of the type referred to in paragraph (1) above on its own motion within 30 days of the date of an award.

(3) Any correction or interpretation of an award shall be in writing and shall comply with the requirements of Article 36.

Article 42 — Additional Award

Within 30 days of receiving an award, a party may, upon notice to the other party, request the Arbitral Tribunal to make an additional award on claims presented in the arbitration but not determined in the award. If the Arbitral Tribunal considers the request justified, it shall make the additional award within 60 days of receipt of the request. When deemed necessary, the Board may extend this 60 day time limit.

Costs of the Arbitration

Article 43 — Costs of the Arbitration

(1) The Costs of the Arbitration consist of:

(i) the Fees of the Arbitral Tribunal;

(ii) the Administrative Fee; and

(iii) the expenses of the Arbitral Tribunal and the SCC.
(2) Before making the final award, the Arbitral Tribunal shall request the Board to finally determine the Costs of the Arbitration. The Board shall finally determine the Costs of the Arbitration in accordance with the Schedule of Costs (Appendix III) in force on the date of commencement of the arbitration pursuant to Article 4.
(3) If the arbitration is terminated before the final award is made pursuant to Article 39, the Board shall finally determine the Costs of the Arbitration having regard to when the arbitration terminates, the work performed by the Arbitral Tribunal and other relevant circumstances.
(4) The Arbitral Tribunal shall include in the final award the Costs of the Arbitration as finally determined by the Board and specify the individual fees and expenses of each member of the Arbitral Tribunal and the SCC.
(5) Unless otherwise agreed by the parties, the Arbitral Tribunal shall, at the request of a party, apportion the Costs of the Arbitration between the parties, having regard to the outcome of the case and other relevant circumstances.
(6) The parties are jointly and severally liable to the arbitrator(s) and to the SCC for the Costs of the Arbitration.

Article 44 — Costs Incurred by a Party

Unless otherwise agreed by the parties, the Arbitral Tribunal may in the final award upon the request of a party, order one party to pay any reasonable costs incurred by another party, including costs for legal representation, having regard to the outcome of the case and other relevant circumstances.

Article 45 — Advance on Costs

(1) The Board shall determine an amount to be paid by the parties as an Advance on Costs.
(2) The Advance on Costs shall correspond to the estimated amount of the Costs of Arbitration pursuant to Article 43(1).
(3) Each party shall pay half of the Advance on Costs, unless separate advances are determined. Where counterclaims or set-offs are submitted, the Board may decide that each of the parties shall pay the advances on costs corresponding to its claim. Upon a request from the Arbitral Tribunal or if otherwise deemed necessary, the Board may order parties to pay additional advances during the course of the arbitration.
(4) If a party fails to make a required payment, the Secretariat shall give the other party an opportunity to do so within a specified period of time. If the required payment is not made, the Board shall dismiss the case in whole or

in part. If the other party makes the required payment, the Arbitral Tribunal may, at the request of such party, make a separate award for reimbursement of the payment.

(5) At any stage during the arbitration or after the Award has been made, the Board may draw on the Advance on Costs to cover the Costs of the Arbitration.

(6) The Board may decide that part of the Advance on Costs may be provided in the form of a bank guarantee or other form of security.

General Rules

Article 46 — Confidentiality

Unless otherwise agreed by the parties, the SCC and the Arbitral Tribunal shall maintain the confidentiality of the arbitration and the award.

Article 47 — Enforcement

In all matters not expressly provided for in these Rules, the SCC, the Arbitral Tribunal and the parties shall act in the spirit of these Rules and shall make every reasonable effort to ensure that all awards are legally enforceable.

Article 48 — Exclusion of Liability

Neither the SCC nor the arbitrator(s) are liable to any party for any act or omission in connection with the arbitration unless such act or omission constitutes willful misconduct or gross negligence.

Appendix I
Organisation

Article 1 — About the SCC

The Arbitration Institute of the Stockholm Chamber of Commerce (the "SCC") is a body providing administrative services in relation to the settlement of disputes. The SCC is part of the Stockholm Chamber of Commerce, but is independent in exercising its functions in the administration of disputes. The SCC is composed of a board of directors (the "Board") and a secretariat (the "Secretariat").

Article 2 — Function of the SCC

The SCC does not itself decide disputes. The function of the SCC is to:

(i) administer domestic and international disputes in accordance with the SCC Rules and other procedures or rules agreed upon by the parties; and

(ii) provide information concerning arbitration and mediation matters.

Article 3 — The Board

The Board shall be composed of one chairperson, a maximum of three vice-chairpersons and a maximum of 12 additional members. The Board shall include both Swedish and non-Swedish nationals.

Article 4 — Appointment of the Board

The Board shall be appointed by the Board of Directors of the Stockholm Chamber of Commerce (the "Board of Directors"). The members of the Board shall be appointed for a period of three years and are eligible for re-appointment in their respective capacities for one further three year period only, unless exceptional circumstances apply.

Article 5 — Removal of a Member of the Board

In exceptional circumstances, the Board of Directors may remove a member of the Board. If a member resigns or is removed during a term of office, the Board of Directors shall appoint a new member for the remainder of the term.

Article 6 — Function of the Board

The function of the Board is to take the decisions required of the SCC in administering disputes under the SCC Rules and any other rules or procedures agreed upon by the parties. Such decisions include decisions on the jurisdiction of the SCC, determination of advances on costs, appointment of arbitrators, decisions upon challenges to arbitrators, removal of arbitrators and the fixing of arbitration costs.

Article 7 — Decisions by the Board

Two members of the Board form a quorum. If a majority is not attained, the Chairperson has the casting vote. The Chairperson or a Vice-Chairperson may to take decisions on behalf of the Board in urgent matters. A committee of the Board may be appointed to take certain decisions on behalf of the Board. The Board may delegate decisions to the Secretariat, including decisions on advances on costs, extension of time for rendering an award, dismissal for non-payment of registration fee, release of arbitrators and fixing of arbitration costs. Decisions by the Board are final.

Article 8 — The Secretariat

The Secretariat acts under the direction of a Secretary General. The Secretariat carries out the functions assigned to it under the SCC Rules. The Secretariat may also take decisions delegated to it by the Board.

Article 9 — Procedures

The SCC shall maintain the confidentiality of the arbitration and the award and shall deal with the arbitration in an impartial, practical and expeditious manner.

Appendix II
Emergency Arbitrator

Article 1 — Emergency Arbitrator

(1) A party may apply for the appointment of an Emergency Arbitrator until the case has been referred to an Arbitral Tribunal pursuant to Article 18 of the Arbitration Rules.

(2) The powers of the Emergency Arbitrator shall be those set out in Article 32 (1)-(3) of the Arbitration Rules. Such powers terminate when the case has been referred to an Arbitral Tribunal pursuant to Article 18 of the Arbitration Rules or when an emergency decision ceases to be binding according to Article 9 (4) of this Appendix.

Article 2 — Application for the Appointment of an Emergency Arbitrator

An application for the appointment of an Emergency Arbitrator shall include:

(i) a statement of the names and addresses, telephone and facsimile numbers and e-mail addresses of the parties and their counsel;

(ii) a summary of the dispute;

(iii) a statement of the interim relief sought and the reasons therefor;

(iv) a copy or description of the arbitration agreement or clause on the basis of which the dispute is to be settled;

(v) comments on the seat of the emergency proceedings, the applicable law (s) and the language(s) of the proceedings; and

(vi) proof of payment of the costs for the emergency proceedings pursuant to Article 10 (1)-(2) of this Appendix.

Article 3 — Notice
As soon as an application for the appointment of an Emergency Arbitrator has been received, the Secretariat shall send the application to the other party.

Article 4 — Appointment of the Emergency Arbitrator
(1) The Board shall seek to appoint an Emergency Arbitrator within 24 hours of receipt of the application for the appointment of an Emergency Arbitrator.
(2) An Emergency Arbitrator shall not be appointed if the SCC manifestly lacks jurisdiction over the dispute.
(3) Article 15 of the Arbitration Rules applies except that a challenge must be made within 24 hours from when the circumstances giving rise to the challenge of an Emergency Arbitrator became known to the party.
(4) An Emergency Arbitrator may not act as an arbitrator in any future arbitration relating to the dispute, unless otherwise agreed by the parties.

Article 5 — Seat of the Emergency Proceedings
The seat of the emergency proceedings shall be that which has been agreed upon by the parties as the seat of the arbitration. If the seat of the arbitration has not been agreed by the parties, the Board shall determine the seat of the emergency proceedings.

Article 6 — Referral to the Emergency Arbitrator
Once an Emergency Arbitrator has been appointed, the Secretariat shall promptly refer the application to the Emergency Arbitrator.

Article 7 — Conduct of the Emergency Proceedings
Article 19 of the Arbitration Rules shall apply to the emergency proceedings, taking into account the urgency inherent in such proceedings.

Article 8 — Emergency Decisions on Interim Measures
(1) Any emergency decision on interim measures shall be made not later than 5 days from the date upon which the application was referred to the Emergency Arbitrator pursuant to Article 6 of this Appendix. The Board may extend this time limit upon a reasoned request from the Emergency Arbitrator, or if otherwise deemed necessary.
(2) Any emergency decision on interim measures shall:
(i) be made in writing;
(ii) state the date when it was made, the seat of the emergency proceedings and the reasons upon which the decision is based; and
(iii) be signed by the Emergency Arbitrator.
(3) The Emergency Arbitrator shall promptly deliver a copy of the emergency decision to each of the parties and to the SCC.

Article 9 — Binding Effect of Emergency Decisions

(1) An emergency decision shall be binding on the parties when rendered.

(2) The emergency decision may be amended or revoked by the Emergency Arbitrator upon a reasoned request by a party.

(3) By agreeing to arbitration under the Arbitration Rules, the parties undertake to comply with any emergency decision without delay.

(4) The emergency decision ceases to be binding if:

(i) the Emergency Arbitrator or an Arbitral Tribunal so decides;

(ii) an Arbitral Tribunal makes a final award;

(iii) arbitration is not commenced within 30 days from the date of the emergency decision; or

(iv) the case is not referred to an Arbitral Tribunal within 90 days from the date of the emergency decision.

(5) An Arbitral Tribunal is not bound by the decision(s) and reasons of the Emergency Arbitrator.

Article 10 — Costs of the Emergency Proceedings

(1) The party applying for the appointment of an Emergency Arbitrator shall pay the costs of the emergency proceedings upon filing the application.

(2) The costs of the emergency proceedings include:

(i) the fee of the Emergency Arbitrator which amounts to EUR 12,000; and

(ii) the application fee which amounts to EUR 3,000.

(3) Upon a request from the Emergency Arbitrator or if otherwise deemed appropriate, the Board may decide to increase or reduce the costs having regard to the nature of the case, the work performed by the Emergency Arbitrator and the SCC, and other relevant circumstances.

(4) If payment of the costs of the emergency proceedings is not made in due time, the Secretariat shall dismiss the application.

(5) At the request of a party, the costs of the emergency proceedings may be apportioned between the parties by an Arbitral Tribunal in a final award.

Appendix III
Schedule of Costs
Arbitration Costs

Article 1 — Registration Fee

(1) The Registration Fee referred to in Article 3 of the Arbitration Rules amounts to EUR 1,500.

(2) The Registration Fee is non-refundable and constitutes a part of the Administrative Fee in Article 3 below. The Registration Fee shall be credited to the Advance on Costs to be paid by the Claimant pursuant to

Article 45 of the Arbitration Rules.

Article 2 — Fees of the Arbitral Tribunal

(1) The Board shall determine the fee of a Chairperson or sole arbitrator based on the amount in dispute in accordance with the table below.

(2) Co-arbitrators shall each receive 60 per cent of the fee of the Chairperson. After consultation with the Arbitral Tribunal, the Board may decide that a different percentage shall apply.

(3) The amount in dispute shall be the aggregate value of all claims, counterclaims and set-offs. Where the amount in dispute cannot be ascertained, the Board shall determine the Fees of the Arbitral Tribunal taking all relevant circumstances into account.

(4) In exceptional circumstances, the Board may deviate from the amounts set out in the table.

Article 3 — Administrative Fee

(1) The Administrative Fee shall be determined in accordance with the table below.

(2) The amount in dispute shall be the aggregate value of all claims, counterclaims and set-offs. Where the amount in dispute cannot be ascertained, the Board shall determine the Administrative Fee taking all relevant circumstances into account.

(3) In exceptional circumstances, the Board may deviate from the amounts set out in the table.

Article 4 — Expenses

In addition to the Fees of the arbitrator(s) and the Administrative Fee, the Board shall fix an amount to cover any reasonable expenses incurred by the arbitrator(s) and the SCC. The expenses of the arbitrator(s) may include the fee and expenses of any expert appointed by the Arbitral Tribunal pursuant to Article 29 of the Arbitration Rules.

Arbitrator's Fees[1]

Amount in Dispute (EUR)	Fee of Chairman/Sole Arbitrator	
	Minimum (EUR)	Maximum (EUR)
to 25 000	2 500	5 500
from 25 001 to 50 000	2 500 + 2 % on the amount above 25 000	5 500 + 14 % on the amount above 25 000
from 50 001 to 100 000	3 000 + 2 % on the amount above 50 000	9 000 + 4 % on the amount above 50 000
from 100 001 to 500 000	4 000 + 1 % on the amount above 100 000	11 000 + 5 % on the amount above 100 000
from 500 001 to 1 000 000	8 000 + 0,8 % on the amount above 500 000	31 000 + 2,4 % on the amount above 500 000
from 1 000 001 to 2 000 000	12 000 + 0,5 % on the amount above 1 000 000	43 000 +2,5 % on the amount above 1 000 000
from 2 000 001 to 5 000 000	17 000 + 0,2 % on the amount above 2 000 000	68 000 + 0,8 % on the amount above 2 000 000
from 5 000 001 to 10 000 000	23 000 + 0,1 % on the amount above 5 000 000	92 000 + 0,68 % on the amount above 5 000 000
from 10 000 001 to 50 000 000	28 000 + 0,03 % on the amount above 10 000 000	126 000 + 0,15 % on the amount above 10 000 000
from 50 000 001 to 75 000 000	40 000 + 0,02 % on the amount above 50 000 000	186 000 + 0,16 % on the amount above 50 000 000
from 75 000 001 to 100 000 000	45 000 + 0,012 % on the amount above 75 000 000	226 000 + 0,02 % on the amount above 75 000 000
from 100 000 001	To be determined by the Board	To be determined by the Board

[1] The Costs of the Arbitration may easily be calculated at <www.sccinstitute.com >.

Administrative Fee[2]

Amount in dispute (EUR)	Administrative Fee (EUR)
Up to 25 000	1 500
from 25 001 to 50 000	1 500 + 4 % on the amount above 25 000
from 50 001 to 100 000	2 500 + 2 % on the amount above 50 000
from 100 001 to 500 000	3 500 + 1,6 % on the amount above 100 000
from 500 001 to 1 000 000	9 900 + 0,8 % on the amount above 500 000
from 1 000 001 to 2 000 000	13 900 + 0,5 % on the amount above 1 000 000
from 2 000 001 to 5 000 000	18 900 + 0,1 % on the amount above 2 000 000
from 5 000 001 to 10 000 000	21 900 + 0,14 % on the amount above 5 000 000
from 10 000 001 to	28 900 + 0,02 % on the amount above 10 000 000
from 50 000 001 to	36 900 + 0,02 % on the amount above 50 000 000
from 75 000 001	41 900 + 0,01 % on the amount above 75 000 000
	Maximum 60 000

[2] The Costs of the Arbitration may easily be calculated at <www.sccinstitute.com>.

ARBITRATION RULES OF THE SINGAPORE INTERNATIONAL ARBITRATION CENTRE (SIAC) *

1 — Scope of Application and Interpretation

1.1 Where parties have agreed to refer their disputes to SIAC for arbitration, the parties shall be deemed to have agreed that the arbitration shall be conducted and administered in accordance with these Rules. If any of these Rules is in conflict with a mandatory provision of the applicable law of the arbitration from which the parties cannot derogate, that provision shall prevail.

1.2 These Rules shall come into force on 1 April 2013 and, unless the parties have agreed otherwise, shall apply to any arbitration which is commenced on or after that date.

1.3 From 1 April 2013, the SIAC Rules (4th edition, 1 July 2010) are amended as follows.

a. In Rule 1.3:

The definitions of "Board", "Chairman" and "Committee of the Board" are deleted and the following are substituted:

"Board" means the Court;

"Chairman" means the President;

"Committee of the Board" means the Court;

b. The following definitions are inserted after the definition of "Committee of the Board":

"Committee of the Court" means a committee consisting of not less than two members of the Court appointed by the President (which may include the President);

"Court" means the Court of Arbitration of SIAC and includes a Committee of the Court;

"President" means the President of the Court and includes a Vice President and the Registrar;

1.4 From 1 April 2013, the SIAC Rules (3rd edition, 1 July 2007) are amended as follows.

a. In Rule 1.2:

The definition of "Chairman" is deleted and the following is substituted:

"Chairman" means the President;

b. The following definitions are inserted after the definition of "Chairman":

"Committee of the Court" means a committee consisting of not less than two members of the Court appointed by the President (which may include the President);

"Court" means the Court of Arbitration of SIAC and includes a Committee of the Court;

"President" means the President of the Court and includes a Vice President

* For a commentary on the SIAC Arbitration Rules, see Lucy Reed, Mark Mangan and John Choong, *A Guide to the SIAC Arbitration Rules* (Oxford University Press, 2014) and John Savage, *The SIAC and International Arbitration in Singapore* (Kluwer Law International, October 2015) (forthcoming).

and the Registrar;
1.5 In these Rules
"Award" includes a partial or final award and an award of an Emergency Arbitrator;
"Committee of the Court" means a committee consisting of not less than two members of the Court appointed by the President (which may include the President);
"Court" means the Court of Arbitration of SIAC and includes a Committee of the Court;
"President" means the President of the Court and includes a Vice President and the Registrar;
"Registrar" means the Registrar of the Court and includes any Deputy Registrar;
"SIAC" means the Singapore International Arbitration Centre; and
"Tribunal" includes a sole arbitrator or all the arbitrators where more than one is appointed.
Any pronoun shall be understood to be gender-neutral; and
Any singular noun shall be understood to refer to the plural in the appropriate circumstances.

2 — Notice, Calculation of Periods of Time

2.1 For the purposes of these Rules, any notice, communication or proposal, shall be in writing. Any such written communication may be delivered or sent by registered postal or courier service or transmitted by any form of electronic communication (including electronic mail and facsimile) or delivered by any other means that provides a record of its delivery. It is deemed to have been received if it is delivered (i) to the addressee personally, (ii) to his habitual residence, place of business or designated address, (iii) to any address agreed by the parties, (iv) according to the practice of the parties in prior dealings, or (v) if none of these can be found after making reasonable inquiry, then at the addressee's last-known residence or place of business.

2.2 The notice, communication, or proposal is deemed to have been received on the day it is delivered.

2.3 For the purposes of calculating any period of time under these Rules, such period shall begin to run on the day following the day when a notice, communication or proposal is received. If the last day of such period is not a business day at the place of receipt pursuant to Rule 2.1, the period is extended until the first business day which follows. Non-business days occurring during the running of the period of time are included in

---

See also, SIAC, *Singapore Arbitral Awards* (LexisNexis, 2012).

calculating the period.

2.4 The parties shall file with the Registrar a copy of any notice, communication or proposal concerning the arbitral proceedings.

2.5 Except as provided in these Rules, the Registrar may at any time extend or shorten any time limits prescribed under these Rules.

3 — Notice of Arbitration

3.1 A party wishing to commence an arbitration (the "Claimant") shall file with the Registrar a Notice of Arbitration which shall comprise:

a. a demand that the dispute be referred to arbitration;

b. the names, address(es), telephone number(s), facsimile number(s) and electronic mail address(es), if known, of the parties to the arbitration and their representatives, if any;

c. a reference to the arbitration clause or the separate arbitration agreement that is invoked and a copy of it;

d. a reference to the contract (or other instrument [e.g., investment treaty]) out of or in relation to which the dispute arises and where possible, a copy of it;

e. a brief statement describing the nature and circumstances of the dispute, specifying the relief claimed and, where possible, an initial quantification of the claim amount;

f. a statement of any matters which the parties have previously agreed as to the conduct of the arbitration or with respect to which the Claimant wishes to make a proposal;

g. a proposal for the number of arbitrator(s) if this is not specified in the arbitration agreement;

h. unless the parties have agreed otherwise, the nomination of an arbitrator if the arbitration agreement provides for three arbitrators, or a proposal for a sole arbitrator if the arbitration agreement provides for a sole arbitrator;

i. any comment as to the applicable rules of law;

j. any comment as to the language of the arbitration;

and

k. payment of the requisite filing fee.

3.2 The Notice of Arbitration may also include the Statement of Claim referred to in Rule 17.2.

3.3 The date of receipt of the complete Notice of Arbitration by the Registrar shall be deemed the date of commencement of the arbitration. For the avoidance of doubt, the Notice of Arbitration is deemed to be complete when all the requirements of Rule 3.1 are fulfilled or when the Registrar determines that there has been substantial compliance with such requirements. SIAC shall notify the parties on the commencement of arbitration.

3.4 The Claimant shall at the same time send a copy of the Notice of Arbitration to the Respondent, and it shall notify the Registrar that it has done so, specifying the mode of service employed and the date of service.

4 — Response to the Notice of Arbitration

4.1 The Respondent shall send to the Claimant a Response within 14 days of receipt of the Notice of Arbitration. The Response shall contain:

a. a confirmation or denial of all or part of the claims;

b. a brief statement describing the nature and circumstances of any counterclaim, specifying the relief claimed and, where possible, an initial quantification of the counterclaim amount;

c. any comment in response to any statements contained in the Notice of Arbitration under Rules 3.1(f), (g), (h), (i) and (j) or any comment with respect to the matters covered in such rules; and

d. unless the parties have agreed otherwise, the nomination of an arbitrator if the arbitration agreement provides for three arbitrators or, if the arbitration agreement provides for a sole arbitrator, agreement with Claimant's proposal for a sole arbitrator or a counter-proposal.

4.2 The Response may also include the Statement of Defence and a Statement of Counterclaim, as referred to in Rules 17.3 and 17.4.

4.3 The Respondent shall at the same time send a copy of the Response to the Registrar, together with the payment of the requisite filing fee for any counterclaim, and shall notify the Registrar of the mode of service of the Response employed and the date of service.

5 — Expedited Procedure

5.1 Prior to the full constitution of the Tribunal, a party may apply to the Registrar in writing for the arbitral proceedings to be conducted in accordance with the Expedited Procedure under this Rule where any of the following criteria is satisfied:

a. the amount in dispute does not exceed the equivalent amount of S$5,000,000, representing the aggregate of the claim, counterclaim and any set-off defence;

b. the parties so agree; or

c. in cases of exceptional urgency.

5.2 When a party has applied to the Registrar under Rule 5.1, and when the President determines, after considering the views of the parties, that the arbitral proceedings shall be conducted in accordance with the Expedited Procedure, the following procedure shall apply:

a. The Registrar may shorten any time limits under these Rules;
b. The case shall be referred to a sole arbitrator, unless the President determines otherwise;
c. Unless the parties agree that the dispute shall be decided on the basis of documentary evidence only, the Tribunal shall hold a hearing for the examination of all witnesses and expert witnesses as well as for any argument;
d. The award shall be made within six months from the date when the Tribunal is constituted unless, in exceptional circumstances, the Registrar extends the time; and
e. The Tribunal shall state the reasons upon which the award is based in summary form, unless the parties have agreed that no reasons are to be given.

6 — Number and Appointment of Arbitrators

6.1 A sole arbitrator shall be appointed unless the parties have agreed otherwise or unless it appears to the Registrar, giving due regard to any proposals by the parties, the complexity, the quantum involved or other relevant circumstances of the dispute, that the dispute warrants the appointment of three arbitrators.

6.2 If the parties have agreed that any arbitrator is to be appointed by one or more of the parties, or by any third person including the arbitrators already appointed, that agreement shall be treated as an agreement to nominate an arbitrator under these Rules.

6.3 In all cases, the arbitrators nominated by the parties, or by any third person including the arbitrators already appointed, shall be subject to appointment by the President in his discretion.

6.4 The President shall appoint an arbitrator as soon as practicable. Any decision by the President to appoint an arbitrator under these Rules shall be final and not subject to appeal.

6.5 The President may appoint any nominee whose appointment has already been suggested or proposed by any party.

6.6 The terms of appointment of each arbitrator shall be fixed by the Registrar in accordance with these Rules and Practice Notes for the time being in force, or in accordance with the agreement of the parties.

7 — Sole Arbitrator

7.1 If a sole arbitrator is to be appointed, either party may propose to the other the names of one or more persons, one of whom would serve as the sole arbitrator. Where the parties have reached an agreement on the nomination of a sole arbitrator, Rule 6.3 shall apply.

7.2 If within 21 days after receipt by the Registrar of the Notice of Arbitration, the parties have not reached an agreement on the nomination of a sole arbitrator, or if at any time either party so requests, the President shall make the appointment as soon as practicable.

8 — Three Arbitrators

8.1 If three arbitrators are to be appointed, each party shall nominate one arbitrator.

8.2 If a party fails to make a nomination within 14 days after receipt of a party's nomination of an arbitrator, or in the manner otherwise agreed by the parties, the President shall proceed to appoint the arbitrator on its behalf.

8.3 Unless the parties have agreed upon another procedure for appointing the third arbitrator, or if such agreed procedure does not result in a nomination within the time limit fixed by the parties or by the Registrar, the third arbitrator, who shall act as the presiding arbitrator, shall be appointed by the President.

9 — Multi-party Appointment of Arbitrator(s)

9.1 Where there are more than two parties in the arbitration, and three arbitrators are to be appointed, the Claimant(s) shall jointly nominate one arbitrator and the Respondent(s) shall jointly nominate one arbitrator. In the absence of both such joint nominations having been made within 28 days of receipt by the Registrar of the Notice of Arbitration or within the period agreed by the parties or set by the Registrar, the President shall appoint all three arbitrators and shall designate one of them to act as the presiding arbitrator.

9.2 Where there are more than two parties in the arbitration, and one arbitrator is to be appointed, all parties are to agree on an arbitrator. In the absence of such a joint nomination having been made within 28 days of receipt by the Registrar of the Notice of Arbitration or within the period agreed by the parties or set by the Registrar, the President shall appoint the arbitrator.

10 — Qualifications of Arbitrators

10.1 Any arbitrator, whether or not nominated by the parties, conducting an arbitration under these Rules shall be and remain at all times independent and impartial, and shall not act as advocate for any party.

10.2 In making an appointment under these Rules, the President shall have due regard to any qualifications required of the arbitrator by the agreement of the parties and to such considerations as are likely to secure the appointment of an independent and impartial arbitrator.

10.3 The President shall also consider whether the arbitrator has sufficient availability to determine the case in a prompt and efficient manner appropriate to the nature of the arbitration.

10.4 An arbitrator shall disclose to the parties and to the Registrar any circumstance that may give rise to justifiable doubts as to his impartiality or independence as soon as reasonably practicable and in any event before appointment by the President.

10.5 An arbitrator shall immediately disclose to the parties, to the other arbitrators and to the Registrar any circumstance of a similar nature that may arise during the arbitration.

10.6 If the parties have agreed on any qualifications required of an arbitrator, the arbitrator shall be deemed to meet such qualifications unless a party states that the arbitrator is not so qualified within 14 days after receipt by that party of the notification of the nomination of the arbitrator. In the event of such a challenge, the procedure for challenge and replacement of an arbitrator in Rules 11 to 14 shall apply.

10.7 No party or anyone acting on its behalf shall have any *ex parte* communication relating to the case with any arbitrator or with any candidate for appointment as party-nominated arbitrator, except to advise the candidate of the general nature of the controversy and of the anticipated proceedings and to discuss the candidate's qualifications, availability or independence in relation to the parties, or to discuss the suitability of candidates for selection as a third arbitrator where the parties or party-designated arbitrators are to participate in that selection. No party or anyone acting on its behalf shall have any *ex parte* communication relating to the case with any candidate for presiding arbitrator.

11 — Challenge of Arbitrators

11.1 Any arbitrator may be challenged if circumstances exist that give rise to justifiable doubts as to the arbitrator's impartiality or independence or if the arbitrator does not possess any requisite qualification on which the parties have agreed.

11.2 A party may challenge the arbitrator nominated by him only for reasons of which he becomes aware after the appointment has been made.

12 — Notice of Challenge

12.1 Subject to Rule 10.6, a party who intends to challenge an arbitrator shall send a notice of challenge within 14 days after the receipt of the notice of appointment of the arbitrator who is being challenged or within 14 days after the circumstances mentioned in Rule 11.1 or 11.2 became known to that party.

12.2 The notice of challenge shall be filed with the Registrar and shall be sent simultaneously to the other party, the arbitrator who is being challenged and the other members of the Tribunal. The notice of challenge shall be in writing and shall state the reasons for the challenge. The Registrar may order a suspension of the arbitration until the challenge is resolved.

12.3 When an arbitrator is challenged by one party, the other party may agree to the challenge. The challenged arbitrator may also withdraw from his office. In neither case does this imply acceptance of the validity of the grounds for the challenge.

12.4 In instances referred to in Rule 12.3, the procedure provided in Rules 6, 7, 8 or 9, as the case may be, shall be used for the appointment of the substitute arbitrator, even if during the process of appointing the challenged arbitrator, a party had failed to exercise his right to nominate. The time limits provided in those Rules shall commence from the date of receipt of the agreement of the other party to the challenge or the challenged arbitrator's withdrawal.

13 — Decision on Challenge

13.1 If, within 7 days of receipt of the notice of challenge, the other party does not agree to the challenge and the arbitrator who is being challenged does not withdraw voluntarily, the Court shall decide the challenge.

13.2 If the Court sustains the challenge, a substitute arbitrator shall be appointed in accordance with the procedure provided in Rules 6, 7, 8 or 9, as the case may be, even if during the process of appointing the challenged arbitrator, a party had failed to exercise his right to nominate. The time limits provided in those Rules shall commence from the date of the Registrar's notification to the parties of the decision by the Court.

13.3 If the Court rejects the challenge, the arbitrator shall continue with the arbitration. Unless the Registrar ordered the suspension of the arbitration pursuant to Rule 12.2, pending the determination of the challenge by the Court, the challenged arbitrator shall be entitled to proceed in the arbitration.

13.4 The Court may fix the costs of the challenge and may direct by whom and how such costs should be borne.

13.5 The Court's decision made under this Rule shall be final and not subject to appeal.

14 — Replacement of an Arbitrator

14.1 In the event of the death, resignation or removal of an arbitrator during the course of the arbitral proceedings, a substitute arbitrator shall be appointed in accordance with the procedure applicable to the nomination and appointment of the arbitrator being replaced.

14.2 In the event that an arbitrator refuses or fails to act or in the event of a de jure or de facto impossibility of him performing his functions or that he is not fulfilling his functions in accordance with the Rules or within prescribed time limits, the procedure for challenge and replacement of an arbitrator provided in Rules 11 to 13 and 14.1 shall apply.

14.3 After consulting with the parties, the President may in his discretion remove an arbitrator who refuses or fails to act, or in the event of a *de jure* or *de facto* impossibility of him performing his functions, or if he is not fulfilling his functions in accordance with the Rules or within the prescribed time limits.

15 — Repetition of Hearings in the Event of Replacement of an Arbitrator

If under Rules 12 to 14 the sole or presiding arbitrator is replaced, any hearings held previously shall be repeated unless otherwise agreed by the parties. If any other arbitrator is replaced, such prior hearings may be repeated at the discretion of the Tribunal after consulting with the parties. If the Tribunal has issued an interim or partial award, any hearings related solely to that award shall not be repeated, and the award shall remain in effect.

16 — Conduct of the Proceedings

16.1 The Tribunal shall conduct the arbitration in such manner as it considers appropriate, after consulting with the parties, to ensure the fair, expeditious, economical and final determination of the dispute.

16.2 The Tribunal shall determine the relevance, materiality and admissibility of all evidence. Evidence need not be admissible in law.

16.3 As soon as practicable after the appointment of all arbitrators, the Tribunal shall conduct a preliminary meeting with the parties, in person or by any other means, to discuss the procedures that will be most appropriate and efficient for the case.

16.4 The Tribunal may in its discretion direct the order of proceedings, bifurcate proceedings, exclude cumulative or irrelevant testimony or other evidence and direct the parties to focus their presentations on issues the decision of which could dispose of all or part of the case.

16.5 A presiding arbitrator may make procedural rulings alone, subject to revision by the Tribunal.

16.6 All statements, documents or other information supplied to the Tribunal and the Registrar by one party shall simultaneously be communicated to the other party.

17 — Submissions by the Parties

17.1 Unless the Tribunal determines otherwise, the submission of written statements shall proceed as set out in this Rule.

17.2 Unless already submitted pursuant to Rule 3.2, the Claimant shall, within a period of time to be determined by the Tribunal, send to the Respondent and the Tribunal a Statement of Claim setting out in full detail:

a. a statement of facts supporting the claim;

b. the legal grounds or arguments supporting the claim;

and

c. the relief claimed together with the amount of all quantifiable claims.

17.3 Unless already submitted pursuant to Rule 4.2, the Respondent shall, within a period of time to be determined by the Tribunal, send to the Claimant a Statement of Defence setting out its full defence to the Statement of Claim, including without limitation, the facts and contentions of law on which it relies. The Statement of Defence shall also state any counterclaim, which shall comply with the requirements of Rule 17.2.

17.4 If a counterclaim is made, the Claimant shall, within a period of time to be determined by the Tribunal, send to the Respondent a Statement of Defence to the Counterclaim stating in full detail which of the facts and contentions of law in the Statement of Counterclaim it admits or denies, on what grounds it denies the claims or contentions, and on what other facts and contentions of law it relies.

17.5 A party may amend its claim, counterclaim or other submissions unless the Tribunal considers it inappropriate to allow such amendment having regard to the delay in making it or prejudice to the other party or any other circumstances. However, a claim or counterclaim may not be amended in such a manner that the amended claim or counterclaim falls outside the scope of the arbitration agreement.

17.6 The Tribunal shall decide which further submissions shall be required from the parties or may be presented by them. The Tribunal shall fix the periods of time for communicating such submissions.

17.7 All submissions referred to in this Rule shall be accompanied by copies of all supporting documents which have not previously been submitted by any party.

17.8 If the Claimant fails within the time specified to submit its Statement of Claim, the Tribunal may issue an order for the termination of the arbitral proceedings or give such other directions as may be appropriate.

17.9 If the Respondent fails to submit a Statement of Defence, or if at any point any party fails to avail itself of the opportunity to present its case in the manner directed by the Tribunal, the Tribunal may proceed with the arbitration.

18 — Seat of Arbitration

18.1 The parties may agree on the seat of arbitration. Failing such an agreement, the seat of arbitration shall be Singapore, unless the Tribunal determines, having regard to all the circumstances of the case, that another seat is more appropriate.

18.2 The Tribunal may hold hearings and meetings by any means it considers expedient or appropriate and at any location it considers convenient or appropriate.

19 — Language of Arbitration

19.1 Unless the parties have agreed otherwise, the Tribunal shall determine the language to be used in the proceedings.

19.2 If a document is written in a language other than the language(s) of the arbitration, the Tribunal, or if the Tribunal has not been established, the Registrar, may order that party to submit a translation in a form to be determined by the Tribunal or the Registrar.

20 — Party Representatives

Any party may be represented by legal practitioners or any other representatives.

21 — Hearings

21.1 Unless the parties have agreed on documents-only arbitration, the Tribunal shall, if either party so requests or the Tribunal so decides, hold a hearing for the presentation of evidence and/or for oral submissions on the merits of the dispute, including without limitation any issue as to jurisdiction.

21.2 The Tribunal shall fix the date, time and place of any meeting or hearing and shall give the parties reasonable notice.

21.3 If any party to the proceedings fails to appear at a hearing without showing sufficient cause for such failure, the Tribunal may proceed with the arbitration and may make the award based on the submissions and evidence before it.

21.4 Unless the parties agree otherwise, all meetings and hearings shall be in private, and any recordings, transcripts, or documents used shall remain confidential.

22 — Witnesses

22.1 Before any hearing, the Tribunal may require any party to give notice of the identity of witnesses, including expert witnesses, whom it intends to produce, the subject matter of their testimony and its relevance to the issues.

22.2 The Tribunal has discretion to allow, refuse or limit the appearance of witnesses.

22.3 Any witness who gives oral evidence may be questioned by each of the parties, their representatives and the Tribunal in such manner as the Tribunal shall determine.

22.4 The Tribunal may direct the testimony of witnesses to be presented in written form, either as signed statements or sworn affidavits or any other form of recording. Subject to Rule 22.2, any party may request that such a witness should attend for oral examination. If the witness fails to attend, the Tribunal may place such weight on the written testimony as it thinks fit, disregard it or exclude it altogether.

22.5 It shall be permissible for any party or its representatives to interview any witness or potential witness (that may be presented by that party) prior to his appearance at any hearing.

23 — Tribunal-Appointed Experts

23.1 Unless the parties have agreed otherwise, the Tribunal:

a. may following consultation with the parties, appoint an expert to report on specific issues; and

b. may require a party to give such expert any relevant information, or to produce or provide access to any relevant documents, goods or property for inspection.

23.2 Any expert so appointed shall submit a report in writing to the Tribunal. Upon receipt of such a written report, the Tribunal shall deliver a copy of the report to the parties and invite the parties to submit written comments on the report.

23.3 Unless the parties have agreed otherwise, if the Tribunal considers it necessary, any such expert shall, after delivery of his written report, participate in a hearing. At the hearing, the parties shall have the opportunity to question him.

24 — Additional Powers of the Tribunal

In addition to the powers specified in these Rules and not in derogation of the mandatory rules of law applicable to the arbitration, the Tribunal shall have the power to:

a. order the correction of any contract, but only to the extent required to rectify any mistake which it determines to have been made by all the parties to that contract. This is subject to the condition that the proper law of the contract allows rectification of such contract;

b. upon the application of a party, allow one or more third parties to be joined in the arbitration, provided that such person is a party to the arbitration agreement, with the written consent of such third party, and thereafter make a single final award or separate awards in respect of all parties;

c. except as provided in Rules 28.2 and 29.5, extend or abbreviate any time limits provided by these Rules or by its directions;

d. conduct such enquiries as may appear to the Tribunal to be necessary or expedient;

e. order the parties to make any property or item available for inspection;

f. order the preservation, storage, sale or disposal of any property or item which is or forms part of the subject-matter of the dispute;

g. order any party to produce to the Tribunal and to the other parties for inspection, and to supply copies of, any document in their possession or control which the Tribunal considers relevant to the case and material to its outcome;

h. issue an award for unpaid costs of the arbitration;

i. direct any party to give evidence by affidavit or in any other form;

j. direct any party to ensure that any award which may be made in the arbitral proceedings is not rendered ineffectual by the dissipation of assets by a party;

k. order any party to provide security for legal or other costs in any manner the Tribunal thinks fit;

l. order any party to provide security for all or part of any amount in dispute in the arbitration;

m. proceed with the arbitration notwithstanding the failure or refusal of any party to comply with these Rules or with the Tribunal's orders or directions or any partial award or to attend any meeting or hearing, and to impose such sanctions as the Tribunal deems appropriate;

n. decide, where appropriate, any issue not expressly or impliedly raised in the submissions filed under Rule 17 provided such issue has been clearly brought to the notice of the other party and that other party has been given adequate opportunity to respond;

o. determine the law applicable to the arbitral proceedings;
and

p. determine any claim of legal or other privilege.

25 — Jurisdiction of the Tribunal

25.1 If a party objects to the existence or validity of the arbitration agreement or to the competence of SIAC to administer an arbitration before the Tribunal is appointed, the Registrar shall determine if reference of such an objection is to be made to the Court. If the Registrar so determines, the

Court shall decide if it is *prima facie* satisfied that a valid arbitration agreement under the Rules may exist. The proceedings shall be terminated if the Court is not so satisfied. Any decision by the Registrar or the Court is without prejudice to the power of the Tribunal to rule on its own jurisdiction.

25.2 The Tribunal shall have the power to rule on its own jurisdiction, including any objections with respect to the existence, termination or validity of the arbitration agreement. For that purpose, an arbitration agreement which forms part of a contract shall be treated as an agreement independent of the other terms of the contract. A decision by the Tribunal that the contract is null and void shall not entail *ipso jure* the invalidity of the arbitration agreement.

25.3 A plea that the Tribunal does not have jurisdiction shall be raised not later than in the Statement of Defence or in a Statement of Defence to a Counterclaim. A plea that the Tribunal is exceeding the scope of its jurisdiction shall be raised promptly after the Tribunal has indicated its intention to decide on the matter alleged to be beyond the scope of its jurisdiction. In either case the Tribunal may nevertheless admit a late plea under this Rule if it considers the delay justified. A party is not precluded from raising such a plea by the fact that he has nominated, or participated in the nomination of, an arbitrator.

25.4 The Tribunal may rule on a plea referred to in Rule 25.3 either as a preliminary question or in an award on the merits.

25.5 A party may rely on a claim or defence for the purpose of a set-off to the extent permitted by the applicable law.

26 — Interim and Emergency Relief

26.1 The Tribunal may, at the request of a party, issue an order or an award granting an injunction or any other interim relief it deems appropriate. The Tribunal may order the party requesting interim relief to provide appropriate security in connection with the relief sought.

26.2 A party in need of emergency interim relief prior to the constitution of the Tribunal may apply for such relief pursuant to the procedures set forth in Schedule 1.

26.3 A request for interim relief made by a party to a judicial authority prior to the constitution of the Tribunal, or in exceptional circumstances thereafter, is not incompatible with these Rules.

27 — Applicable law, *amiable compositeur*

27.1 The Tribunal shall apply the rules of law designated by the parties as applicable to the substance of the dispute. Failing such designation by the parties, the Tribunal shall apply the law which it determines to be appropriate.

27.2 The Tribunal shall decide as *amiable compositeur* or *ex aequo et bono* only if the parties have expressly authorised the Tribunal to do so.

27.3 In all cases, the Tribunal shall decide in accordance with the terms of the contract, if any, and shall take into account any usage of trade applicable to the transaction.

28 — The Award

28.1 The Tribunal shall, after consulting with the parties, declare the proceedings closed if it is satisfied that the parties have no further relevant and material evidence to produce or submission to make. The Tribunal may, on its own motion or upon application of a party but before any award is made, reopen the proceedings.

28.2 Before making any award, the Tribunal shall submit it in draft form to the Registrar. Unless the Registrar extends time or the parties agree otherwise, the Tribunal shall submit the draft award to the Registrar within 45 days from the date on which the Tribunal declares the proceedings closed. The Registrar may, as soon as practicable, suggest modifications as to the form of the award and, without affecting the Tribunal's liberty of decision, may also draw its attention to points of substance. No award shall be made by the Tribunal until it has been approved by the Registrar as to its form.

28.3 The Tribunal may make separate awards on different issues at different times.

28.4 If any arbitrator fails to cooperate in the making of the award, having been given a reasonable opportunity to do so, the remaining arbitrators shall proceed in his absence.

28.5 Where there is more than one arbitrator, the Tribunal shall decide by a majority. Failing a majority decision, the presiding arbitrator alone shall make the award for the Tribunal.

28.6 The award shall be delivered to the Registrar, who shall transmit certified copies to the parties upon the full settlement of the costs of arbitration.

28.7 The Tribunal may award simple or compound interest on any sum which is the subject of the arbitration at such rates as the parties may have agreed or, in the absence of such agreement, as the Tribunal determines to be appropriate, in respect of any period which the Tribunal determines to be appropriate.

28.8 In the event of a settlement, if any party so requests, the Tribunal may render a consent award recording the settlement. If the parties do not require a consent award, the parties shall confirm to the Registrar that a settlement has been reached. The Tribunal shall be discharged and the arbitration concluded upon payment of any outstanding costs of arbitration.

28.9 Subject to Rule 29 and Schedule 1, by agreeing to arbitration under these Rules, the parties undertake to carry out the award immediately and without delay, and they also irrevocably waive their rights to any form of appeal, review or recourse to any state court or other judicial authority insofar as such waiver may be validly made and the parties further agree that an award shall be final and binding on the parties from the date it is made.

28.10 SIAC may publish any award with the names of the parties and other identifying information redacted.

29 — Correction of Awards and Additional Awards

29.1 Within 30 days of receipt of an award, a party may, by written notice to the Registrar and to any other party, request the Tribunal to correct in the award any error in computation, any clerical or typographical error or any error of a similar nature. Any other party may comment on such request within 15 days of its receipt. If the Tribunal considers the request to be justified, it shall make the correction within 30 days of receipt of the request. Any correction, made in the original award or in a separate memorandum, shall constitute part of the award.

29.2 The Tribunal may correct any error of the type referred to in Rule 29.1 on its own initiative within 30 days of the date of the award.

29.3 Within 30 days of receipt of an award, a party may, by written notice to the Registrar and to any other party, request the Tribunal to make an additional award as to claims presented in the arbitral proceedings but not dealt with in the award. Any other party may comment on such request within 15 days of its receipt. If the Tribunal considers the request to be justified, it shall make the additional award within 45 days of receipt of the request.

29.4 Within 30 days of the receipt of an award, a party may, by written notice to the Registrar and to any other party, request that the Tribunal give an interpretation of the award. Any other party may comment on such request within 15 days of its receipt. If the Tribunal considers the request to be justified, it shall give the interpretation in writing within 45 days after the receipt of the request. The interpretation shall form part of the award.

29.5 The Registrar may extend the time limits in this Rule.

29.6 The provisions of Rule 28 shall apply in the same manner with the necessary or appropriate changes in relation to a correction of an award and to any additional award made.

30 — Fees and Deposits

30.1 The Tribunal's fees and SIAC's fees shall be ascertained in accordance with the Schedule of Fees in force at the time of commencement of the arbitration. Alternative methods of determining the Tribunal's fees may be agreed by the parties prior to the constitution of the Tribunal.

30.2 The Registrar shall fix the advances on costs of the arbitration. Unless the Registrar directs otherwise, 50% of such advances shall be payable by the Claimant and the remaining 50% of such advances shall be payable by the Respondent. The Registrar may fix separate advances on costs for claims and counterclaims, respectively.

30.3 Where the amount of the claim or the counterclaim is not quantifiable at the time payment is due, a provisional estimate of the costs of the arbitration shall be made by the Registrar. Such estimate may be based on the nature of the controversy and the circumstances of the case. This may be adjusted in light of such information as may subsequently become available.

30.4 The Registrar may from time to time direct parties to make further advances towards costs of the arbitration incurred or to be incurred on behalf of or for the benefit of the parties.

30.5 If a party fails to make the advances or deposits directed, the Registrar may, after consultation with the Tribunal and the parties, direct the Tribunal to suspend work and set a time limit on the expiry of which the relevant claims or counterclaims shall be considered as withdrawn without prejudice to the party reintroducing the same claims or counterclaims in another proceeding.

30.6 Parties are jointly and severally liable for the costs of the arbitration. Any party is free to pay the whole of the advances or deposits on costs of the arbitration in respect of the claim or the counterclaim should the other party fail to pay its share. The Tribunal or the Registrar may suspend its work, in whole or in part, should the advances or deposits directed under this Rule remain either wholly or in part unpaid. On the application of a party, the Tribunal may issue an award for unpaid costs pursuant to Rule 24 (h).

30.7 If the arbitration is settled or disposed of without a hearing, the costs of arbitration shall be finally determined by the Registrar. The Registrar shall have regard to all the circumstances of the case, including the stage of proceedings at which the arbitration is settled or disposed of. In the event that the costs of arbitration determined are less than the deposits made, there shall be a refund in such proportions as the parties may agree, or failing an agreement, in the same proportions as the deposits were made.

30.8 All advances shall be made to and held by SIAC. Any interest which may accrue on such deposits shall be retained by SIAC.

31 — Costs of the Arbitration

31.1 The Tribunal shall specify in the award, the total amount of the costs of the arbitration. Unless the parties have agreed otherwise, the Tribunal shall determine in the award the apportionment of the costs of the arbitration among the parties.

31.2 The term "costs of the arbitration" includes:

a. the Tribunal's fees and expenses;

b. SIAC's administrative fees and expenses; and

c. the costs of expert advice and of other assistance required by the Tribunal.

32 — Tribunal's Fees and Expenses

32.1 The fees of the Tribunal shall be fixed by the Registrar in accordance with the Schedule of Fees and the stage of the proceedings at which the arbitration ended. In exceptional circumstances, the Registrar may allow an additional fee over that prescribed in the Schedule of Fees to be paid.

32.2 The Tribunal's reasonable out-of-pocket expenses necessarily incurred and other allowances shall be reimbursed in accordance with the applicable Practice Note.

33 — Party's Legal and Other Costs

The Tribunal shall have the authority to order in its award that all or a part of the legal or other costs of a party be paid by another party.

34 — Exclusion of Liability

34.1 SIAC, including the President, members of its Court, directors, officers, employees or any arbitrator, shall not be liable to any person for any negligence, act or omission in connection with any arbitration governed by these Rules.

34.2 SIAC, including the President, members of its Court, directors, officers, employees or any arbitrator, shall not be under any obligation to make any statement in connection with any arbitration governed by these Rules. No party shall seek to make the President, any member of the Court, director, officer, employee or arbitrator act as a witness in any legal proceedings in connection with any arbitration governed by these Rules.

35 — Confidentiality

35.1 The parties and the Tribunal shall at all times treat all matters relating to the proceedings and the award as confidential.

35.2 A party or any arbitrator shall not, without the prior written consent of all the parties, disclose to a third party any such matter except:
a. for the purpose of making an application to any competent court of any State to enforce or challenge the award;
b. pursuant to the order of or a subpoena issued by a court of competent jurisdiction;
c. for the purpose of pursuing or enforcing a legal right or claim;
d. in compliance with the provisions of the laws of any State which are binding on the party making the disclosure;
e. in compliance with the request or requirement of any regulatory body or other authority; or
f. pursuant to an order by the Tribunal on application by a party with proper notice to the other parties.
35.3 In this Rule, "matters relating to the proceedings" means the existence of the proceedings, and the pleadings, evidence and other materials in the arbitration proceedings and all other documents produced by another party in the proceedings or the award arising from the proceedings, but excludes any matter that is otherwise in the public domain.
35.4 The Tribunal has the power to take appropriate measures, including issuing an order or award for sanctions or costs, if a party breaches the provisions of this Rule.

36 — Decisions of the President, the Court and the Registrar

36.1 Subject to Rule 25.1, the decisions of the President, the Court and the Registrar with respect to all matters relating to an arbitration shall be conclusive and binding upon the parties and the Tribunal. The President, the Court and the Registrar shall not be required to provide reasons for such decisions.
36.2 Subject to Rule 25.1, the parties shall be taken to have waived any right of appeal or review in respect of any decisions of the President, the Court and the Registrar to any state court or other judicial authority.

37 — General Provisions

37.1 A party who knows that any provision or requirement under these Rules has not been complied with and proceeds with the arbitration without promptly stating its objection shall be deemed to have waived its right to object.
37.2 In all matters not expressly provided for in these Rules, the President, the Court, the Registrar and the Tribunal shall act in the spirit of these Rules and shall make every reasonable effort to ensure the fair, expeditious and economical conclusion of the arbitration and the enforceability of any

award.

37.3 The Registrar may from time to time issue Practice Notes to supplement, regulate and implement these Rules for the purpose of facilitating the administration of arbitrations governed by these Rules.

SCHEDULES

Schedule 1

Emergency Arbitrator

1. A party in need of emergency relief may, concurrent with or following the filing of a Notice of Arbitration but prior to the constitution of the Tribunal, make an application for emergency interim relief. The party shall notify the Registrar and all other parties in writing of the nature of the relief sought and the reasons why such relief is required on an emergency basis. The application shall also set forth the reasons why the party is entitled to such relief. Such notice must include a statement certifying that all other parties have been notified or an explanation of the steps taken in good faith to notify other parties. The application shall also be accompanied by payment of any fees set by the Registrar for proceedings pursuant to this Schedule 1.

2. The President shall, if he determines that SIAC should accept the application, seek to appoint an Emergency Arbitrator within one business day of receipt by the Registrar of such application and payment of any required fee.

3. Prior to accepting appointment, a prospective Emergency Arbitrator shall disclose to the Registrar any circumstance that may give rise to justifiable doubts as to his impartiality or independence. Any challenge to the appointment of the Emergency Arbitrator must be made within one business day of the communication by the Registrar to the parties of the appointment of the Emergency Arbitrator and the circumstances disclosed.

4. An Emergency Arbitrator may not act as an arbitrator in any future arbitration relating to the dispute, unless agreed by the parties.

5. The Emergency Arbitrator shall, as soon as possible but in any event within two business days of appointment, establish a schedule for consideration of the application for emergency relief. Such schedule shall provide a reasonable opportunity to all parties to be heard, but may provide for proceedings by telephone conference or on written submissions as alternatives to a formal hearing. The Emergency Arbitrator shall have the powers vested in the Tribunal pursuant to these Rules, including the authority to rule on his own jurisdiction, and shall resolve any disputes over the application of this Schedule 1.

6. The Emergency Arbitrator shall have the power to order or award any interim relief that he deems necessary. The Emergency Arbitrator shall give reasons for his decision in writing. The Emergency Arbitrator may modify or vacate the interim award or order for good cause shown.

7. The Emergency Arbitrator shall have no further power to act after the Tribunal is constituted. The Tribunal may reconsider, modify or vacate the interim award or order of emergency relief issued by the Emergency Arbitrator. The Tribunal is not bound by the reasons given by the Emergency Arbitrator. Any order or award issued by the Emergency Arbitrator shall, in any event, cease to be binding if the Tribunal is not constituted within 90 days of such order or award or when the Tribunal makes a final award or if the claim is withdrawn.
8. Any interim award or order of emergency relief may be conditioned on provision by the party seeking such relief of appropriate security.
9. An order or award pursuant to this Schedule 1 shall be binding on the parties when rendered. By agreeing to arbitration under these Rules, the parties undertake to comply with such an order or award without delay.
10. The costs associated with any application pursuant to this Schedule 1 shall initially be apportioned by the Emergency Arbitrator, subject to the power of the Tribunal to determine finally the apportionment of such costs.
11. These Rules shall apply as appropriate to any proceeding pursuant to this Schedule 1, taking into account the inherent urgency of such a proceeding. The Emergency Arbitrator may decide in what manner these Rules shall apply as appropriate, and his decision as to such matters is final and not subject to appeal.

Schedule 2
Special Provisions for SIAC Domestic Arbitration Rules

1 — Repeal

The Domestic Arbitration Rules of the Singapore International Arbitration Centre, 2nd Edition, 1 September 2002 (SIAC Domestic Arbitration Rules) are repealed.

2 — Transitional Provision

Where parties have by agreement expressly referred to arbitration under the SIAC Domestic Arbitration Rules, the agreement shall be deemed to be a reference to arbitration under these Rules and to this Schedule.

3 — Summary Award

1. Upon the expiry of the time limit for the filing of Statement of Claim, Statement of Defence and Counterclaim under Rule 17 of these Rules, but not later than 21 days after the expiry, if a party considers that there is no valid defence to its claim or any substantial part of its claim, it may file with the Tribunal and serve on the other party and the Registrar an application for a summary award on the claim or part of the claim. "Claim" in this Article includes a counterclaim.

2. The application shall be accompanied by an affidavit stating the full facts and detailed grounds in support of it.
3. Within 21 days after service of the application and affidavit, the other party must, if it wishes to contest the application, file and serve an affidavit in opposition. The applicant must file any reply affidavit within 14 days from receipt of the opposition. No further affidavit may be filed without leave of the Tribunal.
4. The Tribunal may on hearing the application:
a. make an award summarily; or
b. make an order dismissing the application; or
c. make an order requiring security for the applicant's claim or part of the claim.
5. The Tribunal's award or order shall be made in writing within 21 days after the close of hearing unless extended by the Registrar.
6. Costs referred to in Rules 31, 32 and 33 of these Rules may be awarded in the discretion of the Tribunal.
7. Rules 28.2, 29.1 and 29.2 of these Rules shall apply, with the necessary or appropriate changes, to a summary award made under this Article.
8. Where the application is dismissed, the Tribunal shall proceed to continue with the arbitration.

CHINA INTERNATIONAL ECONOMIC AND TRADE ARBITRATION COMMISSION (CIETAC) ARBITRATION RULES

(Revised and adopted by the China Council for the Promotion of International Trade/China Chamber of International Commerce on November 4, 2014. Effective as of January 1, 2015.)

Chapter I General Provisions

Article 1 — The Arbitration Commission

1. The China International Economic and Trade Arbitration Commission ("CIETAC"), originally named the Foreign Trade Arbitration Commission of the China Council for the Promotion of International Trade and later renamed the Foreign Economic and Trade Arbitration Commission of the China Council for the Promotion of International Trade, concurrently uses as its name the "Arbitration Institute of the China Chamber of International Commerce".

2. Where an arbitration agreement provides for arbitration by the China Council for the Promotion of International Trade/China Chamber of International Commerce, or by the Arbitration Commission or the Arbitration Institute of the China Council for the Promotion of International Trade/China Chamber of International Commerce, or refers to CIETAC's previous names, it shall be deemed that the parties have agreed to arbitration by CIETAC.

Article 2 — Structure and Duties

1. The Chairman of CIETAC shall perform the functions and duties vested in him/her by these Rules while a Vice Chairman may perform the Chairman's functions and duties with the Chairman's authorization.

2. CIETAC has an Arbitration Court (the "Arbitration Court"), which performs its functions in accordance with these Rules under the direction of the authorized Vice Chairman and the President of the Arbitration Court.

3. CIETAC is based in Beijing. It has sub-commissions or arbitration centers (Appendix I). The sub-commissions/arbitration centers are CIETAC's branches, which accept arbitration applications and administer arbitration cases with CIETAC's authorization.

4. A sub-commission/arbitration center has an arbitration court, which performs the functions of the Arbitration Court in accordance with these Rules under the direction of the president of the arbitration court of the sub-commission/arbitration center.

5. Where a case is administered by a sub-commission/arbitration center, the functions and duties vested in the President of the Arbitration Court under these Rules may, by his/her authorization, be performed by the president of the arbitration court of the relevant sub-commission/arbitration center.

6. The parties may agree to submit their disputes to CIETAC or a sub-

commission/arbitration center of CIETAC for arbitration. Where the parties have agreed to arbitration by CIETAC, the Arbitration Court shall accept the arbitration application and administer the case. Where the parties have agreed to arbitration by a sub-commission/arbitration center, the arbitration court of the sub-commission/arbitration center agreed upon by the parties shall accept the arbitration application and administer the case. Where the sub-commission/arbitration center agreed upon by the parties does not exist or its authorization has been terminated, or where the agreement is ambiguous, the Arbitration Court shall accept the arbitration application and administer the case.

In the event of any dispute, a decision shall be made by CIETAC.

Article 3 — Jurisdiction

1. CIETAC accepts cases involving economic, trade and other disputes of a contractual or non-contractual nature, based on an agreement of the parties.

2. The cases referred to in the preceding paragraph include:

(a) international or foreign-related disputes;

(b) disputes related to the Hong Kong Special Administrative Region, the Macao Special Administrative Region and the Taiwan region; and

(c) domestic disputes.

Article 4 — Scope of Application

1. These Rules uniformly apply to CIETAC and its sub-commissions/arbitration centers.

2. Where the parties have agreed to refer their dispute to CIETAC for arbitration, they shall be deemed to have agreed to arbitration in accordance with these Rules.

3. Where the parties agree to refer their dispute to CIETAC for arbitration but have agreed on a modification of these Rules or have agreed on the application of other arbitration rules, the parties' agreement shall prevail unless such agreement is inoperative or in conflict with a mandatory provision of the law applicable to the arbitral proceedings. Where the parties have agreed on the application of other arbitration rules, CIETAC shall perform the relevant administrative duties.

4. Where the parties agree to refer their dispute to arbitration under these Rules without providing the name of the arbitration institution, they shall be deemed to have agreed to refer the dispute to arbitration by CIETAC.

5. Where the parties agree to refer their disputes to arbitration under CIETAC's customized arbitration rules for a specific trade or profession, the parties' agreement shall prevail. However, if the dispute falls outside the scope of the specific rules, these Rules shall apply.

Article 5 — Arbitration Agreement

1. An arbitration agreement means an arbitration clause in a contract or any other form of a written agreement concluded between the parties providing for the settlement of disputes by arbitration.
2. The arbitration agreement shall be in writing. An arbitration agreement is in writing if it is contained in the tangible form of a document such as a contract, letter, telegram, telex, fax, electronic data interchange, or email. An arbitration agreement shall be deemed to exist where its existence is asserted by one party and not denied by the other during the exchange of the Request for Arbitration and the Statement of Defense.
3. Where the law applicable to an arbitration agreement has different provisions as to the form and validity of the arbitration agreement, those provisions shall prevail.
4. An arbitration clause contained in a contract shall be treated as a clause independent and separate from all other clauses of the contract, and an arbitration agreement attached to a contract shall also be treated as independent and separate from all other clauses of the contract. The validity of an arbitration clause or an arbitration agreement shall not be affected by any modification, cancellation, termination, transfer, expiry, invalidity, ineffectiveness, rescission or non-existence of the contract.

Article 6 — Objection to Arbitration Agreement and/or Jurisdiction

1. CIETAC has the power to determine the existence and validity of an arbitration agreement and its jurisdiction over an arbitration case. CIETAC may, where necessary, delegate such power to the arbitral tribunal.
2. Where CIETAC is satisfied by *prima facie* evidence that a valid arbitration agreement exists, it may make a decision based on such evidence that it has jurisdiction over the arbitration case, and the arbitration shall proceed. Such a decision shall not prevent CIETAC from making a new decision on jurisdiction based on facts and/or evidence found by the arbitral tribunal during the arbitral proceedings that are inconsistent with the prima *facie* evidence.
3. Where CIETAC has delegated the power to determine jurisdiction to the arbitral tribunal, the arbitral tribunal may either make a separate decision on jurisdiction during the arbitral proceedings or incorporate the decision in the final arbitral award.
4. Any objection to an arbitration agreement and/or the jurisdiction over an arbitration case shall be raised in writing before the first oral hearing held by the arbitral tribunal. Where a case is to be decided on the basis of documents only, such an objection shall be raised before the submission of

the first substantive defense.
5. The arbitration shall proceed notwithstanding an objection to the arbitration agreement and/or jurisdiction over the arbitration case.
6. The aforesaid objections to and/or decisions on jurisdiction by CIETAC shall include objections to and/or decisions on a party's standing to participate in the arbitration.
7. CIETAC or its authorized arbitral tribunal shall decide to dismiss the case upon finding that CIETAC has no jurisdiction over an arbitration case. Where a case is to be dismissed before the formation of the arbitral tribunal, the decision shall be made by the President of the Arbitration Court. Where the case is to be dismissed after the formation of the arbitral tribunal, the decision shall be made by the arbitral tribunal.

Article 7 — Place of Arbitration

1. Where the parties have agreed on the place of arbitration, the parties' agreement shall prevail.
2. Where the parties have not agreed on the place of arbitration or their agreement is ambiguous, the place of arbitration shall be the domicile of CIETAC or its sub-commission/arbitration center administering the case. CIETAC may also determine the place of arbitration to be another location having regard to the circumstances of the case.
3. The arbitral award shall be deemed as having been made at the place of Arbitration.

Article 8 — Service of Documents and Periods of Time

1. All documents, notices and written materials in relation to the arbitration may be delivered in person or sent by registered mail or express mail, fax, or by any other means considered proper by the Arbitration Court or the arbitral tribunal.
2. The arbitration documents referred to in the preceding Paragraph 1 shall be sent to the address provided by the party itself or by its representative(s), or to an address agreed by the parties. Where a party or its representative(s) has not provided an address or the parties have not agreed on an address, the arbitration documents shall be sent to such party's address as provided by the other party or its representative(s).
3. Any arbitration correspondence to a party or its representative(s) shall be deemed to have been properly served on the party if delivered to the addressee or sent to the addressee's place of business, registration, domicile, habitual residence or mailing address, or where, after reasonable inquiries by the other party, none of the aforesaid addresses can be found, the arbitration correspondence is sent by the Arbitration Court to the

addressee's last known place of business, registration, domicile, habitual residence or mailing address by registered or express mail, or by any other means that can provide a record of the attempt at delivery, including but not limited to service by public notary, entrustment or retention.

4. The periods of time specified in these Rules shall begin on the day following the day when the party receives or should have received the arbitration correspondence, notices or written materials sent by the Arbitration Court.

Article 9 — Good Faith

Arbitration participants shall proceed with the arbitration in good faith.

Article 10 — Waiver of Right to Object

A party shall be deemed to have waived its right to object where it knows or should have known that any provision of, or requirement under, these Rules has not been complied with and yet participates in or proceeds with the arbitral proceedings without promptly and explicitly submitting its objection in writing to such non-compliance.

Chapter II

Arbitral Proceedings

Section 1 Request for Arbitration, Defense and Counterclaim

Article 11 — Commencement of Arbitration

The arbitral proceedings shall commence on the day on which the Arbitration Court receives a Request for Arbitration.

Article 12 — Application for Arbitration

A party applying for arbitration under these Rules shall:

1. Submit a Request for Arbitration in writing signed and/or sealed by the Claimant or its authorized representative(s), which shall, inter alia, include:

(a) the names and addresses of the Claimant and the Respondent, including the zip code, telephone, fax, email, or any other means of electronic telecommunications;

(b) a reference to the arbitration agreement that is invoked;

(c) a statement of the facts of the case and the main issues in dispute;

(d) the claim of the Claimant; and

(e) the facts and grounds on which the claim is based.

2. Attach to the Request for Arbitration the relevant documentary and other evidence on which the Claimant's claim is based.

3. Pay the arbitration fee in advance to CIETAC in accordance with its Arbitration Fee Schedule.

Article 13 — Acceptance of a Case

1. Upon the written application of a party, CIETAC shall accept a case in

accordance with an arbitration agreement concluded between the parties either before or after the occurrence of the dispute, in which it is provided that disputes are to be referred to arbitration by CIETAC.

2. Upon receipt of a Request for Arbitration and its attachments, where after examination the Arbitration Court finds the formalities required for arbitration application to be complete, it shall send a Notice of Arbitration to both parties together with one copy each of these Rules and CIETAC's Panel of Arbitrators. The Request for Arbitration and its attachments submitted by the Claimant shall be sent to the Respondent under the same cover.

3. Where after examination the Arbitration Court finds the formalities required for the arbitration application to be incomplete, it may request the Claimant to complete them within a specified time period. The Claimant shall be deemed not to have submitted a Request for Arbitration if it fails to complete the required formalities within the specified time period. In such a case, the Claimant's Request for Arbitration and its attachments shall not be kept on file by the Arbitration Court.

4. After CIETAC accepts a case, the Arbitration Court shall designate a case manager to assist with the procedural administration of the case.

Article 14 — Multiple Contracts

The Claimant may initiate a single arbitration concerning disputes arising out of or in connection with multiple contracts, provided that:

(a) such contracts consist of a principal contract and its ancillary contract(s), or such contracts involve the same parties as well as legal relationships of the same nature;

(b) the disputes arise out of the same transaction or the same series of transactions; and

(c) the arbitration agreements in such contracts are identical or compatible.

Article 15 — Statement of Defense

1. The Respondent shall file a Statement of Defense in writing within forty-five (45) days from the date of its receipt of the Notice of Arbitration. If the Respondent has justified reasons to request an extension of the time period, the arbitral tribunal shall decide whether to grant an extension. Where the arbitral tribunal has not yet been formed, the decision on whether to grant the extension of the time period shall be made by the Arbitration Court.

2. The Statement of Defense shall be signed and/or sealed by the Respondent or its authorized representative(s), and shall, *inter alia*, include the following contents and attachments:

(a) the name and address of the Respondent, including the zip code,

telephone, fax, email, or any other means of electronic telecommunications;
(b) the defense to the Request for Arbitration setting forth the facts and grounds on which the defense is based; and
(c) the relevant documentary and other evidence on which the defense is based.
3. The arbitral tribunal has the power to decide whether to accept a Statement of Defense submitted after the expiration of the above time period.
4. Failure by the Respondent to file a Statement of Defense shall not affect the conduct of the arbitral proceedings.

Article 16 — Counterclaim

1. The Respondent shall file a counterclaim, if any, in writing within forty-five (45) days from the date of its receipt of the Notice of Arbitration. If the Respondent has justified reasons to request an extension of the time period, the arbitral tribunal shall decide whether to grant an extension. Where the arbitral tribunal has not yet been formed, the decision on whether to grant the extension of the time period shall be made by the Arbitration Court.
2. When filing the counterclaim, the Respondent shall specify the counterclaim in its Statement of Counterclaim and state the facts and grounds on which the counterclaim is based with the relevant documentary and other evidence attached thereto.
3. When filing the counterclaim, the Respondent shall pay an arbitration fee in advance in accordance with the Arbitration Fee Schedule of CIETAC within a specified time period, failing which the Respondent shall be deemed not to have filed any counterclaim.
4. Where the formalities required for filing a counterclaim are found to be complete, the Arbitration Court shall send a Notice of Acceptance of Counterclaim to the parties. The Claimant shall submit its Statement of Defense in writing within thirty (30) days from the date of its receipt of the Notice. If the Claimant has justified reasons to request an extension of the time period, the arbitral tribunal 10 shall decide whether to grant such an extension. Where the arbitral tribunal has not yet been formed, the decision on whether to grant the extension of the time period shall be made by the Arbitration Court.
5. The arbitral tribunal has the power to decide whether to accept a counterclaim or a Statement of Defense submitted after the expiration of the above time period.
6. Failure of the Claimant to file a Statement of Defense to the Respondent's counterclaim shall not affect the conduct of the arbitral

proceedings.

Article 17 — Amendment to Claim or Counterclaim

The Claimant may apply to amend its claim and the Respondent may apply to amend its counterclaim. However, the arbitral tribunal may refuse any such amendment if it considers that the amendment is too late and may delay the arbitral proceedings.

Article 18 — Joinder of Additional Parties

1. During the arbitral proceedings, a party wishing to join an additional party to the arbitration may file the Request for Joinder with CIETAC, based on the arbitration agreement invoked in the arbitration that prima facie binds the additional party. Where the Request for Joinder is filed after the formation of the arbitral tribunal, a decision shall be made by CIETAC after the arbitral tribunal hears from all parties including the additional party if the arbitral tribunal considers the joinder necessary.

The date on which the Arbitration Court receives the Request for Joinder shall be deemed to be the date of the commencement of arbitration against the additional party.

2. The Request for Joinder shall contain the case number of the existing arbitration; the name, address and other means of communication of each of the parties, including the additional party; the arbitration agreement invoked to join the additional party as well as the facts and grounds the request relies upon; and the claim.

The relevant documentary and other evidence on which the request is based shall be attached to the Request for Joinder.

3. Where any party objects to the arbitration agreement and/or jurisdiction over the arbitration with respect to the joinder proceedings, CIETAC has the power to decide on its jurisdiction based on the arbitration agreement and relevant evidence.

4. After the joinder proceedings commence, the conduct of the arbitral proceedings shall be decided by the Arbitration Court if the arbitral tribunal is not formed, or shall be decided by the arbitral tribunal if it has been formed.

5. Where the joinder takes place prior to the formation of the arbitral tribunal, the relevant provisions on party's nominating or entrusting of the Chairman of CIETAC to appoint arbitrator under these Rules shall apply to the additional party. The arbitral tribunal shall be formed in accordance with Article 29 of these Rules.

Where the joinder takes place after the formation of the arbitral tribunal, the arbitral tribunal shall hear from the additional party on the past arbitral

proceedings including the formation of the arbitral tribunal. If the additional party requests to nominate or entrust the Chairman of CIETAC to appoint an arbitrator, both parties shall nominate or entrust the Chairman of CIETAC to appoint arbitrators again. The arbitral tribunal shall be formed in accordance with Article 29 of these Rules.
6. The relevant provisions on the submission of the Statement of Defense and Counterclaim under these Rules shall apply to the additional party. The time period for the additional party to submit its Statement of Defense and Counterclaim shall start counting from the date of its receipt of the Notice of Joinder.
7. CIETAC shall have the power to decide not to join an additional party where the additional party is *prima facie* not bound by the arbitration agreement invoked in the arbitration, or where any other circumstance exists that makes the joinder inappropriate.

Article 19 — Consolidation of Arbitrations

1. At the request of a party, CIETAC may consolidate two or more arbitrations pending under these Rules into a single arbitration if:
(a) all of the claims in the arbitrations are made under the same arbitration agreement;
(b) the claims in the arbitrations are made under multiple arbitration agreements that are identical or compatible and the arbitrations involve the same parties as well as legal relationships of the same nature;
(c) the claims in the arbitrations are made under multiple arbitration agreements that are identical or compatible and the multiple contracts involved consist of a principle contract and its ancillary contract(s); or
(d) all the parties to the arbitrations have agreed to consolidation.
2. In deciding whether to consolidate the arbitrations in accordance with the preceding Paragraph 1, CIETAC shall take into account the opinions of all parties and other relevant factors such as the correlation between the arbitrations concerned, including the nomination and appointment of arbitrators in the separate arbitrations.
3. Unless otherwise agreed by all the parties, the arbitrations shall be consolidated into the arbitration that was first commenced.
4. After the consolidation of arbitrations, the conduct of the arbitral proceedings shall be decided by the Arbitration Court if the arbitral tribunal is not formed, or shall be decided by the arbitral tribunal if it has been formed.

Article 20 — Submission and Exchange of Arbitration Documents

1. All arbitration documents from the parties shall be submitted to the

Arbitration Court.

2. All arbitration documents to be exchanged during the arbitral proceedings shall be exchanged among the arbitral tribunal and the parties by the Arbitration Court unless otherwise agreed by the parties and with the consent of the arbitral tribunal or otherwise decided by the arbitral tribunal.

Article 21 — Copies of Arbitration Documents

When submitting the Request for Arbitration, the Statement of Defense, the Statement of Counterclaim, evidence, and other arbitration documents, the parties shall make their submissions in quintuplicate. Where there are multiple parties, additional copies shall be provided accordingly. Where the party applies for preservation of property or protection of evidence, it shall also provide additional copies accordingly. Where the arbitral tribunal is composed of a sole arbitrator, the number of copies submitted may be reduced by two.

Article 22 — Representation

A party may be represented by its authorized Chinese and/or foreign representative(s) in handling matters relating to the arbitration. In such a case, a Power of Attorney shall be forwarded to the Arbitration Court by the party or its authorized representative(s).

Article 23 — Conservatory and Interim Measures

1. Where a party applies for conservatory measures pursuant to the laws of the People's Republic of China, CIETAC shall forward the party's application to the competent court designated by that party in accordance with the law.

2. In accordance with the applicable law or the agreement of the parties, a party may apply to the Arbitration Court for emergency relief pursuant to the CIETAC Emergency Arbitrator Procedures (Appendix III). The emergency arbitrator may decide to order or award necessary or appropriate emergency measures. The decision of the emergency arbitrator shall be binding upon both parties.

3. At the request of a party, the arbitral tribunal may decide to order or award any interim measure it deems necessary or proper in accordance with the applicable law or the agreement of the parties and may require the requesting party to provide appropriate security in connection with the measure.

Section 2 Arbitrators and the Arbitral Tribunal

Article 24 — Duties of Arbitrator

An arbitrator shall not represent either party, and shall be and remain independent of the parties and treat them equally.

Article 25 — Number of Arbitrators

1. The arbitral tribunal shall be composed of one or three arbitrators.

2. Unless otherwise agreed by the parties or provided by these Rules, the arbitral tribunal shall be composed of three arbitrators.

Article 26 — Nomination or Appointment of Arbitrator

1. CIETAC maintains a Panel of Arbitrators which uniformly applies to itself and all its sub-commissions/arbitration centers. The parties shall nominate arbitrators from the Panel of Arbitrators provided by CIETAC.

2. Where the parties have agreed to nominate arbitrators from outside CIETAC's Panel of Arbitrators, an arbitrator so nominated by the parties or nominated according to the agreement of the parties may act as arbitrator subject to the confirmation by the Chairman of CIETAC.

Article 27 — Three-Arbitrator Tribunal

1. Within fifteen (15) days from the date of receipt of the Notice of Arbitration, the Claimant and the Respondent shall each nominate, or entrust the Chairman of CIETAC to appoint, an arbitrator, failing which the arbitrator shall be appointed by the Chairman of CIETAC.

2. Within fifteen (15) days from the date of the Respondent's receipt of the Notice of Arbitration, the parties shall jointly nominate, or entrust the Chairman of CIETAC to appoint, the third arbitrator, who shall act as the presiding arbitrator.

3. The parties may each recommend one to five arbitrators as candidates for the presiding arbitrator and shall each submit a list of recommended candidates within the time period specified in the preceding Paragraph 2. Where there is only one common candidate on the lists, such candidate shall be the presiding arbitrator jointly nominated by the parties. Where there is more than one common candidate on the lists, the Chairman of CIETAC shall choose the presiding arbitrator from among the common candidates having regard to the circumstances of the case, and he/she shall act as the presiding arbitrator jointly nominated by the parties. Where there is no common candidate on the lists, the presiding arbitrator shall be appointed by the Chairman of CIETAC.

4. Where the parties have failed to jointly nominate the presiding arbitrator according to the above provisions, the presiding arbitrator shall be appointed by the Chairman of CIETAC.

Article 28 — Sole-Arbitrator Tribunal

Where the arbitral tribunal is composed of one arbitrator, the sole arbitrator shall be nominated pursuant to the procedures stipulated in Paragraphs 2, 3 and 4 of Article 27 of these Rules.

Article 29 — Multiple-Party Tribunal

1. Where there are two or more Claimants and/or Respondents in an Arbitration case, the Claimant side and/or the Respondent side, following discussion, shall each jointly nominate or jointly entrust the Chairman of CIETAC to appoint one arbitrator.

2. The presiding arbitrator or the sole arbitrator shall be nominated in accordance with the procedures stipulated in Paragraphs 2, 3 and 4 of Article 27 of these Rules. When making such nomination pursuant to Paragraph 3 of Article 27 of these Rules, the Claimant side and/or the Respondent side, following discussion, shall each submit a list of their jointly agreed candidates.

3. Where either the Claimant side or the Respondent side fails to jointly nominate or jointly entrust the Chairman of CIETAC to appoint one arbitrator within fifteen (15) days from the date of its receipt of the Notice of Arbitration, the Chairman of CIETAC shall appoint all three members of the arbitral tribunal and designate one of them to act as the presiding arbitrator.

Article 30 — Considerations in Appointing Arbitrators

When appointing arbitrators pursuant to these Rules, the Chairman of CIETAC shall take into consideration the law applicable to the dispute, the place of arbitration, the language of arbitration, the nationalities of the parties, and any other factor(s) the Chairman considers relevant.

Article 31 — Disclosure

1. An arbitrator nominated by the parties or appointed by the Chairman of CIETAC shall sign a Declaration and disclose any facts or circumstances likely to give rise to justifiable doubts as to his/her impartiality or independence.

2. If circumstances that need to be disclosed arise during the arbitral proceedings, the arbitrator shall promptly disclose such circumstances in writing.

3. The Declaration and/or the disclosure of the arbitrator shall be submitted to the Arbitration Court to be forwarded to the parties.

Article 32 — Challenge to Arbitrator

1. Upon receipt of the Declaration and/or the written disclosure of an arbitrator, a party wishing to challenge the arbitrator on the grounds of the disclosed facts or circumstances shall forward the challenge in writing within ten (10) days from the date of such receipt. If a party fails to file a challenge within the above time period, it may not subsequently challenge the arbitrator on the basis of the matters disclosed by the arbitrator.

2. A party having justifiable doubts as to the impartiality or independence of an arbitrator may challenge that arbitrator in writing and shall state the facts and reasons on which the challenge is based with supporting evidence.
3. A party may challenge an arbitrator in writing within fifteen (15) days from the date it receives the Notice of Formation of the Arbitral Tribunal. Where a party becomes aware of a reason for a challenge after such receipt, the party may challenge the arbitrator in writing within fifteen (15) days after such reason has become known to it, but no later than the conclusion of the last oral hearing.
4. The challenge by one party shall be promptly communicated to the other party, the arbitrator being challenged and the other members of the arbitral tribunal.
5. Where an arbitrator is challenged by one party and the other party agrees to the challenge, or the arbitrator being challenged voluntarily withdraws from his/her office, such arbitrator shall no longer be a member of the arbitral tribunal. However, in neither case shall it be implied that the reasons for the challenge are sustained.
6. In circumstances other than those specified in the preceding Paragraph 5, the Chairman of CIETAC shall make a final decision on the challenge with or without stating the reasons.
7. An arbitrator who has been challenged shall continue to serve on the arbitral Tribunal until a final decision on the challenge has been made by the Chairman of CIETAC.

Article 33 — Replacement of Arbitrator

1. In the event that an arbitrator is prevented *de jure* or *de facto* from fulfilling his/her functions, or fails to fulfill his/her functions in accordance with the requirements of these Rules or within the time period specified in these Rules, the Chairman of CIETAC shall have the power to replace the arbitrator. Such arbitrator may also voluntarily withdraw from his/her office.
2. The Chairman of CIETAC shall make a final decision on whether or not an arbitrator should be replaced with or without stating the reasons.
3. In the event that an arbitrator is unable to fulfill his/her functions due to challenge or replacement, a substitute arbitrator shall be nominated or appointed within the time period specified by the Arbitration Court according to the same procedure that applied to the nomination or appointment of the arbitrator being challenged or replaced. If a party fails to nominate or appoint a substitute arbitrator accordingly, the substitute arbitrator shall be appointed by the Chairman of CIETAC.

4. After the replacement of an arbitrator, the arbitral tribunal shall decide whether and to what extent the previous proceedings in the case shall be repeated.

Article 34 — Continuation of Arbitration by Majority

After the conclusion of the last oral hearing, if an arbitrator on a three-member tribunal is unable to participate in the deliberations and/or to render the award owing to his/her demise or to his/her removal from CIETAC's Panel of Arbitrators, or for any other reason, the other two arbitrators may request the Chairman of CIETAC to replace that arbitrator pursuant to Article 33 of these Rules. After consulting with the parties and upon the approval of the Chairman of CIETAC, the other two arbitrators may also continue the arbitral proceedings and make decisions, rulings, or render the award. The Arbitration Court shall notify the parties of the above circumstances.

Section 3 Hearing

Article 35 — Conduct of Hearing

1. The arbitral tribunal shall examine the case in any way it deems appropriate unless otherwise agreed by the parties. Under all circumstances, the arbitral tribunal shall act impartially and fairly and shall afford a reasonable opportunity to both parties to present their case.
2. The arbitral tribunal shall hold oral hearings when examining the case. However, the arbitral tribunal may examine the case on the basis of documents only if the parties so agree and the arbitral tribunal consents or the arbitral tribunal deems that oral hearings are unnecessary and the parties so agree.
3. Unless otherwise agreed by the parties, the arbitral tribunal may adopt an inquisitorial or adversarial approach in hearing the case having regard to the circumstances of the case.
4. The arbitral tribunal may hold deliberations at any place or in any manner that it considers appropriate.
5. Unless otherwise agreed by the parties, the arbitral tribunal may, if it considers it necessary, issue procedural orders or question lists, produce terms of reference, or hold pre-hearing conferences, etc. With the authorization of the other members of the arbitral tribunal, the presiding arbitrator may decide on the procedural arrangements for the arbitral proceedings at his/her own discretion.

Article 36 — Place of Oral Hearing

1. Where the parties have agreed on the place of an oral hearing, the case shall be heard at that agreed place except in the circumstances stipulated in

Paragraph 3 of Article 82 of these Rules.
2. Unless otherwise agreed by the parties, the place of oral hearings shall be in Beijing for a case administered by the Arbitration Court or at the domicile of the sub-commission/arbitration center administering the case, or if the arbitral tribunal considers it necessary and with the approval of the President of the Arbitration Court, at another location.

Article 37 — Notice of Oral Hearing

1. Where a case is to be examined by way of an oral hearing, the parties shall be notified of the date of the first oral hearing at least twenty (20) days in advance of the oral hearing. A party having justified reasons may request a postponement of the oral hearing. However, the party shall communicate such request in writing to the arbitral tribunal within five (5) days of its receipt of the notice of the oral hearing. The arbitral tribunal shall decide whether or not to postpone the oral hearing.
2. Where a party has justified reasons for its failure to submit a request for a postponement of the oral hearing in accordance with the preceding Paragraph 1, the arbitral tribunal shall decide whether or not to accept the request.
3. A notice of a subsequent oral hearing, a notice of a postponed oral hearing, as well as a request for postponement of such an oral hearing, shall not be subject to the time periods specified in the preceding Paragraph 1.

Article 38 — Confidentiality

1. Hearings shall be held in camera. Where both parties request an open hearing, the arbitral tribunal shall make a decision.
2. For cases heard in camera, the parties and their representatives, the arbitrators, the witnesses, the interpreters, the experts consulted by the arbitral tribunal, the appraisers appointed by the arbitral tribunal and other relevant persons shall not disclose to any outsider any substantive or procedural matters relating to the case.

Article 39 — Default

1. If the Claimant fails to appear at an oral hearing without showing sufficient cause, or withdraws from an on-going oral hearing without the permission of the arbitral tribunal, the Claimant may be deemed to have withdrawn its application for arbitration. In such a case, if the Respondent has filed a counterclaim, the arbitral tribunal shall proceed with the hearing of the counterclaim and make a default award.
2. If the Respondent fails to appear at an oral hearing without showing sufficient cause, or withdraws from an on-going oral hearing without the permission of the arbitral tribunal, the arbitral tribunal may proceed with the

arbitration and make a default award. In such a case, if the Respondent has filed a counterclaim, the Respondent may be deemed to have withdrawn its counterclaim.

Article 40 — Record of Oral Hearing

1. The arbitral tribunal may arrange for a written and/or an audio-visual record to be made of an oral hearing. The arbitral tribunal may, if it considers it necessary, take minutes of the oral hearing and request the parties and/or their representatives, witnesses and/or other persons involved to sign and/or affix their seals to the written record or the minutes.
2. The written record, the minutes and the audio-visual record of an oral hearing shall be available for use and reference by the arbitral tribunal.
3. At the request of a party, the Arbitration Court may, having regard to the specific circumstances of the arbitration, decide to engage a stenographer to make a stenographic record of an oral hearing, the cost of which shall be advanced by the parties.

Article 41 — Evidence

1. Each party shall bear the burden of proving the facts on which it relies to support its claim, defense or counterclaim and provide the basis for its opinions, arguments and counter-arguments.
2. The arbitral tribunal may specify a time period for the parties to produce evidence and the parties shall produce evidence within the specified time period. The arbitral tribunal may refuse to admit any evidence produced after that time period. If a party experiences difficulties in producing evidence within the specified time period, it may apply for an extension before the end of the period. The arbitral tribunal shall decide whether or not to extend the time period.
3. If a party bearing the burden of proof fails to produce evidence within the specified time period, or if the produced evidence is not sufficient to support its claim or counterclaim, it shall bear the consequences thereof.

Article 42 — Examination of Evidence

1. Where a case is examined by way of an oral hearing, the evidence shall be produced at the oral hearing and may be examined by the parties.
2. Where a case is to be decided on the basis of documents only, or where the evidence is submitted after the hearing and both parties have agreed to examine the evidence by means of writing, the parties may examine the evidence in writing. In such circumstances, the parties shall submit their written opinions on the evidence within the time period specified by the arbitral tribunal.

Article 43 — Investigation and Evidence Collection by the Arbitral Tribunal

1. The arbitral tribunal may undertake investigation and collect evidence as it considers necessary.
2. When investigating and collecting evidence, the arbitral tribunal may notify the parties to be present. In the event that one or both parties fail to be present after being notified, the investigation and collection of evidence shall proceed without being affected.
3. Evidence collected by the arbitral tribunal through its investigation shall be forwarded to the parties for their comments.

Article 44 — Expert's Report and Appraiser's Report

1. The arbitral tribunal may consult experts or appoint appraisers for clarification on specific issues of the case. Such an expert or appraiser may be a Chinese or foreign institution or natural person.
2. The arbitral tribunal has the power to request the parties, and the parties are also obliged, to deliver or produce to the expert or appraiser any relevant materials, documents, property, or physical objects for examination, inspection or appraisal by the expert or appraiser.
3. Copies of the expert's report and the appraiser's report shall be forwarded to the parties for their comments. At the request of either party and with the approval of the arbitral tribunal, the expert or appraiser shall participate in an oral hearing and give explanations on the report when the arbitral tribunal considers it necessary.

Article 45 — Suspension of the Arbitral Proceedings

1. Where the parties jointly or separately request a suspension of the arbitral proceedings, or under circumstances where such suspension is necessary, the arbitral proceedings may be suspended.
2. The arbitral proceedings shall resume as soon as the reason for the suspension disappears or the suspension period ends.
3. The arbitral tribunal shall decide whether to suspend or resume the arbitral proceedings. Where the arbitral tribunal has not yet been formed, the decision shall be made by the President of the Arbitration Court.

Article 46 — Withdrawal and Dismissal

1. A party may withdraw its claim or counterclaim in its entirety. In the event that the Claimant withdraws its claim in its entirety, the arbitral tribunal may proceed with its examination of the counterclaim and render an arbitral award thereon. In the event that the Respondent withdraws its counterclaim in its entirety, the arbitral tribunal may proceed with the examination of the claim and render an arbitral award thereon.

2. A party may be deemed to have withdrawn its claim or counterclaim if the arbitral proceedings cannot proceed for reasons attributable to that party.
3. A case may be dismissed if the claim and counterclaim have been withdrawn in their entirety. Where a case is to be dismissed prior to the formation of the arbitral tribunal, the President of the Arbitration Court shall make a decision on the dismissal. Where a case is to be dismissed after the formation of the arbitral tribunal, the arbitral tribunal shall make the decision.
4. The seal of CIETAC shall be affixed to the Dismissal Decision referred to in the preceding Paragraph 3 and Paragraph 7 of Article 6 of these Rules.

Article 47 — Combination of Conciliation with Arbitration

1. Where both parties wish to conciliate, or where one party wishes to conciliate and the other party's consent has been obtained by the arbitral tribunal, the arbitral tribunal may conciliate the dispute during the arbitral proceedings. The parties may also settle their dispute by themselves.
2. With the consents of both parties, the arbitral tribunal may conciliate the case in a manner it considers appropriate.
3. During the process of conciliation, the arbitral tribunal shall terminate the conciliation proceedings if either party so requests or if the arbitral tribunal considers that further conciliation efforts will be futile.
4. The parties shall sign a settlement agreement where they have reached settlement through conciliation by the arbitral tribunal or by themselves.
5. Where the parties have reached a settlement agreement through conciliation by the arbitral tribunal or by themselves, they may withdraw their claim or counterclaim, or request the arbitral tribunal to render an arbitral award or a conciliation statement in accordance with the terms of the settlement agreement.
6. Where the parties request for a conciliation statement, the conciliation statement shall clearly set forth the claims of the parties and the terms of the settlement agreement. It shall be signed by the arbitrators, sealed by CIETAC, and served upon both parties.
7. Where conciliation is not successful, the arbitral tribunal shall resume the arbitral proceedings and render an arbitral award.
8. Where the parties wish to conciliate their dispute but do not wish to have conciliation conducted by the arbitral tribunal, CIETAC may, with the consents of both parties, assist the parties to conciliate the dispute in a manner and procedure it considers appropriate.
9. Where conciliation is not successful, neither party may invoke any opinion, view or statement, and any proposal or proposition expressing

acceptance or opposition by either party or by the arbitral tribunal in the process of conciliation as grounds for any claim, defense or counterclaim in the subsequent arbitral proceedings, judicial proceedings, or any other proceedings.

10. Where the parties have reached a settlement agreement by themselves through negotiation or conciliation before the commencement of an arbitration, either party may, based on an arbitration agreement concluded between them that provides for arbitration by CIETAC and the settlement agreement, request CIETAC to constitute an arbitral tribunal to render an arbitral award in accordance with the terms of the settlement agreement. Unless otherwise agreed by the parties, the Chairman of CIETAC shall appoint a sole arbitrator to form such an arbitral tribunal, which shall examine the case in a procedure it considers appropriate and render an award in due course. The specific procedure and time period for rendering the award shall not be subject to other provisions of these Rules.

Chapter III
Arbitral Award

Article 48 — Time Period for Rendering Award

1. The arbitral tribunal shall render an arbitral award within six (6) months from the date on which the arbitral tribunal is formed.
2. Upon the request of the arbitral tribunal, the President of the Arbitration Court may extend the time period if he/she considers it truly necessary and the reasons for the extension truly justified.
3. Any suspension period shall be excluded when calculating the time period in the preceding Paragraph 1.

Article 49 — Making of Award

1. The arbitral tribunal shall independently and impartially render a fair and reasonable arbitral award based on the facts of the case and the terms of the contract, in accordance with the law, and with reference to international practices.
2. Where the parties have agreed on the law applicable to the merits of their dispute, the parties' agreement shall prevail. In the absence of such an agreement or where such agreement is in conflict with a mandatory provision of the law, the arbitral tribunal shall determine the law applicable to the merits of the dispute.
3. The arbitral tribunal shall state in the award the claims, the facts of the dispute, the reasons on which the award is based, the result of the award, the allocation of the arbitration costs, and the date on which and the place at which the award is made. The facts of the dispute and the reasons on which

the award is based may not be stated in the award if the parties have so agreed, or if the award is made in accordance with the terms of a settlement agreement between the parties. The arbitral tribunal has the power to fix in the award the specific time period for the parties to perform the award and the liabilities for failure to do so within the specified time period.
4. The seal of CIETAC shall be affixed to the arbitral award.
5. Where a case is examined by an arbitral tribunal composed of three arbitrators, the award shall be rendered by all three arbitrators or a majority of the arbitrators. A written dissenting opinion shall be kept with the file and may be appended to the award. Such dissenting opinion shall not form a part of the award.
6. Where the arbitral tribunal cannot reach a majority opinion, the arbitral award shall be rendered in accordance with the presiding arbitrator's opinion. The written opinions of the other arbitrators shall be kept with the file and may be appended to the award. Such written opinions shall not form a part of the award.
7. Unless the arbitral award is made in accordance with the opinion of the presiding arbitrator or the sole arbitrator and signed by the same, the arbitral award shall be signed by a majority of the arbitrators. An arbitrator who has a dissenting opinion may or may not sign his/her name on the award.
8. The date on which the award is made shall be the date on which the award comes into legal effect.
9. The arbitral award is final and binding upon both parties. Neither party may bring a lawsuit before a court or make a request to any other organization for revision of the award.

Article 50 — Partial Award

1. Where the arbitral tribunal considers it necessary, or where a party so requests and the arbitral tribunal agrees, the arbitral tribunal may first render a partial award on any part of the claim before rendering the final award. A partial award is final and binding upon both parties.
2. Failure of either party to perform a partial award shall neither affect the arbitral proceedings nor prevent the arbitral tribunal from making the final award.

Article 51 — Scrutiny of Draft Award

The arbitral tribunal shall submit its draft award to CIETAC for scrutiny before signing the award. CIETAC may bring to the attention of the arbitral tribunal issues addressed in the award on the condition that the arbitral tribunal's independence in rendering the award is not affected.

Article 52 — Allocation of Fees

1. The arbitral tribunal has the power to determine in the arbitral award the arbitration fees and other expenses to be paid by the parties to CIETAC.
2. The arbitral tribunal has the power to decide in the arbitral award, having regard to the circumstances of the case, that the losing party shall compensate the winning party for the expenses reasonably incurred by it in pursuing the case. In deciding whether or not the winning party's expenses incurred in pursuing the case are reasonable, the arbitral tribunal shall take into consideration various factors such as the outcome and complexity of the case, the workload of the winning party and/or its representative(s), the amount in dispute, etc.

Article 53 — Correction of Award

1. Within a reasonable time after the award is made, the arbitral tribunal may, on its own initiative, make corrections in writing of any clerical, typographical or calculation errors, or any errors of a similar nature contained in the award.
2. Within thirty (30) days from its receipt of the arbitral award, either party may request the arbitral tribunal in writing for a correction of any clerical, typographical or calculation errors, or any errors of a similar nature contained in the award. If such an error does exist in the award, the arbitral tribunal shall make the correction in writing within thirty (30) days of its receipt of the written request for the correction.
3. The above written correction shall form a part of the arbitral award and shall be subject to the provisions in Paragraphs 4 to 9 of Article 49 of these Rules.

Article 54 — Additional Award

1. Where any matter which should have been decided by the arbitral tribunal was omitted from the arbitral award, the arbitral tribunal may, on its own initiative, make an additional award within a reasonable time after the award is made.
2. Either party may, within thirty (30) days from its receipt of the arbitral award, request the arbitral tribunal in writing for an additional award on any claim or counterclaim which was advanced in the arbitral proceedings but was omitted from the award. If such an omission does exist, the arbitral tribunal shall make an additional award within thirty (30) days of its receipt of the written request.
3. Such additional award shall form a part of the arbitral award and shall be subject to the provisions in Paragraphs 4 to 9 of Article 49 of these Rules.

Article 55 — Performance of Award

1. The parties shall perform the arbitral award within the time period specified in the award. If no time period is specified in the award, the parties shall perform the award immediately.
2. Where one party fails to perform the award, the other party may apply to a competent court for enforcement of the award in accordance with the law.

Chapter IV
Summary Procedure

Article 56 — Application

1. Unless otherwise agreed by the parties, the Summary Procedure shall apply to any case where the amount in dispute does not exceed RMB 5,000,000; or where the amount in dispute exceeds RMB 5,000,000, yet one party applies for arbitration under the Summary Procedure and the other party agrees in writing; or where both parties have agreed to apply the Summary Procedure.
2. Where there is no monetary claim or the amount in dispute is not clear, CIETAC shall determine whether or not to apply the Summary Procedure after full consideration of relevant factors, including but not limited to the complexity of the case and the interests involved.

Article 57 — Notice of Arbitration

Where after examination the Claimant's arbitration application is accepted for arbitration under the Summary Procedure, the Arbitration Court shall send a Notice of Arbitration to both parties.

Article 58 — Formation of the Arbitral Tribunal

Unless otherwise agreed by the parties, a sole-arbitrator tribunal shall be formed in accordance with Article 28 of these Rules to hear a case under the Summary Procedure.

Article 59 — Defense and Counterclaim

1. The Respondent shall submit its Statement of Defense, evidence and other supporting documents within twenty (20) days of its receipt of the Notice of Arbitration. Counterclaim, if any, shall also be filed with evidence and supporting documents within such time period.
2. The Claimant shall file its Statement of Defense to the Respondent's counterclaim within twenty (20) days of its receipt of the counterclaim and its attachments.
3. If a party has justified reasons to request an extension of the time period, the arbitral tribunal shall decide whether to grant such extension. Where the arbitral tribunal has not yet been formed, such decision shall be made by the Arbitration Court.

Article 60 — Conduct of Hearing

The arbitral tribunal may examine the case in the manner it considers appropriate. The arbitral tribunal may decide whether to examine the case solely on the basis of the written materials and evidence submitted by the parties or to hold an oral hearing.

Article 61 — Notice of Oral Hearing

1. For a case examined by way of an oral hearing, after the arbitral tribunal has fixed a date for the first oral hearing, the parties shall be notified of the date at least fifteen (15) days in advance of the oral hearing. A party having justified reasons may request a postponement of the oral hearing. However, the party shall communicate such request in writing to the arbitral tribunal within three (3) days of its receipt of the notice of the oral hearing. The arbitral tribunal shall decide whether or not to postpone the oral hearing.
2. If a party has justified reasons for failure to submit a request for a postponement of the oral hearing in accordance with the preceding Paragraph 1, the arbitral tribunal shall decide whether to accept such a request.
3. A notice of a subsequent oral hearing, a notice of a postponed oral hearing, as well as a request for postponement of such oral hearing, shall not be subject to the time periods specified in the preceding Paragraph 1.

Article 62 — Time Period for Rendering Award

1. The arbitral tribunal shall render an arbitral award within three (3) months from the date on which the arbitral tribunal is formed.
2. Upon the request of the arbitral tribunal, the President of the Arbitration Court may extend the time period if he/she considers it truly necessary and the reasons for the extension truly justified.
3. Any suspension period shall be excluded when calculating the time period in the preceding Paragraph 1.

Article 63 — Change of Procedure

The Summary Procedure shall not be affected by any amendment to the claim or by the filing of a counterclaim. Where the amount in dispute of the amended claim or that of the counterclaim exceeds RMB 5,000,000, the Summary Procedure shall continue to apply unless the parties agree or the arbitral tribunal decides that a change to the general procedure is necessary.

Article 64 — Context Reference

The relevant provisions in the other Chapters of these Rules shall apply to matters not covered in this Chapter.

Chapter V Special Provisions for Domestic Arbitration

Article 65 — Application

1. The provisions of this Chapter shall apply to domestic arbitration cases.
2. The provisions of the Summary Procedure in Chapter IV shall apply if a domestic arbitration case falls within the scope of Article 56 of these Rules.

Article 66 — Acceptance of a Case

1. Upon receipt of a Request for Arbitration, where the Arbitration Court finds the Request to meet the requirements specified in Article 12 of these Rules, the Arbitration Court shall notify the parties accordingly within five (5) days from its receipt of the Request. Where a Request for Arbitration is found not to be in conformity with the requirements, the Arbitration Court shall notify the party in writing of its refusal of acceptance with reasons stated.
2. Upon receipt of a Request for Arbitration, where after examination, the Arbitration Court finds the Request not to be in conformity with the formality requirements specified in Article 12 of these Rules, it may request the Claimant to comply with the requirements within a specified time period.

Article 67 — Formation of the Arbitral Tribunal

The arbitral tribunal shall be formed in accordance with the provisions of Articles 25, 26, 27, 28, 29 and 30 of these Rules.

Article 68 — Defense and Counterclaim

1. Within twenty (20) days from the date of its receipt of the Notice of Arbitration, the Respondent shall submit its Statement of Defense, evidence and other supporting documents. Counterclaim, if any, shall also be filed with evidence and other supporting documents within the time period.
2. The Claimant shall file its Statement of Defense to the Respondent's counterclaim within twenty (20) days from the date of its receipt of the counterclaim and its attachments.
3. If a party has justified reasons to request an extension of the time period, the arbitral tribunal shall decide whether to grant such extension. Where the arbitral tribunal has not yet been formed, such decision shall be made by the Arbitration Court.

Article 69 — Notice of Oral Hearing

1. For a case examined by way of an oral hearing, after the arbitral tribunal has fixed a date for the first oral hearing, the parties shall be notified of the date at least fifteen (15) days in advance of the oral hearing. A party having justified reason may request a postponement of the oral hearing. However, the party shall communicate such request in writing to the arbitral tribunal

within three (3) days of its receipt of the notice of the oral hearing. The arbitral tribunal shall decide whether or not to postpone the oral hearing.
2. If a party has justified reasons for failure to submit a request for a postponement of the oral hearing in accordance with the preceding Paragraph 1, the arbitral tribunal shall decide whether to accept such a request.
3. A notice of a subsequent oral hearing, a notice of a postponed oral hearing, as well as a request for postponement of such oral hearing, shall not be subject to the time periods specified in the preceding Paragraph 1.

Article 70 — Record of Oral Hearing

1. The arbitral tribunal shall make a written record of the oral hearing. Any party or participant in the arbitration may apply for a correction upon finding any omission or mistake in the record regarding its own statements. If the application is refused by the arbitral tribunal, it shall nevertheless be recorded and kept with the file.
2. The written record shall be signed or sealed by the arbitrator(s), the recorder, the parties, and any other participant in the arbitration.

Article 71 — Time Period for Rendering Award

1. The arbitral tribunal shall render an arbitral award within four (4) months from the date on which the arbitral tribunal is formed.
2. Upon the request of the arbitral tribunal, the President of the Arbitration Court may extend the time period if he/she considers it truly necessary and the reasons for the extension truly justified.
3. Any suspension period shall be excluded when calculating the time period in the preceding Paragraph 1.

Article 72 — Context Reference

The relevant provisions in the other Chapters of these Rules, with the exception of Chapter VI, shall apply to matters not covered in this Chapter.

Chapter VI
Special Provisions for Hong Kong Arbitration

Article 73 — Application

1. CIETAC has established the CIETAC Hong Kong Arbitration Center in the Hong Kong Special Administrative Region. The provisions of this Chapter shall apply to arbitration cases accepted and administered by the CIETAC Hong Kong Arbitration Center.
2. Where the parties have agreed to submit their disputes to the CIETAC Hong Kong Arbitration Center for arbitration or to CIETAC for arbitration in Hong Kong, the CIETAC Hong Kong Arbitration Center shall accept the arbitration application and administer the case.

Article 74 — Place of Arbitration and Law Applicable to the Arbitral Proceedings

Unless otherwise agreed by the parties, for an arbitration administered by the CIETAC Hong Kong Arbitration Center, the place of arbitration shall be Hong Kong, the law applicable to the arbitral proceedings shall be the arbitration law of Hong Kong, and the arbitral award shall be a Hong Kong award.

Article 75 — Decision on Jurisdiction

Any objection to an arbitration agreement and/or the jurisdiction over an arbitration case shall be raised in writing no later than the submission of the first substantive defense.

The arbitral tribunal shall have the power to determine the existence and validity of the arbitration agreement and its jurisdiction over the arbitration case.

Article 76 — Nomination or Appointment of Arbitrator

The CIETAC Panel of Arbitrators in effect shall be recommended in arbitration cases administered by the CIETAC Hong Kong Arbitration Center. The parties may nominate arbitrators from outside the CIETAC's Panel of Arbitrators. An arbitrator so nominated shall be subject to the confirmation of the Chairman of CIETAC.

Article 77 — Interim Measures and Emergency Relief

1. Unless otherwise agreed by the parties, the arbitral tribunal has the power to order appropriate interim measures at the request of a party.

2. Where the arbitral tribunal has not yet been formed, a party may apply for emergency relief pursuant to the CIETAC Emergency Arbitrator Procedures (Appendix III).

Article 78 — Seal on Award

The seal of the CIETAC Hong Kong Arbitration Center shall be affixed to the arbitral award.

Article 79 — Arbitration Fees

The CIETAC Arbitration Fee Schedule III (Appendix II) shall apply to the arbitration cases accepted and administered in accordance with this Chapter.

Article 80 — Context Reference

The relevant provisions in the other Chapters of these Rules, with the exception of Chapter V, shall apply to matters not covered in this Chapter.

Chapter VII
Supplementary Provisions

Article 81 — Language

1. Where the parties have agreed on the language of arbitration, their

agreement shall prevail. In the absence of such agreement, the language of arbitration to be used in the proceedings shall be Chinese. CIETAC may also designate another language as the language of arbitration having regard to the circumstances of the case.

2. If a party or its representative(s) or witness(es) requires interpretation at an oral hearing, an interpreter may be provided either by the Arbitration Court or by the party.

3. The arbitral tribunal or the Arbitration Court may, if it considers it necessary, require the parties to submit a corresponding translation of their documents and evidence into Chinese or other languages.

Article 82 — Arbitration Fees and Costs

1. Apart from the arbitration fees charged in accordance with its Arbitration Fee Schedule, CIETAC may charge the parties for any other additional and reasonable actual costs, including but not limited to arbitrators' special remuneration, their travel and accommodation expenses incurred in dealing with the case, engagement fees of stenographers, as well as the costs and expenses of experts, appraisers or interpreters appointed by the arbitral tribunal. The Arbitration Court shall, after hearing from the arbitrator and the party concerned, determine the arbitrator's special remuneration with reference to the standards of arbitrators' fees and expenses set forth in the CIETAC Arbitration Fee Schedule III (Appendix II).

2. Where a party has nominated an arbitrator but fails to advance a deposit for such actual costs as the special remuneration, travel and accommodation expenses of the nominated arbitrator within the time period specified by CIETAC, the party shall be deemed not to have nominated the arbitrator.

3. Where the parties have agreed to hold an oral hearing at a place other than the domicile of CIETAC or its relevant sub-commission/arbitration center, they shall advance a deposit for the actual costs such as travel and accommodation expenses incurred thereby. In the event that the parties fail to do so within the time period specified by CIETAC, the oral hearing shall be held at the domicile of CIETAC or its relevant sub-commission/ arbitration center.

4. Where the parties have agreed to use two or more than two languages as the languages of arbitration, or where the parties have agreed on a three-arbitrator tribunal in a case where the Summary Procedure shall apply in accordance with Article 56 of these Rules, CIETAC may charge the parties for any additional and reasonable costs.

Article 83 — Interpretation

1. The headings of the articles in these Rules shall not be construed as

interpretations of the contents of the provisions contained therein.
2. These Rules shall be interpreted by CIETAC.

Article 84 — Coming into Force

These Rules shall be effective as of January 1, 2015. For cases administered by CIETAC or its sub-commissions/arbitration centers before these Rules come into force, the Arbitration Rules effective at the time of acceptance shall apply, or where both parties agree, these Rules shall apply.

Appendix I

Directory of China International Economic and Trade Arbitration Commission and its Sub-commissions/Arbitration Centers

China International Economic and Trade Arbitration Commission (CIETAC)

Add: 6/F, CCOIC Building, No.2 Huapichang Hutong, Xicheng District, Beijing, 10035, P.R. China
Tel: 86 10 82217788
Fax: 86 10 82217766/64643500
E-mail: info@cietac.org
Website: http://www.cietac.org

South China Office, Arbitration Court of CIETAC

Add: 14A01, Anlian Plaza, No.4018, Jintian Road, Futian District, Shenzhen, 518026, Guangdong Province, P.R.China
Tel: 86 755 82796739
Fax: 86 755 23964130
E-mail: infosz@cietac.org
Website: http://www.cietac.org

Shanghai Office, Arbitration Court of CIETAC

Add: 18/F, Tomson Commercial Building, 710 Dongfang Road, Pudong, New Area, Shanghai 200122, P.R. China
Tel: 86 21 60137688
Fax: 86 21 60137689
E-Mail: infosh@cietac.org
Website: http://www.cietac.org

CIETAC Tianjin International Economic and Financial Arbitration Center(Tianjin Sub-commission)

Add: 4/F, E2-ABC, Financial Street, No.20 Guangchangdong Road, Tianjin

Economic-Technological Development Zone, Tianjin 300457, P.R.China
Tel: 86 22 66285688
Fax: 86 22 66285678
Email: tianjin@cietac.org
Website: http://www.cietac-tj.org

CIETAC Southwest Sub-Commission
Add: 1/F, Bld B, Caifu 3, Caifu Garden, Cai fu Zhongxin, Yubei,Chongqing, 401121,China
Tel: 86 23 86871307
Fax: 86 23 86871190
Email: cietac-sw@cietac.org
Website: http://www.cietac-sw.org

CIETAC Hong Kong Arbitration Center
Add: Unit 4705, 47th Floor, Far East Finance Center, No.16 Harcourt Road, Hong Kong.
Tel: 852 25298066
Fax: 852 25298266
Email: hk@cietac.org
Website: http://www.cietachk.org

Appendix II
China International Economic and Trade Arbitration Commission
Arbitration Fee Schedule I

See Arbitration Fee Schedule (page 234).
When a case is accepted, an additional amount of RMB 10,000 shall be charged as the registration fee, which shall include the expenses for examining the application for arbitration, initiating the arbitral proceedings, computerizing management and filing documents.
The amount in dispute referred to in this Schedule shall be based on the sum of money claimed by the Claimant. If the amount claimed is different from the actual amount in dispute, the actual amount in dispute shall be the basis for calculation.
Where the amount in dispute is not ascertained at the time of applying for arbitration, or where special circumstances exist, the amount of the arbitration fee shall be determined by CIETAC.
Where the arbitration fee is to be charged in a foreign currency, the amount

in the foreign currency shall be equivalent to the corresponding amount in RMB as specified in this Schedule.

Apart from charging the arbitration fee according to this Schedule, CIETAC may also collect other additional and reasonable actual expenses pursuant to the relevant provisions of the Arbitration Rules.

China International Economic and Trade Arbitration Commission Arbitration Fee Schedule II

See Registration Fee Schedule (page 235).

See Handling Fee Schedule (page 236).

The amount in dispute referred to in this Schedule shall be based on the sum of money claimed by the Claimant. If the amount claimed is different from the actual amount in dispute, the actual amount in dispute shall be the basis for calculation.

Where the amount in dispute is not ascertained at the time of applying for arbitration, or where special circumstances exist, the amount of the arbitration fee deposit shall be determined by CIETAC in consideration of the specific rights and interests involved in the dispute.

Apart from charging the arbitration fee according to this Schedule, CIETAC may also collect other additional and reasonable actual expenses pursuant to the relevant provisions of the Arbitration Rules.

China International Economic and Trade Arbitration Commission Arbitration Fee Schedule III

I. Registration Fee

When submitting a Request for Arbitration to the CIETAC Hong Kong Arbitration Center, the Claimant shall pay a registration fee of HKD 8,000, which shall include the expenses for examining the application for arbitration, initiating the arbitral proceedings, computerizing management, filing documents and labor costs. The registration fee is not refundable.

II. Administrative Fee

1. Administrative Fee Table

See Administrative Fee Table (page 237).

2. The administrative fee includes the remuneration of the case manager and the costs of using oral hearing rooms of CIETAC and/or its sub-commissions/arbitration centers.

3. Claims and counterclaims are aggregated for the determination of the amount in dispute. Where the amount in dispute is not ascertained at the time of applying for arbitration, or where special circumstances exist, the amount of the administrative fee shall be determined by CIETAC taking into account the circumstances of the case.

4. Apart from charging the administrative fee according to this Table, the CIETAC Hong Kong Arbitration Center may also collect other additional and reasonable actual expenses pursuant to the relevant provisions of the Arbitration Rules, including but not limited to translation fees, written record fees, and the costs of using oral hearing rooms other than those of CIETAC and/or its sub-commissions/arbitration centers.
5. Where the registration fee and the administrative fee are to be charged in a currency other than HKD, the CIETAC Hong Kong Arbitration Center shall charge an amount of the foreign currency equivalent to the corresponding amount in HKD as specified in this Table.
III. Arbitrator's Fees and Expenses
A. Arbitrator's Fees and Expenses (Based on the Amount in Dispute)
1. Arbitrator's Fees Table
See Arbitrator's Fees Table (page 238).
2. Unless otherwise stipulated in this Schedule, the arbitrator's fees shall be determined by CIETAC in accordance with the above Table taking into account the circumstances of the case. The arbitrator's expenses shall include all reasonable actual expenses incurred from the arbitrator's arbitration activities.
3. The arbitrator's fees may exceed the corresponding maximum amount listed in the Table provided that the parties so agree in writing or CIETAC so determines under exceptional circumstances.
4. The parties shall advance the payment of the arbitrator's fees and expenses determined by CIETAC to the CIETAC Hong Kong Arbitration Center. Subject to the approval of the CIETAC Hong Kong Arbitration Center, the parties may pay the arbitrator's fees and expenses in installments. The parties shall be jointly and severally liable for the payment of the arbitrator's fees and expenses.
5. Claims and counterclaims are aggregated for the determination of the amount in dispute. Where the amount in dispute is not ascertainable, or where special circumstances exist, the amount of the arbitrator's fees shall be determined by CIETAC taking into account the circumstances of the case.
B. Arbitrator's Fees and Expenses (Based on an Hourly Rate)
1. Where the parties have agreed in writing that the arbitrator's fees and expenses are to be based on an hourly rate, their agreement shall prevail. The arbitrator is entitled to fees based on an hourly rate for all the reasonable efforts devoted in the arbitration. The arbitrator's expenses shall include all reasonable actual expenses incurred from the arbitrator's

arbitration activities.

2. Where a party applies for the Emergency Arbitrator Procedures, the emergency arbitrator's fees shall be based on an hourly rate.

3. The hourly rate for each co-arbitrator shall be the rate agreed upon by that co-arbitrator and the nominating party. The hourly rate for a sole or presiding arbitrator shall be the rate agreed upon by that arbitrator and both parties. Where the hourly rate cannot be agreed upon, or the arbitrator is appointed by the Chairman of CIETAC, the hourly rate of the arbitrator shall be determined by CIETAC. The hourly rate for the emergency arbitrator shall be determined by CIETAC.

4. An agreed or determined hourly rate shall not exceed the maximum rate fixed by CIETAC as provided on the website of the CIETAC Hong Kong Arbitration Center on the date of the submission of the Request for Arbitration. The arbitrator's fees may exceed the fixed maximum rate provided that the parties so agree in writing or CIETAC so determines under exceptional circumstances.

5. The parties shall advance the payment of the arbitrator's fees and expenses to the CIETAC Hong Kong Arbitration Center, which amount shall be fixed by the latter. The parties shall be jointly and severally liable for the payment of the arbitrator's fees and expenses.

C. Miscellaneous

1. In accordance with the decision of the arbitral tribunal, the CIETAC Hong Kong Arbitration Center shall have a lien over the award rendered by the tribunal so as to secure the payment of the outstanding fees for the arbitrators and all the expenses due. After all such fees and expenses have been paid in full jointly or by one of the parties, the CIETAC Hong Kong Arbitration Center shall release such award to the parties according to the decision of the arbitral tribunal.

Where the arbitrator's fees and expenses are to be charged in a currency other than HKD, the CIETAC Hong Kong Arbitration Center shall charge an amount of the foreign currency equivalent to the corresponding amount in HKD as specified in this Schedule.

Appendix III

China International Economic and Trade Arbitration Commission Emergency Arbitrator Procedures

Article 1 — Application for the Emergency Arbitrator Procedures

1. A party requiring emergency relief may apply for the Emergency Arbitrator Procedures based upon the applicable law or the agreement of the parties.

2. The party applying for the Emergency Arbitrator Procedures (the "Applicant") shall submit its Application for the Emergency Arbitrator Procedures to the Arbitration Court or the arbitration court of the relevant sub-commission/arbitration center of CIETAC administering the case prior to the formation of the arbitral tribunal.
3. The Application for the Emergency Arbitrator Procedures shall include the following information:
(a) the names and other basic information of the parties involved in the Application;
(b) a description of the underlying dispute giving rise to the Application and the reasons why emergency relief is required;
(c) a statement of the emergency measures sought and the reasons why the applicant is entitled to such emergency relief;
(d) other necessary information required to apply for the emergency relief; and
(e) comments on the applicable law and the language of the Emergency Arbitrator Procedures.
When submitting its Application, the Applicant shall attach the relevant documentary and other evidence on which the Application is based, including but not limited to the arbitration agreement and any other agreements giving rise to the underlying dispute.
The Application, evidence and other documents shall be submitted in triplicate. Where there are multiple parties, additional copies shall be provided accordingly.
4. The Applicant shall advance the costs for the Emergency Arbitrator Procedures.
5. Where the parties have agreed on the language of arbitration, such language shall be the language of the Emergency Arbitrator Procedures. In the absence of such agreement, the language of the Procedures shall be determined by the Arbitration Court.

Article 2 — Acceptance of Application and Appointment of the Emergency Arbitrator

After a preliminary review on the basis of the Application, the arbitration agreement and relevant evidence submitted by the Applicant, the Arbitration Court shall decide whether the Emergency Arbitrator Procedures shall apply. If the Arbitration Court decides to apply the Emergency Arbitrator Procedures, the President of the Arbitration Court shall appoint an emergency arbitrator within one (1) day from his/her receipt of both the Application and the advance payment of the costs for the

Emergency Arbitrator Procedures.
2. Once the emergency arbitrator has been appointed by the President of the Arbitration Court, the Arbitration Court shall promptly transmit the Notice of Acceptance and the Applicant's application file to the appointed emergency arbitrator and the party against whom the emergency measures are sought, meanwhile copying the Notice of Acceptance to the arbitration and the Chairman of CIETAC.

Article 3 — Disclosure and Challenge of the Emergency Arbitrator

1. An emergency arbitrator shall not represent either party, and shall be and remain independent of the parties and treat them equally.
2. Upon acceptance of the appointment, an emergency arbitrator shall sign a Declaration and disclose to the Arbitration Court any facts or circumstances likely to give rise to justifiable doubts as to his/her impartiality or independence. If circumstances that need to be disclosed arise during the Emergency Arbitrator Procedures, the emergency arbitrator shall promptly disclose such circumstances in writing.
3. The Declaration and/or the disclosure of the emergency arbitrator shall be communicated to the parties by the Arbitration Court.
4. Upon receipt of the Declaration and/or the written disclosure of an emergency arbitrator, a party wishing to challenge the arbitrator on the grounds of the facts or circumstances disclosed by the emergency arbitrator shall forward the challenge in writing within two (2) days from the date of such receipt. If a party fails to file a challenge within the above time period, it may not subsequently challenge the emergency arbitrator on the basis of the matters disclosed by the emergency arbitrator.
5. A party which has justifiable doubts as to the impartiality or independence of the appointed emergency arbitrator may challenge that emergency arbitrator in writing and shall state the facts and reasons on which the challenge is based with supporting evidence.
6. A party may challenge an emergency arbitrator in writing within two (2) days from the date of its receipt of the Notice of Acceptance. Where a party becomes aware of a reason for a challenge after such receipt, the party may challenge the emergency arbitrator in writing within two (2) days after such reason has become known, but no later than the formation of the arbitral tribunal.
7. The President of the Arbitration Court shall make a final decision on the challenge of the emergency arbitrator. If the challenge is accepted, the President of the Arbitration Court shall reappoint an emergency arbitrator within one (1) day from the date of the decision confirming the challenge,

and copy the decision to the Chairman of CIETAC. The emergency arbitrator who has been challenged shall continue to perform his/her functions until a final decision on the challenge has been made.
The disclosure and challenge proceedings shall apply equally to the reappointed emergency arbitrator.
8. Unless otherwise agreed by the parties, the emergency arbitrator shall not accept nomination or appointment to act as a member of the arbitral tribunal in any arbitration relating to the underlying dispute.

Article 4 — Place of the Emergency Arbitrator Proceedings

Unless otherwise agreed by the parties, the place of the emergency arbitrator proceedings shall be the place of arbitration, which is determined in accordance with Article 7 of the Arbitration Rules.

Article 5 — The Emergency Arbitrator Proceedings

1. The emergency arbitrator shall establish a procedural timetable for the emergency arbitrator proceedings within a time as short as possible, best within two (2) days from his/her acceptance of the appointment. The emergency arbitrator shall conduct the proceedings in the manner the emergency arbitrator considers to be appropriate, taking into account the nature and the urgency of the emergency relief, and shall ensure that each party has a reasonable opportunity to present its case.
2. The emergency arbitrator may order the provision of appropriate security by the party seeking the emergency relief as the precondition of taking emergency measures.
3. The power of the emergency arbitrator and the emergency arbitrator proceedings shall cease on the date of the formation of the arbitral tribunal.
4. The emergency arbitrator proceedings shall not affect the right of the parties to seek interim measures from a competent court pursuant to the applicable law.

Article 6 — Decision of the Emergency Arbitrator

1. The emergency arbitrator has the power to make a decision to order or award necessary emergency relief, and shall make every reasonable effort to ensure that the decision is valid.
2. The decision of the emergency arbitrator shall be made within fifteen (15) days from the date of that arbitrator's acceptance of the appointment. The President of the Arbitration Court may extend the time period upon the request of the emergency arbitrator only if the President of the Arbitration Court considers it reasonable.
3. The decision of the emergency arbitrator shall state the reasons for taking the emergency measures, be signed by the emergency arbitrator and

stamped with the seal of the Arbitration Court or the arbitration court of its relevant sub-commission/arbitration center.
4. The decision of the emergency arbitrator shall be binding upon both parties. A party may seek enforcement of the decision from a competent court pursuant to the relevant law provisions of the enforcing state or region. Upon a reasoned request of a party, the emergency arbitrator or the arbitral tribunal to be formed may modify, suspend or terminate the decision.
5. The emergency arbitrator may decide to dismiss the application of the Applicant and terminate the emergency arbitrator proceedings, if hat arbitrator considers that circumstances exist where emergency measures are unnecessary or unable to be taken for various reasons.
6. The decision of the emergency arbitrator shall cease to be binding:
(a) if the emergency arbitrator or the arbitral tribunal terminates the decision of the emergency arbitrator;
(b) if the President of the Arbitration Court decides to accept a challenge against the emergency arbitrator;
(c) upon the rendering of a final award by the arbitral tribunal, unless the arbitral tribunal decides that the decision of the emergency arbitrator shall continue to be effective;
(d) upon the Applicant's withdrawal of all claims before the rendering of a final award;
(e) if the arbitral tribunal is not formed within ninety (90) days from the date of the decision of the emergency arbitrator. This period of time may be extended by agreement of the parties or by the Arbitration Court under circumstances it considers appropriate; or
(f) if the arbitration proceedings have been suspended for sixty (60) consecutive days after the formation of the arbitral tribunal.

Article 7 — Costs of the Emergency Arbitrator Proceedings

1. The Applicant shall advance ean amount of RMB 30,000as the costs of the emergency arbitrator proceedings, consisting of the remuneration of the emergency arbitrator and the administrative fee of CIETAC. The Arbitration Court may require the Applicant to advance any other additional and reasonable actual costs.
A party applying to the CIETAC Hong Kong Arbitration Center for emergency relief shall advance the costs of the emergency arbitrator proceedings in accordance with the CIETAC Arbitration Fee Schedule III (Appendix II).
2. The emergency arbitrator shall determine in its decision in what

proportion the costs of the emergency arbitrator proceedings shall be borne by the parties, subject to the power of the arbitral tribunal to finally determine the allocation of such costs at the request of a party.
3. The Arbitration Court may fix the amount of the costs of the emergency arbitrator proceedings refundable to the Applicant if such proceedings terminate before the emergency arbitrator has made a decision.

Article 8 — Miscellaneous

These rules for the Emergency Arbitrator Procedures shall be interpreted by CIETAC.

Arbitration Fee Schedule[1]

Amount in Dispute (RMB)	Arbitration Fee (RMB)
Up to 1,000,000	4% of the amount, minimum 10,000
From 1,000,001 to 2,000,000	40,000 + 3.5% of the amount over 1,000,000
From 2,000,001 to 5,000,000	75,000 + 2.5% of the amount over 2,000,000
From 5,000,001 to 10,000,000	150,000 + 1.5% of the amount over 5,000,000
From 10,000,001 to 50,000,000	225,000 + 1% of the amount over 10,000,000
From 50,000,001 to 100,000,000	625,000 + 0.5% of the amount over 50,000,000
From 100,000,001 to 500,000,000	875,000 + 0.48% of the amount over 100,000,000
From 500,000,001 to 1,000,000,000	2,795,000 + 0.47% of the amount over 500,000,000
From 1,000,000,001 to 2,000,000,000	5,145,000 + 0.46% of the amount over 1,000,000,000
Over 2,000,000,001	9,745,000 + 0.45% of the amount over 2,000,000,000,

[1] This fee schedule applies to arbitration cases accepted under Item (a) and (b), Paragraph 2 of Article 3 of the Arbitration Rules.

Registration Fee Table[2]

Amount in Dispute (RMB)	Registration Fee (RMB)
Up to 1,000	Minimum 100
From 1,001 to 50,000	100 + 5% of the amount over 1,000
From 50,001 to 100,000	2,550 + 4% of the amount over 50,000
From 100,001 to 200,000	4,550 + 3% of the amount over 100,000
From 200,001 to 500,000	7,550 + 2% of the amount over 200,000
From 500,001 to 1,000,000	13,550 + 1% of the amount over 500,000
Over 1,000,001	18,550 + 0.5% of the amount over 1,000,000

[2] This fee schedule applies to arbitration cases accepted under Item (c), Paragraph 2 of Article 3 of the Arbitration Rules.

Handling Fee Table[3]

Amount in Dispute (RMB)	Handling Fee (RMB)
Up to 200,000	Minimum 6,000
From 200,001 to 500,000	6,000 + 2% of the amount over 200,000
From 500,001 to 1,000,000	12,000 + 1.5% of the amount over 500,000
From 1,000,001 to 2,000,000	19,500 + 0.5% of the amount over 1,000,000
From 2,000,001 to 5,000,000	24,500 + 0.45% of the amount over 2,000,000
From 5,000,001 to 10,000,000	38,000 + 0.4% of the amount over 5,000,000
From 10,000,001 to 20,000,000	58,000 + 0.3% of the amount over 10,000,000
From 20,000,001 to 40,000,000	88,000 + 0.2% of the amount over 20,000,000
From 40,000,001 to 100,000,000	128,000 + 0.15% of the amount over 40,000,000
From 100,000,001 to 500,000,000	218,000 + 0.13% of the amount over 100,000,000
Over 500,000,000	738,000 + 0.12% of the amount over 500,000,000

[3] This fee schedule applies to arbitration cases accepted under Item (a) and (b), Paragraph 2 of Article 3 of the Arbitration Rules.

Administrative Fee Table[4]

Amount in Dispute (RMB)	Administrative Fee (RMB)
Up to 500,000	16,000
From 500,000 to 1,000,000	16,000 + 0.78% of the amount over 500,000
From 1,000,001 to 5,000,000	19,900 + 0.65% of the amount over 1,000,000
From 5,000,001 to 10,000,000	45,900 + 0.38% of the amount over 5,000,000
From 10,000,001 to 20,000,000	64,900 + 0.22% of the amount over 10,000,000
From 20,000,001 to 40,000,000	86,900 + 0.15% of the amount over 20,000,000
From 40,000,001 to 80,000,000	116,900 + 0.08% of the amount over 40,000,000
From 80,000,001 to 200,000,000	148,900 + 0.052% of the amount over 80,000,000
From 200,000,001 to 400,000,000	211,300 + 0.04% of the amount over 200,000,000
Over 400,000,001	291,300

[4] This fee schedule applies to arbitration cases administered by the CIETAC Hong Kong Arbitration Center under Chapter VI of the Arbitration Rules.

Arbitrator's Fees Table[5]

Amount in Dispute	Arbitrator's fee (HDK, per arbitrator)	
(HKD)	Minimum	Maximum
Up to 500,000	15,000	60,000
From 500,001 to 1,000,000	15,000 + 2.30% of the amount over 500,000	60,000 + 8.50% of the amount over 500,000
From 1,000,001 to 5,000,000	26,500 + 0.80% of the amount over 1,000,000	102,500 + 4.3% of the amount over 1,000,000
From 5,000,001 to 10,000,000	58,500 + 0.60% of the amount over 5,000,000	274,500 + 2.30%of the amount over 5,000,000
From 10,000,001 to 20,000,000	88,500 + 0.35% of the amount over 10,000,000	389,500 + 1.00%ofthe amount over 10,000,000
From 20,000, 001 to 40,000,000	123,500 + 0.20% of the amount over 20,000,000	489,500 + 0.65% of the amount over 40,000,000
From 40,000,001 to 80,000,000	165,500 + 0.07% of the amount over 40,000,000	619,500 + 0.35% of the amount over 40,000,000
From 80,000,001 to 200,000,000	191,500 + 0.05% of the amount over 80,000,000	795,500 + 0.25% of the amount over 80,000,000
From 200,000,001 to 400,000,000	251,500 + 0.03% of the amount over 200,000,000	1,059,500 + 0.15% of the amount over 200,000,000
From 400,000,001 to 600,000,000	311,500 + 0.02% of the amount over 400,000,000	1,359,500 + 0.10% of the amount over 400,000,000
From 600,000,001 to 750,000,000	351,500 + 0.01% of the amount over 600,000,000	1,599,500 + 0.10% of the amount over 600,000,000
Over 750,000,000	366,500 + 0.008% of the amount over 750,000,000	1,749,500 + 0.06% of the amount over 750,000,000

[5] This fee schedule applies to arbitration cases administered by the CIETAC Hong Kong Arbitration Center under Chapter VI of the Arbitration Rules.

CIVIL EVIDENCE ACT 1995 *
(CHAPTER 38)

An Act to provide for the admissibility of hearsay evidence, the proof of certain documentary evidence and the admissibility and proof of official actuarial tables in civil proceedings; and for connected purposes. [8th November 1995]

Be it enacted by the Queen's most Excellent Majesty, by and with the advice and consent of the Lords Spiritual and Temporal, and Commons, in this present Parliament assembled, and by the authority of the same, as follows:

Admissibility of Hearsay Evidence

1 — Admissibility of Hearsay Evidence

(1) In civil proceedings evidence shall not be excluded on the ground that it is hearsay.

(2) In this Act

(a) "hearsay" means a statement made otherwise than by a person while giving oral evidence in the proceedings which is tendered as evidence of the matters stated; and

(b) references to hearsay include hearsay of whatever degree.

(3) Nothing in this Act affects the admissibility of evidence admissible apart from this section.

(4) The provisions of sections 2 to 6 (safeguards and supplementary provisions relating to hearsay evidence) do not apply in relation to hearsay evidence admissible apart from this section, notwithstanding that it may also be admissible by virtue of this section.

Safeguards in Relation to Hearsay Evidence

2 — Notice of Proposal to Adduce Hearsay Evidence

(1) A party proposing to adduce hearsay evidence in civil proceedings shall, subject to the following provisions of this section, give to the other party or parties to the proceedings

(a) such notice (if any) of that fact, and

(b) on request, such particulars of or relating to the evidence, as is reasonable and practicable in the circumstances for the purpose of enabling him or them to deal with any matters arising from its being hearsay.

(2) Provision may be made by rules of court

(a) specifying classes of proceedings or evidence in relation to which subsection (1) does not apply, and

(b) as to the manner in which (including the time within which) the duties imposed by that subsection are to be complied with in the cases where it does apply.

(3) Subsection (1) may also be excluded by agreement of the parties; and

* For further guidance on the Civil Evidence Act 1995, see Maurice Kay and others (eds), *Blackstone's Civil Practice 2013: The Commentary* (Oxford University Press, 2012) and Peter Hibbert, *Civil Evidence for Practitioners* (4th edn, Sweet & Maxwell, 2014).

compliance with the duty to give notice may in any case be waived by the person to whom notice is required to be given.

(4) A failure to comply with subsection (1), or with rules under subsection (2)(b), does not affect the admissibility of the evidence but may be taken into account by the court

(a) in considering the exercise of its powers with respect to the course of proceedings and costs, and

(b) as a matter adversely affecting the weight to be given to the evidence in accordance with section 4.

3 — Power to Call Witness for Cross-examination on Hearsay Statement

Rules of court may provide that where a party to civil proceedings adduces hearsay evidence of a statement made by a person and does not call that person as a witness, any other party to the proceedings may, with the leave of the court, call that person as a witness and cross-examine him on the statement as if he had been called by the first-mentioned party and as if the hearsay statement were his evidence in chief.

4 — Considerations Relevant to Weighing of Hearsay Evidence

(1) In estimating the weight (if any) to be given to hearsay evidence in civil proceedings the court shall have regard to any circumstances from which any inference can reasonably be drawn as to the reliability or otherwise of the evidence.

(2) Regard may be had, in particular, to the following

(a) whether it would have been reasonable and practicable for the party by whom the evidence was adduced to have produced the maker of the original statement as a witness;

(b) whether the original statement was made contemporaneously with the occurrence or existence of the matters stated;

(c) whether the evidence involves multiple hearsay;

(d) whether any person involved had any motive to conceal or misrepresent matters;

(e) whether the original statement was an edited account, or was made in collaboration with another or for a particular purpose;

(f) whether the circumstances in which the evidence is adduced as hearsay are such as to suggest an attempt to prevent proper evaluation of its weight.

Supplementary Provisions as to Hearsay Evidence

5 — Competence and Credibility

(1) Hearsay evidence shall not be admitted in civil proceedings if or to the extent that it is shown to consist of, or to be proved by means of, a

statement made by a person who at the time he made the statement was not competent as a witness.

For this purpose "not competent as a witness" means suffering from such mental or physical infirmity, or lack of understanding, as would render a person incompetent as a witness in civil proceedings; but a child shall be treated as competent as a witness if he satisfies the requirements of section 96(2)(a) and (b) of the M1Children Act 1989 (conditions for reception of unsworn evidence of child).

(2) Where in civil proceedings hearsay evidence is adduced and the maker of the original statement, or of any statement relied upon to prove another statement, is not called as a witness

(a) evidence which if he had been so called would be admissible for the purpose of attacking or supporting his credibility as a witness is admissible for that purpose in the proceedings; and

(b) evidence tending to prove that, whether before or after he made the statement, he made any other statement inconsistent with it is admissible for the purpose of showing that he had contradicted himself.

Provided that evidence may not be given of any matter of which, if he had been called as a witness and had denied that matter in cross-examination, evidence could not have been adduced by the cross-examining party.

6 — Previous Statements of Witnesses

(1) Subject as follows, the provisions of this Act as to hearsay evidence in civil proceedings apply equally (but with any necessary modifications) in relation to a previous statement made by a person called as a witness in the proceedings.

(2) A party who has called or intends to call a person as a witness in civil proceedings may not in those proceedings adduce evidence of a previous statement made by that person, except

(a) with the leave of the court, or

(b) for the purpose of rebutting a suggestion that his evidence has been fabricated.

This shall not be construed as preventing a witness statement (that is, a written statement of oral evidence which a party to the proceedings intends to lead) from being adopted by a witness in giving evidence or treated as his evidence.

(3) Where in the case of civil proceedings section 3, 4 or 5 of the Criminal Procedure Act1865 applies, which make provision as to

(a) how far a witness may be discredited by the party producing him,

(b) the proof of contradictory statements made by a witness, and

(c) cross-examination as to previous statements in writing, this Act does not authorise the adducing of evidence of a previous inconsistent or contradictory statement otherwise than in accordance with those sections.
This is without prejudice to any provision made by rules of court under section 3 above (power to call witness for cross-examination on hearsay statement).
(4) Nothing in this Act affects any of the rules of law as to the circumstances in which, where a person called as a witness in civil proceedings is cross-examined on a document used by him to refresh his memory, that document may be made evidence in the proceedings.
(5) Nothing in this section shall be construed as preventing a statement of any description referred to above from being admissible by virtue of section 1 as evidence of the matters stated.
7 — Evidence Formerly Admissible at Common Law
(1) The common law rule effectively preserved by section 9(1) and (2)(a) of the Civil Evidence Act 1968 (admissibility of admissions adverse to a party) is superseded by the provisions of this Act.
(2) The common law rules effectively preserved by section 9(1) and (2)(b) to (d) of the Civil Evidence Act 1968, that is, any rule of law whereby in civil proceedings
(a) published works dealing with matters of a public nature (for example, histories, scientific works, dictionaries and maps) are admissible as evidence of facts of a public nature stated in them,
(b) public documents (for example, public registers, and returns made under public authority with respect to matters of public interest) are admissible as evidence of facts stated in them, or
(c) records (for example, the records of certain courts, treaties, Crown grants, pardons and commissions) are admissible as evidence of facts stated in them,
shall continue to have effect.
(3) The common law rules effectively preserved by section 9(3) and (4) of the Civil Evidence Act 1968, that is, any rule of law whereby in civil proceedings
(a) evidence of a person's reputation is admissible for the purpose of proving his good or bad character, or
(b) evidence of reputation or family tradition is admissible
(i) for the purpose of proving or disproving pedigree or the existence of a marriage, or
(ii) for the purpose of proving or disproving the existence of any public or

general right or of identifying any person or thing, shall continue to have effect in so far as they authorise the court to treat such evidence as proving or disproving that matter.

Where any such rule applies, reputation or family tradition shall be treated for the purposes of this Act as a fact and not as a statement or multiplicity of statements about the matter in question.

(4) The words in which a rule of law mentioned in this section is described are intended only to identify the rule and shall not be construed as altering it in any way.

Other Matters

8 — Proof of Statements Contained in Documents

(1) Where a statement contained in a document is admissible as evidence in civil proceedings, it may be proved

(a) by the production of that document, or

(b) whether or not that document is still in existence, by the production of a copy of that document or of the material part of it,

authenticated in such manner as the court may approve.

(2) It is immaterial for this purpose how many removes there are between a copy and the original.

9 — Proof of Records of Business or Public Authority

(1) A document which is shown to form part of the records of a business or public authority may be received in evidence in civil proceedings without further proof.

(2) A document shall be taken to form part of the records of a business or public authority if there is produced to the court a certificate to that effect signed by an officer of the business or authority to which the records belong.

For this purpose

(a) a document purporting to be a certificate signed by an officer of a business or public authority shall be deemed to have been duly given by such an officer and signed by him; and

(b) a certificate shall be treated as signed by a person if it purports to bear a facsimile of his signature.

(3) The absence of an entry in the records of a business or public authority may be proved in civil proceedings by affidavit of an officer of the business or authority to which the records belong.

(4) In this section

"records" means records in whatever form;

"business" includes any activity regularly carried on over a period of time, whether for profit or not, by any body (whether corporate or not) or by an individual;

"officer" includes any person occupying a responsible position in relation to the relevant activities of the business or public authority or in relation to its records; and

"public authority" includes any public or statutory undertaking, any government department and any person holding office under Her Majesty.

(5) The court may, having regard to the circumstances of the case, direct that all or any of the above provisions of this section do not apply in relation to a particular document or record, or description of documents or records.

10 — Admissibility and Proof of Ogden Tables

(1) The actuarial tables (together with explanatory notes) for use in personal injury and fatal accident cases issued from time to time by the Government Actuary's Department are admissible in evidence for the purpose of assessing, in an action for personal injury, the sum to be awarded as general damages for future pecuniary loss.

(2) They may be proved by the production of a copy published by Her Majesty's Stationery Office.

(3) For the purposes of this section

(a) "personal injury" includes any disease and any impairment of a person's physical or mental condition; and

(b) "action for personal injury" includes an action brought by virtue of the Law Reform (Miscellaneous Provisions) Act 1934 or the Fatal Accidents Act 1976.

General

11 — Meaning of "civil proceedings"

In this Act "civil proceedings" means civil proceedings, before any tribunal, in relation to which the strict rules of evidence apply, whether as a matter of law or by agreement of the parties.

References to "the court" and "rules of court" shall be construed accordingly.

12 — Provisions as to Rules of Court

(1) Any power to make rules of court regulating the practice or procedure of the court in relation to civil proceedings includes power to make such provision as may be necessary or expedient for carrying into effect the provisions of this Act.

(2) Any rules of court made for the purposes of this Act as it applies in relation to proceedings in the High Court apply, except in so far as their operation is excluded by agreement, to arbitration proceedings to which this

Act applies, subject to such modifications as may be appropriate.

Any question arising as to what modifications are appropriate shall be determined, in default of agreement, by the arbitrator or umpire, as the case may be.

13 — Interpretation

In this Act

civil proceedings	has the meaning given by section 11 and "court" and "rules of court" shall be construed in accordance with that section;
document	means anything in which information of any description is recorded, and "copy", in relation to a document, means anything onto which information recorded in the document has been copied, by whatever means and whether directly or indirectly;
hearsay	shall be construed in accordance with section 1(2);
oral evidence	includes evidence which, by reason of a defect of speech or hearing, a person called as a witness gives in writing or by signs;
the original statement,	in relation to hearsay evidence, means the underlying statement (if any) by (a) in the case of evidence of fact, a person having personal knowledge of that fact, or (b) in the case of evidence of opinion, the person whose opinion it is; and "statement" means any representation of fact or opinion, however made.

14 — Savings

(1) Nothing in this Act affects the exclusion of evidence on grounds other than that it is hearsay.

This applies whether the evidence falls to be excluded in pursuance of any enactment or rule of law, for failure to comply with rules of court or an order of the court, or otherwise.

(2) Nothing in this Act affects the proof of documents by means other than

those specified in section 8 or 9.
(3) Nothing in this Act affects the operation of the following enactments
(a) section 2 of the Documentary Evidence Act 1868 (mode of proving certain official documents);
(b) section 2 of the Documentary Evidence Act 1882 (documents printed under the superintendence of Stationery Office);
(c) section 1 of the Evidence (Colonial Statutes) Act 1907 (proof of statutes of certain legislatures);
(d) section 1 of the Evidence (Foreign, Dominion and Colonial Documents) Act 1933 (proof and effect of registers and official certificates of certain countries);
(e) section 5 of the Oaths and Evidence (Overseas Authorities and Countries) Act 1963 (provision in respect of public registers of other countries).

15 — Consequential Amendments and Repeals

(1) The enactments specified in Schedule 1 are amended in accordance with that Schedule, the amendments being consequential on the provisions of this Act.
(2) The enactments specified in Schedule 2 are repealed to the extent specified.

16 — Short title, Commencement and Extent

(1) This Act may be cited as the Civil Evidence Act 1995.
(2) The provisions of this Act come into force on such day as the Lord Chancellor may appoint by order made by statutory instrument, and different days may be appointed for different provisions and for different purposes.
(3) Subject to subsection (3A), the provisions of this Act shall not apply in relation to proceedings begun before commencement.
(3A) Transitional provisions for the application of the provisions of this Act to proceedings begun before commencement may be made by rules of court or practice directions.
(4) This Act extends to England and Wales.
(5) Section 10 (admissibility and proof of Ogden Tables) also extends to Northern Ireland.
As it extends to Northern Ireland, the following shall be substituted for subsection (3)(b)
"(b) "action for personal injury" includes an action brought by virtue of the Law Reform (Miscellaneous Provisions) (Northern Ireland) Act 1937 or the Fatal Accidents (Northern Ireland) Order 1977."

(6) The provisions of Schedules 1 and 2 (consequential amendments and repeals) have the same extent as the enactments respectively amended or repealed.

SCHEDULES

Schedule 1

Consequential Amendment (Section 15(1))*

Army Act 1955 (c.18)

1 — For section 62 of the Army Act 1955 (making of false documents) substitute

"62 Making of false documents.

(1) A person subject to military law who

(a) makes an official document which is to his knowledge false in a material particular, or

(b) makes in any official document an entry which is to his knowledge false in a material particular, or

(c) tampers with the whole or any part of an official document (whether by altering it, destroying it, suppressing it, removing it or otherwise), or

(d) with intent to deceive, fails to make an entry in an official document, is liable on conviction by court-martial to imprisonment for a term not exceeding two years or any less punishment provided by this Act.

(2) For the purposes of this section

(a) a document is official if it is or is likely to be made use of, in connection with the performance of his functions as such, by a person who holds office under, or is in the service of, the Crown; and .

(b) a person who has signed or otherwise adopted as his own a document made by another shall be treated, as well as that other, as the maker of the document.

(3) In this section "document" means anything in which information of any description is recorded.".

Air Force Act 1955 (c.19)

2 — For section 62 of the Air Force Act 1955 (making of false documents) substitute

"62 Making of false documents.

(1) A person subject to air-force law who

(a) makes an official document which is to his knowledge false in a material particular, or

(b) makes in any official document an entry which is to his knowledge false in a material particular, or

(c) tampers with the whole or any part of an official document (whether by

---

* Annotations:
Extent Information E2 The provisions of Schedule 1 are co-existive with the enactments they amend, see s.16(6).

altering it, destroying it, suppressing it, removing it or otherwise), or
(d) with intent to deceive, fails to make an entry in an official document, is liable on conviction by court-martial to imprisonment for a term not exceeding two years or any less punishment provided by this Act.
(2) For the purposes of this section
(a) a document is official if it is or is likely to be made use of, in connection with the performance of his functions as such, by a person who holds office under, or is in the service of, the Crown; and
(b) a person who has signed or otherwise adopted as his own a document made by another shall be treated, as well as that other, as the maker of the document.
(3) In this section "document" means anything in which information of any description is recorded.".

Naval Discipline Act 1957 (c.53)

3 — For section 35 of the Naval Discipline Act 1957 (making of false documents) substitute
"35 Falsification of documents.
(1) A person subject to this Act who
(a) makes an official document which is to his knowledge false in a material particular, or
(b) makes in any official document an entry which is to his knowledge false in a material particular, or
(c) tampers with the whole or any part of an official document (whether by altering it, destroying it, suppressing it, removing it or otherwise), or
(d)with intent to deceive, fails to make an entry in an official document, is liable to imprisonment for a term not exceeding two years or any less punishment authorised by this Act.
(2) For the purposes of this section
(a) a document is official if it is or is likely to be made use of, in connection with the performance of his functions as such, by a person who holds office under, or is in the service of, the Crown; and
(b) a person who has signed or otherwise adopted as his own a document made by another shall be treated, as well as that other, as the maker of the document.
(3) In this section "document" means anything in which information of any description is recorded.".

Gaming Act 1968 (c.65)

4 — Sch. 1 para. 4 repealed (1.9.2007) by Gambling Act 2005 (c. 19), ss. 356(4), 358(1), Sch. 17; S.I.2006/3272, art. 2(4) (with Sch. 4 (as amended

(29.4.2007) by S.I. 2007/1157, arts. 7-12 and as amended (16.8.2007) by S.I. 2007/2169, arts. 7-11))

Vehicle and Driving Licences Act 1969 (c.27)

5 — (1) Section 27 of the Vehicle and Driving Licences Act 1969 (admissibility of records as evidence) is amended as follows.

(2) For subsection (2) substitute "(2) In subsection (1) of this section "document" means anything in which information of any description is recorded; "copy", in relation to a document, means anything onto which information recorded in the document has been copied, by whatever means and whether directly or indirectly; and "statement" means any representation of fact, however made.".

(3) In subsection (4)(b), for the words from "for the references" to the end substitute "for the definitions of' "document", "copy" and "statement" there were substituted "document" and "statement" have the same meanings as in section 17(3) of the Law Reform (Miscellaneous Provisions) (Scotland) Act 1968, and the reference to a copy of a document shall be construed in accordance with section 17(4) of that Act, but nothing in this paragraph shall be construed as limiting to civil proceedings the references to proceedings in subsection (1)'. "

Taxes Management Act 1970 (c.9)

6 — Sch. 1 para. 6 omitted (1.4.2009) by virtue of the Finance Act 2008 (c. 9), s. 113, Sch. 36 para. 92(d);S.I. 2009/404, art. 2

Civil Evidence Act 1972 (c.30)

7 — (1) Section 5 of the Civil Evidence Act 1972 (interpretation and application of Act) is amended as follows

(2) For subsection (1) (meaning of "civil proceedings" and "court") substitute

"(1) In this Act "civil proceedings" means civil proceedings, before any tribunal, in relation to which the strict rules of evidence apply, whether as a matter of law or by agreement of the parties; and references to "the court" shall be construed accordingly.".

(3) For subsection (2) (application of High Court or county court rules to certain other civil proceedings) substitute

"(2)The rules of court made for the purposes of the application of sections 2 and 4 of this Act to proceedings in the High Court apply, except in so far as their application is excluded by agreement, to proceedings before tribunals other than the ordinary courts of law, subject to such modifications as may be appropriate.

Any question arising as to what modifications are appropriate shall be determined, in default of agreement, by the tribunal.".

International Carriage of Perishable Foodstuffs Act 1976 (c.58)

8 — In section 15 of the International Carriage of Perishable Foodstuffs Act 1976 (admissibility of records as evidence), for subsection (2) substitute

"(2) In this section as it has effect in England and Wales "document" means anything in which information of any description is recorded; "copy", in relation to a document, means anything onto which information recorded in the document has been copied, by whatever means and whether directly or indirectly; and "statement" means any representation of fact, however made.

(2A) In this section as it has effect in Scotland, "document" and "statement" have the same meanings as in section 17(3) of the Law Reform (Miscellaneous Provisions) (Scotland) Act 1968, and the reference to a copy of a document shall be construed in accordance with section 17(4) of that Act.

(2B) In this section as it has effect in Northern Ireland, "document" and "statement" have the same meanings as in section 6(1) of the Civil Evidence Act (Northern Ireland) 1971, and the reference to a copy of a document shall be construed in accordance with section 6(2) of that Act.

(2C) Nothing in subsection (2A) or (2B) above shall be construed as limiting to civil proceedings the references to proceedings in subsection (1) above.".

Police and Criminal Evidence Act 1984 (c.60)

9 — (1) The Police and Criminal Evidence Act 1984 is amended as follows.

(2) In section 72(1) (interpretation of provisions relating to documentary evidence), for the definition of "copy" and "statement" substitute ""copy", in relation to a document, means anything onto which information recorded in the document has been copied, by whatever means and whether directly or indirectly, and "statement" means any representation of fact, however made; and".

(3) In section 118(1) (general interpretation), in the definition of "document", for "has the same meaning as in Part I of the Civil Evidence Act 1968" substitute "means anything in which information of any description is recorded.".

Companies Act 1985 (c.6)

10 — Sch. 1 para. 10 repealed (14.4.2000) by 1999 c. 23, s. 67(3), Sch. 6 (with Sch. 7 paras. 3(3), 5(2)); S.I.2000/1034, art. 2(c), Sch.

Finance Act 1985 (c.54)

11 — (1) Section 10 of the Finance Act 1985 (production of computer

records, etc.) is amended as follows.
(2) Sch. 1 para. 11(2)-(4) omitted (21.7.2008) by virtue of the Finance Act 2008 (c. 9), s. 114(8)(c)
(3) ....
(4) ....
(5) Omit subsection (7) (adaptation of references to Civil Evidence Act 1968).

Criminal Justice Act 1988 (c.33)

12 — Sch. 1 para. 12 repealed (4.4.2005) by Criminal Justice Act 2003 (c. 44), ss. 332, 336(3), Sch. 37 Pt. 6;S.I. 2005/950, art. 2, Sch. 1 para 44(3) (subject to Sch. 2 (as amended (29.7.2005) by S.I. 2005/2122, art.2 and as amended (14.7.2008) by Criminal Justice and Immigration Act 2008 (c. 4), ss. 148, 149, 153,Sch. 26 para. 78, Sch. 28 Pt. 2; S.I. 2008/1586, art. 2(1), Sch. 1 paras. 48(s), 50(2)(d) and as amended(30.11.2009) by S.I. 2009/3111art. 2(d)-(f)))

Finance Act 1988 (c.39)

13 — (1) Section 127 of the Finance Act 1988 (production of computer records, etc.) is amended as follows.
(2) Sch. 1 para. 12 repealed (4.4.2005) by Criminal Justice Act 2003 (c. 44), ss. 332, 336(3), Sch. 37 Pt. 6;S.I. 2005/950, art. 2, Sch. 1 para 44(3) (subject to Sch. 2 (as amended (29.7.2005) by S.I. 2005/2122, art.2 and as amended (14.7.2008) by Criminal Justice and Immigration Act 2008 (c. 4), ss. 148, 149, 153,Sch. 26 para. 78, Sch. 28 Pt. 2; S.I. 2008/1586, art. 2(1), Sch. 1paras. 48(s), 50(2)(d) and as amended(30.11.2009) by S.I. 2009/3111art. 2 (d)-(f)))
(3) ....
(4) Omit subsection (5) (adaptation of references to Civil Evidence Act 1968).

Housing Act 1988 (c.50)

14 — In section 97 of the Housing Act 1988 (information, etc. for applicant), for subsection (4) substitute
"(4) In this section "document" means anything in which information of any description is recorded; and in relation to a document in which information is recorded otherwise than in legible form any reference to sight of the document is to sight of the information in legible form.".

Road Traffic Offenders Act 1988 (c.53)

15 — In section 13 of the Road Traffic Offenders Act 1988 (admissibility of records as evidence), for subsection (3) substitute
"(3) In the preceding subsections, except in Scotland "copy", in relation to a

document, means anything onto which information recorded in the document has been copied, by whatever means and whether directly or indirectly; "document" means anything in which information of any description is recorded; and "statement" means any representation of fact, however made.

(3A) In Scotland, in the preceding subsections "document" and "statement" have the same meanings as in section 17(3) of the Law Reform (Miscellaneous Provisions) (Scotland) Act 1968, and the reference to a copy of a document shall be construed in accordance with section 17(4) of that Act; but nothing in this subsection shall be construed as limiting to civil proceedings the references to proceedings in subsection (2) above.".

Children Act 1989 (c.41)

16 — In section 96(7) of the Children Act 1989 (evidence given by, or with respect to, children: interpretation), for the definition of "civil proceedings" and "court" substitute ""civil proceedings" means civil proceedings, before any tribunal, in relation to which the strict rules of evidence apply, whether as a matter of law or by agreement of the parties, and references to "the court" shall be construed accordingly;".

Leasehold Reform, Housing and Urban Development Act 1993 (c.28)

17 — In section 11(9) of the Leasehold Reform, Housing and Urban Development Act1993 (right of qualifying tenant to certain information: interpretation), for the definition of "document" substitute ""document" means anything in which information of any description is recorded, and in relation to a document in which information is recorded otherwise than in legible form any reference to sight of the document is to sight of the information in legible form;".

Finance Act 1993 (c.34)

18 — Sch. 1 para. 18 omitted (1.4.2010) by virtue of The Finance Act 2009, Section 96 and Schedule 48(Appointed Day, Savings and Consequential Amendments) Order 2009 (S.I. 2009/ 3054), art. 3, {Sch. para. 16(c)}

Vehicle Excise and Registration Act 1994 (c.22)

19 — In section 52 of the Vehicle Excise and Registration Act 1994 (admissibility of records as evidence), for subsections (3) to (5) substitute

"(3) In this section as it has effect in England and Wales "document" means anything in which information of any description is recorded; "copy", in relation to a document, means anything onto which information recorded in the document has been copied, by whatever means and whether directly or indirectly; and "statement" means any representation of fact, however made.

(4) In this section as it has effect in Scotland, "document" and "statement" have the same meanings as in section 17(3) of the Law Reform (Miscellaneous Provisions) (Scotland) Act 1968, and the reference to a copy of a document shall be construed in accordance with section 17(4) of that Act.

(5) In this section as it has effect in Northern Ireland, "document" and "statement" have the same meanings as in section 6(1) of the Civil Evidence Act (Northern Ireland) 1971, and the reference to a copy of a document shall be construed in accordance with section 6(2) of that Act.

(6) Nothing in subsection (4) or (5) limits to civil proceedings the references to proceedings in subsection (1).".

Value Added Tax Act 1994 (c.23)

20 — In section 96(1) of the Value Added Tax Act 1994 (general interpretative provisions), at the appropriate places insert "document" means anything in which information of any description is recorded; and "copy", in relation to a document, means anything onto which information recorded in the document has been copied, by whatever means and whether directly or indirectly.

Schedule 2 *
Repeals

Chapter	Short Title	Extent of repeal
1938 c. 28.	Evidence Act 1938.	Sections 1 and 2. Section 6(1) except the words from "Proceedings" to "references". Section 6(2)(b).
1968 c. 64.	Civil Evidence Act 1968.	Part I.
1971 c. 33.	Armed Forces Act 1971.	Section 26.
1972 c. 30.	Civil Evidence Act 1972.	Section 1. Section 2(1) and (2). In section 2(3)(b), the words from "by virtue of section 2"to "out-of-court statements)". In section 3(1), the words "Part I of the Civil Evidence Act 1968 or". In section 6(3), the words "1 and", in both places where they occur.
1975 c. 63.	Inheritance (Provision for Family and Dependants) Act 1975.	Section 21.
1979 c. 2.	Customs and Excise Management Act 1979.	Section 75A (6)(a). Section 118A (6)(a).
1980 c. 43.	Magistrates' Courts Act 1980.	In Schedule 7, paragraph 75.
1984 c. 28.	County Courts Act 1984.	In Schedule 2, paragraphs 33and 34.
1985 c. 54.	Finance Act 1985.	Section 10(7).
1986 c. 21.	Armed Forces Act 1986.	Section 3.
1988 c. 39.	Finance Act 1988.	Section 127(5).
1990 c. 26.	Gaming (Amendment)	In the Schedule, paragraph 2 (7).

* Annotations:
Extent Information E2 The provisions of Schedule 2 are co-existive with the enactments they amend, see s.16(6).

1994 c. 9.	Finance Act 1994.	Section 22(2)(a). In Schedule 7, paragraph 1(6)(a).
1994 c. 23.	Value Added Tax Act 1994.	Section 96(6) and (7). In Schedule 11, paragraph 6(6)(a).
1995 c. 4.	Finance Act 1995.	In Schedule 4, paragraph 38.

CONVENTION ON THE RECOGNITION AND ENFORCEMENT OF FOREIGN ARBITRAL AWARDS (1958) *

Article I

1. This Convention shall apply to the recognition and enforcement of arbitral awards made in the territory of a State other than the State where the recognition and enforcement of such awards are sought, and arising out of differences between persons, whether physical or legal. It shall also apply to arbitral awards not considered as domestic awards in the State where their recognition and enforcement are sought.
2. The term "arbitral awards" shall include not only awards made by arbitrators appointed for each case but also those made by permanent arbitral bodies to which the parties have submitted.
3. When signing, ratifying or acceding to this Convention, or notifying extension under Article X hereof, any State may on the basis of reciprocity declare that it will apply the Convention to the recognition and enforcement of awards made only in the territory of another Contracting State. It may also declare that it will apply the Convention only to differences arising out of legal relationships, whether contractual or not, which are considered as commercial under the national law of the State making such declaration.

Article II

1. Each Contracting State shall recognize an agreement in writing under which the parties undertake to submit to arbitration all or any differences which have arisen or which may arise between them in respect of a defined legal relationship, whether contractual or not, concerning a subject matter capable of settlement by arbitration.
2. The term "agreement in writing" shall include an arbitral clause in a contract or an arbitration agreement, signed by the parties or contained in an exchange of letters or telegrams.
3. The court of a Contracting State, when seized of an action in a matter in respect of which the parties have made an agreement within the meaning of this article, shall, at the request of one of the parties, refer the parties to arbitration, unless it finds that the said agreement is null and void, inoperative or incapable of being performed.

Article III

Each Contracting State shall recognize arbitral awards as binding and enforce them in accordance with the rules of procedure of the territory where the award is relied upon, under the conditions laid down in the following articles. There shall not be imposed substantially more onerous conditions or higher fees or charges on the recognition or enforcement of arbitral awards to which this Convention applies than are imposed on the recognition or enforcement of domestic arbitral awards.

---

* For a commentary on the New York Convention, see Herbert Kronke and others (eds), *Recognition and Enforcement of Foreign Arbitral Awards: A Global Commentary on the New York Convention* (Kluwer Law International, 2010) and Reinmar Wolff (ed), *The New York Convention: Commentary*

Article IV

1. To obtain the recognition and enforcement mentioned in the preceding article, the party applying for recognition and enforcement shall, at the time of application, supply:

(a) The duly authenticated original award or a duly certified copy thereof;

(b) The original agreement referred to in Article II or a duly certified copy thereof.

2. If the said award or agreement is not made in an official language of the country in which the award is relied upon, the party applying for recognition and enforcement of the award shall produce a translation of these documents into such language. The translation shall be certified by an official or sworn translator or by a diplomatic or consular agent.

Article V

1. Recognition and enforcement of the award may be refused, at the request of the party against whom it is invoked, only if that party furnishes to the competent authority where the recognition and enforcement is sought, proof that:

(a) The parties to the agreement referred to in Article II were, under the law applicable to them, under some incapacity, or the said agreement is not valid under the law to which the parties have subjected it or, failing any indication thereon, under the law of the country where the award was made; or

(b) the party against whom the award is invoked was not given proper notice of the appointment of the arbitrator or of the arbitration proceedings or was otherwise unable to present his case; or

(c) The award deals with a difference not contemplated by or not falling within the terms of the submission to arbitration, or it contains decisions on matters beyond the scope of the submission to arbitration, provided that, if the decisions on matters submitted to arbitration can be separated from those not so submitted, that part of the award which contains decisions on matters submitted to arbitration may be recognized and enforced; or

(d) The composition of the arbitral authority or the arbitral procedure was not in accordance with the agreement of the parties, or, failing such agreement, was not in accordance with the law of the country where the arbitration took place; or

(e) The award has not yet become binding on the parties or has been set aside or suspended by a competent authority of the country in which, or under the law of which, that award was made.

2. Recognition and enforcement of an arbitral award may also be refused if

(Beck/Hart, 2012). See also, online platform on the New York Convention <http://www.newyorkconvention1958.org/>.

the competent authority in the country where recognition and enforcement is sought finds that:
(a) The subject matter of the difference is not capable of settlement by arbitration under the law of that country; or
(b) The recognition or enforcement of the award would be contrary to the public policy of that country.

Article VI

If an application for the setting aside or suspension of the award has been made to a competent authority referred to in Article V(1)(e), the authority before which the award is sought to be relied upon may, if it considers it proper, adjourn the decision on the enforcement of the award and may also, on the application of the party claiming enforcement of the award, order the other party to give suitable security.

Article VII

1. The provisions of the present Convention shall not affect the validity of multilateral or bilateral agreements concerning the recognition and enforcement of arbitral awards entered into by the Contracting States nor deprive any interested party of any right he may have to avail himself of an arbitral award in the manner and to the extent allowed by the law or the treaties of the country where such award is sought to be relied upon.
2. The Geneva Protocol on Arbitration Clauses of 1923 and the Geneva Convention on the Execution of Foreign Arbitral Awards of 1927 shall cease to have effect between Contracting States on their becoming bound and to the extent that they become bound, by this Convention.

Article VIII

1. This Convention shall be open until 31 December 1958 for signature on behalf of any Member of the United Nations and also on behalf of any other State which is or hereafter becomes a member of any specialized agency of the United Nations, or which is or hereafter becomes a party to the Statute of the International Court of Justice, or any other State to which an invitation has been addressed by the General Assembly of the United Nations.
2. This Convention shall be ratified and the instrument of ratification shall be deposited with the Secretary-General of the United Nations.

Article IX

1. This Convention shall be open for accession to all States referred to in Article VIII.
2. Accession shall be effected by the deposit of an instrument of accession with the Secretary-General of the United Nations.

Article X

1. Any State may, at the time of signature, ratification or accession, declare that this Convention shall extend to all or any of the territories for the international relations of which it is responsible. Such a declaration shall take effect when the Convention enters into force for the State concerned.
2. At any time thereafter any such extension shall be made by notification addressed to the Secretary-General of the United Nations and shall take effect as from the ninetieth day after the day of receipt by the Secretary-General of the United Nations of this notification, or as from the date of entry into force of the Convention for the State concerned, whichever is the later.
3. With respect to those territories to which this Convention is not extended at the time of signature, ratification or accession, each State concerned shall consider the possibility of taking the necessary steps in order to extend the application of this Convention to such territories, subject, where necessary for constitutional reasons, to the consent of the Governments of such territories.

Article XI

In the case of a federal or non-unitary State, the following provisions shall apply:

(a) With respect to those articles of this Convention that come within the legislative jurisdiction of the federal authority, the obligations of the federal Government shall to this extent be the same as those of Contracting States which are not federal States;

(b) With respect to those articles of this Convention that come within the legislative jurisdiction of constituent states or provinces which are not, under the constitutional system of the federation, bound to take legislative action, the federal Government shall bring such articles with a favourable recommendation to the notice of the appropriate authorities of constituent states or provinces at the earliest possible moment;

(c) A federal State Party to this Convention shall, at the request of any other Contracting State transmitted through the Secretary-General of the United Nations, supply a statement of the law and practice of the federation and its constituent units in regard to any particular provision of this Convention, showing the extent to which effect has been given to that provision by legislative or other action.

Article XII

1. This Convention shall come into force on the ninetieth day following the date of deposit of the third instrument of ratification or accession.

2. For each State ratifying or acceding to this Convention after the deposit of the third instrument of ratification or accession, this Convention shall enter into force on the ninetieth day after deposit by such State of its instrument of ratification or accession.

Article XIII

1. Any Contracting State may denounce this Convention by a written notification to the Secretary-General of the United Nations. Denunciation shall take effect one year after the date of receipt of the notification by the Secretary-General.

2. Any State which has made a declaration or notification under Article X may, at any time thereafter, by notification to the Secretary-General of the United Nations, declare that this Convention shall cease to extend to the territory concerned one year after the date of the receipt of the notification by the Secretary-General.

3. This Convention shall continue to be applicable to arbitral awards in respect of which recognition or enforcement proceedings have been instituted before the denunciation takes effect.

Article XIV

A Contracting State shall not be entitled to avail itself of the present Convention against other Contracting States except to the extent that it is itself bound to apply the Convention.

Article XV

The Secretary-General of the United Nations shall notify the States contemplated in Article VIII of the following:

(a) Signatures and ratifications in accordance with Article VIII;

(b) Accessions in accordance with Article IX;

(c) Declarations and notifications under Articles I, X, and XI;

(d) The date upon which this Convention enters into force in accordance with Article XII;

(e) Denunciations and notifications in accordance with Article XIII.

Article XVI

1. This Convention, of which the Chinese, English, French, Russian and Spanish texts shall be equally authentic, shall be deposited in the archives of the United Nations.

2. The Secretary-General of the United Nations shall transmit a certified copy of this Convention to the States contemplated in Article VIII.

FRENCH CODE OF CIVIL PROCEDURE (BOOK IV: ARBITRATION) *

Title I Domestic Arbitration[1]
Chapter I
The Arbitration Agreement

Article 1442

An arbitration agreement may be in the form of an arbitration clause or a submission agreement.

An arbitration clause is an agreement by which the parties to one or more contracts undertake to submit to arbitration disputes which may arise in relation to such contract(s).

A submission agreement is an agreement by which the parties to a dispute submit such dispute to arbitration.

Article 1443

In order to be valid, an arbitration agreement shall be in writing. It can result from an exchange of written communications or be contained in a document to which reference is made in the main agreement.

Article 1444

An arbitration agreement shall designate, including by reference to arbitration rules, the arbitrator or arbitrators, or provide for a procedure for their appointment. Alternatively, Articles 1451 through 1454 shall apply.

Article 1445

In order to be valid, a submission agreement shall define the subject matter of the dispute.

*****Article 1446**

Parties may submit their dispute to arbitration even where proceedings are already pending before a court.

*****Article 1447**

An arbitration agreement is independent of the contract to which it relates. It shall not be affected if such contract is void.

If an arbitration clause is void, it shall be deemed not written.

Article 1448

*** When a dispute subject to an arbitration agreement is brought before a court, such court shall decline jurisdiction, except if an arbitral tribunal has not yet been seized of the dispute and if the arbitration agreement is manifestly void or manifestly not applicable.

*** A court may not decline jurisdiction on its own motion.

Any stipulation contrary to the present article shall be deemed not written.

*****Article 1449**

The existence of an arbitration agreement, insofar as the arbitral tribunal has not yet been constituted, shall not preclude a party from applying to a court

---

* Translated by Emmanuel Gaillard, Nanou Leleu-Knobil and Daniela Pellarini of Shearman & Sterling LLP. For a commentary on the French Arbitration Act, see Laurent Gouiffès and Lara

for measures relating to the taking of evidence or provisional or conservatory measures.
Subject to the provisions governing conservatory attachments and judicial security, application shall be made to the President of the *Tribunal de grande instance* or of the *Tribunal de commerce* who shall rule on the measures relating to the taking of evidence in accordance with the provisions of Article 145[2] and, where the matter is urgent, on the provisional or conservatory measures requested by the parties to the arbitration agreement.

Chapter II
The Arbitral Tribunal

Article 1450

Only a natural person having full capacity to exercise his or her rights may act as an arbitrator.
Where an arbitration agreement designates a legal person, such person shall only have the power to administer the arbitration.

Article 1451

An arbitral tribunal shall be composed of a sole arbitrator or an uneven number of arbitrators.
If an arbitration agreement provides for an even number of arbitrators, an additional arbitrator shall be appointed.
If the parties cannot agree on the appointment of the additional arbitrator, he or she shall be appointed by the other arbitrators within one month of having accepted their mandate or, if they fail to do so, by the judge acting in support of the arbitration (*juge d'appui*) referred to in Article 1459.

*****Article 1452**

If the parties have not agreed on the procedure for appointing the arbitrator (s):
(1) Where there is to be a sole arbitrator and if the parties fail to agree on the arbitrator, he or she shall be appointed by the person responsible for administering the arbitration or, where there is no such person, by the judge acting in support of the arbitration;
(2) Where there are to be three arbitrators, each party shall appoint an arbitrator and the two arbitrators so appointed shall appoint a third arbitrator. If a party fails to appoint an arbitrator within one month following receipt of a request to that effect by the other party, or if the two arbitrators fail to agree on the third arbitrator within one month of having accepted their mandate, the person responsible for administering the arbitration or, where there is no such person, the judge acting in support of

---

Kozyreff, 'Commentary on the New French International Arbitration Law: Towards Quicker and More Efficient Arbitration Proceedings' (2012) 18 Columbia Journal of European Law 45.
[1] See page 276. [2] *Ibid.*

the arbitration, shall appoint the third arbitrator.

***__Article 1453__

If there are more than two parties to the dispute and they fail to agree on the procedure for constituting the arbitral tribunal, the person responsible for administering the arbitration or, where there is no such person, the judge acting in support of the arbitration, shall appoint the arbitrator(s).

***__Article 1454__

Any other dispute relating to the constitution of an arbitral tribunal shall be resolved, if the parties cannot agree, by the person responsible for administering the arbitration or, where there is no such person, by the judge acting in support of the arbitration.

***__Article 1455__

If an arbitration agreement is manifestly void or manifestly not applicable, the judge acting in support of the arbitration shall declare that no appointment need be made.

***__Article 1456__

The constitution of an arbitral tribunal shall be complete upon the arbitrators' acceptance of their mandate. As of that date, the tribunal is seized of the dispute.

Before accepting a mandate, an arbitrator shall disclose any circumstance that may affect his or her independence or impartiality. He or she also shall disclose promptly any such circumstance that may arise after accepting the mandate.

If the parties cannot agree on the removal of an arbitrator, the issue shall be resolved by the person responsible for administering the arbitration or, where there is no such person, by the judge acting in support of the arbitration to whom application must be made within one month following the disclosure or the discovery of the fact at issue.

***__Article 1457__

Arbitrators shall carry out their mandate until it is completed, unless they are legally incapacitated or there is a legitimate reason for them to refuse to act or to resign.

If there is disagreement as to the materiality of the reason invoked, the matter shall be resolved by the person responsible for administering the arbitration or, where there is no such person, by the judge acting in support of the arbitration to whom application must be made within one month following such incapacity, refusal to act or resignation.

***__Article 1458__

An arbitrator may only be removed with the unanimous consent of the parties. Where there is no unanimous consent, the provisions of the final paragraph of Article 1456 shall apply.

Article 1459

The judge acting in support of the arbitration shall be the President of a *Tribunal de grande instance.*

However, the President of a Tribunal de commerce shall have jurisdiction to rule on applications made on the basis of Articles 1451 through 1454 if there is an express provision to that effect in the arbitration agreement. In that case, he or she may apply Article 1455.

The arbitration agreement shall determine which court has territorial jurisdiction, failing which, jurisdiction shall lie with the court of the place where the seat of the arbitral tribunal has been set. Where the arbitration agreement is silent, territorial jurisdiction shall lie with the court of the place where the party or one of the parties resisting the application resides or, if that party does not reside in France, with the court of the place where the applicant resides.

***Article 1460**

Application to the judge acting in support of the arbitration shall be made either by a party or by the arbitral tribunal or one of its members.

Such application shall be made, heard and decided as for expedited proceedings (*référé*).

The judge acting in support of the arbitration shall rule by way of an order against which no recourse can be had. However, such order may be appealed where the judge holds that no appointment need be made for one of the reasons stated in Article 1455.

Article 1461

Subject to the provisions of Article 1456, paragraph 1, any stipulation contrary to the rules set forth in the present chapter shall be deemed not written.

Chapter III
The Arbitral Proceedings

***Article 1462**

A dispute shall be submitted to the arbitral tribunal either jointly by the parties or by the most diligent party.

Article 1463

If an arbitration agreement does not specify a time limit, the duration of the arbitral tribunal's mandate shall be limited to six months as of the date on which the tribunal is seized of the dispute.

*** The statutory or contractual time limit may be extended by agreement between the parties or, where there is no such agreement, by the judge acting in support of the arbitration.

Article 1464

Unless otherwise agreed by the parties, the arbitral tribunal shall define the procedure to be followed in the arbitration. It is under no obligation to abide by the rules governing court proceedings.

However, the fundamental principles governing court proceedings set forth in Articles 4, 10, Article 11, paragraph 1, Article 12, paragraphs 2 and 3, Articles 13 through 21, 23 and 23-1 shall apply.

*** Both parties and arbitrators shall act diligently and in good faith in the conduct of the proceedings.

Subject to legal requirements, and unless otherwise agreed by the parties, arbitral proceedings shall be confidential.

*****Article 1465**

The arbitral tribunal has exclusive jurisdiction to rule on objections to its jurisdiction.

*****Article 1466**

A party which, knowingly and without a legitimate reason, fails to object to an irregularity before the arbitral tribunal in a timely manner shall be deemed to have waived its right to avail itself of such irregularity.

*****Article 1467**

The arbitral tribunal shall take all necessary steps concerning evidentiary and procedural matters, unless the parties authorise it to delegate such tasks to one of its members.

The arbitral tribunal may call upon any person to provide testimony. Witnesses shall not be sworn in.

If a party is in possession of an item of evidence, the arbitral tribunal may enjoin that party to produce it, determine the manner in which it is to be produced and, if necessary, attach penalties to such injunction.

*****Article 1468**

The arbitral tribunal may order upon the parties any conservatory or provisional measures that it deems appropriate, set conditions for such measures and, if necessary, attach penalties to such order. However, only courts may order conservatory attachments and judicial security.

The arbitral tribunal has the power to amend or add to any provisional or conservatory measure that it has granted.

*****Article 1469**

If one of the parties to arbitral proceedings intends to rely on an official (*acte authentique*) or private (*acte sous seing privé*) deed to which it was

not a party, or on evidence held by a third party, it may, upon leave of the arbitral tribunal, have that third party summoned before the President of the *Tribunal de grande instance* for the purpose of obtaining a copy thereof (*expédition*) or the production of the deed or item of evidence.
Articles 42 through 48 shall determine which *Tribunal de grande instance* has territorial jurisdiction in this regard.
Application shall be made, heard and decided as for expedited proceedings (*référé*).
If the president considers the application well-founded, he or she shall order that the relevant original, copy or extract of the deed or item of evidence be issued or produced, under such conditions and guarantees as he or she determines, and, if necessary, attach penalties to such order.
Such order is not readily enforceable.
It may be appealed within fifteen days following service (*signification*) of the order.

*****Article 1470**

Unless otherwise stipulated, the arbitral tribunal shall have the power to rule on a request for verification of handwriting or claim of forgery in accordance with Articles 287 through 294 and Article 299.
Where an incidental claim of forgery of official documents is raised, Article 313 shall apply.

Article 1471

Abatement of proceedings shall be governed by Articles 369 through 372.

*****Article 1472**

Where necessary, the arbitral tribunal may stay the proceedings. The proceedings shall be stayed for the period of time set forth in the stay order or until such time as the event prescribed in the order has occurred.
The arbitral tribunal may, as the circumstances require, lift or shorten the stay.

Article 1473

Unless otherwise stipulated, arbitral proceedings shall also be stayed in the event of the death, legal incapacity, refusal to act, resignation, challenge or removal of an arbitrator, and until such time as a substitute arbitrator has accepted his or her mandate.
The substitute arbitrator shall be appointed in accordance with the procedure agreed upon by the parties or, failing that, in accordance with the procedure followed for the appointment of the original arbitrator.

Article 1474

An abatement or stay of the proceedings shall not put an end to the arbitral

tribunal's mandate.
The arbitral tribunal may ask the parties to report any steps taken towards resuming the proceedings or putting an end to the situation having caused the abatement or stay. If the parties fail to take action, the tribunal may terminate the proceedings.

Article 1475

The arbitral proceedings shall resume at the stage reached before the abatement or stay, once the underlying causes for such abatement or stay cease to exist.
When the proceedings resume, and by way of an exception to Article 1463, the arbitral tribunal may extend the duration of the proceedings for a period not exceeding six months.

Article 1476

The arbitral tribunal shall set the date on which the award is to be rendered.
During the course of the deliberations, no claim may be made, no argument raised nor evidence produced, except at the request of the arbitral tribunal.

Article 1477

Arbitral proceedings shall come to an end upon expiration of the time limit set for the arbitration.

Chapter IV
The Arbitral Award

Article 1478

The arbitral tribunal shall decide the dispute in accordance with the law, unless the parties have empowered it to rule as *amiable compositeur*.

*****Article 1479**

The arbitral tribunal's deliberations shall be confidential.

Article 1480

The arbitral award shall be made by majority decision.
It shall be signed by all the arbitrators.
If a minority among them refuses to sign, the award shall so state and shall have the same effect as if it had been signed by all the arbitrators.

*****Article 1481**

The arbitral award shall state:
(1) the full names of the parties, as well as their domicile or corporate headquarters;
(2) if applicable, the names of the counsel or other persons who represented or assisted the parties;
(3) the names of the arbitrators who made it;
(4) the date on which it was made;

(5) the place where the award was made.

***Article 1482**

The arbitral award shall succinctly set forth the respective claims and arguments of the parties.

The award shall state the reasons upon which it is based.

Article 1483

An arbitral award which fails to comply with the provisions of Article 1480, the provisions of Article 1481 regarding the names of the arbitrators and the date of the award, and those contained in Article 1482 regarding the reasons for the award, shall be void.

However, no omission or inaccuracy in the particulars required for the award to be valid shall render the award void if it can be established, through the case record or any other means, that it does, in fact, comply with the relevant legal requirements.

Article 1484

*** As soon as it is made, an arbitral award shall be *res judicata* with regard to the claims adjudicated in that award.

*** The award may be declared provisionally enforceable.

The award shall be notified by service (*signification*) unless the parties agree otherwise.

Article 1485

*** Once an award is made, the arbitral tribunal shall no longer be vested with the power to rule on the claims adjudicated in that award.

*** However, on application of a party, the arbitral tribunal may interpret the award, rectify clerical errors and omissions, or make an additional award where it failed to rule on a claim. The arbitral tribunal shall rule after having heard the parties or having given them the opportunity to be heard.

If the arbitral tribunal cannot be reconvened and if the parties cannot agree on the constitution of a new tribunal, this power shall vest in the court which would have had jurisdiction had there been no arbitration.

***Article 1486**

Applications under Article 1485, paragraph 2, shall be filed within three months of notification of the award.

Unless otherwise agreed, the decision amending the award or the additional award shall be made within three months of application to the arbitral tribunal. This time limit may be extended in accordance with Article 1463, paragraph 2.

The decision amending the award or the additional award shall be notified in the same manner as the initial award.

Chapter V
Exequatur

Article 1487

An arbitral award may only be enforced by virtue of an enforcement order (*exequatur*) issued by the *Tribunal de grande instance* of the place where the award was made.

Exequatur proceedings shall not be adversarial.

Application for *exequatur* shall be filed by the most diligent party with the Court Registrar, together with the original award and arbitration agreement, or duly authenticated copies of such documents.

The enforcement order shall be affixed to the original or, if the original is not produced, to a duly authenticated copy of the arbitral award, as per the previous paragraph.

Article 1488

No enforcement order may be granted where an award is manifestly contrary to public policy.

An order denying enforcement shall state the reasons upon which it is based.

Chapter VI
Recourse
Section 1 Appeal

Article 1489

An arbitral award shall not be subject to appeal, unless otherwise agreed by the parties.

Article 1490

An appeal may seek to obtain either the reversal or the setting aside of an award.

The court shall rule in accordance with the law or as *amiable compositeur*, within the limits of the arbitral tribunal's mandate.

Section 2 Actions to Set Aside

Article 1491

An action to set aside an award may be brought except where the parties have agreed that the award may be appealed.

Any provision to the contrary shall be deemed not written.

Article 1492

An award may only be set aside where:

(1) the arbitral tribunal wrongly upheld or declined jurisdiction; or

(2) the arbitral tribunal was not properly constituted; or

(3) the arbitral tribunal ruled without complying with the mandate conferred

upon it; or
(4) due process was violated; or
(5) the award is contrary to public policy; or
(6) the award failed to state the reasons upon which it is based, the date on which it was made, the names or signatures of the arbitrator(s) having made the award; or where the award was not made by majority decision.

Article 1493

When a court sets aside an arbitral award, it shall rule on the merits within the limits of the arbitrator's mandate, unless otherwise agreed by the parties.

Section 3 Appeals And Actions To Set Aside – Common Provisions

Article 1494

Appeals and actions to set aside shall be brought before the Court of Appeal of the place where the award was made.

Such recourse can be had as soon as the award is rendered. If no application is made within one month following notification of the award, recourse shall no longer be admissible.

Article 1495

Appeals and actions to set aside shall be brought, heard and decided in accordance with the rules applicable to adversarial proceedings set forth in Articles 900 through 930-1.

Article 1496

Unless an arbitral award is provisionally enforceable, enforcement shall be stayed until expiration of the time limit set for appeals or actions to set aside, or upon the filing of an appeal or action to set aside during this period.

Article 1497

The first president ruling in expedited proceedings (*référé*) or, once the matter is referred to him or her, the judge assigned to the case (*conseiller de la mise en état*) may:

(1) if the award is provisionally enforceable and where enforcement may lead to manifestly excessive consequences, stay or set conditions for enforcement of the award; or
(2) if the award is not provisionally enforceable, order that the award or any part thereof be provisionally enforceable.

Article 1498

If an award is provisionally enforceable or if it has been made provisionally enforceable as per Article 1497(2), the first president or, once the matter is referred to him or her, the judge assigned to the case may grant enforcement (*exequatur*) of the arbitral award.

A decision denying an appeal or an application to set aside an award shall be deemed an enforcement order of the arbitral award or the parts thereof that were not overturned by the court.

Section 4 Recourse Against Orders Granting or Denying Enforcement

Article 1499

No recourse may be had against an order granting enforcement of an award. However, an appeal or an action to set aside an award shall be deemed to constitute recourse against the order of the judge having ruled on enforcement or shall bring an end to said judge's jurisdiction, as regards the parts of the award which are challenged.

Article 1500

An order denying enforcement may be appealed within one month following service (*signification*) thereof.

If it is appealed, and if one of the parties so requests, the Court of Appeal shall rule on an appeal or application to set aside the award, provided that the time limit for such appeal or application has not expired.

Section 5 Other Means of Recourse

Article 1501

Third parties may challenge an arbitral award by petitioning the court which would have had jurisdiction had there been no arbitration, subject to the provisions of Article 588, paragraph 1.

Article 1502

*** Application for revision of an arbitral award may be made in the circumstances provided in Article 595 for court judgments,[3] and under the conditions set forth in Articles 594, 596, 597 and 601 through 603.

*** Application shall be made to the arbitral tribunal.

However, if the arbitral tribunal cannot be reconvened, application shall be made to the Court of Appeal which would have had jurisdiction to hear other forms of recourse against the award.

*****Article 1503**

No *opposition*[4] may be filed against an arbitral award, nor may the Cour de Cassation be petitioned to quash the award.

Title II

International Arbitration

Article 1504

An arbitration is international when international trade interests are at stake.

Article 1505

In international arbitration, and unless otherwise stipulated, the judge acting in support of the arbitration shall be the President of the *Tribunal de grande*

[3] See page 276.

[4] *Ibid.*

instance of Paris when:
(1) the arbitration takes place in France; or
(2) the parties have agreed that French procedural law shall apply to the arbitration; or
(3) the parties have expressly granted jurisdiction to French courts over disputes relating to the arbitral procedure; or
(4) one of the parties is exposed to a risk of a denial of justice.

Article 1506

Unless the parties have agreed otherwise, and subject to the provisions of the present Title, the following Articles shall apply to international arbitration:
(1) 1446, 1447, 1448 (paragraphs 1 and 2) and 1449, regarding the arbitration agreement;
(2) 1452 through 1458 and 1460 regarding the constitution of the arbitral tribunal and the procedure governing application to the judge acting in support of the arbitration;
(3) 1462, 1463 (paragraph 2), 1464 (paragraph 3), 1465 through 1470 and 1472 regarding arbitral proceedings;
(4) 1479, 1481, 1482, 1484 (paragraphs 1 and 2), 1485 (paragraphs 1 and 2) and 1486 regarding arbitral awards;
(5) 1502 (paragraphs 1 and 2) and 1503 regarding means of recourse other than appeals or actions to set aside.

Chapter I
International Arbitration Agreements

Article 1507

An arbitration agreement shall not be subject to any requirements as to its form.

Article 1508

An arbitration agreement may designate the arbitrator(s) or provide for the procedure for their appointment, directly or by reference to arbitration rules or to procedural rules.

Chapter II
Arbitral Proceedings and Awards

Article 1509

An arbitration agreement may define the procedure to be followed in the arbitral proceedings, directly or by reference to arbitration rules or to procedural rules.

Unless the arbitration agreement provides otherwise, the arbitral tribunal shall define the procedure as required, either directly or by reference to arbitration rules or to procedural rules.

Article 1510

Irrespective of the procedure adopted, the arbitral tribunal shall ensure that the parties are treated equally and shall uphold the principle of due process.

Article 1511

The arbitral tribunal shall decide the dispute in accordance with the rules of law chosen by the parties or, where no such choice has been made, in accordance with the rules of law it considers appropriate.

In either case, the arbitral tribunal shall take trade usages into account.

Article 1512

The arbitral tribunal shall rule as *amiable compositeur* if the parties have empowered it to do so.

Article 1513

Unless the arbitration agreement provides otherwise, the award shall be made by majority decision. It shall be signed by all the arbitrators.

However, if a minority among them refuses to sign, the others shall so state in the award.

If there is no majority, the chairman of the arbitral tribunal shall rule alone. Should the other arbitrators refuse to sign, the chairman shall so state in the award, which only he or she shall sign.

An award made under the circumstances described in either of the two preceding paragraphs shall have the same effect as if it had been signed by all the arbitrators or made by majority decision.

Chapter III

Recognition and Enforcement of Arbitral Awards Made Abroad or in International Arbitration

Article 1514

An arbitral award shall be recognised or enforced in France if the party relying on it can prove its existence and if such recognition or enforcement is not manifestly contrary to international public policy.

Article 1515

The existence of an arbitral award shall be proven by producing the original award, together with the arbitration agreement, or duly authenticated copies of such documents.

If such documents are in a language other than French, the party applying for recognition or enforcement shall produce a translation. The applicant may be requested to provide a translation by a translator whose name appears on a list of court experts or a translator accredited by the administrative or judicial authorities of another Member State of the

European Union, a Contracting Party to the European Economic Area Agreement or the Swiss Confederation.

Article 1516

An arbitral award may only be enforced by virtue of an enforcement order (*exequatur*) issued by the *Tribunal de grande instance* of the place where the award was made or by the *Tribunal de grande instance* of Paris if the award was made abroad.

Exequatur proceedings shall not be adversarial.

Application for exequatur shall be filed by the most diligent party with the Court Registrar, together with the original award and arbitration agreement, or duly authenticated copies of such documents.

Article 1517

The enforcement order shall be affixed to the original or, if the original is not produced, to a duly authenticated copy of the arbitral award, as per the final paragraph of Article 1516.

Where an arbitral award is in a language other than French, the enforcement order shall also be affixed to the translation produced as per Article 1515.

An order denying enforcement of an arbitral award shall state the reasons upon which it is based.

Chapter IV
Recourse
Section 1 Awards Made in France

Article 1518

The only means of recourse against an award made in France in an international arbitration is an action to set aside.

Article 1519

An action to set aside shall be brought before the Court of Appeal of the place where the award was made.

Such recourse can be had as soon as the award is rendered. If no application is made within one month following notification of the award, recourse shall no longer be admissible.

The award shall be notified by service (*signification*), unless otherwise agreed by the parties.

Article 1520

An award may only be set aside where:

(1) the arbitral tribunal wrongly upheld or declined jurisdiction; or

(2) the arbitral tribunal was not properly constituted; or

(3) the arbitral tribunal ruled without complying with the mandate conferred upon it; or

(4) due process was violated; or
(5) recognition or enforcement of the award is contrary to international public policy.

Article 1521

The first president or, once the matter is referred to him or her, the judge assigned to the case (*conseiller de la mise en état*) may grant enforcement (*exequatur*) of the award.

Article 1522

By way of a specific agreement the parties may, at any time, expressly waive their right to bring an action to set aside.

Where such right has been waived, the parties nonetheless retain their right to appeal an enforcement order on one of the grounds set forth in Article 1520.

Such appeal shall be brought within one month following notification of the award bearing the enforcement order. The award bearing the enforcement order shall be notified by service (*signification*), unless otherwise agreed by the parties.

Article 1523

An order denying recognition or enforcement of an international arbitral award made in France may be appealed.

The appeal shall be brought within one month following service (*signification*) of the order.

If the order is appealed, and if one of the parties so requests, the Court of Appeal shall rule on an action to set aside unless the parties have waived the right to bring such action or the time limit to bring such action has expired.

Article 1524

No recourse may be had against an order granting enforcement of an award, except as provided in Article 1522, paragraph 2.

However, an action to set aside an award shall be deemed to constitute recourse against the order of the judge having ruled on enforcement or shall bring an end to said judge's jurisdiction, as regards the parts of the award which are challenged.

Section 2 Awards Made Abroad

Article 1525

An order granting or denying recognition or enforcement of an arbitral award made abroad may be appealed.

The appeal shall be brought within one month following service (*signification*) of the order.

However, the parties may agree on other means of notification when an

appeal is brought against an award bearing an enforcement order.
The Court of Appeal may only deny recognition or enforcement of an arbitral award on the grounds listed in Article 1520.

Section 3 Awards Made in France and Abroad – Common Provisions

Article 1526

Neither an action to set aside an award nor an appeal against an enforcement order shall suspend enforcement of an award.
However, the first president ruling in expedited proceedings (*référé*) or, once the matter is referred to him or her, the judge assigned to the matter (*conseiller de la mise en état*), may stay or set conditions for enforcement of an award where enforcement could severely prejudice the rights of one of the parties.

Article 1527

Appeals against orders granting or denying enforcement and actions to set aside awards shall be brought, heard and decided in accordance with the rules applicable to adversarial proceedings set forth in Articles 900 through 930-1.
A decision denying an appeal or application to set aside an award shall be deemed an enforcement order of the arbitral award or of the parts of the award that were not overturned by the court.

---

[1] Articles or paragraphs preceded by three asterisks (***) also apply to international arbitration.

[2] Article 145 provides as follows: "If, before legal proceedings commence, there is a legitimate reason to preserve or establish evidence upon which the resolution of a dispute may depend, measures relating to the taking of evidence may be ordered, upon the request of any concerned party, by way of a petition to a court or expedited proceedings."

[3] Article 595 provides as follows: "An application for revision of a judgment may be made only where:

1. it comes to light, after the judgment is handed down, that it was obtained fraudulently by the party in whose favour it was rendered;
2. decisive evidence that had been withheld by another party is recovered after the judgment was handed down;
3. the judgment is based on documents that have since been proven or have been held by a court to be false;
4. the judgment is based on affidavits, testimonies or oaths that have been held by a court to be false.

In all four cases, an application for revision shall be admissible only where the applicant was not able, through no fault of his or her own, to raise such objection before the judgment became res judicata."

[4] *Opposition* is a form of recourse under French law, available when a judgment is rendered by default because a defendant was not properly notified of a hearing. The defendant can then "oppose" the judgment.

HONG KONG ARBITRATION ORDINANCE (CHAPTER 609) *

Long title An Ordinance to reform the law relating to arbitration, and to provide for related and consequential matters.

Part 1
Preliminary

Section 1 — Short Title and Commencement

(1) This Ordinance may be cited as the Arbitration Ordinance.

(2) Omitted as spent.

Section 2 — Interpretation

(1) In this Ordinance

arbitral tribunal (仲裁庭)	means a sole arbitrator or a panel of arbitrators, and includes an umpire;
arbitration (仲裁)	means any arbitration, whether or not administered by a permanent arbitral institution;
arbitration agreement (仲裁協議)	has the same meaning as in section 19;
arbitrator (仲裁員),	except in sections 23, 24, 30, 31, 32 and 65 and section 1 of Schedule 2, includes an umpire;
claimant (申索人)	means a person who makes a claim or a counter-claim in an arbitration;
Commission (貿法委)	means the United Nations Commission on International Trade Law;
Convention award (公約裁決)	means an arbitral award made in a State or the territory of a State, other than China or any part of China, which is a party to the New York Convention;
Court (原訟法庭)	means the Court of First Instance of the High Court;
dispute (爭議)	includes a difference;
function (職能)	includes a power and a duty;
HKIAC (香港國際仲裁中心)	means the Hong Kong International Arbitration Centre, a company incorporated in Hong Kong under the Companies Ordinance (Cap 32) as in force at the time of the incorporation and limited by guarantee; (Amended 28 of 2012 ss. 912 & 920)
interim measure (臨時措施)	(a) if it is granted by an arbitral tribunal, has the same meaning as in section 35

* For a commentary on the Arbitration Ordinance, see Geoffrey Ma and Denis Brock (eds), *Arbitration in Hong Kong: A Practical Guide* (3rd ed, Sweet & Maxwell, 2014).

	(1) and (2); or (b) if it is granted by a court, has the same meaning as in section 45(9),
and interim measure of protection (臨時保全措施)	is to be construed accordingly;
Macao (澳門)	means the Macao Special Administrative Region; (Added 7 of 2013 s. 3)
Macao award (澳門裁決)	means an arbitral award made in Macao in accordance with the arbitration law of Macao;
the Mainland (內地)	means any part of China other than Hong Kong, Macao and Taiwan;
Mainland award (內地裁決)	means an arbitral award made in the Mainland by a recognized Mainland a arbitral authority in accordance with the Arbitration Law of the People's Republic of China;
mediation (調解)	includes conciliation;
New York Convention (《紐約公約》)	means the Convention on the Recognition and Enforcement of Foreign Arbitral Awards done at New York on 10 June 1958;
party (一方、方)	(a) means a party to an arbitration agreement; or (b) in relation to any arbitral or court proceedings, means a party to the proceedings;
recognized Mainland arbitral authority (認可內地仲裁當局)	means an arbitral authority that is specified in the list of recognized Mainland arbitral authorities published by the Secretary for Justice under section 97;
repealed Ordinance (《舊有條例》)	means the Arbitration Ordinance (Cap 341) repealed by section 109;
respondent (被申請人)	means a person against whom a claim or a counterclaim is made in an

arbitration;

UNCITRAL Model Law (《貿法委示範法》) means the UNCITRAL Model Law on International Commercial Arbitration as adopted by the Commission on 21 June 1985 and as amended by the Commission on 7 July 2006, the full text of which is set out in Schedule 1.

(2) If
(a) a provision of this Ordinance refers to the fact that the parties have agreed, or in any other way refers to an agreement of the parties, the agreement includes any arbitration rules referred to in that agreement; or
(b) a provision of this Ordinance provides that the parties may agree, the agreement, if any, may include any arbitration rules by referring to those rules in that agreement.
(3) If
(a) a provision of this Ordinance (other than sections 53 and 68) refers to a claim, that provision also applies to a counter-claim; or
(b) a provision of this Ordinance (other than section 53) refers to a defence, that provision also applies to a defence to a counter-claim.
(4) A note located in the text of this Ordinance, a section heading of any provision of this Ordinance or a heading of any provision of the UNCITRAL Model Law is for reference only and has no legislative effect.
(5) If the Chinese equivalent of an English expression used in any provision of this Ordinance is different from the Chinese equivalent of the same English expression used in any provision of the UNCITRAL Model Law, those Chinese equivalents are to be treated as being identical in effect.

Section 3 — Object and Principles of this Ordinance

(1) The object of this Ordinance is to facilitate the fair and speedy resolution of disputes by arbitration without unnecessary expense.
(2) This Ordinance is based on the principles
(a) that, subject to the observance of the safeguards that are necessary in the public interest, the parties to a dispute should be free to agree on how the dispute should be resolved; and
(b) that the court should interfere in the arbitration of a dispute only as expressly provided for in this Ordinance.

Section 4 — UNCITRAL Model Law to Have Force of Law in Hong Kong

The provisions of the UNCITRAL Model Law that are expressly stated in this Ordinance as having effect have the force of law in Hong Kong subject to the modifications and supplements as expressly provided for in this Ordinance.

Section 5 — Arbitrations to which this Ordinance Applies

(1) Subject to subsection (2), this Ordinance applies to an arbitration under an arbitration agreement, whether or not the agreement is entered into in Hong Kong, if the place of arbitration is in Hong Kong.

(2) If the place of arbitration is outside Hong Kong, only this Part, sections 20 and 21, Part 3A, sections 45, 60 and 61 and Part 10 apply to the arbitration.

(3) If any other Ordinance provides that this Ordinance applies to an arbitration under that other Ordinance, this Ordinance (other than sections 20(2), (3) and (4), 22(1), 58 and 74(8) and (9)) applies to an arbitration under that other Ordinance, subject to the following

(a) a reference in article 16(1) of the UNCITRAL Model Law, given effect to by section 34, to any objections with respect to the existence or validity of the arbitration agreement is to be construed as any objections with respect to the application of that other Ordinance to the dispute in question;

(b) that other Ordinance is deemed to have expressly provided that, subject to paragraph (c), all the provisions in Schedule 2 apply; and

(c) section 2 of Schedule 2 (if applicable) only applies so as to authorize 2 or more arbitral proceedings under the same Ordinance to be consolidated or to be heard at the same time or one immediately after another.

(4) Subsection (3) has effect, in relation to an arbitration under any other Ordinance, only in so far as this Ordinance is consistent with

(a) that other Ordinance; and

(b) any rules or procedures authorized or recognized by that other Ordinance.

Section 6 — Application

This Ordinance applies to the Government and the Offices set up by the Central People's Government in the Hong Kong Special Administrative Region.

Part 2
General Provisions

Section 7 — Article 1 of UNCITRAL Model Law (Scope of application)

Section 5 has effect in substitution for article 1 of the UNCITRAL Model Law.

Section 8 — Article 2 of UNCITRAL Model Law (Definitions and rules of interpretation)

(1) Section 2 has effect in substitution for article 2 of the UNCITRAL Model Law.

(2) For the purposes of subsection (1), a reference to this Ordinance in section 2 (other than section 2(5)) is to be construed as including the UNCITRAL Model Law.

(3) In the provisions of the UNCITRAL Model Law

(a) a reference to this State is to be construed as Hong Kong;

(b) a reference to a State is to be construed as including Hong Kong;

(c) a reference to different States is to be construed as including Hong Kong and any other place;

(d) a reference to an article is to be construed as an article of the UNCITRAL Model Law; and

(e) (other than in article 2A of the UNCITRAL Model Law, given effect to by section 9) a reference to this Law is to be construed as this Ordinance.

Section 9 — Article 2A of UNCITRAL Model Law (International origin and general principles)

Article 2A of the UNCITRAL Model Law, the text of which is set out below, has effect

> "Article 2A. International origin and general principles
>
> (1) In the interpretation of this Law, regard is to be had to its international origin and to the need to promote uniformity in its application and the observance of good faith.
>
> (2) Questions concerning matters governed by this Law which are not expressly settled in it are to be settled in conformity with the general principles on which this Law is based.".

Section 10 — Article 3 of UNCITRAL Model Law (Receipt of written communications)

(1) Article 3 of the UNCITRAL Model Law, the text of which is set out below, has effect

> "Article 3. Receipt of written communications
>
> (1) Unless otherwise agreed by the parties:
>
> (a) any written communication is deemed to have been received if it is delivered to the addressee personally or if it is delivered at his place of business, habitual residence or mailing address; if none of these can be found after making a reasonable inquiry, a written communication is deemed to have been received if it is sent to the addressee's last-known place of business, habitual residence or

mailing address by registered letter or any other means which provides a record of the attempt to deliver it;

(b) the communication is deemed to have been received on the day it is so delivered.

(2) The provisions of this article do not apply to communications in court proceedings.".

(2) Without affecting subsection (1), if a written communication (other than communications in court proceedings) is sent by any means by which information can be recorded and transmitted to the addressee, the communication is deemed to have been received on the day it is so sent.

(3) Subsection (2) applies only if there is a record of receipt of the communication by the addressee.

Section 11 — Article 4 of UNCITRAL Model Law (Waiver of right to object)

Article 4 of the UNCITRAL Model Law, the text of which is set out below, has effect

"Article 4. Waiver of right to object

A party who knows that any provision of this Law from which the parties may derogate or any requirement under the arbitration agreement has not been complied with and yet proceeds with the arbitration without stating his objection to such non-compliance without undue delay or, if a time-limit is provided therefore, within such period of time, shall be deemed to have waived his right to object.".

Section 12 — Article 5 of UNCITRAL Model Law (Extent of court intervention)

Article 5 of the UNCITRAL Model Law, the text of which is set out below, has effect

"Article 5. Extent of court intervention

In matters governed by this Law, no court shall intervene except where so provided in this Law.".

Section 13 — Article 6 of UNCITRAL Model Law (Court or other authority for certain functions of arbitration assistance and supervision)

(1) Subsections (2) to (6) have effect in substitution for article 6 of the UNCITRAL Model Law.

(2) The functions of the court or other authority referred to in article 11(3) or (4) of the UNCITRAL Model Law, given effect to by section 24, are to be performed by the HKIAC.

(3) The HKIAC may, with the approval of the Chief Justice, make rules to facilitate the performance of its functions under section 23(3), 24 or 32(1).
(4) The functions of the court or other authority referred to in
(a) article 13(3) of the UNCITRAL Model Law, given effect to by section 26; or
(b) article 14(1) of the UNCITRAL Model Law, given effect to by section 27,
are to be performed by the Court.
(5) The functions of the court referred to in
(a) article 16(3) of the UNCITRAL Model Law, given effect to by section 34; or
(b) article 34(2) of the UNCITRAL Model Law, given effect to by section 81,
are to be performed by the Court.
(6) The functions of the competent court referred to in article 27 of the UNCITRAL Model Law, given effect to by section 55, are to be performed by the Court.

Section 14 — Application of Limitation Ordinance and other limitation enactments to arbitrations

(1) The Limitation Ordinance (Cap 347) and any other Ordinance relating to the limitation of actions ("limitation enactments") apply to arbitrations as they apply to actions in the court.
(2) For the purposes of subsection (1), a reference in a limitation enactment to bringing an action is to be construed as, in relation to an arbitration, commencing the arbitral proceedings.
(3) Despite any term in an arbitration agreement to the effect that no cause of action may accrue in respect of any matter required by the agreement to be submitted to arbitration until an award is made under the agreement, the cause of action is, for the purposes of the limitation enactments (whether in their application to arbitrations or to other proceedings), deemed to accrue in respect of that matter at the time when it would have accrued but for that term.
(4) If a court orders that an award is to be set aside, the period between
(a) the commencement of the arbitral proceedings; and
(b) the date of the order of the court setting aside the award, must be excluded in computing the time prescribed by a limitation enactment for the commencement of proceedings (including arbitral proceedings) with respect to the matter submitted to arbitration.

Section 15 — Reference of Interpleader Issue to Arbitration by Court
(1) If
(a) relief by way of interpleader is granted by a court; and
(b) there is an arbitration agreement between the claimants in the interpleader proceedings in respect of any issue between those claimants, the court granting the relief must, subject to subsection (2), direct that the issue is to be determined in accordance with the agreement.
(2) The court may refuse to make a direction under subsection (1) if the circumstances are such that legal proceedings brought by a claimant in respect of the issue would not be stayed.
(3) If the court refuses to make a direction under subsection (1), any provision of the arbitration agreement that an award is a condition precedent to the bringing of legal proceedings in respect of the issue does not affect the determination of the issue by the court.
(4) A direction of the court under subsection (1) is not subject to appeal.
(5) The leave of the court making a decision under subsection (2) is required for any appeal from that decision.
Section 16 — Proceedings to be Heard Otherwise Than in Open Court
(1) Subject to subsection (2), proceedings under this Ordinance in the court are to be heard otherwise than in open court.
(2) The court may order those proceedings to be heard in open court
(a) on the application of any party; or
(b) if, in any particular case, the court is satisfied that those proceedings ought to be heard in open court.
(3) An order of the court under subsection (2) is not subject to appeal.
Section 17 — Restrictions on Reporting of Proceedings Heard Otherwise Than in Open Court
(1) This section applies to proceedings under this Ordinance in the court heard otherwise than in open court ("closed court proceedings").
(2) A court in which closed court proceedings are being heard must, on the application of any party, make a direction as to what information, if any, relating to the proceedings may be published.
(3) A court must not make a direction permitting information to be published unless
(a) all parties agree that the information may be published; or
(b) the court is satisfied that the information, if published, would not reveal any matter (including the identity of any party) that any party reasonably wishes to remain confidential.
(4) Despite subsection (3), if

(a) a court gives a judgment in respect of closed court proceedings; and
(b) the court considers that judgment to be of major legal interest,
the court must direct that reports of the judgment may be published in law reports and professional publications.
(5) If a court directs under subsection (4) that reports of a judgment may be published, but any party reasonably wishes to conceal any matter in those reports (including the fact that the party was such a party), the court must, on the application of the party
(a) make a direction as to the action to be taken to conceal that matter in those reports; and
(b) if the court considers that a report published in accordance with the direction made under paragraph (a) would still be likely to reveal that matter, direct that the report may not be published until after the end of a period, not exceeding 10 years, that the court may direct.
(6) A direction of the court under this section is not subject to appeal.

Section 18 — Disclosure of Information Relating to Arbitral Proceedings and Awards Prohibited

(1) Unless otherwise agreed by the parties, no party may publish, disclose or communicate any information relating to
(a) the arbitral proceedings under the arbitration agreement; or
(b) an award made in those arbitral proceedings.
(2) Nothing in subsection (1) prevents the publication, disclosure or communication of information referred to in that subsection by a party
(a) if the publication, disclosure or communication is made
(i) to protect or pursue a legal right or interest of the party; or
(ii) to enforce or challenge the award referred to in that subsection, in legal proceedings before a court or other judicial authority in or outside Hong Kong;
(b) if the publication, disclosure or communication is made to any government body, regulatory body, court or tribunal and the party is obliged by law to make the publication, disclosure or communication; or
(c) if the publication, disclosure or communication is made to a professional or any other adviser of any of the parties.

Part 3

Arbitration Agreement

Section 19 — Article 7 of UNCITRAL Model Law (Definition and form of arbitration agreement)

(1) Option I of Article 7 of the UNCITRAL Model Law, the text of which is set out below, has effect

"Option I
Article 7. Definition and form of arbitration agreement
(1) "Arbitration agreement" is an agreement by the parties to submit to arbitration all or certain disputes which have arisen or which may arise between them in respect of a defined legal relationship, whether contractual or not. An arbitration agreement may be in the form of an arbitration clause in a contract or in the form of a separate agreement.
(2) The arbitration agreement shall be in writing.
(3) An arbitration agreement is in writing if its content is recorded in any form, whether or not the arbitration agreement or contract has been concluded orally, by conduct, or by other means.
(4) The requirement that an arbitration agreement be in writing is met by an electronic communication if the information contained therein is accessible so as to be useable for subsequent reference; "electronic communication" means any communication that the parties make by means of data messages; "data message" means information generated, sent, received or stored by electronic, magnetic, optical or similar means, including, but not limited to, electronic data interchange (EDI), electronic mail, telegram, telex or telecopy.
(5) Furthermore, an arbitration agreement is in writing if it is contained in an exchange of statements of claim and defence in which the existence of an agreement is alleged by one party and not denied by the other.
(6) The reference in a contract to any document containing an arbitration clause constitutes an arbitration agreement in writing, provided that the reference is such as to make that clause part of the contract.".

(2) Without affecting subsection (1), an arbitration agreement is in writing if
(a) the agreement is in a document, whether or not the document is signed by the parties to the agreement; or
(b) the agreement, although made otherwise than in writing, is recorded by one of the parties to the agreement, or by a third party, with the authority of each of the parties to the agreement.
(3) A reference in an agreement to a written form of arbitration clause constitutes an arbitration agreement if the reference is such as to make that clause part of the agreement.

Section 20 — Article 8 of UNCITRAL Model Law (Arbitration agreement and substantive claim before court)

(1) Article 8 of the UNCITRAL Model Law, the text of which is set out below, has effect

> "Article 8. Arbitration agreement and substantive claim before court
>
> (1) A court before which an action is brought in a matter which is the subject of an arbitration agreement shall, if a party so requests not later than when submitting his first statement on the substance of the dispute, refer the parties to arbitration unless it finds that the agreement is null and void, inoperative or incapable of being performed.
>
> (2) Where an action referred to in paragraph (1) of this article has been brought, arbitral proceedings may nevertheless be commenced or continued, and an award may be made, while the issue is pending before the court.".

(2) If a dispute in the matter which is the subject of an arbitration agreement involves a claim or other dispute that is within the jurisdiction of the Labour Tribunal established by section 3 (Establishment of tribunal) of the Labour Tribunal Ordinance (Cap 25), the court before which an action has been brought may, if a party so requests, refer the parties to arbitration if it is satisfied that

(a) there is no sufficient reason why the parties should not be referred to arbitration in accordance with the arbitration agreement; and

(b) the party requesting arbitration was ready and willing at the time the action was brought to do all things necessary for the proper conduct of the arbitration, and remains so.

(3) Subsection (1) has effect subject to section 15 (Arbitration agreements) of the Control of Exemption Clauses Ordinance (Cap 71).

(4) If the court refuses to refer the parties to arbitration, any provision of the arbitration agreement that an award is a condition precedent to the bringing of legal proceedings in respect of any matter is of no effect in relation to those proceedings.

(5) If the court refers the parties in an action to arbitration, it must make an order staying the legal proceedings in that action.

(6) In the case of Admiralty proceedings

(a) the reference of the parties to arbitration and an order for the stay of those proceedings may, despite subsections (1) and (5), be made conditional on the giving of security for the satisfaction of any award made in the arbitration; or

(b) if the court makes an order under subsection (5) staying those proceedings, the court may (where property has been arrested, or bail or other security has been given to prevent or obtain release from arrest, in those proceedings) order that the property arrested, or the bail or security given, be retained as security for the satisfaction of any award made in the arbitration.

(7) Subject to any provision made by rules of court and to any necessary modifications, the same law and practice apply to the property, bail or security retained in pursuance of an order under subsection (6) as would apply if the property, bail or security retained were held for the purposes of proceedings in the court making the order.

(8) A decision of the court to refer the parties to arbitration under

(a) article 8 of the UNCITRAL Model Law, given effect to by subsection (1); or

(b) subsection (2),

is not subject to appeal.

(9) The leave of the court making a decision to refuse to refer the parties to arbitration under

(a) article 8 of the UNCITRAL Model Law, given effect to by subsection (1); or

(b) subsection (2),

is required for any appeal from that decision.

(10) A decision or order of the court under subsection (6) is not subject to appeal.

Section 21 — Article 9 of UNCITRAL Model Law (Arbitration agreement and interim measures by court)

Article 9 of the UNCITRAL Model Law, the text of which is set out below, has effect

> "Article 9. Arbitration agreement and interim measures by court
> It is not incompatible with an arbitration agreement for a party to request, before or during arbitral proceedings, from a court an interim measure of protection and for a court to grant such measure.".

Section 22 — Whether Agreement Discharged by Death of a Party

(1) Unless otherwise agreed by the parties, an arbitration agreement is not discharged by the death of a party and may be enforced by or against the personal representatives of that party.

(2) Subsection (1) does not affect the operation of any enactment or rule of law by virtue of which a substantive right or obligation is extinguished by death.

Part 3A
Enforcement of Emergency Relief

Section 22A — Interpretation

In this Part emergency arbitrator (緊急仲裁員) means an emergency arbitrator appointed under the arbitration rules (including the arbitration rules of a permanent arbitral institution) agreed to or adopted by the parties to deal with the parties' applications for emergency relief before an arbitral tribunal is constituted.

Section 22B — Enforcement of Emergency Relief Granted by Emergency Arbitrator

(1) Any emergency relief granted, whether in or outside Hong Kong, by an emergency arbitrator under the relevant arbitration rules is enforceable in the same manner as an order or direction of the Court that has the same effect, but only with the leave of the Court.

(2) The Court may not grant leave to enforce any emergency relief granted outside Hong Kong unless the party seeking to enforce it can demonstrate that it consists only of one or more temporary measures (including an injunction) by which the emergency arbitrator orders a party to do one or more of the following

(a) maintain or restore the status quo pending the determination of the dispute concerned;

(b) take action that would prevent, or refrain from taking action that is likely to cause, current or imminent harm or prejudice to the arbitral process itself;

(c) provide a means of preserving assets out of which a subsequent award made by an arbitral tribunal may be satisfied;

(d) preserve evidence that may be relevant and material to resolving the dispute;

(e) give security in connection with anything to be done under paragraph (a), (b), (c) or (d);

(f) give security for the costs of the arbitration.

(3) If leave is granted under subsection (1), the Court may enter judgment in terms of the emergency relief.

(4) A decision of the Court to grant or refuse to grant leave under subsection (1) is not subject to appeal.

Part 4
Composition of Arbitral Tribunal
Division 1. Arbitrators

Section 23 — Article 10 of UNCITRAL Model Law (Number of arbitrators)

(1) Article 10(1) of the UNCITRAL Model Law, the text of which is set out below, has effect

"Article 10. Number of arbitrators

(1) The parties are free to determine the number of arbitrators.

(2) [Not applicable]".

(2) For the purposes of subsection (1), the freedom of the parties to determine the number of arbitrators includes the right of the parties to authorize a third party, including an institution, to make that determination.

(3) Subject to section 1 of Schedule 2 (if applicable), if the parties fail to agree on the number of arbitrators, the number of arbitrators is to be either 1 or 3 as decided by the HKIAC in the particular case.

Section 24 — Article 11 of UNCITRAL Model Law (Appointment of arbitrators)

(1) Article 11 of the UNCITRAL Model Law, the text of which is set out below, has effect subject to section 13(2) and (3)

"Article 11. Appointment of arbitrators

(1) No person shall be precluded by reason of his nationality from acting as an arbitrator, unless otherwise agreed by the parties.

(2) The parties are free to agree on a procedure of appointing the arbitrator or arbitrators, subject to the provisions of paragraphs (4) and (5) of this article.

(3) Failing such agreement,

(a) in an arbitration with three arbitrators, each party shall appoint one arbitrator, and the two arbitrators thus appointed shall appoint the third arbitrator; if a party fails to appoint the arbitrator within thirty days of receipt of a request to do so from the other party, or if the two arbitrators fail to agree on the third arbitrator within thirty days of their appointment, the appointment shall be made, upon request of a party, by the court or other authority specified in article 6;

(b) in an arbitration with a sole arbitrator, if the parties are unable to agree on the arbitrator, he shall be appointed, upon request of a party, by the court or other authority specified in article 6.

(4) Where, under an appointment procedure agreed upon by the parties,

(a) a party fails to act as required under such procedure, or
(b) the parties, or two arbitrators, are unable to reach an agreement expected of them under such procedure, or
(c) a third party, including an institution, fails to perform any function entrusted to it under such procedure, any party may request the court or other authority specified in article 6 to take the necessary measure, unless the agreement on the appointment procedure provides other means for securing the appointment.
(5) A decision on a matter entrusted by paragraph (3) or (4) of this article to the court or other authority specified in article 6 shall be subject to no appeal. The court or other authority, in appointing an arbitrator, shall have due regard to any qualifications required of the arbitrator by the agreement of the parties and to such considerations as are likely to secure the appointment of an independent and impartial arbitrator and, in the case of a sole or third arbitrator, shall take into account as well the advisability of appointing an arbitrator of a nationality other than those of the parties.".

(2) In an arbitration with an even number of arbitrators
(a) if the parties have not agreed on a procedure for appointing the arbitrators under article 11(2) of the UNCITRAL Model Law, given effect to by subsection (1), each party is to appoint the same number of arbitrators; or
(b) if
(i) a party fails to act as required under an appointment procedure agreed upon by the parties; or
(ii) in the case of paragraph (a), a party fails to appoint the appropriate number of arbitrators under that paragraph within 30 days of receipt of a request to do so from the other party,
the HKIAC must make the necessary appointment upon a request to do so from any party.
(3) In an arbitration with an uneven number of arbitrators greater than 3
(a) if the parties have not agreed on a procedure for appointing the arbitrators under article 11(2) of the UNCITRAL Model Law, given effect to by subsection (1)
(i) each party is to appoint the same number of arbitrators; and
(ii) unless otherwise agreed by the parties,
the HKIAC must appoint the remaining arbitrator or arbitrators; or
(b) if
(i) a party fails to act as required under an appointment procedure agreed

upon by the parties; or

(ii) in the case of paragraph (a), a party fails to appoint the appropriate number of arbitrators under that paragraph within 30 days of receipt of a request to do so from the other party, the HKIAC must make the necessary appointment upon a request to do so from any party.

(4) In any other case (in particular, if there are more than 2 parties) article 11(4) of the UNCITRAL Model Law, given effect to by subsection (1), applies as in the case of a failure to agree on an appointment procedure.

(5) If any appointment of an arbitrator is made by the HKIAC by virtue of this Ordinance, the appointment

(a) has effect as if it were made with the agreement of all parties; and

(b) is subject to article 11(5) of the UNCITRAL Model Law, given effect to by subsection (1).

Section 25 — Article 12 of UNCITRAL Model Law (Grounds for challenge)

Article 12 of the UNCITRAL Model Law, the text of which is set out below, has effect

"Article 12. Grounds for challenge

(1) When a person is approached in connection with his possible appointment as an arbitrator, he shall disclose any circumstances likely to give rise to justifiable doubts as to his impartiality or independence. An arbitrator, from the time of his appointment and throughout the arbitral proceedings, shall without delay disclose any such circumstances to the parties unless they have already been informed of them by him.

(2) An arbitrator may be challenged only if circumstances exist that give rise to justifiable doubts as to his impartiality or independence, or if he does not possess qualifications agreed to by the parties. A party may challenge an arbitrator appointed by him, or in whose appointment he has participated, only for reasons of which he becomes aware after the appointment has been made.".

Section 26 — Article 13 of UNCITRAL Model Law (Challenge procedure)

(1) Article 13 of the UNCITRAL Model Law, the text of which is set out below, has effect subject to section 13(4)

"Article 13. Challenge procedure

(1) The parties are free to agree on a procedure for challenging an arbitrator, subject to the provisions of paragraph (3) of this article.

(2) Failing such agreement, a party who intends to challenge an arbitrator shall, within fifteen days after becoming aware of the constitution of the arbitral tribunal or after becoming aware of any circumstance referred to in article 12(2), send a written statement of the reasons for the challenge to the arbitral tribunal. Unless the challenged arbitrator withdraws from his office or the other party agrees to the challenge, the arbitral tribunal shall decide on the challenge.

(3) If a challenge under any procedure agreed upon by the parties or under the procedure of paragraph (2) of this article is not successful, the challenging party may request, within thirty days after having received notice of the decision rejecting the challenge, the court or other authority specified in article 6 to decide on the challenge, which decision shall be subject to no appeal; while such a request is pending, the arbitral tribunal, including the challenged arbitrator, may continue the arbitral proceedings and make an award.".

(2) During the period that a request for the Court to decide on a challenge is pending, the Court may refuse to grant leave under section 84 for the enforcement of any award made during that period by the arbitral tribunal that includes the challenged arbitrator.

(3) An arbitrator who is challenged under article 13(2) of the UNCITRAL Model Law, given effect to by subsection (1), is entitled, if the arbitrator considers it appropriate in the circumstances of the challenge, to withdraw from office as an arbitrator.

(4) The mandate of a challenged arbitrator terminates under article 13 of the UNCITRAL Model Law, given effect to by subsection (1), if

(a) the arbitrator withdraws from office;

(b) the parties agree to the challenge;

(c) the arbitral tribunal upholds the challenge and no request is made for the Court to decide on the challenge; or

(d) the Court, upon request to decide on the challenge, upholds the challenge.

(5) If the Court upholds the challenge, the Court may set aside the award referred to in subsection (2).

Section 27 — Article 14 of UNCITRAL Model Law (Failure or impossibility to act)

Article 14 of the UNCITRAL Model Law, the text of which is set out below, has effect subject to section 13(4)

"Article 14. Failure or impossibility to act

(1) If an arbitrator becomes de jure or de facto unable to perform his functions or for other reasons fails to act without undue delay, his mandate terminates if he withdraws from his office or if the parties agree on the termination. Otherwise, if a controversy remains concerning any of these grounds, any party may request the court or other authority specified in article 6 to decide on the termination of the mandate, which decision shall be subject to no appeal.

(2) If, under this article or article 13(2), an arbitrator withdraws from his office or a party agrees to the termination of the mandate of an arbitrator, this does not imply acceptance of the validity of any ground referred to in this article or article 12(2).".

Section 28 — Article 15 of UNCITRAL Model Law (Appointment of substitute arbitrator)

Article 15 of the UNCITRAL Model Law, the text of which is set out below, has effect

"Article 15. Appointment of substitute arbitrator

Where the mandate of an arbitrator terminates under article 13 or 14 or because of his withdrawal from office for any other reason or because of the revocation of his mandate by agreement of the parties or in any other case of termination of his mandate, a substitute arbitrator shall be appointed according to the rules that were applicable to the appointment of the arbitrator being replaced.".

Section 29 — Death of Arbitrator or Person Appointing Arbitrator

(1) The authority of an arbitrator is personal and the mandate of the arbitrator terminates on the arbitrator's death.

(2) Unless otherwise agreed by the parties, the death of the person by whom an arbitrator was appointed does not revoke the arbitrator's authority.

Section 30 — Appointment of Umpire

In an arbitration with an even number of arbitrators, the arbitrators may, unless otherwise agreed by the parties, appoint an umpire at any time after they are themselves appointed.

Section 31 — Functions of Umpire in Arbitral Proceedings

(1) The parties are free to agree what the functions of an umpire are to be and, in particular

(a) whether the umpire is to attend the arbitral proceedings; and

(b) when, and the extent to which, the umpire is to replace the arbitrators as the arbitral tribunal with the power to make orders, directions and awards.

(2) If or to the extent that there is no such agreement of the parties, the

arbitrators are free to agree on the functions of the umpire.
(3) Subsections (4) to (11) apply subject to any agreement of the parties or the arbitrators.
(4) After an umpire is appointed, the umpire must attend the arbitral proceedings.
(5) The umpire must be supplied with the same documents and other materials as are supplied to the arbitrators.
(6) Orders, directions and awards are to be made by the arbitrators unless, subject to subsection (9), the arbitrators cannot agree on a matter relating to the dispute submitted to arbitration.
(7) If the arbitrators cannot agree on a matter relating to the dispute submitted to arbitration, they must forthwith give notice of that fact in writing to the parties and the umpire, in which case the umpire is to replace the arbitrators as the arbitral tribunal with the power to make orders, directions and awards, in respect of that matter only, subject to subsection (9)(b), as if the umpire were the sole arbitrator.
(8) If the arbitrators cannot agree on a matter relating to the dispute submitted to arbitration but
(a) they fail to give notice of that fact; or
(b) any of them fails to join in the giving of notice, any party may apply to the Court which may decide that the umpire is to replace the arbitrators as the arbitral tribunal with the power to make orders, directions and awards, in respect of that matter only, as if the umpire were the sole arbitrator.
(9) Despite the replacement by the umpire as the arbitral tribunal in respect of a matter, on which the arbitrators cannot agree, relating to the dispute submitted to arbitration, the arbitrators may
(a) still make orders, directions and awards in respect of the other matters relating to the dispute if they consider that it would save costs by doing so; or
(b) refer the entirety of the dispute to the umpire for arbitration.
(10) For the purposes of this section, the arbitrators cannot agree on a matter relating to the dispute submitted to arbitration if any one of the arbitrators, in that arbitrator's view, disagrees with the other arbitrator or any of the other arbitrators over that matter.
(11) A decision of the Court under subsection (8) is not subject to appeal.

Division 2. Mediators

Section 32 — Appointment of Mediator

(1) If
(a) any arbitration agreement provides for the appointment of a mediator by

a person who is not one of the parties; and
(b) that person
(i) refuses to make the appointment; or
(ii) does not make the appointment within the time specified in the arbitration agreement or, if no time is so specified, within a reasonable time after being requested by any party to make the appointment,
the HKIAC may, on the application of any party, appoint a mediator.
(2) An appointment made by the HKIAC under subsection (1) is not subject to appeal.
(3) If any arbitration agreement provides for the appointment of a mediator and further provides that the person so appointed is to act as an arbitrator in the event that no settlement acceptable to the parties can be reached in the mediation proceedings
(a) no objection may be made against the person's acting as an arbitrator, or against the person's conduct of the arbitral proceedings, solely on the ground that the person had acted previously as a mediator in connection with some or all of the matters relating to the dispute submitted to arbitration; or
(b) if the person declines to act as an arbitrator, any other person appointed as an arbitrator is not required first to act as a mediator unless it is otherwise expressed in the arbitration agreement.

Section 33 — Power of Arbitrator to Act as Mediator

(1) If all parties consent in writing, and for so long as no party withdraws the party's consent in writing, an arbitrator may act as a mediator after the arbitral proceedings have commenced.
(2) If an arbitrator acts as a mediator, the arbitral proceedings must be stayed to facilitate the conduct of the mediation proceedings.
(3) An arbitrator who is acting as a mediator
(a) may communicate with the parties collectively or separately; and
(b) must treat the information obtained by the arbitrator from a party as confidential, unless otherwise agreed by that party or unless subsection (4) applies.
(4) If
(a) confidential information is obtained by an arbitrator from a party during the mediation proceedings conducted by the arbitrator as a mediator; and
(b) those mediation proceedings terminate without reaching a settlement acceptable to the parties, the arbitrator must, before resuming the arbitral proceedings, disclose to all other parties as much of that information as the arbitrator considers is material to the arbitral proceedings.

(5) No objection may be made against the conduct of the arbitral proceedings by an arbitrator solely on the ground that the arbitrator had acted previously as a mediator in accordance with this section.

Part 5

Jurisdiction of Arbitral Tribunal

Section 34 — Article 16 of UNCITRAL Model Law (Competence of arbitral tribunal to rule on its jurisdiction)

(1) Article 16 of the UNCITRAL Model Law, the text of which is set out below, has effect subject to section 13(5)

"Article 16. Competence of arbitral tribunal to rule on its jurisdiction

(1) The arbitral tribunal may rule on its own jurisdiction, including any objections with respect to the existence or validity of the arbitration agreement. For that purpose, an arbitration clause which forms part of a contract shall be treated as an agreement independent of the other terms of the contract. A decision by the arbitral tribunal that the contract is null and void shall not entail *ipso jure* the invalidity of the arbitration clause.

(2) A plea that the arbitral tribunal does not have jurisdiction shall be raised not later than the submission of the statement of defence. A party is not precluded from raising such a plea by the fact that he has appointed, or participated in the appointment of, an arbitrator. A plea that the arbitral tribunal is exceeding the scope of its authority shall be raised as soon as the matter alleged to be beyond the scope of its authority is raised during the arbitral proceedings. The arbitral tribunal may, in either case, admit a later plea if it considers the delay justified.

(3) The arbitral tribunal may rule on a plea referred to in paragraph (2) of this article either as a preliminary question or in an award on the merits. If the arbitral tribunal rules as a preliminary question that it has jurisdiction, any party may request, within thirty days after having received notice of that ruling, the court specified in article 6 to decide the matter, which decision shall be subject to no appeal; while such a request is pending, the arbitral tribunal may continue the arbitral proceedings and make an award.".

(2) The power of the arbitral tribunal to rule on its own jurisdiction under subsection (1) includes the power to decide as to

(a) whether the tribunal is properly constituted; or

(b) what matters have been submitted to arbitration in accordance with the arbitration agreement.

(3) If a dispute is submitted to arbitration in accordance with an arbitration agreement and a party
(a) makes a counter-claim arising out of the same dispute; or
(b) relies on a claim arising out of that dispute for the purposes of a set-off,
the arbitral tribunal has jurisdiction to decide on the counter-claim or the claim so relied on only to the extent that the subject matter of that counter-claim or that claim falls within the scope of the same arbitration agreement.
(4) A ruling of the arbitral tribunal that it does not have jurisdiction to decide a dispute is not subject to appeal.
(5) Despite section 20, if the arbitral tribunal rules that it does not have jurisdiction to decide a dispute, the court must, if it has jurisdiction, decide that dispute.

Part 6
Interim Measures and Preliminary Orders
Division 1. Interim Measures

Section 35 — Article 17 of UNCITRAL Model Law (Power of arbitral tribunal to order interim measures)

(1) Article 17 of the UNCITRAL Model Law, the text of which is set out below, has effect

> "Article 17. Power of arbitral tribunal to order interim measures
> (1) Unless otherwise agreed by the parties, the arbitral tribunal may, at the request of a party, grant interim measures.
> (2) An interim measure is any temporary measure, whether in the form of an award or in another form, by which, at any time prior to the issuance of the award by which the dispute is finally decided, the arbitral tribunal orders a party to:
> (a) Maintain or restore the status quo pending determination of the dispute;
> (b) Take action that would prevent, or refrain from taking action that is likely to cause, current or imminent harm or prejudice to the arbitral process itself;
> (c) Provide a means of preserving assets out of which a subsequent award may be satisfied; or
> (d) Preserve evidence that may be relevant and material to the resolution of the dispute.".

(2) An interim measure referred to in article 17 of the UNCITRAL Model Law, given effect to by subsection (1), is to be construed as including an injunction but not including an order under section 56.
(3) If an arbitral tribunal has granted an interim measure, the tribunal may,

on the application of any party, make an award to the same effect as the interim measure.

Section 36 — Article 17A of UNCITRAL Model Law (Conditions for granting interim measures)

Article 17A of the UNCITRAL Model Law, the text of which is set out below, has effect

"Article 17A. Conditions for granting interim measures

(1) The party requesting an interim measure under article 17(2)(a), (b) and (c) shall satisfy the arbitral tribunal that:

(a) Harm not adequately reparable by an award of damages is likely to result if the measure is not ordered, and such harm substantially outweighs the harm that is likely to result to the party against whom the measure is directed if the measure is granted; and

(b) There is a reasonable possibility that the requesting party will succeed on the merits of the claim. The determination on this possibility shall not affect the discretion of the arbitral tribunal in making any subsequent determination.

(2) With regard to a request for an interim measure under article 17 (2)(d), the requirements in paragraphs (1)(a) and (b) of this article shall apply only to the extent the arbitral tribunal considers appropriate.".

Division 2. Preliminary Orders

Section 37 — Article 17B of UNCITRAL Model Law (Applications for preliminary orders and conditions for granting preliminary orders)

Article 17B of the UNCITRAL Model Law, the text of which is set out below, has effect

"Article 17B. Applications for preliminary orders and conditions for granting preliminary orders

(1) Unless otherwise agreed by the parties, a party may, without notice to any other party, make a request for an interim measure together with an application for a preliminary order directing a party not to frustrate the purpose of the interim measure requested.

(2) The arbitral tribunal may grant a preliminary order provided it considers that prior disclosure of the request for the interim measure to the party against whom it is directed risks frustrating the purpose of the measure.

(3) The conditions defined under article 17A apply to any preliminary order, provided that the harm to be assessed under article 17A(1)(a), is the harm likely to result from the order being granted or not.".

Section 38 — Article 17C of UNCITRAL Model Law (Specific regime for preliminary orders)

Article 17C of the UNCITRAL Model Law, the text of which is set out below, has effect

"Article 17C. Specific regime for preliminary orders

(1) Immediately after the arbitral tribunal has made a determination in respect of an application for a preliminary order, the arbitral tribunal shall give notice to all parties of the request for the interim measure, the application for the preliminary order, the preliminary order, if any, and all other communications, including by indicating the content of any oral communication, between any party and the arbitral tribunal in relation thereto.

(2) At the same time, the arbitral tribunal shall give an opportunity to any party against whom a preliminary order is directed to present its case at the earliest practicable time.

(3) The arbitral tribunal shall decide promptly on any objection to the preliminary order.

(4) A preliminary order shall expire after twenty days from the date on which it was issued by the arbitral tribunal. However, the arbitral tribunal may issue an interim measure adopting or modifying the preliminary order, after the party against whom the preliminary order is directed has been given notice and an opportunity to present its case.

(5) A preliminary order shall be binding on the parties but shall not be subject to enforcement by a court. Such a preliminary order does not constitute an award.".

Division 3. Provisions Applicable to Interim Measures and Preliminary Orders

Section 39 — Article 17D of UNCITRAL Model Law (Modification, suspension, termination)

Article 17D of the UNCITRAL Model Law, the text of which is set out below, has effect

"Article 17D. Modification, suspension, termination

The arbitral tribunal may modify, suspend or terminate an interim measure or a preliminary order it has granted, upon application of any party or, in exceptional circumstances and upon prior notice to the parties, on the arbitral tribunal's own initiative.".

Section 40 — Article 17E of UNCITRAL Model Law (Provision of security)

Article 17E of the UNCITRAL Model Law, the text of which is set out below, has effect

"Article 17E. Provision of security

(1) The arbitral tribunal may require the party requesting an interim measure to provide appropriate security in connection with the measure.

(2) The arbitral tribunal shall require the party applying for a preliminary order to provide security in connection with the order unless the arbitral tribunal considers it inappropriate or unnecessary to do so.".

Section 41 — Article 17F of UNCITRAL Model Law (Disclosure)

Article 17F of the UNCITRAL Model Law, the text of which is set out below, has effect

"Article 17F. Disclosure

(1) The arbitral tribunal may require any party promptly to disclose any material change in the circumstances on the basis of which the measure was requested or granted.

(2) The party applying for a preliminary order shall disclose to the arbitral tribunal all circumstances that are likely to be relevant to the arbitral tribunal's determination whether to grant or maintain the order, and such obligation shall continue until the party against whom the order has been requested has had an opportunity to present its case. Thereafter, paragraph (1) of this article shall apply.".

Section 42 — Article 17G of UNCITRAL Model Law (Costs and damages)

Article 17G of the UNCITRAL Model Law, the text of which is set out below, has effect

"Article 17G. Costs and damages

The party requesting an interim measure or applying for a preliminary order shall be liable for any costs and damages caused by the measure or the order to any party if the arbitral tribunal later determines that, in the circumstances, the measure or the order should not have been granted. The arbitral tribunal may award such costs and damages at any point during the proceedings.".

Division 4. Recognition and Enforcement of Interim Measures

Section 43 — Article 17H of UNCITRAL Model Law (Recognition and enforcement)

Section 61 has effect in substitution for article 17H of the UNCITRAL Model Law.

Section 44 — Article 17I of UNCITRAL Model Law (Grounds for refusing recognition or enforcement)

Article 17I of the UNCITRAL Model Law does not have effect.

Division 5. Court-ordered Interim Measures

Section 45 — Article 17J of UNCITRAL Model Law (Court-ordered interim measures)

(1) Article 17J of the UNCITRAL Model Law does not have effect.

(2) On the application of any party, the Court may, in relation to any arbitral proceedings which have been or are to be commenced in or outside Hong Kong, grant an interim measure.

(3) The powers conferred by this section may be exercised by the Court irrespective of whether or not similar powers may be exercised by an arbitral tribunal under section 35 in relation to the same dispute.

(4) The Court may decline to grant an interim measure under subsection (2) on the ground that

(a) the interim measure sought is currently the subject of arbitral proceedings; and

(b) the Court considers it more appropriate for the interim measure sought to be dealt with by the arbitral tribunal.

(5) In relation to arbitral proceedings which have been or are to be commenced outside Hong Kong, the Court may grant an interim measure under subsection (2) only if

(a) the arbitral proceedings are capable of giving rise to an arbitral award (whether interim or final) that may be enforced in Hong Kong under this Ordinance or any other Ordinance; and

(b) the interim measure sought belongs to a type or description of interim measure that may be granted in Hong Kong in relation to arbitral proceedings by the Court.

(6) Subsection (5) applies even if

(a) the subject matter of the arbitral proceedings would not, apart from that subsection, give rise to a cause of action over which the Court would have jurisdiction; or

(b) the order sought is not ancillary or incidental to any arbitral proceedings in Hong Kong.

(7) In exercising the power under subsection (2) in relation to arbitral proceedings outside Hong Kong, the Court must have regard to the fact that the power is
(a) ancillary to the arbitral proceedings outside Hong Kong; and
(b) for the purposes of facilitating the process of a court or arbitral tribunal outside Hong Kong that has primary jurisdiction over the arbitral proceedings.
(8) The Court has the same power to make any incidental order or direction for the purposes of ensuring the effectiveness of an interim measure granted in relation to arbitral proceedings outside Hong Kong as if the interim measure were granted in relation to arbitral proceedings in Hong Kong.
(9) An interim measure referred to in subsection (2) means an interim measure referred to in article 17(2) of the UNCITRAL Model Law, given effect to by section 35(1), as if
(a) a reference to the arbitral tribunal in that article were the court; and
(b) a reference to arbitral proceedings in that article were court proceedings, and is to be construed as including an injunction but not including an order under section 60.
(10) A decision, order or direction of the Court under this section is not subject to appeal.

Part 7

Conduct of Arbitral Proceedings

Section 46 — Article 18 of UNCITRAL Model Law (Equal treatment of parties)

(1) Subsections (2) and (3) have effect in substitution for article 18 of the UNCITRAL Model Law.
(2) The parties must be treated with equality.
(3) When conducting arbitral proceedings or exercising any of the powers conferred on an arbitral tribunal by this Ordinance or by the parties to any of those arbitral proceedings, the arbitral tribunal is required
(a) to be independent;
(b) to act fairly and impartially as between the parties, giving them a reasonable opportunity to present their cases and to deal with the cases of their opponents; and
(c) to use procedures that are appropriate to the particular case, avoiding unnecessary delay or expense, so as to provide a fair means for resolving the dispute to which the arbitral proceedings relate.

Section 47 — Article 19 of UNCITRAL Model Law (Determination of rules of procedure)

(1) Article 19(1) of the UNCITRAL Model Law, the text of which is set out below, has effect

"Article 19. Determination of rules of procedure

(1) Subject to the provisions of this Law, the parties are free to agree on the procedure to be followed by the arbitral tribunal in conducting the proceedings.

(2) [Not applicable]".

(2) If or to the extent that there is no such agreement of the parties, the arbitral tribunal may, subject to the provisions of this Ordinance, conduct the arbitration in the manner that it considers appropriate.

(3) When conducting arbitral proceedings, an arbitral tribunal is not bound by the rules of evidence and may receive any evidence that it considers relevant to the arbitral proceedings, but it must give the weight that it considers appropriate to the evidence adduced in the arbitral proceedings.

Section 48 — Article 20 of UNCITRAL Model Law (Place of arbitration)

Article 20 of the UNCITRAL Model Law, the text of which is set out below, has effect

"Article 20. Place of arbitration

(1) The parties are free to agree on the place of arbitration. Failing such agreement, the place of arbitration shall be determined by the arbitral tribunal having regard to the circumstances of the case, including the convenience of the parties.

(2) Notwithstanding the provisions of paragraph (1) of this article, the arbitral tribunal may, unless otherwise agreed by the parties, meet at any place it considers appropriate for consultation among its members, for hearing witnesses, experts or the parties, or for inspection of goods, other property or documents.".

Section 49 — Article 21 of UNCITRAL Model Law (Commencement of arbitral proceedings)

(1) Article 21 of the UNCITRAL Model Law, the text of which is set out below, has effect

"Article 21. Commencement of arbitral proceedings

Unless otherwise agreed by the parties, the arbitral proceedings in respect of a particular dispute commence on the date on which a request for that dispute to be referred to arbitration is received by the respondent.".

(2) A request referred to in article 21 of the UNCITRAL Model Law, given effect to by subsection (1), has to be made by way of a written communication as referred to in section 10.

Section 50 — Article 22 of UNCITRAL Model Law (Language)

Article 22 of the UNCITRAL Model Law, the text of which is set out below, has effect

"Article 22. Language

(1) The parties are free to agree on the language or languages to be used in the arbitral proceedings. Failing such agreement, the arbitral tribunal shall determine the language or languages to be used in the proceedings. This agreement or determination, unless otherwise specified therein, shall apply to any written statement by a party, any hearing and any award, decision or other communication by the arbitral tribunal.

(2) The arbitral tribunal may order that any documentary evidence shall be accompanied by a translation into the language or languages agreed upon by the parties or determined by the arbitral tribunal.".

Section 51 — Article 23 of UNCITRAL Model Law (Statements of claim and defence)

Article 23 of the UNCITRAL Model Law, the text of which is set out below, has effect

"Article 23. Statements of claim and defence

(1) Within the period of time agreed by the parties or determined by the arbitral tribunal, the claimant shall state the facts supporting his claim, the points at issue and the relief or remedy sought, and the respondent shall state his defence in respect of these particulars, unless the parties have otherwise agreed as to the required elements of such statements. The parties may submit with their statements all documents they consider to be relevant or may add a reference to the documents or other evidence they will submit.

(2) Unless otherwise agreed by the parties, either party may amend or supplement his claim or defence during the course of the arbitral proceedings, unless the arbitral tribunal considers it inappropriate to allow such amendment having regard to the delay in making it.".

Section 52 — Article 24 of UNCITRAL Model Law (Hearings and written proceedings)

Article 24 of the UNCITRAL Model Law, the text of which is set out below, has effect

"Article 24. Hearings and written proceedings

(1) Subject to any contrary agreement by the parties, the arbitral tribunal shall decide whether to hold oral hearings for the presentation of evidence or for oral argument, or whether the proceedings shall be conducted on the basis of documents and other materials. However, unless the parties have agreed that no hearings shall be held, the arbitral tribunal shall hold such hearings at an appropriate stage of the proceedings, if so requested by a party.

(2) The parties shall be given sufficient advance notice of any hearing and of any meeting of the arbitral tribunal for the purposes of inspection of goods, other property or documents.

(3) All statements, documents or other information supplied to the arbitral tribunal by one party shall be communicated to the other party. Also any expert report or evidentiary document on which the arbitral tribunal may rely in making its decision shall be communicated to the parties.".

Section 53 — Article 25 of UNCITRAL Model Law (Default of a party)

(1) Article 25 of the UNCITRAL Model Law, the text of which is set out below, has effect

"Article 25. Default of a party

Unless otherwise agreed by the parties, if, without showing sufficient cause,

(a) the claimant fails to communicate his statement of claim in accordance with article 23(1), the arbitral tribunal shall terminate the proceedings;

(b) the respondent fails to communicate his statement of defence in accordance with article 23(1), the arbitral tribunal shall continue the proceedings without treating such failure in itself as an admission of the claimant's allegations;

(c) any party fails to appear at a hearing or to produce documentary evidence, the arbitral tribunal may continue the proceedings and make the award on the evidence before it.".

(2) Unless otherwise agreed by the parties, subsections (3) and (4) apply except in relation to an application for security for costs.

(3) If, without showing sufficient cause, a party fails to comply with any order or direction of the arbitral tribunal, the tribunal may make a peremptory order to the same effect, prescribing the time for compliance with it that the arbitral tribunal considers appropriate.

(4) If a party fails to comply with a peremptory order, then without affecting section 61, the arbitral tribunal may

(a) direct that the party is not entitled to rely on any allegation or material which was the subject matter of the peremptory order;
(b) draw any adverse inferences that the circumstances may justify from the non-compliance;
(c) make an award on the basis of any materials which have been properly provided to the arbitral tribunal; or
(d) make any order that the arbitral tribunal thinks fit as to the payment of the costs of the arbitration incurred in consequence of the non-compliance.

Section 54 — Article 26 of UNCITRAL Model Law (Expert appointed by arbitral tribunal)

(1) Article 26 of the UNCITRAL Model Law, the text of which is set out below, has effect

"Article 26. Expert appointed by arbitral tribunal

(1) Unless otherwise agreed by the parties, the arbitral tribunal
(a) may appoint one or more experts to report to it on specific issues to be determined by the arbitral tribunal;
(b) may require a party to give the expert any relevant information or to produce, or to provide access to, any relevant documents, goods or other property for his inspection.

(2) Unless otherwise agreed by the parties, if a party so requests or if the arbitral tribunal considers it necessary, the expert shall, after delivery of his written or oral report, participate in a hearing where the parties have the opportunity to put questions to him and to present expert witnesses in order to testify on the points at issue.".

(2) Without affecting article 26 of the UNCITRAL Model Law, given effect to by subsection (1), in assessing the amount of the costs of arbitral proceedings (other than the fees and expenses of the tribunal) under section 74
(a) the arbitral tribunal may appoint assessors to assist it on technical matters, and may allow any of those assessors to attend the proceedings; and
(b) the parties must be given a reasonable opportunity to comment on any information, opinion or advice offered by any of those assessors.

Section 55 — Article 27 of UNCITRAL Model Law (Court assistance in taking evidence)

(1) Article 27 of the UNCITRAL Model Law, the text of which is set out below, has effect

"Article 27. Court assistance in taking evidence

The arbitral tribunal or a party with the approval of the arbitral tribunal may request from a competent court of this State assistance in taking evidence. The court may execute the request within its competence and according to its rules on taking evidence.".

(2) The Court may order a person to attend proceedings before an arbitral tribunal to give evidence or to produce documents or other evidence.

(3) The powers conferred by this section may be exercised by the Court irrespective of whether or not similar powers may be exercised by an arbitral tribunal under section 56 in relation to the same dispute.

(4) A decision or order of the Court made in the exercise of its power under this section is not subject to appeal.

(5) Section 81 (Warrant or order to bring up prisoner to give evidence) of the Evidence Ordinance (Cap 8) applies as if a reference to any proceedings, either criminal or civil, in that section were any arbitral proceedings.

Section 56 — General Powers Exercisable by Arbitral Tribunal

(1) Unless otherwise agreed by the parties, when conducting arbitral proceedings, an arbitral tribunal may make an order

(a) requiring a claimant to give security for the costs of the arbitration;

(b) directing the discovery of documents or the delivery of interrogatories;

(c) directing evidence to be given by affidavit; or

(d) in relation to any relevant property

(i) directing the inspection, photographing, preservation, custody, detention or sale of the relevant property by the arbitral tribunal, a party to the arbitral proceedings or an expert; or

(ii) directing samples to be taken from, observations to be made of, or experiments to be conducted on the relevant property.

(2) An arbitral tribunal must not make an order under subsection (1)(a) only on the ground that the claimant is

(a) a natural person who is ordinarily resident outside Hong Kong;

(b) a body corporate

(i) incorporated under the law of a place outside Hong Kong; or

(ii) the central management and control of which is exercised outside Hong Kong; or

(c) an association

(i) formed under the law of a place outside Hong Kong; or

(ii) the central management and control of which is exercised outside Hong Kong.

(3) An arbitral tribunal

(a) must, when making an order under subsection (1)(a), specify the period

within which the order has to be complied with; and
(b) may extend that period or an extended period.
(4) An arbitral tribunal may make an award dismissing a claim or stay a claim if it has made an order under subsection (1)(a) but the order has not been complied with within the period specified under subsection (3)(a) or extended under subsection (3)(b).
(5) Despite section 35(2), sections 39 to 42 apply, if appropriate, to an order under subsection (1)(d) as if a reference to an interim measure in those sections were an order under that subsection.
(6) Property is a relevant property for the purposes of subsection (1)(d) if
(a) the property is owned by or is in the possession of a party to the arbitral proceedings; and
(b) the property is the subject of the arbitral proceedings, or any question relating to the property has arisen in the arbitral proceedings.
(7) Unless otherwise agreed by the parties, an arbitral tribunal may, when conducting arbitral proceedings, decide whether and to what extent it should itself take the initiative in ascertaining the facts and the law relevant to those arbitral proceedings.
(8) Unless otherwise agreed by the parties, an arbitral tribunal may
(a) administer oaths to, or take the affirmations of, witnesses and parties;
(b) examine witnesses and parties on oath or affirmation; or
(c) direct the attendance before the arbitral tribunal of witnesses in order to give evidence or to produce documents or other evidence.
(9) A person is not required to produce in arbitral proceedings any document or other evidence that the person could not be required to produce in civil proceedings before a court.

Section 57 — Arbitral Tribunal May Limit Amount of Recoverable Costs

(1) Unless otherwise agreed by the parties, an arbitral tribunal may direct that the recoverable costs of arbitral proceedings before it are limited to a specified amount.
(2) Subject to subsection (3), the arbitral tribunal may make or vary a direction either
(a) on its own initiative; or
(b) on the application of any party.
(3) A direction may be made or varied at any stage of the arbitral proceedings but, for the limit of the recoverable costs to be taken into account, this must be done sufficiently in advance of
(a) the incurring of the costs to which the direction or the variation relates;

or
(b) the taking of the steps in the arbitral proceedings which may be affected by the direction or the variation.
(4) In this section
(a) a reference to costs is to be construed as the parties' own costs; and
(b) a reference to arbitral proceedings includes any part of those arbitral proceedings.
Section 58 — Power to Extend Time for Arbitral Proceedings
(1) This section applies to an arbitration agreement that provides for a claim to be barred or for a claimant's right to be extinguished unless the claimant, before the time or within the period specified in the agreement, takes a step
(a) to commence arbitral proceedings; or
(b) to commence any other dispute resolution procedure that must be exhausted before arbitral proceedings may be commenced.
(2) On the application of any party to such an arbitration agreement, an arbitral tribunal may make an order extending the time or period referred to in subsection (1).
(3) An application may be made only after a claim has arisen and after exhausting any available arbitral procedures for obtaining an extension of time.
(4) An arbitral tribunal may make an order under this section extending the time or period referred to in subsection (1) only if it is satisfied
(a) that
(i) the circumstances were such as to be outside the reasonable contemplation of the parties when they entered into the arbitration agreement; and
(ii) it would be just to extend the time or period; or
(b) that the conduct of any party makes it unjust to hold the other party to the strict terms of the agreement.
(5) An arbitral tribunal may extend the time or period referred to in subsection (1), or the time or period extended under subsection (4), for a further period and on the terms that it thinks fit, and the tribunal may do so even though that time or period or the extended time or period has expired.
(6) This section does not affect the operation of section 14 or any other enactment that limits the period for commencing arbitral proceedings.
(7) The power conferred on an arbitral tribunal by this section is exercisable by the Court if at the relevant time there is not in existence an arbitral tribunal that is capable of exercising that power.
(8) An order of the Court made in exercise of its power conferred by

subsection (7) is not subject to appeal.

Section 59 — Order to be Made in Case of Delay in Pursuing Claims in Arbitral Proceedings

(1) Unless otherwise expressed in an arbitration agreement, a party who has a claim under the agreement must, after the commencement of the arbitral proceedings, pursue that claim without unreasonable delay.

(2) Without affecting article 25 of the UNCITRAL Model Law, given effect to by section 53(1), the arbitral tribunal

(a) may make an award dismissing a party's claim; and

(b) may make an order prohibiting the party from commencing further arbitral proceedings in respect of the claim,

if it is satisfied that the party has unreasonably delayed in pursuing the claim in the arbitral proceedings.

(3) The arbitral tribunal may make an award or order either

(a) on its own initiative; or

(b) on the application of any other party.

(4) For the purposes of subsection (2), delay is unreasonable if

(a) it gives rise, or is likely to give rise, to a substantial risk that the issues in the claim will not be resolved fairly; or

(b) it has caused, or is likely to cause, serious prejudice to any other party.

(5) The power conferred on an arbitral tribunal by this section is exercisable by the Court if there is not in existence an arbitral tribunal that is capable of exercising that power.

(6) An award or order made by the Court in exercise of its power conferred by subsection (5) is not subject to appeal.

Section 60 — Special Powers of Court in Relation to Arbitral Proceedings

(1) On the application of any party, the Court may, in relation to any arbitral proceedings which have been or are to be commenced in or outside Hong Kong, make an order

(a) directing the inspection, photographing, preservation, custody, detention or sale of any relevant property by the arbitral tribunal, a party to the arbitral proceedings or an expert; or

(b) directing samples to be taken from, observations to be made of, or experiments to be conducted on any relevant property.

(2) Property is a relevant property for the purposes of subsection (1) if the property is the subject of the arbitral proceedings, or any question relating to the property has arisen in the arbitral proceedings.

(3) The powers conferred by this section may be exercised by the Court

irrespective of whether or not similar powers may be exercised by an arbitral tribunal under section 56 in relation to the same dispute.
(4) The Court may decline to make an order under this section in relation to a matter referred to in subsection (1) on the ground that
(a) the matter is currently the subject of arbitral proceedings; and
(b) the Court considers it more appropriate for the matter to be dealt with by the arbitral tribunal.
(5) An order made by the Court under this section may provide for the cessation of that order, in whole or in part, when the arbitral tribunal makes an order for the cessation.
(6) In relation to arbitral proceedings which have been or are to be commenced outside Hong Kong, the Court may make an order under subsection (1) only if the arbitral proceedings are capable of giving rise to an arbitral award (whether interim or final) that may be enforced in Hong Kong under this Ordinance or any other Ordinance.
(7) Subsection (6) applies even if
(a) the subject matter of the arbitral proceedings would not, apart from that subsection, give rise to a cause of action over which the Court would have jurisdiction; or
(b) the order sought is not ancillary or incidental to any arbitral proceedings in Hong Kong.
(8) In exercising the power under subsection (1) in relation to arbitral proceedings outside Hong Kong, the Court must have regard to the fact that the power is
(a) ancillary to the arbitral proceedings outside Hong Kong; and
(b) for the purposes of facilitating the process of a court or arbitral tribunal outside Hong Kong that has primary jurisdiction over the arbitral proceedings.
(9) Subject to subsection (10), an order or decision of the Court under this section is not subject to appeal.
(10) The leave of the Court is required for any appeal from an order of the Court under subsection (1) for the sale of any relevant property.

Section 61 — Enforcement of Orders and Directions of Arbitral Tribunal

(1) An order or direction made, whether in or outside Hong Kong, in relation to arbitral proceedings by an arbitral tribunal is enforceable in the same manner as an order or direction of the Court that has the same effect, but only with the leave of the Court.
(2) Leave to enforce an order or direction made outside Hong Kong is not to

be granted, unless the party seeking to enforce it can demonstrate that it belongs to a type or description of order or direction that may be made in Hong Kong in relation to arbitral proceedings by an arbitral tribunal.

(3) If leave is granted under subsection (1), the Court may enter judgment in terms of the order or direction.

(4) A decision of the Court to grant or refuse to grant leave under subsection (1) is not subject to appeal.

(5) An order or direction referred to in this section includes an interim measure.

Section 62 — Power of Court to Order Recovery of Arbitrator's Fees

(1) Where an arbitrator's mandate terminates under article 13 of the UNCITRAL Model Law, given effect to by section 26, or under article 14 of the UNCITRAL Model Law, given effect to by section 27, then on the application of any party, the Court, in its discretion and having regard to the conduct of the arbitrator and any other relevant circumstances

(a) may order that the arbitrator is not entitled to receive the whole or part of the arbitrator's fees or expenses; and

(b) may order that the arbitrator must repay the whole or part of the fees or expenses already paid to the arbitrator.

(2) An order of the Court under subsection (1) is not subject to appeal.

Section 63 — Representation and Preparation Work

Section 44 (Penalty for unlawfully practicing as a barrister or notary public), section 45 (Unqualified person not to act as solicitor) and section 47 (Unqualified person not to prepare certain instruments, etc.) of the Legal Practitioners Ordinance (Cap 159) do not apply to

(a) arbitral proceedings;

(b) the giving of advice and the preparation of documents for the purposes of arbitral proceedings; or

(c) any other thing done in relation to arbitral proceedings, except where it is done in connection with court proceedings

(i) arising out of an arbitration agreement; or

(ii) arising in the course of, or resulting from, arbitral proceedings.

Part 8

Making of Award and Termination of Proceedings

Section 64 — Article 28 of UNCITRAL Model Law (Rules applicable to substance of dispute)

Article 28 of the UNCITRAL Model Law, the text of which is set out below, has effect

"Article 28. Rules applicable to substance of dispute

(1) The arbitral tribunal shall decide the dispute in accordance with such rules of law as are chosen by the parties as applicable to the substance of the dispute. Any designation of the law or legal system of a given State shall be construed, unless otherwise expressed, as directly referring to the substantive law of that State and not to its conflict of laws rules.

(2) Failing any designation by the parties, the arbitral tribunal shall apply the law determined by the conflict of laws rules which it considers applicable.

(3) The arbitral tribunal shall decide *ex aequo et bono* or as *amiable compositeur* only if the parties have expressly authorized it to do so.

(4) In all cases, the arbitral tribunal shall decide in accordance with the terms of the contract and shall take into account the usages of the trade applicable to the transaction.".

Section 65 — Article 29 of UNCITRAL Model Law (Decision-making by panel of arbitrators)

Article 29 of the UNCITRAL Model Law, the text of which is set out below, has effect

"Article 29. Decision-making by panel of arbitrators

In arbitral proceedings with more than one arbitrator, any decision of the arbitral tribunal shall be made, unless otherwise agreed by the parties, by a majority of all its members. However, questions of procedure may be decided by a presiding arbitrator, if so authorized by the parties or all members of the arbitral tribunal.".

Section 66 — Article 30 of UNCITRAL Model Law (Settlement)

(1) Article 30 of the UNCITRAL Model Law, the text of which is set out below, has effect

"Article 30. Settlement

(1) If, during arbitral proceedings, the parties settle the dispute, the arbitral tribunal shall terminate the proceedings and, if requested by the parties and not objected to by the arbitral tribunal, record the settlement in the form of an arbitral award on agreed terms.

(2) An award on agreed terms shall be made in accordance with the provisions of article 31 and shall state that it is an award. Such an award has the same status and effect as any other award on the merits of the case.".

(2) If, in a case other than that referred to in article 30 of the UNCITRAL Model Law, given effect to by subsection (1), the parties to an arbitration agreement settle their dispute and enter into an agreement in writing

containing the terms of settlement ("settlement agreement"), the settlement agreement is, for the purposes of its enforcement, to be treated as an arbitral award.

Section 67 — Article 31 of UNCITRAL Model Law (Form and contents of award)

(1) Article 31 of the UNCITRAL Model Law, the text of which is set out below, has effect

"Article 31. Form and contents of award

(1) The award shall be made in writing and shall be signed by the arbitrator or arbitrators. In arbitral proceedings with more than one arbitrator, the signatures of the majority of all members of the arbitral tribunal shall suffice, provided that the reason for any omitted signature is stated.

(2) The award shall state the reasons upon which it is based, unless the parties have agreed that no reasons are to be given or the award is an award on agreed terms under article 30.

(3) The award shall state its date and the place of arbitration as determined in accordance with article 20(1). The award shall be deemed to have been made at that place.

(4) After the award is made, a copy signed by the arbitrators in accordance with paragraph (1) of this article shall be delivered to each party.".

(2) Article 31(4) of the UNCITRAL Model Law, given effect to by subsection (1), has effect subject to section 77.

Section 68 — Article 32 of UNCITRAL Model Law (Termination of proceedings)

Article 32 of the UNCITRAL Model Law, the text of which is set out below, has effect

"Article 32. Termination of proceedings

(1) The arbitral proceedings are terminated by the final award or by an order of the arbitral tribunal in accordance with paragraph (2) of this article.

(2) The arbitral tribunal shall issue an order for the termination of the arbitral proceedings when:

(a) the claimant withdraws his claim, unless the respondent objects thereto and the arbitral tribunal recognizes a legitimate interest on his part in obtaining a final settlement of the dispute;

(b) the parties agree on the termination of the proceedings;

(c) the arbitral tribunal finds that the continuation of the proceedings has for any other reason become unnecessary or impossible.

(3) The mandate of the arbitral tribunal terminates with the termination of the arbitral proceedings, subject to the provisions of articles 33 and 34(4).".

Section 69 — Article 33 of UNCITRAL Model Law (Correction and interpretation of award; additional award)

(1) Article 33 of the UNCITRAL Model Law, the text of which is set out below, has effect

"Article 33. Correction and interpretation of award; additional award

(1) Within thirty days of receipt of the award, unless another period of time has been agreed upon by the parties:

(a) a party, with notice to the other party, may request the arbitral tribunal to correct in the award any errors in computation, any clerical or typographical errors or any errors of similar nature;

(b) if so agreed by the parties, a party, with notice to the other party, may request the arbitral tribunal to give an interpretation of a specific point or part of the award. If the arbitral tribunal considers the request to be justified, it shall make the correction or give the interpretation within thirty days of receipt of the request. The interpretation shall form part of the award.

(2) The arbitral tribunal may correct any error of the type referred to in paragraph (1)(a) of this article on its own initiative within thirty days of the date of the award.

(3) Unless otherwise agreed by the parties, a party, with notice to the other party, may request, within thirty days of receipt of the award, the arbitral tribunal to make an additional award as to claims presented in the arbitral proceedings but omitted from the award. If the arbitral tribunal considers the request to be justified, it shall make the additional award within sixty days.

(4) The arbitral tribunal may extend, if necessary, the period of time within which it shall make a correction, interpretation or an additional award under paragraph (1) or (3) of this article.

(5) The provisions of article 31 shall apply to a correction or interpretation of the award or to an additional award.".

(2) The arbitral tribunal has the power to make other changes to an arbitral award which are necessitated by or consequential on

(a) the correction of any error in the award; or

(b) the interpretation of any point or part of the award, under article 33 of the UNCITRAL Model Law, given effect to by subsection (1).

(3) The arbitral tribunal may review an award of costs within 30 days of the date of the award if, when making the award, the tribunal was not aware of any information relating to costs (including any offer for settlement) which it should have taken into account.
(4) On a review under subsection (3), the arbitral tribunal may confirm, vary or correct the award of costs.

Section 70 — Award of Remedy or Relief

(1) Subject to subsection (2), an arbitral tribunal may, in deciding a dispute, award any remedy or relief that could have been ordered by the Court if the dispute had been the subject of civil proceedings in the Court.
(2) Unless otherwise agreed by the parties, the arbitral tribunal has the same power as the Court to order specific performance of any contract, other than a contract relating to land or any interest in land.

Section 71 — Awards on Different Aspects of Matters

Unless otherwise agreed by the parties, an arbitral tribunal may make more than one award at different times on different aspects of the matters to be determined.

Section 72 — Time for Making Award

(1) Unless otherwise agreed by the parties, an arbitral tribunal has the power to make an award at any time.
(2) The time, if any, limited for making an award, whether under this Ordinance or otherwise, may from time to time be extended by order of the Court on the application of any party, whether that time has expired or not.
(3) An order of the Court under subsection (2) is not subject to appeal.

Section 73 — Effect of award

(1) Unless otherwise agreed by the parties, an award made by an arbitral tribunal pursuant to an arbitration agreement is final and binding both on
(a) the parties; and
(b) any person claiming through or under any of the parties.
(2) Subsection (1) does not affect the right of a person to challenge the award
(a) as provided for in section 26 or 81, section 4 or 5 of Schedule 2, or any other provision of this Ordinance; or
(b) otherwise by any available arbitral process of appeal or review.

Section 74 — Arbitral Tribunal May Award Costs of Arbitral Proceedings

(1) An arbitral tribunal may include in an award directions with respect to the costs of arbitral proceedings (including the fees and expenses of the tribunal).

(2) The arbitral tribunal may, having regard to all relevant circumstances (including the fact, if appropriate, that a written offer of settlement of the dispute concerned has been made), direct in the award under subsection (1) to whom and by whom and in what manner the costs are to be paid
(3) The arbitral tribunal may also, in its discretion, order costs (including the fees and expenses of the tribunal) to be paid by a party in respect of a request made by any of the parties for an order or direction (including an interim measure).
(4) The arbitral tribunal may direct that the costs ordered under subsection (3) are to be paid forthwith or at the time that the tribunal may otherwise specify.
(5) Subject to section 75, the arbitral tribunal must
(a) assess the amount of costs to be awarded or ordered to be paid under this section (other than the fees and expenses of the tribunal); and
(b) award or order those costs (including the fees and expenses of the tribunal).
(6) Subject to subsection (7), the arbitral tribunal is not obliged to follow the scales and practices adopted by the court on taxation when assessing the amount of costs (other than the fees and expenses of the tribunal) under subsection (5).
(7) The arbitral tribunal
(a) must only allow costs that are reasonable having regard to all the circumstances; and
(b) unless otherwise agreed by the parties, may allow costs incurred in the preparation of the arbitral proceedings prior to the commencement of the arbitration.
(8) A provision of an arbitration agreement to the effect that the parties, or any of the parties, must pay their own costs in respect of arbitral proceedings arising under the agreement is void.
(9) A provision referred to in subsection (8) is not void if it is part of an agreement to submit to arbitration a dispute that had arisen before the agreement was made.

Section 75 — Taxation of Costs of Arbitral Proceedings (Other than Fees and Expenses of Arbitral Tribunal)

(1) Without affecting section 74(1) and (2), if the parties have agreed that the costs of arbitral proceedings are to be taxed by the court, then unless the arbitral tribunal otherwise directs in an award, the award is deemed to have included the tribunal's directions that the costs (other than the fees and expenses of the tribunal) are to be taxed by the court on the party and party

basis in accordance with rule 28(2) of Order 62 of the Rules of the High Court (Cap 4 sub. leg. A). (Amended 7 of 2013 s. 7)

(2) On taxation by the court, the arbitral tribunal must make an additional award of costs reflecting the result of such taxation.

(3) A decision of the court on taxation is not subject to appeal.

(4) This section does not apply to costs ordered to be paid under section 74 (3).

Section 76 — Costs in Respect of Unqualified Person

Section 50 (No costs for unqualified person) of the Legal Practitioners Ordinance (Cap 159) does not apply to the recovery of costs in an arbitration.

Section 77 — Determination of Arbitral Tribunal's Fees and Expenses in case of Dispute

(1) An arbitral tribunal may refuse to deliver an award to the parties unless full payment of the fees and expenses of the tribunal is made.

(2) If the arbitral tribunal refuses to deliver an award to the parties under subsection (1), a party may apply to the Court, which

(a) may order the tribunal to deliver the award on the payment into the Court by the applicant of

(i) the fees and expenses demanded; or

(ii) a lesser amount that the Court may specify;

(b) may order that the amount of the fees and expenses payable to the tribunal is to be determined by the means and on the terms that the Court may direct; and

(c) may order that

(i) the fees and expenses as determined under paragraph (b) to be payable are to be paid to the tribunal out of the money paid into the Court; and

(ii) the balance of the money paid into the Court, if any, is to be paid out to the applicant.

(3) For the purposes of subsection (2)

(a) the amount of the fees and expenses payable is the amount which the applicant is liable to pay

(i) under section 78; or

(ii) under any agreement relating to the payment of the arbitrators; and

(b) the fees and expenses of

(i) an expert appointed under article 26 of the UNCITRAL Model Law, given effect to by section 54(1); or

(ii) an assessor appointed under section 54(2),

are to be treated as the fees and expenses of the arbitral tribunal.

(4) No application under subsection (2) may be made if

(a) there is any available arbitral process for appeal or review of the amount of the fees or expenses demanded; or

(b) the total amount of the fees and expenses demanded has been fixed by a written agreement between a party and the arbitrators.

(5) Subsections (1) to (4) also apply to any arbitral or other institution or person vested by the parties with powers in relation to the delivery of the arbitral tribunal's award.

(6) If subsections (1) to (4) so apply under subsection (5), the references to the fees and expenses of the arbitral tribunal are to be construed as including the fees and expenses of that institution or person.

(7) If an application is made to the Court under subsection (2), enforcement of the award (when delivered to the parties), but only in so far as it relates to the fees or expenses of the arbitral tribunal, must be stayed until the application has been disposed of under this section.

(8) An arbitrator is entitled to appear and be heard on any determination under this section.

(9) If the amount of the fees and expenses determined under subsection (2) (b) is different from the amount previously awarded by the arbitral tribunal, the tribunal must amend the previous award to reflect the result of the determination.

(10) An order of the Court under this section is not subject to appeal.

Section 78 — Liability to Pay Fees and Expenses of Arbitral Tribunal

(1) The parties to proceedings before an arbitral tribunal are jointly and severally liable to pay to the tribunal reasonable fees and expenses, if any, of the tribunal that are appropriate in the circumstances.

(2) Subsection (1) has effect subject to any order of the Court made under section 62 or any other relevant provision of this Ordinance.

(3) This section does not affect

(a) the liability of the parties as among themselves to pay the costs of the arbitral proceedings; or

(b) any contractual right or obligation relating to payment of the fees and expenses of the arbitral tribunal.

(4) In this section, a reference to an arbitral tribunal includes

(a) a member of the tribunal who has ceased to act; and

(b) an umpire who has not yet replaced members of the tribunal.

Section 79 — Arbitral Tribunal May Award Interest

(1) Unless otherwise agreed by the parties, an arbitral tribunal may, in the arbitral proceedings before it, award simple or compound interest from the

dates, at the rates, and with the rests that the tribunal considers appropriate, subject to section 80, for any period ending not later than the date of payment

(a) on money awarded by the tribunal in the arbitral proceedings;

(b) on money claimed in, and outstanding at the commencement of, the arbitral proceedings but paid before the award is made; or

(c) on costs awarded or ordered by the tribunal in the arbitral proceedings.

(2) Subsection (1) does not affect any other power of an arbitral tribunal to award interest.

(3) A reference in subsection (1)(a) to money awarded by the tribunal includes an amount payable in consequence of a declaratory award by the tribunal.

Section 80 — Interest on Money or Costs Awarded or Ordered in Arbitral Proceedings

(1) Interest is payable on money awarded by an arbitral tribunal from the date of the award at the judgment rate, except when the award otherwise provides.

(2) Interest is payable on costs awarded or ordered by an arbitral tribunal from

(a) the date of the award or order on costs; or

(b) the date on which costs ordered are directed to be paid forthwith,

at the judgment rate, except when the award or order on costs otherwise provides.

(3) In this section, "judgment rate" (判定利率) means the rate of interest determined by the Chief Justice under section 49(1)(b) (Interest on judgments) of the High Court Ordinance (Cap 4).

Part 9

Recourse Against Award

Section 81 — Article 34 of UNCITRAL Model Law (Application for setting aside as exclusive recourse against arbitral award)

(1) Article 34 of the UNCITRAL Model Law, the text of which is set out below, has effect subject to section 13(5)

> "Article 34. Application for setting aside as exclusive recourse against arbitral award
>
> (1) Recourse to a court against an arbitral award may be made only by an application for setting aside in accordance with paragraphs (2) and (3) of this article.
>
> (2) An arbitral award may be set aside by the court specified in article 6 only if:

(a) the party making the application furnishes proof that:

(i) a party to the arbitration agreement referred to in article 7 was under some incapacity; or the said agreement is not valid under the law to which the parties have subjected it or, failing any indication thereon, under the law of this State; or

(ii) the party making the application was not given proper notice of the appointment of an arbitrator or of the arbitral proceedings or was otherwise unable to present his case; or

(iii) the award deals with a dispute not contemplated by or not falling within the terms of the submission to arbitration, or contains decisions on matters beyond the scope of the submission to arbitration, provided that, if the decisions on matters submitted to arbitration can be separated from those not so submitted, only that part of the award which contains decisions on matters not submitted to arbitration may be set aside; or

(iv) the composition of the arbitral tribunal or the arbitral procedure was not in accordance with the agreement of the parties, unless such agreement was in conflict with a provision of this Law from which the parties cannot derogate, or, failing such agreement, was not in accordance with this Law; or

(b) the court finds that:

(i) the subject-matter of the dispute is not capable of settlement by arbitration under the law of this State; or

(ii) the award is in conflict with the public policy of this State.

(3) An application for setting aside may not be made after three months have elapsed from the date on which the party making that application had received the award or, if a request had been made under article 33, from the date on which that request had been disposed of by the arbitral tribunal.

(4) The court, when asked to set aside an award, may, where appropriate and so requested by a party, suspend the setting aside proceedings for a period of time determined by it in order to give the arbitral tribunal an opportunity to resume the arbitral proceedings or to take such other action as in the arbitral tribunal's opinion will eliminate the grounds for setting aside."

(2) Subsection (1) does not affect

(a) the power of the Court to set aside an arbitral award under section 26(5);

(b) the right to challenge an arbitral award under section 4 of Schedule 2 (if applicable); or

(c) the right to appeal against an arbitral award on a question of law under section 5 of Schedule 2 (if applicable).
(3) Subject to subsection (2)(c), the Court does not have jurisdiction to set aside or remit an arbitral award on the ground of errors of fact or law on the face of the award.
(4) The leave of the Court is required for any appeal from a decision of the Court under article 34 of the UNCITRAL Model Law, given effect to by subsection (1).

Part 10
Recognition and Enforcement of Awards
Division 1. Enforcement of Arbitral Awards

Section 82 — Article 35 of UNCITRAL Model Law (Recognition and enforcement)
Article 35 of the UNCITRAL Model Law does not have effect.

Section 83 — Article 36 of UNCITRAL Model Law (Grounds for refusing recognition or enforcement)
Article 36 of the UNCITRAL Model Law does not have effect.

Section 84 — Enforcement of Arbitral Awards
(1) Subject to section 26(2), an award, whether made in or outside Hong Kong, in arbitral proceedings by an arbitral tribunal is enforceable in the same manner as a judgment of the Court that has the same effect, but only with the leave of the Court.
(2) If leave is granted under subsection (1), the Court may enter judgment in terms of the award.
(3) The leave of the Court is required for any appeal from a decision of the Court to grant or refuse leave to enforce an award under subsection (1).

Section 85 — Evidence to be Produced for Enforcement of Arbitral Awards
The party seeking to enforce an arbitral award, whether made in or outside Hong Kong, which is not a Convention award, Mainland award or Macao award, must produce (Amended 7 of 2013 s. 9)
(a) the duly authenticated original award or a duly certified copy of it;
(b) the original arbitration agreement or a duly certified copy of it; and
(c) if the award or agreement is not in either or both of the official languages, a translation of it in either official language certified by an official or sworn translator or by a diplomatic or consular agent. (Replaced 7 of 2013 s. 9)

Section 86 — Refusal of Enforcement of Arbitral Awards
(1) Enforcement of an award referred to in section 85 may be refused if the

person against whom it is invoked proves
(a) that a party to the arbitration agreement was under some incapacity (under the law applicable to that party); (Replaced 7 of 2013 s. 10)
(b) that the arbitration agreement was not valid
(i) under the law to which the parties subjected it; or
(ii) (if there was no indication of the law to which the arbitration agreement was subjected) under the law of the country where the award was made;
(c) that the person
(i) was not given proper notice of the appointment of the arbitrator or of the arbitral proceedings; or
(ii) was otherwise unable to present the person's case;
(d) subject to subsection (3), that the award
(i) deals with a difference not contemplated by or not falling within the terms of the submission to arbitration; or
(ii) contains decisions on matters beyond the scope of the submission to arbitration;
(e) that the composition of the arbitral authority or the arbitral procedure was not in accordance with
(i) the agreement of the parties; or
(ii) (if there was no agreement) the law of the country where the arbitration took place; or
(f) that the award
(i) has not yet become binding on the parties; or
(ii) has been set aside or suspended by a competent authority of the country in which, or under the law of which, it was made.
(2) Enforcement of an award referred to in section 85 may also be refused if
(a) the award is in respect of a matter which is not capable of settlement by arbitration under the law of Hong Kong;
(b) it would be contrary to public policy to enforce the award; or
(c) for any other reason the court considers it just to do so.
(3) If an award referred to in section 85 contains, apart from decisions on matters submitted to arbitration (*arbitral decisions*), decisions on matters not submitted to arbitration (*unrelated decisions*), the award may be enforced only in so far as it relates to the arbitral decisions that can be separated from the unrelated decisions. (Replaced 7 of 2013 s. 10)
(4) If an application for setting aside or suspending an award referred to in section 85 has been made to a competent authority as mentioned in subsection (1)(f), the court before which enforcement of the award is sought (Amended 7 of 2013 s .10)

(a) may, if it thinks fit, adjourn the proceedings for the enforcement of the award; and
(b) may, on the application of the party seeking to enforce the award, order the person against whom the enforcement is invoked to give security.
(5) A decision or order of the court under subsection (4) is not subject to appeal.

Division 2. Enforcement of Convention Awards

Section 87 — Enforcement of Convention Awards

(1) A Convention award is, subject to this Division, enforceable in Hong Kong either
(a) by action in the Court; or
(b) in the same manner as an award to which section 84 applies, and that section applies to a Convention award accordingly as if a reference in that section to an award were a Convention award. (Amended 7 of 2013 s. 11)
(2) A Convention award which is enforceable as mentioned in subsection (1) is to be treated as binding for all purposes on the parties, and may accordingly be relied on by any of them by way of defence, set off or otherwise in any legal proceedings in Hong Kong. (Replaced 7 of 2013 s. 11)
(3) A reference in this Division to enforcement of a Convention award is to be construed as including reliance on a Convention award.

Section 88 — Evidence to be Produced for Enforcement of Convention Awards

The party seeking to enforce a Convention award must produce
(a) the duly authenticated original award or a duly certified copy of it;
(b) the original arbitration agreement or a duly certified copy of it; and
(c) if the award or agreement is not in either or both of the official languages, a translation of it in either official language certified by an official or sworn translator or by a diplomatic or consular agent. (Replaced 7 of 2013 s. 12)

Section 89 — Refusal of Enforcement of Convention Awards

(1) Enforcement of a Convention award may not be refused except as mentioned in this section. (Amended 7 of 2013 s. 13)
(2) Enforcement of a Convention award may be refused if the person against whom it is invoked proves
(a) that a party to the arbitration agreement was under some incapacity (under the law applicable to that party); (Replaced 7 of 2013 s. 13)
(b) that the arbitration agreement was not valid
(i) under the law to which the parties subjected it; or

(ii) (if there was no indication of the law to which the arbitration agreement was subjected) under the law of the country where the award was made;
(c) that the person
(i) was not given proper notice of the appointment of the arbitrator or of the arbitral proceedings; or
(ii) was otherwise unable to present the person's case;
(d) subject to subsection (4), that the award
(i) deals with a difference not contemplated by or not falling within the terms of the submission to arbitration; or
(ii) contains decisions on matters beyond the scope of the submission to arbitration;
(e) that the composition of the arbitral authority or the arbitral procedure was not in accordance with
(i) the agreement of the parties; or
(ii) (if there was no agreement) the law of the country where the arbitration took place; or
(f) that the award
(i) has not yet become binding on the parties; or
(ii) has been set aside or suspended by a competent authority of the country in which, or under the law of which, it was made.
(3) Enforcement of a Convention award may also be refused if
(a) the award is in respect of a matter which is not capable of settlement by arbitration under the law of Hong Kong; or
(b) it would be contrary to public policy to enforce the award.
(4) If a Convention award contains, apart from decisions on matters submitted to arbitration (arbitral decisions), decisions on matters not submitted to arbitration (unrelated decisions), the award may be enforced only in so far as it relates to the arbitral decisions that can be separated from the unrelated decisions. (Replaced 7 of 2013 s. 13)
(5) If an application for setting aside or suspending a Convention award has been made to a competent authority as mentioned in subsection (2)(f), the court before which enforcement of the award is sought (Amended 7 of 2013 s. 13)
(a) may, if it thinks fit, adjourn the proceedings for the enforcement of the award; and
(b) may, on the application of the party seeking to enforce the award, order the person against whom the enforcement is invoked to give security.
(6) A decision or order of the court under subsection (5) is not subject to appeal.

Section 90 — Order for Declaring Party to New York Convention

(1) The Chief Executive in Council may, by order in the Gazette, declare that any State or territory that

(a) is a party to the New York Convention; and

(b) is specified in the order, is a party to that Convention.

(2) An order under subsection (1), while in force, is conclusive evidence that the State or territory specified in it is a party to the New York Convention.

(3) Subsections (1) and (2) do not affect any other method of proving that a State or territory is a party to the New York Convention.

Section 91 — Saving of Rights to Enforce Convention awards

This Division does not affect any right to enforce or rely on a Convention award otherwise than under this Division.

Division 3. Enforcement of Mainland Awards

Section 92 — Enforcement of Mainland Awards

(1) A Mainland award is, subject to this Division, enforceable in Hong Kong either

(a) by action in the Court; or

(b) in the same manner as an award to which section 84 applies, and that section applies to a Mainland award accordingly as if a reference in that section to an award were a Mainland award. (Amended 7 of 2013 s. 14)

(2) A Mainland award which is enforceable as mentioned in subsection (1) is to be treated as binding for all purposes on the parties, and may accordingly be relied on by any of them by way of defence, set off or otherwise in any legal proceedings in Hong Kong. (Replaced 7 of 2013 s. 14)

(3) A reference in this Division to enforcement of a Mainland award is to be construed as including reliance on a Mainland award.

Section 93 — Restrictions on Enforcement of Mainland Awards

(1) A Mainland award is not, subject to subsection (2), enforceable under this Division if an application has been made on the Mainland for enforcement of the award.

(2) If a Mainland award is not fully satisfied by way of enforcement proceedings taken in the Mainland, or in any other place other than Hong Kong, that part of the award which is not satisfied in those proceedings is enforceable under this Division. (Replaced 7 of 2013 s. 15)

Section 94 — Evidence to be Produced for Enforcement of Mainland Awards

The party seeking to enforce a Mainland award must produce

(a) the duly authenticated original award or a duly certified copy of it;

(b) the original arbitration agreement or a duly certified copy of it; and

(c) if the award or agreement is not in either or both of the official languages, a translation of it in either official language certified by an official or sworn translator or by a diplomatic or consular agent. (Replaced 7 of 2013 s. 16)

Section 95 — Refusal of Enforcement of Mainland Awards

(1) Enforcement of a Mainland award may not be refused except as mentioned in this section. (Amended 7 of 2013 s. 17)

(2) Enforcement of a Mainland award may be refused if the person against whom it is invoked proves

(a) that a party to the arbitration agreement was under some incapacity (under the law applicable to that party); (Replaced 7 of 2013 s. 17)

(b) that the arbitration agreement was not valid

(i) under the law to which the parties subjected it; or

(ii) (if there was no indication of the law to which the arbitration agreement was subjected) under the law of the Mainland;

(c) that the person

(i) was not given proper notice of the appointment of the arbitrator or of the arbitral proceedings; or

(ii) was otherwise unable to present the person's case;

(d) subject to subsection (4), that the award

(i) deals with a difference not contemplated by or not falling within the terms of the submission to arbitration; or

(ii) contains decisions on matters beyond the scope of the submission to arbitration;

(e) that the composition of the arbitral authority or the arbitral procedure was not in accordance with

(i) the agreement of the parties; or

(ii) (if there was no agreement) the law of the Mainland; or

(f) that the award

(i) has not yet become binding on the parties; or

(ii) has been set aside or suspended by a competent authority of the Mainland or under the law of the Mainland.

(3) Enforcement of a Mainland award may also be refused if

(a) the award is in respect of a matter which is not capable of settlement by arbitration under the law of Hong Kong; or

(b) it would be contrary to public policy to enforce the award.

(4) If a Mainland award contains, apart from decisions on matters submitted to arbitration (*arbitral decisions*), decisions on matters not submitted to arbitration (*unrelated decisions*), the award may be enforced only in so far as it relates to the arbitral decisions that can be separated from the unrelated decisions. (Replaced 7 of 2013 s. 17)

Section 96 — Mainland Awards to Which Certain Provisions of This Division do not Apply

(1) Subject to subsection (2), this Division has effect with respect to the enforcement of Mainland awards.

(2) If

(a) a Mainland award was at any time before 1 July 1997 a Convention award within the meaning of Part IV of the repealed Ordinance as then in force; and

(b) the enforcement of that award had been refused at any time before the commencement of section 5 of the Arbitration (Amendment) Ordinance 2000 (2 of 2000) under section 44 of the repealed Ordinance as then in force,

then sections 92 to 95 have no effect with respect to the enforcement of that award.

Section 97 — Publication of List of Recognized Mainland Arbitral Authorities

(1) The Secretary for Justice must, by notice in the Gazette, publish a list of recognized Mainland arbitral authorities supplied from time to time to the Government by the Legislative Affairs Office of the State Council of the People's Republic of China through the Hong Kong and Macao Affairs Office of the State Council.

(2) A list published under subsection (1) is not subsidiary legislation.

Section 98 — Saving of Certain Mainland Awards

Despite the fact that enforcement of a Mainland award had been refused in Hong Kong at any time during the period between 1 July 1997 and the commencement of section 5 of the Arbitration (Amendment) Ordinance 2000 (2 of 2000) under the repealed Ordinance as then in force, the award is, subject to section 96(2), enforceable under this Division as if enforcement of the award had not previously been so refused.

Division 4. Enforcement of Macao Awards

Section 98A — Enforcement of Macao Awards

(1) A Macao award is, subject to this Division, enforceable in Hong Kong

either
(a) by action in the Court; or
(b) in the same manner as an award to which section 84 applies, and that section applies to a Macao award accordingly as if a reference in that section to an award were a Macao award.
(2) A Macao award which is enforceable as mentioned in subsection (1) is to be treated as binding for all purposes on the parties, and may accordingly be relied on by any of them by way of defence, set off or otherwise in any legal proceedings in Hong Kong.
(3) A reference in this Division to enforcement of a Macao award is to be construed as including reliance on a Macao award.

Section 98B — Enforcement of Macao Awards Partially Satisfied

If a Macao award is not fully satisfied by way of enforcement proceedings taken in Macao, or in any other place other than Hong Kong, that part of the award which is not satisfied in those proceedings is enforceable under this Division.

Section 98C — Evidence to be Produced for Enforcement of Macao Awards

The party seeking to enforce a Macao award must produce
(a) the duly authenticated original award or a duly certified copy of it;
(b) the original arbitration agreement or a duly certified copy of it; and
(c) if the award or agreement is not in either or both of the official languages, a translation of it in either official language certified by an official or sworn translator or by a diplomatic or consular agent.

Section 98D — Refusal of Enforcement of Macao Awards

(1) Enforcement of a Macao award may not be refused except as mentioned in this section.
(2) Enforcement of a Macao award may be refused if the person against whom it is invoked proves
(a) that a party to the arbitration agreement was under some incapacity (under the law applicable to that party);
(b) that the arbitration agreement was not valid
(i) under the law to which the parties subjected it; or
(ii) (if there was no indication of the law to which the arbitration agreement was subjected) under the law of Macao;
(c) that the person
(i) was not given proper notice of the appointment of the arbitrator or of the arbitral proceedings; or
(ii) was otherwise unable to present the person's case;

(d) subject to subsection (4), that the award
(i) deals with a difference not contemplated by or not falling within the terms of the submission to arbitration; or
(ii) contains decisions on matters beyond the scope of the submission to arbitration;
(e) that the composition of the arbitral authority or the arbitral procedure was not in accordance with
(i) the agreement of the parties; or
(ii) (if there was no agreement) the law of Macao; or
(f) that the award
(i) has not yet become binding on the parties; or
(ii) has been set aside or suspended by a competent authority of Macao or under the law of Macao.
(3) Enforcement of a Macao award may also be refused if
(a) the award is in respect of a matter which is not capable of settlement by arbitration under the law of Hong Kong; or
(b) it would be contrary to public policy to enforce the award.
(4) If a Macao award contains, apart from decisions on matters submitted to arbitration (arbitral decisions), decisions on matters not submitted to arbitration (unrelated decisions), the award may be enforced only in so far as it relates to the arbitral decisions that can be separated from the unrelated decisions.
(5) If an application for setting aside or suspending a Macao award has been made to a competent authority as mentioned in subsection (2)(f), the court before which enforcement of the award is sought
(a) may, if it thinks fit, adjourn the proceedings for the enforcement of the award; and
(b) may, on the application of the party seeking to enforce the award, order the person against whom the enforcement is invoked to give security.
(6) A decision or order of the court under subsection (5) is not subject to appeal.

Part 11

Provisions That May be Expressly Opted for or Automatically Apply

Section 99 — Arbitration Agreements May Provide Expressly for Opt-in Provisions

An arbitration agreement may provide expressly that any or all of the following provisions are to apply
(a) section 1 of Schedule 2;
(b) section 2 of Schedule 2;

(c) section 3 of Schedule 2;
(d) sections 4 and 7 of Schedule 2;
(e) sections 5, 6 and 7 of Schedule 2.

Section 100 — Opt-in Provisions Automatically Apply in Certain Cases

All the provisions in Schedule 2 apply, subject to section 102, to

(a) an arbitration agreement entered into before the commencement of this Ordinance which has provided that arbitration under the agreement is a domestic arbitration; or

(b) an arbitration agreement entered into at any time within a period of 6 years after the commencement of this Ordinance which provides that arbitration under the agreement is a domestic arbitration.

Section 101 — Opt-in Provisions that Automatically Apply Under Section 100 Deemed to Apply to Hong Kong Construction Subcontracting Cases

(1) If

(a) all the provisions in Schedule 2 apply under section 100(a) or (b) to an arbitration agreement, in any form referred to in section 19, included in a construction contract;

(b) the whole or any part of the construction operations to be carried out under the construction contract ("relevant operation") is subcontracted to any person under another construction contract ("subcontract"); and

(c) that subcontract also includes an arbitration agreement ("subcontracting parties' arbitration agreement") in any form referred to in section 19, then all the provisions in Schedule 2 also apply, subject to section 102, to the subcontracting parties' arbitration agreement.

(2) Unless the subcontracting parties' arbitration agreement is an arbitration agreement referred to in section 100(a) or (b), subsection (1) does not apply if

(a) the person to whom the whole or any part of the relevant operation is subcontracted under the subcontract is

(i) a natural person who is ordinarily resident outside Hong Kong;

(ii) a body corporate

(A) incorporated under the law of a place outside Hong Kong; or

(B) the central management and control of which is exercised outside Hong Kong; or

(iii) an association

(A) formed under the law of a place outside Hong Kong; or

(B) the central management and control of which is exercised outside Hong Kong;

(b) the person to whom the whole or any part of the relevant operation is subcontracted under the subcontract has no place of business in Hong Kong; or

(c) a substantial part of the relevant operation which is subcontracted under the subcontract is to be performed outside Hong Kong.

(3) If

(a) all the provisions in Schedule 2 apply to a subcontracting parties' arbitration agreement under subsection (1);

(b) the whole or any part of the relevant operation that is subcontracted under the subcontract is further subcontracted to another person under a further construction contract ("further subcontract"); and

(c) that further subcontract also includes an arbitration agreement in any form referred to in section 19, subsection (1) has effect subject to subsection (2), and all the provisions in Schedule 2 apply, subject to section 102, to the arbitration agreement so included in that further subcontract as if that further subcontract were a subcontract under subsection (1).

(4) In this section

"construction contract" (建造合約) has the meaning given to it by section 2 (1) of the Construction Industry Council Ordinance (Cap 587);

"construction operations" (建造工程) has the meaning given to it by Schedule 1 to the Construction Industry Council Ordinance (Cap 587).

Section 102 — Circumstances Under Which Opt-in Provisions not Automatically Apply

Sections 100 and 101 do not apply if

(a) the parties to the arbitration agreement concerned so agree in writing; or

(b) the arbitration agreement concerned has provided expressly that

(i) section 100 or 101 does not apply; or

(ii) any of the provisions in Schedule 2 applies or does not apply.

Section 103 — Application of Provisions Under this Part

If there is any conflict or inconsistency between any provision that applies under this Part and any other provision of this Ordinance, the first-mentioned provision prevails, to the extent of the conflict or inconsistency, over that other provision.

Part 12

Miscellaneous

Section 104 — Arbitral Tribunal or Mediator to be Liable for Certain Acts and Omissions

(1) An arbitral tribunal or mediator is liable in law for an act done or omitted to be done by

(a) the tribunal or mediator; or

(b) an employee or agent of the tribunal or mediator,

in relation to the exercise or performance, or the purported exercise or performance, of the tribunal's arbitral functions or the mediator's functions only if it is proved that the act was done or omitted to be done dishonestly.

(2) An employee or agent of an arbitral tribunal or mediator is liable in law for an act done or omitted to be done by the employee or agent in relation to the exercise or performance, or the purported exercise or performance, of the tribunal's arbitral functions or the mediator's functions only if it is proved that the act was done or omitted to be done dishonestly.

(3) In this section, "mediator" (調解員) means a mediator appointed under section 32 or referred to in section 33.

Section 105 — Appointors and Administrators to be Liable Only for Certain Acts and Omissions

(1) A person

(a) who appoints an arbitral tribunal or mediator; or

(b) who exercises or performs any other function of an administrative nature in connection with arbitral or mediation proceedings, is liable in law for the consequences of doing or omitting to do an act in the exercise or performance, or the purported exercise or performance, of the function only if it is proved that the act was done or omitted to be done dishonestly.

(2) Subsection (1) does not apply to an act done or omitted to be done by

(a) a party to the arbitral or mediation proceedings; or

(b) a legal representative or adviser of the party,

in the exercise performance, or the purported exercise or performance, of a function of an administrative nature in connection with those proceedings.

(3) An employee or agent of a person who has done or omitted to do an act referred to in subsection (1) is liable in law for the consequence of the act done or omission made only if it is proved that

(a) the act was done or omission was made dishonestly; and

(b) the employee or agent was a party to the dishonesty.

(4) Neither a person referred to in subsection (1) nor an employee or agent of the person is liable in law for the consequences of any act done or omission made by

(a) the arbitral tribunal or mediator concerned; or

(b) an employee or agent of the tribunal or mediator, in the exercise or performance, or the purported exercise or performance, of the tribunal's arbitral functions or the mediator's functions merely because the person, employee or agent has exercised or performed a function referred to in that subsection.

(5) In this section

"appoint" (委任) includes nominate and designate;

"mediator" (調解員) has the same meaning as in section 104, and "mediation proceedings" (調解程序) is to be construed accordingly.

Section 106 — Rules of Court

(1) The power to make rules of court under section 54 (Rules of court) of the High Court Ordinance (Cap 4) includes power to make rules of court for

(a) the making of an application for an interim measure under section 45(2) or an order under section 60(1); or

(b) the service out of the jurisdiction of an application for the interim measure or order.

(2) Any rules made by virtue of this section may include the incidental, supplementary and consequential provisions that the authority making the rules considers necessary or expedient.

Section 107 — Making an Application, etc. under This Ordinance

An application, request or appeal to the court under this Ordinance is, unless otherwise expressed, to be made in accordance with the Rules of the High Court (Cap 4 sub. leg. A).

Section 108 — Decision, etc. of Court under This Ordinance

A decision, determination, direction or award of the Court under this Ordinance is to be treated as a judgment of the Court for the purposes of section 14 (Appeals in civil matters) of the High Court Ordinance (Cap 4).

Part 13

Repeal, Savings and Transitional Provisions

Section 109 — (Omitted as spent)

(Omitted as spent)

Section 110 — Effect of Repeal on Subsidiary Legislation

Any subsidiary legislation made under the repealed Ordinance and in force at the commencement of this Ordinance, so far as it is not inconsistent with this Ordinance, continues in force and has the like effect for all purposes as if made under this Ordinance.

Section 111 — Savings and Transitional Provisions

Schedule 3 provides for the savings and transitional arrangements that apply on, or relate to, the commencement of this Ordinance.

Part 14

Consequential and Related Amendments

Section 112 — (Omitted as spent)

(Omitted as spent)

SCHEDULES

Schedule 1

UNCITRAL Model Law *

Schedule 2

Provisions That May be Expressly Opted for or Automatically Apply

1 — Sole Arbitrator

Despite section 23, any dispute arising between the parties to an arbitration agreement is to be submitted to a sole arbitrator for arbitration.

2 — Consolidation of Arbitrations

(1) If, in relation to 2 or more arbitral proceedings, it appears to the Court

(a) that a common question of law or fact arises in both or all of them;

(b) that the rights to relief claimed in those arbitral proceedings are in respect of or arise out of the same transaction or series of transactions; or

(c) that for any other reason it is desirable to make an order under this section,

the Court may, on the application of any party to those arbitral proceedings

(d) order those arbitral proceedings

(i) to be consolidated on such terms as it thinks just; or

(ii) to be heard at the same time or one immediately after another; or

(e) order any of those arbitral proceedings to be stayed until after the determination of any other of them.

(2) If the Court orders arbitral proceedings to be consolidated under subsection (1)(d)(i) or to be heard at the same time or one immediately after another under subsection (1)(d)(ii), the Court has the power

(a) to make consequential directions as to the payment of costs in those arbitral proceedings; and

(b) If

(i) all parties to those arbitral proceedings are in agreement as to the choice of arbitrator for those arbitral proceedings, to appoint that arbitrator; or

(ii) the parties cannot agree as to the choice of arbitrator for those arbitral proceedings, to appoint an arbitrator for those arbitral proceedings (and, in the case of arbitral proceedings to be heard at the same time or one immediately after another, to appoint the same arbitrator for those arbitral proceedings).

(3) If the Court makes an appointment of an arbitrator under subsection (2) for the arbitral proceedings to be consolidated or to be heard at the same time or one immediately after another, any appointment of any other arbitrator that has been made for any of those arbitral proceedings ceases to have effect for all purposes on and from the appointment under subsection

---

* See UNCITRAL Model Law on International Commercial Arbitration, pp. 643-659.

(2).
(4) The arbitral tribunal hearing the arbitral proceedings that are consolidated under subsection (1)(d)(i) has the power under sections 74 and 75 in relation to the costs of those arbitral proceedings.
(5) If 2 or more arbitral proceedings are heard at the same time or one immediately after another under subsection (1)(d)(ii), the arbitral tribunal
(a) has the power under sections 74 and 75 only in relation to the costs of those arbitral proceedings that are heard by it; and
(b) accordingly, does not have the power to order a party to any of those arbitral proceedings that are heard at the same time or one immediately after another to pay the costs of a party to any other of those proceedings unless the arbitral tribunal is the same tribunal hearing all of those arbitral proceedings.
(6) An order, direction or decision of the Court under this section is not subject to appeal.

3 — Decision of Preliminary Question of Law by Court

(1) The Court may, on the application of any party to arbitral proceedings, decide any question of law arising in the course of the arbitral proceedings.
(2) An application under subsection (1) may not be made except
(a) with the agreement in writing of all the other parties to the arbitral proceedings; or
(b) with the permission in writing of the arbitral tribunal.
(3) The application must
(a) identify the question of law to be decided; and
(b) state the grounds on which it is said that the question should be decided by the Court.
(4) The Court must not entertain an application under subsection (1) unless it is satisfied that the decision of the question of law might produce substantial savings in costs to the parties.
(5) The leave of the Court or the Court of Appeal is required for any appeal from a decision of the Court under subsection (1).

4 — Challenging Arbitral Award on Ground of Serious Irregularity

(1) A party to arbitral proceedings may apply to the Court challenging an award in the arbitral proceedings on the ground of serious irregularity affecting the tribunal, the arbitral proceedings or the award.
(2) Serious irregularity means an irregularity of one or more of the following kinds which the Court considers has caused or will cause substantial injustice to the applicant
(a) failure by the arbitral tribunal to comply with section 46;

(b) the arbitral tribunal exceeding its powers (otherwise than by exceeding its jurisdiction);
(c) failure by the arbitral tribunal to conduct the arbitral proceedings in accordance with the procedure agreed by the parties;
(d) failure by the arbitral tribunal to deal with all the issues that were put to it;
(e) any arbitral or other institution or person vested by the parties with powers in relation to the arbitral proceedings or the award exceeding its powers;
(f) failure by the arbitral tribunal to give, under section 69, an interpretation of the award the effect of which is uncertain or ambiguous;
(g) the award being obtained by fraud, or the award or the way in which it was procured being contrary to public policy;
(h) failure to comply with the requirements as to the form of the award; or
(i) any irregularity in the conduct of the arbitral proceedings, or in the award which is admitted by the arbitral tribunal or by any arbitral or other institution or person vested by the parties with powers in relation to the arbitral proceedings or the award.
(3) If there is shown to be serious irregularity affecting the arbitral tribunal, the arbitral proceedings or the award, the Court may by order
(a) remit the award to the arbitral tribunal, in whole or in part, for reconsideration;
(b) set aside the award, in whole or in part; or
(c) declare the award to be of no effect, in whole or in part.
(4) If the award is remitted to the arbitral tribunal, in whole or in part, for reconsideration, the tribunal must make a fresh award in respect of the matters remitted
(a) within 3 months of the date of the order for remission; or
(b) within a longer or shorter period that the Court may direct.
(5) The Court must not exercise its power to set aside an award or to declare an award to be of no effect, in whole or in part, unless it is satisfied that itwould be inappropriate to remit the matters in question to the arbitral tribunal for reconsideration.
(6) The leave of the Court or the Court of Appeal is required for any appeal from a decision, order or direction of the Court under this section.
(7) Section 7 of this Schedule also applies to an application or appeal under this section.

5 — Appeal Against Arbitral Award on Question of Law

(1) Subject to section 6 of this Schedule, a party to arbitral proceedings may

appeal to the Court on a question of law arising out of an award made in the arbitral proceedings.
(2) An agreement to dispense with the reasons for an arbitral tribunal's award is to be treated as an agreement to exclude the Court's jurisdiction under this section.
(3) The Court must decide the question of law which is the subject of the appeal on the basis of the findings of fact in the award.
(4) The Court must not consider any of the criteria set out in section 6(4)(c) (i) or (ii) of this Schedule when it decides the question of law under subsection (3).
(5) On hearing an appeal under this section, the Court may by order
(a) confirm the award;
(b) vary the award;
(c) remit the award to the arbitral tribunal, in whole or in part, for reconsideration in the light of the Court's decision; or
(d) set aside the award, in whole or in part.
(6) If the award is remitted to the arbitral tribunal, in whole or in part, for reconsideration, the tribunal must make a fresh award in respect of the matters remitted
(a) within 3 months of the date of the order for remission; or
(b) within a longer or shorter period that the Court may direct.
(7) The Court must not exercise its power to set aside an award, in whole or in part, unless it is satisfied that it would be inappropriate to remit the matters in question to the arbitral tribunal for reconsideration.
(8) The leave of the Court or the Court of Appeal is required for any further appeal from an order of the Court under subsection (5).
(9) Leave to further appeal must not be granted unless
(a) the question is one of general importance; or
(b) the question is one which, for some other special reason, should be considered by the Court of Appeal.
(10) Sections 6 and 7 of this Schedule also apply to an appeal or further appeal under this section.

6 — Application for Leave to Appeal Against Arbitral Award on Question of Law

(1) An appeal under section 5 of this Schedule on a question of law may not be brought by a party to arbitral proceedings except
(a) with the agreement of all the other parties to the arbitral proceedings; or
(b) with the leave of the Court.
(2) An application for leave to appeal must

(a) identify the question of law to be decided; and
(b) state the grounds on which it is said that leave to appeal should be granted.
(3) The Court must determine an application for leave to appeal without a hearing unless it appears to the Court that a hearing is required.
(4) Leave to appeal is to be granted only if the Court is satisfied
(a) that the decision of the question will substantially affect the rights of one or more of the parties;
(b) that the question is one which the arbitral tribunal was asked to decide; and
(c) that, on the basis of the findings of fact in the award
(i) the decision of the arbitral tribunal on the question is obviously wrong; or
(ii) the question is one of general importance and the decision of the arbitral tribunal is at least open to serious doubt.
(5) The leave of the Court or the Court of Appeal is required for any appeal from a decision of the Court to grant or refuse leave to appeal.
(6) Leave to appeal from such a decision of the Court must not be granted unless
(a) the question is one of general importance; or
(b) the question is one which, for some other special reason, should be considered by the Court.

7 — Supplementary Provisions on Challenge to or Appeal Against Arbitral Award

(1) An application or appeal under section 4, 5 or 6 of this Schedule may not be brought if the applicant or appellant has not first exhausted
(a) any available recourse under section 69; and
(b) any available arbitral process of appeal or review.
(2) If, on an application or appeal, it appears to the Court that the award
(a) does not contain the arbitral tribunal's reasons for the award; or
(b) does not set out the arbitral tribunal's reasons for the award in sufficient detail to enable the Court properly to consider the application or appeal, the Court may order the tribunal to state the reasons for the award in sufficient detail for that purpose.
(3) If the Court makes an order under subsection (2), it may make a further order that it thinks fit with respect to any additional costs of the arbitration resulting from its order.
(4) The Court
(a) may order the applicant or appellant to give security for the costs of the

application or appeal; and
(b) may, if the order is not complied with, direct that the application or appeal is to be dismissed.
(5) The power to order security for costs must not be exercised only on the ground that the applicant or appellant is
(a) a natural person who is ordinarily resident outside Hong Kong;
(b) a body corporate
(i) incorporated under the law of a place outside Hong Kong; or
(ii) the central management and control of which is exercised outside Hong Kong; or
(c) an association
(i) formed under the law of a place outside Hong Kong; or
(ii) the central management and control of which is exercised outside Hong Kong.
(6) The Court
(a) may order that any money payable under the award is to be paid into the Court or otherwise secured pending the determination of the application or appeal; and
(b) may, if the order is not complied with, direct that the application or appeal is to be dismissed.
(7) The Court or the Court of Appeal may impose conditions to the same or similar effect as an order under subsection (4) or (6) on granting leave to appeal under section 4, 5 or 6 of this Schedule.
(8) Subsection (7) does not affect the general discretion of the Court or the Court of Appeal to grant leave subject to conditions.
(9) An order, direction or decision of the Court or the Court of Appeal under this section is not subject to appeal.

Schedule 3

Savings and Transitional Provisions

1 — Conduct of Arbitral and Related Proceedings

(1) If an arbitration
(a) has commenced under article 21 of the UNCITRAL Model Law as defined in section 2(1) of the repealed Ordinance before the commencement of this Ordinance; or
(b) has been deemed to be commenced under section 31(1) of the repealed Ordinance before the commencement of this Ordinance,
that arbitration and all related proceedings, including (where the award made in that arbitration has been set aside) arbitral proceedings resumed after the setting aside of the award, are to be governed by the repealed

Ordinance as if this Ordinance had not been enacted.

(2) If an arbitration has commenced under any other Ordinance amended by this Ordinance before the commencement of this Ordinance, that arbitration and all related proceedings, including (where the award made in that arbitration has been set aside) arbitral proceedings resumed after the setting aside of the award, are to be governed by that other Ordinance in force immediately before the commencement of this Ordinance as if this Ordinance had not been enacted.

2 — Appointment of Arbitrators

(1) Subject to subsection (2), the appointment of an arbitrator made before the commencement of this Ordinance is, after the commencement of this Ordinance, to continue to have effect as if this Ordinance had not been enacted.

(2) The enactment of this Ordinance does not revive the appointment of any arbitrator whose mandate has terminated before the commencement of this Ordinance.

3 — Settlement Agreements

If the parties to an arbitration agreement have entered into a settlement agreement under section 2C of the repealed Ordinance before the commencement of this Ordinance, that settlement agreement may be enforced in accordance with that section as if this Ordinance had not been enacted.

4 — Appointment of Members of the Appointment Advisory Board

The appointment of a member of the Appointment Advisory Board established under rule 3 of the Arbitration (Appointment of Arbitrators and Umpires) Rules (Cap 341 sub. leg. B)* made before the commencement of this Ordinance is, after the commencement of this Ordinance, to continue to have effect until the expiry of the term of that appointment as if this Ordinance had not been enacted.

Schedule 4

Omitted as spent

---

* Now Cap 609 sub. leg. B.

HONG KONG INTERNATIONAL ARBITRATION CENTRE ADMINISTERED ARBITRATION RULES *

Section I General Rules

Article 1 — Scope of Application

1.1 These Rules shall govern arbitrations where an arbitration agreement (whether entered into before or after a dispute has arisen) either: (a) provides for these Rules to apply; or (b) subject to Articles 1.2 and 1.3 below, provides for arbitration "administered by HKIAC" or words to similar effect.

1.2 Nothing in these Rules shall prevent parties to a dispute or arbitration agreement from naming HKIAC as appointing authority, or from requesting certain administrative services from HKIAC, without subjecting the arbitration to the provisions contained in these Rules. For the avoidance of doubt, these Rules shall not govern arbitrations where an arbitration agreement provides for arbitration under other rules, including other rules adopted by HKIAC from time to time.

1.3 Subject to Article 1.4, these Rules shall come into force on 1 November 2013 and, unless the parties have agreed otherwise, shall apply to all arbitrations falling within Article 1.1 in which the Notice of Arbitration is submitted on or after that date.

1.4 The provisions contained in Articles 23.1, 28, 29 and Schedule 4 shall not apply if the arbitration agreement was concluded before the date on which these Rules came into force, unless otherwise agreed by the parties.

Article 2 — Notices and Calculation of Periods of Time

2.1 Any notice or other written communication pursuant to these Rules shall be deemed to be received by a party or arbitrator or by HKIAC if:

(a) delivered by hand, registered post or courier service to

(i) the address of the addressee or its representative as notified in writing in the arbitration; or

(ii) in the absence of (i), to the address specified in any applicable agreement between the relevant parties; or

(iii) in the absence of (i) or (ii), to any address which the addressee holds out to the world at the time of such delivery; or

(iv) in the absence of (i), (ii) or (iii), to any last known address of the addressee; or

(b) transmitted by facsimile, email or any other means of telecommunication that provides a record of its transmission, including the time and date, to:

(i) the facsimile number or email address (or equivalent) of that person or its representative as notified in the arbitration;

or

* For a commentary on the HKIAC Arbitration Rules, see Michael J. Moser and Chiann Bao, *Guide to the HKIAC Arbitration Rules* (Oxford University Press, 2015) (forthcoming).

(ii) in the absence of (i), to the facsimile number or email address (or equivalent) specified in any applicable agreement between the relevant parties; or
(iii) in the absence of (i) and (ii), to any facsimile number or email address (or equivalent) which the addressee holds out to the world at the time of such transmission.
2.2 Any such notice or written communication shall be deemed to be received on the earliest day when it is delivered pursuant to paragraph (a) above or transmitted pursuant to paragraph (b) above. For this purpose, the date shall be determined according to the local time at the place of receipt. Where such notice or written communication is being delivered or transmitted to more than one party, or more than one arbitrator, such notice or written communication shall be deemed to be received when it is delivered or transmitted pursuant to paragraph (a) or (b) above to the last intended recipient.
2.3 For the purposes of calculating a period of time under these Rules, such period shall begin to run on the day following the day when a notice, notification, communication or proposal is received or deemed to be received. If the last day of such period is an official holiday or a non-business day at the place of receipt, the period shall be extended until the first business day which follows. Official holidays or non-business days occurring during the running of the period of time shall be included in calculating the period.
2.4 If the circumstances of the case so justify, HKIAC may amend the time limits provided for in these Rules, as well as any time limits that it has set. HKIAC shall not amend any time limits set by the arbitral tribunal unless it directs otherwise.

Article 3 — Interpretation of Rules

3.1 HKIAC shall have the power to interpret all provisions of these Rules. The arbitral tribunal shall interpret the Rules insofar as they relate to its powers and duties hereunder. In the event of any inconsistency between such interpretation and any interpretation by HKIAC, the arbitral tribunal's interpretation shall prevail.
3.2 HKIAC has no obligation to give reasons for any decision it makes in respect of any arbitration commenced under these Rules. All decisions made by HKIAC under these Rules are final and, to the extent permitted by any applicable law, not subject to appeal.
3.3 References in the Rules to "HKIAC" are to the Council of HKIAC or any committee, sub-committee or other body or person specifically

designated by it to perform the functions referred to herein, or, where applicable, to the Secretary General of HKIAC for the time being and other staff members of the Secretariat of HKIAC.

3.4 References in the Rules to "Claimant" include one or more claimants and references to "Respondent" include one or more respondents.

3.5 References to "additional party" include one or more additional parties and references to "party" or "parties" include claimants, respondents or additional parties.

3.6 References in the Rules to the "arbitral tribunal" include one or more arbitrators. Such references do not include an Emergency Arbitrator as defined at paragraph 1 of Schedule 4.

3.7 References in the Rules to "witness" include one or more witnesses and references to "expert" include one or more experts.

3.8 References in the Rules to "claim" or "counterclaim" include any claim or claims by any party against any other party. References to "defence" include any defence or defences by any party to any claim or counterclaim submitted by any other party, including any defence for the purpose of a set-off.

3.9 References in the Rules to "award" include, inter alia, an interim, interlocutory, partial or final award, save for any award made by an Emergency Arbitrator as referred to in Schedule 4.

3.10 References in the Rules to the "seat" of arbitration shall mean the place of arbitration as referred to in Article 20.1 of the UNCITRAL Model Law on International Commercial Arbitration as adopted on 21 June 1985 and as amended on 7 July 2006.

3.11 These Rules include all Schedules attached thereto as amended from time to time by HKIAC, in force on the date the Notice of Arbitration is submitted.

3.12 HKIAC may from time to time issue practice notes to supplement, regulate and implement these Rules for the purpose of facilitating the administration of arbitrations governed by these Rules.

3.13 English is the original language of these Rules. In the event of any discrepancy or inconsistency between the English version and the version in any other language, the English version shall prevail.

Section II Commencement of the Arbitration

Article 4 — Notice of Arbitration

4.1 The party initiating recourse to arbitration (hereinafter called the "Claimant") shall submit a Notice of Arbitration in writing to HKIAC at its address, facsimile number or email address.

4.2 An arbitration shall be deemed to commence on the date on which a copy of the Notice of Arbitration is received by HKIAC. For the avoidance of doubt, this date shall be determined in accordance with the provisions of Articles 2.1 and 2.2.
4.3 The Notice of Arbitration shall include the following:
(a) a demand that the dispute be referred to arbitration;
(b) the names and (in so far as known) the addresses, telephone and facsimile numbers, and email addresses of the parties and of their counsel;
(c) a copy of the arbitration agreement(s) invoked;
(d) a reference to the contract(s) or other legal instrument(s) out of or in relation to which the dispute arises;
(e) a description of the general nature of the claim and an indication of the amount involved, if any;
(f) the relief or remedy sought;
(g) a proposal as to the number of arbitrators (i.e. one or three), if the parties have not previously agreed thereon;
(h) the Claimant's proposal regarding the designation of a sole arbitrator under Article 7, or the Claimant's designation of an arbitrator under Article 8; and
(i) confirmation that copies of the Notice of Arbitration and any exhibits included therewith have been or are being served simultaneously on all other parties (hereinafter called the "Respondent") by one or more means of service to be identified in such confirmation.
4.4 The Notice of Arbitration shall be accompanied by payment, by cheque or transfer to the account of HKIAC, of the Registration Fee as required by Schedule 1.
4.5 The Notice of Arbitration shall be submitted in the language of the arbitration as agreed by the parties. If no agreement has been reached between the parties, the Notice of Arbitration shall be submitted in either English or Chinese.
4.6 The Notice of Arbitration may also include the Statement of Claim referred to in Article 16.
4.7 If the Notice of Arbitration is incomplete or if the Registration Fee is not paid, HKIAC may request the Claimant to remedy the defect within an appropriate period of time. If the Claimant complies with such directions within the applicable time limit, the arbitration shall be deemed to have commenced under Article 4.2 on the date the initial version was received by HKIAC. If the Claimant fails to comply, the Notice of Arbitration shall be deemed not to have been validly submitted and the arbitration shall be

deemed not to have commenced under Article 4.2 without prejudice to the Claimant's right to submit the same claim at a later date in a subsequent Notice of Arbitration.

4.8 The Claimant shall notify and lodge documentary verification with HKIAC of the date of receipt by the Respondent of the Notice of Arbitration and any exhibits included therewith.

Article 5 — Answer to the Notice of Arbitration

5.1 Within 30 days from receipt of the Notice of Arbitration, the Respondent shall submit to HKIAC an Answer to the Notice of Arbitration. This Answer to the Notice of Arbitration shall include the following:

(a) the name, address, telephone and facsimile numbers, and email address of the Respondent and of its counsel (if different from the description contained in the Notice of Arbitration);

(b) any plea that an arbitral tribunal constituted under these Rules lacks jurisdiction;

(c) the Respondent's comments on the particulars set forth in the Notice of Arbitration, pursuant to Article 4.3(e);

(d) the Respondent's answer to the relief or remedy sought in the Notice of Arbitration, pursuant to Article 4.3(f);

(e) the Respondent's proposal as to the number of arbitrators (i.e. one or three), if the parties have not previously agreed thereon;

(f) the parties' joint designation of a sole arbitrator under Article 7 or the Respondent's designation of an arbitrator under Article 8; and

(g) confirmation that copies of the Answer to the Notice of Arbitration and any exhibits included therewith have been or are being served simultaneously on all other parties to the arbitration by one or more means of service to be identified in such confirmation.

5.2 The Answer to the Notice of Arbitration shall be submitted in the language of the arbitration as agreed by the parties. If no agreement has been reached between the parties, the Answer to the Notice of Arbitration shall be submitted in either English or Chinese.

5.3 The Answer to the Notice of Arbitration may also include the Statement of Defence referred to in Article 17, if the Notice of Arbitration contained the Statement of Claim referred to in Article 16.

5.4 Any counterclaim or set-off defence shall to the extent possible be raised with the Respondent's Answer to the Notice of Arbitration, which should include in relation to any such counterclaim or set-off defence:

(a) a reference to the contract(s) or other legal instrument(s) out of or in relation to which it arises;

(b) a description of the general nature of the counterclaim and/or set-off defence and an indication of the amount involved, if any;
(c) the relief or remedy sought.
5.5 If no counterclaim or set-off defence is raised with the Respondent's Answer to the Notice of Arbitration, or if there is no indication of the amount of the counterclaim or set-off, HKIAC shall rely upon the information provided by the Claimant pursuant to Article 4.3(e) for its determination of:
(a) HKIAC's Administrative Fees referred to in Article 33.1(f) and Schedule 1;
(b) the arbitral tribunal's fees (where Article 10.1(b) and Schedule 3 applies); and
(c) whether the provisions of Article 41 (the "Expedited Procedure") may be applicable.
5.6 Once the Registration Fee has been paid and the arbitral tribunal has been confirmed, HKIAC shall transmit the file to the arbitral tribunal.

Section III The Arbitral Tribunal

Article 6 — Number of Arbitrators

6.1 If the parties have not agreed upon the number of arbitrators, HKIAC shall decide whether the case shall be referred to a sole arbitrator or to three arbitrators, taking into account the circumstances of the case.
6.2 Where a case is handled under an Expedited Procedure in accordance with Article 41, the provisions of Article 41.2(a) and (b) shall apply.

Article 7 — Appointment of a Sole Arbitrator

7.1 Unless the parties have agreed otherwise and subject to Articles 9, 10, 11.1 to 11.4:
(a) where the parties have agreed that the dispute shall be referred to a sole arbitrator, they shall jointly designate the sole arbitrator within 30 days from the date when the Notice of Arbitration was received by the Respondent;
(b) where the parties have not agreed upon the number of arbitrators and HKIAC has decided that the dispute shall be referred to a sole arbitrator, the parties shall jointly designate the sole arbitrator within 30 days from the date when HKIAC's decision was received by the last of them.
7.2 If the parties fail to designate the sole arbitrator within the applicable time limit, HKIAC shall appoint the sole arbitrator.

Article 8 — Appointment of Three Arbitrators

8.1 Where a dispute between two parties is referred to three arbitrators, the arbitral tribunal shall be constituted as follows unless the parties have agreed otherwise:

(a) where the parties have agreed that the dispute shall be referred to three arbitrators, each party shall designate, in the Notice of Arbitration and the Answer to the Notice of Arbitration, respectively, one arbitrator. If either party fails to designate an arbitrator, HKIAC shall appoint the arbitrator;
(b) where the parties have not agreed upon the number of arbitrators and HKIAC has decided that the dispute shall be referred to three arbitrators, the Claimant shall designate an arbitrator within 15 days from receipt of HKIAC's decision, and the Respondent shall designate an arbitrator within 15 days from receipt of notification of the Claimant's designation. If a party fails to designate an arbitrator, HKIAC shall appoint the arbitrator;
(c) the two arbitrators so appointed shall designate a third arbitrator who shall act as the presiding arbitrator of the arbitral tribunal. Failing such designation within 30 days from the confirmation of the second arbitrator, HKIAC shall appoint the presiding arbitrator.
8.2 Where there are more than two parties to the arbitration and the dispute is to be referred to three arbitrators, the arbitral tribunal shall be constituted as follows unless the parties have agreed otherwise:
(a) the Claimant or group of Claimants shall designate an arbitrator and the Respondent or group of Respondents shall designate an arbitrator in accordance with the procedure in Article 8.1(a) or (b), as applicable;
(b) if the parties have designated arbitrators in accordance with Article 8.2 (a), the procedure in Article 8.1(c) shall apply to the designation of the presiding arbitrator;
(c) In the event of any failure to designate arbitrators under Article 8.2(a) or if the parties do not all agree in writing that they represent two separate sides (as Claimant(s) and Respondent(s) respectively) for the purposes of designating arbitrators, HKIAC may appoint all members of the arbitral tribunal without regard to any party's designation.
8.3 Appointment of the arbitral tribunal pursuant to Article 8.1 or 8.2 shall be subject to Articles 9, 10 and 11.1 to 11.4.

Article 9 — Confirmation of the Arbitral Tribunal

9.1 All designations of any arbitrator, whether made by the parties or the arbitrators, are subject to confirmation by HKIAC, upon which the appointments shall become effective.
9.2 The designation of an arbitrator shall be confirmed on the terms of:
(a) Schedule 2; or
(b) Schedule 3;
as applicable, in accordance with Article 10 and subject to any variations agreed by all parties and any changes HKIAC considers appropriate.

Article 10 — Fees and Expenses of the Arbitral Tribunal

10.1 The fees and expenses of the arbitral tribunal shall be determined according to either:

(a) an hourly rate in accordance with Schedule 2, including the terms and conditions contained therein; or

(b) the schedule of fees based on the sum in dispute referred to in Schedule 3, including the terms and conditions contained therein.

The parties shall agree the method for determining the fees and expenses of the arbitral tribunal, and shall inform HKIAC of the applicable method within 30 days of the date on which the Respondent receives the Notice of Arbitration. If the parties fail to agree on the applicable method, the arbitral tribunal's fees and expenses shall be determined in accordance with the terms of Schedule 2.

10.2 Where the fees of the arbitral tribunal are to be determined in accordance with Schedule 2,

(a) the applicable rate for each co-arbitrator shall be the rate agreed between that co-arbitrator and the designating party;

(b) the applicable rate for a sole or presiding arbitrator shall be the rate agreed between that arbitrator and the parties,

subject to paragraphs 9.3 and 9.5 of Schedule 2. Where the parties fail to agree the rate of an arbitrator, HKIAC may determine the rate.

10.3 Where the fees of the arbitral tribunal are determined in conformity with Schedule 3, such fees shall be fixed by HKIAC in accordance with that Schedule and the following rules:

(a) the fees of the arbitral tribunal shall be reasonable in amount, taking into account the amount in dispute, the complexity of the subject-matter, the time spent by the arbitral tribunal and any secretary appointed under Article 13.4, and any other circumstances of the case, including, but not limited to, the discontinuation of the arbitration in case of settlement or for any other reason;

(b) where a case is referred to three arbitrators, HKIAC, at its discretion, shall have the right to increase the total fees up to a maximum which shall normally not exceed three times the fees of a sole arbitrator;

(c) the arbitral tribunal's fees may exceed the amounts calculated in accordance with Schedule 3 where in the opinion of HKIAC there are exceptional circumstances, which shall include but shall not be limited to the parties conducting the arbitration in a manner not reasonably contemplated by the arbitral tribunal at the time of appointment.

Article 11 — Qualifications and Challenge of the Arbitral Tribunal

11.1 An arbitral tribunal confirmed under these Rules shall be and remain at all times impartial and independent of the parties.

11.2 Subject to Article 11.3, as a general rule, where the parties to an arbitration under these Rules are of different nationalities, a sole arbitrator or the presiding arbitrator of an arbitral tribunal shall not have the same nationality as any party unless specifically agreed otherwise by all parties in writing.

11.3 Notwithstanding the general rule in Article 11.2, in appropriate circumstances and provided that none of the parties objects within a time limit set by HKIAC, the sole arbitrator or the presiding arbitrator of the arbitral tribunal may be of the same nationality as any of the parties.

11.4 Before confirmation, a prospective arbitrator shall (a) sign a statement confirming his or her availability to decide the dispute and his or her impartiality and independence; and (b) disclose any circumstances likely to give rise to justifiable doubts as to his or her impartiality or independence. An arbitrator, once confirmed and throughout the arbitration, shall disclose without delay any such circumstances to the parties unless they have already been informed by him or her of these circumstances.

11.5 No party or its representatives shall have any *ex parte* communication relating to the arbitration with any arbitrator, or with any candidate to be designated as arbitrator by a party, except to advise the candidate of the general nature of the dispute, to discuss the candidate's qualifications, availability, impartiality or independence, or to discuss the suitability of candidates for the designation of a third arbitrator, where the parties or party -designated arbitrators are to designate that arbitrator. No party or its representatives shall have any *ex parte* communication relating to the arbitration with any candidate for the presiding arbitrator.

11.6 Any arbitrator may be challenged if circumstances exist that give rise to justifiable doubts as to the arbitrator's impartiality or independence, or if the arbitrator does not possess qualifications agreed by the parties, or if the arbitrator becomes de jure or de facto unable to perform his or her functions or for other reasons fails to act without undue delay. A party may challenge the arbitrator designated by it or in whose appointment it has participated only for reasons of which it becomes aware after the designation has been made.

11.7 A party who intends to challenge an arbitrator shall send notice of its challenge within 15 days after the confirmation of that arbitrator has been notified to the challenging party or within 15 days after that party became aware or ought reasonably to have become aware of the circumstances mentioned in Article 11.6.

11.8 The challenge shall be notified to HKIAC, all other parties, the arbitrator who is challenged and the other members of the arbitral tribunal. The notification shall be in writing and shall state the reasons for the challenge.

11.9 Unless the arbitrator being challenged withdraws or the non-challenging party agrees to the challenge within 15 days from receipt of the notice of challenge, HKIAC shall decide on the challenge. Pending the determination of the challenge, the arbitral tribunal (including the challenged arbitrator) may continue the arbitration.

11.10 If an arbitrator withdraws or a party agrees to a challenge under Article 11.9, no acceptance of the validity of any ground referred to in Article 11.6 shall be implied.

Article 12 — Replacement of an Arbitrator

12.1 Subject to Articles 12.2, 27.11 and 28.6, where an arbitrator dies, has been successfully challenged, has been otherwise removed or has resigned, a substitute arbitrator shall be appointed pursuant to the rules that were applicable to the appointment of the arbitrator being replaced. These rules shall apply even if during the process of appointing the arbitrator being replaced, a party had failed to exercise its right to designate or to participate in the appointment.

12.2 If, at the request of a party, HKIAC determines that, in view of the exceptional circumstances of the case, it would be justified for a party to be deprived of its right to designate a substitute arbitrator, HKIAC may, after giving an opportunity to the parties and the remaining arbitrators to express their views:

(a) appoint the substitute arbitrator; or

(b) after the proceedings are declared closed under Article 30.1, authorise the other arbitrators to proceed with the arbitration and make any decision or award.

12.3 If an arbitrator is replaced, the arbitration shall resume at the stage where the arbitrator was replaced or ceased to perform his or her functions, unless the arbitral tribunal decides otherwise.

Section IV Conduct of Arbitration

Article 13 — General Provisions

13.1 Subject to these Rules, the arbitral tribunal shall adopt suitable procedures for the conduct of the arbitration in order to avoid unnecessary delay or expense, having regard to the complexity of the issues and the amount in dispute, and provided that such procedures ensure equal treatment of the parties and afford the parties a reasonable opportunity to present their case.

13.2 At an early stage of the arbitration and in consultation with the parties, the arbitral tribunal shall prepare a provisional timetable for the arbitration, which shall be provided to the parties and HKIAC.

13.3 Subject to Article 11.5, all documents or information supplied to the arbitral tribunal by one party shall at the same time be communicated by that party to the other parties and HKIAC.

13.4 The arbitral tribunal may, after consulting with the parties, appoint a secretary. The secretary shall remain at all times impartial and independent of the parties, and shall disclose any circumstances likely to give rise to justifiable doubts as to his or her impartiality or independence prior to his or her appointment. A secretary, once appointed and throughout the arbitration, shall disclose without delay any such circumstances to the parties unless they have already been informed by him or her of these circumstances.

13.5 The arbitral tribunal and the parties shall do everything necessary to ensure the fair and efficient conduct of the arbitration.

13.6 The parties may be represented by persons of their choice, subject to Article 13.5. The names, addresses, telephone and facsimile numbers, and email addresses of party representatives shall be communicated in writing to the other parties and HKIAC. The arbitral tribunal or HKIAC may require proof of authority of any party representatives.

13.7 In all matters not expressly provided for in these Rules, HKIAC, the arbitral tribunal and the parties shall act in the spirit of these Rules.

13.8 The arbitral tribunal shall make every reasonable effort to ensure that an award is valid.

Article 14 — Seat and Venue of the Arbitration

14.1 The parties may agree on the seat of arbitration. Where there is no agreement as to the seat, the seat of arbitration shall be Hong Kong, unless the arbitral tribunal determines, having regard to the circumstances of the case, that another seat is more appropriate.

14.2 Unless the parties have agreed otherwise, the arbitral tribunal may meet at any location outside of the seat of arbitration which it considers appropriate for consultation among its members, hearing witnesses, experts or the parties, or the inspection of goods, other property or documents. The arbitration shall nonetheless be treated for all purposes as an arbitration conducted at the seat.

Article 15 — Language

15.1 Subject to agreement by the parties, the arbitral tribunal shall, promptly after its appointment, determine the language or languages of the arbitration. This determination shall apply to the Statement of Claim, the Statement of Defence, any further written statements, any award, and, if oral hearings take place, to the language or languages to be used in such hearings.

15.2 The arbitral tribunal may order that any documents annexed to the Statement of Claim or Statement of Defence, and any supplementary documents or exhibits submitted in the course of the arbitration, delivered in their original language, shall be accompanied by a translation into the language or languages of the arbitration agreed upon by the parties or determined by the arbitral tribunal.

Article 16 — Statement of Claim

16.1 Unless the Statement of Claim was contained in the Notice of Arbitration (or the Claimant elects to treat the Notice of Arbitration as the Statement of Claim), the Claimant shall communicate its Statement of Claim in writing to all other parties and to each member of the arbitral tribunal within a period of time to be determined by the arbitral tribunal.

16.2 The Statement of Claim shall include the following particulars:

(a) the names, addresses, telephone and facsimile numbers and email addresses of the parties;

(b) a statement of the facts supporting the claim;

(c) the points at issue;

(d) the legal arguments supporting the claim; and

(e) the relief or remedy sought.

16.3 The Claimant shall annex to its Statement of Claim all documents on which it relies.

16.4 The arbitral tribunal may vary any of the requirements referred to in Article 16 as it considers fit.

Article 17 — Statement of Defence

17.1 Unless the Statement of Defence was contained in the Answer to the Notice of Arbitration (or the Respondent elects to treat the Answer to the Notice of Arbitration as the Statement of Defence), the Respondent shall communicate its Statement of Defence in writing to all other parties and to each member of the arbitral tribunal within a period of time to be determined by the arbitral tribunal.

17.2 The Statement of Defence shall reply to the particulars of the Statement of Claim (set out in Article 16.2(b), (c) and (d)). If the

Respondent has raised an objection to the jurisdiction or to the proper constitution of the arbitral tribunal, the Statement of Defence shall contain the factual and legal basis of such objection.
17.3 Where there is a counterclaim or a set-off defence, the Statement of Defence shall also include the following particulars:
(a) a statement of the facts supporting the counterclaim or set-off defence;
(b) the points at issue;
(c) the legal arguments supporting the counterclaim or set-off defence; and
(d) the relief or remedy sought.
17.4 The Respondent shall annex to its Statement of Defence all documents on which it relies.
17.5 The arbitral tribunal may vary any of the requirements referred to in Article 17 as it considers fit.

Article 18 — Amendments to the Claim or Defence

18.1 During the course of the arbitration a party may amend or supplement its claim or defence unless the arbitral tribunal considers it inappropriate to allow such amendment having regard to the circumstances of the case. However, a claim or defence may not be amended in such a manner that the amended claim or defence falls outside the jurisdiction of the arbitral tribunal.
18.2 HKIAC may adjust its Administrative Fees and the arbitral tribunal's fees (where appropriate) if a party amends its claim or defence.

Article 19 — Jurisdiction of the Arbitral Tribunal

19.1 The arbitral tribunal may rule on its own jurisdiction under these Rules, including any objections with respect to the existence, validity or scope of the arbitration agreement(s).
19.2 The arbitral tribunal shall have the power to determine the existence or the validity of the contract of which an arbitration clause forms a part. For the purposes of Article 19, an arbitration clause which forms part of a contract and which provides for arbitration under these Rules shall be treated as an agreement independent of the other terms of the contract. A decision by the arbitral tribunal that the contract is null and void shall not necessarily entail the invalidity of the arbitration clause.
19.3 A plea that the arbitral tribunal does not have jurisdiction shall be raised if possible in the Answer to the Notice of Arbitration, and shall be raised no later than in the Statement of Defence referred to in Article 17, or, with respect to a counterclaim, in the Reply to the Counterclaim. A party is not precluded from raising such a plea by the fact that it has designated, or participated in the designation of, an arbitrator. A plea that the arbitral

tribunal is exceeding the scope of its authority shall be raised as soon as the matter alleged to be beyond the scope of its authority is raised during the arbitration. The arbitral tribunal may, in either case, admit a later plea if it considers the delay justified.

19.4 If a question arises as to the existence, validity or scope of the arbitration agreement(s) or to the competence of HKIAC to administer an arbitration before the constitution of the arbitral tribunal, HKIAC may decide whether and to what extent the arbitration shall proceed. The arbitration shall proceed if and to the extent that HKIAC is satisfied, prima facie, that an arbitration agreement under the Rules may exist. Any question as to the jurisdiction of the arbitral tribunal shall be decided by the arbitral tribunal once confirmed pursuant to Article 19.1.

19.5 HKIAC's decision pursuant to Article 19.4 is without prejudice to the admissibility or merits of any party's pleas.

Article 20 — Further Written Statements

The arbitral tribunal shall decide which further written statements, if any, in addition to the Statement of Claim and the Statement of Defence, shall be required from the parties or may be presented by them and shall set the periods of time for communicating such statements.

Article 21 — Periods of Time

The periods of time set by the arbitral tribunal for the communication of written statements (including the Statement of Claim and Statement of Defence) should not exceed 45 days. However, the arbitral tribunal may, even in circumstances where the relevant period has already expired, extend time limits if it concludes that an extension is justified.

Article 22 — Evidence and Hearings

22.1 Each party shall have the burden of proving the facts relied on to support its claim or defence.

22.2 The arbitral tribunal shall determine the admissibility, relevance, materiality and weight of the evidence, including whether to apply strict rules of evidence.

22.3 At any time during the arbitration the arbitral tribunal may allow or require a party to produce documents, exhibits or other evidence that the arbitral tribunal determines to be relevant to the case and material to its outcome. The arbitral tribunal shall have the power to admit or exclude any documents, exhibits or other evidence.

22.4 The arbitral tribunal shall decide whether to hold oral hearings for the presentation of evidence or for oral arguments, or whether the arbitration shall be conducted on the basis of documents and other materials. The arbitral tribunal shall hold such hearings at an appropriate stage of the arbitration, if so requested by a party or if it considers fit. In the event of an oral hearing, the arbitral tribunal shall give the parties adequate advance notice of the relevant date, time and place.

22.5 Any person may be a witness or an expert. If a witness or expert is to be heard, each party shall communicate to the arbitral tribunal and to the other party the name and address of the witness or expert it intends to present, and the subject upon and the language in which such witness or expert will give his or her testimony, within such time as shall be agreed or as shall be specified by the arbitral tribunal.

22.6 The arbitral tribunal may make directions for the translation of oral statements made at a hearing and for a record of the hearing if it deems that either is necessary in the circumstances of the case.

22.7 Hearings shall be held in private unless the parties agree otherwise. The arbitral tribunal may require any witness or expert to leave the hearing room at any time during the hearing. The arbitral tribunal is free to determine the manner in which a witness or expert is examined.

Article 23 — Interim Measures of Protection and Emergency Relief

23.1 A party may apply for urgent interim or conservatory relief (the "Emergency Relief") prior to the constitution of the arbitral tribunal pursuant to the procedures set out in Schedule 4 (the "Emergency Arbitrator Procedures").

23.2 At the request of either party, the arbitral tribunal may order any interim measures it deems necessary or appropriate.

23.3 An interim measure, whether in the form of an order or award or in another form, is any temporary measure ordered by the arbitral tribunal at any time prior to the issuance of the award by which the dispute is finally decided, that a party, for example and without limitation:

(a) maintain or restore the status quo pending determination of the dispute;

(b) take action that would prevent, or refrain from taking action that is likely to cause, current or imminent harm or prejudice to the arbitral process itself;

(c) provide a means of preserving assets out of which a subsequent award may be satisfied; or

(d) preserve evidence that may be relevant and material to the resolution of the dispute.

23.4 When deciding a party's request for an interim measure under Article 23.2, the arbitral tribunal shall take into account the circumstances of the case. Relevant factors may include, but are not limited to:

(a) harm not adequately reparable by an award of damages is likely to result if the measure is not ordered, and such harm substantially outweighs the harm that is likely to result to the party against whom the measure is directed if the measure is granted; and

(b) there is a reasonable possibility that the requesting party will succeed on the merits of the claim. The determination on this possibility shall not affect the discretion of the arbitral tribunal in making any subsequent determination.

23.5 The arbitral tribunal may modify, suspend or terminate an interim measure it has granted, upon application of any party or, in exceptional circumstances and upon prior notice to the parties, on the arbitral tribunal's own initiative.

23.6 The arbitral tribunal may require the party requesting an interim measure to provide appropriate security in connection with the measure.

23.7 The arbitral tribunal may require any party promptly to disclose any material change in the circumstances on the basis of which an interim measure was requested or granted.

23.8 The party requesting an interim measure may be liable for any costs and damages caused by the measure to any party if the arbitral tribunal later determines that, in the circumstances then prevailing, the measure should not have been granted. The arbitral tribunal may award such costs and damages at any point during the arbitration.

23.9 A request for interim measures addressed by any party to a competent judicial authority shall not be deemed incompatible with the arbitration agreement(s), or as a waiver thereof.

Article 24 — Security for Costs

The arbitral tribunal may make an order requiring a party to provide security for the costs of the arbitration.

Article 25 — Tribunal-Appointed Experts

25.1 To assist it in the assessment of evidence, the arbitral tribunal, after consulting with the parties, may appoint one or more experts. The arbitral tribunal may meet privately with any tribunal-appointed expert. Such expert shall report to the arbitral tribunal, in writing, on specific issues to be determined by the arbitral tribunal. The arbitral tribunal shall establish terms of reference for the expert, and shall communicate a copy of the expert's terms of reference to the parties and HKIAC.

25.2 The parties shall give the expert any relevant information or produce for his or her inspection any relevant documents or goods that he or she may require of them. Any dispute between a party and such expert as to the relevance of the required information or production shall be referred to the arbitral tribunal for decision.

25.3 Upon receipt of the expert's report, the arbitral tribunal shall send a copy of the report to the parties who shall be given the opportunity to express, in writing, their opinions on the report. The parties shall be entitled to examine any document on which the expert has relied in his or her report.

25.4 At the request of either party the expert, after delivery of the report, shall attend a hearing at which the parties shall have the opportunity to be present and to examine the expert. At this hearing either party may present experts in order to testify on the points at issue. The provisions of Articles 22.2 to 22.7 shall be applicable to such proceedings.

25.5 The provisions of Article 11 shall apply by analogy to any expert appointed by the arbitral tribunal.

Article 26 — Default

26.1 If, within the period of time set by the arbitral tribunal, the Claimant has failed to communicate its Statement of Claim without showing sufficient cause for such failure, the arbitral tribunal shall issue an order for the termination of the arbitration unless the Respondent has brought a counterclaim and wishes the arbitration to continue, in which case the tribunal may proceed with the arbitration in respect of the counterclaim.

26.2 If, within the period of time set by the arbitral tribunal, the Respondent has failed to communicate its Statement of Defence without showing sufficient cause for such failure, the arbitral tribunal may proceed with the arbitration.

26.3 If one of the parties, duly notified under these Rules, fails to present its case in accordance with these Rules including as directed by the arbitral tribunal, without showing sufficient cause for such failure, the arbitral tribunal may proceed with the arbitration and make an award on the basis of the evidence before it.

Article 27 — Joinder of Additional Parties

27.1 The arbitral tribunal shall have the power to allow an additional party to be joined to the arbitration provided that, prima facie, the additional party is bound by an arbitration agreement under these Rules giving rise to the arbitration, including any arbitration under Article 28 or 29.

27.2 The arbitral tribunal's decision pursuant to Article 27.1 is without prejudice to its power to subsequently decide any question as to its jurisdiction arising from such decision.

27.3 A party wishing to join an additional party to the arbitration shall submit a Request for Joinder to HKIAC. HKIAC may fix a time limit for the submission of a Request for Joinder.

27.4 The Request for Joinder shall include the following:
(a) the case reference of the existing arbitration;
(b) the names and addresses, telephone and facsimile numbers, and email addresses of each of the parties, including the additional party;
(c) a request that the additional party be joined to the arbitration;
(d) a reference to the contract(s) or other legal instrument(s) out of or in relation to which the request arises;
(e) a statement of the facts supporting the request;
(f) the points at issue;
(g) the legal arguments supporting the request;
(h) the relief or remedy sought; and
(i) confirmation that copies of the Request for Joinder and any exhibits included therewith have been or are being served simultaneously on all other parties and the arbitral tribunal, where applicable, by one or more means of service to be identified in such confirmation.
A copy of the contract(s), and of the arbitration agreement(s) if not contained in the contract(s), shall be annexed to the Request for Joinder.
27.5 Within 15 days of receiving the Request for Joinder, the additional party shall submit to HKIAC an Answer to the Request for Joinder. The Answer to the Request for Joinder shall include the following:
(a) the name, address, telephone and facsimile numbers, and email address of the additional party and its counsel (if different from the description contained in the Request for Joinder);
(b) any plea that the arbitral tribunal has been improperly constituted and/or lacks jurisdiction over the additional party;
(c) the additional party's comments on the particulars set forth in the Request for Joinder, pursuant to Article 27.4(a) to (g);
(d) the additional party's answer to the relief or remedy sought in the Request for Joinder, pursuant to Article 27.4(h);
(e) details of any claims by the additional party against any other party to the arbitration; and
(f) confirmation that copies of the Answer to the Request for Joinder and any exhibits included therewith have been or are being served simultaneously on all other parties and the arbitral tribunal, where applicable, by one or more means of service to be identified in such confirmation.
27.6 A third party wishing to be joined as an additional party to the arbitration shall submit a Request for Joinder to HKIAC. The provisions of Article 27.4 shall apply to such Request for Joinder.

27.7 Within 15 days of receiving a Request for Joinder pursuant to Article 27.3 or 27.6, the parties shall submit their comments on the Request for Joinder to HKIAC. Such comments may include (without limitation) the following particulars:
(a) any plea that the arbitral tribunal lacks jurisdiction over the additional party;
(b) comments on the particulars set forth in the Request for Joinder, pursuant to Article 27.4(a) to (g);
(c) answer to the relief or remedy sought in the Request for Joinder pursuant to Article 27.4(h);
(d) details of any claims against the additional party; and
(e) confirmation that copies of the comments have been or are being served simultaneously on all other parties and the arbitral tribunal, where applicable, by one or more means of service to be identified in such confirmation.
27.8 Where HKIAC receives a Request for Joinder before the date on which the arbitral tribunal is confirmed, HKIAC may decide whether, prima facie, the additional party is bound by an arbitration agreement under these Rules giving rise to the arbitration, including any arbitration under Article 28 or 29. If so, HKIAC may join the additional party to the arbitration. Any question as to the jurisdiction of the arbitral tribunal arising from HKIAC's decision under this Article 27.8 shall be decided by the arbitral tribunal once confirmed, pursuant to Article 19.1.
27.9 HKIAC's decision pursuant to Article 27.8 is without prejudice to the admissibility or merits of any party's pleas.
27.10 Where an additional party is joined to the arbitration, the date on which the Request for Joinder is received by HKIAC shall be deemed to be the date on which the arbitration in respect of the additional party commences.
27.11 Where an additional party is joined to the arbitration before the date on which the arbitral tribunal is confirmed, all parties to the arbitration shall be deemed to have waived their right to designate an arbitrator, and HKIAC may revoke the appointment of any arbitrators already designated or confirmed. In these circumstances, HKIAC shall appoint the arbitral tribunal.
27.12 The revocation of the appointment of an arbitrator under Article 27.11 is without prejudice to:
(a) the validity of any act done or order made by that arbitrator before his or her appointment was revoked; and

(b) his or her entitlement to be paid his or her fees and expenses subject to Schedule 2 or 3 as applicable.

27.13 The parties waive any objection, on the basis of any decision to join an additional party to the arbitration, to the validity and/or enforcement of any award made by the arbitral tribunal in the arbitration, in so far as such waiver can validly be made.

27.14 HKIAC may adjust its Administrative Fees and the arbitral tribunal's fees (where appropriate) after a Request for Joinder has been submitted.

Article 28 — Consolidation of Arbitrations

28.1 HKIAC shall have the power, at the request of a party (the "Request for Consolidation") and after consulting with the parties and any confirmed arbitrators, to consolidate two or more arbitrations pending under these Rules where:

(a) the parties agree to consolidate; or

(b) all of the claims in the arbitrations are made under the same arbitration agreement; or

(c) the claims are made under more than one arbitration agreement, a common question of law or fact arises in both or all of the arbitrations, the rights to relief claimed are in respect of, or arise out of, the same transaction or series of transactions, and HKIAC finds the arbitration agreements to be compatible.

28.2 The party making the request shall provide copies of the Request for Consolidation to all other parties and to any confirmed arbitrators.

28.3 In deciding whether to consolidate, HKIAC shall take into account the circumstances of the case. Relevant factors may include, but are not limited to, whether one or more arbitrators have been designated or confirmed in more than one of the arbitrations, and if so, whether the same or different arbitrators have been confirmed.

28.4 Where HKIAC decides to consolidate two or more arbitrations, the arbitrations shall be consolidated into the arbitration that commenced first, unless all parties agree or HKIAC decides otherwise taking into account the circumstances of the case. HKIAC shall provide copies of such decision to all parties and to any confirmed arbitrators in all arbitrations.

28.5 The consolidation of two or more arbitrations is without prejudice to the validity of any act done or order made by a court in support of the relevant arbitration before it was consolidated.

28.6 Where HKIAC decides to consolidate two or more arbitrations, the parties to all such arbitrations shall be deemed to have waived their right to designate an arbitrator, and HKIAC may revoke the appointment of any arbitrators already designated or confirmed. In these circumstances, HKIAC shall appoint the arbitral tribunal in respect of the consolidated proceedings.

28.7 The revocation of the appointment of an arbitrator under Article 28.6 is without prejudice to:

(a) the validity of any act done or order made by that arbitrator before his or her appointment was revoked;

(b) his or her entitlement to be paid his or her fees and expenses subject to Schedule 2 or 3 as applicable; and

(c) the date when any claim or defence was raised for the purpose of applying any limitation bar or any similar rule or provision.

28.8 The parties waive any objection, on the basis of HKIAC's decision to consolidate, to the validity and/or enforcement of any award made by the arbitral tribunal in the consolidated proceedings, in so far as such waiver can validly be made.

28.9 HKIAC may adjust its Administrative Fees and the arbitral tribunal's fees (where appropriate) after a Request for Consolidation has been submitted.

Article 29 — Single Arbitration under Multiple Contracts

29.1 Claims arising out of or in connection with more than one contract may be made in a single arbitration, provided that:

(a) all parties to the arbitration are bound by each arbitration agreement giving rise to the arbitration;

(b) a common question of law or fact arises under each arbitration agreement giving rise to the arbitration;

(c) the rights to relief claimed are in respect of, or arise out of, the same transaction or series of transactions; and

(d) the arbitration agreements under which those claims are made are compatible.

29.2 The parties waive any objection, on the basis of the commencement of a single arbitration under Article 29, to the validity and/or enforcement of any award made by the arbitral tribunal in the arbitration, in so far as such waiver can validly be made.

Article 30 — Closure of Proceedings

30.1 When it is satisfied that the parties have had a reasonable opportunity to present their case, the arbitral tribunal shall declare the proceedings closed. Thereafter, no further submission or argument may be made, or evidence produced, unless the tribunal reopens the proceedings in accordance with Article 30.2.

30.2 The arbitral tribunal may, if it considers it necessary owing to exceptional circumstances, decide, on its own initiative or upon application of a party, to reopen the proceedings at any time before the award is made.

Article 31 — Waiver

A party who knows or ought reasonably to know that any provision of, or requirement arising under, these Rules (including the arbitration agreement (s)) has not been complied with and yet proceeds with the arbitration without promptly stating its objection to such non-compliance, shall be deemed to have waived its right to object.

Section V Awards, Decisions and Orders of the Arbitral Tribunal

Article 32 — Decisions

32.1 When there is more than one arbitrator, any award or other decision of the arbitral tribunal shall be made by a majority of the arbitrators. If there is no majority, the award shall be made by the presiding arbitrator alone.

32.2 With the prior agreement of all members of the arbitral tribunal, the presiding arbitrator may make procedural rulings alone.

Article 33 — Costs of the Arbitration

33.1 The arbitral tribunal shall determine the costs of the arbitration in its award. The term "costs of the arbitration" includes only:

(a) the fees of the arbitral tribunal, as determined in accordance with Article 10;

(b) the reasonable travel and other expenses incurred by the arbitral tribunal;

(c) the reasonable costs of expert advice and of other assistance required by the arbitral tribunal;

(d) the reasonable travel and other expenses of witnesses and experts;

(e) the reasonable costs for legal representation and assistance if such costs were claimed during the arbitration;

(f) the Registration Fee and Administrative Fees payable to HKIAC in accordance with Schedule 1.

33.2 The arbitral tribunal may apportion all or part of the costs of the arbitration referred to in Article 33.1 between the parties if it determines that apportionment is reasonable, taking into account the circumstances of the case.

33.3 With respect to the costs of legal representation and assistance referred to in Article 33.1(e), the arbitral tribunal, taking into account the circumstances of the case, may direct that the recoverable costs of the arbitration, or any part of the arbitration, shall be limited to a specified amount.

33.4 Where arbitrations are consolidated pursuant to Article 28, the arbitral tribunal in the consolidated arbitration shall allocate the costs of the arbitration in accordance with Article 33.2 and 33.3. Such costs shall include, but shall not be limited to, the fees of any arbitral tribunal designated or confirmed and any other costs incurred in an arbitration that was subsequently consolidated into another arbitration.

33.5 When the arbitral tribunal issues an order for the termination of the arbitration or makes an award on agreed terms, it or HKIAC shall determine the costs of the arbitration referred to in Article 33.1, in the text of that order or award.

Article 34 — Form and Effect of the Award

34.1 The arbitral tribunal may make a single award or separate awards regarding different issues at different times and in respect of all parties involved in the arbitration in the form of interim, interlocutory, partial or final awards. If appropriate, the arbitral tribunal may also issue interim awards on costs.

34.2 Awards shall be made in writing and shall be final and binding on the parties and any person claiming through or under any of the parties. The parties and any such person shall be deemed to have waived their rights to any form of recourse or defence in respect of enforcement and execution of any award, in so far as such waiver can validly be made.

34.3 The parties undertake to comply without delay with any award or order made by the arbitral tribunal, including any award or order made in any consolidated proceedings under Article 28 or any arbitration under Article 29.

34.4 An award shall state the reasons upon which it is based unless the parties have agreed that no reasons are to be given.

34.5 An award shall be signed by the arbitral tribunal. It shall state the date on which it was made and the seat of arbitration as determined under Article 14 and shall be deemed to have been made at the seat of the arbitration. Where there are three arbitrators and any of them fails to sign, the award shall state the reason for the absence of the signature(s).

34.6 Subject to any lien, originals of the award signed by the arbitrators and affixed with the seal of HKIAC shall be communicated to the parties and HKIAC by the arbitral tribunal. HKIAC shall be supplied with an original copy of the award.

Article 35 — Applicable Law, *Amiable Compositeur*

35.1 The arbitral tribunal shall decide the substance of the dispute in accordance with the rules of law agreed upon by the parties. Any designation of the law or legal system of a given jurisdiction shall be

construed, unless otherwise expressed, as directly referring to the substantive law of that jurisdiction and not to its conflict of laws rules. Failing such designation by the parties, the arbitral tribunal shall apply the rules of law which it determines to be appropriate.
35.2 The arbitral tribunal shall decide as *amiable compositeur* or *ex aequo et bono* only if the parties have expressly agreed that the arbitral tribunal should do so.
35.3 In all cases, the arbitral tribunal shall decide the case in accordance with the terms of the relevant contract(s) and may take into account the usages of the trade applicable to the transaction(s).

Article 36 — Settlement or Other Grounds for Termination

36.1 If, before the award is made, the parties agree on a settlement of the dispute, the arbitral tribunal shall either issue an order for the termination of the arbitration or, if requested by both parties and accepted by the arbitral tribunal, record the settlement in the form of an arbitral award on agreed terms. The arbitral tribunal is not obliged to give reasons for such an award.
36.2 If, before the award is made, the continuation of the arbitration becomes unnecessary or impossible for any reason not mentioned in Article 36.1, the arbitral tribunal shall issue an order for the termination of the arbitration. The arbitral tribunal shall issue such an order unless a party raises a justifiable objection, having been given a reasonable opportunity to comment upon the proposed course of action.
36.3 Copies of the order for termination of the arbitration or of the arbitral award on agreed terms, signed by the arbitral tribunal, shall be communicated by the arbitral tribunal to the parties and HKIAC. Where an arbitral award on agreed terms is made, the provisions of Articles 34.2, 34.3, 34.5 and 34.6 shall apply.

Article 37 — Correction of the Award

37.1 Within 30 days after receipt of the award, either party, with notice to the other party, may request the arbitral tribunal to correct in the award any errors in computation, any clerical or typographical errors, or any errors of similar nature. The arbitral tribunal may set a time limit, normally not exceeding 15 days, for the other party to comment on such request.
37.2 The arbitral tribunal shall make any corrections it considers appropriate within 30 days after receipt of the request but may extend such period of time if necessary.
37.3 The arbitral tribunal may within 30 days after the date of the award make such corrections on its own initiative.
37.4 The arbitral tribunal has the power to make any further correction to

the award which is necessitated by or consequential on (a) the interpretation of any point or part of the award under Article 38; or (b) the issue of any additional award under Article 39.

37.5 Such corrections shall be in writing, and the provisions of Articles 34.2 to 34.6 shall apply.

Article 38 — Interpretation of the Award

38.1 Within 30 days after receipt of the award, either party, with notice to the other party, may request that the arbitral tribunal give an interpretation of the award. The arbitral tribunal may set a time limit, normally not exceeding 15 days, for the other party to comment on such request.

38.2 Any interpretation considered appropriate by the arbitral tribunal shall be given in writing within 30 days after receipt of the request but the tribunal may extend such period of time if necessary.

38.3 The arbitral tribunal has the power to give any further interpretation of the award which is necessitated by or consequential on (a) the correction of any error in the award under Article 37; or (b) the issue of any additional award under Article 39.

38.4 Any interpretation given under Article 38 shall form part of the award and the provisions of Articles 34.2 to 34.6 shall apply.

Article 39 — Additional Award

39.1 Within 30 days after receipt of the award, either party, with notice to the other party, may request the arbitral tribunal to make an additional award as to claims presented in the arbitration but omitted from the award. The arbitral tribunal may set a time limit, normally not exceeding 30 days, for the other party to comment on such request.

39.2 If the arbitral tribunal considers the request for an additional award to be justified, it shall make the additional award within 60 days after receipt of the request but may extend such period of time if necessary.

39.3 The arbitral tribunal has the power to make an additional award which is necessitated by or consequential on (a) the correction of any error in the award under Article 37; or (b) the interpretation of any point or part of the award under Article 38.

39.4 When an additional award is made, the provisions of Articles 34.2 to 34.6 shall apply.

Article 40 — Deposits for Costs

40.1 As soon as practicable after receipt of the Notice of Arbitration by the Respondent, HKIAC shall, in principle, request the Claimant and the Respondent each to deposit with HKIAC an equal amount as an advance for the costs referred to in Article 33.1, paragraphs (a), (b), (c) and (f). HKIAC

shall provide a copy of such request to the arbitral tribunal.
40.2 Where a Respondent submits a counterclaim, or it otherwise appears appropriate in the circumstances, HKIAC may request separate deposits.
40.3 During the course of the arbitration HKIAC may request the parties to make supplementary deposits with HKIAC. HKIAC shall provide a copy of such request(s) to the arbitral tribunal.
40.4 If the required deposits are not paid in full to HKIAC within 30 days after receipt of the request, HKIAC shall so inform the parties in order that one or another of them may make the required payment. If such payment is not made, the arbitral tribunal may order the suspension or termination of the arbitration or continue with the arbitration on such basis and in respect of such claim or counterclaim as the tribunal considers fit.
40.5 In its final award, the arbitral tribunal shall render an account to the parties of the deposits received by HKIAC. Any unexpended balance shall be returned to the parties by HKIAC.
40.6 HKIAC shall place the deposit(s) made by the parties in interest bearing deposit account(s) at a reputable licensed Hong Kong deposit-taking institution. In selecting the account(s), HKIAC shall have due regard to the possible need to make the deposited funds available immediately.

Section VI Other Provisions

Article 41 — Expedited Procedure

41.1 Prior to the constitution of the arbitral tribunal, a party may apply to HKIAC in writing for the arbitration to be conducted in accordance with Article 41.2 where:
(a) the amount in dispute representing the aggregate of any claim and counterclaim (or any set-off defence) does not exceed HKD 25,000,000 (twenty-five million Hong Kong Dollars); or
(b) the parties so agree; or
(c) in cases of exceptional urgency.
41.2 When HKIAC, after considering the views of the parties, grants an application made pursuant to Article 41.1, the arbitral proceedings shall be conducted in accordance with an Expedited Procedure based upon the foregoing provisions of these Rules, subject to the following changes:
(a) the case shall be referred to a sole arbitrator, unless the arbitration agreement provides for three arbitrators;
(b) if the arbitration agreement provides for three arbitrators, HKIAC shall invite the parties to agree to refer the case to a sole arbitrator. If the parties do not agree, the case shall be referred to three arbitrators;
(c) HKIAC may shorten the time limits provided for in the Rules, as well as

any time limits that it has set;

(d) after the submission of the Answer to the Notice of Arbitration, the parties shall in principle be entitled to submit one Statement of Claim and one Statement of Defence (and Counterclaim) and, where applicable, one Statement of Defence in reply to the Counterclaim;

(e) the arbitral tribunal shall decide the dispute on the basis of documentary evidence only, unless it decides that it is appropriate to hold one or more hearings;

(f) the award shall be made within six months from the date when HKIAC transmitted the file to the arbitral tribunal. In exceptional circumstances, HKIAC may extend this time limit;

(g) the arbitral tribunal shall state the reasons upon which the award is based in summary form, unless the parties have agreed that no reasons are to be given.

41.3 Unless the parties agree otherwise, the Expedited Procedure contained in Article 41 shall not apply to any consolidated proceedings under Article 28 or to any arbitration commenced under Article 29.

Article 42 — Confidentiality

42.1 Unless otherwise agreed by the parties, no party may publish, disclose or communicate any information relating to:

(a) the arbitration under the arbitration agreement(s); or

(b) an award made in the arbitration.

42.2 The provisions of Article 42.1 also apply to the arbitral tribunal, any Emergency Arbitrator appointed in accordance with Schedule 4, expert, witness, secretary of the arbitral tribunal and HKIAC.

42.3 The provisions in Article 42.1 do not prevent the publication, disclosure or communication of information referred to in Article 42.1 by a party:

(a) (i) to protect or pursue a legal right or interest of the party; or

(ii) to enforce or challenge the award referred to in Article 42.1;

in legal proceedings before a court or other judicial authority;

(b) to any government body, regulatory body, court or tribunal where the party is obliged by law to make the publication, disclosure or communication; or

(c) to a professional or any other adviser of any of the parties, including any actual or potential witness or expert.

42.4 The deliberations of the arbitral tribunal are confidential.

42.5 An award may be published, whether in its entirety or in the form of excerpts or a summary, only under the following conditions:

(a) a request for publication is addressed to HKIAC;
(b) all references to the parties' names are deleted; and
(c) no party objects to such publication within the time limit fixed for that purpose by HKIAC. In the case of an objection, the award shall not be published.

Article 43 — Exclusion of Liability

43.1 None of the Council of HKIAC nor any committee, sub-commitee or other body or person specifically designated by it to perform the functions referred to in these Rules, nor the Secretary General of HKIAC or other staff members of the Secretariat of HKIAC, the arbitral tribunal, any Emergency Arbitrator, tribunal-appointed expert or secretary of the arbitral tribunal shall be liable for any act or omission in connection with an arbitration conducted under these Rules, save where such act was done or omitted to be done dishonestly.

43.2 After the award has been made and the possibilities of correction, interpretation and additional awards referred to in Articles 37 to 39 have lapsed or been exhausted, neither HKIAC nor the arbitral tribunal, any Emergency Arbitrator, tribunal-appointed expert or secretary of the arbitral tribunal shall be under an obligation to make statements to any person about any matter concerning the arbitration, nor shall a party seek to make any of these persons a witness in any legal or other proceedings arising out of the arbitration.

SCHEDULES

Schedule 1

Registration and Administrative Fee *

1 — Registration Fee

1.1 When submitting a Notice of Arbitration, the Claimant shall pay a Registration Fee in the amount set by HKIAC, as stated on HKIAC's website on the date the Notice of Arbitration is submitted.

1.2 If the Claimant fails to pay the Registration Fee, HKIAC shall not proceed with the arbitration subject to Article 4.7 of the Rules.

1.3 The Registration Fee is not refundable.

2 — HKIAC's Administrative Fees

2.1 HKIAC's Administrative Fee shall be determined in accordance with the following table:

See Table 1 (page 380).

2.2 Claims and counterclaims are aggregated for the determination of the amount in dispute. The same rule applies to any set-off defence, unless the arbitral tribunal, after consulting with the parties, concludes that such set-off defence will not require significant additional work.

2.3 An interest claim shall not be taken into account for the calculation of the amount in dispute. However, when the interest claim exceeds the amounts claimed in principal, the interest claim alone shall be considered in calculating the amount in dispute.

2.4 Pursuant to Articles 18.2, 27.14 or 28.9 or where in the opinion of HKIAC there are exceptional circumstances, HKIAC's Administrative Fees may exceed the amounts calculated in accordance with paragraph 2.1.

2.5 If the amount in dispute is not quantified, HKIAC's Administrative Fees shall be fixed by HKIAC, taking into account the circumstances of the case.

2.6 Amounts in currencies other than Hong Kong Dollars shall be converted into Hong Kong Dollars at the rate of exchange published by HSBC Bank on the date the Notice of Arbitration is submitted or at the time any new claim, set-off defence or amendment to a claim or defence is filed.

Schedule 2

Arbitral Tribunal's Fees, Expenses, Terms and Conditions *

1 — Scope of Application and Interpretation

1.1 Subject to Article 9.2 of the Rules, this Schedule shall apply to arbitrations in which the arbitral tribunal's fees and expenses are to be determined in accordance with Article 10.1(a) of the Rules and to the appointment of an Emergency Arbitrator under Schedule 4.

1.2 HKIAC may interpret the terms of this Schedule as well as the scope of

* (All amounts are in Hong Kong Dollars hereinafter "HKD"). [Effective 1 November, 2013]

application of the Schedule as it considers appropriate.

1.3 This Schedule is supplemented by the Practice Note on Arbitral Tribunal's Fees, Expenses, Terms and Conditions Based on Schedule 2 and Hourly Rates in force on the date the Notice of Arbitration is submitted.

2 — Payments to Arbitral Tribunal

2.1 Payments to the arbitral tribunal shall generally be made by HKIAC from funds deposited by the parties in accordance with Article 40 of the Rules. HKIAC may direct the parties, in such proportions as it considers appropriate, to make one or more interim or final payments to the arbitral tribunal.

2.2 If insufficient funds are held at the time a payment is required, the invoice for the payment may be submitted to the parties for settlement by them direct.

2.3 Payments to the arbitral tribunal shall be made in Hong Kong Dollars unless the tribunal directs otherwise.

2.4 The parties are jointly and severally liable for the fees and expenses of an arbitrator, irrespective of which party appointed the arbitrator.

3 — Arbitral Tribunal's Expenses

3.1 The arbitral tribunal shall be reimbursed for its reasonable expenses in accordance with the Practice Note referred to at paragraph 1.3.

3.2 The expenses of the arbitral tribunal shall not be included in the arbitral tribunal's fees charged by reference to hourly rates under paragraph 9 of this Schedule.

4 — Administrative Expenses

The parties shall be responsible for expenses reasonably incurred and relating to administrative and support services engaged for the purposes of the arbitration, including, but not limited to, the cost of hearing rooms, interpreters and transcription services. Such expenses may be paid directly from the deposits referred to in Article 40 of the Rules as and when they are incurred.

5 — Fees and Expenses Payable to Replaced Arbitrators

Where an arbitrator is replaced pursuant to Article 12, 27 or 28 of the Rules, HKIAC shall decide the amount of fees and expenses to be paid for the replaced arbitrator's services (if any), having taken into account the circumstances of the case, including, but not limited to, the applicable method for determining the arbitrator's fees, work done by the arbitrator in connection with the arbitration, and the complexity of the subject-matter.

6 — Fees and Expenses of Secretary to Arbitral Tribunal

Where the arbitral tribunal appoints a secretary in accordance with Article

---

* Based on Hourly Rate [Effective 1 November, 2013]

13.4 of the Rules, such secretary shall be remunerated at a rate which shall not exceed the rate set by HKIAC, as stated on HKIAC's website on the date the Notice of Arbitration is submitted. The secretary's fees and expenses shall be charged separately. The arbitral tribunal shall determine the total fees and expenses of a secretary under Article 33.1(c) of the Rules.

7 — Lien on Award

HKIAC and the arbitral tribunal shall have a lien over any awards issued by the tribunal to secure the payment of their outstanding fees and expenses, and may accordingly refuse to release any such awards to the parties until all such fees and expenses have been paid in full, whether jointly or by one or other of the parties.

8 — Governing Law

The terms of this Schedule and any non-contractual obligation arising out of or in connection with them shall be governed by and construed in accordance with Hong Kong law.

9 — Arbitral Tribunal's Fee Rates

9.1 An arbitrator shall be remunerated at an hourly rate for all work reasonably carried out in connection with the arbitration.

9.2 Subject to paragraphs 9.3 and 9.4 of this Schedule, the rate referred to in paragraph 9.1 is to be agreed in accordance with Article 10.2 of the Rules. An arbitrator shall agree in writing upon fee rates in accordance with paragraph 9 of this Schedule prior to the confirmation of his or her appointment by HKIAC in accordance with Article 9 of the Rules.

9.3 An arbitrator's agreed hourly rate shall not exceed a rate set by HKIAC, as stated on HKIAC's website on the date the Notice of Arbitration is submitted.

9.4 Subject to paragraph 9.3, an arbitrator may review and increase his or her agreed hourly rate by no more than 10% on each anniversary of the confirmation of his or her appointment by HKIAC.

9.5 Higher rates may be charged if expressly agreed in writing by all parties to the arbitration or if HKIAC so determines in exceptional circumstances.

9.6 If an arbitrator is required to travel for the purposes of fulfilling obligations as an arbitrator, the arbitrator shall be entitled to charge and to be reimbursed for:

(a) time spent travelling but not working at a rate of 50% of the agreed hourly rate; and

(b) time spent working whilst travelling at the full agreed hourly rate.

10 — Cancellation Fees

10.1 All hearings booked shall be paid for, subject to the following

conditions:
(a) if a booking is cancelled at the request of the arbitral tribunal, it will not be charged;
(b) if a booking is cancelled at the request of a party less than 30 days before the day booked it shall be paid at a daily rate of 75% of eight times the applicable hourly rate;
(c) if a booking is cancelled at the request of a party less than 60 days but more than 30 days before the day booked it shall be paid at a daily rate of 50% of eight times the applicable hourly rate;
(d) if a booking is cancelled at the request of a party more than 60 days before the day booked it will not be charged; and
(e) in all cases referred to above credit will be given against all time spent on the case during the day(s) booked.

10.2 Where hearing days are cancelled or postponed other than by agreement of all parties, this may be taken into account when considering any subsequent allocation of costs.

Schedule 3

Arbitral Tribunal's Fees, Expenses, Terms and Conditions *

1 — Scope of Application and Interpretation

1.1 Subject to paragraph 1.2 below and Article 9.2 of the Rules, this Schedule applies to arbitrations in which the arbitral tribunal's fees and expenses are to be determined in accordance with Article 10.1(b) of the Rules.

1.2 This Schedule shall not apply to the appointment of an Emergency Arbitrator under Schedule 4.

1.3 HKIAC may interpret the terms of this Schedule as well as the scope of application of the Schedule as it considers appropriate.

1.4 This Schedule is supplemented by the Practice Note on Arbitral Tribunal's Fees, Expenses, Terms and Conditions Based on Schedule 3 and the Sum in Dispute in force on the date the Notice of Arbitration is submitted.

2 — Payments to Arbitral Tribunal

2.1 Payments to the arbitral tribunal shall generally be made by HKIAC from funds deposited by the parties in accordance with Article 40 of the Rules. HKIAC may direct the parties, in such proportions as it considers appropriate, to make one or more interim or final payments to the arbitral tribunal.

2.2 If insufficient funds are held at the time a payment is required, the invoice for the payment may be submitted to the parties for settlement by

* Based on sum in dispute. (All amounts are in Hong Kong Dollars hereinafter "HKD".) [Effective 1 November, 2013]

them direct.

2.3 Payments to the arbitral tribunal shall be made in Hong Kong Dollars unless the tribunal directs otherwise.

2.4 The parties are jointly and severally liable for the fees and expenses of an arbitrator, irrespective of which party appointed the arbitrator.

3 — Arbitral Tribunal's Expenses

3.1 The arbitral tribunal shall be reimbursed for its reasonable expenses in accordance with the Practice Note referred to at paragraph 1.4.

3.2 The expenses of the arbitral tribunal shall not be included in the determination of fees charged in accordance with paragraph 6 of this Schedule.

4 — Administrative Expenses

The parties shall be responsible for expenses reasonably incurred and relating to administrative and support services engaged for the purposes of the arbitration, including, but not limited to, the cost of hearing rooms, interpreters and transcription services. Such expenses may be paid directly from the deposits referred to in Article 40 of the Rules as and when they are incurred.

5 — Fees and Expenses Payable to Replaced Arbitrators

Where an arbitrator is replaced pursuant to Article 12, 27 or 28 of the Rules, HKIAC shall decide the amount of fees and expenses to be paid for the replaced arbitrator's services (if any), having taken into account the circumstances of the case, including, but not limited to, the applicable method for determining the arbitrator's fees, work done by the arbitrator in connection with the arbitration, and the complexity of the subject-matter.

6 — Determination of Arbitral Tribunal's Fees

6.1 The arbitral tribunal's fees shall be calculated in accordance with the following table. The fees calculated in accordance with the table represent the maximum amount payable to one arbitrator.

See Table 2 (page 381).

6.2 The arbitral tribunal's fees shall cover the activities of the arbitral tribunal from the time the file is transmitted to it until the last award.

6.3 Claims and counterclaims are added for the determination of the amount in dispute. The same rule applies to any set-off defence, unless the arbitral tribunal, after consulting with the parties, concludes that such set-off defence will not require significant additional work.

6.4 An interest claim shall not be taken into account for the calculation of the amount in dispute. However, when the interest claim exceeds the amounts claimed in principal, the interest claim alone shall be considered in calculating the amount in dispute.

6.5 Pursuant to Articles 10.3(c), 18.2, 27.14 or 28.9 or in other exceptional circumstances, the arbitral tribunal's fees may exceed the amounts calculated in accordance with paragraph 6.1.

6.6 If the amount in dispute is not quantified, the arbitral tribunal's fees shall be fixed by HKIAC, taking into account the circumstances of the case.

7 — Lien on Award

HKIAC and the arbitral tribunal shall have a lien over any awards issued by the tribunal to secure the payment of their outstanding fees and expenses, and may accordingly refuse to release any such awards to the parties until all such fees and expenses have been paid in full, whether jointly or by one or other of the parties.

8 — Governing Law

The terms of this Schedule and any non-contractual obligation arising out of or in connection with it shall be governed by and construed in accordance with Hong Kong law.

Schedule 4
Emergency Arbitrator Procedures *

1. A party requiring Emergency Relief may, concurrent with or following the filing of a Notice of Arbitration but prior to the constitution of the arbitral tribunal, submit an application (the "Application") for the appointment of an emergency arbitrator (the "Emergency Arbitrator") to HKIAC.

2. The Application shall be submitted in accordance with any of the means specified in Article 2.1 of the Rules. The Application shall include the following information:

(a) the names and (in so far as known) the addresses, telephone and facsimile numbers, and email addresses of the parties to the Application and of their counsel;

(b) a description of the circumstances giving rise to the Application and of the underlying dispute referred to arbitration;

(c) a statement of the Emergency Relief sought;

(d) the reasons why the applicant needs the Emergency Relief on an urgent basis that cannot await the constitution of an arbitral tribunal;

(e) the reasons why the applicant is entitled to such Emergency Relief;

(f) any relevant agreement(s) and, in particular, the arbitration agreement(s);

(g) comments on the language, the seat of the Emergency Relief proceedings, and the applicable law;

(h) confirmation of payment, by cheque or transfer to the account of

* [Effective 1 November, 2013]

HKIAC, of the amount referred to in paragraph 6 of this Schedule (the "Application Deposit"); and
(i) confirmation that copies of the Application and any exhibits included therewith have been or are being served simultaneously on all other parties to the arbitration by one or more means of service to be identified in such confirmation.

3. The Application may contain such other documents or information as the applicant considers appropriate or as may contribute to the efficient examination of the Application.

4. Two copies of the Application shall be provided, one copy for the Emergency Arbitrator and one copy for HKIAC.

5. If HKIAC determines that it should accept the Application, HKIAC shall seek to appoint an Emergency Arbitrator within two days after receipt of both the Application and the Application Deposit.

6. The Application Deposit is the amount set by HKIAC, as stated on HKIAC's website on the date the Application is submitted. The Application Deposit consists of HKIAC's administrative expenses and the Emergency Arbitrator's fees and expenses. The Emergency Arbitrator's fees shall be determined by HKIAC by reference to his or her hourly rate subject to the terms set out in Schedule 2. HKIAC may, at any time during the Emergency Relief proceedings, decide to increase the Emergency Arbitrator's fees or HKIAC's administrative expenses, taking into account, inter alia, the nature of the case and the nature and amount of work performed by the Emergency Arbitrator and HKIAC. If the party which submitted the Application fails to pay the increased fees and/or expenses within the time limit fixed by HKIAC, the Application shall be dismissed.

7. Once the Emergency Arbitrator has been appointed, HKIAC shall so notify the parties to the Application and shall transmit the file to the Emergency Arbitrator. Thereafter, all written communications from the parties shall be submitted directly to the Emergency Arbitrator with a copy to the other party to the Application and HKIAC. A copy of any written communications from the Emergency Arbitrator to the parties shall also be copied to HKIAC.

8. Article 11 of the Rules shall apply to the Emergency Arbitrator, except that the time limits set out in Articles 11.7 and 11.9 are shortened to three days.

9. Where an Emergency Arbitrator dies, has been successfully challenged, has been otherwise removed, or has resigned, HKIAC shall seek to appoint a substitute Emergency Arbitrator within two days. If an Emergency

Arbitrator withdraws or a party agrees to terminate an Emergency Arbitrator's appointment under paragraph 8 of this Schedule, no acceptance of the validity of any ground referred to in Article 11.6 of the Rules shall be implied. If the Emergency Arbitrator is replaced, the Emergency Relief proceedings shall resume at the stage where the Emergency Arbitrator was replaced or ceased to perform his or her functions, unless the substitute Emergency Arbitrator decides otherwise.

10. If the parties have agreed on the seat of arbitration, such seat shall be the seat of the Emergency Relief proceedings. Where the parties have not agreed on the seat of arbitration, and without prejudice to the arbitral tribunal's determination of the seat of arbitration pursuant to Article 14.1 of the Rules, the seat of the Emergency Relief proceedings shall be Hong Kong.

11. Taking into account the urgency inherent in the Emergency Relief proceedings and ensuring that each party has a reasonable opportunity to be heard on the Application, the Emergency Arbitrator may conduct such proceedings in such a manner as the Emergency Arbitrator considers appropriate. The Emergency Arbitrator shall have the power to rule on objections that the Emergency Arbitrator has no jurisdiction, including any objections with respect to the existence, validity or scope of the arbitration clause(s) or of the separate arbitration agreement(s), and shall resolve any disputes over the applicability of this Schedule.

12. Any decision, order or award of the Emergency Arbitrator on the Application (the "Emergency Decision") shall be made within fifteen days from the date on which HKIAC transmitted the file to the Emergency Arbitrator. This period of time may be extended by agreement of the parties or, in appropriate circumstances, by HKIAC.

13. The Emergency Decision may be made even if in the meantime the file has been transmitted to the arbitral tribunal.

14. Any Emergency Decision shall:

(a) be made in writing;

(b) state the date when it was made and summary reasons upon which the Emergency Decision is based (including a determination on whether the Application is admissible under Article 23.1 of the Rules and whether the Emergency Arbitrator has jurisdiction to grant the Emergency Relief); and

(c) be signed by the Emergency Arbitrator.

15. Any Emergency Decision shall fix the costs of the Emergency Relief proceedings and decide which of the parties shall bear them or in what proportion they shall be borne by the parties, subject always to the power of

the arbitral tribunal to determine finally the apportionment of such costs in accordance with Article 33 of the Rules. The costs of the Emergency Relief proceedings include HKIAC's administrative expenses, the Emergency Arbitrator's fees and expenses and the reasonable and other legal costs incurred by the parties for the Emergency Relief proceedings.

16. Any Emergency Decision shall have the same effect as an interim measure granted pursuant to Article 23 of the Rules and shall be binding on the parties when rendered. By agreeing to arbitration under these Rules, the parties undertake to comply with any Emergency Decision without delay.

17. The Emergency Arbitrator shall be entitled to order the provision of appropriate security by the party seeking Emergency Relief.

18. Any Emergency Decision may, upon a reasoned request by a party, be modified, suspended or terminated by the Emergency Arbitrator or the arbitral tribunal (once constituted).

19. Any Emergency Decision ceases to be binding:

(a) if the Emergency Arbitrator or the arbitral tribunal so decides;

(b) upon the arbitral tribunal rendering a final award, unless the arbitral tribunal expressly decides otherwise;

(c) upon the withdrawal of all claims or the termination of the arbitration before the rendering of a final award; or

(d) if the arbitral tribunal is not constituted within 90 days from the date of the Emergency Decision. This period of time may be extended by agreement of the parties or, in appropriate circumstances, by HKIAC.

20. Subject to paragraph 13 of this Schedule, the Emergency Arbitrator shall have no further power to act once the arbitral tribunal is constituted.

21. The Emergency Arbitrator may not act as arbitrator in any arbitration relating to the dispute that gave rise to the Application and in respect of which the Emergency Arbitrator has acted, unless otherwise agreed by the parties to the arbitration.

22. The Emergency Arbitrator Procedures are not intended to prevent any party from seeking urgent interim or conservatory measures from a competent judicial authority at any time.

23. In all matters not expressly provided for in this Schedule, the Emergency Arbitrator shall act in the spirit of the Rules.

24. The Emergency Arbitrator shall make every reasonable effort to ensure that an Emergency Decision is valid.

Table 1

Sum in Dispute (in HKD)		Administrative Fee (in HKD)
Up to	400,000	14,800
From To	400,001 800,000	14,800 + 0.800% of amt. over 400,000
From To	800,001 4,000,000	18,000 + 0.700% of amt. over 800,000
From To	4,000,001 8,000,000	40,400 + 0.460% of amt. over 4,000, 000
From To	8,000,001 16,000,000	58,800 + 0.260% of amt. over 8,000,000
From To	16,000,001 40,000,000	79,600 + 0.152% of amt. over 16,000,000
From To	40,000,001 80,000,000	116,080 + 0.081% of amt. over 40,000,000
From To	80,000,001 240,000,000	148,480 + 0.052% of amt. over 80,000,000
From To	240,000,001 400,000,000	231,680 + 0.037% of amt. over 240,000,000
Over	400,000,000	290,880

Table 2

Sum in Dispute (in HKD)		Administrative Fee (in HKD)
Up to	400,000	11.000% of amount in dispute
From To	400,001 800,000	44,000 + 10.000% of amt. over 400,000
From To	800,001 4,000,000	84,000 + 5.300% of amt. over 800,000
From To	4,000,001 8,000,000	253,600 + 3.780% of amt. over 4,000, 000
From To	8,000,001 16,000,000	404,800 + 1.730% of amt. over 8,000,000
From To	16,000,001 40,000,000	543,200 + 1.060% of amt. over 16,000,000
From To	40,000,001 80,000,000	797,600 + 0.440% of amt. over 40,000,000
From To	80,000,001 240,000,000	973,600 + 0.250% of amt. over 80,000,000
From To	240,000,001 400,000,000	1,373,600 + 0.228% of amt. over 240,000,000
From To	400,000,001 600,000,000	1,738,400 + 0.101% of amt. over 400,000,000
From To	600,000,001 800,000,000	1,940,400 + 0.067% of amt. over 600,000,0000
From To	800,000,001 4,000,000,000	2,074,400 + 0.044% of amt. over 800,000,000
Over	4,000,000,000	3,482,,400 + 0.025% of amt. Over 4,000,000,000 Maximum of 12,574,000

IBA GUIDELINES FOR DRAFTING INTERNATIONAL ARBITRATION CLAUSES *

I. Introduction

1. The purpose of these Guidelines is to provide a succinct and accessible approach to the drafting of international arbitration clauses. Poorly drafted arbitration clauses may be unenforceable and often cause unnecessary cost and delay. By considering these Guidelines, contract drafters should be able to ensure that their arbitration clauses are effective and adapted to their needs.

2. The Guidelines are divided into five sections (in addition to this introduction). The first section offers basic guidelines on what to do and not to do. The second section addresses optional elements that should be considered when drafting arbitration clauses. The third section addresses multi-tier dispute resolution clauses providing for negotiation, mediation and arbitration. The fourth section discusses the drafting of arbitration clauses for multiparty contracts, and the fifth section considers the drafting of arbitration clauses in situations involving multiple, but related contracts.

II. Basic Drafting Guidelines

Guideline 1: The parties should decide between institutional and *ad hoc* arbitration.

Comments:

3. The first choice facing parties drafting an arbitration clause is whether to opt for institutional or *ad hoc* arbitration.

4. In institutional (or administered) arbitration, an arbitral institution provides assistance in running the arbitral proceedings in exchange for a fee. The institution can assist with practical matters such as organizing hearings and handling communications with and payments to the arbitrators. The institution can also provide services such as appointing an arbitrator if a party defaults, deciding a challenge against an arbitrator and scrutinizing the award. The institution does not decide the merits of the parties' dispute, however. This is left entirely to the arbitrators.

5. Institutional arbitration may be beneficial for parties with little experience in international arbitration. The institution may contribute significant procedural 'know how' that helps the arbitration run effectively, and may even be able to assist when the parties have failed to anticipate something when drafting their arbitration clause. The services provided by an arbitral institution are often worth the relatively low administrative fee charged.

6. If parties choose administered arbitration, they should seek a reputable institution, usually one with an established track record of administering international cases. The major arbitral institutions can administer

* For a commentary on the IBA Guidelines for Drafting Arbitration Clauses, see Paul Friedland and Damien Nyer, 'Drafting Arbitration Clauses Before and After a Dispute' in Lawrence W. Newman and Michael J. Radine (eds), *Soft Law in International Arbitration* (Juris, 2014).

arbitrations around the world, and the arbitral proceedings do not need to take place in the city where the institution is headquartered.

7. In *ad hoc* (or non-administered) arbitration, the burden of running the arbitral proceedings falls entirely on the parties and, once they have been appointed, the arbitrators. As explained below (Guideline 2), the parties can facilitate their task by selecting a set of arbitration rules designed for use in *ad hoc* arbitration. Although no arbitral institution is involved in running the arbitral proceedings, as explained below (Guideline 6), there still is a need to designate a neutral third party (known as an 'appointing authority') to select arbitrators and deal with possible vacancies if the parties cannot agree.

Guideline 2: The parties should select a set of arbitration rules and use the model clause recommended for these arbitration rules as a starting point.

Comments:

8. The second choice facing parties drafting an arbitration clause is selection of a set of arbitration rules. The selected arbitration rules will provide the procedural framework for the arbitral proceedings. If the parties do not incorporate an established set of rules, many procedural issues that may arise during arbitral proceedings should be addressed in the arbitration clause itself, an effort that is rarely desirable and should be undertaken with specialized advice.

9. When the parties have opted for institutional arbitration, the choice of arbitration rules should always coincide with that of the arbitral institution. When the parties have opted for *ad hoc* arbitration, the parties can select arbitration rules developed for non-administered arbitration, eg, the Arbitration Rules developed by the United Nations Commission on International Trade Law ('UNCITRAL'). Even if they do so, the parties should designate an arbitral institution (or another neutral entity) as the appointing authority for selection of the arbitrators (see paragraphs 31-32 below).

10. Once a set of arbitration rules is selected, the parties should use the model clause recommended by the institution or entity that authored the rules as a starting point for drafting their arbitration clause. The parties can add to the model clause, but should rarely subtract from it. By doing so, the parties will ensure that all the elements required to make an arbitration agreement valid, enforceable and effective are present. They will ensure that arbitration is unambiguously established as the exclusive dispute resolution method under their contract and that the correct names of the arbitral

institution and rules are used (thus avoiding confusion or dilatory tactics when a dispute arises). The parties should assure that language added to a model clause is consistent with the selected arbitration rules.

Recommended clause:

11. For an institutional arbitration clause, the website of the chosen institution should be accessed in order to use the model clause proposed by the institution as a basis for drafting the arbitration clause. Some institutions have also developed clauses that are specific to certain industries (eg, shipping).

12. For an *ad hoc* arbitration designating a set of rules, the website of the entity that issues such rules should be accessed in order to use the entity's model clause as a basis for drafting the arbitration clause.

13. In those instances where contracting parties agree to *ad hoc* arbitration without designating a set of rules, the following clause can be used for two-party contracts:

All disputes arising out of or in connection with this agreement, including any question regarding its existence, validity or termination, shall be finally resolved by arbitration.

The place of arbitration shall be [city, country].

The language of the arbitration shall be [...].

The arbitration shall be commenced by a request for arbitration by the claimant, delivered to the respondent. The request for arbitration shall set out the nature of the claim(s) and the relief requested.

The arbitral tribunal shall consist of three arbitrators, one selected by the claimant in the request for arbitration, the second selected by the respondent within [30] days of receipt of the request for arbitration, and the third, who shall act as presiding arbitrator, selected by the two parties within [30] days of the selection of the second arbitrator. If any arbitrators are not selected within these time periods, [the designated appointing authority] shall, upon the request of any party, make the selection(s).

If a vacancy arises, the vacancy shall be filled by the method by which that arbitrator was originally appointed, provided, however, that, if a vacancy arises during or after the hearing on the merits, the remaining two arbitrators may proceed with the arbitration and render an award.

The arbitrators shall be independent and impartial. Any challenge of an arbitrator shall be decided by [the designated appointing authority].

The procedure to be followed during the arbitration shall be agreed by the parties or, failing such agreement, determined by the arbitral tribunal after consultation with the parties.

The arbitral tribunal shall have the power to rule on its own jurisdiction, including any objections with respect to the existence, validity or effectiveness of the arbitration agreement.
The arbitral tribunal may make such ruling in a preliminary decision on jurisdiction or in an award on the merits, as it considers appropriate in the circumstances.
Default by any party shall not prevent the arbitral tribunal from proceeding to render an award. The arbitral tribunal may make its decisions by a majority. In the event that no majority is possible, the presiding arbitrator may make the decision(s) as if acting as a sole arbitrator.
If the arbitrator appointed by a party fails or refuses to participate, the two other arbitrators may proceed with the arbitration and render an award if they determine that the failure or refusal to participate was unjustified.
Any award of the arbitral tribunal shall be final and binding on the parties. The parties undertake to carry out any award without delay and shall be deemed to have waived their right to any form of recourse insofar as such waiver can validly be made. Enforcement of any award may be sought in any court of competent jurisdiction.

Guideline 3: Absent special circumstances, the parties should not attempt to limit the scope of disputes subject to arbitration and should define this scope broadly.

Comments:

14. The scope of an arbitration clause refers to the type and ambit of disputes that are subject to arbitration. Absent particular circumstances compelling otherwise, the scope of an arbitration clause should be defined broadly to cover not only all disputes 'arising out of' the contract, but also all disputes 'in connection with' (or 'relating to') the contract. Less inclusive language invites arguments about whether a given dispute is subject to arbitration.

15. In certain circumstances, the parties may have good reasons to exclude some disputes from the scope of the arbitration clause. For example, it may be appropriate to refer pricing and technical disputes under certain contracts to expert determination rather than to arbitration. As another example, licensors may justifiably wish to retain the option to seek orders of specific performance and other injunctive relief directly from the courts in case of infringement of their intellectual property rights or to submit decisions on the ownership or validity of these rights to courts.

16. The parties should bear in mind that, even when drafted carefully, exclusions may not avoid preliminary arguments over whether a given

dispute is subject to arbitration. A claim may raise some issues that fall within the scope of the arbitration clause and others that do not. To use one of the above examples, a dispute over the ownership or validity of intellectual property rights under a licensing agreement may also involve issues of non-payment, breach and so forth, which could give rise to intractable jurisdictional problems in situations where certain disputes have been excluded from arbitration.

Recommended clause:

17. The parties will ensure that the scope of their arbitration clause is broad by using the model clause associated with the selected arbitration rules.

18. If the parties do not use a model clause, the following clause should be used:

All disputes arising out of or in connection with this agreement, including any question regarding its existence, validity or termination, shall be finally resolved by arbitration under [selected arbitration rules].

19. Exceptionally, if there are special circumstances and the parties wish to limit the scope of disputes subject to arbitration, the following clause can be used: Except for matters that are specifically excluded from arbitration hereunder, all disputes arising out of or in connection with this agreement, including any question regarding its existence, validity or termination, shall be finally resolved by arbitration under [selected arbitration rules].

The following matters are specifically excluded from arbitration hereunder: [...].

Guideline 4: The parties should select the place of arbitration. This selection should be based on both practical and juridical considerations.

Comments:

20. The selection of the place (or 'seat') of arbitration involves obvious practical considerations: neutrality, availability of hearing facilities, proximity to the witnesses and evidence, the parties' familiarity with the language and culture, willingness of qualified arbitrators to participate in proceedings in that place. The place of arbitration may also influence the profile of the arbitrators, especially if not appointed by the parties. Convenience should not be the decisive factor, however, as under most rules the tribunal is free to meet and hold hearings in places other than the designated place of arbitration.

21. The place of arbitration is the juridical home of the arbitration. Close attention must be paid to the legal regime of the chosen place of arbitration because this choice has important legal consequences under most national

arbitration legislations as well as under some arbitration rules. While the place of arbitration does not determine the law governing the contract and the merits (see paragraphs 42-46 below), it does determine the law (arbitration law or *lex arbitri*) that governs certain procedural aspects of the arbitration, eg, the powers of arbitrators and the judicial oversight of the arbitral process. Moreover, the courts at the place of arbitration can be called upon to provide assistance (eg, by appointing or replacing arbitrators, by ordering provisional and conservatory measures, or by assisting with the taking of evidence), and may also interfere with the conduct of the arbitration (eg, by ordering a stay of the arbitral proceedings). Further, these courts have jurisdiction to hear challenges against the award at the end of the arbitration; awards set aside at the place of arbitration may not be enforceable elsewhere. Even if the award is not set aside, the place of arbitration may affect the enforceability of the award under applicable international treaties.

22. As a general rule, the parties should set the place of arbitration in a jurisdiction (i) that is a party to the 1958 Convention on the Recognition and Enforcement of Foreign Arbitral Awards (known as the New York Convention), (ii) whose law is supportive of arbitration and permits arbitration of the subject matter of the contract, and (iii) whose courts have a track record of issuing unbiased decisions that are supportive of the arbitral process.

23. An arbitration clause that fails to specify the place of arbitration will be effective, though undesirable. The arbitral institution, if there is one, or the arbitrators, will choose for the parties if they cannot agree on a place of arbitration after a dispute has arisen. (In *ad hoc* arbitration, however, if difficulties arise with the appointment of the arbitrators and no place of arbitration is selected, the parties may be unable to proceed with the arbitration unless courts in some country are willing to assist.) The parties should not leave such a critical decision to others.

24. The parties should specify in their arbitration clause the 'place of arbitration', rather than the place of the 'hearing'. By designating only the place of the hearing, the parties leave it uncertain whether they have designated the 'place of arbitration' for the purposes of applicable laws and treaties. Moreover, by designating the place of the hearing in the arbitration clause, the parties deprive the arbitrators of desired flexibility to hold hearings in other places, as may be convenient.

Recommended Clause:

25. The place of arbitration shall be [city, country].

Guideline 5: The parties should specify the number of arbitrators.

Comments:

26. The parties should specify the number of arbitrators (ordinarily one or three and, in any case, an odd number). The number of arbitrators has an impact on the overall cost, the duration and, on occasion, the quality of the arbitral proceedings. Proceedings before a three-member tribunal will almost inevitably be lengthier and more expensive than those before a sole arbitrator. A three-member tribunal may be better equipped, however, to address complex issues of fact and law, and may reduce the risk of irrational or unfair results. The parties may also desire the increased control of the process afforded by each having the opportunity to select an arbitrator.

27. If the parties do not specify the number of arbitrators (and cannot agree on this once a dispute has arisen), the arbitral institution, if there is one, will make the decision for them, generally on the basis of the amount in dispute and the perceived complexity of the case. In *ad hoc* arbitration, the selected arbitration rules, if any, will ordinarily specify whether one or three arbitrators are to be appointed absent contrary agreement. Where the parties have not selected such a set of arbitration rules, it is especially important to specify the number of arbitrators in the clause itself.

28. Parties may remain deliberately silent as to the number of arbitrators, reasoning that the choice between a one- or three-member tribunal will be better made if and when a dispute arises. While the opportunity to decide this question after a dispute arises is an advantage, the corresponding disadvantage is that the proceedings may be delayed if the parties disagree on the number of arbitrators, particularly in the *ad hoc* context. On balance, it is recommended to specify the number of arbitrators in advance in the arbitration clause itself.

Recommended Clause:

29. There shall be [one or three] arbitrator[s].

Guideline 6: The parties should specify the method of selection and replacement of arbitrators and, when *ad hoc* arbitration is chosen, should select an appointing authority.

Comments:

30. Both institutional and *ad hoc* arbitration rules provide default mechanisms for selecting and replacing arbitrators. When they have incorporated such set of rules, the parties may be content to rely on the default mechanism set forth in the rules. The parties may also agree on an alternative method. For example, many arbitration rules provide for the chairperson of a three-member tribunal to be selected by the two co-

arbitrators or by the institution. Parties often prefer to attempt to select the chairperson themselves in the first instance. If the parties decide to depart from the default mechanism, they should use language consistent with the terminology of the applicable arbitration rules. For example, under certain institutional rules, the parties 'nominate' arbitrators, and only the institution is empowered to 'appoint' them. When the parties have not incorporated a set of arbitration rules, it is crucial that they spell out the method for selecting and replacing arbitrators in the arbitration clause itself.

31. The need to designate an appointing authority in the context of *ad hoc* arbitration constitutes a significant difference between drafting an institutional arbitration clause and drafting an *ad hoc* arbitration clause. In institutional arbitration, the institution is available to select or replace arbitrators when the parties fail to do so. There is no such institution in *ad hoc* arbitration. It is, therefore, critical that the parties designate an 'appointing authority' in the *ad hoc* context, to select or replace arbitrators in the event the parties fail to do so. Absent such a choice, the courts at the place of arbitration may be willing to make the necessary appointments and replacement. (Under the UNCITRAL Rules, the Secretary General of the Permanent Court of Arbitration designates the appointing authority if the parties have failed to do so in their arbitration clause.)

32. The appointing authority may be an arbitral institution, a court, a trade or professional association, or another neutral entity. The parties should select an office or title (eg, the president of an arbitral institution, the chief judge of a court, or the chair of a trade or professional association) rather than an individual (as such individual may be unable to act when called upon to do so). The parties should also make sure that the selected authority will agree to perform its duties if and when called upon to do so.

33. Significant time may be wasted at the outset of the proceedings if no time limits are specified for the appointment of the arbitrators. Such time limits are ordinarily set in arbitration rules. Parties that have agreed to incorporate such rules thus need not concern themselves with this issue, unless they wish to depart from the appointment mechanism set forth in the rules. When the parties have not agreed to incorporate a set of arbitration rules, it is important to set such time limits in the arbitration clause itself.

34. When a tribunal is comprised of three arbitrators, it sometimes occurs that one arbitrator resigns, refuses to cooperate or otherwise fails to participate in the proceedings at a late and critical juncture (eg, during the deliberations). In those circumstances, replacement may not be an option as it would overly delay and disrupt the proceedings. Absent specific

authorization, however, the remaining two arbitrators may not be able to render a valid and enforceable award. Most (but not all) arbitration rules therefore permit the other two arbitrators in such a situation to continue the proceedings as a 'truncated' tribunal and to issue an award. When the parties do not select a set of arbitration rules (or where the selected arbitration rules do not address the issue), the parties can authorize in the arbitration clause a 'truncated' tribunal to proceed to render an award.

Recommended Clauses:

35. When institutional arbitration is chosen, and the institutional rules do not provide for all arbitrator selections and replacements to be made by the parties in the first instance, and the parties wish to make their own selections, the following clause can be used:

There shall be three arbitrators, one selected by the initiating party in the request for arbitration, the second selected by the other party within [30] days of receipt of the request for arbitration, and the third, who shall act as [chairperson or presiding arbitrator], selected by the two parties within [30] days of the selection of the second arbitrator. If any arbitrators are not selected within these time periods, the [institution] shall make the selection (s). If replacement of an arbitrator becomes necessary, replacement shall be done by the same method(s) as above.

36. When non-administered arbitration is chosen, the parties can provide for a method of selection and replacement of arbitrators by choosing a set of *ad hoc* arbitration rules, eg, the UNCITRAL Arbitration Rules.

37. The clause proposed above for *ad hoc* arbitration without a set of arbitration rules (see paragraph 13 above) sets forth a comprehensive mechanism to select and replace the members of a three-member tribunal and includes provisions permitting a truncated tribunal to proceed to render an award without the participation of an obstructive or defaulting arbitrator.

38. In similar circumstances, but where the parties wish to submit their dispute to a sole arbitrator, the parties can amend the clause proposed in paragraph 13 above and use the following language:

There shall be one arbitrator, selected jointly by the parties. If the arbitrator is not selected within [30] days of the receipt of the request for arbitration, the [designated appointing authority] shall make the selection.

Guideline 7: The parties should specify the language of arbitration.

Comments:

39. Arbitration clauses in contracts between parties whose languages differ, or whose shared language differs from that of the place of arbitration, should ordinarily specify the language of arbitration. In making this choice,

the parties should consider not only the language of the contract and of the related documentation, but also the likely effect of their choice on the pool of qualified arbitrators and counsel. Absent a choice in the arbitration clause, it is for the arbitrators to determine the language of arbitration. It is likely that the arbitrators will choose the language of the contract or, if different, of the correspondence exchanged by the parties. Leaving this decision to the arbitrators could cause unnecessary cost and delay.

40. Contract drafters are often tempted to provide for more than one language of arbitration. The parties should carefully consider whether to do so. Multi-lingual arbitration, while workable (there are numerous examples of proceedings conducted in both English and Spanish, for example), may present challenges depending on the languages chosen. There may be difficulties in finding arbitrators who are able to conduct arbitration proceedings in two languages, and the required translation and interpretation may add to the costs and delays of the proceedings. A solution may be to specify one language of arbitration, but to provide that documents may be submitted in another language (without translation).

Recommended Clause:

41. The language of the arbitration shall be [...].

Guideline 8: The parties should ordinarily specify the rules of law governing the contract and any subsequent disputes.

Comments:

42. In international transactions, it is important for the parties to select in their contract the rules of law that govern the contract and any subsequent disputes (the 'substantive law').

43. The choice of substantive law should be set forth in a clause separate from the arbitration clause or should be addressed together with arbitration in a clause which makes clear that the clause serves a dual purpose, eg, captioning the clause 'Governing Law and Arbitration [or Dispute Resolution].' This is so because issues can arise under the substantive law during the performance of the contract independent of any arbitral dispute.

44. By choosing the substantive law, the parties do not choose the procedural or arbitration law. Such law, absent a contrary agreement, is ordinarily that of the place of arbitration (see paragraph 21 above). Although the parties can agree otherwise, it is rarely advisable to do so.

45. Sometimes parties do not choose a national legal system as the substantive law. Instead, they choose *lex mercatoria* or other a-national rules of law. In other cases, they empower the arbitral tribunal to determine the dispute on the basis of what is fair and reasonable (*ex aequo et bono*).

Care should be taken before selecting these options. While appropriate in certain situations (eg, when the parties cannot agree on a national law), they may create difficulties by virtue of the relative uncertainty as to their content or impact on the outcome. As it is difficult to ascertain in advance the rules that will ultimately be applied by the arbitrators when the parties select these alternatives to national laws, resolving disputes may become more complex, uncertain and costly.

Recommended Clause:

46. The following clause can be used to select the substantive law:

This agreement is governed by, and all disputes arising under or in connection with this agreement shall be resolved in accordance with, [selected law or rules of law].

III. Drafting Guidelines for Optional Elements

47. Arbitration being a matter of agreement, contracting parties have the opportunity in their arbitration clause to tailor the process to their specific needs. There are numerous options that contracting parties can consider. This section sets out and comments upon the few that the parties should consider during the negotiation of an arbitration clause. By setting out these options, these Guidelines do not thereby suggest that these optional elements need to be included in an arbitration clause.

Option 1: The authority of the arbitral tribunal and of the courts with respect to provisional and conservatory measures.

Comments:

48. It is rarely necessary to provide in the arbitration clause that the arbitral tribunal or the courts or both have the authority to order provisional and conservatory measures pending decision on the merits. The arbitral tribunal and the courts ordinarily have the authority to do so, subject to various conditions, even where the arbitration clause is silent in this respect. The authority of the arbitral tribunal rests with the arbitration rules and the relevant arbitration law. That of the courts rests with the relevant arbitration law.

49. When the governing arbitration law restricts the availability of provisional or conservatory relief, however, or when the availability of provisional and conservatory relief is of special concern (eg, because trade secrets or other confidential information are involved), the parties may want to make the authority of the arbitral tribunal and the courts explicit in the arbitration clause.

50. When the availability of provisional and conservatory relief is of special concern, the parties may also want to modify restrictive aspects of the

applicable arbitration rules. For example, certain institutional rules restrict the right of the parties to apply to the courts for provisional and conservatory relief once the arbitral tribunal is appointed. Under other arbitration rules, the arbitral tribunal is authorized to order provisional and conservatory measures with respect to 'the subject matter of the dispute', which leaves uncertain whether the arbitral tribunal can order measures to preserve the position of the parties (eg, injunction, security for costs) or the integrity of the arbitral process (eg, freezing orders, anti-suit injunctions).

Recommended clauses:

51. The following clause can be used to make explicit the authority of the arbitral tribunal with respect to provisional and conservatory relief:

Except as otherwise specifically limited in this agreement, the arbitral tribunal shall have the power to grant any remedy or relief that it deems appropriate, whether provisional or final, including but not limited to conservatory relief and injunctive relief, and any such measures ordered by the arbitral tribunal shall, to the extent permitted by applicable law, be deemed to be a final award on the subject matter of the measures and shall be enforceable as such.

52. The following clause can be added to the above clause, or used independently, to specify that resort to courts for provisional and conservatory measures is not precluded by the arbitration agreement:

Each party retains the right to apply to any court of competent jurisdiction for provisional and/or conservatory relief, including prearbitral attachments or injunctions, and any such request shall not be deemed incompatible with the agreement to arbitrate or a waiver of the right to arbitrate.

53. The following clause can be added to the clause recommended at paragraph 51 above, or used independently, to limit the parties' right to resort to the courts for provisional and conservatory relief after the arbitral tribunal is constituted:

Each party has the right to apply to any court of competent jurisdiction for provisional and/or conservatory relief, including pre-arbitral attachments or injunctions, and any such request shall not be deemed incompatible with the agreement to arbitrate or a waiver of the right to arbitrate, provided however that, after the arbitral tribunal is constituted, the arbitral tribunal shall have sole jurisdiction to consider applications for provisional and/or conservatory relief, and any such measures ordered by the arbitral tribunal may be specifically enforced by any court of competent jurisdiction.

54. If, in exceptional circumstances, the parties consider that *ex parte* provisional relief by the arbitral tribunal may be needed, they should so

specify and amend the clause recommended at paragraph 51 above by adding '(including *ex parte*)' after the word 'provisional'. Even with such addition, however, *ex parte* remedies ordered by the arbitral tribunal may not be enforceable under the relevant arbitration law.

Option 2: Document production.

Comments:

55. While the extent document production and information exchange in international arbitration varies from case to case and from arbitrator to arbitrator, parties are usually required to produce identified documents (including internal documents) that are shown to be relevant and material to the dispute. Other features particular to 'discovery' in some jurisdictions, such as depositions and interrogatories, are ordinarily absent. The IBA has developed a set of rules, the IBA Rules on the Taking of Evidence in International Arbitration (the 'IBA Rules'), designed to reflect this standard practice. These rules, which address production of both paper documents and electronically-stored information, are often used by international arbitral tribunals, expressly or not, as guidance.

56. The parties have three primary options regarding information or document production. They can say nothing about it and be content to rely on the default provisions of the governing arbitration law, which ordinarily leaves the question to the discretion of the arbitrators. They can adopt the IBA Rules. They can devise their own standards (bearing in mind that extensive document production is likely to have a major impact on the length and cost of the proceedings).

57. A difficulty that may arise in the context of document production in international arbitration is the issue of which rules should govern whether certain documents are exempt from production due to privilege. When, in the rare instance, contracting parties can foresee at the contract drafting stage that issues of privilege may arise and be of consequence, the parties may want to specify in their arbitration clause the principles that will govern all such questions. Article 9 of the IBA Rules provides guidance in this respect.

Recommended Clauses:

58. The following clause can be used to incorporate the IBA Rules either as a mandatory standard or, alternatively, for guidance purpose only:

[In addition to the authority conferred upon the arbitral tribunal by the [arbitration rules]], the arbitral tribunal shall have the authority to order production of documents [in accordance with] [taking guidance from] the IBA Rules on the Taking of Evidence in International Arbitration [as

current on the date of this agreement/the commencement of the arbitration].
59. The following clause can be used if the parties wish to specify the principles that will govern issues of privilege with respect to document disclosure:
All contentions that a document or communication is privileged and, as such, exempt from production in the arbitration, shall be resolved by the arbitral tribunal in accordance with Article 9 of the IBA Rules on the Taking of Evidence in International Arbitration.
Option 3: Confidentiality issues.
Comments:
60. Parties frequently assume that arbitration proceedings are confidential. While arbitration is private, in many jurisdictions parties are under no duty to keep the existence or content of the arbitration proceedings confidential. Few national laws or arbitration rules impose confidentiality obligations on the parties. Where a general duty is recognized, it is often subject to exceptions.
61. Parties concerned about confidentiality should, therefore, address this issue in their arbitration clause. In doing so, the parties should avoid absolute requirements because disclosure may be required by law, to protect or pursue a legal right or to enforce or challenge an award in subsequent judicial proceedings. The parties should also anticipate that the preparation of their claims, defenses and counterclaims may require disclosure of confidential information to non-parties (witnesses and experts).
62. Conversely, given the common assumption that arbitration proceedings are confidential, where the parties do not wish to be bound by any confidentiality duties, the parties should expressly say so in their arbitration clause.
Recommended Clauses:
63. Some arbitration rules set forth confidentiality obligations, and the parties will accordingly impose such obligations upon themselves if they agree to arbitrate under these rules.
64. The following clause imposes confidentiality obligations upon the parties:
The existence and content of the arbitral proceedings and any rulings or award shall be kept confidential by the parties and members of the arbitral tribunal except (i) to the extent that disclosure may be required of a party to fulfil a legal duty, protect or pursue a legal right, or enforce or challenge an award in bona fide legal proceedings before a state court or other judicial authority, (ii) with the consent of all parties, (iii) where needed for the

preparation or presentation of a claim or defense in this arbitration, (iv) where such information is already in the public domain other than as a result of a breach of this clause, or (v) by order of the arbitral tribunal upon application of a party.

65. The following clause may be used where the parties do not wish to be bound by any confidentiality obligation:

The parties shall be under no confidentiality obligation with respect to arbitration hereunder except as may be imposed by mandatory provisions of law.

Option 4: Allocation of costs and fees.

Comments:

66. Costs (eg, arbitrators' fees and expenses and, if applicable, institutional fees) and lawyers' fees can be substantial in international arbitration. It is rarely possible to predict how the arbitral tribunal will allocate these costs and fees, if at all, at the end of the proceedings. Domestic approaches diverge widely (from no allocation at all to full recovery by the prevailing party), and arbitrators have wide discretion in this respect.

67. Given these uncertainties, the parties may wish to address the issue of costs and fees in their arbitration clause (bearing in mind that such provisions may not be enforceable in certain jurisdictions). The parties have several options. They may merely confirm that the arbitrators can allocate costs and fees as they see fit. They may provide that the arbitrators make no allocation of costs and fees. They may try to ensure that costs and fees are allocated to the 'winner' or the 'prevailing party' on the merits, or that the arbitrators are to allocate costs and fees in proportion to success or failure. The parties should avoid absolute language ('shall') in drafting such a clause, as the identification of the 'winner' or the 'prevailing party' may be difficult and the clause may needlessly constrain the arbitrators in their allocation of costs and fees.

68. The parties may also wish to consider whether to allow compensation for the time spent by management, in-house counsel, experts and witnesses, as this issue is often uncertain in international arbitration.

Recommended Clauses:

69. The following clause can be used to ensure that the arbitrators have discretion to allocate both costs and fees (or to reaffirm such discretion if the designated arbitration rules include a provision to this effect):

The arbitral tribunal may include in its award an allocation to any party of such costs and expenses, including lawyers' fees [and costs and expenses of management, in-house counsel, experts and witnesses], as the arbitral tribunal shall deem reasonable.

70. The following clause provides for allocation of costs and fees to the 'prevailing' party:

The arbitral tribunal may award its costs and expenses, including lawyers' fees, to the prevailing party, if any and as determined by the arbitral tribunal in its discretion.

71. The following clause provides for allocation of costs and fees in proportion to success:

The arbitral tribunal may include in their award an allocation to any party of such costs and expenses, including lawyers' fees [and costs and expenses of management, in-house counsel, experts and witnesses], as the arbitral tribunal shall deem reasonable. In making such allocation, the arbitral tribunal shall consider the relative success of the parties on their claims and counterclaims and defenses.

72. The following clause can be used to ensure that the arbitrators do not allocate costs and fees:

All costs and expenses of the arbitral tribunal [and of the arbitral institution] shall be borne by the parties equally. Each party shall bear all costs and expenses (including of its own counsel, experts and witnesses) involved in preparing and presenting its case.

Option 5: Qualifications required of arbitrators.

Comments:

73. An advantage of arbitration, as compared to national court proceedings, is that the parties select the arbitrators and can, therefore, choose individuals with expertise or knowledge relevant to their dispute.

74. It is usually not advisable, however, to specify in the arbitration clause the qualifications required of arbitrators. The parties are ordinarily in a better position at the time of a dispute to know whether expertise is required, and if so, which, and each remains free at that time to appoint an arbitrator with the desired qualifications. Specifying qualification requirements in the arbitration clause may also drastically reduce the pool of available arbitrators. Further, a party intent on delaying the proceedings may challenge arbitrators on the basis of the qualification requirements.

75. If the parties nonetheless wish to specify such qualifications in the arbitration clause, they should avoid overly specific requirements, as the arbitration agreement may be unenforceable if, when a dispute arises, the parties are unable to identify suitable candidates who both meet the qualification requirements and are available to act as arbitrators.

76. Parties sometimes specify that the sole arbitrator or, in the case of a

three-member panel, the presiding arbitrator shall not share a common nationality with any of the parties. In institutional arbitration, such qualification requirement is often superfluous, as arbitral institutions ordinarily apply such practice in making appointments. In *ad hoc* arbitration, however, the parties may want so to specify in their arbitration clause.

Recommended Clauses:

77. The qualifications of arbitrators can be specified by adding the following to the arbitration clause:

[Each arbitrator][The presiding arbitrator] shall be [a lawyer/an accountant].

Or

[Each arbitrator][The presiding arbitrator] shall have experience in [specific industry].

Or

[The arbitrators][The presiding arbitrator] shall not be of the same nationality as any of the parties.

Option 6: Time limits.

Comments:

78. Parties sometimes try to save costs and time by providing in the arbitration clause that the award be made within a fixed period from the commencement of arbitration (a process known as 'fast-tracking'). Fast-tracking can save costs, but parties can rarely know at the time of drafting the arbitration clause whether every dispute liable to arise under the contract will be appropriate for resolution within the prescribed period. An award that is not rendered within the prescribed period may be unenforceable or may attract unnecessary challenges.

79. If, despite these considerations, the parties wish to set time limits in the arbitration clause, the tribunal should be allowed to extend these time limits to avoid the risk of an unenforceable award.

Recommended Clauses:

80. The following clause can be used to set time limits:

The award shall be rendered within [...] months of the appointment of [the sole arbitrator] [the chairperson], unless the arbitral tribunal determines, in a reasoned decision, that the interest of justice or the complexity of the case requires that such limit be extended.

Option 7: Finality of arbitration.

Comments:

81. An advantage of arbitration is that arbitral awards are final and not subject to appeal. In most jurisdictions, awards can be challenged only for

lack of jurisdiction, serious procedural defects or unfairness, and cannot be reviewed on the merits. Most arbitration rules reinforce the finality of arbitration by providing that awards are final and that the parties waive any recourse against them.

82. When the arbitration clause does not incorporate a set of arbitration rules, or where the incorporated rules do not contain finality and waiver of recourse language, it is prudent to specify in the arbitration clause that awards are final and not subject to recourse. Even where the parties incorporate arbitration rules that contain such language, it may still be advisable to repeat this language in the arbitration clause if the parties anticipate that the award may need to be enforced or otherwise scrutinized in jurisdictions that view arbitration with suspicion. When adding a waiver of recourse to the arbitration clause, the parties should review the law of the seat of arbitration to determine the scope of what is being waived, and the language required under the *lex arbitri.*

83. Parties are sometimes tempted to expand the scope of judicial review by, for example, allowing review of the merits. It is rarely advisable, and often not open to the parties, to do so. If the parties nonetheless wish to expand the scope of judicial review, specialized advice should be sought and the law at the place of arbitration should be reviewed carefully.

Recommended Clauses:

84. When the parties wish to emphasize the finality of arbitration and to waive any recourse against the award, the following language can be added to the arbitration clause, subject to any requirement imposed by the *lex arbitri:*

Any award of the arbitral tribunal shall be final and binding on the parties. The parties undertake to comply fully and promptly with any award without delay and shall be deemed to have waived their right to any form of recourse insofar as such waiver can validly be made.

85. When, in the exceptional case, the parties wish to expand the scope of judicial review and allow appeals on the merits, the parties should seek advice as to their power to do so in the relevant jurisdiction. Where enforceable, the following sentence can be considered:

The parties shall have the right to seek judicial review of the tribunal's award in the courts of [selected jurisdiction] in accordance with the standard of appellate review applicable to decisions of courts of first instance in such jurisdiction(s).

IV. Drafting Guidelines for Multi-Tier Dispute Resolution Clauses

86. It is common for dispute resolution clauses in international contracts to

provide for negotiation, mediation or some other form of alternative dispute resolution as preliminary steps before arbitration. Construction contracts, for example, sometimes require disputes to be submitted to a standing dispute board before they can be referred to arbitration. These clauses, known as multi-tier clauses, present specific drafting challenges.

Multi-Tier Guideline 1: The clause should specify a period of time for negotiation or mediation, triggered by a defined and undisputable event (ie, a written request), after which either party can resort to arbitration.

Comments:

87. A multi-tier clause that requires negotiation or mediation before arbitration may be deemed to create a condition precedent to arbitration. To minimize the risk that a party will use negotiation or mediation in order to gain delay or other tactical advantage, the clause should specify a time period beyond which the dispute can be submitted to arbitration, and this time period should generally be short. In specifying such time period, the parties should be aware that commencing negotiation or mediation may not be sufficient to suspend the prescription or limitation periods.

88. The period of time for negotiation or mediation should be triggered by a defined and indisputable event, such as a written request to negotiate or mediate under the clause or the appointment of a mediator. It is not advisable to define the triggering event by reference to a written notice of the dispute because a mere written exchange about the dispute might then be sufficient to trigger the deadline.

Recommended Clauses:

89. See the clauses recommended below at paragraphs 94-96.

Multi-Tier Guideline 2: The clause should avoid the trap of rendering arbitration permissive, not mandatory.

Comments:

90. Parties drafting multi-tier dispute resolution clauses often inadvertently leave ambiguous their intent to arbitrate disputes that cannot be resolved by negotiation or mediation. This happens when the parties provide that disputes not resolved by negotiation or mediation 'may' be submitted to arbitration.

Recommended Clauses:

91. See the clauses recommended below at paragraphs 94-96.

Multi-Tier Guideline 3: The clause should define the disputes to be submitted to negotiation or mediation and to arbitration in identical terms.

Comments:

92. Multi-tier dispute resolution clauses sometimes do not define in identical terms the disputes that are subject to negotiation or mediation as a first step and those subject to arbitration. Such ambiguities may suggest that some disputes can be submitted to arbitration immediately without going through negotiation or mediation as a first step.

93. The broad reference to 'disputes' in the clauses recommended below should cover counterclaims. Such counterclaims would thus need to go through the several steps and could not be raised for the first time in the arbitration. If the parties wish to preserve the right to raise counterclaims for the first time in the arbitration, they should so specify in their arbitration clause.

Recommended Clauses:

94. The following clause provides for mandatory negotiation as a first step:

The parties shall endeavor to resolve amicably by negotiation all disputes arising out of or in connection with this agreement, including any question regarding its existence, validity or termination. Any such dispute which remains unresolved [30] days after either party requests in writing negotiation under this clause or within such other period as the parties may agree in writing, shall be finally settled under the [designated set of arbitration rules] by [one or three] arbitrator[s] appointed in accordance with the said Rules. The place of arbitration shall be [city, country]. The language of arbitration shall be [...].

[All communications during the negotiation are confidential and shall be treated as made in the course of compromise and settlement negotiations for purposes of applicable rules of evidence and any additional confidentiality and professional secrecy protections provided by applicable law.]

95. The following clause provides for mandatory mediation as a first step:

The parties shall endeavor to resolve amicably by mediation under the [designated set of mediation rules] all disputes arising out of or in connection with this agreement, including any question regarding its existence, validity or termination. Any such dispute not settled pursuant to the said Rules within [45] days after appointment of the mediator or within such other period as the parties may agree in writing, shall be finally settled under the [designated set of arbitration rules] by [one or three] arbitrator[s] appointed in accordance with the said Rules. The place of arbitration shall be [city, country]. The language of arbitration shall be [...].

[All communications during the mediation are confidential and shall be treated as made in the course of compromise and settlement negotiations for purposes of applicable rules of evidence and any additional confidentiality and professional secrecy protections provided by applicable law.]

96. The following clause provides for both mandatory negotiation and mediation sequentially before arbitration:

All disputes arising out of or in connection with this agreement, including any question regarding its existence, validity or termination ('Dispute'), shall be resolved in accordance with the procedures specified below, which shall be the sole and exclusive procedures for the resolution of any such Dispute.

(A) Negotiation

The parties shall endeavor to resolve any Dispute amicably by negotiation between executives who have authority to settle the Dispute [and who are at a higher level of management than the persons with direct responsibility for administration or performance of this agreement].

(B) Mediation

Any Dispute not resolved by negotiation in accordance with paragraph (A) within [30] days after either party requested in writing negotiation under paragraph (A), or within such other period as the parties may agree in writing, shall be settled amicably by mediation under the [designated set of mediation rules].

(C) Arbitration

Any Dispute not resolved by mediation in accordance with paragraph (B) within [45] days after appointment of the mediator, or within such other period as the parties may agree in writing, shall be finally settled under the [designated set of arbitration rules] by [one or three] arbitrator[s] appointed in accordance with the said Rules. The place of arbitration shall be [...]. The language of arbitration shall be [...].

[All communications during the negotiation and mediation pursuant to paragraphs (A) and (B) are confidential and shall be treated as made in the course of compromise and settlement negotiations for purposes of applicable rules of evidence and any additional confidentiality and professional secrecy protections provided by applicable law.]

V. Drafting Guidelines for Multiparty Arbitration Clauses

97. International contracts often involve more than two parties. Parties drafting arbitration clauses for these contracts may fail to realize the specific drafting difficulties that result from the multiplicity of parties. In

particular, one cannot always rely on the model clauses of arbitral institutions, as these are ordinarily drafted with two parties in mind and may need to be adapted to be workable in a multiparty context. Specialized advice should generally be sought to draft such clauses.

Multiparty Guideline 1: The clause should address the consequences of the multiplicity of parties for the appointment of the arbitral tribunal.

Comments:

98. In a multiparty context, it is often not workable to provide that 'each party' appoints an arbitrator. There is an easy solution if the parties are content to provide for a sole arbitrator: in such case, the parties can provide that the sole arbitrator is to be appointed jointly by the parties or, absent agreement, by the institution or appointing authority. Where there are to be three arbitrators, a solution is to provide that the three arbitrators be appointed jointly by the parties or, absent agreement on all, by the institution or appointing authority.

99. Alternatively, the arbitration clause can require that the parties on each 'side' make joint appointments. This option is available when it can be anticipated at the drafting stage that certain contracting parties will have aligned interests. The overriding requirement is, however, that all parties be treated equally in the appointment process. This means in practice that, when two or more parties on one side fail to agree on an arbitrator, the institution or appointing authority will appoint all arbitrators, as the parties on one side would otherwise have had the opportunity to pick their arbitrator while the others not. This is the solution that has been adopted in some institutional arbitration rules.

Recommended Clauses:

100. The clause recommended below at paragraph 105 specifies a mechanism for appointing arbitrators in a multiparty context.

Multiparty Guideline 2: The clause should address the procedural complexities (intervention, joinder) arising from the multiplicity of parties.

Comments:

101. Procedural complexities may abound in the multiparty context. One is that of intervention: a contracting party that is not party to an arbitration commenced under the clause may wish to intervene in the proceedings. Another is that of joinder: a contracting party that is named as respondent may wish to join another contracting party that has not been named as respondent in the proceedings.

102. An arbitration clause would be workable even if it failed to address

these complexities. Such clause would, however, leave open the possibility of overlapping proceedings, conflicting decisions and associated delays, costs and uncertainties.

103. There is no easy way to address these complexities. A multiparty arbitration clause should be carefully drafted with regard to the particular circumstances, and specialized advice should usually be sought. As a general rule, the clause should provide that notice of any proceedings commenced under the clause be given to each contracting party regardless of whether that contracting party is named as respondent. There should be a clear time period after that notice for each contracting party to intervene or join other contracting parties in the proceedings, and no arbitrator should be appointed before the expiry of that time period.

104. Alternatively, the parties can opt to arbitrate under institutional rules that provide for intervention and joinder, bearing in mind that these rules may give wide discretion to the institution in this respect.

Recommended Clauses:

105. The following provision provides for intervention and joinder of other parties to the same agreement:

All disputes arising out of or in connection with this agreement, including any question regarding its existence, validity or termination, shall be finally resolved by arbitration under [selected arbitration rules], except as they may be modified herein or by mutual agreement of the parties.

The place of arbitration shall be [city, country]. The language of arbitration shall be [...]. There shall be three arbitrators, selected as follows.

In the event that the request for arbitration names only one claimant and one respondent, and no party has exercised its right to joinder or intervention in accordance with the paragraphs below, the claimant and the respondent shall each appoint one arbitrator within [15] days after the expiry of the period during which parties can exercise their right to joinder or intervention. If either party fails to appoint an arbitrator as provided, then, upon the application of any party, that arbitrator shall be appointed by [the designated arbitral institution]. The two arbitrators shall appoint the third arbitrator, who shall act as presiding arbitrator. If the two arbitrators fail to appoint the presiding arbitrator within [45] days of the appointment of the second arbitrator, the presiding arbitrator shall be appointed by [the designated arbitral institution/appointing authority].

In the event that more than two parties are named in the request for arbitration or at least one contracting party exercises its right to joinder or intervention in accordance with the paragraphs below, the claimant(s) shall jointly appoint one arbitrator and the respondent(s) shall jointly appoint the other arbitrator, both within [15] days after the expiry of the period during which parties can exercise their right to joinder or intervention. If the parties fail to appoint an arbitrator as provided above, [the designated arbitral institution/appointing authority] shall, upon the request of any party, appoint all three arbitrators and designate one of them to act as presiding arbitrator. If the claimant(s) and the respondent(s) appoint the arbitrators as provided above, the two arbitrators shall appoint the third arbitrator, who shall act as presiding arbitrator. If the two arbitrators fail to appoint the third arbitrator within [45] days of the appointment of the second arbitrator, the presiding arbitrator shall be appointed by [the designated arbitral institution/ appointing authority].

Any party to this agreement may, either separately or together with any other party to this agreement, initiate arbitration proceedings pursuant to this clause by sending a request for arbitration to all other parties to this agreement [and to the designated arbitral institution, if any].

Any party to this agreement may intervene in any arbitration proceedings hereunder by submitting a written notice of claim, counterclaim or cross-claim against any party to this agreement, provided that such notice is also sent to all other parties to this agreement [and to the designated arbitral institution, if any] within [30] days from the receipt by such intervening party of the relevant request for arbitration or notice of claim, counterclaim or cross-claim.

Any party to this agreement named as respondent in a request for arbitration, or a notice of claim, counterclaim or cross-claim, may join any other party to this agreement in any arbitration proceedings hereunder by submitting a written notice of claim, counterclaim or cross-claim against that party, provided that such notice is also sent to all other parties to this agreement [and to the designated arbitral institution, if any] within [30] days from the receipt by such respondent of the relevant request for arbitration or notice of claim, counterclaim or cross-claim.

Any joined or intervening party shall be bound by any award rendered by the arbitral tribunal even if such party chooses not to participate in the arbitration proceedings.

VI. Drafting Guidelines for Multi-Contract Arbitration Clauses

106. It is common for a single international transaction to involve several related contracts. Drafting arbitration clauses in a multi-contract setting presents specific challenges.

Multi-Contract Guideline 1: The arbitration clauses in the related contracts should be compatible.

Comments:

107. The parties should avoid specifying different dispute resolution mechanisms in their related contracts (eg, arbitration under different sets of rules or in different places), lest they run the risk of fragmenting future disputes. An arbitral tribunal appointed under the first contract may not have jurisdiction to consider a dispute that raises questions about the second contract, thus inviting parallel proceedings.

108. Assuming the parties want consistent decisions and wish to avoid parallel proceedings, a straightforward solution is to establish a stand-alone dispute resolution protocol, which is signed by all the parties and then incorporated by reference in all related contracts. If it is impractical to conclude such a protocol, the parties should ensure that the arbitration clauses in the related contract are identical or complementary. It is especially important that the arbitration clauses specify the same set of rules, place of arbitration and number of arbitrators. To avoid difficulties when proceedings are consolidated, the same substantive law and language of arbitration should also be specified. The parties should also make clear that a tribunal appointed under one contract has jurisdiction to consider and decide issues related to the other related contracts.

Recommended Clause:

109. If the parties do not wish to, or cannot, establish a stand-alone dispute resolution protocol, the following provision should be added to the arbitration clause in each related contract:

The parties agree that an arbitral tribunal appointed hereunder or under [the related agreement(s)] may exercise jurisdiction with respect to both this agreement and [the related agreement(s)].

Multi-Contract Guideline 2: The parties should consider whether to provide for consolidation of arbitral proceedings commenced under the related contracts.

Comments:

110. A procedural complexity that arises in a multi-contract setting is that of consolidation. Different arbitrations may be commenced under related contracts at different times. It may, or may not, be in the parties' interest to have these arbitrations dealt with in a single consolidated arbitration. In some situations, the parties may reason that one single consolidated arbitration would be more efficient and cost-effective. In other circumstances, the parties may have reasons to keep the arbitrations

separated.

111. If the parties wish to permit consolidation of related arbitrations, they should say so in the arbitration clause. Courts in some jurisdiction have discretion to order consolidation of related arbitration proceedings, but ordinarily will not do so absent parties' agreement. Where the courts at the place of arbitration have no such power, or where the parties do not wish to rely on judicial discretion, the parties should also spell out in the clause the procedure for consolidating related proceedings. The applicable arbitration rules, if any, and the law of the place of arbitration should be reviewed carefully, as they may constrain the parties' ability to consolidate arbitral proceedings. Conversely, in some jurisdictions, the parties may want to exclude the possibility of consolidation (or class arbitration).

112. Specialized advice is required when the related contracts also involve more than two parties. Drafting consolidation provisions in a multiparty context is especially intricate. An obvious difficulty is that each party must be treated equally with respect to the appointment of the arbitrators. A workable, but less than ideal, solution is to provide for all appointments to be made by the institution or appointing authority. The parties should also be aware that a consolidation clause may, in some jurisdictions, be read as consent to class-action arbitration.

Recommended Clauses:

113. The following provision provides for consolidation of related arbitrations between the same two parties:

The parties consent to the consolidation of arbitrations commenced hereunder and/or under [the related agreements] as follows. If two or more arbitrations are commenced hereunder and/or [the related agreements], any party named as claimant or respondent in any of these arbitrations may petition any arbitral tribunal appointed in these arbitrations for an order that the several arbitrations be consolidated in a single arbitration before that arbitral tribunal (a 'Consolidation Order'). In deciding whether to make such a Consolidation Order, that arbitral tribunal shall consider whether the several arbitrations raise common issues of law or facts and whether to consolidate the several arbitrations would serve the interests of justice and efficiency.

If before a Consolidation Order is made by an arbitral tribunal with respect to another arbitration, arbitrators have already been appointed in that other arbitration, their appointment terminates upon the making of such Consolidation Order and they are deemed to be *functus officio*. Such termination is without prejudice to: (i) the validity of any acts done or orders made by them prior to the termination, (ii) their entitlement to be paid their proper fees and disbursements, (iii) the date when any claim or defense was raised for the purpose of applying any limitation bar or any like rule or provision, (iv) evidence adduced and admissible before termination, which evidence shall be admissible in arbitral proceedings after the Consolidation Order, and (v) the parties' entitlement to legal and other costs incurred before termination.

In the event of two or more conflicting Consolidation Orders, the Consolidation Order that was made first inime shall prevail.

IBA GUIDELINES ON CONFLICTS OF INTEREST IN INTERNATIONAL ARBITRATION

Part I
General Standards Regarding Impartiality, Independence and Disclosure

1 — General Principle

Every arbitrator shall be impartial and independent of the parties at the time of accepting an appointment to serve and shall remain so until the final award has been rendered or them proceedings have otherwise finally terminated.

Explanation to General Standard 1:

A fundamental principle underlying these Guidelines is that each arbitrator must be impartial and independent of the parties at the time he or she accepts an appointment to act as arbitrator, and must remain so during the entire course of the arbitration proceeding, including the time period for the correction or interpretation of a final award under the relevant rules, assuming such time period is known or readily ascertainable.

The question has arisen as to whether this obligation should extend to the period during which the award may be challenged before the relevant courts. The decision taken is that this obligation should not extend in this manner, unless the final award may be referred back to the original Arbitral Tribunal under the relevant applicable law or relevant institutional rules. Thus, the arbitrator's obligation in this regard ends when the Arbitral Tribunal has rendered the final award, and any correction or interpretation as may be permitted under the relevant rules has been issued, or the time for seeking the same has elapsed, the proceedings have been finally terminated (for example, because of a settlement), or the arbitrator otherwise no longer has jurisdiction.

If, after setting aside or other proceedings, the dispute is referred back to the same Arbitral Tribunal, a fresh round of disclosure and review of potential conflicts of interests may be necessary.

2 — Conflicts of Interest

(a) An arbitrator shall decline to accept an appointment or, if the arbitration has already been commenced, refuse to continue to act as an arbitrator, if he or she has any doubt as to his or her ability to be impartial or independent.

(b) The same principle applies if facts or circumstances exist, or have arisen since the appointment, which, from the point of view of a reasonable third person having knowledge of the relevant facts and circumstances, would give rise to justifiable doubts as to the arbitrator's impartiality or independence, unless the parties have accepted the arbitrator in accordance with the requirements set out in General Standard 4.

(c) Doubts are justifiable if a reasonable third
person, having knowledge of the relevant facts and circumstances, would reach the conclusion that there is a likelihood that the arbitrator may be influenced by factors other than the merits of the case as presented by the parties in reaching his or her decision.
(d) Justifiable doubts necessarily exist as to the arbitrator's impartiality or independence in any of the situations described in the Non-Waivable Red List.

Explanation to General Standard 2:

(a) If the arbitrator has doubts as to his or her ability to be impartial and independent, the arbitrator must decline the appointment. This standard should apply regardless of the stage of the proceedings. This is a basic principle that is spelled out in these Guidelines in order to avoid confusion and to foster confidence in the arbitral process.
(b) In order for standards to be applied as consistently as possible, the test for disqualification is an objective one. The wording 'impartiality or independence' derives from the widely adopted Article 12 of the United Nations Commission on International Trade Law (UNCITRAL) Model Law, and the use of an appearance test based on justifiable doubts as to the impartiality or independence of the arbitrator, as provided in Article 12(2) of the UNCITRAL Model Law, is to be applied objectively (a 'reasonable third person test'). Again, as described in the Explanation to General Standard 3(e), this standard applies regardless of the stage of the proceedings.
(c) Laws and rules that rely on the standard of justifiable doubts often do not define that standard. This General Standard is intended to provide some context for making this determination.
(d) The Non-Waivable Red List describes circumstances that necessarily raise justifiable doubts as to the arbitrator's impartiality or independence. For example, because no one is allowed to be his or her own judge, there cannot be identity between an arbitrator and a party. The parties, therefore, cannot waive the conflict of interest arising in such a situation.

3 —Disclosure by the Arbitrator

(a) If facts or circumstances exist that may, in the eyes of the parties, give rise to doubts as to the arbitrator's impartiality or independence, the arbitrator shall disclose such facts or circumstances to the parties, the arbitration institution or other appointing authority (if any, and if so required by the applicable institutional rules) and the co-arbitrators, if any, prior to accepting his or her appointment or, if thereafter, as soon as he or

she learns of them.
(b) An advance declaration or waiver in relation to possible conflicts of interest arising from facts and circumstances that may arise in the future does not discharge the arbitrator's ongoing duty of disclosure under General Standard 3(a).
(c) It follows from General Standards 1 and 2(a) that an arbitrator who has made a disclosure considers himself or herself to be impartial and independent of the parties, despite the disclosed facts, and, therefore, capable of performing his or her duties as arbitrator. Otherwise, he or she would have declined the nomination or appointment at the outset, or resigned.
(d) Any doubt as to whether an arbitrator should disclose certain facts or circumstances should be resolved in favour of disclosure.
(e) When considering whether facts or circumstances exist that should be disclosed, the arbitrator shall not take into account whether the arbitration is at the beginning or at a later stage.

Explanation to General Standard 3:

(a) The arbitrator's duty to disclose under General Standard 3(a) rests on the principle that the parties have an interest in being fully informed of any facts or circumstances that may be relevant in their view. Accordingly, General Standard 3(d) provides that any doubt as to whether certain facts or circumstances should be disclosed should be resolved in favour of disclosure. However, situations that, such as those set out in the Green List, could never lead to disqualification under the objective test set out in General Standard 2, need not be disclosed. As reflected in General Standard 3(c), a disclosure does not imply that the disclosed facts are such as to disqualify the arbitrator under General Standard 2. The duty of disclosure under General Standard 3(a) is ongoing in nature.
(b) The IBA Arbitration Committee has considered the increasing use by prospective arbitrators of declarations in respect of facts or circumstances that may arise in the future, and the possible conflicts of interest that may result, sometimes referred to as 'advance waivers'. Such declarations do not discharge the arbitrator's ongoing duty of disclosure under General Standard 3(a). The Guidelines, however, do not otherwise take a position as to the validity and effect of advance declarations or waivers, because the validity and effect of any advance declaration or waiver must be assessed in view of the specific text of the advance declaration or waiver, the particular circumstances at hand and the applicable law.
(c) A disclosure does not imply the existence of a conflict of interest. An

arbitrator who has made a disclosure to the parties considers himself or herself to be impartial and independent of the parties, despite the disclosed facts, or else he or she would have declined the nomination, or resigned. An arbitrator making a disclosure thus feels capable of performing his or her duties. It is the purpose of disclosure to allow the parties to judge whether they agree with the evaluation of the arbitrator and, if they so wish, to explore the situation further. It is hoped that the promulgation of this General Standard will eliminate the misconception that disclosure itself implies doubts sufficient to disqualify the arbitrator, or even creates a presumption in favour of disqualification. Instead, any challenge should only be successful if an objective test, as set forth in General Standard 2 above, is met. Under Comment 5 of the Practical Application of the General Standards, a failure to disclose certain facts and circumstances that may, in the eyes of the parties, give rise to doubts as to the arbitrator's impartiality or independence, does not necessarily mean that a conflict of interest exists, or that a disqualification should ensue.

(d) In determining which facts should be disclosed, an arbitrator should take into account all circumstances known to him or her. If the arbitrator finds that he or she should make a disclosure, but that professional secrecy rules or other rules of practice or professional conduct prevent such disclosure, he or she should not accept the appointment, or should resign.

(e) Disclosure or disqualification (as set out in General Standards 2 and 3) should not depend on the particular stage of the arbitration. In order to determine whether the arbitrator should disclose, decline the appointment or refuse to continue to act, the facts and circumstances alone are relevant, not the current stage of the proceedings, or the consequences of the withdrawal. As a practical matter, arbitration institutions may make a distinction depending on the stage of the arbitration. Courts may likewise apply different standards. Nevertheless, no distinction is made by these Guidelines depending on the stage of the arbitral proceedings. While there are practical concerns, if an arbitrator must withdraw after the arbitration has commenced, a distinction based on the stage of the arbitration would be inconsistent with the General Standards.

4 — Waiver by the Parties

(a) If, within 30 days after the receipt of any disclosure by the arbitrator, or after a party otherwise learns of facts or circumstances that could constitute a potential conflict of interest for an arbitrator, a party does not raise an express objection with regard to that arbitrator, subject to paragraphs (b) and (c) of this General Standard, the party is deemed to have waived any potential conflict of interest in respect of the arbitrator based on such facts or circumstances and may not raise any objection based on such facts or circumstances at a later stage.

(b) However, if facts or circumstances exist as described in the Non-Waivable Red List, any waiver by a party (including any declaration or advance waiver, such as that contemplated in General Standard 3(b)), or any agreement by the parties to have such a person serve as arbitrator, shall be regarded as invalid.

(c) A person should not serve as an arbitrator when a conflict of interest, such as those exemplified in the Waivable Red List, exists. Nevertheless, such a person may accept appointment as arbitrator, or continue to act as an arbitrator, if the following conditions are met:

(i) all parties, all arbitrators and the arbitration institution, or other appointing authority (if any), have full knowledge of the conflict of interest; and

(ii) all parties expressly agree that such a person may serve as arbitrator, despite the conflict of interest.

(d) An arbitrator may assist the parties in reaching a settlement of the dispute, through conciliation, mediation or otherwise, at any stage of the proceedings. However, before doing so, the arbitrator should receive an express agreement by the parties that acting in such a manner shall not disqualify the arbitrator from continuing to serve as arbitrator. Such express agreement shall be considered to be an effective waiver of any potential conflict of interest that may arise from the arbitrator's participation in such a process, or from information that the arbitrator may learn in the process. If the assistance by the arbitrator does not lead to the final settlement of the case, the parties remain bound by their waiver. However, consistent with General Standard 2(a) and notwithstanding such agreement, the arbitrator shall resign if, as a consequence of his or her involvement in the settlement process, the arbitrator develops doubts as to his or her ability to remain impartial or independent in the future course of the arbitration.

Explanation to General Standard 4:

(a) Under General Standard 4(a), a party is deemed to have waived any potential conflict of interest, if such party has not raised an objection in respect of such conflict of interest within 30 days. This time limit should run from the date on which the party learns of the relevant facts or circumstances, including through the disclosure process.

(b) General Standard 4(b) serves to exclude from the scope of General Standard 4(a) the facts and circumstances described in the Non-Waivable

Red List. Some arbitrators make declarations that seek waivers from the parties with respect to facts or circumstances that may arise in the future. Irrespective of any such waiver sought by the arbitrator, as provided in General Standard 3(b), facts and circumstances arising in the course of the arbitration should be disclosed to the parties by virtue of the arbitrator's ongoing duty of disclosure.
(c) Notwithstanding a serious conflict of interest, such as those that are described by way of example in the Waivable Red List, the parties may wish to engage such a person as an arbitrator. Here, party autonomy and the desire to have only impartial and independent arbitrators must be balanced. Persons with a serious conflict of interest, such as those that are described by way of example in the Waivable Red List, may serve as arbitrators only if the parties make fully informed, explicit waivers.
(d) The concept of the Arbitral Tribunal assisting the parties in reaching a settlement of their dispute in the course of the arbitration proceedings is well-established in some jurisdictions, but not in others. Informed consent by the parties to such a process prior to its beginning should be regarded as an effective waiver of a potential conflict of interest. Certain jurisdictions may require such consent to be in writing and signed by the parties. Subject to any requirements of applicable law, express consent may be sufficient and may be given at a hearing and reflected in the minutes or transcript of the proceeding. In addition, in order to avoid parties using an arbitrator as mediator as a means of disqualifying the arbitrator, the General Standard makes clear that the waiver should remain effective, if the mediation is unsuccessful. In giving their express consent, the parties should realise the consequences of the arbitrator assisting them in a settlement process, including the risk of the resignation of the arbitrator.

5 — Scope

(a) These Guidelines apply equally to tribunal chairs, sole arbitrators and co -arbitrators, howsoever appointed.
(b) Arbitral or administrative secretaries and assistants, to an individual arbitrator or the Arbitral Tribunal, are bound by the same duty of independence and impartiality as arbitrators, and it is the responsibility of the Arbitral Tribunal to ensure that such duty is respected at all stages of the arbitration.

Explanation to General Standard 5:

(a) Because each member of an Arbitral Tribunal has an obligation to be impartial and independent, the General Standards do not distinguish between sole arbitrators, tribunal chairs, party-appointed arbitrators or arbitrators appointed by an institution.

(b) Some arbitration institutions require arbitral or administrative secretaries and assistants to sign a declaration of independence and impartiality. Whether or not such a requirement exists, arbitral or administrative secretaries and assistants to the Arbitral Tribunal are bound by the same duty of independence and impartiality (including the duty of disclosure) as arbitrators, and it is the responsibility of the Arbitral Tribunal to ensure that such duty is respected at all stages of the arbitration. Furthermore, this duty applies to arbitral or administrative secretaries and assistants to either the Arbitral Tribunal or individual members of the Arbitral Tribunal.

6 — Relationships

(a) The arbitrator is in principle considered to bear the identity of his or her law firm, but when considering the relevance of facts or circumstances to determine whether a potential conflict of interest exists, or whether disclosure should be made, the activities of an arbitrator's law firm, if any, and the relationship of the arbitrator with the law firm, should be considered in each individual case. The fact that the activities of the arbitrator's firm involve one of the parties shall not necessarily constitute a source of such conflict, or a reason for disclosure. Similarly, if one of the parties is a member of a group with which the arbitrator's firm has a relationship, such fact should be considered in each individual case, but shall not necessarily constitute by itself a source of a conflict of interest, or a reason for disclosure.

(b) If one of the parties is a legal entity, any legal or physical person having a controlling influence on the legal entity, or a direct economic interest in, or a duty to indemnify a party for, the award to be rendered in the arbitration, may be considered to bear the identity of such party.

Explanation to General Standard 6:

(a) The growing size of law firms should be taken into account as part of today's reality in international arbitration. There is a need to balance the interests of a party to appoint the arbitrator of its choice, who may be a partner at a large law firm, and the importance of maintaining confidence in the impartiality and independence of international arbitrators. The arbitrator must, in principle, be considered to bear the identity of his or her law firm, but the activities of the arbitrator's firm should not automatically create a conflict of interest. The relevance of the activities of the arbitrator's firm, such as the nature, timing and scope of the work by the law firm, and the relationship of the arbitrator with the law firm, should be considered in each case. General Standard 6(a) uses the term 'involve' rather than 'acting for' because the relevant connections with a party may include activities other than representation on a legal matter. Although barristers' chambers should not be equated with law firms for the purposes of conflicts, and no general standard is proffered for barristers' chambers, disclosure may be warranted in view of the relationships among barristers, parties or counsel. When a party to an arbitration is a member of a group of companies, special questions regarding conflicts of interest arise. Because individual corporate structure arrangements vary widely, a catch-all rule is not appropriate. Instead, the particular circumstances of an affiliation with another entity within the same group of companies, and the relationship of that entity with the arbitrator's law firm, should be considered in each individual case.

(b) When a party in international arbitration is a legal entity, other legal and physical persons may have a controlling influence on this legal entity, or a direct economic interest in, or a duty to indemnify a party for, the award to be rendered in the arbitration. Each situation should be assessed individually, and General Standard 6(b) clarifies that such legal persons and individuals may be considered effectively to be that party. Third-party funders and insurers in relation to the dispute may have a direct economic interest in the award, and as such may be considered to be the equivalent of the party. For these purposes, the terms 'third-party funder' and 'insurer' refer to any person or entity that is contributing funds, or other material support, to the prosecution or defence of the case and that has a direct economic interest in, or a duty to indemnify a party for, the award to be rendered in the arbitration.

7 — Duty of the Parties and the Arbitrator

(a) A party shall inform an arbitrator, the Arbitral Tribunal, the other parties and the arbitration institution or other appointing authority (if any) of any relationship, direct or indirect, between the arbitrator and the party (or another company of the same group of companies, or an individual having a controlling influence on the party in the arbitration), or between the arbitrator and any person or entity with a direct economic interest in, or a duty to indemnify a party for, the award to be rendered in the arbitration. The party shall do so on its own initiative at the earliest opportunity.

(b) A party shall inform an arbitrator, the Arbitral Tribunal, the other parties and the arbitration institution or other appointing authority (if any) of the identity of its counsel appearing in the arbitration, as well as of any relationship, including membership of the same barristers' chambers, between its counsel and the arbitrator. The party shall do so on its own initiative at the earliest opportunity, and upon any change in its counsel

team.
(c) In order to comply with General Standard 7(a), a party shall perform reasonable enquiries and provide any relevant information available to it.
(d) An arbitrator is under a duty to make reasonable enquiries to identify any conflict of interest, as well as any facts or circumstances that may reasonably give rise to doubts as to his or her impartiality or independence. Failure to disclose a conflict is not excused by lack of knowledge, if the arbitrator does not perform such reasonable enquiries.

Explanation to General Standard 7:

(a) The parties are required to disclose any relationship with the arbitrator. Disclosure of such relationships should reduce the risk of an unmeritorious challenge of an arbitrator's impartiality or independence based on information learned after the appointment. The parties' duty of disclosure of any relationship, direct or indirect, between the arbitrator and the party (or another company of the same group of companies, or an individual having a controlling influence on the party in the arbitration) has been extended to relationships with persons or entities having a direct economic interest in the award to be rendered in the arbitration, such as an entity providing funding for the arbitration, or having a duty to indemnify a party for the award.
(b) Counsel appearing in the arbitration, namely the persons involved in the representation of the parties in the arbitration, must be identified by the parties at the earliest opportunity. A party's duty to disclose the identity of counsel appearing in the arbitration extends to all members of that party's counsel team and arises from the outset of the proceedings.
(c) In order to satisfy their duty of disclosure, the parties are required to investigate any relevant information that is reasonably available to them. In addition, any party to an arbitration is required, at the outset and on an ongoing basis during the entirety of the proceedings, to make a reasonable effort to ascertain and to disclose available information that, applying the general standard, might affect the arbitrator's impartiality or independence.
(d) In order to satisfy their duty of disclosure under the Guidelines, arbitrators are required to investigate any relevant information that is reasonably available to them.

Part II

Practical Application of the General Standards

1. If the Guidelines are to have an important practical influence, they should address situations that are likely to occur in today's arbitration practice and should provide specific guidance to arbitrators, parties, institutions and

courts as to which situations do or do not constitute conflicts of interest, or should or should not be disclosed. For this purpose, the Guidelines categorise situations that may occur in the following Application Lists. These lists cannot cover every situation. In all cases, the General Standards should control the outcome.

2. The Red List consists of two parts: 'a Non-Waivable Red List' (see General Standards 2(d) and 4(b)); and 'a Waivable Red List' (see General Standard 4(c)). These lists are non-exhaustive and detail specific situations that, depending on the facts of a given case, give rise to justifiable doubts as to the arbitrator's impartiality and independence. That is, in these circumstances, an objective conflict of interest exists from the point of view of a reasonable third person having knowledge of the relevant facts and circumstances (see General Standard 2(b)). The Non-Waivable Red List includes situations deriving from the overriding principle that no person can be his or her own judge. Therefore, acceptance of such a situation cannot cure the conflict. The Waivable Red List covers situations that are serious but not as severe. Because of their seriousness, unlike circumstances described in the Orange List, these situations should be considered waivable, but only if and when the parties, being aware of the conflict of interest situation, expressly state their willingness to have such a person act as arbitrator, as set forth in General Standard 4(c).

3. The Orange List is a non-exhaustive list of specific situations that, depending on the facts of a given case, may, in the eyes of the parties, give rise to doubts as to the arbitrator's impartiality or independence. The Orange List thus reflects situations that would fall under General Standard 3 (a), with the consequence that the arbitrator has a duty to disclose such situations. In all these situations, the parties are deemed to have accepted the arbitrator if, after disclosure, no timely objection is made, as established in General Standard 4(a).

4. Disclosure does not imply the existence of a conflict of interest; nor should it by itself result either in a disqualification of the arbitrator, or in a presumption regarding disqualification. The purpose of the disclosure is to inform the parties of a situation that they may wish to explore further in order to determine whether objectively – that is, from the point of view of a reasonable third person having knowledge of the relevant facts and circumstances – there are justifiable doubts as to the arbitrator's impartiality or independence. If the conclusion is that there are no justifiable doubts, the arbitrator can act. Apart from the situations covered by the Non-Waivable Red List, he or she can also act if there is no timely objection by the parties

or, in situations covered by the Waivable Red List, if there is a specific acceptance by the parties in accordance with General Standard 4(c). If a party challenges the arbitrator, he or she can nevertheless act, if the authority that rules on the challenge decides that the challenge does not meet the objective test for disqualification.

5. A later challenge based on the fact that an arbitrator did not disclose such facts or circumstances should not result automatically in non-appointment, later disqualification or a successful challenge to any award. Nondisclosure cannot by itself make an arbitrator partial or lacking independence: only the facts or circumstances that he or she failed to disclose can do so.

6. Situations not listed in the Orange List or falling outside the time limits used in some of the Orange List situations are generally not subject to disclosure. However, an arbitrator needs to assess on a case-by-case basis whether a given situation, even though not mentioned in the Orange List, is nevertheless such as to give rise to justifiable doubts as to his or her impartiality or independence. Because the Orange List is a non-exhaustive list of examples, there may be situations not mentioned, which, depending on the circumstances, may need to be disclosed by an arbitrator. Such may be the case, for example, in the event of repeat past appointments by the same party or the same counsel beyond the three-year period provided for in the Orange List, or when an arbitrator concurrently acts as counsel in an unrelated case in which similar issues of law are raised. Likewise, an appointment made by the same party or the same counsel appearing before an arbitrator, while the case is ongoing, may also have to be disclosed, depending on the circumstances. While the Guidelines do not require disclosure of the fact that an arbitrator concurrently serves, or has in the past served, on the same Arbitral Tribunal with another member of the tribunal, or with one of the counsel in the current proceedings, an arbitrator should assess on a case-by-case basis whether the fact of having frequently served as counsel with, or as an arbitrator on, Arbitral Tribunals with another member of the tribunal may create a perceived imbalance within the tribunal. If the conclusion is 'yes', the arbitrator should consider a disclosure.

7. The Green List is a non-exhaustive list of specific situations where no appearance and no actual conflict of interest exists from an objective point of view. Thus, the arbitrator has no duty to disclose situations falling within the Green List. As stated in the Explanation to General Standard 3(a), there should be a limit to disclosure, based on reasonableness; in some situations, an objective test should prevail over the purely subjective test of 'the eyes'

of the parties.

8. The borderline between the categories that comprise the Lists can be thin. It can be debated whether a certain situation should be on one List instead of another. Also, the Lists contain, for various situations, general terms such as 'significant' and 'relevant'. The Lists reflect international principles and best practices to the extent possible. Further definition of the norms, which are to be interpreted reasonably in light of the facts and circumstances in each case, would be counterproductive.

1. Non-Waivable Red List

1.1 There is an identity between a party and the arbitrator, or the arbitrator is a legal representative or employee of an entity that is a party in the arbitration.

1.2 The arbitrator is a manager, director or member of the supervisory board, or has a controlling influence on one of the parties or an entity that has a direct economic interest in the award to be rendered in the arbitration.

1.3 The arbitrator has a significant financial or personal interest in one of the parties, or the outcome of the case.

1.4 The arbitrator or his or her firm regularly advises the party, or an affiliate of the party, and the arbitrator or his or her firm derives significant financial income therefrom.

2. Waivable Red List

2.1 Relationship of the arbitrator to the dispute

2.1.1 The arbitrator has given legal advice, or provided an expert opinion, on the dispute to a party or an affiliate of one of the parties.

2.1.2 The arbitrator had a prior involvement in the dispute.

2.2 Arbitrator's direct or indirect interest in the dispute

2.2.1 The arbitrator holds shares, either directly or indirectly, in one of the parties, or an affiliate of one of the parties, this party or an affiliate being privately held.

2.2.2 A close family member[1] of the arbitrator has a significant financial interest in the outcome of the dispute.

2.2.3 The arbitrator, or a close family member of the arbitrator, has a close relationship with a non-party who may be liable to recourse on the part of the unsuccessful party in the dispute.

2.3 Arbitrator's relationship with the parties or counsel

2.3.1 The arbitrator currently represents or advises one of the parties, or an affiliate of one of the parties.

2.3.2 The arbitrator currently represents or advises the lawyer or law firm acting as counsel for one of the parties.

[1] See page 424.

2.3.3 The arbitrator is a lawyer in the same law firm as the counsel to one of the parties.
2.3.4 The arbitrator is a manager, director or member of the supervisory board, or has a controlling influence in an affiliate[2] of one of the parties, if the affiliate is directly involved in the matters in dispute in the arbitration.
2.3.5 The arbitrator's law firm had a previous but terminated involvement in the case without the arbitrator being involved himself or herself.
2.3.6 The arbitrator's law firm currently has a significant commercial relationship with one of the parties, or an affiliate of one of the parties.
2.3.7 The arbitrator regularly advises one of the parties, or an affiliate of one of the parties, but neither the arbitrator nor his or her firm derives a significant financial income therefrom.
2.3.8 The arbitrator has a close family relationship with one of the parties, or with a manager, director or member of the supervisory board, or any person having a controlling influence in one of the parties, or an affiliate of one of the parties, or with a counsel representing a party.
2.3.9 A close family member of the arbitrator has a significant financial or personal interest in one of the parties, or an affiliate of one of the parties.

3. Orange List

3.1 Previous services for one of the parties or other involvement in the case
3.1.1 The arbitrator has, within the past three years, served as counsel for one of the parties, or an affiliate of one of the parties, or has previously advised or been consulted by the party, or an affiliate of the party, making the appointment in an unrelated matter, but the arbitrator and the party, or the affiliate of the party, have no ongoing relationship.
3.1.2 The arbitrator has, within the past three years, served as counsel against one of the parties, or an affiliate of one of the parties, in an unrelated matter.
3.1.3 The arbitrator has, within the past three years, been appointed as arbitrator on two or more occasions by one of the parties, or an affiliate of one of the parties.[3]
3.1.4 The arbitrator's law firm has, within the past three years, acted for or against one of the parties, or an affiliate of one of the parties, in an unrelated matter without the involvement of the arbitrator.
3.1.5 The arbitrator currently serves, or has served within the past three years, as arbitrator in another arbitration involving one of the parties, or an affiliate of one of the parties.
3.2 Current services for one of the parties
3.2.1 The arbitrator's law firm is currently rendering services to one of the

[2] See page 424.
[3] *Ibid.*

parties, or to an affiliate of one of the parties, without creating a significant commercial relationship for the law firm and without the involvement of the arbitrator.

3.2.2 A law firm or other legal organisation that shares significant fees or other revenues with the arbitrator's law firm renders services to one of the parties, or an affiliate of one of the parties, before the Arbitral Tribunal.

3.3.3 The arbitrator or his or her firm represents a party, or an affiliate of one of the parties to the arbitration, on a regular basis, but such representation does not concern the current dispute.

3.3 Relationship between an arbitrator and another arbitrator or counsel

3.3.1 The arbitrator and another arbitrator are lawyers in the same law firm.

3.3.2 The arbitrator and another arbitrator, or the counsel for one of the parties, are members of the same barristers' chambers.

3.3.3 The arbitrator was, within the past three years, a partner of, or otherwise affiliated with, another arbitrator or any of the counsel in the arbitration.

3.3.4 A lawyer in the arbitrator's law firm is an arbitrator in another dispute involving the same party or parties, or an affiliate of one of the parties.

3.3.5 A close family member of the arbitrator is a partner or employee of the law firm representing one of the parties, but is not assisting with the dispute.

3.3.6 A close personal friendship exists between an arbitrator and a counsel of a party.

3.3.7 Enmity exists between an arbitrator and counsel appearing in the arbitration.

3.3.8 The arbitrator has, within the past three years, been appointed on more than three occasions by the same counsel, or the same law firm.

3.3.9 The arbitrator and another arbitrator, or counsel for one of the parties in the arbitration, currently act or have acted together within the past three years as cocounsel.

3.4 Relationship between arbitrator and party and others involved in the arbitration

3.4.1 The arbitrator's law firm is currently acting adversely to one of the parties, or an affiliate of one of the parties.

3.4.2 The arbitrator has been associated with a party, or an affiliate of one of the parties, in a professional capacity, such as a former employee or partner.

3.4.3 A close personal friendship exists between an arbitrator and a manager or director or a member of the supervisory board of: a party; an entity that has a direct economic interest in the award to be rendered in the arbitration; or any person having a controlling influence, such as a controlling shareholder interest, on one of the parties or an affiliate of one of the parties or a witness or expert.

3.4.4 Enmity exists between an arbitrator and a manager or director or a member of the supervisory board of: a party; an entity that has a direct economic interest in the award; or any person having a controlling influence in one of the parties or an affiliate of one of the parties or a witness or expert.

3.4.5 If the arbitrator is a former judge, he or she has, within the past three years, heard a significant case involving one of the parties, or an affiliate of one of the parties.

3.5 Other circumstances

3.5.1 The arbitrator holds shares, either directly or indirectly, that by reason of number or denomination constitute a material holding in one of the parties, or an affiliate of one of the parties, this party or affiliate being publicly listed.

3.5.2 The arbitrator has publicly advocated a position on the case, whether in a published paper, or speech, or otherwise.

3.5.3 The arbitrator holds a position with the appointing authority with respect to the dispute.

3.5.4 The arbitrator is a manager, director or member of the supervisory board, or has a controlling influence on an affiliate of one of the parties, where the affiliate is not directly involved in the matters in dispute in the arbitration.

4. Green List

4.1 Previously expressed legal opinions

4.1.1 The arbitrator has previously expressed a legal opinion (such as in a law review article or public lecture) concerning an issue that also arises in the arbitration (but this opinion is not focused on the case).

4.2 Current services for one of the parties

4.2.1 A firm, in association or in alliance with the arbitrator's law firm, but that does not share significant fees or other revenues with the arbitrator's law firm, renders services to one of the parties, or an affiliate of one of the parties, in an unrelated matter.

4.3 Contacts with another arbitrator, or with counsel for one of the parties

4.3.1 The arbitrator has a relationship with another arbitrator, or with the counsel for one of the parties, through membership in the same professional association, or social or charitable organisation, or through a social media network.

4.3.2 The arbitrator and counsel for one of the parties have previously served together as arbitrators.

4.3.3 The arbitrator teaches in the same faculty or school as another arbitrator or counsel to one of the parties, or serves as an officer of a professional association or social or charitable organisation with another arbitrator or counsel for one of the parties.

4.3.4 The arbitrator was a speaker, moderator or organiser in one or more conferences, or participated in seminars or working parties of a professional, social or charitable organisation, with another arbitrator or counsel to the parties.

4.4 Contacts between the arbitrator and one of the parties

4.4.1 The arbitrator has had an initial contact with a party, or an affiliate of a party (or their counsel) prior to appointment, if this contact is limited to the arbitrator's availability and qualifications to serve, or to the names of possible candidates for a chairperson, and did not address the merits or procedural aspects of the dispute, other than to provide the arbitrator with a basic understanding of the case.

4.4.2 The arbitrator holds an insignificant amount of shares in one of the parties, or an affiliate of one of the parties, which is publicly listed.

4.4.3 The arbitrator and a manager, director or member of the supervisory board, or any person having a controlling influence on one of the parties, or an affiliate of one of the parties, have worked together as joint experts, or in another professional capacity, including as arbitrators in the same case.

4.4.4 The arbitrator has a relationship with one of the parties or its affiliates through a social media network.

---

[1] Throughout the Application Lists, the term 'close family member' refers to a: spouse, sibling, child, parent or life partner, in addition to any other family member with whom a close relationship exists.

[2] Throughout the Application Lists, the term 'affiliate' encompasses all companies in a group of companies, including the parent company.

[3] It may be the practice in certain types of arbitration, such as maritime, sports or commodities arbitration, to draw arbitrators from a smaller or specialised pool of individuals. If in such fields it is the custom and practice for parties to frequently appoint the same arbitrator in different cases, no disclosure of this fact is required, where all parties in the arbitration should be familiar with such custom and practice.

IBA GUIDELINES ON PARTY REPRESENTATION IN INTERNATIONAL ARBITRATION *

Preamble

The IBA Arbitration Committee established the Task Force on Counsel Conduct in International Arbitration (the 'Task Force') in 2008.

The mandate of the Task Force was to focus on issues of counsel conduct and party representation in international arbitration that are subject to, or informed by, diverse and potentially conflicting rules and norms. As an initial inquiry, the Task Force undertook to determine whether such differing norms and practises may undermine the fundamental fairness and integrity of international arbitral proceedings and whether international guidelines on party representation in international arbitration may assist parties, counsel and arbitrators. In 2010, the Task Force commissioned a survey (the 'Survey') in order to examine these issues. Respondents to the Survey expressed support for the development of international guidelines for party representation.

The Task Force proposed draft guidelines to the IBA Arbitration Committee's officers in October 2012. The Committee then reviewed the draft guidelines and consulted with experienced arbitration practitioners, arbitrators and arbitral institutions. The draft guidelines were then submitted to all members of the IBA Arbitration Committee for consideration.

Unlike in domestic judicial settings, in which counsel are familiar with, and subject, to a single set of professional conduct rules, party representatives in international arbitration may be subject to diverse and potentially conflicting bodies of domestic rules and norms. The range of rules and norms applicable to the representation of parties in international arbitration may include those of the party representative's home jurisdiction, the arbitral seat, and the place where hearings physically take place. The Survey revealed a high degree of uncertainty among respondents regarding what rules govern party representation in international arbitration. The potential for confusion may be aggravated when individual counsel working collectively, either within a firm or through a co-counsel relationship, are themselves admitted to practise in multiple jurisdictions that have conflicting rules and norms.

In addition to the potential for uncertainty, rules and norms developed for domestic judicial litigation may be ill-adapted to international arbitral proceedings. Indeed, specialised practises and procedures have been developed in international arbitration to accommodate the legal and cultural differences among participants and the complex, multinational nature of the disputes. Domestic professional conduct rules and norms, by contrast, are developed to apply in specific legal cultures consistent with established

* For a commentary on the IBA Guidelines on Party Representation in International Arbitration, see Edna Sussman, 'Ethics in International Arbitration, Soft Law Guidance for Arbitrators and Party Representatives' in Lawrence W. Newman and Michael J. Radine (eds), *Soft Law in International*

national procedures.

The IBA Guidelines on Party Representation in International Arbitration (the 'Guidelines') are inspired by the principle that party representatives should act with integrity and honesty and should not engage in activities designed to produce unnecessary delay or expense, including tactics aimed at obstructing the arbitration proceedings.

As with the International Principles on Conduct for the Legal Profession, adopted by the IBA on 28 May 2011, the Guidelines are not intended to displace otherwise applicable mandatory laws, professional or disciplinary rules, or agreed arbitration rules that may be relevant or applicable to matters of party representation. They are also not intended to vest arbitral tribunals with powers otherwise reserved to bars or other professional bodies.

The use of the term guidelines rather than rules is intended to highlight their contractual nature. The parties may thus adopt the Guidelines or a portion thereof by agreement. Arbitral tribunals may also apply the Guidelines in their discretion, subject to any applicable mandatory rules, if they determine that they have the authority to do so.

The Guidelines are not intended to limit the flexibility that is inherent in, and a considerable advantage of, international arbitration, and parties and arbitral tribunals may adapt them to the particular circumstances of each arbitration.

Definitions

In the IBA Guidelines on Party Representation in International Arbitration:

Arbitral Tribunal or Tribunal	means a sole Arbitrator or a panel of Arbitrators in the arbitration;
Arbitrator	means an arbitrator in the arbitration;
Document	means a writing, communication, picture, drawing, program or data of any kind, whether recorded or maintained on paper or by electronic, audio, visual or any other means;
Domestic Bar or Bar	means the national or local authority or authorities responsible for the regulation

Arbitration (Juris, 2014).

	of the professional conduct of lawyers;
Evidence	means documentary evidence and written and oral testimony.
Ex Parte Communications	means oral or written communications between a Party Representative and an Arbitrator or prospective Arbitrator without the presence or knowledge of the opposing Party or Parties;
Expert	means a person or organisation appearing before an Arbitral Tribunal to provide expert analysis and opinion on specific issues determined by a Party or by the Arbitral Tribunal;
Expert Report	means a written statement by an Expert;
Guidelines	mean these IBA Guidelines on Party Representation in International Arbitration, as they may be revised or amended from time to time;
Knowingly	means with actual knowledge of the fact in question;
Misconduct	means a breach of the present Guidelines or any other conduct that the Arbitral Tribunal determines to be contrary to the duties of a Party Representative;
Party	means a party to the arbitration;
Party-Nominated Arbitrator	means an Arbitrator who is nominated or appointed by one or more Parties;
Party Representative or Representative	means any person, including a

	Party's employee, who appears in an arbitration on behalf of a Party and makes submissions, arguments or representations to the Arbitral Tribunal on behalf of such Party, other than in the capacity as a Witness or Expert, and whether or not legally qualified or admitted to a Domestic Bar;
Presiding Arbitrator	means an arbitrator who is either a sole Arbitrator or the chairperson of the Arbitral Tribunal;
Request to Produce	means a written request by a Party that another Party produce Documents;
Witness	means a person appearing before an Arbitral Tribunal to provide testimony of fact;
Witness Statement	means a written statement by a Witness recording testimony.

Application of Guidelines

1. The Guidelines shall apply where and to the extent that the Parties have so agreed, or the Arbitral Tribunal, after consultation with the Parties, wishes to rely upon them after having determined that it has the authority to rule on matters of Party representation to ensure the integrity and fairness of the arbitral proceedings.

2. In the event of any dispute regarding the meaning of the Guidelines, the Arbitral Tribunal should interpret them in accordance with their overall purpose and in the manner most appropriate for the particular arbitration.

3. The Guidelines are not intended to displace otherwise applicable mandatory laws, professional or disciplinary rules, or agreed arbitration rules, in matters of Party representation. The Guidelines are also not intended to derogate from the arbitration agreement or to undermine either a Party representative's primary duty of loyalty to the party whom he or she represents or a Party representative's paramount obligation to present such Party's case to the Arbitral Tribunal.

Comments to Guidelines 1–3

As explained in the Preamble, the Parties and Arbitral Tribunals may benefit from guidance in matters of Party Representation, in particular in order to address instances where differing norms and expectations may threaten the integrity and fairness of the arbitral proceedings.

By virtue of these Guidelines, Arbitral Tribunals need not, in dealing with such issues, and subject to applicable mandatory laws, be limited by a choice-of-law rule or private international law analysis to choosing among national or domestic professional conduct rules. Instead, these Guidelines offer an approach designed to account for the multi-faceted nature of international arbitral proceedings.

These Guidelines shall apply where and to the extent that the Parties have so agreed. Parties may adopt these Guidelines, in whole or in part, in their arbitration agreement or at any time subsequently.

An Arbitral Tribunal may also apply, or draw inspiration from, the Guidelines, after having determined that it has the authority to rule on matters of Party representation in order to ensure the integrity and fairness of the arbitral proceedings. Before making such determination, the Arbitral Tribunal should give the Parties an opportunity to express their views.

These Guidelines do not state whether Arbitral Tribunals have the authority to rule on matters of Party representation and to apply the Guidelines in the absence of an agreement by the Parties to that effect. The Guidelines neither recognise nor exclude the existence of such authority. It remains for the Tribunal to make a determination as to whether it has the authority to rule on matters of Party representation and to apply the Guidelines.

A Party Representative, acting within the authority granted to it, acts on behalf of the Party whom he or she represents. It follows therefore that an obligation or duty bearing on a Party Representative is an obligation or duty of the represented Party, who may ultimately bear the consequences of the misconduct of its Representative.

Party Representation

4. Party Representatives should identify themselves to the other Party or Parties and the Arbitral Tribunal at the earliest opportunity. A Party should promptly inform the Arbitral Tribunal and the other Party or Parties of any change in such representation.

5. Once the Arbitral Tribunal has been constituted, a person should not accept representation of a Party in the arbitration when a relationship exists between the person and an Arbitrator that would create a conflict of interest, unless none of the Parties objects after proper disclosure.

6. The Arbitral Tribunal may, in case of breach of Guideline 5, take measures appropriate to safeguard the integrity of the proceedings, including the exclusion of the new Party Representative from participating in all or part of the arbitral proceedings.

Comments to Guidelines 4–6

Changes in Party representation in the course of the arbitration may, because of conflicts of interest between a newly-appointed Party Representative and one or more of the Arbitrators, threaten the integrity of the proceedings. In such case, the Arbitral Tribunal may, if compelling circumstances so justify, and where it has found that it has the requisite authority, consider excluding the new Representative from participating in all or part of the arbitral proceedings. In assessing whether any such conflict of interest exists, the Arbitral Tribunal may rely on the IBA Guidelines on Conflicts of Interest in International Arbitration.

Before resorting to such measure, it is important that the Arbitral Tribunal give the Parties an opportunity to express their views about the existence of a conflict, the extent of the Tribunal's authority to act in relation to such conflict, and the consequences of the measure that the Tribunal is contemplating.

Communications with Arbitrators

7. Unless agreed otherwise by the Parties, and subject to the exceptions below, a Party Representative should not engage in any Ex Parte Communications with an Arbitrator concerning the arbitration.

8. It is not improper for a Party Representative to have Ex Parte Communications in the following circumstances:

(a) A Party Representative may communicate with a prospective Party-Nominated Arbitrator to determine his or her expertise, experience, ability, availability, willingness and the existence of potential conflicts of interest.

(b) A Party Representative may communicate with a prospective or appointed Party-Nominated Arbitrator for the purpose of the selection of the Presiding Arbitrator.

(c) A Party Representative may, if the Parties are in agreement that such a communication is permissible, communicate with a prospective Presiding Arbitrator to determine his or her expertise, experience, ability, availability, willingness and the existence of potential conflicts of interest.

(d) While communications with a prospective Party-Nominated Arbitrator or Presiding Arbitrator may include a general description of the dispute, a Party Representative should not seek the views of the prospective Party Nominated Arbitrator or Presiding Arbitrator on the substance of the dispute.

Comments to Guidelines 7–8

Guidelines 7–8 deal with communications between a Party Representative and an Arbitrator or potential Arbitrator concerning the arbitration.

The Guidelines seek to reflect best international practices and, as such, may depart from potentially diverging domestic arbitration practices that are more restrictive or, to the contrary, permit broader Ex Parte Communications.

Ex Parte Communications, as defined in these Guidelines, may occur only in defined circumstances, and a Party Representative should otherwise refrain from any such communication. The Guidelines do not seek to define when the relevant period begins or ends. Any communication that takes place in the context of, or in relation to, the constitution of the Arbitral Tribunal is covered.

Ex Parte Communications with a prospective Arbitrator (Party-Nominated or Presiding Arbitrator) should be limited to providing a general description of the dispute and obtaining information regarding the suitability of the potential Arbitrator, as described in further detail below. A Party Representative should not take the opportunity to seek the prospective Arbitrator's views on the substance of the dispute.

The following discussion topics are appropriate in pre-appointment communications in order to assess the prospective Arbitrator's expertise, experience, ability, availability, willingness and the existence of potential conflicts of interest: (a) the prospective Arbitrator's publications, including books, articles and conference papers or engagements; (b) any activities of the prospective Arbitrator and his or her law firm or organisation within which he or she operates, that may raise justifiable doubts as to the prospective Arbitrator's independence or impartiality; (c) a description of the general nature of the dispute; (d) the terms of the arbitration agreement, and in particular any agreement as to the seat, language, applicable law and rules of the arbitration; (e) the identities of the Parties, Party Representatives, Witnesses, Experts and interested parties; and (f) the anticipated timetable and general conduct of the proceedings.

Applications to the Arbitral Tribunal without the presence or knowledge of the opposing Party or Parties may be permitted in certain circumstances, if the parties so agreed, or as permitted by applicable law. Such may be the case, in particular, for interim measures.

Finally, a Party Representative may communicate with the Arbitral Tribunal if the other Party or Parties fail to participate in a hearing or proceedings and are not represented.

Submissions to the Arbitral Tribunal

9. A Party Representative should not make any knowingly false submission of fact to the Arbitral Tribunal.

10. In the event that a Party Representative learns that he or she previously made a false submission of fact to the Arbitral Tribunal, the Party Representative should, subject to countervailing considerations of confidentiality and privilege, promptly correct such submission.

11. A Party Representative should not submit Witness or Expert evidence that he or she knows to be false. If a Witness or Expert intends to present or presents evidence that a Party Representative knows or later discovers to be false, such Party Representative should promptly advise the Party whom he or she represents of the necessity of taking remedial measures and of the consequences of failing to do so. Depending upon the circumstances, and subject to countervailing considerations of confidentiality and privilege, the Party Representative should promptly take remedial measures, which may include one or more of the following:

(a) advise the Witness or Expert to testify truthfully;

(b) take reasonable steps to deter the Witness or Expert from submitting false evidence;

(c) urge the Witness or Expert to correct or withdraw the false evidence;

(d) correct or withdraw the false evidence;

(e) withdraw as Party Representative if the circumstances so warrant.

Comments to Guidelines 9–11

Guidelines 9–11 concern the responsibility of a Party Representative when making submissions and tendering evidence to the Arbitral Tribunal. This principle is sometimes referred to as the duty of candour or honesty owed to the Tribunal.

The Guidelines identify two aspects of the responsibility of a Party Representative: the first relates to submissions of fact made by a Party Representative (Guidelines 9 and 10), and the second concerns the evidence given by a Witness or Expert (Guideline 11).

With respect to submissions to the Arbitral Tribunal, these Guidelines contain two limitations to the principles set out for Party Representatives. First, Guidelines 9 and 10 are restricted to false submissions of fact. Secondly, the Party Representative must have actual knowledge of the false nature of the submission, which may be inferred from the circumstances.

Under Guideline 10, a Party Representative should promptly correct any false submissions of fact previously made to the Tribunal, unless prevented from doing so by countervailing considerations of confidentiality and privilege. Such principle also applies, in case of a change in representation, to a newly-appointed Party Representative who becomes aware that his or her predecessor made a false submission.

With respect to legal submissions to the Tribunal, a Party Representative may argue any construction of a law a contract, a treaty or any authority that he or she believes is reasonable.

Guideline 11 addresses the presentation of evidence to the Tribunal that a Party Representative knows to be false. A Party Representative should not offer knowingly false evidence or testimony. A Party Representative therefore should not assist a Witness or Expert or seek to influence a Witness or Expert to give false evidence to the Tribunal in oral testimony or written Witness Statements or Expert Reports.

The considerations outlined for Guidelines 9 and 10 apply equally to Guideline 11. Guideline 11 is more specific in terms of the remedial measures that a Party Representative may take in the event that the Witness or Expert intends to present or presents evidence that the Party Representative knows or later discovers to be false. The list of remedial measures provided in Guideline 11 is not exhaustive. Such remedial measures may extend to the Party Representative's withdrawal from the case, if the circumstances so warrant. Guideline 11 acknowledges, by using the term 'may', that certain remedial measures, such as correcting or withdrawing false Witness or Expert evidence may not be compatible with the ethical rules bearing on counsel in some jurisdictions.

Information Exchange and Disclosure

12. When the arbitral proceedings involve or are likely to involve Document production, a Party Representative should inform the client of the need to preserve, so far as reasonably possible, Documents, including electronic Documents that would otherwise be deleted in accordance with a Document retention policy or in the ordinary course of business, which are potentially relevant to the arbitration.

13. A Party Representative should not make any Request to Produce, or any objection to a Request to Produce, for an improper purpose, such as to harass or cause unnecessary delay.

14. A Party Representative should explain to the Party whom he or she represents the necessity of producing, and potential consequences of failing to produce, any Document that the Party or Parties have undertaken, or been ordered, to produce.

15. A Party Representative should advise the Party whom he or she

represents to take, and assist such Party in taking, reasonable steps to ensure that: (i) a reasonable search is made for Documents that a Party has undertaken, or been ordered, to produce; and (ii) all non-privileged, responsive Documents are produced.

16. A Party Representative should not suppress or conceal, or advise a Party to suppress or conceal, Documents that have been requested by another Party or that the Party whom he or she represents has undertaken, or been ordered, to produce.

17. If, during the course of an arbitration, a Party Representative becomes aware of the existence of a Document that should have been produced, but was not produced, such Party Representative should advise the Party whom he or she represents of the necessity of producing the Document and the consequences of failing to do so.

Comments to Guidelines 12–17

The IBA addressed the scope of Document production in the IBA Rules on the Taking of Evidence in International Arbitration (see Articles 3 and 9). Guidelines 12–17 concern the conduct of Party Representatives in connection with Document production.

Party Representatives are often unsure whether and to what extent their respective domestic standards of professional conduct apply to the process of preserving, collecting and producing documents in international arbitration. It is common for Party Representatives in the same arbitration proceeding to apply different standards. For example, one Party Representative may consider him- or her-self obligated to ensure that the Party whom he or she represents undertakes a reasonable search for, and produces, all responsive, non-privileged Documents, while another Party Representative may view Document production as the sole responsibility of the Party whom he or she represents. In these circumstances, the disparity in access to information or evidence may undermine the integrity and fairness of the arbitral proceedings.

The Guidelines are intended to address these difficulties by suggesting standards of conduct in international arbitration. They may not be necessary in cases where Party Representatives share similar expectations with respect to their role in relation to Document production or in cases where Document production is not done or is minimal.

The Guidelines are intended to foster the taking of objectively reasonable steps to preserve, search for and produce Documents that a Party has an obligation to disclose.

Under Guidelines 12–17, a Party Representative should, under the given circumstances, advise the Party whom he or she represents to: (i) identify those persons within the Party's control who might possess Documents potentially relevant to the arbitration, including electronic Documents; (ii) notify such persons of the need to preserve and not destroy any such Documents; and (iii) suspend or otherwise make arrangements to override any Document retention or other policies/practises whereby potentially relevant Documents might be destroyed in the ordinary course of business.

Under Guidelines 12–17, a Party Representative should, under the given circumstances, advise the Party whom he or she represents to, and assist such Party to: (i) put in place a reasonable and proportionate system for collecting and reviewing Documents within the possession of persons within the Party's control in order to identify Documents that are relevant to the arbitration or that have been requested by another Party; and (ii) ensure that the Party Representative is provided with copies of, or access to, all such Documents.

While Article 3 of the IBA Rules on the Taking of Evidence in International Arbitration requires the production of Documents relevant to the case and material to its outcome, Guideline 12 refers only to potentially relevant Documents because its purpose is different: when a Party Representative advises the Party whom he or she represents to preserve evidence, such Party Representative is typically not at that stage in a position to assess materiality, and the test for preserving and collecting Documents therefore should be potential relevance to the case at hand.

Finally, a Party Representative should not make a Request to Produce, or object to a Request to Produce, when such request or objection is only aimed at harassing, obtaining documents for purposes extraneous to the arbitration, or causing unnecessary delay (Guideline 13).

Witnesses and Experts

18. Before seeking any information from a potential Witness or Expert, a Party Representative should identify himself or herself, as well as the Party he or she represents, and the reason for which the information is sought.

19. A Party Representative should make any potential Witness aware that he or she has the right to inform or instruct his or her own counsel about the contact and to discontinue the communication with the Party Representative.

20. A Party Representative may assist Witnesses in the preparation of Witness Statements and Experts in the preparation of Expert Reports.

21. A Party Representative should seek to ensure that a Witness Statement reflects the Witness's own account of relevant facts, events and

circumstances.

22. A Party Representative should seek to ensure that an Expert Report reflects the Expert's own analysis and opinion.

23. A Party Representative should not invite or encourage a Witness to give false evidence.

24. A Party Representative may, consistent with the principle that the evidence given should reflect the Witness's own account of relevant facts, events or circumstances, or the Expert's own analysis or opinion, meet or interact with Witnesses and Experts in order to discuss and prepare their prospective testimony.

25. A Party Representative may pay, offer to pay, or acquiesce in the payment of:

(a) expenses reasonably incurred by a Witness or Expert in preparing to testify or testifying at a hearing;

(b) reasonable compensation for the loss of time incurred by a Witness in testifying and preparing to testify; and

(c) reasonable fees for the professional services of a Party-appointed Expert.

Comments to Guidelines 18–25

Guidelines 18–25 are concerned with interactions between Party Representatives and Witnesses and Experts. The interaction between Party Representatives and Witnesses is also addressed in Guidelines 9–11 concerning Submissions to the Arbitral Tribunal.

Many international arbitration practitioners desire more transparent and predictable standards of conduct with respect to relations with Witnesses and Experts in order to promote the principle of equal treatment among Parties. Disparate practises among jurisdictions may create inequality and threaten the integrity of the arbitral proceedings.

The Guidelines are intended to reflect best international arbitration practise with respect to the preparation of Witness and Expert testimony.

When a Party Representative contacts a potential Witness, he or she should disclose his or her identity and the reason for the contact before seeking any information from the potential Witness (Guideline 18). A Party Representative should also make the potential Witness aware of his or her right to inform or instruct counsel about this contact and involve such counsel in any further communication (Guideline 19).

Domestic professional conduct norms in some jurisdictions require higher standards with respect to contacts with potential Witnesses who are known to be represented by counsel. For example, some common law jurisdictions maintain a prohibition against contact by counsel with any potential Witness whom counsel knows to be represented in respect of the particular arbitration.

If a Party Representative determines that he or she is subject to a higher standard than the standard prescribed in these Guidelines, he or she may address the situation with the other Party and/or the Arbitral Tribunal.

As provided by Guideline 20, a Party Representative may assist in the preparation of Witness Statements and Expert Reports, but should seek to ensure that a Witness Statement reflects the Witness's own account of relevant facts, events and circumstances (Guideline 21), and that any Expert Report reflects the Expert's own views, analysis and conclusions (Guideline 22).

A Party Representative should not invite or encourage a Witness to give false evidence (Guideline 23).

As part of the preparation of testimony for the arbitration, a Party Representative may meet with Witnesses and Experts (or potential Witnesses and Experts) to discuss their prospective testimony. A Party Representative may also help a Witness in preparing his or her own Witness Statement or Expert Report. Further, a Party Representative may assist a Witness in preparing for their testimony in direct and cross-examination, including through practise questions and answers (Guideline 24). This preparation may include a review of the procedures through which testimony will be elicited and preparation of both direct testimony and cross -examination. Such contacts should however not alter the genuineness of the Witness or Expert evidence, which should always reflect the Witness's own account of relevant facts, events or circumstances, or the Expert's own analysis or opinion.

Finally, Party Representatives may pay, offer to pay or acquiesce in the payment of reasonable compensation to a Witness for his or her time and a reasonable fee for the professional services of an Expert (Guideline 25).

Remedies for Misconduct

26. If the Arbitral Tribunal, after giving the Parties notice and a reasonable opportunity to be heard, finds that a Party Representative has committed Misconduct, the Arbitral Tribunal, as appropriate, may:

(a) admonish the Party Representative;

(b) draw appropriate inferences in assessing the evidence relied upon, or the legal arguments advanced by, the Party Representative;

(c) consider the Party Representative's Misconduct in apportioning the costs of the arbitration, indicating, if appropriate, how and in what amount the Party Representative's Misconduct leads the Tribunal to a different

apportionment of costs;
(d) take any other appropriate measure in order to preserve the fairness and integrity of the proceedings.
27. In addressing issues of Misconduct, the Arbitral Tribunal should take into account:
(a) the need to preserve the integrity and fairness of the arbitral proceedings and the enforceability of the award;
(b) the potential impact of a ruling regarding Misconduct on the rights of the Parties;
(c) the nature and gravity of the Misconduct, including the extent to which the misconduct affects the conduct of the proceedings;
(d) the good faith of the Party Representative;
(e) relevant considerations of privilege and confidentiality; and
(f) the extent to which the Party represented by the Party Representative knew of, condoned, directed, or participated in, the Misconduct.

Comments to Guidelines 26–27

Guidelines 26–27 articulate potential remedies to address Misconduct by a Party Representative.

Their purpose is to preserve or restore the fairness and integrity of the arbitration.

The Arbitral Tribunal should seek to apply the most proportionate remedy or combination of remedies in light of the nature and gravity of the Misconduct, the good faith of the Party Representative and the Party whom he or she represents, the impact of the remedy on the Parties' rights, and the need to preserve the integrity, effectiveness and fairness of the arbitration and the enforceability of the award.

Guideline 27 sets forth a list of factors that is neither exhaustive nor binding, but instead reflects an overarching balancing exercise to be conducted in addressing matters of Misconduct by a Party Representative in order to ensure that the arbitration proceed in a fair and appropriate manner.

Before imposing any remedy in respect of alleged Misconduct, it is important that the Arbitral Tribunal gives the Parties and the impugned Representative the right to be heard in relation to the allegations made.

IBA RULES ON THE TAKING OF EVIDENCE IN INTERNATIONAL ARBITRATION *

Preamble

1. These IBA Rules on the Taking of Evidence in International Arbitration are intended to provide an efficient, economical and fair process for the taking of evidence in international arbitrations, particularly those between Parties from different legal traditions. They are designed to supplement the legal provisions and the institutional, *ad hoc* or other rules that apply to the conduct of the arbitration.
2. Parties and Arbitral Tribunals may adopt the IBA Rules of Evidence, in whole or in part, to govern arbitration proceedings, or they may vary them or use them as guidelines in developing their own procedures. The Rules are not intended to limit the flexibility that is inherent in, and an advantage of, international arbitration, and Parties and Arbitral Tribunals are free to adapt them to the particular circumstances of each arbitration.
3. The taking of evidence shall be conducted on the principles that each Party shall act in good faith and be entitled to know, reasonably in advance of any Evidentiary Hearing or any fact or merits determination, the evidence on which the other Parties rely.

Definitions

In the IBA Rules of Evidence:

Arbitral Tribunal	means a sole arbitrator or a panel of arbitrators;
Claimant	means the Party or Parties who commenced the arbitration and any Party who, through joinder or otherwise, becomes aligned with such Party or Parties;
Document	means a writing, communication, picture, drawing, program or data of any kind, whether recorded or maintained on paper or by electronic, audio, visual or any other means;
Evidentiary Hearing	means any hearing, whether or not held on consecutive days, at which the Arbitral Tribunal, whether in person, by teleconference,

* For a commentary on the IBA Rules on the Taking of Evidence, see IBA Working Party, 'Commentary on the revised text of the 2010 IBA Rules on the Taking of Evidence in International Arbitration'. See also, Tobias Zuberbühler, Dieter Hofmann, Christian Oetiker and Thomas Rohner

	videoconference or other method, receives oral or other evidence;
Expert Report	means a written statement by a Tribunal-Appointed Expert or a Party-Appointed Expert;
General Rules	mean the institutional, *ad hoc* or other rules that apply to the conduct of the arbitration;
IBA Rules of Evidence or Rules	means these IBA Rules on the Taking of Evidence in International Arbitration, as they may be revised or amended from time to time;
Party	means a party to the arbitration;
Party-Appointed Expert	means a person or organization appointed by a Party in order to report on specific issues determined by the Party;
Request to Produce	means a written request by a Party that another Party produce Documents;
Respondent	means the Party or Parties against whom the Claimant made its claim, and any Party who, through joinder or otherwise, becomes aligned with such Party or Parties, and includes a Respondent making a counterclaim;
Tribunal-Appointed Expert	means a person or organization appointed by the Arbitral Tribunal in order to report to it on specific issues determined by the Arbitral Tribunal;
and	
Witness Statement	means a written statement of testimony by a witness of fact.

Sellier, *IBA Rules of Evidence: Commentary on the IBA Rules on the Taking of Evidence in International Arbitration* (European Law Publishers, 2012) and Peter Ashford, *The IBA Rules on the Taking of Evidence in International Arbitration: A Guide* (Cambridge University Press, 2014).

Article 1 — Scope of Application

1. Whenever the Parties have agreed or the Arbitral Tribunal has determined to apply the IBA Rules of Evidence, the Rules shall govern the taking of evidence, except to the extent that any specific provision of them may be found to be in conflict with any mandatory provision of law determined to be applicable to the case by the Parties or by the Arbitral Tribunal.
2. Where the Parties have agreed to apply the IBA Rules of Evidence, they shall be deemed to have agreed, in the absence of a contrary indication, to the version as current on the date of such agreement.
3. In case of conflict between any provisions of the IBA Rules of Evidence and the General Rules, the Arbitral Tribunal shall apply the IBA Rules of Evidence in the manner that it determines best in order to accomplish the purposes of both the General Rules and the IBA Rules of Evidence, unless the Parties agree to the contrary.
4. In the event of any dispute regarding the meaning of the IBA Rules of Evidence, the Arbitral Tribunal shall interpret them according to their purpose and in the manner most appropriate for the particular arbitration.
5. Insofar as the IBA Rules of Evidence and the General Rules are silent on any matter concerning the taking of evidence and the Parties have not agreed otherwise, the Arbitral Tribunal shall conduct the taking of evidence as it deems appropriate, in accordance with the general principles of the IBA Rules of Evidence.

Article 2 — Consultation on Evidentiary Issues

1. The Arbitral Tribunal shall consult the Parties at the earliest appropriate time in the proceedings and invite them to consult each other with a view to agreeing on an efficient, economical and fair process for the taking of evidence.
2. The consultation on evidentiary issues may address the scope, timing and manner of the taking of evidence, including:

(a) the preparation and submission of Witness Statements and Expert Reports;

(b) the taking of oral testimony at any Evidentiary Hearing;

(c) the requirements, procedure and format applicable to the production of Documents;

(d) the level of confidentiality protection to be afforded to evidence in the arbitration; and

(e) the promotion of efficiency, economy and conservation of resources in connection with the taking of evidence.

3. The Arbitral Tribunal is encouraged to identify to the Parties, as soon as

it considers it to be appropriate, any issues:
(a) that the Arbitral Tribunal may regard as relevant to the case and material to its outcome; and/or
(b) for which a preliminary determination may be appropriate.

Article 3 — Documents

1. Within the time ordered by the Arbitral Tribunal, each Party shall submit to the Arbitral Tribunal and to the other Parties all Documents available to it on which it relies, including public Documents and those in the public domain, except for any Documents that have already been submitted by another Party.

2. Within the time ordered by the Arbitral Tribunal, any Party may submit to the Arbitral Tribunal and to the other Parties a Request to Produce.

3. A Request to Produce shall contain:
(a) (i) a description of each requested Document sufficient to identify it, or
(ii) a description in sufficient detail (including subject matter) of a narrow and specific requested category of Documents that are reasonably believed to exist; in the case of Documents maintained in electronic form, the requesting Party may, or the Arbitral Tribunal may order that it shall be required to, identify specific files, search terms, individuals or other means of searching for such Documents in an efficient and economical manner;
(b) a statement as to how the Documents requested are relevant to the case and material to its outcome; and
(c) (i) a statement that the Documents requested are not in the possession, custody or control of the requesting Party or a statement of the reasons why it would be unreasonably burdensome for the requesting Party to produce such Documents, and
(ii) a statement of the reasons why the requesting Party assumes the Documents requested are in the possession, custody or control of another Party.

4. Within the time ordered by the Arbitral Tribunal, the Party to whom the Request to Produce is addressed shall produce to the other Parties and, if the Arbitral Tribunal so orders, to it, all the Documents requested in its possession, custody or control as to which it makes no objection.

5. If the Party to whom the Request to Produce is addressed has an objection to some or all of the Documents requested, it shall state the objection in writing to the Arbitral Tribunal and the other Parties within the time ordered by the Arbitral Tribunal. The reasons for such objection shall be any of those set forth in Article 9.2 or a failure to satisfy any of the requirements of Article 3.3.

6. Upon receipt of any such objection, the Arbitral Tribunal may invite the relevant Parties to consult with each other with a view to resolving the objection.
7. Either Party may, within the time ordered by the Arbitral Tribunal, request the Arbitral Tribunal to rule on the objection. The Arbitral Tribunal shall then, in consultation with the Parties and in timely fashion, consider the Request to Produce and the objection. The Arbitral Tribunal may order the Party to whom such Request is addressed to produce any requested Document in its possession, custody or control as to which the Arbitral Tribunal determines that (i) the issues that the requesting Party wishes to prove are relevant to the case and material to its outcome; (ii) none of the reasons for objection set forth in Article 9.2 applies; and (iii) the requirements of Article 3.3 have been satisfied. Any such Document shall be produced to the other Parties and, if the Arbitral Tribunal so orders, to it.
8. In exceptional circumstances, if the propriety of an objection can be determined only by review of the Document, the Arbitral Tribunal may determine that it should not review the Document. In that event, the Arbitral Tribunal may, after consultation with the Parties, appoint an independent and impartial expert, bound to confidentiality, to review any such Document and to report on the objection. To the extent that the objection is upheld by the Arbitral Tribunal, the expert shall not disclose to the Arbitral Tribunal and to the other Parties the contents of the Document reviewed.
9. If a Party wishes to obtain the production of Documents from a person or organisation who is not a Party to the arbitration and from whom the Party cannot obtain the Documents on its own, the Party may, within the time ordered by the Arbitral Tribunal, ask it to take whatever steps are legally available to obtain the requested Documents, or seek leave from the Arbitral Tribunal to take such steps itself. The Party shall submit such request to the Arbitral Tribunal and to the other Parties in writing, and the request shall contain the particulars set forth in Article 3.3, as applicable. The Arbitral Tribunal shall decide on this request and shall take, authorize the requesting Party to take, or order any other Party to take, such steps as the Arbitral Tribunal considers appropriate if, in its discretion, it determines that (i) the Documents would be relevant to the case and material to its outcome, (ii) the requirements of Article 3.3, as applicable, have been satisfied and (iii) none of the reasons for objection set forth in Article 9.2 applies.
10. At any time before the arbitration is concluded, the Arbitral Tribunal may (i) request any Party to produce Documents, (ii) request any Party to use its best efforts to take or (iii) itself take, any step that it considers

appropriate to obtain Documents from any person or organisation. A Party to whom such a request for Documents is addressed may object to the request for any of the reasons set forth in Article 9.2. In such cases, Article 3.4 to Article 3.8 shall apply correspondingly.

11. Within the time ordered by the Arbitral Tribunal, the Parties may submit to the Arbitral Tribunal and to the other Parties any additional Documents on which they intend to rely or which they believe have become relevant to the case and material to its outcome as a consequence of the issues raised in Documents, Witness Statements or Expert Reports submitted or produced, or in other submissions of the Parties.

12. With respect to the form of submission or production of Documents:

(a) copies of Documents shall conform to the originals and, at the request of the Arbitral Tribunal, any original shall be presented for inspection;

(b) Documents that a Party maintains in electronic form shall be submitted or produced in the form most convenient or economical to it that is reasonably usable by the recipients, unless the Parties agree otherwise or, in the absence of such agreement, the Arbitral Tribunal decides otherwise;

(c) a Party is not obligated to produce multiple copies of Documents which are essentially identical unless the Arbitral Tribunal decides otherwise; and

(d) translations of Documents shall be submitted together with the originals and marked as translations with the original language identified.

13. Any Document submitted or produced by a Party or non-Party in the arbitration and not otherwise in the public domain shall be kept confidential by the Arbitral Tribunal and the other Parties, and shall be used only in connection with the arbitration. This requirement shall apply except and to the extent that disclosure may be required of a Party to fulfil a legal duty, protect or pursue a legal right, or enforce or challenge an award in bona fide legal proceedings before a state court or other judicial authority. The Arbitral Tribunal may issue orders to set forth the terms of this confidentiality. This requirement shall be without prejudice to all other obligations of confidentiality in the arbitration.

14. If the arbitration is organised into separate issues or phases (such as jurisdiction, preliminary determinations, liability or damages), the Arbitral Tribunal may, after consultation with the Parties, schedule the submission of Documents and Requests to Produce separately for each issue or phase.

Article 4 — Witnesses of Fact

1. Within the time ordered by the Arbitral Tribunal, each Party shall identify the witnesses on whose testimony it intends to rely and the subject matter of that testimony.

2. Any person may present evidence as a witness, including a Party or a Party's officer, employee or other representative.
3. It shall not be improper for a Party, its officers, employees, legal advisors or other representatives to interview its witnesses or potential witnesses and to discuss their prospective testimony with them.
4. The Arbitral Tribunal may order each Party to submit within a specified time to the Arbitral Tribunal and to the other Parties Witness Statements by each witness on whose testimony it intends to rely, except for those witnesses whose testimony is sought pursuant to Articles 4.9 or 4.10. If Evidentiary Hearings are organised into separate issues or phases (such as jurisdiction, preliminary determinations, liability or damages), the Arbitral Tribunal or the Parties by agreement may schedule the submission of Witness Statements separately for each issue or phase.
5. Each Witness Statement shall contain:
(a) the full name and address of the witness, a statement regarding his or her present and past relationship (if any) with any of the Parties, and a description of his or her background, qualifications, training and experience, if such a description may be relevant to the dispute or to the contents of the statement;
(b) a full and detailed description of the facts, and the source of the witness's information as to those facts, sufficient to serve as that witness's evidence in the matter in dispute. Documents on which the witness relies that have not already been submitted shall be provided;
(c) a statement as to the language in which the Witness Statement was originally prepared and the language in which the witness anticipates giving testimony at the Evidentiary Hearing;
(d) an affirmation of the truth of the Witness Statement; and
(e) the signature of the witness and its date and place.
6. If Witness Statements are submitted, any Party may, within the time ordered by the Arbitral Tribunal, submit to the Arbitral Tribunal and to the other Parties revised or additional Witness Statements, including statements from persons not previously named as witnesses, so long as any such revisions or additions respond only to matters contained in another Party's Witness Statements, Expert Reports or other submissions that have not been previously presented in the arbitration.
7. If a witness whose appearance has been requested pursuant to Article 8.1 fails without a valid reason to appear for testimony at an Evidentiary Hearing, the Arbitral Tribunal shall disregard any Witness Statement related to that Evidentiary Hearing by that witness unless, in exceptional

circumstances, the Arbitral Tribunal decides otherwise.
8. If the appearance of a witness has not been requested pursuant to Article 8.1, none of the other Parties shall be deemed to have agreed to the correctness of the content of the Witness Statement.
9. If a Party wishes to present evidence from a person who will not appear voluntarily at its request, the Party may, within the time ordered by the Arbitral Tribunal, ask it to take whatever steps are legally available to obtain the testimony of that person, or seek leave from the Arbitral Tribunal to take such steps itself. In the case of a request to the Arbitral Tribunal, the Party shall identify the intended witness, shall describe the subjects on which the witness's testimony is sought and shall state why such subjects are relevant to the case and material to its outcome. The Arbitral Tribunal shall decide on this request and shall take, authorize the requesting Party to take or order any other Party to take, such steps as the Arbitral Tribunal considers appropriate if, in its discretion, it determines that the testimony of that witness would be relevant to the case and material to its outcome.
10. At any time before the arbitration is concluded, the Arbitral Tribunal may order any Party to provide for, or to use its best efforts to provide for, the appearance for testimony at an Evidentiary Hearing of any person, including one whose testimony has not yet been offered. A Party to whom such a request is addressed may object for any of the reasons set forth in Article 9.2.

Article 5 — Party-Appointed Experts

1. A Party may rely on a Party-Appointed Expert as a means of evidence on specific issues. Within the time ordered by the Arbitral Tribunal, (i) each Party shall identify any Party-Appointed Expert on whose testimony it intends to rely and the subject-matter of such testimony; and (ii) the Party-Appointed Expert shall submit an Expert Report.
2. The Expert Report shall contain:
(a) the full name and address of the Party-Appointed Expert, a statement regarding his or her present and past relationship (if any) with any of the Parties, their legal advisors and the Arbitral Tribunal, and a description of his or her background, qualifications, training and experience;
(b) a description of the instructions pursuant to which he or she is providing his or her opinions and conclusions;
(c) a statement of his or her independence from the Parties, their legal advisors and the Arbitral Tribunal;
(d) a statement of the facts on which he or she is basing his or her expert opinions and conclusions;

(e) his or her expert opinions and conclusions, including a description of the methods, evidence and information used in arriving at the conclusions. Documents on which the Party-Appointed Expert relies that have not already been submitted shall be provided;
(f) if the Expert Report has been translated, a statement as to the language in which it was originally prepared, and the language in which the Party-Appointed Expert anticipates giving testimony at the Evidentiary Hearing;
(g) an affirmation of his or her genuine belief in the opinions expressed in the Expert Report;
(h) the signature of the Party-Appointed Expert and its date and place; and
(i) if the Expert Report has been signed by more than one person, an attribution of the entirety or specific parts of the Expert Report to each author.
3. If Expert Reports are submitted, any Party may, within the time ordered by the Arbitral Tribunal, submit to the Arbitral Tribunal and to the other Parties revised or additional Expert Reports, including reports or statements from persons not previously identified as Party-Appointed Experts, so long as any such revisions or additions respond only to matters contained in another Party's Witness Statements, Expert Reports or other submissions that have not been previously presented in the arbitration.
4. The Arbitral Tribunal in its discretion may order that any Party-Appointed Experts who will submit or who have submitted Expert Reports on the same or related issues meet and confer on such issues. At such meeting, the Party-Appointed Experts shall attempt to reach agreement on the issues within the scope of their Expert Reports, and they shall record in writing any such issues on which they reach agreement, any remaining areas of disagreement and the reasons therefore.
5. If a Party-Appointed Expert whose appearance has been requested pursuant to Article 8.1 fails without a valid reason to appear for testimony at an Evidentiary Hearing, the Arbitral Tribunal shall disregard any Expert Report by that Party-Appointed Expert related to that Evidentiary Hearing unless, in exceptional circumstances, the Arbitral Tribunal decides otherwise.
6. If the appearance of a Party-Appointed Expert has not been requested pursuant to Article 8.1, none of the other Parties shall be deemed to have agreed to the correctness of the content of the Expert Report.

Article 6 — Tribunal-Appointed Experts

1. The Arbitral Tribunal, after consulting with the Parties, may appoint one or more independent Tribunal-Appointed Experts to report to it on specific

issues designated by the Arbitral Tribunal. The Arbitral Tribunal shall establish the terms of reference for any Tribunal-Appointed Expert Report after consulting with the Parties. A copy of the final terms of reference shall be sent by the Arbitral Tribunal to the Parties.

2. The Tribunal-Appointed Expert shall, before accepting appointment, submit to the Arbitral Tribunal and to the Parties a description of his or her qualifications and a statement of his or her independence from the Parties, their legal advisors and the Arbitral Tribunal. Within the time ordered by the Arbitral Tribunal, the Parties shall inform the Arbitral Tribunal whether they have any objections as to the Tribunal-Appointed Expert's qualifications and independence. The Arbitral Tribunal shall decide promptly whether to accept any such objection. After the appointment of a Tribunal-Appointed Expert, a Party may object to the expert's qualifications or independence only if the objection is for reasons of which the Party becomes aware after the appointment has been made. The Arbitral Tribunal shall decide promptly what, if any, action to take.

3. Subject to the provisions of Article 9.2, the Tribunal-Appointed Expert may request a Party to provide any information or to provide access to any Documents, goods, samples, property, machinery, systems, processes or site for inspection, to the extent relevant to the case and material to its outcome. The authority of a Tribunal-Appointed Expert to request such information or access shall be the same as the authority of the Arbitral Tribunal. The Parties and their representatives shall have the right to receive any such information and to attend any such inspection. Any disagreement between a Tribunal-Appointed Expert and a Party as to the relevance, materiality or appropriateness of such a request shall be decided by the Arbitral Tribunal, in the manner provided in Articles 3.5 through 3.8. The Tribunal-Appointed Expert shall record in the Expert Report any non-compliance by a Party with an appropriate request or decision by the Arbitral Tribunal and shall describe its effects on the determination of the specific issue.

4. The Tribunal-Appointed Expert shall report in writing to the Arbitral Tribunal in an Expert Report. The Expert Report shall contain:

(a) the full name and address of the Tribunal-Appointed Expert, and a description of his or her background, qualifications, training and experience;

(b) a statement of the facts on which he or she is basing his or her expert opinions and conclusions;

(c) his or her expert opinions and conclusions, including a description of the methods, evidence and information used in arriving at the conclusions.

Documents on which the Tribunal-Appointed Expert relies that have not already been submitted shall be provided;

(d) if the Expert Report has been translated, a statement as to the language in which it was originally prepared, and the language in which the Tribunal-Appointed Expert anticipates giving testimony at the Evidentiary Hearing;

(e) an affirmation of his or her genuine belief in the opinions expressed in the Expert Report;

(f) the signature of the Tribunal-Appointed Expert and its date and place; and

(g) if the Expert Report has been signed by more than one person, an attribution of the entirety or specific parts of the Expert Report to each author.

5. The Arbitral Tribunal shall send a copy of such Expert Report to the Parties. The Parties may examine any information, Documents, goods, samples, property, machinery, systems, processes or site for inspection that the Tribunal-Appointed Expert has examined and any correspondence between the Arbitral Tribunal and the Tribunal-Appointed Expert. Within the time ordered by the Arbitral Tribunal, any Party shall have the opportunity to respond to the Expert Report in a submission by the Party or through a Witness Statement or an Expert Report by a Party-Appointed Expert. The Arbitral Tribunal shall send the submission, Witness Statement or Expert Report to the Tribunal-Appointed Expert and to the other Parties.

6. At the request of a Party or of the Arbitral Tribunal, the Tribunal-Appointed Expert shall be present at an Evidentiary Hearing. The Arbitral Tribunal may question the Tribunal-Appointed Expert, and he or she may be questioned by the Parties or by any Party-Appointed Expert on issues raised in his or her Expert Report, the Parties' submissions or Witness Statement or the Expert Reports made by the Party-Appointed Experts pursuant to Article 6.5.

7. Any Expert Report made by a Tribunal-Appointed Expert and its conclusions shall be assessed by the Arbitral Tribunal with due regard to all circumstances of the case.

8. The fees and expenses of a Tribunal-Appointed Expert, to be funded in a manner determined by the Arbitral Tribunal, shall form part of the costs of the arbitration.

Article 7 — Inspection

Subject to the provisions of Article 9.2, the Arbitral Tribunal may, at the request of a Party or on its own motion, inspect or require the inspection by a Tribunal-Appointed Expert or a Party-Appointed Expert of any site, property, machinery or any other goods, samples, systems, processes or Documents, as it deems appropriate. The Arbitral Tribunal shall, in consultation with the Parties, determine the timing and arrangement for the inspection. The Parties and their representatives shall have the right to attend any such inspection.

Article 8 — Evidentiary Hearing

1. Within the time ordered by the Arbitral Tribunal, each Party shall inform the Arbitral Tribunal and the other Parties of the witnesses whose appearance it requests. Each witness (which term includes, for the purposes of this Article, witnesses of fact and any experts) shall, subject to Article 8.2, appear for testimony at the Evidentiary Hearing if such person's appearance has been requested by any Party or by the Arbitral Tribunal. Each witness shall appear in person unless the Arbitral Tribunal allows the use of videoconference or similar technology with respect to a particular witness.

2. The Arbitral Tribunal shall at all times have complete control over the Evidentiary Hearing. The Arbitral Tribunal may limit or exclude any question to, answer by or appearance of a witness, if it considers such question, answer or appearance to be irrelevant, immaterial, unreasonably burdensome, duplicative or otherwise covered by a reason for objection set forth in Article 9.2. Questions to a witness during direct and re-direct testimony may not be unreasonably leading.

3. With respect to oral testimony at an Evidentiary Hearing:

(a) the Claimant shall ordinarily first present the testimony of its witnesses, followed by the Respondent presenting the testimony of its witnesses;

(b) following direct testimony, any other Party may question such witness, in an order to be determined by the Arbitral Tribunal. The Party who initially presented the witness shall subsequently have the opportunity to ask additional questions on the matters raised in the other Parties' questioning;

(c) thereafter, the Claimant shall ordinarily first present the testimony of its Party-Appointed Experts, followed by the Respondent presenting the testimony of its Party-Appointed Experts. The Party who initially presented the Party-Appointed Expert shall subsequently have the opportunity to ask additional questions on the matters raised in the other Parties' questioning;

(d) the Arbitral Tribunal may question a Tribunal-Appointed Expert, and he or she may be questioned by the Parties or by any Party-Appointed Expert, on issues raised in the Tribunal-Appointed Expert Report, in the Parties' submissions or in the Expert Reports made by the Party-Appointed Experts;

(e) if the arbitration is organised into separate issues or phases (such as jurisdiction, preliminary determinations, liability and damages), the Parties may agree or the Arbitral Tribunal may order the scheduling of testimony separately for each issue or phase;
(f) the Arbitral Tribunal, upon request of a Party or on its own motion, may vary this order of proceeding, including the arrangement of testimony by particular issues or in such a manner that witnesses be questioned at the same time and in confrontation with each other (witness conferencing);
(g) the Arbitral Tribunal may ask questions to a witness at any time.
4. A witness of fact providing testimony shall first affirm, in a manner determined appropriate by the Arbitral Tribunal, that he or she commits to tell the truth or, in the case of an expert witness, his or her genuine belief in the opinions to be expressed at the Evidentiary Hearing. If the witness has submitted a Witness Statement or an Expert Report, the witness shall confirm it. The Parties may agree or the Arbitral Tribunal may order that the Witness Statement or Expert Report shall serve as that witness's direct testimony.
5. Subject to the provisions of Article 9.2, the Arbitral Tribunal may request any person to give oral or written evidence on any issue that the Arbitral Tribunal considers to be relevant to the case and material to its outcome. Any witness called and questioned by the Arbitral Tribunal may also be questioned by the Parties.

Article 9 — Admissibility and Assessment of Evidence

1. The Arbitral Tribunal shall determine the admissibility, relevance, materiality and weight of evidence.
2. The Arbitral Tribunal shall, at the request of a Party or on its own motion, exclude from evidence or production any Document, statement, oral testimony or inspection for any of the following reasons:
(a) lack of sufficient relevance to the case or materiality to its outcome;
(b) legal impediment or privilege under the legal or ethical rules determined by the Arbitral Tribunal to be applicable;
(c) unreasonable burden to produce the requested evidence;
(d) loss or destruction of the Document that has been shown with reasonable likelihood to have occurred;
(e) grounds of commercial or technical confidentiality that the Arbitral Tribunal determines to be compelling;
(f) grounds of special political or institutional sensitivity (including evidence that has been classified as secret by a government or a public international institution) that the Arbitral Tribunal determines to be

compelling; or

(g) considerations of procedural economy, proportionality, fairness or equality of the Parties that the Arbitral Tribunal determines to be compelling.

3. In considering issues of legal impediment or privilege under Article 9.2 (b), and insofar as permitted by any mandatory legal or ethical rules that are determined by it to be applicable, the Arbitral Tribunal may take into account:

(a) any need to protect the confidentiality of a Document created or statement or oral communication made in connection with and for the purpose of providing or obtaining legal advice;

(b) any need to protect the confidentiality of a Document created or statement or oral communication made in connection with and for the purpose of settlement negotiations;

(c) the expectations of the Parties and their advisors at the time the legal impediment or privilege is said to have arisen;

(d) any possible waiver of any applicable legal impediment or privilege by virtue of consent, earlier disclosure, affirmative use of the Document, statement, oral communication or advice contained therein, or otherwise; and

(e) the need to maintain fairness and equality as between the Parties, particularly if they are subject to different legal or ethical rules.

4. The Arbitral Tribunal may, where appropriate, make necessary arrangements to permit evidence to be presented or considered subject to suitable confidentiality protection.

5. If a Party fails without satisfactory explanation to produce any Document requested in a Request to Produce to which it has not objected in due time or fails to produce any Document ordered to be produced by the Arbitral Tribunal, the Arbitral Tribunal may infer that such document would be adverse to the interests of that Party.

6. If a Party fails without satisfactory explanation to make available any other relevant evidence, including testimony, sought by one Party to which the Party to whom the request was addressed has not objected in due time or fails to make available any evidence, including testimony, ordered by the Arbitral Tribunal to be produced, the Arbitral Tribunal may infer that such evidence would be adverse to the interests of that Party.

7. If the Arbitral Tribunal determines that a Party has failed to conduct itself in good faith in the taking of evidence, the Arbitral Tribunal may, in addition to any other measures available under these Rules, take such failure

into account in its assignment of the costs of the arbitration, including costs arising out of or in connection with the taking of evidence.

ICC RULES OF ARBITRATION
Rules of Arbitration of the International Chamber of Commerce *

Introductory Provisions

Article 1 — International Court of Arbitration

1. The International Court of Arbitration (the "Court") of the International Chamber of Commerce (the "ICC") is the independent arbitration body of the ICC. The statutes of the Court are set forth in Appendix I.
2. The Court does not itself resolve disputes. It administers the resolution of disputes by arbitral tribunals, in accordance with the Rules of Arbitration of the ICC (the "Rules"). The Court is the only body authorized to administer arbitrations under the Rules, including the scrutiny and approval of awards rendered in accordance with the Rules. It draws up its own internal rules, which are set forth in Appendix II (the "Internal Rules").
3. The President of the Court (the "President") or, in the President's absence or otherwise at the President's request, one of its Vice-Presidents shall have the power to take urgent decisions on behalf of the Court, provided that any such decision is reported to the Court at its next session.
4. As provided for in the Internal Rules, the Court may delegate to one or more committees composed of its members the power to take certain decisions, provided that any such decision is reported to the Court at its next session.
5. The Court is assisted in its work by the Secretariat of the Court (the "Secretariat") under the direction of its Secretary General (the "Secretary General").

Article 2 — Definitions

In the Rules:

(i) "arbitral tribunal" includes one or more arbitrators;

(ii) "claimant" includes one or more claimants, "respondent" includes one or more respondents, and "additional party" includes one or more additional parties;

(iii) "party" or "parties" include claimants, respondents or additional parties;

(iv) "claim" or "claims" include any claim by any party against any other party;

(v) "award" includes, *inter alia*, an interim, partial or final award.

Article 3 — Written Notifications or Communications; Time Limits

1. All pleadings and other written communications submitted by any party, as well as all documents annexed thereto, shall be supplied in a number of copies sufficient to provide one copy for each party, plus one for each arbitrator, and one for the Secretariat. A copy of any notification or communication from the arbitral tribunal to the parties shall be sent to the

---

* For a commentary on the ICC Arbitration Rules, see Jason Fry, Simon Greenberg and Francesca Mazza, *The Secretariat's Guide to ICC Arbitration* (ICC Publication No. 729E, 2012). See also, Jacob Grierson and Annet van Hooft, *Arbitrating under the 2012 ICC Rules: An Introductory User's*

Secretariat.

2. All notifications or communications from the Secretariat and the arbitral tribunal shall be made to the last address of the party or its representative for whom the same are intended, as notified either by the party in question or by the other party. Such notification or communication may be made by delivery against receipt, registered post, courier, email, or any other means of telecommunication that provides a record of the sending thereof.

3. A notification or communication shall be deemed to have been made on the day it was received by the party itself or by its representative, or would have been received if made in accordance with Article 3(2).

4. Periods of time specified in or fixed under the Rules shall start to run on the day following the date a notification or communication is deemed to have been made in accordance with Article 3(3). When the day next following such date is an official holiday, or a non-business day in the country where the notification or communication is deemed to have been made, the period of time shall commence on the first following business day. Official holidays and non-business days are included in the calculation of the period of time. If the last day of the relevant period of time granted is an official holiday or a nonbusiness day in the country where the notification or communication is deemed to have been made, the period of time shall expire at the end of the first following business day.

Commencing the Arbitration

Article 4 — Request for Arbitration

1. A party wishing to have recourse to arbitration under the Rules shall submit its Request for Arbitration (the "Request") to the Secretariat at any of the offices specified in the Internal Rules. The Secretariat shall notify the claimant and respondent of the receipt of the Request and the date of such receipt.

2. The date on which the Request is received by the Secretariat shall, for all purposes, be deemed to be the date of the commencement of the arbitration.

3. The Request shall contain the following information:

a) the name in full, description, address and other contact details of each of the parties;

b) the name in full, address and other contact details of any person(s) representing the claimant in the arbitration;

c) a description of the nature and circumstances of the dispute giving rise to the claims and of the basis upon which the claims are made;

d) a statement of the relief sought, together with the amounts of any quantified claims and, to the extent possible, an estimate of the monetary

---

Guide (Kluwer Law International, 2012) and Yves Derains and Eric A. Schwartz, *A Guide to the ICC Rules of Arbitration* (3rd ed, Kluwer Law International, July 2015) (forthcoming).

value of any other claims;
e) any relevant agreements and, in particular, the arbitration agreement(s);
f) where claims are made under more than one arbitration agreement, an indication of the arbitration agreement under which each claim is made;
g) all relevant particulars and any observations or proposals concerning the number of arbitrators and their choice in accordance with the provisions of Articles 12 and 13, and any nomination of an arbitrator required thereby; and
h) all relevant particulars and any observations or proposals as to the place of the arbitration, the applicable rules of law and the language of the arbitration.

The claimant may submit such other documents or information with the Request as it considers appropriate or as may contribute to the efficient resolution of the dispute.

4. Together with the Request, the claimant shall:
a) submit the number of copies thereof required by Article 3(1); and
b) make payment of the filing fee required by Appendix III ("Arbitration Costs and Fees") in force on the date the Request is submitted.

In the event that the claimant fails to comply with either of these requirements, the Secretariat may fix a time limit within which the claimant must comply, failing which the file shall be closed without prejudice to the claimant's right to submit the same claims at a later date in another Request.

5. The Secretariat shall transmit a copy of the Request and the documents annexed thereto to the respondent for its Answer to the Request once the Secretariat has sufficient copies of the Request and the required filing fee.

Article 5 — Answer to the Request; Counterclaims

1. Within 30 days from the receipt of the Request from the Secretariat, the respondent shall submit an Answer (the "Answer") which shall contain the following information:
a) its name in full, description, address and other contact details;
b) the name in full, address and other contact details of any person(s) representing the respondent in the arbitration;
c) its comments as to the nature and circumstances of the dispute giving rise to the claims and the basis upon which the claims are made;
d) its response to the relief sought;
e) any observations or proposals concerning the number of arbitrators and their choice in light of the claimant's proposals and in accordance with the provisions of Articles 12 and 13, and any nomination of an arbitrator required thereby; and

f) any observations or proposals as to the place of the arbitration, the applicable rules of law and the language of the arbitration.

The respondent may submit such other documents or information with the Answer as it considers appropriate or as may contribute to the efficient resolution of the dispute.

2. The Secretariat may grant the respondent an extension of the time for submitting the Answer, provided the application for such an extension contains the respondent's observations or proposals concerning the number of arbitrators and their choice and, where required by Articles 12 and 13, the nomination of an arbitrator. If the respondent fails to do so, the Court shall proceed in accordance with the Rules.

3. The Answer shall be submitted to the Secretariat in the number of copies specified by Article 3(1).

4. The Secretariat shall communicate the Answer and the documents annexed thereto to all other parties.

5. Any counterclaims made by the respondent shall be submitted with the Answer and shall provide:

a) a description of the nature and circumstances of the dispute giving rise to the counterclaims and of the basis upon which the counterclaims are made;

b) a statement of the relief sought together with the amounts of any quantified counterclaims and, to the extent possible, an estimate of the monetary value of any other counterclaims;

c) any relevant agreements and, in particular, the arbitration agreement(s); and

d) where counterclaims are made under more than one arbitration agreement, an indication of the arbitration agreement under which each counterclaim is made.

The respondent may submit such other documents or information with the counterclaims as it considers appropriate or as may contribute to the efficient resolution of the dispute.

6. The claimant shall submit a reply to any counterclaim within 30 days from the date of receipt of the counterclaims communicated by the Secretariat. Prior to the transmission of the file to the arbitral tribunal, the Secretariat may grant the claimant an extension of time for submitting the reply.

Article 6 — Effect of the Arbitration Agreement

1. Where the parties have agreed to submit to arbitration under the Rules, they shall be deemed to have submitted *ipso facto* to the Rules in

effect on the date of commencement of the arbitration, unless they have agreed to submit to the Rules in effect on the date of their arbitration agreement.

2. By agreeing to arbitration under the Rules, the parties have accepted that the arbitration shall be administered by the Court.

3. If any party against which a claim has been made does not submit an Answer, or raises one or more pleas concerning the existence, validity or scope of the arbitration agreement or concerning whether all of the claims made in the arbitration may be determined together in a single arbitration, the arbitration shall proceed and any question of jurisdiction or of whether the claims may be determined together in that arbitration shall be decided directly by the arbitral tribunal, unless the Secretary General refers the matter to the Court for its decision pursuant to Article 6(4).

4. In all cases referred to the Court under Article 6(3), the Court shall decide whether and to what extent the arbitration shall proceed. The arbitration shall proceed if and to the extent that the Court is *prima facie* satisfied that an arbitration agreement under the Rules may exist. In particular:

(i) where there are more than two parties to the arbitration, the arbitration shall proceed between those of the parties, including any additional parties joined pursuant to Article 7, with respect to which the Court is *prima facie* satisfied that an arbitration agreement under the Rules that binds them all may exist; and

(ii) where claims pursuant to Article 9 are made under more than one arbitration agreement, the arbitration shall proceed as to those claims with respect to which the Court is prima facie satisfied (a) that the arbitration agreements under which those claims are made may be compatible, and (b) that all parties to the arbitration may have agreed that those claims can be determined together in a single arbitration.

The Court's decision pursuant to Article 6(4) is without prejudice to the admissibility or merits of any party's plea or pleas.

5. In all matters decided by the Court under Article 6(4), any decision as to the jurisdiction of the arbitral tribunal, except as to parties or claims with respect to which the Court decides that the arbitration cannot proceed, shall then be taken by the arbitral tribunal itself.

6. Where the parties are notified of the Court's decision pursuant to Article 6(4) that the arbitration cannot proceed in respect of some or all of them, any party retains the right to ask any court having jurisdiction whether or not, and in respect of which of them, there is a binding arbitration agreement.

7. Where the Court has decided pursuant to Article 6(4) that the arbitration cannot proceed in respect of any of the claims, such decision shall not prevent a party from reintroducing the same claim at a later date in other proceedings.
8. If any of the parties refuses or fails to take part in the arbitration or any stage thereof, the arbitration shall proceed notwithstanding such refusal or failure.
9. Unless otherwise agreed, the arbitral tribunal shall not cease to have jurisdiction by reason of any allegation that the contract is non-existent or null and void, provided that the arbitral tribunal upholds the validity of the arbitration agreement. The arbitral tribunal shall continue to have jurisdiction to determine the parties' respective rights and to decide their claims and pleas even though the contract itself may be non-existent or null and void.

Multiple Parties, Multiple Contracts and Consolidation

Article 7 — Joinder of Additional Parties

1. A party wishing to join an additional party to the arbitration shall submit its request for arbitration against the additional party (the "Request for Joinder") to the Secretariat. The date on which the Request for Joinder is received by the Secretariat shall, for all purposes, be deemed to be the date of the commencement of arbitration against the additional party. Any such joinder shall be subject to the provisions of Articles 6(3)–6(7) and 9. No additional party may be joined after the confirmation or appointment of any arbitrator, unless all parties, including the additional party, otherwise agree. The Secretariat may fix a time limit for the submission of a Request for Joinder.
2. The Request for Joinder shall contain the following information:
a) the case reference of the existing arbitration;
b) the name in full, description, address and other contact details of each of the parties, including the additional party; and
c) the information specified in Article 4(3) subparagraphs c), d), e) and f).
The party filing the Request for Joinder may submit therewith such other documents or information as it considers appropriate or as may contribute to the efficient resolution of the dispute.
3. The provisions of Articles 4(4) and 4(5) shall apply, *mutatis mutandis*, to the Request for Joinder.
4. The additional party shall submit an Answer in accordance, *mutatis mutandis*, with the provisions of Articles 5(1)–5(4). The additional party

may make claims against any other party in accordance with the provisions of Article 8.

Article 8 — Claims between Multiple Parties

1. In an arbitration with multiple parties, claims may be made by any party against any other party, subject to the provisions of Articles 6(3)–6(7) and 9 and provided that no new claims may be made after the Terms of Reference are signed or approved by the Court without the authorization of the arbitral tribunal pursuant to Article 23(4).

2. Any party making a claim pursuant to Article 8(1) shall provide the information specified in Article 4(3) subparagraphs c), d), e) and f).

3. Before the Secretariat transmits the file to the arbitral tribunal in accordance with Article 16, the following provisions shall apply, *mutatis mutandis*, to any claim made: Article 4(4) subparagraph a); Article 4 (5); Article 5(1) except for subparagraphs a), b), e) and f); Article 5(2); Article 5(3) and Article 5(4). Thereafter, the arbitral tribunal shall determine the procedure for making a claim.

Article 9 — Multiple Contracts

Subject to the provisions of Articles 6(3)–6(7) and 23(4), claims arising out of or in connection with more than one contract may be made in a single arbitration, irrespective of whether such claims are made under one or more than one arbitration agreement under the Rules.

Article 10 — Consolidation of Arbitrations

The Court may, at the request of a party, consolidate two or more arbitrations pending under the Rules into a single arbitration, where:

a) the parties have agreed to consolidation; or

b) all of the claims in the arbitrations are made under the same arbitration agreement; or

c) where the claims in the arbitrations are made under more than one arbitration agreement, the arbitrations are between the same parties, the disputes in the arbitrations arise in connection with the same legal relationship, and the Court finds the arbitration agreements to be compatible.

In deciding whether to consolidate, the Court may take into account any circumstances it considers to be relevant, including whether one or more arbitrators have been confirmed or appointed in more than one of the arbitrations and, if so, whether the same or different persons have been confirmed or appointed.

When arbitrations are consolidated, they shall be consolidated into the arbitration that commenced first, unless otherwise agreed by all parties.

The Arbitral Tribunal

Article 11 — General Provisions

1. Every arbitrator must be and remain impartial and independent of the parties involved in the arbitration.
2. Before appointment or confirmation, a prospective arbitrator shall sign a statement of acceptance, availability, impartiality and independence. The prospective arbitrator shall disclose in writing to the Secretariat any facts or circumstances which might be of such a nature as to call into question the arbitrator's independence in the eyes of the parties, as well as any circumstances that could give rise to reasonable doubts as to the arbitrator's impartiality. The Secretariat shall provide such information to the parties in writing and fix a time limit for any comments from them.
3. An arbitrator shall immediately disclose in writing to the Secretariat and to the parties any facts or circumstances of a similar nature to those referred to in Article 11(2) concerning the arbitrator's impartiality or independence which may arise during the arbitration.
4. The decisions of the Court as to the appointment, confirmation, challenge or replacement of an arbitrator shall be final, and the reasons for such decisions shall not be communicated.
5. By accepting to serve, arbitrators undertake to carry out their responsibilities in accordance with the Rules.
6. Insofar as the parties have not provided otherwise, the arbitral tribunal shall be constituted in accordance with the provisions of Articles 12 and 13.

Article 12 — Constitution of the Arbitral tribunal

Number of Arbitrators

1. The disputes shall be decided by a sole arbitrator or by three arbitrators.
2. Where the parties have not agreed upon the number of arbitrators, the Court shall appoint a sole arbitrator, save where it appears to the Court that the dispute is such as to warrant the appointment of three arbitrators. In such case, the claimant shall nominate an arbitrator within a period of 15 days from the receipt of the notification of the decision of the Court, and the respondent shall nominate an arbitrator within a period of 15 days from the receipt of the notification of the nomination made by the claimant. If a party fails to nominate an arbitrator, the appointment shall be made by the Court.

Sole Arbitrator

3. Where the parties have agreed that the dispute shall be resolved by a sole arbitrator, they may, by agreement, nominate the sole arbitrator for confirmation. If the parties fail to nominate a sole arbitrator within 30 days from the date when the claimant's Request for Arbitration has been received

by the other party, or within such additional time as may be allowed by the Secretariat, the sole arbitrator shall be appointed by the Court.

Three Arbitrators

4. Where the parties have agreed that the dispute shall be resolved by three arbitrators, each party shall nominate in the Request and the Answer, respectively, one arbitrator for confirmation. If a party fails to nominate an arbitrator, the appointment shall be made by the Court.

5 Where the dispute is to be referred to three arbitrators, the third arbitrator, who will act as president of the arbitral tribunal, shall be appointed by the Court, unless the parties have agreed upon another procedure for such appointment, in which case the nomination will be subject to confirmation pursuant to Article 13. Should such procedure not result in a nomination within 30 days from the confirmation or appointment of the co-arbitrators or any other time limit agreed by the parties or fixed by the Court, the third arbitrator shall be appointed by the Court.

6. Where there are multiple claimants or multiple respondents, and where the dispute is to be referred to three arbitrators, the multiple claimants, jointly, and the multiple respondents, jointly, shall nominate an arbitrator for confirmation pursuant to Article 13.

7. Where an additional party has been joined, and where the dispute is to be referred to three arbitrators, the additional party may, jointly with the claimant(s) or with the respondent(s), nominate an arbitrator for confirmation pursuant to Article 13.

8. In the absence of a joint nomination pursuant to Articles 12(6) or 12(7) and where all parties are unable to agree to a method for the constitution of the arbitral tribunal, the Court may appoint each member of the arbitral tribunal and shall designate one of them to act as president. In such case, the Court shall be at liberty to choose any person it regards as suitable to act as arbitrator, applying Article 13 when it considers this appropriate.

Article 13 —Appointment and Confirmation of the Arbitrators

1. In confirming or appointing arbitrators, the Court shall consider the prospective arbitrator's nationality, residence and other relationships with the countries of which the parties or the other arbitrators are nationals and the prospective arbitrator's availability and ability to conduct the arbitration in accordance with the Rules. The same shall apply where the Secretary General confirms arbitrators pursuant to Article 13(2).

2. The Secretary General may confirm as co-arbitrators, sole arbitrators and presidents of arbitral tribunals persons nominated by the parties or pursuant to their particular agreements, provided that the statement they have

submitted contains no qualification regarding impartiality or independence or that a qualified statement regarding impartiality or independence has not given rise to objections. Such confirmation shall be reported to the Court at its next session. If the Secretary General considers that a co-arbitrator, sole arbitrator or president of an arbitral tribunal should not be confirmed, the matter shall be submitted to the Court.

3. Where the Court is to appoint an arbitrator, it shall make the appointment upon proposal of a National Committee or Group of the ICC that it considers to be appropriate. If the Court does not accept the proposal made, or if the National Committee or Group fails to make the proposal requested within the time limit fixed by the Court, the Court may repeat its request, request a proposal from another National Committee or Group that it considers to be appropriate, or appoint directly any person whom it regards as suitable.

4. The Court may also appoint directly to act as arbitrator any person whom it regards as suitable where:

a) one or more of the parties is a state or claims to be a state entity; or

b) the Court considers that it would be appropriate to appoint an arbitrator from a country or territory where there is no National Committee or Group; or

c) the President certifies to the Court that circumstances exist which, in the President's opinion, make a direct appointment necessary and appropriate.

5. The sole arbitrator or the president of the arbitral tribunal shall be of a nationality other than those of the parties. However, in suitable circumstances and provided that none of the parties objects within the time limit fixed by the Court, the sole arbitrator or the president of the arbitral tribunal may be chosen from a country of which any of the parties is a national.

Article 14 — Challenge of Arbitrators

1. A challenge of an arbitrator, whether for an alleged lack of impartiality or independence, or otherwise, shall be made by the submission to the Secretariat of a written statement specifying the facts and circumstances on which the challenge is based.

2. For a challenge to be admissible, it must be submitted by a party either within 30 days from receipt by that party of the notification of the appointment or confirmation of the arbitrator, or within 30 days from the date when the party making the challenge was informed of the facts and circumstances on which the challenge is based if such date is subsequent to the receipt of such notification.

3. The Court shall decide on the admissibility and, at the same time, if necessary, on the merits of a challenge after the Secretariat has afforded an opportunity for the arbitrator concerned, the other party or parties and any other members of the arbitral tribunal to comment in writing within a suitable period of time. Such comments shall be communicated to the parties and to the arbitrators.

Article 15 — Replacement of Arbitrators

1. An arbitrator shall be replaced upon death, upon acceptance by the Court of the arbitrator's resignation, upon acceptance by the Court of a challenge, or upon acceptance by the Court of a request of all the parties.

2. An arbitrator shall also be replaced on the Court's own initiative when it decides that the arbitrator is prevented *de jure* or *de facto* from fulfilling the arbitrator's functions, or that the arbitrator is not fulfilling those functions in accordance with the Rules or within the prescribed time limits.

3. When, on the basis of information that has come to its attention, the Court considers applying Article 15(2), it shall decide on the matter after the arbitrator concerned, the parties and any other members of the arbitral tribunal have had an opportunity to comment in writing within a suitable period of time. Such comments shall be communicated to the parties and to the arbitrators.

4. When an arbitrator is to be replaced, the Court has discretion to decide whether or not to follow the original nominating process. Once reconstituted, and after having invited the parties to comment, the arbitral tribunal shall determine if and to what extent prior proceedings shall be repeated before the reconstituted arbitral tribunal.

5. Subsequent to the closing of the proceedings, instead of replacing an arbitrator who has died or been removed by the Court pursuant to Articles 15(1) or 15(2), the Court may decide, when it considers it appropriate, that the remaining arbitrators shall continue the arbitration. In making such determination, the Court shall take into account the views of the remaining arbitrators and of the parties and such other matters that it considers appropriate in the circumstances.

The Arbitral Proceedings

Article 16 — Transmission of the File to the Arbitral Tribunal

The Secretariat shall transmit the file to the arbitral tribunal as soon as it has been constituted, provided the advance on costs requested by the Secretariat at this stage has been paid.

Article 17 — Proof of Authority

At any time after the commencement of the arbitration, the arbitral tribunal or the Secretariat may require proof of the authority of any party representatives.

Article 18 — Place of the Arbitration

1. The place of the arbitration shall be fixed by the Court, unless agreed upon by the parties.
2. The arbitral tribunal may, after consultation with the parties, conduct hearings and meetings at any location it considers appropriate, unless otherwise agreed by the parties.
3. The arbitral tribunal may deliberate at any location it considers appropriate.

Article 19 — Rules Governing the Proceedings

The proceedings before the arbitral tribunal shall be governed by the Rules and, where the Rules are silent, by any rules which the parties or, failing them, the arbitral tribunal may settle on, whether or not reference is thereby made to the rules of procedure of a national law to be applied to the arbitration.

Article 20 — Language of the Arbitration

In the absence of an agreement by the parties, the arbitral tribunal shall determine the language or languages of the arbitration, due regard being given to all relevant circumstances, including the language of the contract.

Article 21 — Applicable Rules of Law

1. The parties shall be free to agree upon the rules of law to be applied by the arbitral tribunal to the merits of the dispute. In the absence of any such agreement, the arbitral tribunal shall apply the rules of law which it determines to be appropriate.
2. The arbitral tribunal shall take account of the provisions of the contract, if any, between the parties and of any relevant trade usages.
3. The arbitral tribunal shall assume the powers of an *amiable compositeur* or decide *ex aequo et bono* only if the parties have agreed to give it such powers.

Article 22 — Conduct of the Arbitration

1. The arbitral tribunal and the parties shall make every effort to conduct the arbitration in an expeditious and cost-effective manner, having regard to the complexity and value of the dispute.
2. In order to ensure effective case management, the arbitral tribunal, after consulting the parties, may adopt such procedural measures as it considers appropriate, provided that they are not contrary to any agreement of the parties.
3. Upon the request of any party, the arbitral tribunal may make orders

concerning the confidentiality of the arbitration proceedings or of any other matters in connection with the arbitration and may take measures for protecting trade secrets and confidential information.
4. In all cases, the arbitral tribunal shall act fairly and impartially and ensure that each party has a reasonable opportunity to present its case.
5. The parties undertake to comply with any order made by the arbitral tribunal.

Article 23 — Terms of Reference

1. As soon as it has received the file from the Secretariat, the arbitral tribunal shall draw up, on the basis of documents or in the presence of the parties and in the light of their most recent submissions, a document defining its Terms of Reference. This document shall include the following particulars:
a) the names in full, description, address and other contact details of each of the parties and of any person(s) representing a party in the arbitration;
b) the addresses to which notifications and communications arising in the course of the arbitration may be made;
c) a summary of the parties' respective claims and of the relief sought by each party, together with the amounts of any quantified claims and, to the extent possible, an estimate of the monetary value of any other claims;
d) unless the arbitral tribunal considers it inappropriate, a list of issues to be determined;
e) the names in full, address and other contact details of each of the arbitrators;
f) the place of the arbitration; and
g) particulars of the applicable procedural rules and, if such is the case, reference to the power conferred upon the arbitral tribunal to act as *amiable compositeur* or to decide *ex aequo et bono.*
2. The Terms of Reference shall be signed by the parties and the arbitral tribunal. Within two months of the date on which the file has been transmitted to it, the arbitral tribunal shall transmit to the Court the Terms of Reference signed by it and by the parties. The Court may extend this time limit pursuant to a reasoned request from the arbitral tribunal or on its own initiative if it decides it is necessary to do so.
3. If any of the parties refuses to take part in the drawing up of the Terms of Reference or to sign the same, they shall be submitted to the Court for approval. When the Terms of Reference have been signed in accordance with Article 23(2) or approved by the Court, the arbitration shall proceed.
4. After the Terms of Reference have been signed or approved by the Court,

no party shall make new claims which fall outside the limits of the Terms of Reference unless it has been authorized to do so by the arbitral tribunal, which shall consider the nature of such new claims, the stage of the arbitration and other relevant circumstances.

Article 24 — Case Management Conference and Procedural Timetable

1. When drawing up the Terms of Reference or as soon as possible thereafter, the arbitral tribunal shall convene a case management conference to consult the parties on procedural measures that may be adopted pursuant to Article 22(2). Such measures may include one or more of the case management techniques described in Appendix IV.
2. During or following such conference, the arbitral tribunal shall establish the procedural timetable that it intends to follow for the conduct of the arbitration. The procedural timetable and any modifications thereto shall be communicated to the Court and the parties.
3. To ensure continued effective case management, the arbitral tribunal, after consulting the parties by means of a further case management conference or otherwise, may adopt further procedural measures or modify the procedural timetable.
4. Case management conferences may be conducted through a meeting in person, by video conference, telephone or similar means of communication. In the absence of an agreement of the parties, the arbitral tribunal shall determine the means by which the conference will be conducted. The arbitral tribunal may request the parties to submit case management proposals in advance of a case management conference and may request the attendance at any case management conference of the parties in person or through an internal representative.

Article 25 — Establishing the Facts of the Case

1. The arbitral tribunal shall proceed within as short a time as possible to establish the facts of the case by all appropriate means.
2. After studying the written submissions of the parties and all documents relied upon, the arbitral tribunal shall hear the parties together in person if any of them so requests or, failing such a request, it may of its own motion decide to hear them.
3. The arbitral tribunal may decide to hear witnesses, experts appointed by the parties or any other person, in the presence of the parties, or in their absence provided they have been duly summoned.
4. The arbitral tribunal, after having consulted the parties, may appoint one or more experts, define their terms of reference and receive their reports. At the request of a party, the parties shall be given the opportunity to question

at a hearing any such expert.
5. At any time during the proceedings, the arbitral tribunal may summon any party to provide additional evidence.
6. The arbitral tribunal may decide the case solely on the documents submitted by the parties unless any of the parties requests a hearing.

Article 26 — Hearings

1. When a hearing is to be held, the arbitral tribunal, giving reasonable notice, shall summon the parties to appear before it on the day and at the place fixed by it.
2. If any of the parties, although duly summoned, fails to appear without valid excuse, the arbitral tribunal shall have the power to proceed with the hearing.
3. The arbitral tribunal shall be in full charge of the hearings, at which all the parties shall be entitled to be present. Save with the approval of the arbitral tribunal and the parties, persons not involved in the proceedings shall not be admitted.
4. The parties may appear in person or through duly authorized representatives. In addition, they may be assisted by advisers.

Article 27 — Closing of the Proceedings and Date for Submission of Draft Awards

As soon as possible after the last hearing concerning matters to be decided in an award or the filing of the last authorized submissions concerning such matters, whichever is later, the arbitral tribunal shall:

a) declare the proceedings closed with respect to the matters to be decided in the award; and

b) inform the Secretariat and the parties of the date by which it expects to submit its draft award to the Court for approval pursuant to Article 33.

After the proceedings are closed, no further submission or argument may be made, or evidence produced, with respect to the matters to be decided in the award, unless requested or authorized by the arbitral tribunal.

Article 28 — Conservatory and Interim Measures

1. Unless the parties have otherwise agreed, as soon as the file has been transmitted to it, the arbitral tribunal may, at the request of a party, order any interim or conservatory measure it deems appropriate. The arbitral tribunal may make the granting of any such measure subject to appropriate security being furnished by the requesting party. Any such measure shall take the form of an order, giving reasons, or of an award, as the arbitral tribunal considers appropriate.
2. Before the file is transmitted to the arbitral tribunal, and in appropriate

circumstances even thereafter, the parties may apply to any competent judicial authority for interim or conservatory measures. The application of a party to a judicial authority for such measures or for the implementation of any such measures ordered by an arbitral tribunal shall not be deemed to be an infringement or a waiver of the arbitration agreement and shall not affect the relevant powers reserved to the arbitral tribunal.
Any such application and any measures taken by the judicial authority must be notified without delay to the Secretariat. The Secretariat shall inform the arbitral tribunal thereof.

Article 29 — Emergency Arbitrator

1. A party that needs urgent interim or conservatory measures that cannot await the constitution of an arbitral tribunal ("Emergency Measures") may make an application for such measures pursuant to the Emergency Arbitrator Rules in Appendix V. Any such application shall be accepted only if it is received by the Secretariat prior to the transmission of the file to the arbitral tribunal pursuant to Article 16 and irrespective of whether the party making the application has already submitted its Request for Arbitration.
2. The emergency arbitrator's decision shall take the form of an order. The parties undertake to comply with any order made by the emergency arbitrator.
3. The emergency arbitrator's order shall not bind the arbitral tribunal with respect to any question, issue or dispute determined in the order. The arbitral tribunal may modify, terminate or annul the order or any modification thereto made by the emergency arbitrator.
4. The arbitral tribunal shall decide upon any party's requests or claims related to the emergency arbitrator proceedings, including the reallocation of the costs of such proceedings and any claims arising out of or in connection with the compliance or non-compliance with the order.
5. Articles 29(1)–29(4) and the Emergency Arbitrator Rules set forth in Appendix V (collectively the "Emergency Arbitrator Provisions") shall apply only to parties that are either signatories of the arbitration agreement under the Rules that is relied upon for the application or successors to such signatories.
6. The Emergency Arbitrator Provisions shall not apply if:

a) the arbitration agreement under the Rules was concluded before the date on which the Rules came into force;

b) the parties have agreed to opt out of the Emergency Arbitrator Provisions; or

c) the parties have agreed to another pre-arbitral procedure that provides for the granting of conservatory, interim or similar measures.

7. The Emergency Arbitrator Provisions are not intended to prevent any party from seeking urgent interim or conservatory measures from a competent judicial authority at any time prior to making an application for such measures, and in appropriate circumstances even thereafter, pursuant to the Rules. Any application for such measures from a competent judicial authority shall not be deemed to be an infringement or a waiver of the arbitration agreement. Any such application and any measures taken by the judicial authority must be notified without delay to the Secretariat.

Awards

Article 30 — Time Limit for the Final Award

1. The time limit within which the arbitral tribunal must render its final award is six months. Such time limit shall start to run from the date of the last signature by the arbitral tribunal or by the parties of the Terms of Reference or, in the case of application of Article 23(3), the date of the notification to the arbitral tribunal by the Secretariat of the approval of the Terms of Reference by the Court. The Court may fix a different time limit based upon the procedural timetable established pursuant to Article 24(2).

2. The Court may extend the time limit pursuant to a reasoned request from the arbitral tribunal or on its own initiative if it decides it is necessary to do so.

Article 31 — Making of the Award

1. When the arbitral tribunal is composed of more than one arbitrator, an award is made by a majority decision. If there is no majority, the award shall be made by the president of the arbitral tribunal alone.

2. The award shall state the reasons upon which it is based.

3. The award shall be deemed to be made at the place of the arbitration and on the date stated therein.

Article 32 — Award by Consent

If the parties reach a settlement after the file has been transmitted to the arbitral tribunal in accordance with Article 16, the settlement shall be recorded in the form of an award made by consent of the parties, if so requested by the parties and if the arbitral tribunal agrees to do so.

Article 33 — Scrutiny of the Award by the Court

Before signing any award, the arbitral tribunal shall submit it in draft form to the Court. The Court may lay down modifications as to the form of the award and, without affecting the arbitral tribunal's liberty of decision, may also draw its attention to points of substance. No award shall be rendered by the arbitral tribunal until it has been approved by the Court as to its form.

Article 34 — Notification, Deposit and Enforceability of the Award

1. Once an award has been made, the Secretariat shall notify to the parties the text signed by the arbitral tribunal, provided always that the costs of the arbitration have been fully paid to the ICC by the parties or by one of them.
2. Additional copies certified true by the Secretary General shall be made available on request and at any time to the parties, but to no one else.
3. By virtue of the notification made in accordance with Article 34(1), the parties waive any other form of notification or deposit on the part of the arbitral tribunal.
4. An original of each award made in accordance with the Rules shall be deposited with the Secretariat.
5. The arbitral tribunal and the Secretariat shall assist the parties in complying with whatever further formalities may be necessary.
6. Every award shall be binding on the parties. By submitting the dispute to arbitration under the Rules, the parties undertake to carry out any award without delay and shall be deemed to have waived their right to any form of recourse insofar as such waiver can validly be made.

Article 35 — Correction and Interpretation of the Award; Remission of Awards

1. On its own initiative, the arbitral tribunal may correct a clerical, computational or typographical error, or any errors of similar nature contained in an award, provided such correction is submitted for approval to the Court within 30 days of the date of such award.
2. Any application of a party for the correction of an error of the kind referred to in Article 35(1), or for the interpretation of an award, must be made to the Secretariat within 30 days of the receipt of the award by such party, in a number of copies as stated in Article 3(1). After transmittal of the application to the arbitral tribunal, the latter shall grant the other party a short time limit, normally not exceeding 30 days, from the receipt of the application by that party, to submit any comments thereon. The arbitral tribunal shall submit its decision on the application in draft form to the Court not later than 30 days following the expiration of the time limit for the receipt of any comments from the other party or within such other period as the Court may decide.
3. A decision to correct or to interpret the award shall take the form of an addendum and shall constitute part of the award. The provisions of Articles 31, 33 and 34 shall apply *mutatis mutandis*.
4. Where a court remits an award to the arbitral tribunal, the provisions of

Articles 31, 33, 34 and this Article 35 shall apply *mutatis mutandis* to any addendum or award made pursuant to the terms of such remission. The Court may take any steps as may be necessary to enable the arbitral tribunal to comply with the terms of such remission and may fix an advance to cover any additional fees and expenses of the arbitral tribunal and any additional ICC administrative expenses.

Costs

Article 36 — Advance to Cover the Costs of the Arbitration

1. After receipt of the Request, the Secretary General may request the claimant to pay a provisional advance in an amount intended to cover the costs of the arbitration until the Terms of Reference have been drawn up. Any provisional advance paid will be considered as a partial payment by the claimant of any advance on costs fixed by the Court pursuant to this Article 36.

2. As soon as practicable, the Court shall fix the advance on costs in an amount likely to cover the fees and expenses of the arbitrators and the ICC administrative expenses for the claims which have been referred to it by the parties, unless any claims are made under Article 7 or 8 in which case Article 36(4) shall apply. The advance on costs fixed by the Court pursuant to this Article 36(2) shall be payable in equal shares by the claimant and the respondent.

3. Where counterclaims are submitted by the respondent under Article 5 or otherwise, the Court may fix separate advances on costs for the claims and the counterclaims. When the Court has fixed separate advances on costs, each of the parties shall pay the advance on costs corresponding to its claims.

4 Where claims are made under Article 7 or 8, the Court shall fix one or more advances on costs that shall be payable by the parties as decided by the Court. Where the Court has previously fixed any advance on costs pursuant to this Article 36, any such advance shall be replaced by the advance(s) fixed pursuant to this Article 36(4), and the amount of any advance previously paid by any party will be considered as a partial payment by such party of its share of the advance(s) on costs as fixed by the Court pursuant to this Article 36(4).

5. The amount of any advance on costs fixed by the Court pursuant to this Article 36 may be subject to readjustment at any time during the arbitration In all cases, any party shall be free to pay any other party's share of any advance on costs should such other party fail to pay its share.

6. When a request for an advance on costs has not been complied with, and

after consultation with the arbitral tribunal, the Secretary General may direct the arbitral tribunal to suspend its work and set a time limit, which must be not less than 15 days, on the expiry of which the relevant claims shall be considered as withdrawn. Should the party in question wish to object to this measure, it must make a request within the aforementioned period for the matter to be decided by the Court. Such party shall not be prevented, on the ground of such withdrawal, from reintroducing the same claims at a later date in another proceeding.

7. If one of the parties claims a right to a set-off with regard to any claim, such set-off shall be taken into account in determining the advance to cover the costs of the arbitration in the same way as a separate claim insofar as it may require the arbitral tribunal to consider additional matters.

Article 37 — Decision as to the Costs of the Arbitration

1. The costs of the arbitration shall include the fees and expenses of the arbitrators and the ICC administrative expenses fixed by the Court, in accordance with the scale in force at the time of the commencement of the arbitration, as well as the fees and expenses of any experts appointed by the arbitral tribunal and the reasonable legal and other costs incurred by the parties for the arbitration.

2. The Court may fix the fees of the arbitrators at a figure higher or lower than that which would result from the application of the relevant scale should this be deemed necessary due to the exceptional circumstances of the case.

3. At any time during the arbitral proceedings, the arbitral tribunal may make decisions on costs, other than those to be fixed by the Court, and order payment.

4. The final award shall fix the costs of the arbitration and decide which of the parties shall bear them or in what proportion they shall be borne by the parties.

5. In making decisions as to costs, the arbitral tribunal may take into account such circumstances as it considers relevant, including the extent to which each party has conducted the arbitration in an expeditious and cost-effective manner.

6. In the event of the withdrawal of all claims or the termination of the arbitration before the rendering of a final award, the Court shall fix the fees and expenses of the arbitrators and the ICC administrative expenses. If the parties have not agreed upon the allocation of the costs of the arbitration or other relevant issues with respect to costs, such matters shall be decided by the arbitral tribunal. If the arbitral tribunal has not been constituted at the

time of such withdrawal or termination, any party may request the Court to proceed with the constitution of the arbitral tribunal in accordance with the Rules so that the arbitral tribunal may make decisions as to costs.

Miscellaneous

Article 38 — Modified Time Limits

1. The parties may agree to shorten the various time limits set out in the Rules. Any such agreement entered into subsequent to the constitution of an arbitral tribunal shall become effective only upon the approval of the arbitral tribunal.
2. The Court, on its own initiative, may extend any time limit which has been modified pursuant to Article 38(1) if it decides that it is necessary to do so in order that the arbitral tribunal and the Court may fulfil their responsibilities in accordance with the Rules.

Article 39 — Waiver

A party which proceeds with the arbitration without raising its objection to a failure to comply with any provision of the Rules, or of any other rules applicable to the proceedings, any direction given by the arbitral tribunal, or any requirement under the arbitration agreement relating to the constitution of the arbitral tribunal or the conduct of the proceedings, shall be deemed to have waived its right to object.

Article 40 — Limitation of Liability

The arbitrators, any person appointed by the arbitral tribunal, the emergency arbitrator, the Court and its members, the ICC and its employees, and the ICC National Committees and Groups and their employees and representatives shall not be liable to any person for any act or omission in connection with the arbitration, except to the extent such limitation of liability is prohibited by applicable law.

Article 41 — General Rule

In all matters not expressly provided for in the Rules, the Court and the arbitral tribunal shall act in the spirit of the Rules and shall make every effort to make sure that the award is enforceable at law.

Appendix I
Statutes of the International Court of Arbitration

Article 1 — Function

1. The function of the International Court of Arbitration of the International Chamber of Commerce (the "Court") is to ensure the application of the Rules of Arbitration of the International Chamber of Commerce, and it has all the necessary powers for that purpose.
2. As an autonomous body, it carries out these functions in complete independence from the ICC and its organs.
3. Its members are independent from the ICC National Committees and Groups.

Article 2 — Composition of the Court

The Court shall consist of a President,[1] Vice Presidents,[2] and members and alternate members (collectively designated as members). In its work it is assisted by its Secretariat (Secretariat of the Court).

Article 3 — Appointment

1. The President is elected by the ICC World Council upon the recommendation of the Executive Board of the ICC.
2. The ICC World Council appoints the Vice-Presidents of the Court from among the members of the Court or otherwise.
3. Its members are appointed by the ICC World Council on the proposal of National Committees or Groups, one member for each National Committee or Group.
4. On the proposal of the President of the Court, the World Council may appoint alternate members.
5. The term of office of all members, including, for the purposes of this paragraph, the President and Vice-Presidents, is three years. If a member is no longer in a position to exercise the member's functions, a successor is appointed by the World Council for the remainder of the term. Upon the recommendation of the Executive Board, the duration of the term of office of any member may be extended beyond three years if the World Council so decides.

Article 4 — Plenary session of the Court

The Plenary Sessions of the Court are presided over by the President or, in the President'' absence, by one of the Vice-Presidents designated by the President. The deliberations shall be valid when at least six members are present. Decisions are taken by a majority vote, the President or Vice-President, as the case may be, having a casting vote in the event of a tie.

---

[1] Referred to as "Chairman of the International Court of Arbitration" in the Constitution of the International Chamber of Commerce. [2] Referred to as "Vice-Chairmen of the International Court of Arbitration" in the Constitution of the International Chamber of Commerce.

Article 5 — Committees
The Court may set up one or more Committees and establish the functions and organization of such Committees.

Article 6 — Confidentiality
The work of the Court is of a confidential nature which must be respected by everyone who participates in that work in whatever capacity. The Court lays down the rules regarding the persons who can attend the meetings of the Court and its Committees and who are entitled to have access to materials related to the work of the Court and its Secretariat.

Article 7 — Modification of the Rules of Arbitration
Any proposal of the Court for a modification of the Rules is laid before the Commission on Arbitration before submission to the Executive Board of the ICC for approval, provided, however, that the Court, in order to take account of developments in information technology, may propose to modify or supplement the provisions of Article 3 of the Rules or any related provisions in the Rules without laying any such proposal before the Commission.

Appendix II
Internal Rules of the International Court of Arbitration

Article 1 — Confidential Character of the Work of the international Court of Arbitration

1. For the purposes of this Appendix, members of the Court include the President and Vice-Presidents of the Court.
2. The sessions of the Court, whether plenary or those of a Committee of the Court, are open only to its members and to the Secretariat.
3. However, in exceptional circumstances, the President of the Court may invite other persons to attend. Such persons must respect the confidential nature of the work of the Court.
4. The documents submitted to the Court, or drawn up by it or the Secretariat in the course of the Court's proceedings, are communicated only to the members of the Court and to the Secretariat and to persons authorized by the President to attend Court sessions.
5. The President or the Secretary General of the Court may authorize researchers undertaking work of an academic nature to acquaint themselves with awards and other documents of general interest, with the exception of memoranda, notes, statements and documents remitted by the parties within the framework of arbitration proceedings.
6. Such authorization shall not be given unless the beneficiary has undertaken to respect the confidential character of the documents made

available and to refrain from publishing anything based upon information contained therein without having previously submitted the text for approval to the Secretary General of the Court.

7. The Secretariat will in each case submitted to arbitration under the Rules retain in the archives of the Court all awards, Terms of Reference and decisions of the Court, as well as copies of the pertinent correspondence of the Secretariat.

8. Any documents, communications or correspondence submitted by the parties or the arbitrators may be destroyed unless a party or an arbitrator requests in writing within a period fixed by the Secretariat the return of such documents, communications or correspondence. All related costs and expenses for the return of those documents shall be paid by such party or arbitrator.

Article 2 — Participation of Members of the International Court of Arbitration in ICC Arbitration

1. The President and the members of the Secretariat of the Court may not act as arbitrators or as counsel in cases submitted to ICC arbitration.

2. The Court shall not appoint Vice-Presidents or members of the Court as arbitrators. They may, however, be proposed for such duties by one or more of the parties, or pursuant to any other procedure agreed upon by the parties, subject to confirmation.

3. When the President, a Vice-President or a member of the Court or of the Secretariat is involved in any capacity whatsoever in proceedings pending before the Court, such person must inform the Secretary General of the Court upon becoming aware of such involvement.

4. Such person must be absent from the Court session whenever the matter is considered by the Court and shall not participate in the discussions or in the decisions of the Court.

5. Such person will not receive any material documentation or information pertaining to such proceedings.

Article 3 — Relations between the Members of the Court and the ICC National Committees and Groups

1. By virtue of their capacity, the members of the Court are independent of the ICC National Committees and Groups which proposed them for appointment by the ICC World Council.

2. Furthermore, they must regard as confidential, vis-à-vis the said National Committees and Groups, any information concerning individual cases with which they have become acquainted in their capacity as members of the Court, except when they have been requested by the President of the Court,

by a Vice-President of the Court authorized by the President of the Court, or by the Court's Secretary General to communicate specific information to their respective National Committees or Groups.

Article 4 — Committee of the Court

1. In accordance with the provisions of Article 1(4) of the Rules and Article 5 of its statutes (Appendix I), the Court hereby establishes a Committee of the Court.

2. The members of the Committee consist of a president and at least two other members. The President of the Court acts as the president of the Committee. In the President's absence or otherwise at the President's request, a Vice-President of the Court or, in exceptional circumstances, another member of the Court may act as president of the Committee.

3. The other two members of the Committee are appointed by the Court from among the Vice-presidents or the other members of the Court. At each Plenary Session the Court appoints the members who are to attend the meetings of the Committee to be held before the next Plenary Session.

4. The Committee meets when convened by its president. Two members constitute a quorum.

5. (a) The Court shall determine the decisions that may be taken by the Committee.

(b) The decisions of the Committee are taken unanimously.

(c) When the Committee cannot reach a decision or deems it preferable to abstain, it transfers the case to the next Plenary Session, making any suggestions it deems appropriate.

(d) The Committee's decisions are brought to the notice of the Court at its next Plenary Session.

Article 5 — Court Secretariat

1. In the Secretary General's absence or otherwise at the Secretary General's request, the Deputy Secretary General and/or the General Counsel shall have the authority to refer matters to the Court, confirm arbitrators, certify true copies of Awards and request the payment of a provisional advance, respectively provided for in Articles 6(3), 13(2), 34(2) and 36(1) of the Rules.

2. The Secretariat may, with the approval of the Court, issue notes and other documents for the information of the parties and the arbitrators, or as necessary for the proper conduct of the arbitral proceedings.

3. Offices of the Secretariat may be established outside the headquarters of the ICC. The Secretariat shall keep a list of offices designated by the Secretary General. Requests for Arbitration may be submitted to the

Secretariat at any of its offices, and the Secretariat's functions under the Rules may be carried out from any of its offices, as instructed by the Secretary General, Deputy Secretary General or General Counsel.

Article 6 — Scrutiny of Arbitral Awards

When the Court scrutinizes draft awards in accordance with Article 33 of the Rules, it considers, to the extent practicable, the requirements of mandatory law at the place of the arbitration.

Appendix III

Arbitration Costs and Fees

Article 1 — Advance on Costs

1. Each request to commence an arbitration pursuant to the Rules must be accompanied by a filing fee of US$ 3,000. Such payment is non-refundable and shall be credited to the claimant's portion of the advance on costs.

2. The provisional advance fixed by the Secretary General according to Article 36(1) of the Rules shall normally not exceed the amount obtained by adding together the ICC administrative expenses, the minimum of the fees (as set out in the scale hereinafter) based upon the amount of the claim and the expected reimbursable expenses of the arbitral tribunal incurred with respect to the drafting of the Terms of Reference. If such amount is not quantified, the provisional advance shall be fixed at the discretion of the Secretary General. Payment by the claimant shall be credited to its share of the advance on costs fixed by the Court.

3. In general, after the Terms of Reference have been signed or approved by the Court and the procedural timetable has been established, the arbitral tribunal shall, in accordance with Article 36(6) of the Rules, proceed only with respect to those claims or counterclaims in regard to which the whole of the advance on costs has been paid.

4. The advance on costs fixed by the Court according to Articles 36(2) or 36 (4) of the Rules comprises the fees of the arbitrator or arbitrators (hereinafter referred to as "arbitrator"), any arbitration-related expenses of the arbitrator and the ICC administrative expenses.

5. Each party shall pay its share of the total advance on costs in cash. However, if a party's share of the advance on costs is greater than US$ 500,000 (the "Threshold Amount"), such party may post a bank guarantee for any amount above the Threshold Amount. The Court may modify the Threshold Amount at any time at its discretion.

6. The Court may authorize the payment of advances on costs, or any party's share thereof, in instalments, subject to such conditions as the Court thinks fit, including the payment of additional ICC administrative expenses.

7. A party that has already paid in full its share of the advance on costs fixed by the Court may, in accordance with Article 36(5) of the Rules, pay the unpaid portion of the advance owed by the defaulting party by posting a bank guarantee.
8. When the Court has fixed separate advances on costs pursuant to Article 36(3) of the Rules, the Secretariat shall invite each party to pay the amount of the advance corresponding to its respective claim(s).
9. When, as a result of the fixing of separate advances on costs, the separate advance fixed for the claim of either party exceeds one half of such global advance as was previously fixed (in respect of the same claims and counterclaims that are the subject of separate advances), a bank guarantee may be posted to cover any such excess amount. In the event that the amount of the separate advance is subsequently increased, at least one half of the increase shall be paid in cash.
10. The Secretariat shall establish the terms governing all bank guarantees which the parties may post pursuant to the above provisions.
11. As provided in Article 36(5) of the Rules, the advance on costs may be subject to readjustment at any time during the arbitration, in particular to take into account fluctuations in the amount in dispute, changes in the amount of the estimated expenses of the arbitrator, or the evolving difficulty or complexity of arbitration proceedings.
12. Before any expertise ordered by the arbitral tribunal can be commenced, the parties, or one of them, shall pay an advance on costs fixed by the arbitral tribunal sufficient to cover the expected fees and expenses of the expert as determined by the arbitral tribunal. The arbitral tribunal shall be responsible for ensuring the payment by the parties of such fees and expenses.
13. The amounts paid as advances on costs do not yield interest for the parties or the arbitrator.

Article 2 — Costs and Fees

1. Subject to Article 37(2) of the Rules, the Court shall fix the fees of the arbitrator in accordance with the scale hereinafter set out or, where the amount in dispute is not stated, at its discretion.
2. In setting the arbitrator's fees, the Court shall take into consideration the diligence and efficiency of the arbitrator, the time spent, the rapidity of the proceedings, the complexity of the dispute and the timeliness of the submission of the draft award, so as to arrive at a figure within the limits specified or, in exceptional circumstances (Article 37(2) of the Rules), at a figure higher or lower than those limits.

3. When a case is submitted to more than one arbitrator, the Court, at its discretion, shall have the right to increase the total fees up to a maximum which shall normally not exceed three times the fees of one arbitrator.
4. The arbitrator's fees and expenses shall be fixed exclusively by the Court as required by the Rules. Separate fee arrangements between the parties and the arbitrator are contrary to the Rules.
5. The Court shall fix the ICC administrative expenses of each arbitration in accordance with the scale hereinafter set out or, where the amount in dispute is not stated, at its discretion. In exceptional circumstances, the Court may fix the ICC administrative expenses at a lower or higher figure than that which would result from the application of such scale, provided that such expenses shall normally not exceed the maximum amount of the scale.
6. At any time during the arbitration, the Court may fix as payable a portion of the ICC administrative expenses corresponding to services that have already been performed by the Court and the Secretariat.
7. The Court may require the payment of administrative expenses in addition to those provided in the scale of administrative expenses as a condition for holding an arbitration in abeyance at the request of the parties or of one of them with the acquiescence of the other.
8. If an arbitration terminates before the rendering of a final award, the Court shall fix the fees and expenses of the arbitrators and the ICC administrative expenses at its discretion, taking into account the stage attained by the arbitral proceedings and any other relevant circumstances.
9. Any amount paid by the parties as an advance on costs exceeding the costs of the arbitration fixed by the Court shall be reimbursed to the parties having regard to the amounts paid.
10. In the case of an application under Article 35(2) of the Rules or of a remission pursuant to Article 35(4) of the Rules, the Court may fix an advance to cover additional fees and expenses of the arbitral tribunal and additional ICC administrative expenses and may make the transmission of such application to the arbitral tribunal subject to the prior cash payment in full to the ICC of such advance. The Court shall fix at its discretion the costs of the procedure following an application or a remission, which shall include any possible fees of the arbitrator and ICC administrative expenses, when approving the decision of the arbitral tribunal.
11. The Secretariat may require the payment of administrative expenses in addition to those provided in the scale of administrative expenses for any expenses arising in relation to a request pursuant to Article 34(5) of the

Rules.

12. When an arbitration is preceded by an attempt at amicable resolution pursuant to the ICC ADR Rules, one half of the ICC administrative expenses paid for such ADR proceedings shall be credited to the ICC administrative expenses of the arbitration.

13. Amounts paid to the arbitrator do not include any possible value added tax (VAT) or other taxes or charges and imposts applicable to the arbitrator's fees. Parties have a duty to pay any such taxes or charges; however, the recovery of any such charges or taxes is a matter solely between the arbitrator and the parties.

14. Any ICC administrative expenses may be subject to value added tax (VAT) or charges of a similar nature at the prevailing rate.

Article 3 — ICC as Appointing Authority

Any request received for an authority of the ICC to act as appointing authority will be treated in accordance with the Rules of ICC as Appointing Authority in UNCITRAL or Other *Ad Hoc* Arbitration Proceedings and shall be accompanied by a non-refundable filing fee of US$ 3,000. No request shall be processed unless accompanied by the said filing fee. For additional services, ICC may at its discretion fix ICC administrative expenses, which shall be commensurate with the services provided and shall normally not exceed the maximum amount of US$ 10,000.

Article 4 — Scales of Administrative Expenses and Arbitrator's Fees

1. The Scales of Administrative Expenses and Arbitrator's Fees set forth below shall be effective as of 1 January 2012 in respect of all arbitrations commenced on or after such date, irrespective of the version of the Rules applying to such arbitrations.

2. To calculate the ICC administrative expenses and the arbitrator's fees, the amounts calculated for each successive tranche of the amount in dispute must be added together, except that where the amount in dispute is over US$ 500 million, a flat amount of US$ 113,215 shall constitute the entirety of the ICC administrative expenses.

3. All amounts fixed by the Court or pursuant to any of the appendices to the Rules are payable in US$ except where prohibited by law, in which case the ICC may apply a different scale and fee arrangement in another currency.

See Table 1 (page 489).
See Table 2 (page 490).
See Table 3 (page 491).

Appendix IV
Case Management Techniques

The following are examples of case management techniques that can be used by the arbitral tribunal and the parties for controlling time and cost. Appropriate control of time and cost is important in all cases. In cases of low complexity and low value, it is particularly important to ensure that time and costs are proportionate to what is at stake in the dispute.

a) Bifurcating the proceedings or rendering one or more partial awards on key issues, when doing so may genuinely be expected to result in a more efficient resolution of the case.

b) Identifying issues that can be resolved by agreement between the parties or their experts.

c) Identifying issues to be decided solely on the basis of documents rather than through oral evidence or legal argument at a hearing.

d) Production of documentary evidence:

(i) requiring the parties to produce with their submissions the documents on which they rely;

(ii) avoiding requests for document production when appropriate in order to control time and cost;

(iii) in those cases where requests for document production are considered appropriate, limiting such requests to documents or categories of documents that are relevant and material to the outcome of the case;

(iv) establishing reasonable time limits for the production of documents;

(v) using a schedule of document production to facilitate the resolution of issues in relation to the production of documents.

e) Limiting the length and scope of written submissions and written and oral witness evidence (both fact witnesses and experts) so as to avoid repetition and maintain a focus on key issues.

f) Using telephone or video conferencing for procedural and other hearings where attendance in person is not essential and use of IT that enables online communication among the parties, the arbitral tribunal and the Secretariat of the Court.

g) Organizing a pre-hearing conference with the arbitral tribunal at which arrangements for a hearing can be discussed and agreed and the arbitral tribunal can indicate to the parties issues on which it would like the parties to focus at the hearing.

h) Settlement of disputes:

(i) informing the parties that they are free to settle all or part of the dispute either by negotiation or through any form of amicable dispute resolution

methods such as, for example, mediation under the ICC ADR Rules;
(ii) where agreed between the parties and the arbitral tribunal, the arbitral tribunal may take steps to facilitate settlement of the dispute, provided that every effort is made to ensure that any subsequent award is enforceable at law.
Additional techniques are described in the ICC publication entitled "Techniques for Controlling Time and Costs in Arbitration".

Appendix V
Emergency Arbitrator Rules

Article 1 — Application for Emergency Measures

1. A party wishing to have recourse to an emergency arbitrator pursuant to Article 29 of the Rules of Arbitration of the ICC (the "Rules") shall submit its Application for Emergency Measures (the "Application") to the Secretariat at any of the offices specified in the Internal Rules of the Court in Appendix II to the Rules.
2. The Application shall be supplied in a number of copies sufficient to provide one copy for each party, plus one for the emergency arbitrator, and one for the Secretariat.
3. The Application shall contain the following information:
a) the name in full, description, address and other contact details of each of the parties;
b) the name in full, address and other contact details of any person(s) representing the applicant;
c) a description of the circumstances giving rise to the Application and of the underlying dispute referred or to be referred to arbitration;
d) a statement of the Emergency Measures sought;
e) the reasons why the applicant needs urgent interim or conservatory measures that cannot await the constitution of an arbitral tribunal;
f) any relevant agreements and, in particular, the arbitration agreement;
g) any agreement as to the place of the arbitration, the applicable rules of law or the language of the arbitration;
h) proof of payment of the amount referred to in Article 7(1) of this Appendix; and
i) any Request for Arbitration and any other submissions in connection with the underlying dispute, which have been filed with the Secretariat by any of the parties to the emergency arbitrator proceedings prior to the making of the Application.
The Application may contain such other documents or information as the applicant considers appropriate or as may contribute to the efficient

examination of the Application.
4. The Application shall be drawn up in the language of the arbitration if agreed upon by the parties or, in the absence of any such agreement, in the language of the arbitration agreement.
5. If and to the extent that the President of the Court (the "President") considers, on the basis of the information contained in the Application, that the Emergency Arbitrator Provisions apply with reference to Article 29(5) and Article 29(6) of the Rules, the Secretariat shall transmit a copy of the Application and the documents annexed thereto to the responding party. If and to the extent that the President considers otherwise, the Secretariat shall inform the parties that the emergency arbitrator proceedings shall not take place with respect to some or all of the parties and shall transmit a copy of the Application to them for information.
6. The President shall terminate the emergency arbitrator proceedings if a Request for Arbitration has not been received by the Secretariat from the applicant within 10 days of the Secretariat's receipt of the Application, unless the emergency arbitrator determines that a longer period of time is necessary.

Article 2 — Appointment of the Emergency Arbitrator; Transmission of the File

1. The President shall appoint an emergency arbitrator within as short a time as possible, normally within two days from the Secretariat's receipt of the Application.
2. No emergency arbitrator shall be appointed after the file has been transmitted to the arbitral tribunal pursuant to Article 16 of the Rules. An emergency arbitrator appointed prior thereto shall retain the power to make an order within the time limit permitted by Article 6(4) of this Appendix.
3. Once the emergency arbitrator has been appointed, the Secretariat shall so notify the parties and shall transmit the file to the emergency arbitrator. Thereafter, all written communications from the parties shall be submitted directly to the emergency arbitrator with a copy to the other party and the Secretariat. A copy of any written communications from the emergency arbitrator to the parties shall be submitted to the Secretariat.
4. Every emergency arbitrator shall be and remain impartial and independent of the parties involved in the dispute.
5. Before being appointed, a prospective emergency arbitrator shall sign a statement of acceptance, availability, impartiality and independence. The Secretariat shall provide a copy of such statement to the parties.
6. An emergency arbitrator shall not act as an arbitrator in any arbitration

relating to the dispute that gave rise to the Application.

Article 3 — Challenge of an Emergency Arbitrator

1. A challenge against the emergency arbitrator must be made within three days from receipt by the party making the challenge of the notification of the appointment or from the date when that party was informed of the facts and circumstances on which the challenge is based if such date is subsequent to the receipt of such notification.

2. The challenge shall be decided by the Court after the Secretariat has afforded an opportunity for the emergency arbitrator and the other party or parties to provide comments in writing within a suitable period of time.

Article 4 — Place of Emergency Arbitrator Proceedings

1. If the parties have agreed upon the place of the arbitration, such place shall be the place of the emergency arbitrator proceedings. In the absence of such agreement, the President shall fix the place of the emergency arbitrator proceedings, without prejudice to the determination of the place of the arbitration pursuant to Article 18(1) of the Rules.

2. Any meetings with the emergency arbitrator may be conducted through a meeting in person at any location the emergency arbitrator considers appropriate or by video conference, telephone or similar means of communication.

Article 5 — Proceedings

1. The emergency arbitrator shall establish a procedural timetable for the emergency arbitrator proceedings within as short a time as possible, normally within two days from the transmission of the file to the emergency arbitrator pursuant to Article 2(3) of this Appendix.

2. The emergency arbitrator shall conduct the proceedings in the manner which the emergency arbitrator considers to be appropriate, taking into account the nature and the urgency of the Application. In all cases, the emergency arbitrator shall act fairly and impartially and ensure that each party has a reasonable opportunity to present its case.

Article 6 — Order

1. Pursuant to Article 29(2) of the Rules, the emergency arbitrator's decision shall take the form of an order (the "Order").

2. In the Order, the emergency arbitrator shall determine whether the Application is admissible pursuant to Article 29(1) of the Rules and whether the emergency arbitrator has jurisdiction to order Emergency Measures.

3. The Order shall be made in writing and shall state the reasons upon which it is based. It shall be dated and signed by the emergency arbitrator.

4. The Order shall be made no later than 15 days from the date on which the

file was transmitted to the emergency arbitrator pursuant to Article 2(3) of this Appendix. The President may extend the time limit pursuant to a reasoned request from the emergency arbitrator or on the President's own initiative if the President decides it is necessary to do so.

5. Within the time limit established pursuant to Article 6(4) of this Appendix, the emergency arbitrator shall send the Order to the parties, with a copy to the Secretariat, by any of the means of communication permitted by Article 3(2) of the Rules that the emergency arbitrator considers will ensure prompt receipt.

6. The Order shall cease to be binding on the parties upon:

a) the President's termination of the emergency arbitrator proceedings pursuant to Article 1(6) of this Appendix;

b) the acceptance by the Court of a challenge against the emergency arbitrator pursuant to Article 3 of this Appendix;

c) the arbitral tribunal's final award, unless the arbitral tribunal expressly decides otherwise; or

d) the withdrawal of all claims or the termination of the arbitration before the rendering of a final award.

7. The emergency arbitrator may make the Order subject to such conditions as the emergency arbitrator thinks fit, including requiring the provision of appropriate security.

8. Upon a reasoned request by a party made prior to the transmission of the file to the arbitral tribunal pursuant to Article 16 of the Rules, the emergency arbitrator may modify, terminate or annul the Order.

Article 7 — Costs of the Emergency Arbitrator Proceedings

1. The applicant must pay an amount of US$ 40,000, consisting of US$ 10,000 for ICC administrative expenses and US$ 30 000 for the emergency arbitrator's fees and expenses. Notwithstanding Article 1(5) of this Appendix, the Application shall not be notified until the payment of US$ 40,000 is received by the Secretariat.

2. The President may, at any time during the emergency arbitrator proceedings, decide to increase the emergency arbitrator's fees or the ICC administrative expenses taking into account, inter alia, the nature of the case and the nature and amount of work performed by the emergency arbitrator, the Court, the President and the Secretariat. If the party which submitted the Application fails to pay the increased costs within the time limit fixed by the Secretariat, the Application shall be considered as withdrawn.

3. The emergency arbitrator's Order shall fix the costs of the emergency arbitrator proceedings and decide which of the parties shall bear them or in

what proportion they shall be borne by the parties.

4. The costs of the emergency arbitrator proceedings include the ICC administrative expenses, the emergency arbitrator's fees and expenses and the reasonable legal and other costs incurred by the parties for the emergency arbitrator proceedings.

5. In the event that the emergency arbitrator proceedings do not take place pursuant to Article 1(5) of this Appendix or are otherwise terminated prior to the making of an Order, the President shall determine the amount to be reimbursed to the applicant, if any. An amount of US$ 5,000 for ICC administrative expenses is non-refundable in all cases.

Article 8 — General Rule

1. The President shall have the power to decide, at the President's discretion, all matters relating to the administration of the emergency arbitrator proceedings not expressly provided for in this Appendix.

2. In the President's absence or otherwise at the President's request, any of the Vice-Presidents of the Court shall have the power to take decisions on behalf of the President.

3. In all matters concerning emergency arbitrator proceedings not expressly provided for in this Appendix, the Court, the President and the emergency arbitrator shall act in the spirit of the Rules and this Appendix.

Table 1

A Administrative Expenses		B Arbitrator's Fees		
		Amount in Dispute (in US Dollars)	Fees	
Amount in Dispute (in US Dollars)	Administrative Expenses		minimum	maximum
up to 50,000	$3,000	up to 50,000	$3,000	18.0200%
from 50,001 to 100,000	4.73%	from 50,001 to 100,000	2.6500%	13.5680%
from 100,001 to 200,000	2.53%	from 100,001 to 200,000	1.4310%	7.6850%
from 200,001 to 500,000	2.09%	from 200,001 to 500,000	1.3670%	6.8370%
from 500,001 to 1,000,000	1.51%	from 500,001 to 1,000,000	0.9540%	4.0280%
from 1,000,001 to 2,000,000	0.95%	from 1,000,001 to 2,000,000	0.6890%	3.6040%
from 2,000,001 to 5,000,000	0.46%	from 2,000,001 to 5,000,000	0.3750%	1.3910%
from 5,000,001 to 10,000,000	0.25%	from 5,000,001 to 10,000,000	0.1280%	0.9100%
from 10,000,001 to 30,000,000	0.10%	from 10,000,001 to 30,000,000	0.0640%	0.2410%
from 30,000,001 to 50,000,000	0.09%	from 30,000,001 to 50,000,000	0.0590%	0.2280%
from 50,000,001 to 80,000,000	0.01%	from 50,000,001 to 80,000,000	0.0330%	0.1570%
from 80,000,001 to 500,000,000	0.0035%	from 80,000,001 to 100,000,000	0.0210%	0.1150%
over 500,000,000	$113,215	from 100,000,001 to 500,000,000	0.0110%	0.0580%
		over 500,000,000	0.0100%	0.0400%

Table 2 *

Amount in dispute (in US Dollars)	**A Administrative expenses (in US Dollars)**
up to 50,000	3,000
from 50,001 to 100,000	3,000 + 4.73% of amt. over 50,000
from 100,001 to 200,000	5,365 + 2.53% of amt. over 100,000
from 200,001 to 500,000	7,895 + 2.09% of amt. over 200,000
from 500,001 to 1,000,000	14,165 + 1.51% of amt. over 500,000
from 1,000,001 to 2,000,000	21,715 + 0.95% of amt. over 1,000,000
from 2,000,001 to 5,000,000	31,215 + 0.46% of amt. over 2,000,000
from 5,000,001 to 10,000,000	45,015 + 0.25% of amt. over 5,000,000
from 10,000,001 to 30,000,000	57,515 + 0.10% of amt. over 10,000,000
from 30,000,001 to 50,000,000	77,515 + 0.09% of amt. over 30,000,000
from 50,000,001 to 80,000,000	95,515 + 0.01% of amt. over 50,000,000
from 80,000,001 to 100,000,000	98,515 + 0.0035% of amt. over 80,000,000
from 100,000,001 to 500,000,000	99,215 + 0.0035% of amt. over 100,000,000
over 500,000,000	113,215

* For illustrative purposes only, the table indicates the resulting administrative expenses in US$ when the proper calculations have been made.

Table 3 **

Amount in Dispute (in US Dollars)	B Arbitrator's Fees (in US Dollars)	
	Minimum	Maximum
up to 50,000	3,000	18.0200% of amount in dispute
from 50,001 to 100,000	3,000 + 2.6500% of amt. over 50,000	9,010 + 13.5680% of amt. over 50,000
from 100,001 to 200,000	4,325 + 1.4310% of amt. over 100,000	15,794 + 7.6850% of amt. over 100,000
from 200,001 to 500,000	5,756 + 1.3670% of amt. over 200,000	23,479 + 6.8370% of amt. over 200,000
from 500,001 to 1,000,000	9,857 + 0.9540% of amt. over 500,000	43,990 + 4.0280% of amt. over 500,000
from 1,000,001 to 2,000,000	14,627 + 0.6890% of amt. over 1,000,000	64,130 + 3.6040% of amt. over 1,000,000
from 2,000,001 to 5,000,000	21,517 + 0.3750% of amt. over 2,000,000	100,170 + 1.3910% of amt. over 2,000,000
from 5,000,001 to 10,000,000	32,767 + 0.1280% of amt. over 5,000,000	141,900 + 0.9100% of amt. over 5,000,000
From 10,000,001 to 30,000,000	39,167 + 0.0640% of amt. over 10,000,000	187,400 + 0.2410% of amt. over 10,000,000
from 30,000,001 to 50,000,000	51,967 + 0.0590% of amt. over 30,000,000	235,600 + 0.2280% of amt. over 30,000,000
from 50,000,001 to 80,000,000	63,767 + 0.0330% of amt. over 50,000,000	281,200 + 0.1570% of amt. over 50,000,000
from 80,000,001 to 100,000,000	73,667 + 0.0210% of amt. over 80,000,000	328,300 + 0.1150% of amt. over 80,000,000
from 100,000,001 to 500,000,000	77,867 + 0.0110% of amt. over 100,000,000	351,300 + 0.0580% of amt. over 100,000,000
over 500,000,000	121,867 + 0.0100% of amt. over 500,000,000	583,300 + 0.0400% of amt. over 500,000,000

** For illustrative purposes only, the table indicates the resulting range of fees in US$ when the proper calculations have been made.

ICC TECHNIQUES FOR CONTROLLING TIME AND COSTS IN ARBITRATION *

Introduction

Costs incurred by the parties constitute the largest part of the total cost of international arbitration proceedings. It follows that if the overall cost of the arbitral proceedings is to be reduced, special emphasis needs to be placed on steps aimed at lowering the costs connected with the parties' presentation of their cases. Such costs are often caused by unnecessarily long and complicated proceedings with unfocused requests for disclosure of documents and unnecessary witness and expert evidence. Costs can also be unnecessarily increased when counsel from different legal backgrounds use procedures familiar to them in a manner that leads to needless duplication.

The increasing and, on occasion, unnecessary complication of the proceedings seems to be the main explanation for the long duration and high cost of many international arbitrations. The longer the proceedings, the more expensive they will be. The 2012 ICC Rules of Arbitration (the "Rules") have expressly addressed these concerns.

These Techniques for Controlling Time and Costs in Arbitration (the "Techniques") are designed to assist arbitral tribunals, parties and their counsel in devising tailor-made procedures for individual arbitrations pursuant to Articles 22-24 of the Rules.

In particular, the Techniques may be of benefit to the parties and the tribunal when preparing the case management conference and seeking agreement on procedures suitable for their case. If the parties cannot reach agreement, the Techniques may also assist the arbitral tribunal in adopting procedures that it considers appropriate, taking into account its obligation to conduct the arbitration in an expeditious and cost-effective manner. The Techniques are freely accessible online on the ICC's website (www.iccwbo.org) and in the ICC Dispute Resolution Library (www.iccdrl.com). They are in no way prescriptive. Rather, they provide suggestions that may assist in arriving at procedures that are efficient and will reduce both cost and time. Certain procedures will be appropriate for one arbitration, but inappropriate for another. There may be other procedures not mentioned here that are well suited to a particular case. In all instances, it is for the parties and the arbitral tribunal to select the procedures that are best suited for the case. The table of contents to this document can serve as a checklist of points to consider.

While the main focus of the Techniques is to provide guidance on the procedure during the arbitration, the first two sections give suggestions on the drafting of arbitration agreements and the initiation of arbitral proceedings.

---

* For a commentary on the ICC Techniques for Controlling Time and Costs in Arbitration, see Thomas J. Stipanowich, 'Soft Law in the Organization and General Conduct of Commercial Arbitration Proceedings' in Lawrence W. Newman and Michael J. Radine (eds), *Soft Law in*

Arbitration Agreement

1 — Keeping clauses simple

Simple, clearly drafted arbitration clauses will avoid uncertainty and disputes over their meaning and effect. They will minimize the risk of time and costs being spent on disputes regarding, for example, the jurisdiction of the arbitral tribunal or the process of appointing arbitrators. In all cases, ensure that the arbitration clause conforms with any relevant applicable laws.

2 — Use of the ICC model clause

Use of the standard ICC arbitration clause is recommended. It provides as follows:

All disputes arising out of or in connection with the present contract shall be finally settled under the Rules of Arbitration of the International Chamber of Commerce by one or more arbitrators appointed in accordance with the said Rules.

Modifications to the standard clause can result in unintended and undesirable consequences and therefore should be made only with great care and for specific purposes. In addition to the standard clause, the parties may wish to specify in separate sentences the place of the arbitration, the language of the arbitration and the rules of law governing the contract. Be cautious about adding to this clause further provisions relating to the procedure for the arbitration.

The Rules permit any party in need of urgent or conservatory measures that cannot await the constitution of an arbitral tribunal to make an application to the ICC International Court of Arbitration (the "Court") for the appointment of an emergency arbitrator to decide upon the request for such measures. The parties should consider whether the Emergency Arbitrator Provisions as set out in Article 29 and Appendix V of the Rules are desirable in their particular situation. If the parties do not want the Emergency Arbitrator Provisions to apply, they must agree to opt out of those provisions and may do so by using the following model clause:

All disputes arising out of or in connection with the present contract shall be finally settled under the Rules of Arbitration of the International Chamber of Commerce by one or more arbitrators appointed in accordance with the said Rules. The Emergency Arbitrator Provisions shall not apply.

3 — Selection and appointment of arbitrators

High-value and complex contracts can give rise to small disputes for which a three-member tribunal may be too expensive. Although parties may desire the certainty of appointing either a one- or a three-member tribunal in their

---

International Arbitration (Juris, 2014).

arbitration agreement, consideration should be given to staying with the standard ICC arbitration clause and providing for one or more arbitrators.

This will enable the ICC to appoint, or the parties to agree on, a sole arbitrator where the specific nature of any subsequent dispute does not warrant a three-member tribunal (Rules, Article 12(2)).

If the parties wish the ICC to select and appoint all members of the arbitral tribunal (see paragraph 11 below), then the following wording can be used: "All arbitrators shall be selected and appointed by the ICC International Court of Arbitration."

Adding special requirements regarding the expertise and qualifications of arbitrators to be appointed will reduce the pool of available arbitrators and may increase the time taken to select a tribunal.

4 — Fast track procedures

Consideration may be given to setting out fast-track procedures in the arbitration clause. Indeed, Article 38(1) of the Rules enables the parties to shorten time limits provided for in the Rules, while Article 38(2) enables the Court to extend those shortened time limits when necessary. Fast-track procedures are designed to enable an arbitration to proceed quickly, given the specific nature of the contract and the disputes that are likely to arise. However, experience shows that in practice it is difficult at the time of drafting the clause to predict with a reasonable degree of certainty the nature of disputes and the procedures that will be suitable for those disputes. Also, disagreements can arise later over the interpretation or application of fast-track clauses. Careful thought should therefore be given before such provisions are included in an arbitration agreement. Once a dispute has arisen, the parties could at that time agree upon a fast-track procedure, if appropriate.

5 — Time limits for rendering the final award

One commonly used provision that can give rise to significant difficulties is the requirement that a final award be produced within a certain number of weeks or months from the commencement of the arbitration. Such specific time limits can create jurisdictional and enforcement problems if it turns out that the time limit specified is unrealistic or not clearly defined.

6 — More detailed arbitration agreement after the dispute has arisen

If the parties agree to submit a dispute to ICC arbitration after the dispute has arisen, they can consider specifying in some detail the procedure for the arbitration, taking into account the nature of the dispute in question. This procedure may include some of the suggestions set out below to control time and costs.

Initiation of Proceedings

Selection of Counsel

7 — Counsel with experience

Consider appointing counsel with the skills necessary for handling the arbitration at hand and who are sensitive to the need for appropriate time and cost efficiency. Such counsel are more likely to be able to work with the arbitral tribunal and the other party's counsel to devise an efficient procedure for the case.

8 — Counsel with time

Ensure that the counsel you have selected has sufficient time to devote to the case.

Selection of Arbitrators

9 — Use of a sole arbitrator

After a dispute has arisen, consider agreeing upon having a sole arbitrator, when appropriate. Generally speaking, a one-member tribunal will be able to act more quickly than a three-member tribunal, since discussions between tribunal members are not needed and diary clashes for hearings will be minimized. A one-member tribunal will obviously also be cheaper.

10 — Arbitrators with time

Whether selecting a sole arbitrator or a three-member tribunal, it is advisable to make sufficient enquiries to ensure that the individuals selected have sufficient time to devote to the case in question. If there is a particular need for speed, this must be made clear to the ICC so that it can be taken into consideration when making any appointments.

11 — Selection and appointment by the ICC

Consider allowing the ICC to select and appoint the arbitral tribunal, whether it be a sole arbitrator or a three-person tribunal. This will generally be the quickest way to constitute the arbitral tribunal if there is no agreement between the parties on the identity of all arbitrators. It will also reduce the risk of challenges, facilitate the constitution of a tribunal having a variety of specialist skills and create a different dynamic within the arbitral tribunal. If the parties wish to have input into the selection of the tribunal by the ICC, they can request that the ICC provide a list of possible arbitrators to be selected in accordance with a procedure to be agreed upon by the parties in consultation with the ICC.

12 — Avoiding objections

Any objection to the appointment of an arbitrator will delay the constitution of the arbitral tribunal. When selecting an arbitrator, give careful thought to whether or not the appointment of that arbitrator might give rise to an objection.

13 — Selecting arbitrators with strong case management skills

A tribunal that is proactive and skilled in case management will be able to play its role in managing the arbitration so as to make it as cost and time effective as possible, given the issues in dispute and the number and nature of the parties. Careful consideration should therefore be given to selecting tribunal members, especially the sole arbitrator or chair.

Request for Arbitration and Answer

14 — Complying with the Rules

The claimant should ensure that the Request for Arbitration includes all of the elements required by Article 4(3), subparagraphs (a)—(h), of the Rules. Failure to do so may make it necessary for the Secretariat to revert to the Claimant before the Request can be forwarded to the Respondent in accordance with Article 4(5). This causes delay. Similarly, when filing its Answer, the Respondent should include all elements required by Article 5 (1), subparagraphs (a)—(f), of the Rules.

15 — Setting out a detailed statement of case

The Rules do not require a Request for Arbitration or an Answer to set out a full statement of case for either the claim or the defence (or, where applicable, a counterclaim). Whether or not a full statement is made in the Request can have an impact on the efficient management of the arbitration. Where the Request does contain detailed particulars of the claim, and a similar approach is taken by the respondent in the Answer, the parties and the arbitral tribunal will be in a position to make informed decisions at a very early stage in the proceedings regarding the procedural measures and case management techniques that are appropriate for the case. This will help to optimize the first case management conference held pursuant to Article 24(1).

16 — Submitting additional information

The Rules expressly allow the parties to submit with a Request or an Answer any further documents or information that may contribute to the efficient resolution of the dispute (see Articles 4(3) and 5(1)). Those provisions allow for the submission of a full statement of case but also allow the parties simply to submit additional useful information. Consideration should be given to exercising this option, whether or not a full statement of case is provided.

Language of the Arbitration

17 — Determination of the language by the arbitral tribunal

If the parties have not agreed on the language of the arbitration, the arbitral tribunal, when determining the language, should consider doing so by means of a procedural order pursuant to Article 20 of the ICC Rules, prior to drawing up the Terms of Reference and after ascertaining the positions of the parties.

18 — Proceedings involving two or more languages

Having two or more languages of the arbitration will normally increase time and cost. Consideration should be given to whether the use of two or more languages truly justifies the additional time and cost. On the other hand, where there is a single language of the arbitration, the use of an additional language should be considered if it would reduce time and cost. For example, where appropriate, the parties can agree that documents, legal materials and witness testimony in a particular language need not be translated into the language of the arbitration.

If the parties have agreed, or the arbitral tribunal has decided, that the arbitration will be conducted in two or more languages, the parties and the arbitral tribunal should consider agreeing upon practical means to avoid duplication. In cases where the members of the arbitral tribunal are fluent in all applicable languages, it may not be necessary for documents to be translated. Consideration should also be given to avoiding having the Terms of Reference, procedural orders and awards in more than one language. If this cannot be avoided, the parties would be well advised to agree upon the language that will prevail.

Establishing the Framework of the Arbitral Proceedings

The Rules call for the framework of the arbitral proceedings to be established in three steps: the Terms of Reference; the case management conference; and the procedural timetable. The paragraphs that follow provide suggestions on how to use each of these steps to optimize time and cost efficiency.

Terms of Reference

19 — Summaries of claims and relief sought

The arbitral tribunal should consider whether it is appropriate for it to draft the summary of claims and/or the relief sought itself, or whether it would assist if each party were to provide a draft summary for inclusion in the Terms of Reference in accordance with Article 23(1), subparagraph (c), of the Rules. In the latter case, the arbitral tribunal should consider requesting the parties to limit their summaries to an appropriate fixed number of pages. Further guidance on preparing Terms of Reference can be found in the article of Serge Lazareff, "Terms of Reference", ICC International Court of Arbitration Bulletin, Vol. 17/No. 1 (2006).[1]

[1] The ICC International Court of Arbitration Bulletin is available from the ICC Bookstore (www.iccbooks.com) and online in the ICC Dispute Resolution Library (www.iccdrl.com).

20 — Empowering the president of the arbitral tribunal on procedural issues

Where there is a three-member tribunal, it may not be necessary for all procedural issues to be decided upon by all three arbitrators. The parties should consider empowering the president of the arbitral tribunal to decide on certain procedural issues alone. In all events, consider authorizing the president to sign procedural orders alone.

21 — Administrative secretary to the arbitral tribunal

Consider whether or not an administrative secretary to the arbitral tribunal would assist in reducing time and cost. If it is decided to use such a secretary, the parties and the arbitral tribunal should take into account the Note of the Secretariat of the Court on the Appointment, Duties and Remuneration of Administrative Secretaries. It is distributed to arbitrators in all cases and is reproduced in the ICC International Court of Arbitration Bulletin, Vol. 23/No. 1 (2012).

22 — Need for a physical meeting

Consider whether it is appropriate to agree upon and sign the Terms of Reference without a physical meeting (e.g. by way of a telephone or video conference). In making that decision, the advantages of having a physical meeting at the start of the proceedings should be weighed against the time and cost involved. The holding of the case management conference should also be taken into account when deciding whether or not to hold a physical meeting (see paragraph 31 below).

23 — Counterparts

If there is no physical meeting for signing the Terms of Reference, the arbitral tribunal should consider having the Terms of Reference signed in counterparts.

24 — Compliance with Article 23(3)

If a party refuses to take part in drawing up the Terms of Reference or refuses to sign them, the arbitral tribunal should make certain that the Terms of Reference to be submitted to the Court for approval pursuant to Article 23(3) of the Rules do not contain any provisions that require the parties' agreement or a decision by the arbitral tribunal.

Case Management Conferences

25 — Timing

Article 24(1) requires the arbitral tribunal to convene a case management conference when drawing up the Terms of Reference or as soon as possible thereafter. Consider whether it is most convenient and efficient to hold the case management conference immediately after the signing of the Terms of

Reference and at the same meeting.

26 — Preparation

For the case management conference to be most effective, the tribunal should consider asking the parties well in advance of the conference to submit joint or separate case management proposals. This will encourage them actively to consider and exchange views on the procedures and case management techniques that may be appropriate for the case. Any joint or separate proposals from the parties, any agreements between the parties, and any suggestions from the tribunal should be discussed at the case management conference. It should be noted that, in accordance with Article 22(2) of the Rules, the arbitral tribunal may not adopt procedural measures that are contrary to an agreement of the parties.

27 — Use of the Techniques

Appendix IV of the Rules sets out examples of available case management techniques. These and additional examples are also contained in this Report. They can be used by the arbitral tribunal and the parties at the case management conference to assist in arriving at the most appropriate procedures for the case (see the section entitled "Subsequent procedure for the arbitration" below).

28 — Providing information in advance of the conference

The more information the arbitral tribunal has about the issues in the case prior to the conference, the better placed it will be to assist the parties in devising a procedure that will deal with the dispute as efficiently as possible. For example, a tribunal that has made itself familiar with the details of the case from the outset can be proactive and give appropriate, tailor-made suggestions on the issues to be addressed in documentary and witness evidence, the areas in which it will be assisted by expert evidence, and the extent to which disclosure of documents by the parties is needed to address the issues in dispute.

29 — Scope

Whenever possible, the procedure for the entire arbitration should be determined at the first case management conference and reflected in the procedural timetable to be established pursuant to Article 24(2) of the Rules. However, it may not always be possible to do so, for example in very complex cases or in cases where insufficient detail has been provided prior to the first case management conference. In such situations, the procedural timetable would lay out the procedure as far as can be done (e.g. through a first round of briefs) and a second case management conference would be held promptly to determine the remainder of the procedure for the arbitration.

30 — Client attendance

Article 24(4) of the Rules expressly allows the arbitral tribunal to request the attendance at the case management conference of the parties in person or through an internal representative. The tribunal should consider requiring such attendance. When clients are present at the case management conference, they can play an active role in the decision-making process. They should be empowered to make case management decisions. Such decisions call for a costbenefit analysis. For example, is an additional round of briefs worth the time and expense? Is a degree of discovery-style document production likely to produce benefits justifying the time and cost?

31 — Need for a physical meeting

As with the drawing up of the Terms of Reference (see paragraph 22 above) and as permitted by Article 24(4), consider whether it is appropriate to hold the case management conference by way of telephone, video conference or similar means of communication that do not involve a physical meeting. If the case management conference is to be held at the same time as the Terms of Reference are signed, consider whether that would justify a physical meeting for both purposes.

32 — Use of discretion in apportionment of costs

Pursuant to Article 37(5) of the Rules, the extent to which each party has conducted the arbitration in an expeditious and cost-effective manner may be taken into account by the arbitral tribunal in determining who shall bear what portion of the costs of the arbitration.

The arbitral tribunal should consider informing the parties at the case management conference that in exercising its discretion to allocate costs pursuant to the Rules, it will take into consideration any unreasonable failure to comply with procedures agreed upon or ordered in the arbitration or any other unreasonable conduct (see paragraph 82 below).

33 — Further case management conferences

Consider holding further case management conferences during the course of the arbitration, as appropriate. Such conferences may be held prior to significant phases in the procedure (e.g. the exchange of witness statements) so as to ensure that the procedure provided for that phase remains appropriate. Short telephone conferences may also be held at regular intervals (e.g. once a month) to enable the arbitral tribunal to check on progress and discuss with the parties any unforeseen procedural issues that have arisen or may shortly arise.

Procedural Timetable

34 — Compliance with the procedural timetable

Consistent with their obligation under Article 22(1) of the Rules to make every effort to conduct the arbitration in an expeditious and cost-effective manner, the arbitrators and the parties should make all reasonable efforts to comply with the procedural timetable. Extensions and revisions of the timetable should be made only when justified. Any revisions should be promptly communicated to the Court and the parties in accordance with Article 24(2) of the Rules.

35 — Need for a hearing

Consider whether or not it is necessary for there to be a hearing in order for the arbitral tribunal to decide the case. If it is possible for the arbitral tribunal to decide the case on documents alone, this will significantly reduce costs and time.

36 — Fixing the hearing date

If a hearing is necessary, then early in the proceedings (ideally at the first case management conference) consider fixing the date for this hearing. This will reduce the likelihood that the arbitral proceedings become drawn out and will enable the procedure leading up to the hearing to be adapted to the time available.

37 — Pre-hearing conference

Consider organizing a conference with the arbitral tribunal, which may be by telephone, to discuss the arrangements for any hearing. At such a prehearing conference, held a suitable time before the hearing itself, the parties and the arbitral tribunal can discuss matters such as time allocation, use of transcripts, translation issues, order of witnesses and other practical arrangements that will facilitate the smooth conduct of the hearing. The arbitral tribunal may consider using the occasion of the pre-hearing conference to indicate to the parties the issues on which it would like them to focus at the forthcoming hearing.

38 — Short and realistic time periods

When deciding upon the length of the final hearing and the amount of time required for all procedural steps leading up to that hearing, choose the shortest times that are realistic. Unrealistically short periods of time are likely to result in longer rather than shorter proceedings, should they need to be rescheduled.

39 — Bifurcation and partial awards

The arbitral tribunal should consider, or the parties could agree on, bifurcating the proceedings or rendering a partial award when doing so may genuinely be expected to result in a more efficient resolution of the case.

40 — Briefing everyone involved in the case

As soon as the proceedings start, parties should give thought to the input that will be needed for each step in the anticipated timetable. Once the timetable is set, the parties should consider precisely what is required of them to comply with the timetable. It will be useful for all relevant personnel to be briefed accordingly (e.g. management within the client organization, witnesses, internal and external lawyers, experts). This will greatly assist in enabling everyone to reserve the time needed to provide input at the relevant point in the procedure and will assist in enabling each party to adhere to deadlines set in the timetable.

Settlement

41 — Arbitral tribunal's role in promoting settlement

The arbitral tribunal should consider informing the parties that they are free to settle all or part of the dispute at any time during the ongoing arbitration, either through direct negotiations or through any form of ADR proceedings. For example, ADR proceedings can be conducted under the ICC ADR Rules, further information on which can be found in the article of Peter Wolrich entitled "ICC ADR Rules: The Latest Addition to ICC's Dispute Resolution Services" in ADR—International Applications, 2001 Special Supplement of the ICC International Court of Arbitration Bulletin.

42 — Settlement initiatives taken with the parties' agreement

The parties may request the arbitral tribunal to suspend the arbitration proceedings for a specific period of time while settlement discussions take place. The parties may also agree that the arbitral tribunal should take other steps to facilitate settlement of their dispute, provided that such steps are not inconsistent with the tribunal's duty under Article 41 of the Rules to make every effort to make sure that its award is enforceable at law.

Subsequent Procedure for the Arbitration

The paragraphs that follow give guidance on the points to be discussed by the parties and the arbitral tribunal at the case management conference. They provide suggestions that may assist in reducing the cost and duration of the proceedings.

Written Submissions

Written submissions come in different forms and are given different names. They include the Request for Arbitration and the Answer, statements of case and defence, memorials and other written arguments, and opening and closing written submissions. These comments apply to written submissions generally.

43 — Setting out the case in full early in the proceedings

If the parties set out their cases in full early in the proceedings, the parties and the arbitral tribunal will be better able to understand the key issues at an early stage. Doing so will help ensure that the procedure defined at the case management conference is efficient and that time and money are not wasted on matters that turn out to be of no direct relevance to the issues to be determined.

44 — Avoiding repetition

Avoid unnecessary repetition of arguments. Once a party has set out its position in full, it should not be necessary to repeat the arguments at later stages (e.g. in pre-hearing memorials, oral submissions or post-hearing memorials), and the arbitral tribunal may direct that there be no such repetition.

45 — Sequential or simultaneous delivery

Consider whether it is more effective for written submissions to be sequential or simultaneous. Whilst simultaneous submissions enable both parties to inform each other of their cases at the same time (and this may make things quicker), it can also result in inefficiency if the parties raise different issues in their submissions and extensive submissions are required in response.

46 — Specifying form and content

Consider specifying the form and content of written submissions. For example, clarify whether the first round of written submissions should or should not be accompanied by witness statements and/or expert reports.

47 — Limiting the length of submissions

Consider agreeing on limiting the length of specific submissions. This can help focus attention on the key issues to be addressed and is likely to save time and cost.

48 — Limiting the number of submissions

Consider limiting the number of rounds of submissions. This may help to avoid repetition and encourage the parties to present all key issues in their first submissions.

Documentary Evidence

49 — Organization of documents

From the outset of the case the parties should consider using a coherent system for numbering or otherwise identifying documents produced in the case. This process can start with the Request for Arbitration and the Answer, and a system for the remainder of the arbitration can be established with the arbitral tribunal at the time of the first case management conference.

50 — Producing documents on which the parties rely

The parties will normally each produce the documents upon which they intend to rely. Each party should consider avoiding requests for production of documents from another party unless such production is relevant and material to the outcome of the case. When the parties have agreed upon non -controversial facts, no documentary evidence should be needed to prove those facts.

51 — Establishing procedure for requests for production

Consider whether requests for production of documents are genuinely necessary. If they are, the parties and the arbitral tribunal should consider establishing a clear and efficient procedure for the submission and exchange of documents. In that regard, they could consider referring to Article 3 of the IBA Rules on the Taking of Evidence in International Arbitration for guidance. In addition, the parties and the arbitral tribunal should consider establishing an appropriate time frame for the production of documents. In most situations, this is likely to be after the parties have set out their cases in full for the first time. If issues concerning the production of electronic documents arise, consider referring to the ICC Commission Report Managing E-Document Production[2] for information and guidance on how to manage such production in an efficient and cost-effective manner

52 — Managing requests for production efficiently

Time and costs associated with requests for production of documents, if any, can further be reduced by agreeing upon one or more of the following:

- Limiting the number of requests;
- Limiting requests to the production of documents (whether in paper or electronic form) that are relevant and material to the outcome of the case;
- Establishing reasonable time limits for the production of documents;
- Using the Schedule of Document Production devised by Alan Redfern (often referred to as the Redfern Schedule) in the form of a chart containing the following four columns:

First Column: identification of the document(s) or categories of documents that have been requested;

Second Column: short description of the reasons for each request;

Third Column: summary of the objections by the other party to the production of the document(s) or categories of documents requested; and

Fourth Column: left blank for the decision of the arbitral tribunal on each

[2] Available in print as ICC Publication 860 and online at <www.iccdrl.com>.

request.

53 — Avoiding duplication

It is common for each of the parties to produce copies of the same documents, appended to their statements of case, witness statements or other written submissions. Avoiding duplication where possible will reduce costs.

54 — Selection of documents to be provided to the arbitral tribunal

It is wasteful to provide the arbitrators with documents that are not material to their determination of the case. In particular, it will usually not be appropriate to send to the arbitral tribunal all documents produced pursuant to production requests. This not only generates unnecessary costs, but also makes it harder for the arbitral tribunal to prepare efficiently.

55 — Keeping hard copies to a minimum

Consider minimizing the volume of paper documents that need to be produced. Exchanging documents in electronic form can reduce costs (see the ICC Commission Report Managing E-Document Production and the 2004 Special Supplement of the ICC International Court of Arbitration Bulletin, Using Technology to Resolve Business Disputes).

56 — Translations

Try to agree how translations of any documents are to be dealt with. Reducing the need for certified translations will help to lower costs. Certified translations may be required only where translation issues emerge from unofficial translations.

57 — Authenticity of documents

Consider providing that documents produced by the parties are deemed to be authentic unless and until such authenticity is challenged by another party.

Correspondence

58 — Correspondence between counsel

Avoid unnecessary correspondence between counsel. The arbitral tribunal may consider informing the parties that the persistent use of such correspondence may be viewed as unreasonable conduct and be taken into consideration by the arbitral tribunal when exercising its discretion in allocating costs pursuant to the Rules (see paragraph 82 below).

59 — Sending correspondence to the arbitral tribunal

Avoid sending correspondence between counsel to the arbitral tribunal unless a decision of the arbitral tribunal is required. Any such correspondence that is addressed to the arbitral tribunal should be copied to the Secretariat in accordance with Article 3(1) of the Rules.

Witness Statements

60 — Limiting the number of witnesses

Every witness adds to the costs, both when a witness statement is prepared and considered and when the witness attends to give oral evidence. Costs can be saved by limiting the number of witnesses to those whose evidence is required on key issues. The arbitral tribunal may assist in identifying those issues on which witness evidence is required and focusing the evidence from witnesses on those issues. This whole process will be facilitated if the parties can reach agreement on non-controversial facts that do not need to be addressed by witness evidence.

61 — Minimizing the number of rounds of witness statements

If there are to be witness statements, consider the timing for the exchange of such statements so as to minimize the number of rounds of statements that are required. For example, consider whether it is preferable for witness statements to be exchanged after all documents on which the parties wish to rely have been produced, so that the witnesses can comment on those documents in a single statement.

Expert evidence

62 — Presumption that expert evidence not required

It is helpful to start with a presumption that expert evidence will not be required. Depart from this presumption only if expert evidence is needed in order to inform the arbitral tribunal on key issues in dispute.

63 — ICC International Centre for Expertise

If either the parties or the arbitral tribunal require assistance in identifying an expert witness, recourse can be had to the ICC International Centre for Expertise pursuant to the ICC Rules for Expertise. Where an ICC arbitral tribunal seeks a proposal from the Centre for a tribunal-appointed expert, the services of the Centre are available at no cost. Further information regarding the operation of the ICC Rules for Expertise and the services of the Centre can be found in Jason Fry, Simon Greenberg, Francesca Mazza, The Secretariat's Guide to ICC Arbitration (ICC Publication 729).[3]

64 — Clarity regarding the subject matter and scope of reports

It is essential for there to be clarity at an early stage (by agreement, if possible) over the subject matter and scope of any expert evidence to be produced. This will help to ensure that the experts appointed by the parties have similar expertise and address the same issues.

65 — Number of experts

Other than in exceptional circumstances, it should not be necessary for there to be more than one expert per party for any particular area of expertise.

---

[3] Available from www.iccbooks.com and online at <www.iccdrl.com>.

66 — Number of reports

Consider agreeing on a limit to the number of rounds of expert reports and consider whether simultaneous or sequential exchange will be more efficient.

67 — Meetings of experts

Experts will often be able to narrow the issues in dispute if they can meet and discuss their views after they have exchanged reports. Consideration should therefore be given to providing that experts shall take steps to agree on issues in advance of any hearing at which their evidence is to be presented. Time and cost can be saved if the experts draw up a list recording the issues on which they have agreed and those on which they disagree.

68 — Use of single expert

Consider whether a single expert appointed either by the arbitral tribunal or jointly by the parties might be more efficient than experts appointed by each party. A single, tribunal-appointed expert may be more efficient in some circumstances. An expert appointed by the arbitral tribunal or jointly by the parties should be given a clear brief and the expert's report should be required by a specified date consistent with the timetable for the arbitration.

Hearings

69 — Minimizing the length and number of hearings

Hearings are expensive and time-consuming. If the length and number of hearings requiring the physical attendance of the arbitral tribunal and the parties are minimized, this will significantly reduce the time and cost of the proceedings.

70 — Choosing the best location for hearings

Pursuant to Article 18(2) of the Rules, hearings do not need to be held at the place of the arbitration. The arbitral tribunal and the parties can select the most efficient place to hold hearings. In some cases, it may be more cost-effective to hold hearings at a location that, for example, is convenient to the majority of the witnesses due to give evidence at that hearing.

71 — Telephone and video conferencing

For procedural hearings in particular, consider the use of telephone and video conferencing, where appropriate. Also, consider whether certain witnesses can give evidence by video link, so as to avoid the need to travel to an evidentiary hearing.

72 — Providing submissions in good time

The arbitral tribunal should be provided with all necessary submissions (e.g. pre-hearing briefs, if any) sufficiently in advance of any hearing to be able to read them, prepare and become fully informed of the issues to be addressed.

73 — Cut-off date for evidence

In advance of any evidentiary hearing, consider setting a cut-off date after which no new documentary evidence will be admitted unless a compelling reason is shown.

74 — Identifying core documents

Consider providing the arbitral tribunal, in advance of any hearing, with a list of the documents it needs to read in preparation for the hearing. Where appropriate, this can be done by preparing and delivering to the arbitral tribunal a bundle of core documents on which the parties rely.

75 — Agenda and timetable

Consider agreeing on an agenda and timetable for all hearings, with an equitable division of time between each of the parties. Consider the use of a chess clock to monitor the fair allocation of time.

76 — Avoiding repetition

Consideration should be given to whether it is necessary to repeat pre-hearing written submissions in opening oral statements. This is sometimes done because of concern that the arbitral tribunal will not have read or digested the written submissions. If the arbitral tribunal has been provided with the documents it needs to read in advance of the hearing and has prepared properly, no such repetition will be necessary.

77 — Need for witnesses to appear

Prior to any hearing, consider whether all witnesses need to give oral evidence. This is a matter on which the parties' counsel can confer and seek to reach agreement.

78 — Use of written statements as direct evidence

Cost and time can be saved by limiting or avoiding direct examination of witnesses. When appropriate, witness statements can substitute for direct examination at a hearing.

79 — Witness conferencing

Witness conferencing is a technique in which two or more fact or expert witnesses presented by one or more of the parties are questioned together on particular topics by the arbitral tribunal and possibly by counsel. Consider whether this technique is appropriate for the arbitration at hand.

80 — Limiting cross-examination

If there is to be cross-examination of witnesses, the arbitral tribunal, after hearing the parties, should consider limiting the time available to each party for such cross-examination.

81 — Closing submissions

Consider whether post-hearing submissions can be avoided in order to save time and cost. However, if post-hearing submissions are required, consider providing for either oral or written closing submissions. The use of both will result in additional time and cost. In order to give focus, the arbitral tribunal should consider providing counsel with a list of questions or issues to be addressed by the parties in the closing submissions. Any written closing submissions should be provided by an agreed date as soon as reasonable following the hearing.

Costs

82 — Using allocation of costs to encourage efficient conduct of the proceedings

The allocation of costs can be a useful tool to encourage efficient behaviour and discourage unreasonable behaviour. Pursuant to Article 37(5) of the Rules, the arbitral tribunal has discretion to award costs in such a manner as it considers appropriate. It is expressly stated that, in making its decisions on costs, the tribunal may take into consideration the extent to which each party has conducted the arbitration in an expeditious and cost-effective manner. The tribunal should consider informing the parties at the outset of the arbitration (e.g. at the case management conference) that it intends to take into account the manner in which each party has conducted the proceedings and to sanction any unreasonable behaviour by a party when deciding on costs. Unreasonable behaviour could include: excessive document requests, excessive legal argument, excessive cross-examination, dilatory tactics, exaggerated claims, failure to comply with procedural orders, unjustified applications for interim relief, and unjustified failure to comply with the procedural timetable.

Deliberations and Awards

83 — Anticipating the time required

Before closing the proceedings, the arbitral tribunal should ensure that time has been reserved in each of the arbitrators' diaries for deliberation promptly thereafter. The arbitral tribunal should promptly comply with Article 27 of the Rules and indicate to the Secretariat and the parties the date by which it expects to submit its draft award to the Court.

84 — Prompt completion of the award

The arbitral tribunal must use its best efforts to submit the draft award as quickly as possible and should follow the guidance on drafting awards in the ICC Award Checklist sent to all arbitrators when the case file is transmitted to them. Further guidance can be found in the article "Drafting

Awards in ICC Arbitrations" by Humphrey LLoyd, Marco Darmon, Jean-Pierre Ancel, Lord Dervaird, Christoph Liebscher and Herman Verbist, published in the ICC International Court of Arbitration Bulletin, Vol. 16/ No. 2 (2005).

Special Considerations

Multiparty and Multi-contract Arbitrations

85 — Conditions imposed by Articles 7–9 of the Rules

Subject to certain conditions set forth in the Rules, Article 7 expressly permits the joinder of additional parties; Article 8 expressly permits claims between multiple parties; and Article 9 expressly permits claims arising out of more than one contract to be brought in a single arbitration, even if the claims are made under more than one arbitration agreement. Clearly, time and cost will be wasted if a party seeks to apply those provisions when the conditions set forth in the Rules are not met. For example, a Request for Joinder pursuant to Article 7 will be successful only if the joined party is bound by the arbitration agreement under which the claims in the arbitration are made; in addition, no additional party may be joined after the confirmation or appointment of any arbitrator, unless otherwise agreed. While Article 9 allows claims to be made in a single arbitration under more than one arbitration agreement, those claims will be sustained only if the different arbitration agreements are compatible. The conditions imposed by Articles 7, 8 and 9 should be carefully studied so as to avoid wasting time and money by making claims that will be rejected or by claiming against parties over whom the tribunal will have no jurisdiction.

86 — Adapting procedures to multiparty and multi-contract cases

The presence of one or more additional parties, the existence of one or more claims between claimants or between respondents, and the existence of claims under more than one contract are likely to complicate the proceedings. Care should be taken at the case management conference to devise tailor-made procedures, appropriate to the specifics of the case at hand, for dealing with the presence of additional parties, cross-claims and multi-contract claims.

Consolidation

87 — Consider consolidating related cases

Article 10 of the Rules provides for the consolidation of two or more separate arbitrations brought under the Rules when all of the parties to those arbitrations consent to the consolidation. Consider whether giving such consent would result in a more efficient resolution of the disputes.

Emergency Arbitrator Proceedings

88 — Issues to consider before initiating emergency arbitrator proceedings

Subject to the conditions set forth in the Rules, the Emergency Arbitrator Provisions allow a party to seek urgent interim or conservatory measures from an emergency arbitrator acting under the Rules. The emergency arbitrator offers an alternative forum to state courts for seeking such relief. In deciding whether to file an Application for Emergency Measures, a party should consider a number of issues: first, whether it is genuinely useful and necessary to spend time and money on seeking to obtain interim or conservatory measures; second, whether an application for Emergency Measures under the Rules is preferable to seeking interim measures in a state court. Furthermore, the party should make sure that the conditions for bringing emergency arbitrator proceedings under the Rules are met. For example, the party making the application must be able to demonstrate that it needs urgent interim or conservatory measures that cannot await the constitution of the arbitral tribunal. Also, emergency arbitrator proceedings may only be brought against a signatory of the arbitration agreement or the signatory's successor. An attempt to bring emergency arbitrator proceedings that do not meet all of the conditions will result in needless expenditure and loss of time.

ICDR GUIDELINES FOR ARBITRATORS CONCERNING EXCHANGES OF INFORMATION *

Introduction

The American Arbitration Association (AAA) and its international arm, the International Centre for Dispute Resolution® (ICDR) are committed to the principle that commercial arbitration, and particularly international commercial arbitration, should provide a simpler, less expensive and more expeditious form of dispute resolution than resort to national courts.

While arbitration must be a fair process, care must also be taken to prevent the importation of procedural measures and devices from different court systems, which may be considered conducive to fairness within those systems, but which are not appropriate to the conduct of arbitrations in an international context and which are inconsistent with an alternative form of dispute resolution that is simpler, less expensive and more expeditious. One of the factors contributing to complexity, expense and delay in recent years has been the migration from court systems into arbitration of procedural devices that allow one party to a court proceeding access to information in the possession of the other, without full consideration of the differences between arbitration and litigation.

The purpose of these guidelines is to make it clear to arbitrators that they have the authority, the responsibility and, in certain jurisdictions, the mandatory duty to manage arbitration proceedings so as to achieve the goal of providing a simpler, less expensive, and more expeditious process. Unless the parties agree otherwise in writing, these guidelines will become effective in all international cases administered by the ICDR commenced after May 31, 2008, and may be adopted at the discretion of the tribunal in pending cases. They will be reflected in amendments incorporated into the next revision of the International Arbitration Rules. They may be adopted in arbitration clauses or by agreement at any time in any other arbitration administered by the AAA.

1 — In General

a. The tribunal shall manage the exchange of information among the parties in advance of the hearings with a view to maintaining efficiency and economy. The tribunal and the parties should endeavor to avoid unnecessary delay and expense while at the same time balancing the goals of avoiding surprise, promoting equality of treatment, and safeguarding each party's opportunity to present its claims and defenses fairly.

b. The parties may provide the tribunal with their views on the appropriate level of information exchange for each case, but the tribunal retains final authority to apply the above standard. To the extent that the Parties wish to depart from this standard, they may do so only on the basis of an express

* For a commentary on the ICDR Guidelines for Arbitrators, see Lawrence W. Newman, 'Disclosure of Documents and Presentation of Evidence in International Arbitration: ICDR Guidelines for Arbitrators Concerning Exchange of Information' in Lawrence W. Newman and Michael J. Radine

agreement among all of them in writing and in consultation with the tribunal.

2 — Documents on which a Party Relies

Parties shall exchange, in advance of the hearing, all documents upon which each intends to rely.

3 — Documents in the Possession of Another Party

a. In addition to any disclosure pursuant to paragraph 2, the tribunal may, upon application, require one party to make available to another party documents in the party's possession, not otherwise available to the party seeking the documents, that are reasonably believed to exist and to be relevant and material to the outcome of the case. Requests for documents shall contain a description of specific documents or classes of documents, along with an explanation of their relevance and materiality to the outcome of the case.

b. The tribunal may condition any exchange of documents subject to claims of commercial or technical confidentiality on appropriate measures to protect such confidentiality.

4 — Electronic Documents

When documents to be exchanged are maintained in electronic form, the party in possession of such documents may make them available in the form (which may be paper copies) most convenient and economical for it, unless the Tribunal determines, on application and for good cause, that there is a compelling need for access to the documents in a different form. Requests for documents maintained in electronic form should be narrowly focused and structured to make searching for them as economical as possible. The Tribunal may direct testing or other means of focusing and limiting any search.

5 — Inspections

The tribunal may, on application and for good cause, require a party to permit inspection on reasonable notice of relevant premises or objects.

6 — Other Procedures

a. Arbitrators should be receptive to creative solutions for achieving exchange of information in ways that avoid costs and delay, consistent with the principle of due process expressed in these Guidelines.

b. Depositions, interrogatories, and requests to admit, as developed in American court procedures, are generally not appropriate procedures for obtaining information in international arbitration.

7 — Privileges and Professional Ethics

The tribunal should respect applicable rules of privilege or professional

(eds), *Soft Law in nternational Arbitration* (Juris, 2014).

ethics and other legal impediments. When the parties, their counsel or their documents would be subject under applicable law to different rules, the tribunal should to the extent possible apply the same rule to both sides, giving preference to the rule that provides the highest level of protection.

8 — Costs and Compliance

a. In resolving any dispute about pre-hearing exchanges of information, the tribunal shall require a requesting party to justify the time and expense that its request may involve, and may condition granting such a request on the payment of part or all of the cost by the party seeking the information. The tribunal may also allocate the costs of providing information among the parties, either in an interim order or in an award.

b. In the event any party fails to comply with an order for information exchange, the tribunal may draw adverse inferences and may take such failure into account in allocating costs.

ICSID RULES OF PROCEDURE FOR ARBITRATION PROCEEDINGS (ARBITRATION RULES) *

Chapter I
Establishment of the Tribunal

Rule 1 — General Obligations

(1) Upon notification of the registration of the request for arbitration, the parties shall, with all possible dispatch, proceed to constitute a Tribunal, with due regard to Section 2 of Chapter IV of the Convention.

(2) Unless such information is provided in the request, the parties shall communicate to the Secretary-General as soon as possible any provisions agreed by them regarding the number of arbitrators and the method of their appointment.

(3) The majority of the arbitrators shall be nationals of States other than the State party to the dispute and of the State whose national is a party to the dispute, unless the sole arbitrator or each individual member of the Tribunal is appointed by agreement of the parties. Where the Tribunal is to consist of three members, a national of either of these States may not be appointed as an arbitrator by a party without the agreement of the other party to the dispute. Where the Tribunal is to consist of five or more members, nationals of either of these States may not be appointed as arbitrators by a party if appointment by the other party of the same number of arbitrators of either of these nationalities would result in a majority of arbitrators of these nationalities.

(4) No person who had previously acted as a conciliator or arbitrator in any proceeding for the settlement of the dispute may be appointed as a member of the Tribunal.

Rule 2 — Method of Constituting the Tribunal in the Absence of Previous Agreement

(1) If the parties, at the time of the registration of the request for arbitration, have not agreed upon the number of arbitrators and the method of their appointment, they shall, unless they agree otherwise, follow the following procedure:

(a) the requesting party shall, within 10 days after the registration of the request, propose to the other party the appointment of a sole arbitrator or of a specified uneven number of arbitrators and specify the method proposed for their appointment;

(b) within 20 days after receipt of the proposals made by the requesting party, the other party shall:

(i) accept such proposals; or

(ii) make other proposals regarding the number of arbitrators and the method of their appointment;

---

* For a commentary on the ICSID Arbitration Rules, see Lucy Reed, Jan Paulsson, Nigel Blackaby, *A Guide to ICSID Arbitration* (2nd edn, Kluwer Law International, 2010). See also, Thomas H. Webster, *Handbook of Investment Arbitration: Commentary, Precedents and Models for ICSID*

(c) within 20 days after receipt of the reply containing any such other proposals, the requesting party shall notify the other party whether it accepts or rejects such proposals.

(2) The communications provided for in paragraph (1) shall be made or promptly confirmed in writing and shall either be transmitted through the Secretary-General or directly between the parties with a copy to the Secretary-General. The parties shall promptly notify the Secretary-General of the contents of any agreement reached.

(3) At any time 60 days after the registration of the request, if no agreement on another procedure is reached, either party may inform the Secretary-General that it chooses the formula provided for in Article 37(2)(b) of the Convention. The Secretary-General shall thereupon promptly inform the other party that the Tribunal is to be constituted in accordance with that Article.

Rule 3 — Appointment of Arbitrators to a Tribunal Constituted in Accordance with Convention Article 37(2)(b)

(1) If the Tribunal is to be constituted in accordance with Article 37(2)(b) of the Convention:

(a) either party shall in a communication to the other party:

(i) name two persons, identifying one of them, who shall not have the same nationality as nor be a national of either party, as the arbitrator appointed by it, and the other as the arbitrator proposed to be the President of the Tribunal; and

(ii) invite the other party to concur in the appointment of the arbitrator proposed to be the President of the Tribunal and to appoint another arbitrator;

(b) promptly upon receipt of this communication the other party shall, in its reply:

(i) name a person as the arbitrator appointed by it, who shall not have the same nationality as nor be a national of either party; and

(ii) concur in the appointment of the arbitrator proposed to be the President of the Tribunal or name another person as the arbitrator proposed to be President;

(c) promptly upon receipt of the reply containing such a proposal, the initiating party shall notify the other party whether it concurs in the appointment of the arbitrator proposed by that party to be the President of the Tribunal.

(2) The communications provided for in this Rule shall be made or promptly confirmed in writing and shall either be transmitted through the

---

Arbitration (Sweet & Maxwell, 2012).

Secretary-General or directly between the parties with a copy to the Secretary-General.

Rule 4 — Appointment of Arbitrators by the Chairman of the Administrative Council

(1) If the Tribunal is not constituted within 90 days after the dispatch by the Secretary-General of the notice of registration, or such other period as the parties may agree, either party may, through the Secretary-General, address to the Chairman of the Administrative Council a request in writing to appoint the arbitrator or arbitrators not yet appointed and to designate an arbitrator to be the President of the Tribunal.

(2) The provision of paragraph (1) shall apply mutatis mutandis in the event that the parties have agreed that the arbitrators shall elect the President of the Tribunal and they fail to do so.

(3) The Secretary-General shall forthwith send a copy of the request to the other party.

(4) The Chairman shall use his best efforts to comply with that request within 30 days after its receipt. Before he proceeds to make an appointment or designation, with due regard to Articles 38 and 40(1) of the Convention, he shall consult both parties as far as possible.

(5) The Secretary-General shall promptly notify the parties of any appointment or designation made by the Chairman.

Rule 5 — Acceptance of Appointments

(1) The party or parties concerned shall notify the Secretary-General of the appointment of each arbitrator and indicate the method of his appointment.

(2) As soon as the Secretary-General has been informed by a party or the Chairman of the Administrative Council of the appointment of an arbitrator, he shall seek an acceptance from the appointee.

(3) If an arbitrator fails to accept his appointment within 15 days, the Secretary-General shall promptly notify the parties, and if appropriate the Chairman, and invite them to proceed to the appointment of another arbitrator in accordance with the method followed for the previous appointment.

Rule 6 — Constitution of the Tribunal

(1) The Tribunal shall be deemed to be constituted and the proceeding to have begun on the date the Secretary-General notifies the parties that all the arbitrators have accepted their appointment.

(2) Before or at the first session of the Tribunal, each arbitrator shall sign a declaration in the following form:

"To the best of my knowledge there is no reason why I should not serve on the Arbitral Tribunal constituted by the International Centre for Settlement of Investment Disputes with respect to a dispute between ____________________and____________________.

I shall keep confidential all information coming to my knowledge as a result of my participation in this proceeding, as well as the contents of any award made by the Tribunal.

I shall judge fairly as between the parties, according to the applicable law, and shall not accept any instruction or compensation with regard to the proceeding from any source except as provided in the Convention on the Settlement of Investment Disputes between States and Nationals of Other States and in the Regulations and Rules made pursuant thereto.

Attached is a statement of (a) my past and present professional, business and other relationships (if any) with the parties and (b) any other circumstance that might cause my reliability for independent judgment to be questioned by a party. I acknowledge that by signing this declaration, I assume a continuing obligation promptly to notify the Secretary-General of the Centre of any such relationship or circumstance that subsequently arises during this proceeding."

Any arbitrator failing to sign a declaration by the end of the first session of the Tribunal shall be deemed to have resigned.

Rule 7 — Replacement of Arbitrators

At any time before the Tribunal is constituted, each party may replace any arbitrator appointed by it and the parties may by common consent agree to replace any arbitrator. The procedure of such replacement shall be in accordance with Rules 1, 5 and 6.

Rule 8 — Incapacity or Resignation of Arbitrators

(1) If an arbitrator becomes incapacitated or unable to perform the duties of his office, the procedure in respect of the disqualification of arbitrators set forth in Rule 9 shall apply.

(2) An arbitrator may resign by submitting his resignation to the other members of the Tribunal and the Secretary-General. If the arbitrator was appointed by one of the parties, the Tribunal shall promptly consider the reasons for his resignation and decide whether it consents thereto. The Tribunal shall promptly notify the Secretary-General of its decision.

Rule 9 — Disqualification of Arbitrators

(1) A party proposing the disqualification of an arbitrator pursuant to Article 57 of the Convention shall promptly, and in any event before the proceeding is declared closed, file its proposal with the Secretary-General, stating its reasons therefor.

(2) The Secretary-General shall forthwith:
(a) transmit the proposal to the members of the Tribunal and, if it relates to a sole arbitrator or to a majority of the members of the Tribunal, to the Chairman of the Administrative Council; and
(b) notify the other party of the proposal.
(3) The arbitrator to whom the proposal relates may, without delay, furnish explanations to the Tribunal or the Chairman, as the case may be.
(4) Unless the proposal relates to a majority of the members of the Tribunal, the other members shall promptly consider and vote on the proposal in the absence of the arbitrator concerned. If those members are equally divided, they shall, through the Secretary-General, promptly notify the Chairman of the proposal, of any explanation furnished by the arbitrator concerned and of their failure to reach a decision.
(5) Whenever the Chairman has to decide on a proposal to disqualify an arbitrator, he shall use his best efforts to take that decision within 30 days after he has received the proposal.
(6) The proceeding shall be suspended until a decision has been taken on the proposal.

Rule 10 — Procedure during a Vacancy on the Tribunal

(1) The Secretary-General shall forthwith notify the parties and, if necessary, the Chairman of the Administrative Council of the disqualification, death, incapacity or resignation of an arbitrator and of the consent, if any, of the Tribunal to a resignation.
(2) Upon the notification by the Secretary-General of a vacancy on the Tribunal, the proceeding shall be or remain suspended until the vacancy has been filled.

Rule 11 — Filling Vacancies on the Tribunal

(1) Except as provided in paragraph (2), a vacancy resulting from the disqualification, death, incapacity or resignation of an arbitrator shall be promptly filled by the same method by which his appointment had been made.
(2) In addition to filling vacancies relating to arbitrators appointed by him, the Chairman of the Administrative Council shall appoint a person from the Panel of Arbitrators:
(a) to fill a vacancy caused by the resignation, without the consent of the Tribunal, of an arbitrator appointed by a party; or
(b) at the request of either party, to fill any other vacancy, if no new appointment is made and accepted within 45 days of the notification of the vacancy by the Secretary-General.

(3) The procedure for filling a vacancy shall be in accordance with Rules 1, 4(4), 4(5), 5 and, mutatis mutandis, 6(2).

Rule 12 — Resumption of Proceeding after Filling a Vacancy

As soon as a vacancy on the Tribunal has been filled, the proceeding shall continue from the point it had reached at the time the vacancy occurred. The newly appointed arbitrator may, however, require that the oral procedure be recommenced, if this had already been started.

Chapter II
Working of the Tribunal

Rule 13 — Sessions of the Tribunal

(1) The Tribunal shall hold its first session within 60 days after its constitution or such other period as the parties may agree. The dates of that session shall be fixed by the President of the Tribunal after consultation with its members and the Secretary-General. If upon its constitution the Tribunal has no President because the parties have agreed that the President shall be elected by its members, the Secretary-General shall fix the dates of that session. In both cases, the parties shall be consulted as far as possible.

(2) The dates of subsequent sessions shall be determined by the Tribunal, after consultation with the Secretary-General and with the parties as far as possible.

(3) The Tribunal shall meet at the seat of the Centre or at such other place as may have been agreed by the parties in accordance with Article 63 of the Convention. If the parties agree that the proceeding shall be held at a place other than the Centre or an institution with which the Centre has made the necessary arrangements, they shall consult with the Secretary-General and request the approval of the Tribunal. Failing such approval, the Tribunal shall meet at the seat of the Centre.

(4) The Secretary-General shall notify the members of the Tribunal and the parties of the dates and place of the sessions of the Tribunal in good time.

Rule 14 — Sittings of the Tribunal

(1) The President of the Tribunal shall conduct its hearings and preside at its deliberations.

(2) Except as the parties otherwise agree, the presence of a majority of the members of the Tribunal shall be required at its sittings.

(3) The President of the Tribunal shall fix the date and hour of its sittings.

Rule 15 — Deliberations of the Tribunal

(1) The deliberations of the Tribunal shall take place in private and remain secret.

(2) Only members of the Tribunal shall take part in its deliberations. No

other person shall be admitted unless the Tribunal decides otherwise.

Rule 16 — Decisions of the Tribunal

(1) Decisions of the Tribunal shall be taken by a majority of the votes of all its members. Abstention shall count as a negative vote.

(2) Except as otherwise provided by these Rules or decided by the Tribunal, it may take any decision by correspondence among its members, provided that all of them are consulted. Decisions so taken shall be certified by the President of the Tribunal.

Rule 17 — Incapacity of the President

If at any time the President of the Tribunal should be unable to act, his functions shall be performed by one of the other members of the Tribunal, acting in the order in which the Secretary-General had received the notice of their acceptance of their appointment to the Tribunal.

Rule 18 — Representation of the Parties

(1) Each party may be represented or assisted by agents, counsel or advocates whose names and authority shall be notified by that party to the Secretary-General, who shall promptly inform the Tribunal and the other party.

(2) For the purposes of these Rules, the expression "party" includes, where the context so admits, an agent, counsel or advocate authorized to represent that party.

Chapter III
General Procedural Provisions

Rule 19 — Procedural Orders

The Tribunal shall make the orders required for the conduct of the proceeding.

Rule 20 — Preliminary Procedural Consultation

(1) As early as possible after the constitution of a Tribunal, its President shall endeavor to ascertain the views of the parties regarding questions of procedure. For this purpose he may request the parties to meet him. He shall, in particular, seek their views on the following matters:

(a) the number of members of the Tribunal required to constitute a quorum at its sittings;

(b) the language or languages to be used in the proceeding;

(c) the number and sequence of the pleadings and the time limits within which they are to be filed;

(d) the number of copies desired by each party of instruments filed by the other;

(e) dispensing with the written or the oral procedure;

(f) the manner in which the cost of the proceeding is to be apportioned; and
(g) the manner in which the record of the hearings shall be kept.
(2) In the conduct of the proceeding the Tribunal shall apply any agreement between the parties on procedural matters, except as otherwise provided in the Convention or the Administrative and Financial Regulations.

Rule 21 — Pre-Hearing Conference

(1) At the request of the Secretary-General or at the discretion of the President of the Tribunal, a pre-hearing conference between the Tribunal and the parties may be held to arrange for an exchange of information and the stipulation of uncontested facts in order to expedite the proceeding.
(2) At the request of the parties, a pre-hearing conference between the Tribunal and the parties, duly represented by their authorized representatives, may be held to consider the issues in dispute with a view to reaching an amicable settlement.

Rule 22 — Procedural Languages

(1) The parties may agree on the use of one or two languages to be used in the proceeding, provided, that, if they agree on any language that is not an official language of the Centre, the Tribunal, after consultation with the Secretary-General, gives its approval. If the parties do not agree on any such procedural language, each of them may select one of the official languages (i.e., English, French and Spanish) for this purpose.
(2) If two procedural languages are selected by the parties, any instrument may be filed in either language. Either language may be used at the hearings, subject, if the Tribunal so requires, to translation and interpretation. The orders and the award of the Tribunal shall be rendered and the record kept in both procedural languages, both versions being equally authentic.

Rule 23 — Copies of Instruments

Except as otherwise provided by the Tribunal after consultation with the parties and the Secretary-General, every request, pleading, application, written observation, supporting documentation, if any, or other instrument shall be filed in the form of a signed original accompanied by the following number of additional copies:
(a) before the number of members of the Tribunal has been determined: five;
(b) after the number of members of the Tribunal has been determined: two more than the number of its members.

Rule 24 — Supporting Documentation

Supporting documentation shall ordinarily be filed together with the instrument to which it relates, and in any case within the time limit fixed for the filing of such instrument.

Rule 25 — Correction of Errors

An accidental error in any instrument or supporting document may, with the consent of the other party or by leave of the Tribunal, be corrected at any time before the award is rendered.

Rule 26 — Time Limits

(1) Where required, time limits shall be fixed by the Tribunal by assigning dates for the completion of the various steps in the proceeding. The Tribunal may delegate this power to its President.

(2) The Tribunal may extend any time limit that it has fixed. If the Tribunal is not in session, this power shall be exercised by its President.

(3) Any step taken after expiration of the applicable time limit shall be disregarded unless the Tribunal, in special circumstances and after giving the other party an opportunity of stating its views, decides otherwise.

Rule 27 — Waiver

A party which knows or should have known that a provision of the Administrative and Financial Regulations, of these Rules, of any other rules or agreement applicable to the proceeding, or of an order of the Tribunal has not been complied with and which fails to state promptly its objections thereto, shall be deemed—subject to Article 45 of the Convention—to have waived its right to object.

Rule 28 — Cost of Proceeding

(1) Without prejudice to the final decision on the payment of the cost of the proceeding, the Tribunal may, unless otherwise agreed by the parties, decide:

(a) at any stage of the proceeding, the portion which each party shall pay, pursuant to Administrative and Financial Regulation 14, of the fees and expenses of the Tribunal and the charges for the use of the facilities of the Centre;

(b) with respect to any part of the proceeding, that the related costs (as determined by the Secretary-General) shall be borne entirely or in a particular share by one of the parties.

(2) Promptly after the closure of the proceeding, each party shall submit to the Tribunal a statement of costs reasonably incurred or borne by it in the proceeding and the Secretary-General shall submit to the Tribunal an account of all amounts paid by each party to the Centre and of all costs incurred by the Centre for the proceeding. The Tribunal may, before the award has been rendered, request the parties and the Secretary-General to

provide additional information concerning the cost of the proceeding.

Chapter IV
Written and Oral Procedures

Rule 29 — Normal Procedures

Except if the parties otherwise agree, the proceeding shall comprise two distinct phases: a written procedure followed by an oral one.

Rule 30 — Transmission of the Request

As soon as the Tribunal is constituted, the Secretary-General shall transmit to each member a copy of the request by which the proceeding was initiated, of the supporting documentation, of the notice of registration and of any communication received from either party in response thereto.

Rule 31 — The Written Procedure

(1) In addition to the request for arbitration, the written procedure shall consist of the following pleadings, filed within time limits set by the Tribunal:

(a) a memorial by the requesting party;

(b) a counter-memorial by the other party; and, if the parties so agree or the Tribunal deems it necessary:

(c) a reply by the requesting party; and

(d) a rejoinder by the other party.

(2) If the request was made jointly, each party shall, within the same time limit determined by the Tribunal, file its memorial and, if the parties so agree or the Tribunal deems it necessary, its reply; however, the parties may instead agree that one of them shall, for the purposes of paragraph (1), be considered as the requesting party.

(3) A memorial shall contain: a statement of the relevant facts; a statement of law; and the submissions. A counter-memorial, reply or rejoinder shall contain an admission or denial of the facts stated in the last previous pleading; any additional facts, if necessary; observations concerning the statement of law in the last previous pleading; a statement of law in answer thereto; and the submissions.

Rule 32 — The Oral Procedure

(1) The oral procedure shall consist of the hearing by the Tribunal of the parties, their agents, counsel and advocates, and of witnesses and experts.

(2) Unless either party objects, the Tribunal, after consultation with the Secretary-General, may allow other persons, besides the parties, their agents, counsel and advocates, witnesses and experts during their testimony, and officers of the Tribunal, to attend or observe all or part of the hearings, subject to appropriate logistical arrangements. The Tribunal shall for such

cases establish procedures for the protection of proprietary or privileged information.

(3) The members of the Tribunal may, during the hearings, put questions to the parties, their agents, counsel and advocates, and ask them for explanations.

Rule 33 — Marshalling of Evidence

Without prejudice to the rules concerning the production of documents, each party shall, within time limits fixed by the Tribunal, communicate to the Secretary-General, for transmission to the Tribunal and the other party, precise information regarding the evidence which it intends to produce and that which it intends to request the Tribunal to call for, together with an indication of the points to which such evidence will be directed.

Rule 34 — Evidence: General Principles

(1) The Tribunal shall be the judge of the admissibility of any evidence adduced and of its probative value.

(2) The Tribunal may, if it deems it necessary at any stage of the proceeding:

(a) call upon the parties to produce documents, witnesses and experts; and

(b) visit any place connected with the dispute or conduct inquiries there.

(3) The parties shall cooperate with the Tribunal in the production of the evidence and in the other measures provided for in paragraph (2). The Tribunal shall take formal note of the failure of a party to comply with its obligations under this paragraph and of any reasons given for such failure.

(4) Expenses incurred in producing evidence and in taking other measures in accordance with paragraph (2) shall be deemed to constitute part of the expenses incurred by the parties within the meaning of Article 61(2) of the Convention.

Rule 35 — Examination of Witnesses and Experts

(1) Witnesses and experts shall be examined before the Tribunal by the parties under the control of its President. Questions may also be put to them by any member of the Tribunal.

(2) Each witness shall make the following declaration before giving his evidence:

"I solemnly declare upon my honour and conscience that I shall speak the truth, the whole truth and nothing but the truth."

(3) Each expert shall make the following declaration before making his statement:

"I solemnly declare upon my honour and conscience that my statement will be in accordance with my sincere belief."

Rule 36 — Witnesses and Experts: Special Rules
Notwithstanding Rule 35 the Tribunal may:
(a) admit evidence given by a witness or expert in a written deposition; and
(b) with the consent of both parties, arrange for the examination of a witness or expert otherwise than before the Tribunal itself. The Tribunal shall define the subject of the examination, the time limit, the procedure to be followed and other particulars. The parties may participate in the examination.
Rule 37 — Visits and Inquiries; Submissions of Non-disputing Parties
(1) If the Tribunal considers it necessary to visit any place connected with the dispute or to conduct an inquiry there, it shall make an order to this effect. The order shall define the scope of the visit or the subject of the inquiry, the time limit, the procedure to be followed and other particulars. The parties may participate in any visit or inquiry.
(2) After consulting both parties, the Tribunal may allow a person or entity that is not a party to the dispute (in this Rule called the "nondisputing party") to file a written submission with the Tribunal regarding a matter within the scope of the dispute. In determining whether to allow such a filing, the Tribunal shall consider, among other things, the extent to which:
(a) the non-disputing party submission would assist the Tribunal in the determination of a factual or legal issue related to the proceeding by bringing a perspective, particular knowledge or insight that is different from that of the disputing parties;
(b) the non-disputing party submission would address a matter within the scope of the dispute;
(c) the non-disputing party has a significant interest in the proceeding.
The Tribunal shall ensure that the non-disputing party submission does not disrupt the proceeding or unduly burden or unfairly prejudice either party, and that both parties are given an opportunity to present their observations on the non-disputing party submission.
Rule 38 — Closure of the Proceeding
(1) When the presentation of the case by the parties is completed, the proceeding shall be declared closed.
(2) Exceptionally, the Tribunal may, before the award has been rendered, reopen the proceeding on the ground that new evidence is forthcoming of such a nature as to constitute a decisive factor, or that there is a vital need for clarification on certain specific points.

Chapter V
Particular Provisions

Rule 39 — Provisional Measures

(1) At any time after the institution of the proceeding, a party may request that provisional measures for the preservation of its rights be recommended by the Tribunal. The request shall specify the rights to be preserved, the measures the recommendation of which is requested, and the circumstances that require such measures.

(2) The Tribunal shall give priority to the consideration of a request made pursuant to paragraph (1).

(3) The Tribunal may also recommend provisional measures on its own initiative or recommend measures other than those specified in a request. It may at any time modify or revoke its recommendations.

(4) The Tribunal shall only recommend provisional measures, or modify or revoke its recommendations, after giving each party an opportunity of presenting its observations.

(5) If a party makes a request pursuant to paragraph (1) before the constitution of the Tribunal, the Secretary-General shall, on the application of either party, fix time limits for the parties to present observations on the request, so that the request and observations may be considered by the Tribunal promptly upon its constitution.

(6) Nothing in this Rule shall prevent the parties, provided that they have so stipulated in the agreement recording their consent, from requesting any judicial or other authority to order provisional measures, prior to or after the institution of the proceeding, for the preservation of their respective rights and interests.

Rule 40 — Ancillary Claims

(1) Except as the parties otherwise agree, a party may present an incidental or additional claim or counter-claim arising directly out of the subject-matter of the dispute, provided that such ancillary claim is within the scope of the consent of the parties and is otherwise within the jurisdiction of the Centre.

(2) An incidental or additional claim shall be presented not later than in the reply and a counter-claim no later than in the countermemorial, unless the Tribunal, upon justification by the party presenting the ancillary claim and upon considering any objection of the other party, authorizes the presentation of the claim at a later stage in the proceeding.

(3) The Tribunal shall fix a time limit within which the party against which an ancillary claim is presented may file its observations thereon.

Rule 41 — Preliminary Objections

(1) Any objection that the dispute or any ancillary claim is not within the jurisdiction of the Centre or, for other reasons, is not within the competence of the Tribunal shall be made as early as possible. A party shall file the objection with the Secretary-General no later than the expiration of the time limit fixed for the filing of the countermemorial, or, if the objection relates to an ancillary claim, for the filing of the rejoinder—unless the facts on which the objection is based are unknown to the party at that time.

(2) The Tribunal may on its own initiative consider, at any stage of the proceeding, whether the dispute or any ancillary claim before it is within the jurisdiction of the Centre and within its own competence.

(3) Upon the formal raising of an objection relating to the dispute, the Tribunal may decide to suspend the proceeding on the merits. The President of the Tribunal, after consultation with its other members, shall fix a time limit within which the parties may file observations on the objection.

(4) The Tribunal shall decide whether or not the further procedures relating to the objection made pursuant to paragraph (1) shall be oral. It may deal with the objection as a preliminary question or join it to the merits of the dispute. If the Tribunal overrules the objection or joins it to the merits, it shall once more fix time limits for the further procedures.

(5) Unless the parties have agreed to another expedited procedure for making preliminary objections, a party may, no later than 30 days after the constitution of the Tribunal, and in any event before the first session of the Tribunal, file an objection that a claim is manifestly without legal merit. The party shall specify as precisely as possible the basis for the objection. The Tribunal, after giving the parties the opportunity to present their observations on the objection, shall, at its first session or promptly thereafter, notify the parties of its decision on the objection. The decision of the Tribunal shall be without prejudice to the right of a party to file an objection pursuant to paragraph (1) or to object, in the course of the proceeding, that a claim lacks legal merit.

(6) If the Tribunal decides that the dispute is not within the jurisdiction of the Centre or not within its own competence, or that all claims are manifestly without legal merit, it shall render an award to that effect.

Rule 42 — Default

(1) If a party (in this Rule called the "defaulting party") fails to appear or to present its case at any stage of the proceeding, the other party may, at any time prior to the discontinuance of the proceeding, request the Tribunal to deal with the questions submitted to it and to render an award.

(2) The Tribunal shall promptly notify the defaulting party of such a request. Unless it is satisfied that that party does not intend to appear or to present its case in the proceeding, it shall, at the same time, grant a period of grace and to this end:

(a) if that party had failed to file a pleading or any other instrument within the time limit fixed therefor, fix a new time limit for its filing; or

(b) if that party had failed to appear or present its case at a hearing, fix a new date for the hearing.

The period of grace shall not, without the consent of the other party, exceed 60 days.

(3) After the expiration of the period of grace or when, in accordance with paragraph (2), no such period is granted, the Tribunal shall resume the consideration of the dispute. Failure of the defaulting party to appear or to present its case shall not be deemed an admission of the assertions made by the other party.

(4) The Tribunal shall examine the jurisdiction of the Centre and its own competence in the dispute and, if it is satisfied, decide whether the submissions made are well-founded in fact and in law. To this end, it may, at any stage of the proceeding, call on the party appearing to file observations, produce evidence or submit oral explanations.

Rule 43 — Settlement and Discontinuance

(1) If, before the award is rendered, the parties agree on a settlement of the dispute or otherwise to discontinue the proceeding, the Tribunal, or the Secretary-General if the Tribunal has not yet been constituted, shall, at their written request, in an order take note of the discontinuance of the proceeding.

(2) If the parties file with the Secretary-General the full and signed text of their settlement and in writing request the Tribunal to embody such settlement in an award, the Tribunal may record the settlement in the form of its award.

Rule 44 — Discontinuance at Request of a Party

If a party requests the discontinuance of the proceeding, the Tribunal, or the Secretary-General if the Tribunal has not yet been constituted, shall in an order fix a time limit within which the other party may state whether it opposes the discontinuance. If no objection is made in writing within the time limit, the other party shall be deemed to have acquiesced in the discontinuance and the Tribunal, or if appropriate the Secretary-General, shall in an order take note of the discontinuance of the proceeding. If objection is made, the proceeding shall continue.

Rule 45 — Discontinuance for Failure of Parties to Act

If the parties fail to take any steps in the proceeding during six consecutive months or such period as they may agree with the approval of the Tribunal, or of the Secretary-General if the Tribunal has not yet been constituted, they shall be deemed to have discontinued the proceeding and the Tribunal, or if appropriate the Secretary-General, shall, after notice to the parties, in an order take note of the discontinuance.

Chapter VI
The Award

Rule 46 — Preparation of the Award

The award (including any individual or dissenting opinion) shall be drawn up and signed within 120 days after closure of the proceeding. The Tribunal may, however, extend this period by a further 60 days if it would otherwise be unable to draw up the award.

Rule 47 — The Award

(1) The award shall be in writing and shall contain:

(a) a precise designation of each party;

(b) a statement that the Tribunal was established under the Convention, and a description of the method of its constitution;

(c) the name of each member of the Tribunal, and an identification of the appointing authority of each;

(d) the names of the agents, counsel and advocates of the parties;

(e) the dates and place of the sittings of the Tribunal;

(f) a summary of the proceeding;

(g) a statement of the facts as found by the Tribunal;

(h) the submissions of the parties;

(i) the decision of the Tribunal on every question submitted to it, together with the reasons upon which the decision is based; and

(j) any decision of the Tribunal regarding the cost of the proceeding.

(2) The award shall be signed by the members of the Tribunal who voted for it; the date of each signature shall be indicated.

(3) Any member of the Tribunal may attach his individual opinion to the award, whether he dissents from the majority or not, or a statement of his dissent.

Rule 48 — Rendering of the Award

(1) Upon signature by the last arbitrator to sign, the Secretary-General shall promptly:

(a) authenticate the original text of the award and deposit it in the archives of the Centre, together with any individual opinions and statements of dissent; and

(b) dispatch a certified copy of the award (including individual opinions and statements of dissent) to each party, indicating the date of dispatch on the original text and on all copies.

(2) The award shall be deemed to have been rendered on the date on which the certified copies were dispatched.

(3) The Secretary-General shall, upon request, make available to a party additional certified copies of the award.

(4) The Centre shall not publish the award without the consent of the parties. The Centre shall, however, promptly include in its publications excerpts of the legal reasoning of the Tribunal.

Rule 49 — Supplementary Decisions and Rectification

(1) Within 45 days after the date on which the award was rendered, either party may request, pursuant to Article 49(2) of the Convention, a supplementary decision on, or the rectification of, the award. Such a request shall be addressed in writing to the Secretary-General. The request shall:

(a) identify the award to which it relates;

(b) indicate the date of the request;

(c) state in detail:

(i) any question which, in the opinion of the requesting party, the Tribunal omitted to decide in the award; and

(ii) any error in the award which the requesting party seeks to have rectified; and

(d) be accompanied by a fee for lodging the request.

(2) Upon receipt of the request and of the lodging fee, the Secretary-General shall forthwith:

(a) register the request;

(b) notify the parties of the registration;

(c) transmit to the other party a copy of the request and of any accompanying documentation; and

(d) transmit to each member of the Tribunal a copy of the notice of registration, together with a copy of the request and of any accompanying documentation.

(3) The President of the Tribunal shall consult the members on whether it is necessary for the Tribunal to meet in order to consider the request. The Tribunal shall fix a time limit for the parties to file their observations on the request and shall determine the procedure for its consideration.

(4) Rules 46-48 shall apply, *mutatis mutandis*, to any decision of the Tribunal pursuant to this Rule.

(5) If a request is received by the Secretary-General more than 45 days after the award was rendered, he shall refuse to register the request and so inform forthwith the requesting party.

Chapter VII

Interpretation, Revision and Annulment of the Award

Rule 50 — The Application

(1) An application for the interpretation, revision or annulment of an award shall be addressed in writing to the Secretary-General and shall:

(a) identify the award to which it relates;

(b) indicate the date of the application;

(c) state in detail:

(i) in an application for interpretation, the precise points in dispute;

(ii) in an application for revision, pursuant to Article 51(1) of the Convention, the change sought in the award, the discovery of some fact of such a nature as decisively to affect the award, and evidence that when the award was rendered that fact was unknown to the Tribunal and to the applicant, and that the applicant's ignorance of that fact was not due to negligence;

(iii) in an application for annulment, pursuant to Article 52(1) of the Convention, the grounds on which it is based. These grounds are limited to the following:

– that the Tribunal was not properly constituted;

– that the Tribunal has manifestly exceeded its powers;

– that there was corruption on the part of a member of the Tribunal;

– that there has been a serious departure from a fundamental rule of procedure;

– that the award has failed to state the reasons on which it is based;

(d) be accompanied by the payment of a fee for lodging the application.

(2) Without prejudice to the provisions of paragraph (3), upon receiving an application and the lodging fee, the Secretary-General shall forthwith:

(a) register the application;

(b) notify the parties of the registration; and

(c) transmit to the other party a copy of the application and of any accompanying documentation.

(3) The Secretary-General shall refuse to register an application for:

(a) revision, if, in accordance with Article 51(2) of the Convention, it is not made within 90 days after the discovery of the new fact and in any event within three years after the date on which the award was rendered (or any subsequent decision or correction);

(b) annulment, if, in accordance with Article 52(2) of the Convention, it is not made:
(i) within 120 days after the date on which the award was rendered (or any subsequent decision or correction) if the application is based on any of the following grounds:
– the Tribunal was not properly constituted;
– the Tribunal has manifestly exceeded its powers;
– there has been a serious departure from a fundamental rule of procedure;
– the award has failed to state the reasons on which it is based;
(ii) in the case of corruption on the part of a member of the Tribunal, within 120 days after discovery thereof, and in any event within three years after the date on which the award was rendered (or any subsequent decision or correction).
(4) If the Secretary-General refuses to register an application for revision, or annulment, he shall forthwith notify the requesting party of his refusal.

Rule 51 — Interpretation or Revision: Further Procedures

(1) Upon registration of an application for the interpretation or revision of an award, the Secretary-General shall forthwith:
(a) transmit to each member of the original Tribunal a copy of the notice of registration, together with a copy of the application and of any accompanying documentation; and
(b) request each member of the Tribunal to inform him within a specified time limit whether that member is willing to take part in the consideration of the application.
(2) If all members of the Tribunal express their willingness to take part in the consideration of the application, the Secretary-General shall so notify the members of the Tribunal and the parties. Upon dispatch of these notices the Tribunal shall be deemed to be reconstituted.
(3) If the Tribunal cannot be reconstituted in accordance with paragraph (2), the Secretary-General shall so notify the parties and invite them to proceed, as soon as possible, to constitute a new Tribunal, including the same number of arbitrators, and appointed by the same method, as the original one.

Rule 52 — Annulment: Further Procedures

(1) Upon registration of an application for the annulment of an award, the Secretary-General shall forthwith request the Chairman of the Administrative Council to appoint an *ad hoc* Committee in accordance with Article 52(3) of the Convention.
(2) The Committee shall be deemed to be constituted on the date the

Secretary-General notifies the parties that all members have accepted their appointment. Before or at the first session of the Committee, each member shall sign a declaration conforming to that set forth in Rule 6(2).

Rule 53 — Rules of Procedure

The provisions of these Rules shall apply mutatis mutandis to any procedure relating to the interpretation, revision or annulment of an award and to the decision of the Tribunal or Committee.

Rule 54 — Stay of Enforcement of the Award

(1) The party applying for the interpretation, revision or annulment of an award may in its application, and either party may at any time before the final disposition of the application, request a stay in the enforcement of part or all of the award to which the application relates. The Tribunal or Committee shall give priority to the consideration of such a request.

(2) If an application for the revision or annulment of an award contains a request for a stay of its enforcement, the Secretary-General shall, together with the notice of registration, inform both parties of the provisional stay of the award. As soon as the Tribunal or Committee is constituted it shall, if either party requests, rule within 30 days on whether such stay should be continued; unless it decides to continue the stay, it shall automatically be terminated.

(3) If a stay of enforcement has been granted pursuant to paragraph (1) or continued pursuant to paragraph (2), the Tribunal or Committee may at any time modify or terminate the stay at the request of either party. All stays shall automatically terminate on the date on which a final decision is rendered on the application, except that a Committee granting the partial annulment of an award may order the temporary stay of enforcement of the unannulled portion in order to give either party an opportunity to request any new Tribunal constituted pursuant to Article 52(6) of the Convention to grant a stay pursuant to Rule 55(3).

(4) A request pursuant to paragraph (1), (2) (second sentence) or (3) shall specify the circumstances that require the stay or its modification or termination. A request shall only be granted after the Tribunal or Committee has given each party an opportunity of presenting its observations.

(5) The Secretary-General shall promptly notify both parties of the stay of enforcement of any award and of the modification or termination of such a stay, which shall become effective on the date on which he dispatches such notification.

Rule 55 — Resubmission of Dispute after an Annulment

(1) If a Committee annuls part or all of an award, either party may request

the resubmission of the dispute to a new Tribunal. Such a request shall be addressed in writing to the Secretary-General and shall:
(a) identify the award to which it relates;
(b) indicate the date of the request;
(c) explain in detail what aspect of the dispute is to be submitted to the Tribunal; and
(d) be accompanied by a fee for lodging the request.
(2) Upon receipt of the request and of the lodging fee, the Secretary-General shall forthwith:
(a) register it in the Arbitration Register;
(b) notify both parties of the registration;
(c) transmit to the other party a copy of the request and of any accompanying documentation; and
(d) invite the parties to proceed, as soon as possible, to constitute a new Tribunal, including the same number of arbitrators, and appointed by the same method, as the original one.
(3) If the original award had only been annulled in part, the new Tribunal shall not reconsider any portion of the award not so annulled. It may, however, in accordance with the procedures set forth in Rule 54, stay or continue to stay the enforcement of the unannulled portion of the award until the date its own award is rendered.
(4) Except as otherwise provided in paragraphs (1)–(3), these Rules shall apply to a proceeding on a resubmitted dispute in the same manner as if such dispute had been submitted pursuant to the Institution Rules.

Chapter VIII
General Provisions

Rule 56 — Final Provisions

(1) The texts of these Rules in each official language of the Centre shall be equally authentic.
(2) These Rules may be cited as the "Arbitration Rules" of the Centre.

LCIA ARBITRATION RULES *

Preamble

Where any agreement, submission or reference howsoever made or evidenced in writing (whether signed or not) provides in whatsoever manner for arbitration under the rules of or by the LCIA, the London Court of International Arbitration, the London Court of Arbitration or the London Court, the parties thereto shall be taken to have agreed in writing that any arbitration between them shall be conducted in accordance with the LCIA Rules or such amended rules as the LCIA may have adopted hereafter to take effect before the commencement of the arbitration and that such LCIA Rules form part of their agreement (collectively, the "Arbitration Agreement"). These LCIA Rules comprise this Preamble, the Articles and the Index, together with the Annex to the LCIA Rules and the Schedule of Costs as both from time to time may be separately amended by the LCIA (the "LCIA Rules").

Article 1 — Request for Arbitration

1.1 Any party wishing to commence an arbitration under the LCIA Rules (the "Claimant") shall deliver to the Registrar of the LCIA Court (the "Registrar") a written request for arbitration (the "Request"), containing or accompanied by:

(i) the full name and all contact details (including postal address, e-mail address, telephone and facsimile numbers) of the Claimant for the purpose of receiving delivery of all documentation in the arbitration; and the same particulars of the Claimant's legal representatives (if any) and of all other parties to the arbitration;

(ii) the full terms of the Arbitration Agreement (excepting the LCIA Rules) invoked by the Claimant to support its claim, together with a copy of any contractual or other documentation in which those terms are contained and to which the Claimant's claim relates;

(iii) a statement briefly summarising the nature and circumstances of the dispute, its estimated monetary amount or value, the transaction(s) at issue and the claim advanced by the Claimant against any other party to the arbitration (each such other party being here separately described as a "Respondent");

(iv) a statement of any procedural matters for the arbitration (such as the arbitral seat, the language(s) of the arbitration, the number of arbitrators, their qualifications and identities) upon which the parties have already agreed in writing or in respect of which the Claimant makes any proposal under the Arbitration Agreement;

(v) if the Arbitration Agreement (or any other written agreement)

* For a commentary on the LCIA Arbitration Rules, see Shai Wade, Phillip Clifford and James Clanchy, *A Commentary on the LCIA Rules* (Sweet & Maxwell, forthcoming).

howsoever calls for any form of party nomination of arbitrators, the full name, postal address, e-mail address, telephone and facsimile numbers of the Claimant's nominee;

(vi) confirmation that the registration fee prescribed in the Schedule of Costs has been or is being paid to the LCIA, without which actual receipt of such payment the Request shall be treated by the Registrar as not having been delivered and the arbitration as not having been commenced under the Arbitration Agreement; and

(vii) confirmation that copies of the Request (including all accompanying documents) have been or are being delivered to all other parties to the arbitration by one or more means to be identified specifically in such confirmation, to be supported then or as soon as possible thereafter by documentary proof satisfactory to the LCIA Court of actual delivery (including the date of delivery) or, if actual delivery is demonstrated to be impossible to the LCIA Court's satisfaction, sufficient information as to any other effective form of notification.

1.2 The Request (including all accompanying documents) may be submitted to the Registrar in electronic form (as e-mail attachments) or in paper form or in both forms. If submitted in paper form, the Request shall be submitted in two copies where a sole arbitrator is to be appointed, or, if the parties have agreed or the Claimant proposes that three arbitrators are to be appointed, in four copies.

1.3 The Claimant may use, but is not required to do so, the standard electronic form available on-line from the LCIA's website for LCIA Requests.

1.4 The date of receipt by the Registrar of the Request shall be treated as the date upon which the arbitration has commenced for all purposes (the "Commencement Date"), subject to the LCIA's actual receipt of the registration fee.

1.5 There may be one or more Claimants (whether or not jointly represented); and in such event, where appropriate, the term "Claimant" shall be so interpreted under the Arbitration Agreement.

Article 2 — Response

2.1 Within 28 days of the Commencement Date, or such lesser or greater period to be determined by the LCIA Court upon application by any party or upon its own initiative (pursuant to Article 22.5), the Respondent shall deliver to the Registrar a written response to the Request (the "Response"), containing or accompanied by:

(i) the Respondent's full name and all contact details (including postal address, e-mail address, telephone and facsimile numbers) for the purpose of receiving delivery of all documentation in the arbitration and the same particulars of its legal representatives (if any);

(ii) confirmation or denial of all or part of the claim advanced by the Claimant in the Request, including the Claimant's invocation of the Arbitration Agreement in support of its claim;

(iii) if not full confirmation, a statement briefly summarising the nature and circumstances of the dispute, its estimated monetary amount or value, the transaction(s) at issue and the defence advanced by the Respondent, and also indicating whether any cross-claim will be advanced by the Respondent against any other party to the arbitration (such cross-claim to include any counterclaim against any Claimant and any other cross-claim against any Respondent);

(iv) a response to any procedural statement for the arbitration contained in the Request under Article 1.1(iv), including the Respondent's own statement relating to the arbitral seat, the language(s) of the arbitration, the number of arbitrators, their qualifications and identities and any other procedural matter upon which the parties have already agreed in writing or in respect of which the Respondent makes any proposal under the Arbitration Agreement;

(v) if the Arbitration Agreement (or any other written agreement) howsoever calls for party nomination of arbitrators, the full name, postal address, e-mail address, telephone and facsimile numbers of the Respondent's nominee; and

(vi) confirmation that copies of the Response (including all accompanying documents) have been or are being delivered to all other parties to the arbitration by one or more means of delivery to be identified specifically in such confirmation, to be supported then or as soon as possible thereafter by documentary proof satisfactory to the LCIA Court of actual delivery (including the date of delivery) or, if actual delivery is demonstrated to be impossible to the LCIA Court's satisfaction, sufficient information as to any other effective form of notification.

2.2 The Response (including all accompanying documents) may be submitted to the Registrar in electronic form (as e-mail attachments) or in paper form or in both forms. If submitted in paper form, the Response shall be submitted in two copies where a sole arbitrator is to be appointed, or, if the parties have agreed or the Respondent proposes that three arbitrators are to be appointed, in four copies.

2.3 The Respondent may use, but is not required to do so, the standard electronic form available on-line from the LCIA's website for LCIA Responses.

2.4 Failure to deliver a Response within time shall constitute an irrevocable waiver of that party's opportunity to nominate or propose any arbitral candidate. Failure to deliver any or any part of a Response within time or at all shall not (by itself) preclude the Respondent from denying any claim or from advancing any defence or cross-claim in the arbitration.

2.5 There may be one or more Respondents (whether or not jointly represented); and in such event, where appropriate, the term "Respondent" shall be so interpreted under the Arbitration Agreement.

Article 3 — LCIA Court and Registrar

3.1 The functions of the LCIA Court under the Arbitration Agreement shall be performed in its name by the President of the LCIA Court (or any of its Vice-Presidents, Honorary Vice-Presidents or former Vice-Presidents) or by a division of three or more members of the LCIA Court appointed by its President or any Vice-President (the "LCIA Court").

3.2 The functions of the Registrar under the Arbitration Agreement shall be performed under the supervision of the LCIA Court by the Registrar or any deputy Registrar.

3.3 All communications in the arbitration to the LCIA Court from any party, arbitrator or expert to the Arbitral Tribunal shall be addressed to the Registrar.

Article 4 — Written Communications and Periods of Time

4.1 Any written communication by the LCIA Court, the Registrar or any party may be delivered personally or by registered postal or courier service or (subject to Article 4.3) by facsimile, e-mail or any other electronic means of telecommunication that provides a record of its transmission, or in any other manner ordered by the Arbitral Tribunal.

4.2 Unless otherwise ordered by the Arbitral Tribunal, if an address has been agreed or designated by a party for the purpose of receiving any communication in regard to the Arbitration Agreement or (in the absence of such agreement or designation) has been regularly used in the parties' previous dealings, any written communication (including the Request and Response) may be delivered to such party at that address, and if so delivered, shall be treated as having been received by such party.

4.3 Delivery by electronic means (including e-mail and facsimile) may only be effected to an address agreed or designated by the receiving party for that purpose or ordered by the Arbitral Tribunal.

4.4 For the purpose of determining the commencement of any time-limit, a written communication shall be treated as having been received by a party on the day it is delivered or, in the case of electronic means, transmitted in accordance with Articles 4.1 to 4.3 (such time to be determined by reference to the recipient's time-zone).

4.5 For the purpose of determining compliance with a time-limit, a written communication shall be treated as having been sent by a party if made or transmitted in accordance with Articles 4.1 to 4.3 prior to or on the date of the expiration of the time-limit.

4.6 For the purpose of calculating a period of time, such period shall begin to run on the day following the day when a written communication is received by the addressee. If the last day of such period is an official holiday or non-business day at the place of that addressee (or the place of the party against whom the calculation of time applies), the period shall be extended until the first business day which follows that last day. Official holidays and non-business days occurring during the running of the period of time shall be included in calculating that period.

Article 5 — Formation of Arbitral Tribunal

5.1 The formation of the Arbitral Tribunal by the LCIA Court shall not be impeded by any controversy between the parties relating to the sufficiency of the Request or the Response. The LCIA Court may also proceed with the arbitration notwithstanding that the Request is incomplete or the Response is missing, late or incomplete.

5.2 The expression the "Arbitral Tribunal" includes a sole arbitrator or all the arbitrators where more than one.

5.3 All arbitrators shall be and remain at all times impartial and independent of the parties; and none shall act in the arbitration as advocate for or representative of any party. No arbitrator shall advise any party on the parties' dispute or the outcome of the arbitration.

5.4 Before appointment by the LCIA Court, each arbitral candidate shall furnish to the Registrar (upon the latter's request) a brief written summary of his or her qualifications and professional positions (past and present); the candidate shall also agree in writing fee-rates conforming to the Schedule of Costs; the candidate shall sign a written declaration stating: (i) whether there are any circumstances currently known to the candidate which are likely to give rise in the mind of any party to any justifiable doubts as to his or her impartiality or independence and, if so, specifying in full such circumstances in the declaration; and (ii) whether the candidate is ready, willing and able to devote sufficient time, diligence and industry to ensure the expeditious and efficient conduct of the arbitration. The candidate shall

furnish promptly such agreement and declaration to the Registrar.
5.5 If appointed, each arbitral candidate shall thereby assume a continuing duty as an arbitrator, until the arbitration is finally concluded, forthwith to disclose in writing any circumstances becoming known to that arbitrator after the date of his or her written declaration (under Article 5.4) which are likely to give rise in the mind of any party to any justifiable doubts as to his or her impartiality or independence, to be delivered to the LCIA Court, any other members of the Arbitral Tribunal and all parties in the arbitration.
5.6 The LCIA Court shall appoint the Arbitral Tribunal promptly after receipt by the Registrar of the Response or, if no Response is received, after 35 days from the Commencement Date (or such other lesser or greater period to be determined by the LCIA Court pursuant to Article 22.5).
5.7 No party or third person may appoint any arbitrator under the Arbitration Agreement: the LCIA Court alone is empowered to appoint arbitrators (albeit taking into account any written agreement or joint nomination by the parties).
5.8 A sole arbitrator shall be appointed unless the parties have agreed in writing otherwise or if the LCIA Court determines that in the circumstances a three-member tribunal is appropriate (or, exceptionally, more than three).
5.9 The LCIA Court shall appoint arbitrators with due regard for any particular method or criteria of selection agreed in writing by the parties. The LCIA Court shall also take into account the transaction(s) at sisue, the nature and circumstances of the dispute, its monetary amount or value, the location and languages of the parties, the number of parties and all other factors which it may consider relevant in the circumstances.
5.10 The President of the LCIA Court shall only be eligible to be appointed as an arbitrator if the parties agree in writing to nominate him or her as the sole or presiding arbitrator; and the Vice Presidents of the LCIA Court and the Chairman of the LCIA Board of Directors (the latter being *ex officio* a member of the LCIA Court) shall only be eligible to be appointed as arbitrators if nominated in writing by a party or parties—provided that no such nominee shall have taken or shall take thereafter any part in any function of the LCIA Court or LCIA relating to such arbitration.

Article 6 — Nationality of Arbitrators

6.1 Where the parties are of different nationalities, a sole arbitrator or the presiding arbitrator shall not have the same nationality as any party unless the parties who are not of the same nationality as the arbitral candidate all agree in writing otherwise.
6.2 The nationality of a party shall be understood to include those of its

controlling shareholders or interests.
6.3 A person who is a citizen of two or more States shall be treated as a national of each State; citizens of the European Union shall be treated as nationals of its different Member States and shall not be treated as having the same nationality; a citizen of a State's overseas territory shall be treated as a national of that territory and not of that State; and a legal person incorporated in a State's overseas territory shall be treated as such and not (by such fact alone) as a national of or a legal person incorporated in that State.

Article 7 — Party and Other Nominations

7.1 If the parties have agreed howsoever that any arbitrator is to be appointed by one or more of them or by any third person (other than the LCIA Court), that agreement shall be treated under the Arbitration Agreement as an agreement to nominate an arbitrator for all purposes. Such nominee may only be appointed by the LCIA Court as arbitrator subject to that nominee's compliance with Articles 5.3 to 5.5; and the LCIA Court shall refuse to appoint any nominee if it determines that the nominee is not so compliant or is otherwise unsuitable.
7.2 Where the parties have howsoever agreed that the Claimant or the Respondent or any third person (other than the LCIA Court) is to nominate an arbitrator and such nomination is not made within time or at all (in the Request, Response or otherwise), the LCIA Court may appoint an arbitrator notwithstanding any absent or late nomination.
7.3 In the absence of written agreement between the Parties, no party may unilaterally nominate a sole arbitrator or presiding arbitrator.

Article 8 — Three or More Parties

8.1 Where the Arbitration Agreement entitles each party howsoever to nominate an arbitrator, the parties to the dispute number more than two and such parties have not all agreed in writing that the disputant parties represent collectively two separate "sides" for the formation of the Arbitral Tribunal (as Claimants on one side and Respondents on the other side, each side nominating a single arbitrator), the LCIA Court shall appoint the Arbitral Tribunal without regard to any party's entitlement or nomination.
8.2 In such circumstances, the Arbitration Agreement shall be treated for all purposes as a written agreement by the parties for the nomination and appointment of the Arbitral Tribunal by the LCIA Court alone.

Article 9A — Expedited Formation of Arbitral Tribunal

9.1 In the case of exceptional urgency, any party may apply to the LCIA Court for the expedited formation of the Arbitral Tribunal under Article 5.

9.2 Such an application shall be made to the Registrar in writing (preferably by electronic means), together with a copy of the Request (if made by a Claimant) or a copy of the Response (if made by a Respondent), delivered or notified to all other parties to the arbitration. The application shall set out the specific grounds for exceptional urgency requiring the expedited formation of the Arbitral Tribunal.

9.3 The LCIA Court shall determine the application as expeditiously as possible in the circumstances. If the application is granted, for the purpose of forming the Arbitral Tribunal the LCIA Court may abridge any period of time under the Arbitration Agreement or other agreement of the parties (pursuant to Article 22.5).

Article 9B — Emergency Arbitrator

9.4 Subject always to Article 9.14 below, in the case of emergency at any time prior to the formation or expedited formation of the Arbitral Tribunal (under Articles 5 or 9A), any party may apply to the LCIA Court for the immediate appointment of a temporary sole arbitrator to conduct emergency proceedings pending the formation or expedited formation of the Arbitral Tribunal (the "Emergency Arbitrator").

9.5 Such an application shall be made to the Registrar in writing (preferably by electronic means), together with a copy of the Request (if made by a Claimant) or a copy of the Response (if made by a Respondent), delivered or notified to all other parties to the arbitration. The application shall set out, together with all relevant documentation: (i) the specific grounds for requiring, as an emergency, the appointment of an Emergency Arbitrator; and (ii) the specific claim, with reasons, for emergency relief. The application shall be accompanied by the applicant's written confirmation that the applicant has paid or is paying to the LCIA the Special Fee under Article 9B, without which actual receipt of such payment the application shall be dismissed by the LCIA Court. The Special Fee shall be subject to the terms of the Schedule of Costs. Its amount is prescribed in the Schedule, covering the fees and expenses of the Emergency Arbitrator and the administrative fees and expenses of the LCIA, with additional charges (if any) of the LCIA Court. After the appointment of the Emergency Arbitrator, the amount of the Special Fee payable by the applicant may be increased by the LCIA Court in accordance with the Schedule. Article 24 shall not apply to any Special Fee paid to the LCIA

9.6 The LCIA Court shall determine the application as soon as possible in the circumstances. If the application is granted, an Emergency Arbitrator shall be appointed by the LCIA Court within three days of the Registrar's receipt of the application (or as soon as possible thereafter). Articles 5.1, 5.7, 5.9, 5.10, 6, 9C, 10 and 16.2 (last sentence) shall apply to such appointment. The Emergency Arbitrator shall comply with the requirements of Articles 5.3, 5.4 and (until the emergency proceedings are finally concluded) Article 5.5.

9.7 The Emergency Arbitrator may conduct the emergency proceedings in any manner determined by the Emergency Arbitrator to be appropriate in the circumstances, taking account of the nature of such emergency proceedings, the need to afford to each party, if possible, an opportunity to be consulted on the claim for emergency relief (whether or not it avails itself of such opportunity), the claim and reasons for emergency relief and the parties' further submissions (if any). The Emergency Arbitrator is not required to hold any hearing with the parties (whether in person, by telephone or otherwise) and may decide the claim for emergency relief on available documentation. In the event of a hearing, Articles 16.3, 19.2, 19.3 and 19.4 shall apply.

9.8 The Emergency Arbitrator shall decide the claim for emergency relief as soon as possible, but no later than 14 days following the Emergency Arbitrator's appointment. This deadline may only be extended by the LCIA Court in exceptional circumstances (pursuant to Article 22.5) or by the written agreement of all parties to the emergency proceedings. The Emergency Arbitrator may make any order or award which the Arbitral Tribunal could make under the Arbitration Agreement (excepting Arbitration and Legal Costs under Articles 28.2 and 28.3); and, in addition, make any order adjourning the consideration of all or any part of the claim for emergency relief to the proceedings conducted by the Arbitral Tribunal (when formed).

9.9 An order of the Emergency Arbitrator shall be made in writing, with reasons. An award of the Emergency Arbitrator shall comply with Article 26.2 and, when made, take effect as an award under Article 26.8 (subject to Article 9.11). The Emergency Arbitrator shall be responsible for delivering any order or award to the Registrar, who shall transmit the same promptly to the parties by electronic means, in addition to paper form (if so requested by any party). In the event of any disparity between electronic and paper forms, the electronic form shall prevail.

9.10 The Special Fee paid shall form a part of the Arbitration Costs under Article 28.2 determined by the LCIA Court (as to the amount of Arbitration Costs) and decided by the Arbitral Tribunal (as to the proportions in which the parties shall bear Arbitration Costs). Any legal or other expenses incurred by any party during the emergency proceedings shall form a part of the Legal Costs under Article 28.3 decided by the Arbitral Tribunal (as to amount and as to payment between the parties of Legal Costs).

9.11 Any order or award of the Emergency Arbitrator (apart from any order adjourning to the Arbitral Tribunal, when formed, any part of the claim for emergency relief) may be confirmed, varied, discharged or revoked, in whole or in part, by order or award made by the Arbitral Tribunal upon application by any party or upon its own initiative.

9.12 Article 9B shall not prejudice any party's right to apply to a state court or other legal Authority for any interim or conservatory measures before the formation of the Arbitration Tribunal; and it shall not be treated as an alternative to or substitute for the exercise of such right. During the emergency proceedings, any application to and any order by such court or authority shall be communicated promptly in writing to the Emergency Arbitrator, the Registrar and all other parties.

9.13 Articles 3.3, 13.1-13.4, 14.4, 14.5, 16, 17, 18, 22.3, 22.4, 23, 28, 29, 30, 31 and 32 and the Annex shall apply to emergency proceedings. In addition to the provisions expressly set out there and in Article 9B above, the Emergency Arbitrator and the parties to the emergency proceedings shall also be guided by other provisions of the Arbitration Agreement, whilst recognising that several such provisions may not be fully applicable or appropriate to emergency proceedings. Wherever relevant, the LCIA Court may abridge under any such provisions any period of time (pursuant to Article 22.5).

9.14 Article 9B shall not apply if either: (i) the parties have concluded their arbitration agreement before 1 October 2014 and the parties have not agreed in writing to 'opt in' to Article 9B; or (ii) the parties have agreed in writing at any time to 'opt out' of Article 9B.

Article 9C — Expedited Appointment of Replacement Arbitrator

9.15 Any party may apply to the LCIA Court for the expedited appointment of a replacement arbitrator under Article 11.

9.16 Such an application shall be made in writing to the Registrar (preferably by electronic means), delivered (or notified) to all other parties to the arbitration; and it shall set out the specific grounds requiring the expedited appointment of the replacement arbitrator.

9.17 The LCIA Court shall determine the application as expeditiously as possible in the circumstances. If the application is granted, for the purpose of expediting the appointment of the replacement arbitrator the LCIA Court may abridge any period of time in the Arbitration Agreement or any other agreement of the parties (pursuant to Article 22.5).

Article 10 — Revocation and Challenges

10.1 The LCIA Court may revoke any arbitrator's appointment upon its own initiative, at the written request of all other members of the Arbitral Tribunal or upon a written challenge by any party if: (i) that arbitrator gives written notice to the LCIA Court of his or her intent to resign as arbitrator, to be copied to all parties and all other members of the Arbitral Tribunal (if any); (ii) that arbitrator falls seriously ill, refuses or becomes unable or unfit to act; or (iii) circumstances exist that give rise to justifiable doubts as to that arbitrator's impartiality or independence.

10.2 The LCIA Court may determine that an arbitrator is unfit to act under Article 10.1 if that arbitrator: (i) acts in deliberate violation of the Arbitration Agreement; (ii) does not act fairly or impartially as between the parties; or (iii) does not conduct or participate in the arbitration with reasonable efficiency, diligence and industry.

10.3 A party challenging an arbitrator under Article 10.1 shall, within 14 days of the formation of the Arbitral Tribunal or (if later) within 14 days of becoming aware of any grounds described in Article 10.1 or 10.2, deliver a written statement of the reasons for its challenge to the LCIA Court, the Arbitral Tribunal and all other parties. A party may challenge an arbitrator whom it has nominated, or in whose appointment it has participated, only for reasons of which it becomes aware after the appointment has been made by the LCIA Court.

10.4 The LCIA Court shall provide to those other parties and the challenged arbitrator a reasonable opportunity to comment on the challenging party's written statement. The LCIA Court may require at any time further information and materials from the challenging party, the challenged arbitrator, other parties and other members of the Arbitral Tribunal (if any).

10.5 If all other parties agree in writing to the challenge within 14 days of receipt of the written statement, the LCIA Court shall revoke that arbitrator's appointment (without reasons).

10.6 Unless the parties so agree or the challenged arbitrator resigns in writing within 14 days of receipt of the written statement, the LCIA Court shall decide the challenge and, if upheld, shall revoke that arbitrator's appointment. The LCIA Court's decision shall be made in writing, with reasons; and a copy shall be transmitted by the Registrar to the parties, the challenged arbitrator and other members of the Arbitral Tribunal (if any). A challenged arbitrator who resigns in writing prior to the LCIA Court's decision shall not be considered as having admitted any part of the written statement.

10.7 The LCIA Court shall determine the amount of fees and expenses (if any) to be paid for the former arbitrator's services, as it may consider appropriate in the circumstances. The LCIA Court may also determine whether, in what amount and to whom any party should pay forthwith the costs of the challenge; and the LCIA Court may also refer all or any part of such costs to the later decision of the Arbitral Tribunal and/or the LCIA Court under Article 28.

Article 11 — Nomination and Replacement

11.1 In the event that the LCIA Court determines that justifiable doubts exist as to any arbitral candidate's suitability, independence or impartiality, or if a nominee declines appointment as arbitrator, or if an arbitrator is to be replaced for any reason, the LCIA Court may determine whether or not to follow the original nominating process for such arbitral appointment.

11.2 The LCIA Court may determine that any opportunity given to a party to make any re-nomination (under the Arbitration Agreement or otherwise) shall be waived if not exercised within 14 days (or such lesser or greater time as the LCIA Court may determine), after which the LCIA Court shall appoint the replacement arbitrator without such re-nomination.

Article 12 — Majority Power to Continue Deliberations

12.1 In exceptional circumstances, where an arbitrator without good cause refuses or persistently fails to participate in the deliberations of an Arbitral Tribunal, the remaining arbitrators jointly may decide (after their written notice of such refusal or failure to the LCIA Court, the parties and the absent arbitrator) to continue the arbitration (including the making of any award) notwithstanding the absence of that other arbitrator, subject to the written approval of the LCIA Court.

12.2 In deciding whether to continue the arbitration, the remaining arbitrators shall take into account the stage of the arbitration, any explanation made by or on behalf of the absent arbitrator for his or her refusal or non-participation, the likely effect upon the legal recognition or enforceability of any award at the seat of the arbitration and such other matters as they consider appropriate in the circumstances. The reasons for such decision shall be stated in any award made by the remaining arbitrators without the participation of the absent arbitrator.

12.3 In the event that the remaining arbitrators decide at any time thereafter not to continue the arbitration without the participation of the absent arbitrator, the remaining arbitrators shall notify in writing the parties and the LCIA Court of such decision; and, in that event, the remaining arbitrators or any party may refer the matter to the LCIA Court for the revocation of the absent arbitrator's appointment and the appointment of a replacement arbitrator under Articles 10 and 11.

Article 13 — Communications between Parties and Arbitral Tribunal

13.1 Following the formation of the Arbitral Tribunal, all communications shall take place directly between the Arbitral Tribunal and the parties (to be copied to the Registrar), unless the Arbitral Tribunal decides that communications should continue to be made through the Registrar.

13.2 Where the Registrar sends any written communication to one party on behalf of the Arbitral Tribunal or the LCIA Court, he or she shall send a copy to each of the other parties.

13.3 Where any party delivers to the Arbitral Tribunal any communication (including statements and documents under Article 15), whether by electronic means or otherwise, it shall deliver a copy to each arbitrator, all other parties and the Registrar; and it shall confirm to the Arbitral Tribunal in writing that it has done or is doing so.

13.4 During the arbitration from the Arbitral Tribunal's formation onwards, no party shall deliberately initiate or attempt to initiate any unilateral contact relating to the arbitration or the parties' dispute with any member of the Arbitral Tribunal or any member of the LCIA Court exercising any function in regard to the arbitration (but not including the Registrar), which has not been disclosed in writing prior to or shortly after the time of such contact to all other parties, all members of the Arbitral Tribunal (if comprised of more than one arbitrator) and the Registrar.

13.5 Prior to the Arbitral Tribunal's formation, unless the parties agree otherwise in writing, any arbitrator, candidate or nominee who is required to participate in the selection of a presiding arbitrator may consult any party in order to obtain the views of that party as to the suitability of any candidate or nominee as presiding arbitrator, provided that such arbitrator, candidate or nominee informs the Registrar of such consultation.

Article 14 — Conduct of Proceedings

14.1 The parties and the Arbitral Tribunal are encouraged to make contact (whether by a hearing in person, telephone conference-call, video conference or exchange of correspondence) as soon as practicable but no later than 21 days from receipt of the Registrar's written notification of the formation of the Arbitral Tribunal.

14.2 The parties may agree on joint proposals for the conduct of their arbitration for consideration by the Arbitral Tribunal. They are encouraged to do so in consultation with the Arbitral Tribunal and consistent with the

Arbitral Tribunal's general duties under the Arbitration Agreement.

14.3 Such agreed proposals shall be made by the parties in writing or recorded in writing by the Arbitral Tribunal at the parties' request and with their authority.

14.4 Under the Arbitration Agreement, the Arbitral Tribunal's general duties at all times during the arbitration shall include:

(i) a duty to act fairly and impartially as between all parties, giving each a reasonable opportunity of putting its case and dealing with that of its opponent(s); and

(ii) a duty to adopt procedures suitable to the circumstances of the arbitration, avoiding unnecessary delay and expense, so as to provide a fair, efficient and expeditious means for the final resolution of the parties' dispute.

14.5 The Arbitral Tribunal shall have the widest discretion to discharge these general duties, subject to such mandatory law(s) or rules of law as the Arbitral Tribunal may decide to be applicable; and at all times the parties shall do everything necessary in good faith for the fair, efficient and expeditious conduct of the arbitration, including the Arbitral Tribunal's discharge of its general duties.

14.6 In the case of an Arbitral Tribunal other than a sole arbitrator, the presiding arbitrator, with the prior agreement of its other members and all parties, may make procedural orders alone.

Article 15 — Written Statements

15.1 Unless the parties have agreed or jointly proposed in writing otherwise or the Arbitral Tribunal should decide differently, the written stage of the arbitration and its procedural time-table shall be as set out in this Article 15.

15.2 Within 28 days of receipt of the Registrar's written notification of the Arbitral Tribunal's formation, the Claimant shall deliver to the Arbitral Tribunal and all other parties either: (i) its written election to have its Request treated as its Statement of Case complying with this Article 15.2; or (ii) its written Statement of Case setting out in sufficient detail the relevant facts and legal submissions on which it relies, together with the relief claimed against all other parties, and all essential documents.

15.3 Within 28 days of receipt of the Claimant's Statement of Case or the Claimant's election to treat the Request as its Statement of Case, the Respondent shall deliver to the Arbitral Tribunal and all other parties either: (i) its written election to have its Response treated as its Statement of Defence and (if applicable) Cross-claim complying with this Article 15.3; or (ii) its written Statement of Defence and (if applicable) Statement of

Cross-claim setting out in sufficient detail the relevant facts and legal submissions on which it relies, together with the relief claimed against all other parties, and all essential documents.

15.4 Within 28 days of receipt of the Respondent's Statement of Defence and (if applicable) Statement of Cross-claim or the Respondent's election to treat the Response as its Statement of Defence and (if applicable) Cross-claim, the Claimant shall deliver to the Arbitral Tribunal and all other parties a written Statement of Reply which, where there are any cross-claims, shall also include a Statement of Defence to Cross-claim in the same manner required for a Statement of Defence, together with all essential documents.

15.5 If the Statement of Reply contains a Statement of Defence to Cross-claim, within 28 days of its receipt the Respondent shall deliver to the Arbitral Tribunal and all other parties its written Statement of Reply to the Defence to Cross-claim, together with all essential documents.

15.6 The Arbitral Tribunal may provide additional directions as to any part of the written stage of the arbitration (including witness statements, submissions and evidence), particularly where there are multiple claimants, multiple respondents or any cross-claim between two or more respondents or between two or more claimants.

15.7 No party may submit any further written statement following the last of these Statements, unless otherwise ordered by the Arbitral Tribunal.

15.8 If the Respondent fails to submit a Statement of Defence or the Claimant a Statement of Defence to Cross-claim, or if at any time any party fails to avail itself of the opportunity to present its written case in the manner required under this Article 15 or otherwise by order of the Arbitral Tribunal, the Arbitral Tribunal may nevertheless proceed with the arbitration (with or without a hearing) and make one or more awards.

15.9 As soon as practicable following this written stage of the arbitration, the Arbitral Tribunal shall proceed in such manner as has been agreed in writing by the parties or pursuant to its authority under the Arbitration Agreement.

15.10 In any event, the Arbitral Tribunal shall seek to make its final award as soon as reasonably possible following the last submission from the parties (whether made orally or in writing), in accordance with a timetable notified to the parties and the Registrar as soon as practicable (if necessary, as revised and re-notified from time to time). When the Arbitral Tribunal (not being a sole arbitrator) establishes a time for what it contemplates shall be the last submission from the parties (whether written or oral), it shall set aside adequate time for deliberations as soon as possible after that last submission and notify the parties of the time it has set aside.

Article 16 — Seat(s) of Arbitration and Place(s) of Hearing

16.1 The parties may agree in writing the seat (or legal place) of their arbitration at any time before the formation of the Arbitral Tribunal and, after such formation, with the prior written consent of the Arbitral Tribunal.

16.2 In default of any such agreement, the seat of the arbitration shall be London (England), unless and until the Arbitral Tribunal orders, in view of the circumstances and after having given the parties a reasonable opportunity to make written comments to the Arbitral Tribunal, that another arbitral seat is more appropriate. Such default seat shall not be considered as a relevant circumstance by the LCIA Court in appointing any arbitrators under Articles 5, 9A, 9B, 9C and 11.

16.3 The Arbitral Tribunal may hold any hearing at any convenient geographical place in consultation with the parties and hold its deliberations at any geographical place of its own choice; and if such place(s) should be elsewhere than the seat of the arbitration, the arbitration shall nonetheless be treated for all purposes as an arbitration conducted at the arbitral seat and any order or award as having been made at that seat.

16.4 The law applicable to the Arbitration Agreement and the arbitration shall be the law applicable at the seat of the arbitration, unless and to the extent that the parties have agreed in writing on the application of other laws or rules of law and such agreement is not prohibited by the law applicable at the arbitral seat.

Article 17 — Language(s) of Arbitration

17.1 The initial language of the arbitration (until the formation of the Arbitral Tribunal) shall be the language or prevailing language of the Arbitration Agreement, unless the parties have agreed in writing otherwise.

17.2 In the event that the Arbitration Agreement is written in more than one language of equal standing, the LCIA Court may, unless the Arbitration Agreement provides that the arbitration proceedings shall be conducted from the outset in more than one language, determine which of those languages shall be the initial language of the arbitration.

17.3 A non-participating or defaulting party shall have no cause for complaint if communications to and from the LCIA Court and Registrar are conducted in the initial language(s) of the arbitration or of the arbitral seat.

17.4 Following the formation of the Arbitral Tribunal, unless the parties have agreed upon the language or languages of the arbitration, the Arbitral Tribunal shall decide upon the language(s) of the arbitration after giving the parties a reasonable opportunity to make written comments and taking into account the initial language(s) of the arbitration and any other matter it may consider appropriate in the circumstances.

17.5 If any document is expressed in a language other than the language(s) of the arbitration and no translation of such document is submitted by the party relying upon the document, the Arbitral Tribunal may order or (if the Arbitral Tribunal has not been formed) the Registrar may request that party to submit a translation of all or any part of that document in any language(s) of the arbitration or of the arbitral seat.

Article 18 — Legal Representatives

18.1 Any party may be represented in the arbitration by one or more authorised legal representatives appearing by name before the Arbitral Tribunal.

18.2 Until the Arbitral Tribunal's formation, the Registrar may request from any party: (i) written proof of the authority granted by that party to any legal representative designated in its Request or Response; and (ii) written confirmation of the names and addresses of all such party's legal representatives in the arbitration. After its formation, at any time, the Arbitral Tribunal may order any party to provide similar proof or confirmation in any form it considers appropriate.

18.3 Following the Arbitral Tribunal's formation, any intended change or addition by a party to its legal representatives shall be notified promptly in writing to all other parties, the Arbitral Tribunal and the Registrar; and any such intended change or addition shall only take effect in the arbitration subject to the approval of the Arbitral Tribunal.

18.4 The Arbitral Tribunal may withhold approval of any intended change or addition to a party's legal representatives where such change or addition could compromise the composition of the Arbitral Tribunal or the finality of any award (on the grounds of possible conflict or other like impediment). In deciding whether to grant or withhold such approval, the Arbitral Tribunal shall have regard to the circumstances, including: the general principle that a party may be represented by a legal representative chosen by that party, the stage which the arbitration has reached, the efficiency resulting from maintaining the composition of the Arbitral Tribunal (as constituted throughout the arbitration) and any likely wasted costs or loss of time resulting from such change or addition.

18.5 Each party shall ensure that all its legal representatives appearing by name before the Arbitral Tribunal have agreed to comply with the general guidelines contained in the Annex to the LCIA Rules, as a condition of such representation. In permitting any legal representative so to appear, a party shall thereby represent that the legal representative has agreed to such compliance.

18.6 In the event of a complaint by one party against another party's legal representative appearing by name before the Arbitral Tribunal (or of such complaint by the Arbitral Tribunal upon its own initiative), the Arbitral Tribunal may decide, after consulting the parties and granting that legal representative a reasonable opportunity to answer the complaint, whether or not the legal representative has violated the general guidelines. If such violation is found by the Arbitral Tribunal, the Arbitral Tribunal may order any or all of the following sanctions against the legal representative: (i) a written reprimand; (ii) a written caution as to future conduct in the arbitration; and (iii) any other measure necessary to fulfil within the arbitration the general duties required of the Arbitral Tribunal under Articles 14.4(i) and (ii).

Article 19 — Oral Hearing(s)

19.1 Any party has the right to a hearing before the Arbitral Tribunal on the parties' dispute at any appropriate stage of the arbitration (as decided by the Arbitral Tribunal), unless the parties have agreed in writing upon a documents-only arbitration. For this purpose, a hearing may consist of several part-hearings (as decided by the Arbitral Tribunal).

19.2 The Arbitral Tribunal shall organise the conduct of any hearing in advance, in consultation with the parties. The Arbitral Tribunal shall have the fullest authority under the Arbitration Agreement to establish the conduct of a hearing, including its date, form, content, procedure, time-limits and geographical place. As to form, a hearing may take place by video or telephone conference or in person (or a combination of all three). As to content, the Arbitral Tribunal may require the parties to address a list of specific questions or issues arising from the parties' dispute.

19.3 The Arbitral Tribunal shall give to the parties reasonable notice in writing of any hearing.

19.4 All hearings shall be held in private, unless the parties agree otherwise in writing.

Article 20 — Witness(es)

20.1 Before any hearing, the Arbitral Tribunal may order any party to give written notice of the identity of each witness that party wishes to call (including rebuttal witnesses), as well as the subject-matter of that witness's testimony, its content and its relevance to the issues in the arbitration.

20.2 Subject to any order otherwise by the Arbitral Tribunal, the testimony of a witness may be presented by a party in written form, either as a signed statement or like document.

20.3 The Arbitral Tribunal may decide the time, manner and form in which these written materials shall be exchanged between the parties and presented to the Arbitral Tribunal; and it may allow, refuse or limit the written and oral testimony of witnesses (whether witnesses of fact or expert witnesses).

20.4 The Arbitral Tribunal and any party may request that a witness, on whose written testimony another party relies, should attend for oral questioning at a hearing before the Arbitral Tribunal. If the Arbitral Tribunal orders that other party to secure the attendance of that witness and the witness refuses or fails to attend the hearing without good cause, the Arbitral Tribunal may place such weight on the written testimony or exclude all or any part thereof altogether as it considers appropriate in the circumstances.

20.5 Subject to the mandatory provisions of any applicable law, rules of law and any order of the Arbitral Tribunal otherwise, it shall not be improper for any party or its legal representatives to interview any potential witness for the purpose of presenting his or her testimony in written form to the Arbitral Tribunal or producing such person as an oral witness at any hearing.

20.6 Subject to any order by the Arbitral Tribunal otherwise, any individual intending to testify to the Arbitral Tribunal may be treated as a witness notwithstanding that the individual is a party to the arbitration or was, remains or has become an officer, employee, owner or shareholder of any party or is otherwise identified with any party.

20.7 Subject to the mandatory provisions of any applicable law, the Arbitral Tribunal shall be entitled (but not required) to administer any appropriate oath to any witness at any hearing, prior to the oral testimony of that witness.

20.8 Any witness who gives oral testimony at a hearing before the Arbitral Tribunal may be questioned by each of the parties under the control of the Arbitral Tribunal. The Arbitral Tribunal may put questions at any stage of such testimony.

Article 21 — Expert(s) to Arbitral Tribunal

21.1 The Arbitral Tribunal, after consultation with the parties, may appoint one or more experts to report in writing to the Arbitral Tribunal and the parties on specific issues in the arbitration, as identified by the Arbitral Tribunal.

21.2 Any such expert shall be and remain impartial and independent of the parties; and he or she shall sign a written declaration to such effect, delivered to the Arbitral Tribunal and copied to all parties.

21.3 The Arbitral Tribunal may require any party at any time to give to such expert any relevant information or to provide access to any relevant documents, goods, samples, property, site or thing for inspection under that party's control on such terms as the Arbitral Tribunal thinks appropriate in the circumstances.

21.4 If any party so requests or the Arbitral Tribunal considers it necessary, the Arbitral Tribunal may order the expert, after delivery of the expert's written report, to participate in a hearing at which the parties shall have a reasonable opportunity to question the expert on the report and to present witnesses in order to testify on relevant issues arising from the report.

21.5 The fees and expenses of any expert appointed by the Arbitral Tribunal under this Article 21 may be paid out of the deposits payable by the parties under Article 24 and shall form part of the Arbitration Costs under Article 28.

Article 22 — Additional Powers

22.1 The Arbitral Tribunal shall have the power, upon the application of any party or (save for sub-paragraphs (viii), (ix) and (x) below) upon its own initiative, but in either case only after giving the parties a reasonable opportunity to state their views and upon such terms (as to costs and otherwise) as the Arbitral Tribunal may decide:

(i) to allow a party to supplement, modify or amend any claim, defence, cross-claim, defence to cross-claim and reply, including a Request, Response and any other written statement, submitted by such party;

(ii) to abridge or extend (even where the period of time has expired) any period of time prescribed under the Arbitration Agreement, any other agreement of the parties or any order made by the Arbitral Tribunal;

(iii) to conduct such enquiries as may appear to the Arbitral Tribunal to be necessary or expedient, including whether and to what extent the Arbitral Tribunal should itself take the initiative in identifying relevant issues and ascertaining relevant facts and the law(s) or rules of law applicable to the Arbitration Agreement, the arbitration and the merits of the parties' dispute;

(iv) to order any party to make any documents, goods, samples, property, site or thing under its control available for inspection by the Arbitral Tribunal, any other party, any expert to such party and any expert to the Tribunal;

(v) to order any party to produce to the Arbitral Tribunal and to other parties documents or copies of documents in their possession, custody or power

which the Arbitral Tribunal decides to be relevant;
(vi) to decide whether or not to apply any strict rules of evidence (or any other rules) as to the admissibility, relevance or weight of any material tendered by a party on any issue of fact or expert opinion; and to decide the time, manner and form in which such material should be exchanged between the parties and presented to the Arbitral Tribunal;
(vii) to order compliance with any legal obligation, payment of compensation for breach of any legal obligation and specific performance of any agreement (including any arbitration agreement or any contract relating to land);
(viii) to allow one or more third persons to be joined in the arbitration as a party provided any such third person and the applicant party have consented to such joinder in writing following the Commencement Date or (if earlier) in the Arbitration Agreement; and 18 thereafter to make a single final award, or separate awards, in respect of all parties so implicated in the arbitration;
(ix) to order, with the approval of the LCIA Court, the consolidation of the arbitration with one or more other arbitrations into a single arbitration subject to the LCIA Rules where all the parties to the arbitrations to be consolidated so agree in writing;
(x) to order, with the approval of the LCIA Court, the consolidation of the arbitration with one or more other arbitrations subject to the LCIA Rules commenced under the same arbitration agreement or any compatible arbitration agreement(s) between the same disputing parties, provided that no arbitral tribunal has yet been formed by the LCIA Court for such other arbitration(s) or, if already formed, that such tribunal(s) is(are) composed of the same arbitrators; and
(xi) to order the discontinuance of the arbitration if it appears to the Arbitral Tribunal that the arbitration has been abandoned by the parties or all claims and any cross-claims withdrawn by the parties, provided that, after fixing a reasonable period of time within which the parties shall be invited to agree or to object to such discontinuance, no party has stated its written objection to the Arbitral Tribunal to such discontinuance upon the expiry of such period of time.
22.2 By agreeing to arbitration under the Arbitration Agreement, the parties shall be treated as having agreed not to apply to any state court or other legal authority for any order available from the Arbitral Tribunal (if formed) under Article 22.1, except with the agreement in writing of all parties.
22.3 The Arbitral Tribunal shall decide the parties' dispute in accordance

with the law(s) or rules of law chosen by the parties as applicable to the merits of their dispute. If and to the extent that the Arbitral Tribunal decides that the parties have made no such choice, the Arbitral Tribunal shall apply the law(s) or rules of law which it considers appropriate.

22.4 The Arbitral Tribunal shall only apply to the merits of the dispute principles deriving from "*ex aequo et bono*", "*amiable composition*" or "honourable engagement" where the parties have so agreed in writing.

22.5 Subject to any order of the Arbitral Tribunal under Article 22.1(ii), the LCIA Court may also abridge or extend any period of time under the Arbitration Agreement or other agreement of the parties (even where the period of time has expired).

22.6 Without prejudice to the generality of Articles 22.1(ix) and (x), the LCIA Court may determine, after giving the parties a reasonable opportunity to state their views, that two or more arbitrations, subject to the LCIA Rules and commenced under the same arbitration agreement between the same disputing parties, shall be consolidated to form one single arbitration subject to the LCIA Rules, provided that no arbitral tribunal has yet been formed by the LCIA Court for any of the arbitrations to be consolidated.

Article 23 — Jurisdiction and Authority

23.1 The Arbitral Tribunal shall have the power to rule upon its own jurisdiction and authority, including any objection to the initial or continuing existence, validity, effectiveness or scope of the Arbitration Agreement.

23.2 For that purpose, an arbitration clause which forms or was intended to form part of another agreement shall be treated as an arbitration agreement independent of that other agreement. A decision by the Arbitral Tribunal that such other agreement is non-existent, invalid or ineffective shall not entail (of itself) the non-existence, invalidity or ineffectiveness of the arbitration clause.

23.3 An objection by a Respondent that the Arbitral Tribunal does not have jurisdiction shall be raised as soon as possible but not later than the time for its Statement of Defence; and a like objection by any party responding to a cross-claiming party shall be raised as soon as possible but not later than thetime for its Statement of Defence to Cross-claim. An objection that the Arbitral Tribunal is exceeding the scope of its authority shall be raised promptly after the Arbitral Tribunal has indicated its intention to act upon the matter alleged to lie beyond its authority. The Arbitral Tribunal may nevertheless admit an untimely objection as to its jurisdiction or authority if

it considers the delay justified in the circumstances.
23.4 The Arbitral Tribunal may decide the objection to its jurisdiction or authority in an award as to jurisdiction or authority or later in an award on the merits, as it considers appropriate in the circumstances.
23.5 By agreeing to arbitration under the Arbitration Agreement, after the formation of the Arbitral Tribunal the parties shall be treated as having agreed not to apply to any state court or other legal authority for any relief regarding the Arbitral Tribunal's jurisdiction or authority, except (i) with the prior agreement in writing of all parties to the arbitration, or (ii) the prior authorisation of the Arbitral Tribunal, or (iii) following the latter's award on the objection to its jurisdiction or authority.
Article 24 — Deposits
24.1 The LCIA Court may direct the parties, in such proportions and at such times as it thinks appropriate, to make one or more payments to the LCIA on account of the Arbitration Costs. Such payments deposited by the parties may be applied by the LCIA Court to pay any item of such Arbitration Costs (including the LCIA's own fees and expenses) in accordance with the LCIA Rules.
24.2 All payments made by parties on account of the Arbitration Costs shall be held by the LCIA in trust under English law in England, to be disbursed or otherwise applied by the LCIA in accordance with the LCIA Rules and invested having regard also to the interests of the LCIA. Each payment made by a party shall be credited by the LCIA with interest at the rate from time to time credited to an overnight deposit of that amount with the bank(s) engaged by the LCIA to manage deposits from time to time; and any surplus income (beyond such interest) shall accrue for the sole benefit of the LCIA. In the event that payments (with such interest) exceed the total amount of the Arbitration Costs at the conclusion of the arbitration, the excess amount shall be returned by the LCIA to the parties as the ultimate default beneficiaries of the trust.
24.3 Save for exceptional circumstances, the Arbitral Tribunal should not proceed with the arbitration without having ascertained from the Registrar that the LCIA is or will be in requisite funds as regards outstanding and future Arbitration Costs.
24.4 In the event that a party fails or refuses to make any payment on account of the Arbitration Costs as directed by the LCIA Court, the LCIA Court may direct the other party or parties to effect a substitute payment to allow the arbitration to proceed (subject to any order or award on Arbitration Costs).

24.5 In such circumstances, the party effecting the substitute payment may request the Arbitral Tribunal to make an order or award in order to recover that amount as a debt immediately due and payable to that party by the defaulting party, together with any interest.

24.6 Failure by a claiming or cross-claiming party to make promptly and in full any required payment on account of Arbitration Costs may be treated by the Arbitral Tribunal as a withdrawal from the arbitration of the claim or cross-claim respectively, thereby removing such claim or cross-claim (as the case may be) from the scope of the Arbitral Tribunal's jurisdiction under the Arbitration Agreement, subject to any terms decided by the Arbitral Tribunal as to the reinstatement of the claim or cross-claim in the event of subsequent payment by the claiming or cross-claiming party. Such a withdrawal shall not preclude the claiming or cross-claiming party from defending as a respondent any claim or cross-claim made by another party.

Article 25 — Interim and Conservatory Measures

25.1 The Arbitral Tribunal shall have the power upon the application of any party, after giving all other parties a reasonable opportunity to respond to such application and upon such terms as the Arbitral Tribunal considers appropriate in the circumstances:

(i) to order any respondent party to a claim or cross-claim to provide security for all or part of the amount in dispute, by way of deposit or bank guarantee or in any other manner;

(ii) to order the preservation, storage, sale or other disposal of any documents, goods, samples, property, site or thing under the control of any party and relating to the subject-matter of the arbitration; and

(iii) to order on a provisional basis, subject to a final decision in an award, any relief which the Arbitral Tribunal would have power to grant in an award, including the payment of money or the disposition of property as between any parties.

Such terms may include the provision by the applicant party of a cross-indemnity, secured in such manner as the Arbitral Tribunal considers appropriate, for any costs or losses incurred by the respondent party in complying with the Arbitral Tribunal's order. Any amount payable under such cross-indemnity and any consequential relief may be decided by the Arbitral Tribunal by one or more awards in the arbitration.

25.2 The Arbitral Tribunal shall have the power upon the application of a party, after giving all other parties a reasonable opportunity to respond to such application, to order any claiming or cross-claiming party to provide or procure security for Legal Costs and Arbitration Costs by way of deposit or bank guarantee or in any other manner and upon such terms as the Arbitral Tribunal considers appropriate in the circumstances. Such terms may include the provision by that other party of a cross-indemnity, itself secured in such manner as the Arbitral Tribunal considers appropriate, for any costs and losses incurred by such claimant or cross-claimant in complying with the Arbitral Tribunal's order. Any amount payable under such cross-indemnity and any consequential relief may be decided by the Arbitral Tribunal by one or more awards in the arbitration. In the event that a claiming or cross-claiming party does not comply with any order to provide security, the Arbitral Tribunal may stay that party's claims or cross-claims or dismiss them by an award.

25.3 The power of the Arbitral Tribunal under Article 25.1 shall not prejudice any party's right to apply to a state court or other legal authority for interim or conservatory measures to similar effect: (i) before the formation of the Arbitral Tribunal; and (ii) after the formation of the Arbitral Tribunal, in exceptional cases and with the Arbitral Tribunal's authorisation, until the final award. After the Commencement Date, any application and any order for such measures before the formation of the Arbitral Tribunal shall be communicated promptly in writing by the applicant party to the Registrar; after its formation, also to the Arbitral Tribunal; and in both cases also to all other parties.

25.4. By agreeing to arbitration under the Arbitration Agreement, the parties shall be taken to have agreed not to apply to any state court or other legal authority for any order for security for Legal Costs or Arbitration Costs.

Article 26 — Award(s)

26.1 The Arbitral Tribunal may make separate awards on different issues at different times, including interim payments on account of any claim or cross -claim (including Legal and Arbitration Costs). Such awards shall have the same status as any other award made by the Arbitral Tribunal.

26.2 The Arbitral Tribunal shall make any award in writing and, unless all parties agree in writing otherwise, shall state the reasons upon which such award is based. The award shall also state the date when the award is made and the seat of the arbitration; and it shall be signed by the Arbitral Tribunal or those of its members assenting to it.

26.3 An award may be expressed in any currency, unless the parties have agreed otherwise.

26.4 Unless the parties have agreed otherwise, the Arbitral Tribunal may order that simple or compound interest shall be paid by any party on any sum awarded at such rates as the Arbitral Tribunal decides to be appropriate (without being bound by rates of interest practised by any state court or other legal authority) in respect of any period which the Arbitral Tribunal decides to be appropriate ending not later than the date upon which the award is complied with.

26.5 Where there is more than one arbitrator and the Arbitral Tribunal fails to agree on any issue, the arbitrators shall decide that issue by a majority. Failing a majority decision on any issue, the presiding arbitrator shall decide that issue.

26.6 If any arbitrator refuses or fails to sign the award, the signatures of the majority or (failing a majority) of the presiding arbitrator shall be sufficient, provided that the reason for the omitted signature is stated in the award by the majority or by the presiding arbitrator.

26.7 The sole or presiding arbitrator shall be responsible for delivering the award to the LCIA Court, which shall transmit to the parties the award authenticated by the Registrar as an LCIA award, provided that all Arbitration Costs have been paid in full to the LCIA in accordance with Articles 24 and 28. Such transmission may be made by any electronic means, in addition to paper form (if so requested by any party). In the event of any disparity between electronic and paper forms, the paper form shall prevail.

26.8 Every award (including reasons for such award) shall be final and binding on the parties. The parties undertake to carry out any award immediately and without any delay (subject only to Article 27); and the parties also waive irrevocably their right to any form of appeal, review or recourse to any state court or other legal authority, insofar as such waiver shall not be prohibited under any applicable law.

26.9 In the event of any final settlement of the parties' dispute, the Arbitral Tribunal may decide to make an award recording the settlement if the parties jointly so request in writing (a "Consent Award"), provided always that such Consent Award shall contain an express statement on its face that it is an award made at the parties' joint request and with their consent. A Consent Award need not contain reasons. If the parties do not jointly request a Consent Award, on written confirmation by the parties to the LCIA Court that a final settlement has been reached, the Arbitral Tribunal shall be discharged and the arbitration proceedings concluded by the LCIA Court, subject to payment by the parties of any outstanding Arbitration Costs in accordance with Articles 24 and 28.

Article 27 — Correction of Award(s) and Additional Award(s)

27.1 Within 28 days of receipt of any award, a party may by written notice to the Registrar (copied to all other parties) request the Arbitral Tribunal to correct in the award any error in computation, any clerical or typographical error, any ambiguity or any mistake of a similar nature. If the Arbitral Tribunal considers the request to be justified, after consulting the parties, it shall make the correction within 28 days of receipt of the request. Any correction shall take the form of a memorandum by the Arbitral Tribunal.

27.2 The Arbitral Tribunal may also correct any error (including any error in computation, any clerical or typographical error or any error of a similar nature) upon its own initiative in the form of a memorandum within 28 days of the date of the award, after consulting the parties.

27.3 Within 28 days of receipt of the final award, a party may by written notice to the Registrar (copied to all other parties), request the Arbitral Tribunal to make an additional award as to any claim or cross-claim presented in the arbitration but not decided in any award. If the Arbitral Tribunal considers the request to be justified, after consulting the parties, it shall make the additional award within 56 days of receipt of the request.

27.4 As to any claim or cross-claim presented in the arbitration but not decided in any award, the Arbitral Tribunal may also make an additional award upon its own initiative within 28 days of the date of the award, after consulting the parties.

27.5 The provisions of Article 26.2 to 26.7 shall apply to any memorandum or additional award made hereunder. A memorandum shall be treated as part of the award.

Article 28 — Arbitration Costs and Legal Costs

28.1 The costs of the arbitration other than the legal or other expenses incurred by the parties themselves (the "Arbitration Costs") shall be determined by the LCIA Court in accordance with the Schedule of Costs. The parties shall be jointly and severally liable to the LCIA and the Arbitral Tribunal for such Arbitration Costs.

28.2 The Arbitral Tribunal shall specify by an award the amount of the Arbitration Costs determined by the LCIA Court (in the absence of a final settlement of the parties' dispute regarding liability for such costs). The Arbitral Tribunal shall decide the proportions in which the parties shall bear such Arbitration Costs. If the Arbitral Tribunal has decided that all or any part of the Arbitration Costs shall be borne by a party other than a party which has already covered such costs by way of a payment to the LCIA under Article 24, the latter party shall have the right to recover the appropriate amount of Arbitration Costs from the former party.

28.3 The Arbitral Tribunal shall also have the power to decide by an award that all or part of the legal or other expenses incurred by a party (the "Legal Costs") be paid by another party. The Arbitral Tribunal shall decide the amount of such Legal Costs on such reasonable basis as it thinks appropriate. The Arbitral Tribunal shall not be required to apply the rates or procedures for assessing such costs practised by any state court or other legal authority.

28.4 The Arbitral Tribunal shall make its decisions on both Arbitration Costs and Legal Costs on the general principle that costs should reflect the parties' relative success and failure in the award or arbitration or under different issues, except where it appears to the Arbitral Tribunal that in the circumstances the application of such a general principle would be inappropriate under the Arbitration Agreement or otherwise. The Arbitral Tribunal may also take into account the parties' conduct in the arbitration, including any co-operation in facilitating the proceedings as to time and cost and any non-co-operation resulting in undue delay and unnecessary expense. Any decision on costs by the Arbitral Tribunal shall be made with reasons in the award containing such decision.

28.5 In the event that the parties have howsoever agreed before their dispute that one or more parties shall pay the whole or any part of the Arbitration Costs or Legal Costs whatever the result of any dispute, arbitration or award, such agreement (in order to be effective) shall be confirmed by the parties in writing after the Commencement Date.

28.6 If the arbitration is abandoned, suspended, withdrawn or concluded, by agreement or otherwise, before the final award is made, the parties shall remain jointly and severally liable to pay to the LCIA and the Arbitral Tribunal the Arbitration Costs determined by the LCIA Court.

28.7 In the event that the Arbitration Costs are less than the deposits received by the LCIA under Article 24, there shall be a refund by the LCIA to the parties in such proportions as the parties may agree in writing, or failing such agreement, in the same proportions and to the same payers as the deposits were paid to the LCIA.

Article 29 — Determinations and Decisions by LCIA Court

29.1 The determinations of the LCIA Court with respect to all matters relating to the arbitration shall be conclusive and binding upon the parties and the Arbitral Tribunal, unless otherwise directed 24 by the LCIA Court. Save for reasoned decisions on arbitral challenges under Article 10, such determinations are to be treated as administrative in nature; and the LCIA Court shall not be required to give reasons for any such determination.

29.2 To the extent permitted by any applicable law, the parties shall be taken to have waived any right of appeal or review in respect of any determination and decision of the LCIA Court to any state court or other legal authority. If such appeal or review takes place due to mandatory provisions of any applicable law or otherwise, the LCIA Court may determine whether or not the arbitration should continue, notwithstanding such appeal or review.

Article 30 — Confidentiality

30.1 The parties undertake as a general principle to keep confidential all awards in the arbitration, together with all materials in the arbitration created for the purpose of the arbitration and all other documents produced by another party in the proceedings not otherwise in the public domain, save and to the extent that disclosure may be required of a party by legal duty, to protect or pursue a legal right, or to enforce or challenge an award in legal proceedings before a state court or other legal authority.

30.2 The deliberations of the Arbitral Tribunal shall remain confidential to its members, save as required by any applicable law and to the extent that disclosure of an arbitrator's refusal to participate in the arbitration is required of the other members of the Arbitral Tribunal under Articles 10, 12, 26 and 27.

30.3 The LCIA does not publish any award or any part of an award without the prior written consent of all parties and the Arbitral Tribunal.

Article 31 — Limitation of Liability

31.1 None of the LCIA (including its officers, members and employees), the LCIA Court (including its President, Vice-Presidents, Honourary Vice-Presidents and members), the Registrar (including any deputy Registrar), any arbitrator, any Emergency Arbitrator and any expert to the Arbitral Tribunal shall be liable to any party howsoever for any act or omission in connection with any arbitration, save: (i) where the act or omission is shown by that party to constitute conscious and deliberate wrongdoing committed by the body or person alleged to be liable to that party; or (ii) to the extent that any part of this provision is shown to be prohibited by any applicable law.

31.2 After the award has been made and all possibilities of any memorandum or additional award under Article 27 have lapsed or been exhausted, neither the LCIA (including its officers, members and employees), the LCIA Court (including its President, Vice-Presidents, Honourary Vice-Presidents and members), the Registrar (including any deputy Registrar), any arbitrator, any Emergency Arbitrator or any expert to the Arbitral Tribunal shall be under any legal obligation to make any statement to any person about any matter concerning the arbitration; nor shall any party seek to make any of these bodies or persons a witness in any legal or other proceedings arising out of the arbitration.

Article 32 — General Rules

32.1 A party who knows that any provision of the Arbitration Agreement has not been complied with and yet proceeds with the arbitration without promptly stating its objection as to such non-compliance to the Registrar (before the formation of the Arbitral Tribunal) or the Arbitral Tribunal (after its formation), shall be treated as having irrevocably waived its right to object for all purposes.

32.2 For all matters not expressly provided in the Arbitration Agreement, the LCIA Court, the LCIA, the Registrar, the Arbitral Tribunal and each of the parties shall act at all times in good faith, respecting the spirit of the Arbitration Agreement, and shall make every reasonable effort to ensure that any award is legally recognised and enforceable at the arbitral seat.

32.3 If and to the extent that any part of the Arbitration Agreement is decided by the Arbitral Tribunal, the Emergency Arbitrator, or any court or other legal authority of competent jurisdiction to be invalid, ineffective or unenforceable, such decision shall not, of itself, adversely affect any order or award by the Arbitral Tribunal or the Emergency Arbitrator or any other part of the Arbitration Agreement which shall remain in full force and effect, unless prohibited by any applicable law.

Index (in alphabetical order)

Arbitral Tribunal:	see Article 5.2;
Arbitration Agreement:	see Preamble;
Arbitration Costs:	see Article 28.1;
Claimant:	see Articles 1.1 & 1.5;
Commencement Date:	see Article 1.4;
Consent Award:	see Article 26.9;
Cross-claim:	see Article 2.1(iii);
Emergency Arbitrator:	see Articles 5.2 & 9.4;
LCIA Court:	see Article 3.1;
LCIA Rules:	See Preamble;
Legal Costs:	see Article 28.3;
Legal Representatives:	see Articles 1.1(i); 2.1(i), 18.1, 18.3 & 18.4;
Registrar:	see Articles 1.1 & 3.2;
Request:	see Article 1.1;
Respondent:	see Articles 1.1(iii) & 2.5;
Response:	see Article 2.1;
Special Fee:	see Article 9.5;
Statement of Case:	see Article 15.2;
Statement of Defence:	see Article 15.3;
Statement of Cross-claim:	see Article 15.3;
Statement of Defence to Cross-claim:	see Article 15.4; and
Statement of Reply:	see Article 15.4.

ANNEX TO THE LCIA RULES

General Guidelines for the Parties' Legal Representatives

(Articles 18.5 and 18.6 of the LCIA Rules)

Paragraph 1: These general guidelines are intended to promote the good and equal conduct of the parties' legal representatives appearing by name within the arbitration. Nothing in these guidelines is intended to derogate from the Arbitration Agreement or to undermine any legal representative's primary duty of loyalty to the party represented in the arbitration or the obligation to present that party's case effectively to the Arbitral Tribunal. Nor shall these guidelines derogate from any mandatory laws, rules of law, professional rules or codes of conduct if and to the extent that any are shown to apply to a legal representative appearing in the arbitration.

Paragraph 2: A legal representative should not engage in activities intended unfairly to obstruct the arbitration or to jeopardise the finality of any award, including repeated challenges to an arbitrator's appointment or to the jurisdiction or authority of the Arbitral Tribunal known to be unfounded by that legal representative.

Paragraph 3: A legal representative should not knowingly make any false statement to the Arbitral Tribunal or the LCIA Court.

Paragraph 4: A legal representative should not knowingly procure or assist in the preparation of or rely upon any false evidence presented to the Arbitral Tribunal or the LCIA Court.

Paragraph 5: A legal representative should not knowingly conceal or assist in the concealment of any document (or any part thereof) which is ordered to be produced by the Arbitral Tribunal.

Paragraph 6: During the arbitration proceedings, a legal representative should not deliberately initiate or attempt to initiate with any member of the Arbitral Tribunal or with any member of the LCIA Court making any determination or decision in regard to the arbitration (but not including the Registrar) any unilateral contact relating to the arbitration or the parties' dispute, which has not been disclosed in writing prior to or shortly after the time of such contact to all other parties, all members of the Arbitral Tribunal (if comprised of more than one arbitrator) and the Registrar in accordance with Article 13.4.

Paragraph 7: In accordance with Articles 18.5 and 18.6, the Arbitral Tribunal may decide whether a legal representative has violated these general guidelines and, if so, how to exercise its discretion to impose any or all of the sanctions listed in Article 18.6.

SINGAPORE INTERNATIONAL ARBITRATION ACT (CHAPTER 143A) *

Part I
Preliminary

1 — Short Title

This Act may be cited as the International Arbitration Act.

Part II
International Commercial Arbitration

2 — Interpretation of Part II

(1) In this Part, unless the context otherwise requires

arbitral tribunal	means a sole arbitrator or a panel of arbitrators or a permanent arbitral institution, and includes an emergency arbitrator appointed pursuant to the rules of arbitration agreed to or adopted by the parties including the rules of arbitration of an institution or organisation;
appointing authority	means the authority designated under section 8(2) or (3);
arbitration agreement	means an arbitration agreement referred to in section 2A;
award	means a decision of the arbitral tribunal on the substance of the dispute and includes any interim, interlocutory or partial award but excludes any orders or directions made under section 12;
Model Law	means the UNCITRAL Model Law on International Commercial Arbitration adopted by the United Nations Commission on International Trade Law on 21st June 1985, the text in English of which is set out in the First Schedule;
party	means a party to an arbitration agreement or, in any case where an arbitration does not involve all of the parties to the arbitration agreement, means a party to the arbitration.

(2) Except so far as the contrary intention appears, a word or expression that is used both in this Part and in the Model Law (whether or not a particular

* For a commentary on the Singapore International Arbitration Act, see Leslie K. H. Chew, *Singapore Arbitration Handbook* (LexisNexis, 2003) and Robert M. Merkin and Johanna Hjalmarsson, *Singapore Arbitration Legislation: Annotated* (Informa, 2009).

meaning is given to it by the Model Law) has, in the Model Law, the same meaning as it has in this Part.
(3) [Deleted by Act 12 of 2012]
(4) [Deleted by Act 12 of 2012]

2A — Definition and Form of Arbitration Agreement

(1) In this Act, "arbitration agreement" means an agreement by the parties to submit to arbitration all or certain disputes which have arisen or which may arise between them in respect of a defined legal relationship, whether contractual or not.
(2) An arbitration agreement may be in the form of an arbitration clause in a contract or in the form of a separate agreement.
(3) An arbitration agreement shall be in writing.
(4) An arbitration agreement is in writing if its content is recorded in any form, whether or not the arbitration agreement or contract has been concluded orally, by conduct or by other means.
(5) The requirement that an arbitration agreement shall be in writing is satisfied by an electronic communication if the information contained therein is accessible so as to be useable for subsequent reference.
(6) Where in any arbitral or legal proceedings, a party asserts the existence of an arbitration agreement in a pleading, statement of case or any other document in circumstances in which the assertion calls for a reply and the assertion is not denied, there shall be deemed to be an effective arbitration agreement as between the parties to the proceedings.
(7) A reference in a contract to any document containing an arbitration clause shall constitute an arbitration agreement in writing if the reference is such as to make that clause part of the contract.
(8) A reference in a bill of lading to a charterparty or other document containing an arbitration clause shall constitute an arbitration agreement in writing if the reference is such as to make that clause part of the bill of lading.
(9) Article 7 of the Model Law shall not apply to this section.
(10) In this section
"data message" means information generated, sent, received or stored by electronic, magnetic, optical or similar means, including, but not limited to, electronic data interchange (EDI), electronic mail, telegram, telex or telecopy;
"electronic communication" means any communication that the parties make by means of data messages.

3 — Model Law to Have Force of Law
(1) Subject to this Act, the Model Law, with the exception of Chapter VIII thereof, shall have the force of law in Singapore.
(2) In the Model Law
"State" means Singapore and any country other than Singapore;
"this State" means Singapore.
4 — Interpretation of Model Law by use of Extrinsic Material
(1) For the purposes of interpreting the Model Law, reference may be made to the documents of
(a) the United Nations Commission on International Trade Law; and
(b) its working group for the preparation of the Model Law, relating to the Model Law.
(2) Subsection (1) shall not affect the application of section 9A of the Interpretation Act (Cap. 1) for the purposes of interpreting this Act.
5 — Application of Part II
(1) This Part and the Model Law shall not apply to an arbitration which is not an international arbitration unless the parties agree in writing that this Part or the Model Law shall apply to that arbitration.
(2) Notwithstanding Article 1(3) of the Model Law, an arbitration is international if
(a) at least one of the parties to an arbitration agreement, at the time of the conclusion of the agreement, has its place of business in any State other than Singapore; or
(b) one of the following places is situated outside the State in which the parties have their places of business:
(i) the place of arbitration if determined in, or pursuant to, the arbitration agreement;
(ii) any place where a substantial part of the obligations of the commercial relationship is to be performed or the place with which the subject-matter of the dispute is most closely connected; or
(c) the parties have expressly agreed that the subject-matter of the arbitration agreement relates to more than one country.
(3) For the purposes of subsection (2)
(a) if a party has more than one place of business, the place of business shall be that which has the closest relationship to the arbitration agreement;
(b) if a party does not have a place of business, a reference to his place of business shall be construed as a reference to his habitual residence.
(4) Notwithstanding any provision to the contrary in the Arbitration Act (Cap. 10), that Act shall not apply to any arbitration to which this Part

applies.

6 — Enforcement of International Arbitration Agreement

(1) Notwithstanding Article 8 of the Model Law, where any party to an arbitration agreement to which this Act applies institutes any proceedings in any court against any other party to the agreement in respect of any matter which is the subject of the agreement, any party to the agreement may, at any time after appearance and before delivering any pleading or taking any other step in the proceedings, apply to that court to stay the proceedings so far as the proceedings relate to that matter.

(2) The court to which an application has been made in accordance with subsection (1) shall make an order, upon such terms or conditions as it may think fit, staying the proceedings so far as the proceedings relate to the matter, unless it is satisfied that the arbitration agreement is null and void, inoperative or incapable of being performed.

(3) Where a court makes an order under subsection (2), the court may, for the purpose of preserving the rights of parties, make such interim or supplementary orders as it may think fit in relation to any property which is the subject of the dispute to which the order under that subsection relates.

(4) Where no party to the proceedings has taken any further step in the proceedings for a period of not less than 2 years after an order staying the proceedings has been made, the court may, on its own motion, make an order discontinuing the proceedings without prejudice to the right of any of the parties to apply for the discontinued proceedings to be reinstated.

(5) For the purposes of this section and sections 7 and 11A

(a) a reference to a party shall include a reference to any person claiming through or under such party;

(b) "court" means the High Court, District Court, Magistrate's Court or any other court in which proceedings are instituted.

7 — Court's Powers on Stay of Proceedings

(1) Where a court stays proceedings under section 6, the court may, if in those proceedings property has been arrested or bail or other security has been given to prevent or obtain release from arrest, order

(a) that the property arrested be retained as security for the satisfaction of any award made on the arbitration; or

(b) that the stay be conditional on the provision of equivalent security for the satisfaction of any such award.

(2) Subject to Rules of Court and to any necessary modification, the same law and practice shall apply in relation to property retained in pursuance of an order under this section as would apply if it were held for the purposes of

proceedings in the court which made the order.

8 — Authorities Specified for Purposes of Article 6 of Model Law

(1) The High Court in Singapore shall be taken to have been specified in Article 6 of the Model Law as courts competent to perform the functions referred to in that Article except for Article 11(3) and (4) of the Model Law.

(2) The Chairman of the Singapore International Arbitration Centre shall be taken to have been specified as the authority competent to perform the functions under Article 11(3) and (4) of the Model Law.

(3) The Chief Justice may, if he thinks fit, by notification published in the Gazette, appoint any other person to exercise the powers of the Chairman of the Singapore International Arbitration Centre under subsection (2).

8A — Application of Limitation Act and Foreign Limitation Periods Act 2012

(1) The Limitation Act (Cap. 163) and the Foreign Limitation Periods Act 2012 shall apply to arbitral proceedings as they apply to proceedings before any court and any reference in both Acts to the commencement of proceedings shall be construed as a reference to the commencement of arbitral proceedings.

(2) The High Court may order that in computing the time prescribed by the Limitation Act or the Foreign Limitation Periods Act 2012 for the commencement of proceedings (including arbitral proceedings) in respect of a dispute which was the subject-matter of

(a) an award which the High Court orders to be set aside or declares to be of no effect; or

(b) the affected part of an award which the High Court orders to be set aside in part or declares to be in part of no effect,

the period between the commencement of the arbitration and the date of the order referred to in paragraph (a) or (b) shall be excluded.

(3) Notwithstanding any term in an arbitration agreement to the effect that no cause of action shall accrue in respect of any matter required by the agreement to be referred until an award is made under the agreement, the cause of action shall, for the purposes of the Limitation Act and the Foreign Limitation Periods Act 2012, be deemed to have accrued in respect of any such matter at the time when it would have accrued but for that term in the agreement.

9 — Number of Arbitrators for Purposes of Article 10 (2) of Model Law

Notwithstanding Article 10(2) of the Model Law, if the number of arbitrators is not determined by the parties, there shall be a single arbitrator.

9A — Default Appointment of Arbitrators

(1) Notwithstanding Article 11(3) of the Model Law, in an arbitration with 3 arbitrators, each party shall appoint one arbitrator, and the parties shall by agreement appoint the third arbitrator.

(2) Where the parties fail to agree on the appointment of the third arbitrator within 30 days of the receipt of the first request by either party to do so, the appointment shall be made, upon the request of a party, by the appointing authority.

10 — Appeal on Ruling of Jurisdiction

(1) This section shall have effect notwithstanding Article 16(3) of the Model Law.

(2) An arbitral tribunal may rule on a plea that it has no jurisdiction at any stage of the arbitral proceedings.

(3) If the arbitral tribunal rules

(a) on a plea as a preliminary question that it has jurisdiction; or

(b) on a plea at any stage of the arbitral proceedings that it has no jurisdiction,

any party may, within 30 days after having received notice of that ruling, apply to the High Court to decide the matter.

(4) An appeal from the decision of the High Court made under Article 16(3) of the Model Law or this section shall lie to the Court of Appeal only with the leave of the High Court.

(5) There shall be no appeal against a refusal for grant of leave of the High Court.

(6) Where the High Court, or the Court of Appeal on appeal, decides that the arbitral tribunal has jurisdiction

(a) the arbitral tribunal shall continue the arbitral proceedings and make an award; and

(b) where any arbitrator is unable or unwilling to continue the arbitral proceedings, the mandate of that arbitrator shall terminate and a substitute arbitrator shall be appointed in accordance with Article 15 of the Model Law.

(7) In making a ruling or decision under this section that the arbitral tribunal has no jurisdiction, the arbitral tribunal, the High Court or the Court of Appeal (as the case may be) may make an award or order of costs of the proceedings, including the arbitral proceedings (as the case may be), against any party.

(8) Where an award of costs is made by the arbitral tribunal under subsection (7), section 21 shall apply with the necessary modifications.

(9) Where an application is made pursuant to Article 16(3) of the Model Law or this section

(a) such application shall not operate as a stay of the arbitral proceedings or of execution of any award or order made in the arbitral proceedings unless the High Court orders otherwise; and

(b) no intermediate act or proceeding shall be invalidated except so far as the High Court may direct.

(10) Where there is an appeal from the decision of the High Court pursuant to subsection (4)

(a) such appeal shall not operate as a stay of the arbitral proceedings or of execution of any award or order made in the arbitral proceedings unless the High Court or the Court of Appeal orders otherwise; and

(b) no intermediate act or proceeding shall be invalidated except so far as the Court of Appeal may direct.

11 — Public Policy and Arbitrability

(1) Any dispute which the parties have agreed to submit to arbitration under an arbitration agreement may be determined by arbitration unless it is contrary to public policy to do so.

(2) The fact that any written law confers jurisdiction in respect of any matter on any court of law but does not refer to the determination of that matter by arbitration shall not, of itself, indicate that a dispute about that matter is not capable of determination by arbitration.

11A — Reference of Interpleader Issue to Arbitration

Where in proceedings before any court relief by way of interpleader is granted and any issue between the claimants is one in respect of which there is an arbitration agreement between them, the court granting the relief may direct the issue between the claimants to be determined in accordance with the agreement.

12 — Powers of Arbitral Tribunal

(1) Without prejudice to the powers set out in any other provision of this Act and in the Model Law, an arbitral tribunal shall have powers to make orders or give directions to any party for

(a) security for costs;

(b) discovery of documents and interrogatories;

(c) giving of evidence by affidavit;

(d) the preservation, interim custody or sale of any property which is or forms part of the subject-matter of the dispute;

(e) samples to be taken from, or any observation to be made of or experiment conducted upon, any property which is or forms part of the

subject-matter of the dispute;
(f) the preservation and interim custody of any evidence for the purposes of the proceedings;
(g) securing the amount in dispute;
(h) ensuring that any award which may be made in the arbitral proceedings is not rendered ineffectual by the dissipation of assets by a party; and
(i) an interim injunction or any other interim measure.
(2) An arbitral tribunal shall, unless the parties to an arbitration agreement have (whether in the arbitration agreement or in any other document in writing) agreed to the contrary, have power to administer oaths to or take affirmations of the parties and witnesses.
(3) An arbitral tribunal shall, unless the parties to an arbitration agreement have (whether in the arbitration agreement or in any other document in writing) agreed to the contrary, have power to adopt if it thinks fit inquisitorial processes.
(4) The power of the arbitral tribunal to order a claimant to provide security for costs as referred to in subsection (1)(a) shall not be exercised by reason only that the claimant is
(a) an individual ordinarily resident outside Singapore; or
(b) a corporation or an association incorporated or formed under the law of a country outside Singapore, or whose central management and control is exercised outside Singapore.
(5) Without prejudice to the application of Article 28 of the Model Law, an arbitral tribunal, in deciding the dispute that is the subject of the arbitral proceedings
(a) may award any remedy or relief that could have been ordered by the High Court if the dispute had been the subject of civil proceedings in that Court;
(b) may award simple or compound interest on the whole or any part of any sum in accordance with section 20(1).
(6) All orders or directions made or given by an arbitral tribunal in the course of an arbitration shall, by leave of the High Court or a Judge thereof, be enforceable in the same manner as if they were orders made by a court and, where leave is so given, judgment may be entered in terms of the order or direction.

12A — Court-ordered Interim Measures

(1) This section shall apply in relation to an arbitration
(a) to which this Part applies; and
(b) irrespective of whether the place of arbitration is in the territory of

Singapore.

(2) Subject to subsections (3) to (6), for the purpose of and in relation to an arbitration referred to in subsection (1), the High Court or a Judge thereof shall have the same power of making an order in respect of any of the matters set out in section 12(1)(c) to (i) as it has for the purpose of and in relation to an action or a matter in the court.

(3) The High Court or a Judge thereof may refuse to make an order under subsection (2) if, in the opinion of the High Court or Judge, the fact that the place of arbitration is outside Singapore or likely to be outside Singapore when it is designated or determined makes it inappropriate to make such order.

(4) If the case is one of urgency, the High Court or a Judge thereof may, on the application of a party or proposed party to the arbitral proceedings, make such orders under subsection (2) as the High Court or Judge thinks necessary for the purpose of preserving evidence or assets.

(5) If the case is not one of urgency, the High Court or a Judge thereof shall make an order under subsection (2) only on the application of a party to the arbitral proceedings (upon notice to the other parties and to the arbitral tribunal) made with the permission of the arbitral tribunal or the agreement in writing of the other parties.

(6) In every case, the High Court or a Judge thereof shall make an order under subsection (2) only if or to the extent that the arbitral tribunal, and any arbitral or other institution or person vested by the parties with power in that regard, has no power or is unable for the time being to act effectively.

(7) An order made by the High Court or a Judge thereof under subsection (2) shall cease to have effect in whole or in part (as the case may be) if the arbitral tribunal, or any such arbitral or other institution or person having power to act in relation to the subject-matter of the order, makes an order which expressly relates to the whole or part of the order under subsection (2).

13 — Witnesses May be Summoned by Subpoena

(1) Any party to an arbitration agreement may take out a subpoena to testify or a subpoena to produce documents.

(2) The High Court or a Judge thereof may order that a subpoena to testify or a subpoena to produce documents shall be issued to compel the attendance before an arbitral tribunal of a witness wherever he may be within Singapore.

(3) The High Court or a Judge thereof may also issue an order under section 38 of the Prisons Act (Cap. 247) to bring up a prisoner for examination

before an arbitral tribunal.

(4) No person shall be compelled under any such subpoena to produce any document which he could not be compelled to produce on the trial of an action.

14 — [Repealed by Act 12 of 2012]

15 — Law of Arbitration other than Model Law

(1) If the parties to an arbitration agreement (whether made before or after 1st November 2001)[1] have expressly agreed either

(a) that the Model Law or this Part shall not apply to the arbitration; or

(b) that the Arbitration Act (Cap. 10) or the repealed Arbitration Act (Cap. 10, 1985 Ed.) shall apply to the arbitration,

then, both the Model Law and this Part shall not apply to that arbitration but the Arbitration Act or the repealed Arbitration Act (if applicable) shall apply to that arbitration.

(2) For the avoidance of doubt, a provision in an arbitration agreement referring to or adopting any rules of arbitration shall not of itself be sufficient to exclude the application of the Model Law or this Part to the arbitration concerned.

15A — Application of Rules of Arbitration

(1) It is hereby declared for the avoidance of doubt that a provision of rules of arbitration agreed to or adopted by the parties, whether before or after the commencement of the arbitration, shall apply and be given effect to the extent that such provision is not inconsistent with a provision of the Model Law or this Part from which the parties cannot derogate.

(2) Without prejudice to subsection (1), subsections (3) to (6) shall apply for the purposes of determining whether a provision of rules of arbitration is inconsistent with the Model Law or this Part.

(3) A provision of rules of arbitration is not inconsistent with the Model Law or this Part merely because it provides for a matter on which the Model Law and this Part is silent.

(4) Rules of arbitration are not inconsistent with the Model Law or this Part merely because the rules are silent on a matter covered by any provision of the Model Law or this Part.

(5) A provision of rules of arbitration is not inconsistent with the Model Law or this Part merely because it provides for a matter which is covered by a provision of the Model Law or this Part which allows the parties to make their own arrangements by agreement but which applies in the absence of such agreement.

(6) The parties may make the arrangements referred to in subsection (5) by

---

[1] Date of commencement of the International Arbitration (Amendment) Act 2001 (Act 38/2001).

agreeing to the application or adoption of rules of arbitration or by providing any other means by which a matter may be decided.

(7) In this section and section 15, "rules of arbitration" means the rules of arbitration agreed to or adopted by the parties including the rules of arbitration of an institution or organisation.

16 — Appointment of Conciliator

(1) Where an agreement provides for the appointment of a conciliator by a person who is not one of the parties and that person refuses to make the appointment or does not make it within the time specified in the agreement or, if no time is so specified, within a reasonable time of being requested by any party to the agreement to make the appointment, the Chairman for the time being of the Singapore International Arbitration Centre may, on the application of any party to the agreement, appoint a conciliator who shall have the like powers to act in the conciliation proceedings as if he had been appointed in accordance with the terms of the agreement.

(2) The Chief Justice may, if he thinks fit, by notification published in the Gazette, appoint any other person to exercise the powers of the Chairman of the Singapore International Arbitration Centre under subsection (1).

(3) Where an arbitration agreement provides for the appointment of a conciliator and further provides that the person so appointed shall act as an arbitrator in the event of the conciliation proceedings failing to produce a settlement acceptable to the parties

(a) no objection shall be taken to the appointment of such person as an arbitrator, or to his conduct of the arbitral proceedings, solely on the ground that he had acted previously as a conciliator in connection with some or all of the matters referred to arbitration;

(b) if such person declines to act as an arbitrator, any other person appointed as an arbitrator shall not be required first to act as a conciliator unless a contrary intention appears in the arbitration agreement.

(4) Unless a contrary intention appears therein, an agreement which provides for the appointment of a conciliator shall be deemed to contain a provision that in the event of the conciliation proceedings failing to produce a settlement acceptable to the parties within 4 months, or such longer period as the parties may agree to, of the date of the appointment of the conciliator or, where he is appointed by name in the agreement, of the receipt by him of written notification of the existence of a dispute, the conciliation proceedings shall thereupon terminate.

(5) For the purposes of this section and section 17

(a) any reference to "conciliator" shall include a reference to any person

who acts as a mediator;
(b) any reference to "conciliation proceedings" shall include a reference to mediation proceedings.

17 — Power of Arbitrator to Act as Conciliator

(1) If all parties to any arbitral proceedings consent in writing and for so long as no party has withdrawn his consent in writing, an arbitrator or umpire may act as a conciliator.

(2) An arbitrator or umpire acting as conciliator

(a) may communicate with the parties to the arbitral proceedings collectively or separately; and

(b) shall treat information obtained by him from a party to the arbitral proceedings as confidential, unless that party otherwise agrees or unless subsection (3) applies.

(3) Where confidential information is obtained by an arbitrator or umpire from a party to the arbitral proceedings during conciliation proceedings and those proceedings terminate without the parties reaching agreement in settlement of their dispute, the arbitrator or umpire shall before resuming the arbitral proceedings disclose to all other parties to the arbitral proceedings as much of that information as he considers material to the arbitral proceedings.

(4) No objection shall be taken to the conduct of arbitral proceedings by a person solely on the ground that that person had acted previously as a conciliator in accordance with this section.

18 — Award by Consent

If the parties to an arbitration agreement reach agreement in settlement of their dispute and the arbitral tribunal has recorded the terms of settlement in the form of an arbitral award on agreed terms in accordance with Article 30 of the Model Law, the award

(a) shall be treated as an award on an arbitration agreement; and

(b) may, by leave of the High Court or a Judge thereof, be enforced in the same manner as a judgment or an order to the same effect, and where leave is so given, judgment may be entered in terms of the award.

19 — Enforcement of Awards

An award on an arbitration agreement may, by leave of the High Court or a Judge thereof, be enforced in the same manner as a judgment or an order to the same effect and, where leave is so given, judgment may be entered in terms of the award.

19A — Awards Made on Different Issues

(1) Unless otherwise agreed by the parties, the arbitral tribunal may make

more than one award at different points in time during the arbitral proceedings on different aspects of the matters to be determined.

(2) The arbitral tribunal may, in particular, make an award relating to

(a) an issue affecting the whole claim; or

(b) a part only of the claim, counter-claim or cross-claim, which is submitted to it for decision.

(3) If the arbitral tribunal makes an award under this section, it shall specify in its award, the issue, or claim or part of a claim, which is the subject-matter of the award.

19B — Effect of Award

(1) An award made by the arbitral tribunal pursuant to an arbitration agreement is final and binding on the parties and on any persons claiming through or under them and may be relied upon by any of the parties by way of defence, set-off or otherwise in any proceedings in any court of competent jurisdiction.

(2) Except as provided in Articles 33 and 34(4) of the Model Law, upon an award being made, including an award made in accordance with section 19A, the arbitral tribunal shall not vary, amend, correct, review, add to or revoke the award.

(3) For the purposes of subsection (2), an award is made when it has been signed and delivered in accordance with Article 31 of the Model Law.

(4) This section shall not affect the right of a person to challenge the award by any available arbitral process of appeal or review or in accordance with the provisions of this Act and the Model Law.

19C — Authentication of Awards and Arbitration Agreements

(1) For the purposes of the enforcement of an award in any Convention country, the Minister may by order appoint such persons holding office in such arbitral institution or other organisation as the Minister may specify in the order, to authenticate any award or arbitration agreement or to certify copies thereof.

(2) Any person appointed under subsection (1)

(a) shall comply with any condition imposed by the Minister; and

(b) shall not, without the written consent of the parties, directly or indirectly disclose any matter, including the identity of any party to the award or arbitration agreement, to any third party.

(3) An award or arbitration agreement or a copy thereof duly authenticated or certified by a person appointed under subsection (1) shall be deemed to have been authenticated or certified by a competent authority in Singapore for the purposes of enforcement in any Convention country.

(4) For the avoidance of doubt, nothing in this section shall
(a) prevent any person from authenticating any award or arbitration agreement or certifying copies thereof in any other manner or method or by any other person, institution or organisation; or
(b) affect the right of a person to challenge or appeal against any award by any available arbitral process of appeal or review, or in accordance with the provisions of this Act and the Model Law.
(5) In this section, "Convention country" has the same meaning as in section 27(1).

20 — Interest on Awards

(1) Subject to subsection (3), unless otherwise agreed by the parties, an arbitral tribunal may, in the arbitral proceedings before it, award simple or compound interest from such date, at such rate and with such rest as the arbitral tribunal considers appropriate, for any period ending not later than the date of payment on the whole or any part of
(a) any sum which is awarded by the arbitral tribunal in the arbitral proceedings;
(b) any sum which is in issue in the arbitral proceedings but is paid before the date of the award; or
(c) costs awarded or ordered by the arbitral tribunal in the arbitral proceedings.
(2) Nothing in subsection (1) shall affect any other power of an arbitral tribunal to award interest.
(3) Where an award directs a sum to be paid, that sum shall, unless the award otherwise directs, carry interest as from the date of the award and at the same rate as a judgment debt.

21 — Taxation of Costs

(1) Any costs directed by an award to be paid shall, unless the award otherwise directs, be taxable by the Registrar of the Singapore International Arbitration Centre (referred to in this section as the Registrar).
(2) Unless the fees of the arbitral tribunal have been fixed by a written agreement or such agreement has provided for determination of the fees by a person or an institution agreed to by the parties, any party to the arbitration may require that such fees be taxed by the Registrar.
(3) A certificate signed by the Registrar on the amount of costs or fees taxed shall form part of the award of the arbitral tribunal.
(4) The Chief Justice may, if he thinks fit, by notification published in the Gazette, appoint any other person to exercise the powers of the Registrar under this section.

22 — Proceedings to be Heard Otherwise Than in Open Court
Proceedings under this Act in any court shall, on the application of any party to the proceedings, be heard otherwise than in open court.

23 — Restrictions on Reporting of Proceedings Heard Otherwise Than in Open Court
(1) This section shall apply to proceedings under this Act in any court heard otherwise than in open court.
(2) A court hearing any proceedings to which this section applies shall, on the application of any party to the proceedings, give directions as to whether any and, if so, what information relating to the proceedings may be published.
(3) A court shall not give a direction under subsection (2) permitting information to be published unless
(a) all parties to the proceedings agree that such information may be published; or
(b) the court is satisfied that the information, if published in accordance with such directions as it may give, would not reveal any matter, including the identity of any party to the proceedings, that any party to the proceedings reasonably wishes to remain confidential.
(4) Notwithstanding subsection (3), where a court gives grounds of decision for a judgment in respect of proceedings to which this section applies and considers that judgment to be of major legal interest, the court shall direct that reports of the judgment may be published in law reports and professional publications but, if any party to the proceedings reasonably wishes to conceal any matter, including the fact that he was such a party, the court shall
(a) give directions as to the action that shall be taken to conceal that matter in those reports; and
(b) if it considers that a report published in accordance with directions given under paragraph (a) would be likely to reveal that matter, direct that no report shall be published until after the end of such period, not exceeding 10 years, as it considers appropriate.

24 — Court May Set Aside Award
Notwithstanding Article 34(1) of the Model Law, the High Court may, in addition to the grounds set out in Article 34(2) of the Model Law, set aside the award of the arbitral tribunal if
(a) the making of the award was induced or affected by fraud or corruption; or
(b) a breach of the rules of natural justice occurred in connection with the

making of the award by which the rights of any party have been prejudiced.

25 — Liability of Arbitrator

An arbitrator shall not be liable for

(a) negligence in respect of anything done or omitted to be done in the capacity of arbitrator; and

(b) any mistake in law, fact or procedure made in the course of arbitral proceedings or in the making of an arbitral award.

25A — Immunity of Appointing Authority and Arbitral Institutions, etc.

(1) The appointing authority, or an arbitral or other institution or person designated or requested by the parties to appoint or nominate an arbitrator, shall not be liable for anything done or omitted in the discharge or purported discharge of that function unless the act or omission is shown to have been in bad faith.

(2) The appointing authority, or an arbitral or other institution or person by whom an arbitrator is appointed or nominated, shall not be liable, by reason only of having appointed or nominated him, for anything done or omitted by the arbitrator, his employees or agents in the discharge or purported discharge of his functions as arbitrator.

(3) This section shall apply to an employee or agent of the appointing authority or of an arbitral or other institution or person as it applies to the appointing authority, institution or person himself.

26 — Transitional Provisions

(1) This Part shall not apply in relation to an international arbitration between parties to an arbitration agreement that was commenced before 27th January 1995 unless the parties have (whether in the agreement or in any other document in writing) otherwise agreed.

(2) Subject to subsection (1), where the arbitral proceedings were commenced before 27 January 1995, the law governing the arbitration agreement and the arbitration shall be the law which would have applied if this Act had not been enacted.

(3) In any written law, agreement in writing or other document, a reference to arbitration under the Arbitration Act (Cap. 10) shall, so far as relevant and unless the contrary intention appears, be construed to include a reference to arbitration under this Act.

(4) For the purposes of this section, arbitral proceedings are to be taken as having commenced on the date of the receipt by the respondent of a request for the dispute to be referred to arbitration, or, where the parties have agreed in writing that any other date is to be taken as the date of commencement of

the arbitral proceedings, then on that date.

Part III
Foreign Awards

27 — Interpretation of Part III

(1) In this Part, unless the context otherwise requires

"agreement in writing" includes an agreement contained in an exchange of letters, telegrams, telefacsimile or in a communication by teleprinter;

"arbitral award" has the same meaning as in the Convention, but also includes an order or a direction made or given by an arbitral tribunal in the course of an arbitration in respect of any of the matters set out in section 12 (1)(c) to (i);

"arbitration agreement" means an agreement in writing of the kind referred to in paragraph 1 of Article II of the Convention;

"Convention" means the Convention on the Recognition and Enforcement of Foreign Arbitral Awards adopted in 1958 by the United Nations Conference on International Commercial Arbitration at its twenty-fourth meeting, the English text of which is set out in the Second Schedule;

"Convention country" means a country (other than Singapore) that is a Contracting State within the meaning of the Convention;

"court" means the High Court in Singapore;

"foreign award" means an arbitral award made in pursuance of an arbitration agreement in the territory of a Convention country other than Singapore.

(2) In this Part, where the context so admits, "enforcement", in relation to a foreign award, includes the recognition of the award as binding for any purpose, and "enforce" and "enforced" have corresponding meanings.

(3) For the purposes of this Part, a body corporate shall be taken to be habitually resident in a country if it is incorporated or has its principal place of business in that country.

28 — Application of Part III

(1) This Part shall apply to arbitration agreements made before 27th January 1995 as it applies to arbitration agreements made on or after that date.

(2) This Part shall not apply to foreign awards made before 19th November 1986.

29 — Recognition and Enforcement of Foreign Awards

(1) Subject to this Part, a foreign award may be enforced in a court either by action or in the same manner as an award of an arbitrator made in Singapore is enforceable under section 19.

(2) Any foreign award which is enforceable under subsection (1) shall be

recognised as binding for all purposes upon the persons between whom it was made and may accordingly be relied upon by any of those parties by way of defence, set-off or otherwise in any legal proceedings in Singapore.

30 — Evidence

(1) In any proceedings in which a person seeks to enforce a foreign award by virtue of this Part, he shall produce to the court

(a) the duly authenticated original award or a duly certified copy thereof;

(b) the original arbitration agreement under which the award purports to have been made, or a duly certified copy thereof;

and

(c) where the award or agreement is in a foreign language, a translation of it in the English language, duly certified in English as a correct translation by a sworn translator or by an official or by a diplomatic or consular agent of the country in which the award was made.

(2) A document produced to a court in accordance with this section shall, upon mere production, be received by the court as prima facie evidence of the matters to which it relates.

31 — Refusal of Enforcement

(1) In any proceedings in which the enforcement of a foreign award is sought by virtue of this Part, the party against whom the enforcement is sought may request that the enforcement be refused, and the enforcement in any of the cases mentioned in subsections (2) and (4) may be refused but not otherwise.

(2) A court so requested may refuse enforcement of a foreign award if the person against whom enforcement is sought proves to the satisfaction of the court that

(a) a party to the arbitration agreement in pursuance of which the award was made was, under the law applicable to him, under some incapacity at the time when the agreement was made;

(b) the arbitration agreement is not valid under the law to which the parties have subjected it or, in the absence of any indication in that respect, under the law of the country where the award was made;

(c) he was not given proper notice of the appointment of the arbitrator or of the arbitration proceedings or was otherwise unable to present his case in the arbitration proceedings;

(d) subject to subsection (3), the award deals with a difference not contemplated by, or not falling within the terms of, the submission to arbitration or contains a decision on the matter beyond the scope of the submission to arbitration;

(e) the composition of the arbitral authority or the arbitral procedure was not in accordance with the agreement of the parties or, failing such agreement was not in accordance with the law of the country where the arbitration took place; or

(f) the award has not yet become binding on the parties to the arbitral award or has been set aside or suspended by a competent authority of the country in which, or under the law of which, the award was made.

(3) When a foreign award referred to in subsection (2)(d) contains decisions on matters not submitted to arbitration but those decisions can be separated from decisions on matters submitted to arbitration, the award may be enforced to the extent that it contains decisions on matters so submitted.

(4) In any proceedings in which the enforcement of a foreign award is sought by virtue of this Part, the court may refuse to enforce the award if it finds that

(a) the subject-matter of the difference between the parties to the award is not capable of settlement by arbitration under the law of Singapore; or

(b) enforcement of the award would be contrary to the public policy of Singapore.

(5) Where, in any proceedings in which the enforcement of a foreign award is sought by virtue of this Part, the court is satisfied that an application for the setting aside or for the suspension of the award has been made to a competent authority of the country in which, or under the law of which, the award was made, the court may and may

(a) if the court considers it proper to do so, adjourn the proceedings or, as the case may be, so much of the proceedings as relates to the award; and

(b) on the application of the party seeking to enforce the award, order the other party to give suitable security.

32 — [Deleted by Act 26/2009]

33 — Enforcement of Awards Under other Provisions of Law

(1) Nothing in this Part shall affect the right of any person to enforce an arbitral award otherwise than as is provided for in this Part.

(2) Notwithstanding section 3(5) of the Reciprocal Enforcement of Commonwealth Judgments Act (Cap. 264), where a foreign award is both enforceable under this Part and registrable as a judgment under that Act, proceedings to enforce the award under this Part may be commenced without any disentitlement to recover any costs of the proceedings, unless otherwise ordered by the court.

(3) Notwithstanding section 7 of the Reciprocal Enforcement of Foreign Judgments Act (Cap. 265), proceedings to enforce a foreign award under

this Part may be commenced where the award is both enforceable under this Part and registrable as a judgment under that Act.

Part IV
General

34 — Act to bind Government

This Act shall bind the Government.

35 — Rules of Court

The Rules Committee constituted under section 80 of the Supreme Court of Judicature Act (Cap. 322) may make Rules of Court regulating the practice and procedure of any court in respect of any matter under this Act.

SCHEDULES
Schedule 1
UNCITRAL Model Law on International Commercial Arbitration[2]
Schedule 2
Convention on the Recognition and Enforcement of Foreign Arbitral Awards 1958[3]

[2] See UNCITRAL Model Law on International Commercial Arbitration, pp. 643-659.
[3] See New York Convention, pp. 256-260.

SWISS RULES OF INTERNATIONAL ARBITRATION *

Section I Introductory Rules

Scope of Application

Article 1

1. These Rules shall govern arbitrations where an agreement to arbitrate refers to these Rules or to the arbitration rules of the Chambers of Commerce and Industry of Basel, Bern, Geneva, Neuchâtel, Ticino, Vaud, Zurich, or any further Chamber of Commerce and Industry that may adhere to these Rules.
2. The seat of arbitration designated by the parties may be in Switzerland or in any other country.
3. This version of the Rules shall come into force on 1 June 2012 and, unless the parties have agreed otherwise, shall apply to all arbitral proceedings in which the Notice of Arbitration is submitted on or after that date.
4. By submitting their dispute to arbitration under these Rules, the parties confer on the Court, to the fullest extent permitted under the law applicable to the arbitration, all of the powers required for the purpose of supervising the arbitral proceedings otherwise vested in the competent judicial authority, including the power to extend the term of office of the arbitral tribunal and to decide on the challenge of an arbitrator on grounds not provided for in these Rules.
5. These Rules shall govern the arbitration, except if one of them is in conflict with a provision of the law applicable to the arbitration from which the parties cannot derogate, in which case that provision shall prevail.

Notice, Calculation of Periods of Time

Article 2

1. For the purposes of these Rules, any notice, including a notification, communication, or proposal, is deemed to have been received if it is delivered to the addressee, or to its habitual residence, place of business, postal or electronic address, or, if none of these can be identified after making a reasonable inquiry, to the addressee's last-known residence or place of business. A notice shall be deemed to have been received on the day it is delivered.
2. A period of time under these Rules shall begin to run on the day following the day when a notice, notification, communication, or proposal is received. If the last day of such a period is an official holiday or a non-business day at the residence or place of business of the addressee, the period is extended until the first business day which follows. Official holidays or nonbusiness days are included in the calculation of a period of

* For a commentary on the Swiss Rules of International Arbitration, see Tobias Zuberbühler, Christoph Müller and Philipp Habegger (eds), *Swiss Rules of International Arbitration: Commentary* (2nd edn, Schulthess Verlag, 2013).

time.

3. If the circumstances so justify, the Court may extend or shorten any time-limit it has fixed or has the authority to fix or amend.

Notice of Arbitration and Answer to the Notice of Arbitration

Article 3

1. The party initiating arbitration (hereinafter called the "Claimant" or, where applicable, the "Claimants") shall submit a Notice of Arbitration to the Secretariat at any of the addresses listed in Appendix A.

2. Arbitral proceedings shall be deemed to commence on the date on which the Notice of Arbitration is received by the Secretariat.

3. The Notice of Arbitration shall be submitted in as many copies as there are other parties (hereinafter called the "Respondent" or, where applicable, the "Respondents"), together with an additional copy for each arbitrator and one copy for the Secretariat, and shall include the following:

(a) A demand that the dispute be referred to arbitration;

(b) The names, addresses, telephone and fax numbers, and e-mail addresses (if any) of the parties and of their representative(s);

(c) A copy of the arbitration clause or the separate arbitration agreement that is invoked;

(d) A reference to the contract or other legal instrument(s) out of, or in relation to, which the dispute arises;

(e) The general nature of the claim and an indication of the amount involved, if any;

(f) The relief or remedy sought;

(g) A proposal as to the number of arbitrators (i.e. one or three), the language, and the seat of the arbitration, if the parties have not previously agreed thereon;

(h) The Claimant's designation of one or more arbitrators, if the parties' agreement so requires;

(i) Confirmation of payment by check or transfer to the relevant account listed in Appendix A of the Registration Fee as required by Appendix B (Schedule of Costs) in force on the date the Notice of Arbitration is submitted.

4. The Notice of Arbitration may also include:

(a) The Claimant's proposal for the appointment of a sole arbitrator referred to in Article 7;

(b) The Statement of Claim referred to in Article 18.

5. If the Notice of Arbitration is incomplete, if the required number of copies or attachments are not submitted, or if the Registration Fee is not

paid, the Secretariat may request the Claimant to remedy the defect within an appropriate period of time. The Secretariat may also request the Claimant to submit a translation of the Notice of Arbitration within the same period of time if it is not submitted in English, German, French, or Italian. If the Claimant complies with such directions within the applicable time-limit, the Notice of Arbitration shall be deemed to have been validly filed on the date on which the initial version was received by the Secretariat.

6. The Secretariat shall provide, without delay, a copy of the Notice of Arbitration together with any exhibits to the Respondent.

7. Within thirty days from the date of receipt of the Notice of Arbitration, the Respondent shall submit to the Secretariat an Answer to the Notice of Arbitration. The Answer to the Notice of Arbitration shall be submitted in as many copies as there are other parties, together with an additional copy for each arbitrator and one copy for the Secretariat, and shall, to the extent possible, include the following:

(a) The name, address, telephone and fax numbers, and e-mail address of the Respondent and of its representative(s);

(b) Any plea that an arbitral tribunal constituted under these Rules lacks jurisdiction;

(c) The Respondent's comments on the particulars set forth in the Notice of Arbitration referred to in Article 3(3)(e);

(d) The Respondent's answer to the relief or remedy sought in the Notice of Arbitration referred to in Article 3(3)(f);

(e) The Respondent's proposal as to the number of arbitrators (i.e. one or three), the language, and the seat of the arbitration referred to in Article 3(3)(g);

(f) The Respondent's designation of one or more arbitrators if the parties' agreement so requires.

8. The Answer to the Notice of Arbitration may also include:

(a) The Respondent's proposal for the appointment of a sole arbitrator referred to in Article 7;

(b) The Statement of Defence referred to in Article 19.

9. Articles 3(5) and (6) are applicable to the Answer to the Notice of Arbitration.

10. Any counterclaim or set-off defence shall in principle be raised with the Answer to the Notice of Arbitration. Article 3(3) is applicable to the counterclaim or set-off defence.

11. If no counterclaim or set-off defence is raised with the Answer to the Notice of Arbitration, or if there is no indication of the amount of the

counterclaim or set-off defence, the Court may rely exclusively on the Notice of Arbitration in order to determine the possible application of Article 42(2) (Expedited Procedure).
12. If the Respondent does not submit an Answer to the Notice of Arbitration, or if the Respondent raises an objection to the arbitration being administered under these Rules, the Court shall administer the case, unless there is manifestly no agreement to arbitrate referring to these Rules.

Consolidation and Joinder

Article 4

1. Where a Notice of Arbitration is submitted between parties already involved in other arbitral proceedings pending under these Rules, the Court may decide, after consulting with the parties and any confirmed arbitrator in all proceedings, that the new case shall be consolidated with the pending arbitral proceedings. The Court may proceed in the same way where a Notice of Arbitration is submitted between parties that are not identical to the parties in the pending arbitral proceedings. When rendering its decision, the Court shall take into account all relevant circumstances, including the links between the cases and the progress already made in the pending arbitral proceedings. Where the Court decides to consolidate the new case with the pending arbitral proceedings, the parties to all proceedings shall be deemed to have waived their right to designate an arbitrator, and the Court may revoke the appointment and confirmation of arbitrators and apply the provisions of Section II (Composition of the Arbitral Tribunal).
2. Where one or more third persons request to participate in arbitral proceedings already pending under these Rules or where a party to pending arbitral proceedings under these Rules requests that one or more third persons participate in the arbitration, the arbitral tribunal shall decide on such request, after consulting with all of the parties, including the person or persons to be joined, taking into account all relevant circumstances.

Section II Composition of the Arbitral Tribunal

Confirmation of Arbitrators

Article 5

1. All designations of an arbitrator made by the parties or the arbitrators are subject to confirmation by the Court, upon which the appointments shall become effective. The Court has no obligation to give reasons when it does not confirm an arbitrator.
2. Where a designation is not confirmed, the Court may either:
(a) invite the party or parties concerned, or, as the case may be, the arbitrators, to make a new designation within a reasonable time-limit; or

(b) in exceptional circumstances, proceed directly with the appointment.

3. In the event of any failure in the constitution of the arbitral tribunal under these Rules, the Court shall have all powers to address such failure and may, in particular, revoke any appointment made, appoint or reappoint any of the arbitrators and designate one of them as the presiding arbitrator.

4. If, before the arbitral tribunal is constituted, the parties agree on a settlement of the dispute, or the continuation of the arbitral proceedings becomes unnecessary or impossible for other reasons, the Secretariat shall give advance notice to the parties that the Court may terminate the proceedings. Any party may request that the Court proceed with the constitution of the arbitral tribunal in accordance with these Rules in order that the arbitral tribunal determine and apportion the costs not agreed upon by the parties.

5. Once the Registration Fee and any Provisional Deposit have been paid in accordance with Appendix B (Schedule of Costs) and all arbitrators have been confirmed, the Secretariat shall transmit the file to the arbitral tribunal without delay.

Number of Arbitrators

Article 6

1. If the parties have not agreed upon the number of arbitrators, the Court shall decide whether the case shall be referred to a sole arbitrator or to a three-member arbitral tribunal, taking into account all relevant circumstances.

2. As a rule, the Court shall refer the case to a sole arbitrator, unless the complexity of the subject matter and/or the amount in dispute justify that the case be referred to a three-member arbitral tribunal.

3. If the arbitration agreement provides for an arbitral tribunal composed of more than one arbitrator, and this appears inappropriate in view of the amount in dispute or of other circumstances, the Court shall invite the parties to agree to refer the case to a sole arbitrator.

4. Where the amount in dispute does not exceed CHF 1,000,000 (one million Swiss francs), Article 42(2) (Expedited Procedure) shall apply.

Appointment of a Sole Arbitrator

Article 7

1. Where the parties have agreed that the dispute shall be referred to a sole arbitrator, they shall jointly designate the sole arbitrator within thirty days from the date on which the Notice of Arbitration was received by the Respondent(s), unless the parties' agreement provides otherwise.

2. Where the parties have not agreed upon the number of arbitrators, they

shall jointly designate the sole arbitrator within thirty days from the date of receipt of the Court's decision that the dispute shall be referred to a sole arbitrator.

3. If the parties fail to designate the sole arbitrator within the applicable time-limit, the Court shall proceed with the appointment.

Appointment of Arbitrators in Bi-party or Multi-party Proceedings

Article 8

1. Where a dispute between two parties is referred to a three-member arbitral tribunal, each party shall designate one arbitrator, unless the parties have agreed otherwise.

2. If a party fails to designate an arbitrator within the time-limit set by the Court or resulting from the arbitration agreement, the Court shall appoint the arbitrator. Unless the parties' agreement provides otherwise, the two arbitrators so appointed shall designate, within thirty days from the confirmation of the second arbitrator, a third arbitrator who shall act as the presiding arbitrator of the arbitral tribunal. Failing such designation, the Court shall appoint the presiding arbitrator.

3. In multi-party proceedings, the arbitral tribunal shall be constituted in accordance with the parties' agreement.

4. If the parties have not agreed upon a procedure for the constitution of the arbitral tribunal in multi-party proceedings, the Court shall set an initial thirty-day time-limit for the Claimant or group of Claimants to designate an arbitrator, and set a subsequent thirty-day time-limit for the Respondent or group of Respondents to designate an arbitrator. If the party or group(s) of parties have each designated an arbitrator, Article 8(2) shall apply to the designation of the presiding arbitrator.

5. Where a party or group of parties fails to designate an arbitrator in multi-party proceedings, the Court may appoint all of the arbitrators, and shall specify the presiding arbitrator.

Independence and Challenge of Arbitrators

Article 9

1. Any arbitrator conducting an arbitration under these Rules shall be and shall remain at all times impartial and independent of the parties.

2. Prospective arbitrators shall disclose to those who approach them in connection with a possible appointment any circumstances likely to give rise to justifiable doubts as to their impartiality or independence. An arbitrator, once designated or appointed, shall disclose such circumstances to the parties, unless they have already been so informed.

Article 10

1. Any arbitrator may be challenged if circumstances exist that give rise to justifiable doubts as to the arbitrator's impartiality or independence.

2. A party may challenge the arbitrator designated by it only for reasons of which it becomes aware after the appointment has been made.

Article 11

1. A party intending to challenge an arbitrator shall send a notice of challenge to the Secretariat within 15 days after the circumstances giving rise to the challenge became known to that party.

2. If, within 15 days from the date of the notice of challenge, all of the parties do not agree to the challenge, or the challenged arbitrator does not withdraw, the Court shall decide on the challenge.

3. The decision of the Court is final and the Court has no obligation to give reasons.

Removal of an Arbitrator

Article 12

1. If an arbitrator fails to perform his or her functions despite a written warning from the other arbitrators or from the Court, the Court may revoke the appointment of that arbitrator.

2. The arbitrator shall first have an opportunity to present his or her position to the Court. The decision of the Court is final and the Court has no obligation to give reasons.

Replacement of an Arbitrator

Article 13

1. Subject to Article 13(2), in all instances in which an arbitrator has to be replaced, a replacement arbitrator shall be designated or appointed pursuant to the procedure provided for in Articles 7 and 8 within the time-limit set by the Court. Such procedure shall apply even if a party or the arbitrators had failed to make the required designation during the initial appointment process.

2. In exceptional circumstances, the Court may, after consulting with the parties and any remaining arbitrators:

(a) directly appoint the replacement arbitrator; or

(b) after the closure of the proceedings, authorise the remaining arbitrator(s) to proceed with the arbitration and make any decision or award.

Article 14

If an arbitrator is replaced, the proceedings shall, as a rule, resume at the stage reached when the arbitrator who was replaced ceased to perform his or her functions, unless the arbitral tribunal decides otherwise.

Section III Arbitral Proceedings

General Provisions

Article 15

1. Subject to these Rules, the arbitral tribunal may conduct the arbitration in such manner as it considers appropriate, provided that it ensures equal treatment of the parties and their right to be heard.
2. At any stage of the proceedings, the arbitral tribunal may hold hearings for the presentation of evidence by witnesses, including expert witnesses, or for oral argument. After consulting with the parties, the arbitral tribunal may also decide to conduct the proceedings on the basis of documents and other materials.
3. At an early stage of the arbitral proceedings, and in consultation with the parties, the arbitral tribunal shall prepare a provisional timetable for the arbitral proceedings, which shall be provided to the parties and, for information, to the Secretariat.
4. All documents or information provided to the arbitral tribunal by one party shall at the same time be communicated by that party to the other parties.
5. The arbitral tribunal may, after consulting with the parties, appoint a secretary. Articles 9 to 11 shall apply to the secretary.
6. The parties may be represented or assisted by persons of their choice.
7. All participants in the arbitral proceedings shall act in good faith, and make every effort to contribute to the efficient conduct of the proceedings and to avoid unnecessary costs and delays. The parties undertake to comply with any award or order made by the arbitral tribunal or emergency arbitrator without delay.
8. With the agreement of each of the parties, the arbitral tribunal may take steps to facilitate the settlement of the dispute before it. Any such agreement by a party shall constitute a waiver of its right to challenge an arbitrator's impartiality based on the arbitrator's participation and knowledge acquired in taking the agreed steps.

Seat of the Arbitration

Article 16

1. If the parties have not determined the seat of the arbitration, or if the designation of the seat is unclear or incomplete, the Court shall determine the seat of the arbitration, taking into account all relevant circumstances, or shall request the arbitral tribunal to determine it.
2. Without prejudice to the determination of the seat of the arbitration, the arbitral tribunal may decide where the proceedings shall be conducted. In

particular, it may hear witnesses and hold meetings for consultation among its members at any place it deems appropriate, having regard to the circumstances of the arbitration.
3. The arbitral tribunal may meet at any place it deems appropriate for the inspection of goods, other property, or documents. The parties shall be given sufficient notice to enable them to be present at such an inspection.
4. The award shall be deemed to be made at the seat of the arbitration.

Language

Article 17

1. Subject to an agreement of the parties, the arbitral tribunal shall, promptly after its appointment, determine the language or languages to be used in the proceedings. This determination shall apply to the Statement of Claim, the Statement of Defence, any further written statements, and to any oral hearings.
2. The arbitral tribunal may order that any documents annexed to the Statement of Claim or Statement of Defence, and any supplementary documents or exhibits submitted in the course of the proceedings in a language other than the language or languages agreed upon by the parties or determined by the arbitral tribunal shall be accompanied by a translation into such language or languages.

Statement of Claim

Article 18

1. Within a period of time to be determined by the arbitral tribunal, and unless the Statement of Claim was contained in the Notice of Arbitration, the Claimant shall communicate its Statement of Claim in writing to the Respondent and to each of the arbitrators. A copy of the contract, and, if it is not contained in the contract, of the arbitration agreement, shall be annexed to the Statement of Claim.
2. The Statement of Claim shall include the following particulars:
(a) The names and addresses of the parties;
(b) A statement of the facts supporting the claim;
(c) The points at issue;
(d) The relief or remedy sought.
3. As a rule, the Claimant shall annex to its Statement of Claim all documents and other evidence on which it relies.

Statement of Defence

Article 19

1. Within a period of time to be determined by the arbitral tribunal, and unless the Statement of Defence was contained in the Answer to the Notice

of Arbitration, the Respondent shall communicate its Statement of Defence in writing to the Claimant and to each of the arbitrators.

2. The Statement of Defence shall reply to the particulars of the Statement of Claim set out in Articles 18(2)(b) to (d). If the Respondent raises an objection to the jurisdiction or to the proper constitution of the arbitral tribunal, the Statement of Defence shall contain the factual and legal basis of such objection. As a rule, the Respondent shall annex to its Statement of Defence all documents and other evidence on which it relies.

3. Articles 18(2)(b) to (d) shall apply to a counterclaim and a claim relied on for the purpose of a set-off.

Amendments to the Claim or Defence

Article 20

1. During the course of the arbitral proceedings, a party may amend or supplement its claim or defence, unless the arbitral tribunal considers it inappropriate to allow such amendment having regard to the delay in making it, the prejudice to the other parties, or any other circumstances. However, a claim may not be amended in such a manner that the amended claim falls outside the scope of the arbitration clause or separate arbitration agreement.

2. The arbitral tribunal may adjust the costs of the arbitration if a party amends or supplements its claims, counterclaims, or defences.

Objections to the Jurisdiction of the Arbitral Tribunal

Article 21

1. The arbitral tribunal shall have the power to rule on any objections to its jurisdiction, including any objection with respect to the existence or validity of the arbitration clause or of the separate arbitration agreement.

2. The arbitral tribunal shall have the power to determine the existence or the validity of the contract of which an arbitration clause forms part. For the purposes of Article 21, an arbitration clause which forms part of a contract and which provides for arbitration under these Rules shall be treated as an agreement independent of the other terms of the contract. A decision by the arbitral tribunal that the contract is null and void shall not entail *ipso jure* the invalidity of the arbitration clause.

3. As a rule, any objection to the jurisdiction of the arbitral tribunal shall be raised in the Answer to the Notice of Arbitration, and in no event later than in the Statement of Defence referred to in Article 19, or, with respect to a counterclaim, in the reply to the counterclaim.

4. In general, the arbitral tribunal should rule on any objection to its jurisdiction as a preliminary question. However, the arbitral tribunal may

proceed with the arbitration and rule on such an objection in an award on the merits.

5. The arbitral tribunal shall have jurisdiction to hear a set-off defence even if the relationship out of which the defence is said to arise is not within the scope of the arbitration clause, or falls within the scope of another arbitration agreement or forum-selection clause.

Further Written Statements

Article 22

The arbitral tribunal shall decide which further written statements, in addition to the Statement of Claim and the Statement of Defence, shall be required from the parties or may be presented by them and shall set the periods of time for communicating such statements.

Periods of Time

Article 23

The periods of time set by the arbitral tribunal for the communication of written statements (including the Statement of Claim and Statement of Defence) should not exceed forty-five days. However, the arbitral tribunal may extend the time-limits if it considers that an extension is justified.

Evidence and Hearings

Article 24

1. Each party shall have the burden of proving the facts relied on to support its claim or defence.

2. The arbitral tribunal shall determine the admissibility, relevance, materiality, and weight of the evidence.

3. At any time during the arbitral proceedings, the arbitral tribunal may require the parties to produce documents, exhibits, or other evidence within a period of time determined by the arbitral tribunal.

Article 25

1. The arbitral tribunal shall give the parties adequate advance notice of the date, time, and place of any oral hearing.

2. Any person may be a witness or an expert witness in the arbitration. It is not improper for a party, its officers, employees, legal advisors, or counsel to interview witnesses, potential witnesses, or expert witnesses.

3. Prior to a hearing and within a period of time determined by the arbitral tribunal, the evidence of witnesses and expert witnesses may be presented in the form of written statements or reports signed by them.

4. At the hearing, witnesses and expert witnesses may be heard and examined in the manner set by the arbitral tribunal. The arbitral tribunal may direct that witnesses or expert witnesses be examined through means

that do not require their physical presence at the hearing (including by videoconference).

5. Arrangements shall be made for the translation of oral statements made at a hearing and for a record of the hearing to be provided if this is deemed necessary by the arbitral tribunal having regard to the circumstances of the case, or if the parties so agree.

6. Hearings shall be held *in camera* unless the parties agree otherwise. The arbitral tribunal may order witnesses or expert witnesses to retire during the testimony of other witnesses or expert witnesses.

Interim Measures of Protection

Article 26

1. At the request of a party, the arbitral tribunal may grant any interim measures it deems necessary or appropriate. Upon the application of any party or, in exceptional circumstances and with prior notice to the parties, on its own initiative, the arbitral tribunal may also modify, suspend or terminate any interim measures granted.

2. Interim measures may be granted in the form of an interim award. The arbitral tribunal shall be entitled to order the provision of appropriate security.

3. In exceptional circumstances, the arbitral tribunal may rule on a request for interim measures by way of a preliminary order before the request has been communicated to any other party, provided that such communication is made at the latest together with the preliminary order and that the other parties are immediately granted an opportunity to be heard.

4. The arbitral tribunal may rule on claims for compensation for any damage caused by an unjustified interim measure or preliminary order.

5. By submitting their dispute to arbitration under these Rules, the parties do not waive any right that they may have under the applicable laws to submit a request for interim measures to a judicial authority. A request for interim measures addressed by any party to a judicial authority shall not be deemed to be incompatible with the agreement to arbitrate, or to constitute a waiver of that agreement.

6. The arbitral tribunal shall have discretion to apportion the costs relating to a request for interim measures in an interim award or in the final award.

Tribunal-Appointed Experts

Article 27

1. The arbitral tribunal, after consulting with the parties, may appoint one or more experts to report to it, in writing, on specific issues to be determined by the arbitral tribunal. A copy of the expert's terms of reference,

established by the arbitral tribunal, shall be communicated to the parties.
2. The parties shall give the expert any relevant information or produce for the expert's inspection any relevant documents or goods that the expert may require of them. Any dispute between a party and the expert as to the relevance of the required information, documents or goods shall be referred to the arbitral tribunal.
3. Upon receipt of the expert's report, the arbitral tribunal shall communicate a copy of the report to the parties, which shall be given the opportunity to express, in writing, their opinion on the report. A party shall be entitled to examine any document on which the expert has relied in the report.
4. At the request of any party, the expert, after delivery of the report, may be heard at a hearing during which the parties shall have the opportunity to be present and to examine the expert. At this hearing, any party may present expert witnesses in order to testify on the points at issue. Article 25 shall be applicable to such proceedings.
5. Articles 9 to 11 shall apply to any expert appointed by the arbitral tribunal.

Default

Article 28

1. If, within the period of time set by the arbitral tribunal, the Claimant has failed to communicate its claim without showing sufficient cause for such failure, the arbitral tribunal shall issue an order for the termination of the arbitral proceedings. If, within the period of time set by the arbitral tribunal, the Respondent has failed to communicate its Statement of Defence without showing sufficient cause for such failure, the arbitral tribunal shall order that the proceedings continue.
2. If one of the parties, duly notified under these Rules, fails to appear at a hearing, without showing sufficient cause for such failure, the arbitral tribunal may proceed with the arbitration.
3. If one of the parties, duly invited to produce documentary or other evidence, fails to do so within the period of time determined by the arbitral tribunal, without showing sufficient cause for such failure, the arbitral tribunal may make the award on the evidence before it.

Closure of Proceedings

Article 29

1. When it is satisfied that the parties have had a reasonable opportunity to present their respective cases on matters to be decided in an award, the arbitral tribunal may declare the proceedings closed with regard to such

matters.

2. The arbitral tribunal may, if it considers it necessary owing to exceptional circumstances, decide, on its own initiative or upon the application of a party, to reopen the proceedings on the matters with regard to which the proceedings were closed pursuant to Article 29(1) at any time before the award on such matters is made.

Waiver of Rules

Article 30

If a party knows that any provision of, or requirement under, these Rules or any other applicable procedural rule has not been complied with and yet proceeds with the arbitration without promptly stating its objection to such non-compliance, it shall be deemed to have waived its right to raise an objection.

Section IV The Award

Decisions

Article 31

1. If the arbitral tribunal is composed of more than one arbitrator, any award or other decision of the arbitral tribunal shall be made by a majority of the arbitrators. If there is no majority, the award shall be made by the presiding arbitrator alone.

2. If authorized by the arbitral tribunal, the presiding arbitrator may decide on questions of procedure, subject to revision by the arbitral tribunal.

Form and Effect of the Award

Article 32

1. In addition to making a final award, the arbitral tribunal may make interim, interlocutory, or partial awards. If appropriate, the arbitral tribunal may also award costs in awards that are not final.

2. The award shall be made in writing and shall be final and binding on the parties.

3. The arbitral tribunal shall state the reasons upon which the award is based, unless the parties have agreed that no reasons are to be given.

4. An award shall be signed by the arbitrators and it shall specify the seat of the arbitration and the date on which the award was made. Where the arbitral tribunal is composed of more than one arbitrator and any of them fails to sign, the award shall state the reason for the absence of the signature.

5. The publication of the award is governed by Article 44.

6. Originals of the award signed by the arbitrators shall be communicated by the arbitral tribunal to the parties and to the Secretariat. The Secretariat

shall retain a copy of the award.

Applicable Law, *Amiable Compositeur*

Article 33

1. The arbitral tribunal shall decide the case in accordance with the rules of law agreed upon by the parties or, in the absence of a choice of law, by applying the rules of law with which the dispute has the closest connection.
2. The arbitral tribunal shall decide as *amiable compositeur* or *ex aequo et bono* only if the parties have expressly authorised the arbitral tribunal to do so.
3. In all cases, the arbitral tribunal shall decide in accordance with the terms of the contract and shall take into account the trade usages applicable to the transaction.

Settlement or Other Grounds for Termination

Article 34

1. If, before the award is made, the parties agree on a settlement of the dispute, the arbitral tribunal shall either issue an order for the termination of the arbitral proceedings or, if requested by the parties and accepted by the arbitral tribunal, record the settlement in the form of an arbitral award on agreed terms. The arbitral tribunal is not obliged to give reasons for such an award.
2. If, before the award is made, the continuation of the arbitral proceedings becomes unnecessary or impossible for any reason not mentioned in Article 34(1), the arbitral tribunal shall give advance notice to the parties that it may issue an order for the termination of the proceedings. The arbitral tribunal shall have the power to issue such an order, unless a party raises justifiable grounds for objection.
3. Copies of the order for termination of the arbitral proceedings or of the arbitral award on agreed terms, signed by the arbitrators, shall be communicated by the arbitral tribunal to the parties and to the Secretariat. Where an arbitral award on agreed terms is made, Articles 32(2) and (4) to (6) shall apply.

Interpretation of the Award

Article 35

1. Within thirty days after the receipt of the award, a party, with notice to the Secretariat and to the other parties, may request that the arbitral tribunal give an interpretation of the award. The arbitral tribunal may set a time-limit, as a rule not exceeding thirty days, for the other parties to comment on the request.
2. The interpretation shall be given in writing within forty-five days after

the receipt of the request. The Court may extend this time limit. The interpretation shall form part of the award and Articles 32(2) to (6) shall apply.

Correction of the Award

Article 36

1. Within thirty days after the receipt of the award, a party, with notice to the Secretariat and to the other parties, may request the arbitral tribunal to correct in the award any errors in computation, any clerical or typographical errors, or any errors of similar nature. The arbitral tribunal may set a time-limit, as a rule not exceeding thirty days, for the other parties to comment on the request.
2. The arbitral tribunal may within thirty days after the communication of the award make such corrections on its own initiative.
3. Such corrections shall be in writing, and Articles 32(2) to (6) shall apply.

Additional Award

Article 37

1. Within thirty days after the receipt of the award, a party, with notice to the Secretariat and the other parties, may request the arbitral tribunal to make an additional award as to claims presented in the arbitral proceedings but omitted from the award. The arbitral tribunal may set a time-limit, as a rule not exceeding thirty days, for the other parties to comment on the request.
2. If the arbitral tribunal considers the request for an additional award to be justified and considers that the omission can be rectified without any further hearings or evidence, it shall complete its award within sixty days after the receipt of the request. The Court may extend this time-limit.
3. Articles 32(2) to (6) shall apply to any additional award.

Costs

Article 38

The award shall contain a determination of the costs of the arbitration. The term "costs" includes only:

(a) The fees of the arbitral tribunal, to be stated separately as to each arbitrator and any secretary, and to be determined by the arbitral tribunal itself in accordance with Articles 39 and 40(3) to (5);

(b) The travel and other expenses incurred by the arbitral tribunal and any secretary;

(c) The costs of expert advice and of other assistance required by the arbitral tribunal;

(d) The travel and other expenses of witnesses, to the extent such expenses

are approved by the arbitral tribunal;
(e) The costs for legal representation and assistance, if such costs were claimed during the arbitral proceedings, and only to the extent that the arbitral tribunal determines that the amount of such costs is reasonable;
(f) The Registration Fee and the Administrative Costs in accordance with Appendix B (Schedule of Costs);
(g) The Registration Fee, the fees and expenses of any emergency arbitrator, and the costs of expert advice and of other assistance required by such emergency arbitrator, determined in accordance with Article 43(9).

Article 39

1. The fees and expenses of the arbitral tribunal shall be reasonable in amount, taking into account the amount in dispute, the complexity of the subject-matter of the arbitration, the time spent and any other relevant circumstances of the case, including the discontinuation of the arbitral proceedings in case of settlement. In the event of a discontinuation of the arbitral proceedings, the fees of the arbitral tribunal may be less than the minimum amount resulting from Appendix B (Schedule of Costs).
2. The fees and expenses of the arbitral tribunal shall be determined in accordance with Appendix B (Schedule of Costs).
3. The arbitral tribunal shall decide on the allocation of its fees among its members. As a rule, the presiding arbitrator shall receive between 40% and 50% and each co-arbitrator between 25% and 30% of the total fees, in view of the time and efforts spent by each arbitrator.

Article 40

1. Except as provided in Article 40(2), the costs of the arbitration shall in principle be borne by the unsuccessful party. However, the arbitral tribunal may apportion any of the costs of the arbitration among the parties if it determines that such apportionment is reasonable, taking into account the circumstances of the case.
2. With respect to the costs of legal representation and assistance referred to in Article 38(e), the arbitral tribunal, taking into account the circumstances of the case, shall be free to determine which party shall bear such costs or may apportion such costs among the parties if it determines that an apportionment is reasonable.
3. If the arbitral tribunal issues an order for the termination of the arbitral proceedings or makes an award on agreed terms, it shall determine the costs of the arbitration referred to in Articles 38 and 39 in the order or award.
4. Before rendering an award, termination order, or decision on a request under Articles 35 to 37, the arbitral tribunal shall submit to the Secretariat a

draft thereof for approval or adjustment by the Court of the determination on costs made pursuant to Articles 38(a) to (c) and (f) and Article 39. Any such approval or adjustment shall be binding upon the arbitral tribunal.

5. No additional costs may be charged by an arbitral tribunal for interpretation, correction, or completion of its award under Articles 35 to 37, unless they are justified by the circumstances.

Deposit of Costs

Article 41

1. The arbitral tribunal, once constituted, and after consulting with the Court, shall request each party to deposit an equal amount as an advance for the costs referred to in Articles 38(a) to (c) and the Administrative Costs referred to in Article 38(f). Any Provisional Deposit paid by a party in accordance with Appendix B (Schedule of Costs) shall be considered as a partial payment of its deposit. The arbitral tribunal shall provide a copy of such request to the Secretariat.

2. Where a Respondent submits a counterclaim, or it otherwise appears appropriate in the circumstances, the arbitral tribunal may in its discretion establish separate deposits.

3. During the course of the arbitral proceedings, the arbitral tribunal may, after consulting with the Court, request supplementary deposits from the parties. The arbitral tribunal shall provide a copy of any such request to the Secretariat.

4. If the required deposits are not paid in full within fifteen days after the receipt of the request, the arbitral tribunal shall notify the parties in order that one or more of them may make the required payment. If such payment is not made, the arbitral tribunal may order the suspension or termination of the arbitral proceedings.

5. In its final award, the arbitral tribunal shall issue to the parties a statement of account of the deposits received. Any unused amount shall be returned to the parties.

Section V Other Provisions

Expedited Procedure

Article 42

1. If the parties so agree, or if Article 42(2) is applicable, the arbitral proceedings shall be conducted in accordance with an Expedited Procedure based upon the foregoing provisions of these Rules, subject to the following changes:

(a) The file shall be transmitted to the arbitral tribunal only upon payment of the Provisional Deposit as required by Section 1.4 of Appendix B

Schedule of Costs);
(b) After the submission of the Answer to the Notice of Arbitration, the parties shall, as a rule, be entitled to submit only a Statement of Claim, a Statement of Defence (and counterclaim) and, where applicable, a Statement of Defence in reply to the counterclaim;
(c) Unless the parties agree that the dispute shall be decided on the basis of documentary evidence only, the arbitral tribunal shall hold a single hearing for the examination of the witnesses and expert witnesses, as well as for oral argument;
(d) The award shall be made within six months from the date on which the Secretariat transmitted the file to the arbitral tribunal. In exceptional circumstances, the Court may extend this time-limit;
(e) The arbitral tribunal shall state the reasons upon which the award is based in summary form, unless the parties have agreed that no reasons are to be given.
2. The following provisions shall apply to all cases in which the amount in dispute, representing the aggregate of the claim and the counterclaim (or any set-off defence), does not exceed CHF 1,000,000 (one million Swiss francs), unless the Court decides otherwise, taking into account all relevant circumstances:
(a) The arbitral proceedings shall be conducted in accordance with the Expedited Procedure set forth in Article 42(1);
(b) The case shall be referred to a sole arbitrator, unless the arbitration agreement provides for more than one arbitrator;
(c) If the arbitration agreement provides for an arbitral tribunal composed of more than one arbitrator, the Secretariat shall invite the parties to agree to refer the case to a sole arbitrator. If the parties do not agree to refer the case to a sole arbitrator, the fees of the arbitrators shall be determined in accordance with Appendix B (Schedule of Costs), but shall in no event be less than the fees resulting from the hourly rate set out in Section 2.8 of Appendix B.

Emergency Relief

Article 43

1. Unless the parties have agreed otherwise, a party requiring urgent interim measures pursuant to Article 26 before the arbitral tribunal is constituted may submit to the Secretariat an application for emergency relief proceedings (hereinafter the "Application"). In addition to the particulars set out in Articles 3(3)(b) to (e), the Application shall include:
(a) A statement of the interim measure(s) sought and the reasons therefor, in

particular the reason for the purported urgency;
(b) Comments on the language, the seat of arbitration, and the applicable law;
(c) Confirmation of payment by check or transfer to the relevant account listed in Appendix A of the Registration Fee and of the deposit for emergency relief proceedings as required by Section 1.6 of Appendix B (Schedule of Costs).
2. As soon as possible after receipt of the Application, the Registration Fee, and the deposit for emergency relief proceedings, the Court shall appoint and transmit the file to a sole emergency arbitrator, unless
(a) there is manifestly no agreement to arbitrate referring to these Rules, or
(b) it appears more appropriate to proceed with the constitution of the arbitral tribunal and refer the Application to it.
3. If the Application is submitted before the Notice of Arbitration, the Court shall terminate the emergency relief proceedings if the Notice of Arbitration is not submitted within ten days from the receipt of the Application. In exceptional circumstances, the Court may extend this time-limit.
4. Articles 9 to 12 shall apply to the emergency arbitrator except that the time-limits set out in Articles 11(1) and (2) are shortened to three days.
5. If the parties have not determined the seat of the arbitration, or if the designation of the seat is unclear or incomplete, the seat of the arbitration for the emergency relief proceedings shall be determined by the Court without prejudice to the determination of the seat of the arbitration pursuant to Article 16(1).
6. The emergency arbitrator may conduct the emergency relief proceedings in such a manner as the emergency arbitrator considers appropriate, taking into account the urgency inherent in such proceedings and ensuring that each party has a reasonable opportunity to be heard on the Application.
7. The decision on the Application shall be made within fifteen days from the date on which the Secretariat transmitted the file to the emergency arbitrator. This period of time may be extended by agreement of the parties or, in appropriate circumstances, by the Court. The decision on the Application may be made even if in the meantime the file has been transmitted to the arbitral tribunal.
8. A decision of the emergency arbitrator shall have the same effects as a decision pursuant to Article 26. Any interim measure granted by the emergency arbitrator may be modified, suspended or terminated by the emergency arbitrator or, after transmission of the file to it, by the arbitral tribunal.

9. The decision on the Application shall include a determination of costs as referred to in Article 38(g). Before rendering the decision on the Application, the emergency arbitrator shall submit to the Secretariat a draft thereof for approval or adjustment by the Court of the determination of costs. The costs shall be payable out of the deposit for emergency relief proceedings. The determination of costs pursuant to Articles 38(d) and (e) and the apportionment of all costs among the parties shall be decided by the arbitral tribunal. If no arbitral tribunal is constituted, the determination of costs pursuant to Articles 38(d) and (e) and the apportionment of all costs shall be decided by the emergency arbitrator in a separate award.
10. Any measure granted by the emergency arbitrator ceases to be binding on the parties either upon the termination of the emergency relief proceedings pursuant to Article 43(3), upon the termination of the arbitral proceedings, or upon the rendering of a final award, unless the arbitral tribunal expressly decides otherwise in the final award.
11. The emergency arbitrator may not serve as arbitrator in any arbitration relating to the dispute in respect of which the emergency arbitrator has acted, unless otherwise agreed by the parties.

Confidentiality

Article 44

1. Unless the parties expressly agree in writing to the contrary, the parties undertake to keep confidential all awards and orders as well as all materials submitted by another party in the framework of the arbitral proceedings not already in the public domain, except and to the extent that a disclosure may be required of a party by a legal duty, to protect or pursue a legal right, or to enforce or challenge an award in legal proceedings before a judicial authority. This undertaking also applies to the arbitrators, the tribunal-appointed experts, the secretary of the arbitral tribunal, the members of the board of directors of the Swiss Chambers' Arbitration Institution, the members of the Court and the Secretariat, and the staff of the individual Chambers.
2. The deliberations of the arbitral tribunal are confidential.
3. An award or order may be published, whether in its entirety or in the form of excerpts or a summary, only under the following conditions:
(a) A request for publication is addressed to the Secretariat;
(b) All references to the parties' names are deleted; and
(c) No party objects to such publication within the time-limit fixed for that purpose by the Secretariat.

Exclusion of Liability
Article 45

1. Neither the members of the board of directors of the Swiss Chambers' Arbitration Institution, the members of the Court and the Secretariat, the individual Chambers or their staff, the arbitrators, the tribunal-appointed experts, nor the secretary of the arbitral tribunal shall be liable for any act or omission in connection with an arbitration conducted under these Rules, except if the act or omission is shown to constitute intentional wrongdoing or gross negligence.
2. After the award or termination order has been made and the possibilities of correction, interpretation and additional awards referred to in Articles 35 to 37 have lapsed or have been exhausted, neither the members of the board of the Swiss Chambers' Arbitration Institution, the members of the Court and the Secretariat, the individual Chambers or their staff, the arbitrators, the tribunal-appointed experts, nor the secretary of the arbitral tribunal shall be under an obligation to make statements to any person about any matter concerning the arbitration. No party shall seek to make any of these persons a witness in any legal or other proceedings arising out of the arbitration.

Appendix A
Offices of the Secretariat of the Arbitration Court

Swiss Chambers' Arbitration Institution Arbitration Court Secretariat

c/o Basel Chamber of Commerce
Aeschenvorstadt 67
P.O. Box
CH-4010 Basel
Telephone: +41 61 270 60 50
Fax: +41 61 270 60 05
E-mail: basel@swissarbitration.org
Bank details: UBS AG, CH-4002 Basel
Account No: 292-10157720.0
Clearing No: 292
Swift Code: UBSWCHZH80A
Iban: CH98 0029 2292 10157720 0

c/o Chamber of Commerce and Industry of Bern
Kramgasse 2
P.O. Box 5464
CH-3001 Bern
Telephone: +41 31 388 87 87
Fax: +41 31 388 87 88
E-mail: bern@swissarbitration.org
Bank details: BEKB
Account No: KK 16 166.151.0.44 HIV Kanton Bern
Clearing No: 790
Swift Code: KBBECH22
Iban: CH35 0079 0016 1661 5104 4

c/o Geneva Chamber of Commerce, Industry and Services
4, Boulevard du Théâtre
P.O. Box 5039
CH-1211 Geneva 11
Telephone: +41 22 819 91 11
Fax: +41 22 819 91 36
E-mail: geneva@swissarbitration.org
Bank details: UBS SA, Rue du Rhône 8, 1204 Genève

Account No: 279-HU108533.1
Clearing No: 279
Swift Code: UBSWCHZH80A
Iban: CH13 0027 9279 HU1085331

c/o Neuchâtel Chamber of Commerce and Industry
4, rue de la Serre
P.O. Box 2012
CH-2001 Neuchâtel
Telephone: +41 32 727 24 27
Fax: +41 32 727 24 28
E-mail: neuchatel@swissarbitration.org
Bank details: BCN, Neuchâtel
Account No: C0029.20.09
Clearing No: 766
Swift Code: BCNNCH22
Iban: CH69 0076 6000 C002 9200 9

c/o Chamber of Commerce and Industry of Ticino
Corso Elvezia 16
P.O. Box 5399
CH-6901 Lugano
Telephone: +41 91 911 51 11
Fax: +41 91 911 51 12
E-mail: lugano@swissarbitration.org
Bank details: Banca della Svizzera Italiana (BSI), Via Magatti 2, CH-6901 Lugano
Account No: A201021A
Clearing No: 8465
Swift Code: BSILCH22
Iban: CH64 0846 5000 0A20 1021 A

c/o Chamber of Commerce and Industry of Vaud
Avenue d'Ouchy 47
P.O. Box 315
CH-1001 Lausanne
Telephone: +41 21 613 35 31
Fax: +41 21 613 35 05
E-mail: lausanne@swissarbitration.org

Bank details: Banque Cantonale Vaudoise, 1001 Lausanne
Account No: CO 5284.78.17
Clearing No: 767
Swift Code: BCVLCH2LXX
Iban: CH44 0076 7000 U528 4781 7

c/o Zurich Chamber of Commerce
Selnaustrasse 32
P.O. Box 3058
CH-8022 Zurich
Telephone: +41 44 217 40 50
Fax: +41 44 217 40 51
E-mail: zurich@swissarbitration.org
Bank details: Credit Suisse, CH-8070 Zurich
Account No: 497380-01
Clearing No: 4835
Swift Code: CRESCHZZ80A
Iban: CH62 0483 5049 7380 0100 0

Appendix B
Schedule of Costs (effective as of 1 June 2012)

(All amounts in this Appendix B are in Swiss francs, hereinafter "CHF").

1. Registration Fee and Deposits

1.1 When submitting a Notice of Arbitration, the Claimant shall pay a non-refundable Registration Fee of

- CHF 4,500 for arbitrations where the amount in dispute does not exceed CHF 2,000,000;
- CHF 6,000 for arbitrations where the amount in dispute is between CHF 2,000,001 and CHF 10,000,000;
- CHF 8,000 for arbitrations where the amount in dispute exceeds CHF 10,000,000.

1.2 If the amount in dispute is not quantified, the Claimant shall pay a non-refundable Registration Fee of CHF 6,000.

1.3 The above provisions shall apply to any counterclaim.

1.4 Under the Expedited Procedure, upon receipt of the Notice of Arbitration, the Court shall request the Claimant to pay a Provisional Deposit of CHF 5,000.

1.5 If the Registration Fee or any Provisional Deposit is not paid, the arbitration shall not proceed with respect to the related claim(s) or counterclaim(s).

1.6 A party applying for Emergency Relief shall pay a non-refundable Registration Fee of CHF 4,500 and a deposit as an advance for the costs of the emergency relief proceedings of CHF 20,000 together with the Application. If the Registration Fee and the deposit are not paid, the Court shall not proceed with the emergency relief proceedings.

1.7 In case of a request for the correction or interpretation of the award or for an additional award made pursuant to Articles 35, 36 or 37, or where a judicial authority remits an award to the arbitral tribunal, the arbitral tribunal may request a supplementary deposit with prior approval of the Court.

2. Fees and Administrative Costs

2.1 The fees referred to in Articles 38(a) and (g) shall cover the activities of the arbitral tribunal and the emergency arbitrator, respectively, from the moment the file is transmitted until the final award, termination order, or decision in emergency relief proceedings.

2.2 Where the amount in dispute exceeds the threshold specified in Section 6 of this Appendix B, Administrative Costs[1] shall be payable to the Swiss Chambers' Arbitration Institution,
in addition to the Registration Fee.

2.3 As a rule, and except for emergency relief proceedings, the fees of the arbitral tribunal and the Administrative Costs shall be computed on the basis of the scale in Section 6 of this Appendix B, taking into account the criteria of Article 39(1). The fees of the arbitral tribunal, the deposits requested pursuant to Article 41, as well as the Administrative Costs may exceed the amounts set out in the scale only in exceptional circumstances and with prior approval of the Court.

2.4 Claims and counterclaims are added for the determination of the amount in dispute. The same rule applies to set-off defences, unless the arbitral tribunal, after consulting with the parties, concludes that such set-off defences will not require significant additional work.

2.5 Interest claims shall not be taken into account for the calculation of the amount in dispute. However, when the interest claims exceed the amount claimed as principal, the interest claims alone shall be taken into account for the calculation of the amount in dispute.

2.6 Amounts in currencies other than the Swiss franc shall be converted into Swiss francs at the rate of exchange applicable at the time the Notice of Arbitration is received by the Secretariat or at the time any new claim,

[1] This is a contribution, in the maximum amount of CHF 50,000, to the Administrative Costs of the Swiss Chambers' Arbitration Institution, in addition to the Registration Fee. In the event of a discontinuation of the arbitral proceedings (Article 39(1)), the Swiss Chambers' Arbitration

counterclaim, set-off defence or amendment to a claim or defence is filed.
2.7 If the amount in dispute is not quantified, the fees of the arbitral tribunal and the Administrative Costs shall be determined by the arbitral tribunal, the calculation of the amount in dispute.
2.8 Where the parties do not agree to refer the case to a sole arbitrator as provided for by Article 42(2) (Expedited Procedure), the fees of the arbitrators shall be determined in accordance with the scale in Section 6 of this Appendix B, but shall not be less than the fees resulting from the application of an hourly rate of CHF 350 (three hundred fifty Swiss francs) for the arbitrators.
2.9 The fees of the emergency arbitrator shall range from CHF 2,000 to CHF 20,000. They may exceed CHF 20,000 only in exceptional circumstances and with the approval of the Court.

3. Expenses

The expenses of the arbitral tribunal and the emergency arbitrator shall cover their reasonable disbursements for the arbitration, such as expenses for travel, accommodation, meals, and any other costs related to the conduct of the proceedings. The Court shall issue general guidelines for the accounting of such expenses.[2]

4. Administration of Deposits

4.1 The Secretariat or, if so requested by the Secretariat, the arbitral tribunal, is to hold the deposits to be paid by the parties in a separate bank account which is solely used for, and clearly identified as relating to, the arbitral proceedings in question.
4.2 With the approval of the Court, part of the deposits may from time to time be released to each member of the arbitral tribunal as an advance on

5. Taxes and Charges Applicable to Fees

Amounts payable to the arbitral tribunal or emergency arbitrator do not include any possible value added taxes (VAT) or other taxes or charges that may be applicable to the fees of a member of the arbitral tribunal or emergency arbitrator. Parties have a duty to pay any such taxes or charges. The recovery of any such taxes or charges is a matter solely between each member of the arbitral or the emergency arbitrator, on the one hand, and the parties, on the other.

Institution may, in its discretion, decide not to charge all or part of the Administrative Costs.
[2] The guidelines are available at <www.swissarbitration.org>.

6. Scale of Arbitrator's Fee and Administrative Costs

6.1 Sole Arbitrator

Amount in Dispute	Administrative costs	Sole Arbitrator	
		Minimum	Maximum
0 – 300,000	–	4% of amount	12% of amount
300,001 – 600,000	–	12,000 + 2% of amount over 300,000	36,000 + 8% of amount over 300,000
600,001 – 1,000,000	–	18,000 + 1.5% of amount over 600,000	60,000 + 6% of amount over 600,000
1,000,001 – 2,000,000	–	24,000 + 0.6% of amount over 1,000,000	84,000 + 3.6% of amount over 1,000,000
2,000,001 – 10,000,000	4,000 + 0.2% of amount over 2,000,000	30,000 + 0.38% of amount over 2,000,000	120,000 + 1.5% of amount over 2,000,000
10,000,001 – 20,000,000	20,000 + 0.1% of amount over 10,000,000	60,400 + 0.3% of amount over 10,000,000	240,000 + 0.6% of amount over 10,000,000
20,000,001 – 50,000,000	30,000 + 0.05% of amount over 20,000,000	90,400 + 0.1% of amount over 20,000,000	300,000 + 0.2% of amount over 20,000,000
50,000,001 – 100,000,000	45,000 + 0.01% of amount over 50,000,000	120,400 + 0.06% of amount over 50,000,000	360,000 + 0.18% of amount over 50,000,000
100,000,001 – 250,000,000	50,000	150,400 + 0.02% of amount over 100,000,000	450,000 + 0.1% of amount over 100,000,000
> 250,000,000	50,000	180,400 + 0.01% of amount over 250,000,000	600,000 + 0.06% of amount over 250,000,000

6. Scale of Arbitrator's Fee and Administrative Costs

6.2 Three Arbitrators[3]

Amount in Dispute	Administrative costs	Sole Arbitrator	
		Minimum	Maximum
0 – 300,000	—	10% of amount	30% of amount
300,001 – 600,000	—	30,000 + 5% of amount over 300,000	90,000 + 20% of amount over 300,000
600,001 – 1,000,000	—	45,000 + 3.75% of amount over 600,000	150,000 + 15% of amount over 600,000
1,000,001 – 2,000,000	—	60,000 + 1.5% of amount over 1,000,000	210,000 + 9% of amount over 1,000,000
2,000,001 – 10,000,000	4,000 + 0.2% of amount over 2,000,000	75,000 + 0.95% of amount over 2,000,000	300,000 + 3.75% of amount over 2,000,000
10,000,001 – 20,000,000	20,000 + 0.1% of amount over 10,000,000	151,000 + 0.75% of amount over 10,000,000	600,000 + 1.5% of amount over 10,000,000
20,000,001 – 50,000,000	30,000 + 0.05% of amount over 20,000,000	226,000 + 0.25% of amount over 20,000,000	750,000 + 0.5% of amount over 20,000,000
50,000,001 – 100,000,000	45,000 + 0.01% of amount over 50,000,000	301,000 + 0.15% of amount over 50,000,000	900,000 + 0.45% of amount over 50,000,000
100,000,001 – 250,000,000	50,000	376,000 + 0.05% of amount over 100,000,000	1,125,000 + 0.25% of amount over 100,000,000
> 250,000,000	50,000	451,000 + 0.025% of amount over 250,000,000	1,500,000 + 0.15% of amount over 250,000,000

[3] The fees of an arbitral tribunal consisting of more than one arbitrator represent those of a sole arbitrator plus 75 % for each additional arbitrator, i.e. 250% of the fees of a sole arbitrator for a three-member tribunal.

UNCITRAL ARBITRATION RULES
(with new article 1, paragraph 4, as adopted in 2013) *

Section I Introductory Rules

Scope of Application

Article 1

1. Where parties have agreed that disputes between them in respect of a defined legal relationship, whether contractual or not, shall be referred to arbitration under the UNCITRAL Arbitration Rules, then such disputes shall be settled in accordance with these Rules subject to such modification as the parties may agree.
2. The parties to an arbitration agreement concluded after 15 August 2010 shall be presumed to have referred to the Rules in effect on the date of commencement of the arbitration, unless the parties have agreed to apply a particular version of the Rules. That presumption does not apply where the arbitration agreement has been concluded by accepting after 15 August 2010 an offer made before that date.
3. These Rules shall govern the arbitration except that where any of these Rules is in conflict with a provision of the law applicable to the arbitration from which the parties cannot derogate, that provision shall prevail.
4. For investor-State arbitration initiated pursuant to a treaty providing for the protection of investments or investors, these Rules include the UNCITRAL Rules on Transparency in Treaty based Investor-State Arbitration ("Rules on Transparency"), subject to article 1 of the Rules on Transparency.

Notice and Calculation of Periods of Time

Article 2

1. A notice, including a notification, communication or proposal, may be transmitted by any means of communication that provides or allows for a record of its transmission.
2. If an address has been designated by a party specifically for this purpose or authorized by the arbitral tribunal, any notice shall be delivered to that party at that address, and if so delivered shall be deemed to have been received. Delivery by electronic means such as facsimile or e-mail may only be made to an address so designated or authorized.
3. In the absence of such designation or authorization, a notice is:

(a) Received if it is physically delivered to the addressee; or

(b) Deemed to have been received if it is delivered at the place of business, habitual residence or mailing address of the addressee.

4. If, after reasonable efforts, delivery cannot be effected in accordance with paragraphs 2 or 3, a notice is deemed to have been received if it is sent to the addressee's last-known place of business, habitual residence or mailing

---

* For a commentary on the UNCITRAL Arbitration Rules, David D. Caron and Lee M. Caplan (eds), *The UNCITRAL Arbitration Rules: A Commentary* (2nd edn, Oxford University Press, 2013) and Clyde Croft, Christopher Kee and Jeff Waincymer (eds), *A Guide to the UNCITRAL Arbitration*

address by registered letter or any other means that provides a record of delivery or of attempted delivery.

5. A notice shall be deemed to have been received on the day it is delivered in accordance with paragraphs 2, 3 or 4, or attempted to be delivered in accordance with paragraph 4. A notice transmitted by electronic means is deemed to have been received on the day it is sent, except that a notice of arbitration so transmitted is only deemed to have been received on the day when it reaches the addressee's electronic address.

6. For the purpose of calculating a period of time under these Rules, such period shall begin to run on the day following the day when a notice is received. If the last day of such period is an official holiday or a non-business day at the residence or place of business of the addressee, the period is extended until the first business day which follows. Official holidays or non-business days occurring during the running of the period of time are included in calculating the period.

Notice of Arbitration

Article 3

1. The party or parties initiating recourse to arbitration (hereinafter called the "claimant") shall communicate to the other party or parties (hereinafter called the "respondent") a notice of arbitration.

2. Arbitral proceedings shall be deemed to commence on the date on which the notice of arbitration is received by the respondent.

3. The notice of arbitration shall include the following:

(a) A demand that the dispute be referred to arbitration;

(b) The names and contact details of the parties;

(c) Identification of the arbitration agreement that is invoked;

(d) Identification of any contract or other legal instrument out of or in relation to which the dispute arises or, in the absence of such contract or instrument, a brief description of the relevant relationship;

(e) A brief description of the claim and an indication of the amount involved, if any;

(f) The relief or remedy sought;

(g) A proposal as to the number of arbitrators, language and place of arbitration, if the parties have not previously agreed thereon.

4. The notice of arbitration may also include:

(a) A proposal for the designation of an appointing authority referred to in article 6, paragraph 1;

(b) A proposal for the appointment of a sole arbitrator referred to in article 8, paragraph 1;

Rules (Cambridge University Press, 2013).

(c) Notification of the appointment of an arbitrator referred to in article 9 or 10.

5. The constitution of the arbitral tribunal shall not be hindered by any controversy with respect to the sufficiency of the notice of arbitration, which shall be finally resolved by the arbitral tribunal.

Response to the Notice of Arbitration

Article 4

1. Within 30 days of the receipt of the notice of arbitration, the respondent shall communicate to the claimant a response to the notice of arbitration, which shall include:

(a) The name and contact details of each respondent;

(b) A response to the information set forth in the notice of arbitration, pursuant to article 3, paragraphs 3 (c) to (g).

2. The response to the notice of arbitration may also include:

(a) Any plea that an arbitral tribunal to be constituted under these Rules lacks jurisdiction;

(b) A proposal for the designation of an appointing authority referred to in article 6, paragraph 1;

(c) A proposal for the appointment of a sole arbitrator referred to in article 8, paragraph 1;

(d) Notification of the appointment of an arbitrator referred to in article 9 or 10;

(e) A brief description of counterclaims or claims for the purpose of a set-off, if any, including where relevant, an indication of the amounts involved, and the relief or remedy sought;

(f) A notice of arbitration in accordance with article 3 in case the respondent formulates a claim against a party to the arbitration agreement other than the claimant.

3. The constitution of the arbitral tribunal shall not be hindered by any controversy with respect to the respondent's failure to communicate a response to the notice of arbitration, or an incomplete or late response to the notice of arbitration, which shall be finally resolved by the arbitral tribunal.

Representation and Assistance

Article 5

Each party may be represented or assisted by persons chosen by it. The names and addresses of such persons must be communicated to all parties and to the arbitral tribunal. Such communication must specify whether the appointment is being made for purposes of representation or assistance. Where a person is to act as a representative of a party, the arbitral tribunal, on its own initiative or at the request of any party, may at any time require proof of authority granted to the representative in such a form as the arbitral tribunal may determine.

Designating and Appointing Authorities

Article 6

1. Unless the parties have already agreed on the choice of an appointing authority, a party may at any time propose the name or names of one or more institutions or persons, including the Secretary-General of the Permanent Court of Arbitration at The Hague (hereinafter called the "PCA"), one of whom would serve as appointing authority.

2. If all parties have not agreed on the choice of an appointing authority within 30 days after a proposal made in accordance with paragraph 1 has been received by all other parties, any party may request the Secretary-General of the PCA to designate the appointing authority.

3. Where these Rules provide for a period of time within which a party must refer a matter to an appointing authority and no appointing authority has been agreed on or designated, the period is suspended from the date on which a party initiates the procedure for agreeing on or designating an appointing authority until the date of such agreement or designation.

4. Except as referred to in article 41, paragraph 4, if the appointing authority refuses to act, or if it fails to appoint an arbitrator within 30 days after it receives a party's request to do so, fails to act within any other period provided by these Rules, or fails to decide on a challenge to an arbitrator within a reasonable time after receiving a party's request to do so, any party may request the Secretary-General of the PCA to designate a substitute appointing authority.

5. In exercising their functions under these Rules, the appointing authority and the Secretary-General of the PCA may require from any party and the arbitrators the information they deem necessary and they shall give the parties and, where appropriate, the arbitrators, an opportunity to present their views in any manner they consider appropriate. All such communications to and from the appointing authority and the Secretary-General of the PCA shall also be provided by the sender to all other parties.

6. When the appointing authority is requested to appoint an arbitrator pursuant to articles 8, 9, 10 or 14, the party making the request shall send to the appointing authority copies of the notice of arbitration and, if it exists, any response to the notice of arbitration.

7. The appointing authority shall have regard to such considerations as are likely to secure the appointment of an independent and impartial arbitrator

and shall take into account the advisability of appointing an arbitrator of a nationality other than the nationalities of the parties.

Section II Composition of the Arbitral Tribunal

Number of Arbitrators

Article 7

1. If the parties have not previously agreed on the number of arbitrators, and if within 30 days after the receipt by the respondent of the notice of arbitration the parties have not agreed that there shall be only one arbitrator, three arbitrators shall be appointed.

2. Notwithstanding paragraph 1, if no other parties have responded to a party's proposal to appoint a sole arbitrator within the time limit provided for in paragraph 1 and the party or parties concerned have failed to appoint a second arbitrator in accordance with article 9 or 10, the appointing authority may, at the request of a party, appoint a sole arbitrator pursuant to the procedure provided for in article 8, paragraph 2, if it determines that, in view of the circumstances of the case, this is more appropriate.

Appointment of Arbitrators (Articles 8 to 10)

Article 8

1. If the parties have agreed that a sole arbitrator is to be appointed and if within 30 days after receipt by all other parties of a proposal for the appointment of a sole arbitrator the parties have not reached agreement thereon, a sole arbitrator shall, at the request of a party, be appointed by the appointing authority.

2. The appointing authority shall appoint the sole arbitrator as promptly as possible. In making the appointment, the appointing authority shall use the following list-procedure, unless the parties agree that the list-procedure should not be used or unless the appointing authority determines in its discretion that the use of the list-procedure is not appropriate for the case:

(a) The appointing authority shall communicate to each of the parties an identical list containing at least three names;

(b) Within 15 days after the receipt of this list, each party may return the list to the appointing authority after having deleted the name or names to which it objects and numbered the remaining names on the list in the order of its preference;

(c) After the expiration of the above period of time the appointing authority shall appoint the sole arbitrator from among the names approved on the lists returned to it and in accordance with the order of preference indicated by the parties;

(d) If for any reason the appointment cannot be made according to this procedure, the appointing authority may exercise its discretion in appointing the sole arbitrator.

Article 9

1. If three arbitrators are to be appointed, each party shall appoint one arbitrator. The two arbitrators thus appointed shall choose the third arbitrator who will act as the presiding arbitrator of the arbitral tribunal.
2. If within 30 days after the receipt of a party's notification of the appointment of an arbitrator the other party has not notified the first party of the arbitrator it has appointed, the first party may request the appointing authority to appoint the second arbitrator.
3. If within 30 days after the appointment of the second arbitrator the two arbitrators have not agreed on the choice of the presiding arbitrator, the presiding arbitrator shall be appointed by the appointing authority in the same way as a sole arbitrator would be appointed under article 8.

Article 10

1. For the purposes of article 9, paragraph 1, where three arbitrators are to be appointed and there are multiple parties as claimant or as respondent, unless the parties have agreed to another method of appointment of arbitrators, the multiple parties jointly, whether as claimant or as respondent, shall appoint an arbitrator.
2. If the parties have agreed that the arbitral tribunal is to be composed of a number of arbitrators other than one or three, the arbitrators shall be appointed according to the method agreed upon by the parties.
3. In the event of any failure to constitute the arbitral tribunal under these Rules, the appointing authority shall, at the request of any party, constitute the arbitral tribunal and, in doing so, may revoke any appointment already made and appoint or reappoint each of the arbitrators and designate one of them as the presiding arbitrator.

Disclosures by and Challenge of Arbitrators (Articles 11 to 13)

Article 11

When a person is approached in connection with his or her possible appointment as an arbitrator, he or she shall disclose any circumstances likely to give rise to justifiable doubts as to his or her impartiality or independence. An arbitrator, from the time of his or her appointment and throughout the arbitral proceedings, shall without delay disclose any such circumstances to the parties and the other arbitrators unless they have already been informed by him or her of these circumstances.

Article 12

1. Any arbitrator may be challenged if circumstances exist that give rise to

justifiable doubts as to the arbitrator's impartiality or independence.
2. A party may challenge the arbitrator appointed by it only for reasons of which it becomes aware after the appointment has been made.
3. In the event that an arbitrator fails to act or in the event of the de jure or de facto impossibility of his or her performing his or her functions, the procedure in respect of the challenge of an arbitrator as provided in article 13 shall apply.

Article 13

1. A party that intends to challenge an arbitrator shall send notice of its challenge within 15 days after it has been notified of the appointment of the challenged arbitrator, or within 15 days after the circumstances mentioned in articles 11 and 12 became known to that party.
2. The notice of challenge shall be communicated to all other parties, to the arbitrator who is challenged and to the other arbitrators. The notice of challenge shall state the reasons for the challenge.
3. When an arbitrator has been challenged by a party, all parties may agree to the challenge. The arbitrator may also, after the challenge, withdraw from his or her office. In neither case does this imply acceptance of the validity of the grounds for the challenge.
4. If, within 15 days from the date of the notice of challenge, all parties do not agree to the challenge or the challenged arbitrator does not withdraw, the party making the challenge may elect to pursue it. In that case, within 30 days from the date of the notice of challenge, it shall seek a decision on the challenge by the appointing authority.

Replacement of an Arbitrator

Article 14

1. Subject to paragraph 2, in any event where an arbitrator has to be replaced during the course of the arbitral proceedings, a substitute arbitrator shall be appointed or chosen pursuant to the procedure provided for in articles 8 to 11 that was applicable to the appointment or choice of the arbitrator being replaced. This procedure shall apply even if during the process of appointing the arbitrator to be replaced, a party had failed to exercise its right to appoint or to participate in the appointment.
2. If, at the request of a party, the appointing authority determines that, in view of the exceptional circumstances of the case, it would be justified for a party to be deprived of its right to appoint a substitute arbitrator, the appointing authority may, after giving an opportunity to the parties and the remaining arbitrators to express their views: (a) appoint the substitute arbitrator; or (b) after the closure of the hearings, authorize the other

arbitrators to proceed with the arbitration and make any decision or award.

Repetition of Hearings in the Event of the Replacement of an Arbitrator

Article 15

If an arbitrator is replaced, the proceedings shall resume at the stage where the arbitrator who was replaced ceased to perform his or her functions, unless the arbitral tribunal decides otherwise.

Exclusion of Liability

Article 16

Save for intentional wrongdoing, the parties waive, to the fullest extent permitted under the applicable law, any claim against the arbitrators, the appointing authority and any person appointed by the arbitral tribunal based on any act or omission in connection with the arbitration.

Section III Arbitral Proceedings

General Provisions

Article 17

1. Subject to these Rules, the arbitral tribunal may conduct the arbitration in such manner as it considers appropriate, provided that the parties are treated with equality and that at an appropriate stage of the proceedings each party is given a reasonable opportunity of presenting its case. The arbitral tribunal, in exercising its discretion, shall conduct the proceedings so as to avoid unnecessary delay and expense and to provide a fair and efficient process for resolving the parties' dispute.
2. As soon as practicable after its constitution and after inviting the parties to express their views, the arbitral tribunal shall establish the provisional timetable of the arbitration. The arbitral tribunal may, at any time, after inviting the parties to express their views, extend or abridge any period of time prescribed under these Rules or agreed by the parties.
3. If at an appropriate stage of the proceedings any party so requests, the arbitral tribunal shall hold hearings for the presentation of evidence by witnesses, including expert witnesses, or for oral argument. In the absence of such a request, the arbitral tribunal shall decide whether to hold such hearings or whether the proceedings shall be conducted on the basis of documents and other materials.
4. All communications to the arbitral tribunal by one party shall be communicated by that party to all other parties. Such communications shall be made at the same time, except as otherwise permitted by the arbitral tribunal if it may do so under applicable law.
5. The arbitral tribunal may, at the request of any party, allow one or more

third persons to be joined in the arbitration as a party provided such person is a party to the arbitration agreement, unless the arbitral tribunal finds, after giving all parties, including the person or persons to be joined, the opportunity to be heard, that joinder should not be permitted because of prejudice to any of those parties. The arbitral tribunal may make a single award or several awards in respect of all parties so involved in the arbitration.

Place of Arbitration

Article 18

1. If the parties have not previously agreed on the place of arbitration, the place of arbitration shall be determined by the arbitral tribunal having regard to the circumstances of the case. The award shall be deemed to have been made at the place of arbitration.

2. The arbitral tribunal may meet at any location it considers appropriate for deliberations. Unless otherwise agreed by the parties, the arbitral tribunal may also meet at any location it considers appropriate for any other purpose, including hearings.

Language

Article 19

1. Subject to an agreement by the parties, the arbitral tribunal shall, promptly after its appointment, determine the language or languages to be used in the proceedings. This determination shall apply to the statement of claim, the statement of defence, and any further written statements and, if oral hearings take place, to the language or languages to be used in such hearings.

2. The arbitral tribunal may order that any documents annexed to the statement of claim or statement of defence, and any supplementary documents or exhibit submitted in the course of the proceedings, delivered in their original language, shall be accompanied by a translation into the language or languages agreed upon by the parties or determined by the arbitral tribunal.

Statement of Claim

Article 20

1. The claimant shall communicate its statement of claim in writing to the respondent and to each of the arbitrators within a period of time to be determined by the arbitral tribunal. The claimant may elect to treat its notice of arbitration referred to in article 3 as a statement of claim, provided that the notice of arbitration also complies with the requirements of paragraphs 2 to 4 of this article.

2. The statement of claim shall include the following particulars:
(a) The names and contact details of the parties;
(b) A statement of the facts supporting the claim;
(c) The points at issue;
(d) The relief or remedy sought;
(e) The legal grounds or arguments supporting the claim.
3. A copy of any contract or other legal instrument out of or in relation to which the dispute arises and of the arbitration agreement shall be annexed to the statement of claim.
4. The statement of claim should, as far as possible, be accompanied by all documents and other evidence relied upon by the claimant, or contain references to them.

Statement of Defence

Article 21

1. The respondent shall communicate its statement of defence in writing to the claimant and to each of the arbitrators within a period of time to be determined by the arbitral tribunal. The respondent may elect to treat its response to the notice of arbitration referred to in article 4 as a statement of defence, provided that the response to the notice of arbitration also complies with the requirements of paragraph 2 of this article.
2. The statement of defence shall reply to the particulars (b) to (e) of the statement of claim (art. 20, para. 2). The statement of defence should, as far as possible, be accompanied by all documents and other evidence relied upon by the respondent, or contain references to them.
3. In its statement of defence, or at a later stage in the arbitral proceedings if the arbitral tribunal decides that the delay was justified under the circumstances, the respondent may make a counterclaim or rely on a claim for the purpose of a set-off provided that the arbitral tribunal has jurisdiction over it.
4. The provisions of article 20, paragraphs 2 to 4, shall apply to a counterclaim, a claim under article 4, paragraph 2 (f), and a claim relied on for the purpose of a set-off.

Amendments to the Claim or Defence

Article 22

During the course of the arbitral proceedings, a party may amend or supplement its claim or defence, including a counterclaim or a claim for the purpose of a set-off, unless the arbitral tribunal considers it inappropriate to allow such amendment or supplement having regard to the delay in making it or prejudice to other parties or any other circumstances. However, a claim or defence, including a counterclaim or a claim for the purpose of a set-off, may not be amended or supplemented in such a manner that the amended or supplemented claim or defence falls outside the jurisdiction of the arbitral tribunal.

Pleas as to the Jurisdiction of the Arbitral Tribunal

Article 23

1. The arbitral tribunal shall have the power to rule on its own jurisdiction, including any objections with respect to the existence or validity of the arbitration agreement. For that purpose, an arbitration clause that forms part of a contract shall be treated as an agreement independent of the other terms of the contract. A decision by the arbitral tribunal that the contract is null shall not entail automatically the invalidity of the arbitration clause.
2. A plea that the arbitral tribunal does not have jurisdiction shall be raised no later than in the statement of defence or, with respect to a counterclaim or a claim for the purpose of a set-off, in the reply to the counterclaim or to the claim for the purpose of a set-off. A party is not precluded from raising such a plea by the fact that it has appointed, or participated in the appointment of, an arbitrator. A plea that the arbitral tribunal is exceeding the scope of its authority shall be raised as soon as the matter alleged to be beyond the scope of its authority is raised during the arbitral proceedings. The arbitral tribunal may, in either case, admit a later plea if it considers the delay justified.
3. The arbitral tribunal may rule on a plea referred to in paragraph 2 either as a preliminary question or in an award on the merits. The arbitral tribunal may continue the arbitral proceedings and make an award, notwithstanding any pending challenge to its jurisdiction before a court.

Further Written Statements

Article 24

The arbitral tribunal shall decide which further written statements, in addition to the statement of claim and the statement of defence, shall be required from the parties or may be presented by them and shall fix the periods of time for communicating such statements.

Periods of Time

Article 25

The periods of time fixed by the arbitral tribunal for the communication of written statements (including the statement of claim and statement of defence) should not exceed 45 days. However, the arbitral tribunal may extend the time limits if it concludes that an extension is justified.

Interim Measures
Article 26

1. The arbitral tribunal may, at the request of a party, grant interim measures.

2. An interim measure is any temporary measure by which, at any time prior to the issuance of the award by which the dispute is finally decided, the arbitral tribunal orders a party, for example and without limitation, to:

(a) Maintain or restore the status quo pending determination of the dispute;

(b) Take action that would prevent, or refrain from taking action that is likely to cause, (i) current or imminent harm or (ii) prejudice to the arbitral process itself;

(c) Provide a means of preserving assets out of which a subsequent award may be satisfied; or

(d) Preserve evidence that may be relevant and material to the resolution of the dispute.

3. The party requesting an interim measure under paragraphs 2 (a) to (c) shall satisfy the arbitral tribunal that:

(a) Harm not adequately reparable by an award of damages is likely to result if the measure is not ordered, and such harm substantially outweighs the harm that is likely to result to the party against whom the measure is directed if the measure is granted; and

(b) There is a reasonable possibility that the requesting party will succeed on the merits of the claim. The determination on this possibility shall not affect the discretion of the arbitral tribunal in making any subsequent determination.

4. With regard to a request for an interim measure under paragraph 2 (d), the requirements in paragraphs 3 (a) and (b) shall apply only to the extent the arbitral tribunal considers appropriate.

5. The arbitral tribunal may modify, suspend or terminate an interim measure it has granted, upon application of any party or, in exceptional circumstances and upon prior notice to the parties, on the arbitral tribunal's own initiative.

6. The arbitral tribunal may require the party requesting an interim measure to provide appropriate security in connection with the measure.

7. The arbitral tribunal may require any party promptly to disclose any material change in the circumstances on the basis of which the interim measure was requested or granted.

8. The party requesting an interim measure may be liable for any costs and damages caused by the measure to any party if the arbitral tribunal later

determines that, in the circumstances then prevailing, the measure should not have been granted. The arbitral tribunal may award such costs and damages at any point during the proceedings.

9. A request for interim measures addressed by any party to a judicial authority shall not be deemed incompatible with the agreement to arbitrate, or as a waiver of that agreement.

Evidence

Article 27

1. Each party shall have the burden of proving the facts relied on to support its claim or defence.

2. Witnesses, including expert witnesses, who are presented by the parties to testify to the arbitral tribunal on any issue of fact or expertise may be any individual, notwithstanding that the individual is a party to the arbitration or in any way related to a party. Unless otherwise directed by the arbitral tribunal, statements by witnesses, including expert witnesses, may be presented in writing and signed by them.

3. At any time during the arbitral proceedings the arbitral tribunal may require the parties to produce documents, exhibits or other evidence within such a period of time as the arbitral tribunal shall determine.

4. The arbitral tribunal shall determine the admissibility, relevance, materiality and weight of the evidence offered.

Hearings

Article 28

1. In the event of an oral hearing, the arbitral tribunal shall give the parties adequate advance notice of the date, time and place thereof.

2. Witnesses, including expert witnesses, may be heard under the conditions and examined in the manner set by the arbitral tribunal.

3. Hearings shall be held in camera unless the parties agree otherwise. The arbitral tribunal may require the retirement of any witness or witnesses, including expert witnesses, during the testimony of such other witnesses, except that a witness, including an expert witness, who is a party to the arbitration shall not, in principle, be asked to retire.

4. The arbitral tribunal may direct that witnesses, including expert witnesses, be examined through means of telecommunication that do not require their physical presence at the hearing (such as videoconference).

Experts Appointed by the Arbitral Tribunal

Article 29

1. After consultation with the parties, the arbitral tribunal may appoint one or more independent experts to report to it, in writing, on specific issues to

be determined by the arbitral tribunal. A copy of the expert's terms of reference, established by the arbitral tribunal, shall be communicated to the parties.
2. The expert shall, in principle before accepting appointment, submit to the arbitral tribunal and to the parties a description of his or her qualifications and a statement of his or her impartiality and independence. Within the time ordered by the arbitral tribunal, the parties shall inform the arbitral tribunal whether they have any objections as to the expert's qualifications, impartiality or independence. The arbitral tribunal shall decide promptly whether to accept any such objections. After an expert's appointment, a party may object to the expert's qualifications, impartiality or independence only if the objection is for reasons of which the party becomes aware after the appointment has been made. The arbitral tribunal shall decide promptly what, if any, action to take.
3. The parties shall give the expert any relevant information or produce for his or her inspection any relevant documents or goods that he or she may require of them. Any dispute between a party and such expert as to the relevance of the required information or production shall be referred to the arbitral tribunal for decision.
4. Upon receipt of the expert's report, the arbitral tribunal shall communicate a copy of the report to the parties, which shall be given the opportunity to express, in writing, their opinion on the report. A party shall be entitled to examine any document on which the expert has relied in his or her report.
5. At the request of any party, the expert, after delivery of the report, may be heard at a hearing where the parties shall have the opportunity to be present and to interrogate the expert. At this hearing, any party may present expert witnesses in order to testify on the points at issue. The provisions of article 28 shall be applicable to such proceedings.

Default

Article 30

1. If, within the period of time fixed by these Rules or the arbitral tribunal, without showing sufficient cause:
(a) The claimant has failed to communicate its statement of claim, the arbitral tribunal shall issue an order for the termination of the arbitral proceedings, unless there are remaining matters that may need to be decided and the arbitral tribunal considers it appropriate to do so;
(b) The respondent has failed to communicate its response to the notice of arbitration or its statement of defence, the arbitral tribunal shall order that

the proceedings continue, without treating such failure in itself as an admission of the claimant's allegations; the provisions of this subparagraph also apply to a claimant's failure to submit a defence to a counterclaim or to a claim for the purpose of a set-off.
2. If a party, duly notified under these Rules, fails to appear at a hearing, without showing sufficient cause for such failure, the arbitral tribunal may proceed with the arbitration.
3. If a party, duly invited by the arbitral tribunal to produce documents, exhibits or other evidence, fails to do so within the established period of time, without showing sufficient cause for such failure, the arbitral tribunal may make the award on the evidence before it.

Closure of Hearings

Article 31

1. The arbitral tribunal may inquire of the parties if they have any further proof to offer or witnesses to be heard or submissions to make and, if there are none, it may declare the hearings closed.
2. The arbitral tribunal may, if it considers it necessary owing to exceptional circumstances, decide, on its own initiative or upon application of a party, to reopen the hearings at any time before the award is made.

Waiver of Right to Object

Article 32

A failure by any party to object promptly to any non-compliance with these Rules or with any requirement of the arbitration agreement shall be deemed to be a waiver of the right of such party to make such an objection, unless such party can show that, under the circumstances, its failure to object was justified.

Section IV The Award

Decisions

Article 33

1. When there is more than one arbitrator, any award or other decision of the arbitral tribunal shall be made by a majority of the arbitrators.
2. In the case of questions of procedure, when there is no majority or when the arbitral tribunal so authorizes, the presiding arbitrator may decide alone, subject to revision, if any, by the arbitral tribunal.

Form and Effect of the Award

Article 34

1. The arbitral tribunal may make separate awards on different issues at different times.
2. All awards shall be made in writing and shall be final and binding on the

parties. The parties shall carry out all awards without delay.
3. The arbitral tribunal shall state the reasons upon which the award is based, unless the parties have agreed that no reasons are to be given.
4. An award shall be signed by the arbitrators and it shall contain the date on which the award was made and indicate the place of arbitration. Where there is more than one arbitrator and any of them fails to sign, the award shall state the reason for the absence of the signature.
5. An award may be made public with the consent of all parties or where and to the extent disclosure is required of a party by legal duty, to protect or pursue a legal right or in relation to legal proceedings before a court or other competent authority.
6. Copies of the award signed by the arbitrators shall be communicated to the parties by the arbitral tribunal.

Applicable Law, *Amiable Compositeur*

Article 35

1. The arbitral tribunal shall apply the rules of law designated by the parties as applicable to the substance of the dispute. Failing such designation by the parties, the arbitral tribunal shall apply the law which it determines to be appropriate.
2. The arbitral tribunal shall decide as *amiable compositeur* or *ex aequo et bono* only if the parties have expressly authorized the arbitral tribunal to do so.
3. In all cases, the arbitral tribunal shall decide in accordance with the terms of the contract, if any, and shall take into account any usage of trade applicable to the transaction.

Settlement or Other Grounds for Termination

Article 36

1. If, before the award is made, the parties agree on a settlement of the dispute, the arbitral tribunal shall either issue an order for the termination of the arbitral proceedings or, if requested by the parties and accepted by the arbitral tribunal, record the settlement in the form of an arbitral award on agreed terms. The arbitral tribunal is not obliged to give reasons for such an award.
2. If, before the award is made, the continuation of the arbitral proceedings becomes unnecessary or impossible for any reason not mentioned in paragraph 1, the arbitral tribunal shall inform the parties of its intention to issue an order for the termination of the proceedings. The arbitral tribunal shall have the power to issue such an order unless there are remaining matters that may need to be decided and the arbitral tribunal considers it

appropriate to do so.
3. Copies of the order for termination of the arbitral proceedings or of the arbitral award on agreed terms, signed by the arbitrators, shall be communicated by the arbitral tribunal to the parties. Where an arbitral award on agreed terms is made, the provisions of article 34, paragraphs 2, 4 and 5, shall apply.

Interpretation of the Award

Article 37

1. Within 30 days after the receipt of the award, a party, with notice to the other parties, may request that the arbitral tribunal give an interpretation of the award.
2. The interpretation shall be given in writing within 45 days after the receipt of the request. The interpretation shall form part of the award and the provisions of article 34, paragraphs 2 to 6, shall apply.

Correction of the Award

Article 38

1. Within 30 days after the receipt of the award, a party, with notice to the other parties, may request the arbitral tribunal to correct in the award any error in computation, any clerical or typographical error, or any error or omission of a similar nature. If the arbitral tribunal considers that the request is justified, it shall make the correction within 45 days of receipt of the request.
2. The arbitral tribunal may within 30 days after the communication of the award make such corrections on its own initiative.
3. Such corrections shall be in writing and shall form part of the award. The provisions of article 34, paragraphs 2 to 6, shall apply.

Additional Award

Article 39

1. Within 30 days after the receipt of the termination order or the award, a party, with notice to the other parties, may request the arbitral tribunal to make an award or an additional award as to claims presented in the arbitral proceedings but not decided by the arbitral tribunal.
2. If the arbitral tribunal considers the request for an award or additional award to be justified, it shall render or complete its award within 60 days after the receipt of the request. The arbitral tribunal may extend, if necessary, the period of time within which it shall make the award.
3. When such an award or additional award is made, the provisions of article 34, paragraphs 2 to 6, shall apply.

Definition of Costs
Article 40

1. The arbitral tribunal shall fix the costs of arbitration in the final award and, if it deems appropriate, in another decision.

2. The term "costs" includes only:

(a) The fees of the arbitral tribunal to be stated separately as to each arbitrator and to be fixed by the tribunal itself in accordance with article 41;

(b) The reasonable travel and other expenses incurred by the arbitrators;

(c) The reasonable costs of expert advice and of other assistance required by the arbitral tribunal;

(d) The reasonable travel and other expenses of witnesses to the extent such expenses are approved by the arbitral tribunal;

(e) The legal and other costs incurred by the parties in relation to the arbitration to the extent that the arbitral tribunal determines that the amount of such costs is reasonable;

(f) Any fees and expenses of the appointing authority as well as the fees and expenses of the Secretary-General of the PCA.

3. In relation to interpretation, correction or completion of any award under articles 37 to 39, the arbitral tribunal may charge the costs referred to in paragraphs 2 (b) to (f), but no additional fees.

Fees and Expenses of Arbitrators
Article 41

1. The fees and expenses of the arbitrators shall be reasonable in amount, taking into account the amount in dispute, the complexity of the subject matter, the time spent by the arbitrators and any other relevant circumstances of the case.

2. If there is an appointing authority and it applies or has stated that it will apply a schedule or particular method for determining the fees for arbitrators in international cases, the arbitral tribunal in fixing its fees shall take that schedule or method into account to the extent that it considers appropriate in the circumstances of the case.

3. Promptly after its constitution, the arbitral tribunal shall inform the parties as to how it proposes to determine its fees and expenses, including any rates it intends to apply. Within 15 days of receiving that proposal, any party may refer the proposal to the appointing authority for review. If, within 45 days of receipt of such a referral, the appointing authority finds that the proposal of the arbitral tribunal is inconsistent with paragraph 1, it shall make any necessary adjustments thereto, which shall be binding upon the arbitral tribunal.

4. (a) When informing the parties of the arbitrators' fees and expenses that have been fixed pursuant to article 40, paragraphs 2 (a) and (b), the arbitral tribunal shall also explain the manner in which the corresponding amounts have been calculated;
(b) Within 15 days of receiving the arbitral tribunal's determination of fees and expenses, any party may refer for review such determination to the appointing authority. If no appointing authority has been agreed upon or designated, or if the appointing authority fails to act within the time specified in these Rules, then the review shall be made by the Secretary-General of the PCA;
(c) If the appointing authority or the Secretary-General of the PCA finds that the arbitral tribunal's determination is inconsistent with the arbitral tribunal's proposal (and any adjustment thereto) under paragraph 3 or is otherwise manifestly excessive, it shall, within 45 days of receiving such a referral, make any adjustments to the arbitral tribunal's determination that are necessary to satisfy the criteria in paragraph 1. Any such adjustments shall be binding upon the arbitral tribunal;
(d) Any such adjustments shall either be included by the arbitral tribunal in its award or, if the award has already been issued, be implemented in a correction to the award, to which the procedure of article 38, paragraph 3, shall apply.
5. Throughout the procedure under paragraphs 3 and 4, the arbitral tribunal shall proceed with the arbitration, in accordance with article 17, paragraph 1.
6. A referral under paragraph 4 shall not affect any determination in the award other than the arbitral tribunal's fees and expenses; nor shall it delay the recognition and enforcement of all parts of the award other than those relating to the determination of the arbitral tribunal's fees and expenses.

Allocation of Costs

Article 42

1. The costs of the arbitration shall in principle be borne by the unsuccessful party or parties. However, the arbitral tribunal may apportion each of such costs between the parties if it determines that apportionment is reasonable, taking into account the circumstances of the case.
2. The arbitral tribunal shall in the final award or, if it deems appropriate, in any other award, determine any amount that a party may have to pay to another party as a result of the decision on allocation of costs.

Deposit of Costs
Article 43

1. The arbitral tribunal, on its establishment, may request the parties to deposit an equal amount as an advance for the costs referred to in article 40, paragraphs 2 (a) to (c).
2. During the course of the arbitral proceedings the arbitral tribunal may request supplementary deposits from the parties.
3. If an appointing authority has been agreed upon or designated, and when a party so requests and the appointing authority consents to perform the function, the arbitral tribunal shall fix the amounts of any deposits or supplementary deposits only after consultation with the appointing authority, which may make any comments to the arbitral tribunal that it deems appropriate concerning the amount of such deposits and supplementary deposits.
4. If the required deposits are not paid in full within 30 days after the receipt of the request, the arbitral tribunal shall so inform the parties in order that one or more of them may make the required payment. If such payment is not made, the arbitral tribunal may order the suspension or termination of the arbitral proceedings.
5. After a termination order or final award has been made, the arbitral tribunal shall render an accounting to the parties of the deposits received and return any unexpended balance to the parties.

UNCITRAL Rules on Transparency in Treaty-based Investor-State Arbitration

Article 1 — Scope of Application

Applicability of the Rules

1. The UNCITRAL Rules on Transparency in Treaty-based Investor-State Arbitration ("Rules on Transparency") shall apply to investor-State arbitration initiated under the UNCITRAL Arbitration Rules pursuant to a treaty providing for the protection of investments or investors ("treaty")* concluded on or after 1 April 2014 unless the Parties to the treaty** have agreed otherwise.
2. In investor-State arbitrations initiated under the UNCITRAL Arbitration Rules pursuant to a treaty concluded before 1 April 2014, these Rules shall apply only when:

(a) The parties to an arbitration (the "disputing parties") agree to their application in respect of that arbitration; or

(b) The Parties to the treaty or, in the case of a multilateral treaty, the State

* See page 642.

** *Ibid.*

of the claimant and the respondent State, have agreed after 1 April 2014 to their application.

Application of the Rules

3. In any arbitration in which the Rules on Transparency apply pursuant to a treaty or to an agreement by the Parties to that treaty:

(a) The disputing parties may not derogate from these Rules, by agreement or otherwise, unless permitted to do so by the treaty;

(b) The arbitral tribunal shall have the power, besides its discretionary authority under certain provisions of these Rules, to adapt the requirements of any specific provision of these Rules to the particular circumstances of the case, after consultation with the disputing parties, if such adaptation is necessary to conduct the arbitration in a practical manner and is consistent with the transparency objective of these Rules.

Discretion and authority of the arbitral tribunal

4. Where the Rules on Transparency provide for the arbitral tribunal to exercise discretion, the arbitral tribunal in exercising such discretion shall take into account:

(a) The public interest in transparency in treaty-based investor-State arbitration and in the particular arbitral proceedings; and

(b) The disputing parties' interest in a fair and efficient resolution of their dispute.

5. These Rules shall not affect any authority that the arbitral tribunal may otherwise have under the UNCITRAL Arbitration Rules to conduct the arbitration in such a manner as to promote transparency, for example by accepting submissions from third persons.

6. In the presence of any conduct, measure or other action having the effect of wholly undermining the transparency objectives of these Rules, the arbitral tribunal shall ensure that those objectives prevail.

Applicable instrument in case of conflict

7. Where the Rules on Transparency apply, they shall supplement any applicable arbitration rules. Where there is a conflict between the Rules on Transparency and the applicable arbitration rules, the Rules on Transparency shall prevail. Notwithstanding any provision in these Rules, where there is a conflict between the Rules on Transparency and the treaty, the provisions of the treaty shall prevail.

8. Where any of these Rules is in conflict with a provision of the law applicable to the arbitration from which the disputing parties cannot derogate, that provision shall prevail.

Application in non-UNCITRAL arbitrations

9. These Rules are available for use in investor-State arbitrations initiated under rules other than the UNCITRAL Arbitration Rules or in *ad hoc* proceedings.

Article 2 — Publication of Information at the Commencement of Arbitral Proceedings

Once the notice of arbitration has been received by the respondent, each of the disputing parties shall promptly communicate a copy of the notice of arbitration to the repository referred to under article 8. Upon receipt of the notice of arbitration from the respondent, or upon receipt of the notice of arbitration and a record of its transmission to the respondent, the repository shall promptly make available to the public information regarding the name of the disputing parties, the economic sector involved and the treaty under which the claim is being made.

Article 3 — Publication of Documents

1. Subject to article 7, the following documents shall be made available to the public: the notice of arbitration, the response to the notice of arbitration, the statement of claim, the statement of defence and any further written statements or written submissions by any disputing party; a table listing all exhibits to the aforesaid documents and to expert reports and witness statements, if such table has been prepared for the proceedings, but not the exhibits themselves; any written submissions by the non-disputing Party (or Parties) to the treaty and by third persons, transcripts of hearings, where available; and orders, decisions and awards of the arbitral tribunal.

2. Subject to article 7, expert reports and witness statements, exclusive of the exhibits thereto, shall be made available to the public, upon request by any person to the arbitral tribunal.

3. Subject to article 7, the arbitral tribunal may decide, on its own initiative or upon request from any person, and after consultation with the disputing parties, whether and how to make available exhibits and any other documents provided to, or issued by, the arbitral tribunal not falling within paragraphs 1 or 2 above. This may include, for example, making such documents available at a specified site.

4. The documents to be made available to the public pursuant to paragraphs 1 and 2 shall be communicated by the arbitral tribunal to the repository referred to under article 8 as soon as possible, subject to any relevant arrangements or time limits for the protection of confidential or protected information prescribed under article 7. The documents to be made available pursuant to paragraph 3 may be communicated by the arbitral tribunal to the

repository referred to under article 8 as they become available and, if applicable, in a redacted form in accordance with article 7. The repository shall make all documents available in a timely manner, in the form and in the language in which it receives them.

5. A person granted access to documents under paragraph 3 shall bear any administrative costs of making those documents available to that person, such as the costs of photocopying or shipping documents to that person, but not the costs of making those documents available to the public through the repository.

Article 4 — Submission by a Third Person

1. After consultation with the disputing parties, the arbitral tribunal may allow a person that is not a disputing party, and not a non-disputing Party to the treaty ("third person(s)"), to file a written submission with the arbitral tribunal regarding a matter within the scope of the dispute.

2. A third person wishing to make a submission shall apply to the arbitral tribunal, and shall, in a concise written statement, which is in a language of the arbitration and complies with any page limits set by the arbitral tribunal:

(a) Describe the third person, including, where relevant, its membership and legal status (e.g., trade association or other non-governmental organization), its general objectives, the nature of its activities and any parent organization (including any organization that directly or indirectly controls the third person);

(b) Disclose any connection, direct or indirect, which the third person has with any disputing party;

(c) Provide information on any government, person or organization that has provided to the third person (i) any financial or other assistance in preparing the submission; or (ii) substantial assistance in either of the two years preceding the application by the third person under this article (e.g. funding around 20 per cent of its overall operations annually);

(d) Describe the nature of the interest that the third person has in the arbitration; and

(e) Identify the specific issues of fact or law in the arbitration that the third person wishes to address in its written submission.

3. In determining whether to allow such a submission, the arbitral tribunal shall take into consideration, among other factors it determines to be relevant:

(a) Whether the third person has a significant interest in the arbitral proceedings; and

(b) The extent to which the submission would assist the arbitral tribunal in

the determination of a factual or legal issue related to the arbitral proceedings by bringing a perspective, particular knowledge or insight that is different from that of the disputing parties.
4. The submission filed by the third person shall:
(a) Be dated and signed by the person filing the submission on behalf of the third person;
(b) Be concise, and in no case longer than as authorized by the arbitral tribunal;
(c) Set out a precise statement of the third person's position on issues; and
(d) Address only matters within the scope of the dispute.
5. The arbitral tribunal shall ensure that any submission does not disrupt or unduly burden the arbitral proceedings, or unfairly prejudice any disputing party.
6. The arbitral tribunal shall ensure that the disputing parties are given a reasonable opportunity to present their observations on any submission by the third person.

Article 5 — Submission by a Non-disputing Party to the Treaty

1. The arbitral tribunal shall, subject to paragraph 4, allow, or, after consultation with the disputing parties, may invite, submissions on issues of treaty interpretation from a non-disputing Party to the treaty.
2. The arbitral tribunal, after consultation with the disputing parties, may allow submissions on further matters within the scope of the dispute from a non-disputing Party to the treaty. In determining whether to allow such submissions, the arbitral tribunal shall take into consideration, among other factors it determines to be relevant, the factors referred to in article 4, paragraph 3, and, for greater certainty, the need to avoid submissions which would support the claim of the investor in a manner tantamount to diplomatic protection.
3. The arbitral tribunal shall not draw any inference from the absence of any submission or response to any invitation pursuant to paragraphs 1 or 2.
4. The arbitral tribunal shall ensure that any submission does not disrupt or unduly burden the arbitral proceedings, or unfairly prejudice any disputing party.
5. The arbitral tribunal shall ensure that the disputing parties are given a reasonable opportunity to present their observations on any submission by a non-disputing Party to the treaty.

Article 6 — Hearings

1. Subject to article 6, paragraphs 2 and 3, hearings for the presentation of evidence or for oral argument ("hearings") shall be public.

2. Where there is a need to protect confidential information or the integrity of the arbitral process pursuant to article 7, the arbitral tribunal shall make arrangements to hold in private that part of the hearing requiring such protection.
3. The arbitral tribunal shall make logistical arrangements to facilitate the public access to hearings (including where appropriate by organizing attendance through video links or such other means as it deems appropriate). However, the arbitral tribunal may, after consultation with the disputing parties, decide to hold all or part of the hearings in private where this becomes necessary for logistical reasons, such as when the circumstances render any original arrangement for public access to a hearing infeasible.

Article 7 — Exceptions to Transparency

Confidential or protected information

1. Confidential or protected information, as defined in paragraph 2 and as identified pursuant to the arrangements referred to in paragraphs 3 and 4, shall not be made available to the public pursuant to articles 2 to 6.
2. Confidential or protected information consists of:
(a) Confidential business information;
(b) Information that is protected against being made available to the public under the treaty;
(c) Information that is protected against being made available to the public, in the case of the information of the respondent State, under the law of the respondent State, and in the case of other information, under any law or rules determined by the arbitral tribunal to be applicable to the disclosure ofsuch information; or
(d) Information the disclosure of which would impede law enforcement.
3. The arbitral tribunal, after consultation with the disputing parties, shall make arrangements to prevent any confidential or protected information from being made available to the public, including by putting in place, as appropriate:
(a) Time limits in which a disputing party, non-disputing Party to the treaty or third person shall give notice that it seeks protection for such information in documents;
(b) Procedures for the prompt designation and redaction of the particular confidential or protected information in such documents; and
(c) Procedures for holding hearings in private to the extent required by article 6, paragraph 2.

Any determination as to whether information is confidential or protected shall be made by the arbitral tribunal after consultation with the disputing parties.

4. Where the arbitral tribunal determines that information should not be redacted from a document, or that a document should not be prevented from being made available to the public, any disputing party, non-disputing Party to the treaty or third person that voluntarily introduced the document into the record shall be permitted to withdraw all or part of the document from the record of the arbitral proceedings.

5. Nothing in these Rules requires a respondent State to make available to the public information the disclosure of which it considers to be contrary to its essential security interests.

Integrity of the arbitral process

6. Information shall not be made available to the public pursuant to articles 2 to 6 where the information, if made available to the public, would jeopardize the integrity of the arbitral process as determined pursuant to paragraph 7.

7. The arbitral tribunal may, on its own initiative or upon the application of a disputing party, after consultation with the disputing parties where practicable, take appropriate measures to restrain or delay the publication of information where such publication would jeopardize the integrity of the arbitral process because it could hamper the collection or production of evidence, lead to the intimidation of witnesses, lawyers acting for disputing parties or members of the arbitral tribunal, or in comparably exceptional circumstances.

Article 8 — Repository of Published Information

The repository of published information under the Rules on Transparency shall be the Secretary-General of the United Nations or an institution named by UNCITRAL.

---

* For the purposes of the Rules on Transparency, a "treaty" shall be understood broadly as encompassing any bilateral or multilateral treaty that contain provisions on the protection of investments or investors and a right for investor to resort to arbitration against Parties to the treaty, including any treaty commonly referred to as a free trade agreement, economic integration agreement, trade and investment framework or cooperation agreement, or bilateral investment treaty.

** For the purposes of the Rules on Transparency, any reference to a "Party to the treaty" or a "State" includes, for example, a regional economic integration organization where it is a Party to the treaty.

UNCITRAL MODEL LAW ON INTERNATIONAL COMMERCIAL ARBITRATION 1985 (with amendments as adopted in 2006) *

Chapter I
General Provisions

Article 1 — Scope of Application[1]

This Law applies to international commercial[2] arbitration, subject to any agreement in force between this State and any other State or States.

(2) The provisions of this Law, except articles 8, 9, 17 H, 17 I, 17 J, 35 and 36, apply only if the place of arbitration is in the territory of this State.

(3) An arbitration is international if:

(a) the parties to an arbitration agreement have, at the time of the conclusion of that agreement, their places of business in different States; or

(b) one of the following places is situated outside the State in which the parties have their places of business:

(i) the place of arbitration if determined in, or pursuant to, the arbitration agreement;

(ii) any place where a substantial part of the obligations of the commercial relationship is to be performed or the place with which the subject-matter of the dispute is most closely connected; or

(c) the parties have expressly agreed that the subject-matter of the arbitration agreement relates to more than one country.

(4) For the purposes of paragraph (3) of this article:

(a) if a party has more than one place of business, the place of business is that which has the closest relationship to the arbitration agreement;

(b) if a party does not have a place of business, reference is to be made to his habitual residence.

(5) This Law shall not affect any other law of this State by virtue of which certain disputes may not be submitted to arbitration or may be submitted to arbitration only according to provisions other than those of this Law.

Article 2 — Definitions and Rules of Interpretation

For the purposes of this Law:

(a) "arbitration" means any arbitration whether or not administered by a permanent arbitral institution;

(b) "arbitral tribunal" means a sole arbitrator or a panel of arbitrators;

(c) "court" means a body or organ of the judicial system of a State;

(d) where a provision of this Law, except article 28, leaves the parties free to determine a certain issue, such freedom includes the right of the parties to authorise a third party, including an institution, to make that determination;

(e) where a provision of this Law refers to the fact that the parties have agreed or that they may agree or in any other way refers to an agreement of the parties, such agreement includes any arbitration rules referred to in that

---

* For a commentary on the UNCITRAL Model Law, see Explanatory Note by the UNCITRAL secretariat on the 1985 Model Law on International Commercial Arbitration as amended in 2006. See also, UNCITRAL 2012 Digest of Case Law on the Model Law on International Commercial

agreement;
(f) where a provision of this Law, other than in articles 25(a) and 32(2)(a), refers to a claim, it also applies to a counter-claim, and where it refers to a defence, it also applies to a defence to such counter-claim.

Article 2A — International Origin and General Principles

(As adopted by the Commission at its thirty-ninth session, in 2006)

(1) In the interpretation of this Law, regard is to be had to its international origin and to the need to promote uniformity in its application and the observance of good faith.

(2) Questions concerning matters governed by this Law which are not expressly settled in it are to be settled in conformity with the general principles on which this Law is based.

Article 3 — Receipt of Written Communications

(1) Unless otherwise agreed by the parties:

(a) any written communication is deemed to have been received if it is delivered to the addressee personally or if it is delivered at his place of business, habitual residence or mailing address; if none of these can be found after making a reasonable inquiry, a written communication is deemed to have been received if it is sent to the addressee's last-known place of business, habitual residence or mailing address by registered letter or any other means which provides a record of the attempt to deliver it;

(b) the communication is deemed to have been received on the day it is so delivered.

(2) The provisions of this article do not apply to communications in court proceedings.

Article 4 — Waiver of Right to Object

A party who knows that any provision of this Law from which the parties may derogate or any requirement under the arbitration agreement has not been complied with and yet proceeds with the arbitration without stating his objection to such non-compliance without undue delay or, if a time-limit is provided therefor, within such period of time, shall be deemed to have waived his right to object.

Article 5 — Extent of Court Intervention

In matters governed by this Law, no court shall intervene except where so provided in this Law.

Article 6 — Court or Other Authority for Certain Functions of Arbitration Assistance and Supervision

The functions referred to in articles 11(3), 11(4), 13(3), 14, 16(3) and 34(2) shall be performed by ... [Each State enacting this model law specifies the

---

Arbitration (1985, with amendments as adopted in 2006). [1] Article headings are for reference purposes only and are not to be used for purposes of interpretation. [2] The term 'commercial' should be given a wide interpretation so as to cover matters arising from all relationships of a commercial

court, courts or, where referred to therein, other authority competent to perform these functions.]

Chapter II
Arbitration Agreement

Option I

Article 7 — Definition and Form of Arbitration Agreement

(As adopted by the Commission at its thirty-ninth session, in 2006)

(1) "Arbitration agreement" is an agreement by the parties to submit to arbitration all or certain disputes which have arisen or which may arise between them in respect of a defined legal relationship, whether contractual or not. An arbitration agreement may be in the form of an arbitration clause in a contract or in the form of a separate agreement.

(2) The arbitration agreement shall be in writing.

(3) An arbitration agreement is in writing if its content is recorded in any form, whether or not the arbitration agreement or contract has been concluded orally, by conduct, or by other means.

(4) The requirement that an arbitration agreement be in writing is met by an electronic communication if the information contained therein is accessible so as to be useable for subsequent reference; "electronic communication" means any communication that the parties make by means of data messages; "data message" means information generated, sent, received or stored by electronic, magnetic, optical or similar means, including, but not limited to, electronic data interchange (EDI), electronic mail, telegram, telex or telecopy.

(5) Furthermore, an arbitration agreement is in writing if it is contained in an exchange of statements of claim and defence in which the existence of an agreement is alleged by one party and not denied by the other.

(6) The reference in a contract to any document containing an arbitration clause constitutes an arbitration agreement in writing, provided that the reference is such as to make that clause part of the contract.

Option II

Article 7 — Definition and Form of Arbitration Agreement

"Arbitration agreement" is an agreement by the parties to submit to arbitration all or certain disputes which have arisen or which may arise between them in respect of a defined legal relationship, whether contractual or not.

Article 8 — Arbitration Agreement and Substantive Claim Before Court

(1) A court before which an action is brought in a matter which is the

---

nature, whether contractual or not. Relationships of a commercial nature include, but are not limited to, the following transactions: any trade transaction for the supply or exchange of goods or services; distribution agreement; commercial representation or agency; factoring; leasing; construction of

subject of an arbitration agreement shall, if a party so requests not later than when submitting his first statement on the substance of the dispute, refer the parties to arbitration unless it finds that the agreement is null and void, inoperative or incapable of being performed.

(2) Where an action referred to in paragraph (1) of this article has been brought, arbitral proceedings may nevertheless be commenced or continued, and an award may be made, while the issue is pending before the court.

Article 9 — Arbitration Agreement and Interim Measures by Court

It is not incompatible with an arbitration agreement for a party to request, before or during arbitral proceedings, from a court an interim measure of protection and for a court to grant such measure.

Chapter III
Arbitration Agreement

Article 10 — Number of Arbitrators

(1) The parties are free to determine the number of arbitrators.

(2) Failing such determination, the number of arbitrators shall be three.

Article 11 — Appointment of Arbitrators

(1) No person shall be precluded by reason of his nationality from acting as an arbitrator, unless otherwise agreed by the parties.

(2) The parties are free to agree on a procedure of appointing the arbitrator or arbitrators, subject to the provisions of paragraphs (4) and (5) of this article.

(3) Failing such agreement,

(a) in an arbitration with three arbitrators, each party shall appoint one arbitrator, and the two arbitrators thus appointed shall appoint the third arbitrator; if a party fails to appoint the arbitrator within thirty days of receipt of a request to do so from the other party, or if the two arbitrators fail to agree on the third arbitrator within thirty days of their appointment, the appointment shall be made, upon request of a party, by the court or other authority specified in article 6;

(b) in an arbitration with a sole arbitrator, if the parties are unable to agree on the arbitrator, he shall be appointed, upon request of a party, by the court or other authority specified in article 6.

(4) Where, under an appointment procedure agreed upon by the parties,

(a) a party fails to act as required under such procedure, or

(b) the parties, or two arbitrators, are unable to reach an agreement expected of them under such procedure, or

(c) a third party, including an institution, fails to perform any function entrusted to it under such procedure, any party may request the court or

---

works; consulting; engineering; licensing; investment; financing; banking; insurance; exploitation agreement or concession; joint venture and other forms of industrial or business co-operation; carriage of goods or passengers by air, sea, rail or road.

other authority specified in article 6 to take the necessary measure, unless the agreement on the appointment procedure provides other means for securing the appointment.

(5) A decision on a matter entrusted by paragraph (3) or (4) of this article to the court or other authority specified in article 6 shall be subject to no appeal. The court or other authority, in appointing an arbitrator, shall have due regard to any qualifications required of the arbitrator by the agreement of the parties and to such considerations as are likely to secure the appointment of an independent and impartial arbitrator and, in the case of a sole or third arbitrator, shall take into account as well the advisability of appointing an arbitrator of a nationality other than those of the parties.

Article 12 — Grounds for Challenge

(1) When a person is approached in connection with his possible appointment as an arbitrator, he shall disclose any circumstances likely to give rise to justifiable doubts as to his impartiality or independence. An arbitrator, from the time of his appointment and throughout the arbitral proceedings, shall without delay disclose any such circumstances to the parties unless they have already been informed of them by him.

(2) An arbitrator may be challenged only if circumstances exist that give rise to justifiable doubts as to his impartiality or independence, or if he does not possess qualifications agreed to by the parties. A party may challenge an arbitrator appointed by him, or in whose appointment he has participated, only for reasons of which he becomes aware after the appointment has been made.

Article 13 — Challenge Procedure

(1) The parties are free to agree on a procedure for challenging an arbitrator, subject to the provisions of paragraph (3) of this article.

(2) Failing such agreement, a party who intends to challenge an arbitrator shall, within fifteen days after becoming aware of the constitution of the arbitral tribunal or after becoming aware of any circumstance referred to in article 12(2), send a written statement of the reasons for the challenge to the arbitral tribunal. Unless the challenged arbitrator withdraws from his office or the other party agrees to the challenge, the arbitral tribunal shall decide on the challenge.

(3) If a challenge under any procedure agreed upon by the parties or under the procedure of paragraph (2) of this article is not successful, the challenging party may request, within thirty days after having received notice of the decision rejecting the challenge, the court or other authority specified in article 6 to decide on the challenge, which decision shall be

subject to no appeal; while such a request is pending, the arbitral tribunal, including the challenged arbitrator, may continue the arbitral proceedings and make an award.

Article 14 — Failure or Impossibility to Act

(1) If an arbitrator becomes *de jure* or *de facto* unable to perform his functions or for other reasons fails to act without undue delay, his mandate terminates if he withdraws from his office or if the parties agree on the termination. Otherwise, if a controversy remains concerning any of these grounds, any party may request the court or other authority specified in article 6 to decide on the termination of the mandate, which decision shall be subject to no appeal.

(2) If, under this article or article 13(2), an arbitrator withdraws from his office or a party agrees to the termination of the mandate of an arbitrator, this does not imply acceptance of the validity of any ground referred to in this article or article 12(2).

Article 15 — Appointment of Substitute Arbitrator

Where the mandate of an arbitrator terminates under article 13 or 14 or because of his withdrawal from office for any other reason or because of the revocation of his mandate by agreement of the parties or in any other case of termination of his mandate, a substitute arbitrator shall be appointed according to the rules that were applicable to the appointment of the arbitrator being replaced.

Chapter IV
Jurisdiction of Arbitral Tribunal

Article 16 — Competence of Arbitral Tribunal to Rule on Its Jurisdiction

(1) The arbitral tribunal may rule on its own jurisdiction, including any objections with respect to the existence or validity of the arbitration agreement. For that purpose, an arbitration clause which forms part of a contract shall be treated as an agreement independent of the other terms of the contract. A decision by the arbitral tribunal that the contract is null and void shall not entail *ipso jure* the invalidity of the arbitration clause.

(2) A plea that the arbitral tribunal does not have jurisdiction shall be raised not later than the submission of the statement of defence. A party is not precluded from raising such a plea by the fact that he has appointed, or participated in the appointment of, an arbitrator. A plea that the arbitral tribunal is exceeding the scope of its authority shall be raised as soon as the matter alleged to be beyond the scope of its authority is raised during the arbitral proceedings. The arbitral tribunal may, in either case, admit a later

plea if it considers the delay justified.

(3) The arbitral tribunal may rule on a plea referred to in paragraph (2) of this article either as a preliminary question or in an award on the merits. If the arbitral tribunal rules as a preliminary question that it has jurisdiction, any party may request, within thirty days after having received notice of that ruling, the court specified in article 6 to decide the matter, which decision shall be subject to no appeal; while such a request is pending, the arbitral tribunal may continue the arbitral proceedings and make an award.

Chapter IV A

Interim Measures and Preliminary Orders

(As adopted by the Commission at its thirty-ninth session, in 2006)

Section 1. Interim Measures

Article 17 — Power of Arbitral Tribunal to Order Interim Measures

(1) Unless otherwise agreed by the parties, the arbitral tribunal may, at the request of a party, grant interim measures.

(2) An interim measure is any temporary measure, whether in the form of an award or in another form, by which, at any time prior to the issuance of the award by which the dispute is finally decided, the arbitral tribunal orders a party to:

(a) Maintain or restore the status quo pending determination of the dispute;

(b) Take action that would prevent, or refrain from taking action that is likely to cause, current or imminent harm or prejudice to the arbitral process itself;

(c) Provide a means of preserving assets out of which a subsequent award may be satisfied; or

(d) Preserve evidence that may be relevant and material to the resolution of the dispute.

Article 17 A — Conditions for Granting Interim Measure

(1) The party requesting an interim measure under article 17(2)(a), (b) and (c) shall satisfy the arbitral tribunal that:

(a) Harm not adequately reparable by an award of damages is likely to result if the measure is not ordered, and such harm substantially outweighs the harm that is likely to result to the party against whom the measure is directed if the measure is granted; and

(b) There is a reasonable possibility that the requesting party will succeed on the merits of the claim. The determination on this possibility shall not affect the discretion of the arbitral tribunal in making any subsequent determination.

(2) With regard to a request for an interim measure under article 17(2)(d),

the requirements in paragraphs (1)(a) and (b) of this article shall apply only to the extent the arbitral tribunal considers appropriate.

Section 2. Preliminary Orders

Article 17 B — Applications for Preliminary Orders and Conditions for Granting Preliminary Orders

(1) Unless otherwise agreed by the parties, a party may, without notice to any other party, make a request for an interim measure together with an application for a preliminary order directing a party not to frustrate the purpose of the interim measure requested.

(2) The arbitral tribunal may grant a preliminary order provided it considers that prior disclosure of the request for the interim measure to the party against whom it is directed risks frustrating the purpose of the measure.

(3) The conditions defined under article 17 A apply to any preliminary order, provided that the harm to be assessed under article 17 A(1)(a), is the harm likely to result from the order being granted or not.

Article 17 C — Specific Regime for Preliminary Orders

(1) Immediately after the arbitral tribunal has made a determination in respect of an application for a preliminary order, the arbitral tribunal shall give notice to all parties of the request for the interim measure, the application for the preliminary order, the preliminary order, if any, and all other communications, including by indicating the content of any oral communication, between any party and the arbitral tribunal in relation thereto.

(2) At the same time, the arbitral tribunal shall give an opportunity to any party against whom a preliminary order is directed to present its case at the earliest practicable time.

(3) The arbitral tribunal shall decide promptly on any objection to the preliminary order.

(4) A preliminary order shall expire after twenty days from the date on which it was issued by the arbitral tribunal. However, the arbitral tribunal may issue an interim measure adopting or modifying the preliminary order, after the party against whom the preliminary order is directed has been given notice and an opportunity to present its case.

(5) A preliminary order shall be binding on the parties but shall not be subject to enforcement by a court. Such a preliminary order does not constitute an award.

Section 3. Provisions Applicable to Interim Measures and Preliminary Orders

Article 17 D — Modification, Suspension, Termination

The arbitral tribunal may modify, suspend or terminate an interim measure or a preliminary order it has granted, upon application of any party or, in exceptional circumstances and upon prior notice to the parties, on the arbitral tribunal's own initiative.

Article 17 E — Provision of Security

(1) The arbitral tribunal may require the party requesting an interim measure to provide appropriate security in connection with the measure.

(2) The arbitral tribunal shall require the party applying for a preliminary order to provide security in connection with the order unless the arbitral tribunal considers it inappropriate or unnecessary to do so.

Article 17 F — Disclosure

(1) The arbitral tribunal may require any party promptly to disclose any material change in the circumstances on the basis of which the measure was requested or granted.

(2) The party applying for a preliminary order shall disclose to the arbitral tribunal all circumstances that are likely to be relevant to the arbitral tribunal's determination whether to grant or maintain the order, and such obligation shall continue until the party against whom the order has been requested has had an opportunity to present its case. Thereafter, paragraph (1) of this article shall apply.

Article 17 G — Costs and Damages

The party requesting an interim measure or applying for a preliminary order shall be liable for any costs and damages caused by the measure or the order to any party if the arbitral tribunal later determines that, in the circumstances, the measure or the order should not have been granted. The arbitral tribunal may award such costs and damages at any point during the proceedings.

Section 4. Recognition and Enforcement of Interim Measures

Article 17 H — Recognition and Enforcement

(1) An interim measure issued by an arbitral tribunal shall be recognised as binding and, unless otherwise provided by the arbitral tribunal, enforced upon application to the competent court, irrespective of the country in which it was issued, subject to the provisions of article 17 I.

(2) The party who is seeking or has obtained recognition or enforcement of an interim measure shall promptly inform the court of any termination, suspension or modification of that interim measure.

(3) The court of the State where recognition or enforcement is sought may, if it considers it proper, order the requesting party to provide appropriate security if the arbitral tribunal has not already made a determination with respect to security or where such a decision is necessary to protect the rights of third parties.

Article 17 I — Grounds for Refusing Recognition and Enforcement[3]

(1) Recognition or enforcement of an interim measure may be refused only:

(a) At the request of the party against whom it is invoked if the court is satisfied that:

(i) Such refusal is warranted on the grounds set forth in article 36(1)(a)(i), (ii), (iii) or (iv); or

(ii) The arbitral tribunal's decision with respect to the provision of security in connection with the interim measure issued by the arbitral tribunal has not been complied with; or

(iii) The interim measure has been terminated or suspended by the arbitral tribunal or, where so empowered, by the court of the State in which the arbitration takes place or under the law of which that interim measure was granted; or

(b) If the court finds that:

(i) The interim measure is incompatible with the powers conferred upon the court unless the court decides to reformulate the interim measure to the extent necessary to adapt it to its own powers and procedures for the purposes of enforcing that interim measure and without modifying its substance; or

(ii) Any of the grounds set forth in article 36(1)(b)(i) or (ii), apply to the recognition and enforcement of the interim measure.

(2) Any determination made by the court on any ground in paragraph (1) of this article shall be effective only for the purposes of the application to recognise and enforce the interim measure. The court where recognition or enforcement is sought shall not, in making that determination, undertake a review of the substance of the interim measure.

Section 5. Court-Ordered Interim Measures

Article 17 J — Court-ordered Interim Measures

A court shall have the same power of issuing an interim measure in relation to arbitration proceedings, irrespective of whether their place is in the territory of this State, as it has in relation to proceedings in courts. The court shall exercise such power in accordance with its own procedures in consideration of the specific features of international arbitration.

---

[3] The conditions set forth in article 17 I are intended to limit the number of circumstances in which the court may refuse to enforce an interim measure. It would not be contrary to the level of harmonization sought to be achieved by these model provisions if a State were to adopt fewer

Chapter V
Conduct of Arbitral Proceedings

Article 18 — Equal Treatment of Parties

The parties shall be treated with equality and each party shall be given a full opportunity of presenting his case.

Article 19 — Determination of Rules of Procedure

(1) Subject to the provisions of this Law, the parties are free to agree on the procedure to be followed by the arbitral tribunal in conducting the proceedings.

(2) Failing such agreement, the arbitral tribunal may, subject to the provisions of this Law, conduct the arbitration in such manner as it considers appropriate. The power conferred upon the arbitral tribunal includes the power to determine the admissibility, relevance, materiality and weight of any evidence.

Article 20 — Place of Arbitration

(1) The parties are free to agree on the place of arbitration. Failing such agreement, the place of arbitration shall be determined by the arbitral tribunal having regard to the circumstances of the case, including the convenience of the parties.

(2) Notwithstanding the provisions of paragraph (1) of this article, the arbitral tribunal may, unless otherwise agreed by the parties, meet at any place it considers appropriate for consultation among its members, for hearing witnesses, experts or the parties, or for inspection of goods, other property or documents.

Article 21 — Commencement of Arbitral Proceedings

Unless otherwise agreed by the parties, the arbitral proceedings in respect of a particular dispute commence on the date on which a request for that dispute to be referred to arbitration is received by the respondent.

Article 22 — Language

(1) The parties are free to agree on the language or languages to be used in the arbitral proceedings. Failing such agreement, the arbitral tribunal shall determine the language or languages to be used in the proceedings. This agreement or determination, unless otherwise specified therein, shall apply to any written statement by a party, any hearing and any award, decision or other communication by the arbitral tribunal.

(2) The arbitral tribunal may order that any documentary evidence shall be accompanied by a translation into the language or languages agreed upon by the parties or determined by the arbitral tribunal.

---

circumstances in which enforcement may be refused.

Article 23 — Statements of Claim and Defence

(1) Within the period of time agreed by the parties or determined by the arbitral tribunal, the claimant shall state the facts supporting his claim, the points at issue and the relief or remedy sought, and the respondent shall state his defence in respect of these particulars, unless the parties have otherwise agreed as to the required elements of such statements. The parties may submit with their statements all documents they consider to be relevant or may add a reference to the documents or other evidence they will submit.

(2) Unless otherwise agreed by the parties, either party may amend or supplement his claim or defence during the course of the arbitral proceedings, unless the arbitral tribunal considers it inappropriate to allow such amendment having regard to the delay in making it.

Article 24 — Hearings and Written Proceedings

(1) Subject to any contrary agreement by the parties, the arbitral tribunal shall decide whether to hold oral hearings for the presentation of evidence or for oral argument, or whether the proceedings shall be conducted on the basis of documents and other materials. However, unless the parties have agreed that no hearings shall be held, the arbitral tribunal shall hold such hearings at an appropriate stage of the proceedings, if so requested by a party.

(2) The parties shall be given sufficient advance notice of any hearing and of any meeting of the arbitral tribunal for the purposes of inspection of goods, other property or documents.

(3) All statements, documents or other information supplied to the arbitral tribunal by one party shall be communicated to the other party. Also any expert report or evidentiary document on which the arbitral tribunal may rely in making its decision shall be communicated to the parties.

Article 25 — Default of a Party

Unless otherwise agreed by the parties, if, without showing sufficient cause,

(a) the claimant fails to communicate his statement of claim in accordance with article 23(1), the arbitral tribunal shall terminate the proceedings;

(b) the respondent fails to communicate his statement of defence in accordance with article 23(1), the arbitral tribunal shall continue the proceedings without treating such failure in itself as an admission of the claimant's allegations;

(c) any party fails to appear at a hearing or to produce documentary evidence, the arbitral tribunal may continue the proceedings and make the award on the evidence before it.

Article 26 — Expert Appointed by Arbitral Tribunal

(1) Unless otherwise agreed by the parties, the arbitral tribunal

(a) may appoint one or more experts to report to it on specific issues to be determined by the arbitral tribunal;

(b) may require a party to give the expert any relevant information or to produce, or to provide access to, any relevant documents, goods or other property for his inspection.

(2) Unless otherwise agreed by the parties, if a party so requests or if the arbitral tribunal considers it necessary, the expert shall, after delivery of his written or oral report, participate in a hearing where the parties have the opportunity to put questions to him and to present expert witnesses in order to testify on the points at issue.

Article 27 — Court Assistance in Taking Evidence

The arbitral tribunal or a party with the approval of the arbitral tribunal may request from a competent court of this State assistance in taking evidence. The court may execute the request within its competence and according to its rules on taking evidence.

Chapter VI
Making of Award and Termination of Proceedings

Article 28 — Rules Applicable to Substance of Dispute

(1) The arbitral tribunal shall decide the dispute in accordance with such rules of law as are chosen by the parties as applicable to the substance of the dispute. Any designation of the law or legal system of a given State shall be construed, unless otherwise expressed, as directly referring to the substantive law of that State and not to its conflict of laws rules.

(2) Failing any designation by the parties, the arbitral tribunal shall apply the law determined by the conflict of laws rules which it considers applicable.

(3) The arbitral tribunal shall decide *ex aequo et bono* or as *amiable compositeur* only if the parties have expressly authorised it to do so.

(4) In all cases, the arbitral tribunal shall decide in accordance with the terms of the contract and shall take into account the usages of the trade applicable to the transaction.

Article 29 — Decision-making by Panel of Arbitrators

In arbitral proceedings with more than one arbitrator, any decision of the arbitral tribunal shall be made, unless otherwise agreed by the parties, by a majority of all its members. However, questions of procedure may be decided by a presiding arbitrator, if so authorised by the parties or all members of the arbitral tribunal.

Article 30 — Settlement

(1) If, during arbitral proceedings, the parties settle the dispute, the arbitral tribunal shall terminate the proceedings and, if requested by the parties and not objected to by the arbitral tribunal, record the settlement in the form of an arbitral award on agreed terms.

(2) An award on agreed terms shall be made in accordance with the provisions of article 31 and shall state that it is an award. Such an award has the same status and effect as any other award on the merits of the case.

Article 31 — Form and Contents of Award

(1) The award shall be made in writing and shall be signed by the arbitrator or arbitrators. In arbitral proceedings with more than one arbitrator, the signatures of the majority of all members of the arbitral tribunal shall suffice, provided that the reason for any omitted signature is stated.

(2) The award shall state the reasons upon which it is based, unless the parties have agreed that no reasons are to be given or the award is an award on agreed terms under article 30.

(3) The award shall state its date and the place of arbitration as determined in accordance with article 20(1). The award shall be deemed to have been made at that place.

(4) After the award is made, a copy signed by the arbitrators in accordance with paragraph (1) of this article shall be delivered to each party.

Article 32 — Termination of Proceedings

(1) The arbitral proceedings are terminated by the final award or by an order of the arbitral tribunal in accordance with paragraph (2) of this article.

(2) The arbitral tribunal shall issue an order for the termination of the arbitral proceedings when:

(a) the claimant withdraws his claim, unless the respondent objects thereto and the arbitral tribunal recognises a legitimate interest on his part in obtaining a final settlement of the dispute;

(b) the parties agree on the termination of the proceedings;

(c) the arbitral tribunal finds that the continuation of the proceedings has for any other reason become unnecessary or impossible.

(3) The mandate of the arbitral tribunal terminates with the termination of the arbitral proceedings, subject to the provisions of articles 33 and 34(4).

Article 33 — Correction and Interpretation of Award; Additional Award

(1) Within thirty days of receipt of the award, unless another period of time has been agreed upon by the parties:

(a) a party, with notice to the other party, may request the arbitral tribunal to correct in the award any errors in computation, any clerical or typographical errors or any errors of similar nature;

(b) if so agreed by the parties, a party, with notice to the other party, may request the arbitral tribunal to give an interpretation of a specific point or part of the award.

If the arbitral tribunal considers the request to be justified, it shall make the correction or give the interpretation within thirty days of receipt of the request. The interpretation shall form part of the award.

(2) The arbitral tribunal may correct any error of the type referred to in paragraph (1)(a) of this article on its own initiative within thirty days of the date of the award.

(3) Unless otherwise agreed by the parties, a party, with notice to the other party, may request, within thirty days of receipt of the award, the arbitral tribunal to make an additional award as to claims presented in the arbitral proceedings but omitted from the award. If the arbitral tribunal considers the request to be justified, it shall make the additional award within sixty days.

(4) The arbitral tribunal may extend, if necessary, the period of time within which it shall make a correction, interpretation or an additional award under paragraph (1) or (3) of this article.

(5) The provisions of article 31 shall apply to a correction or interpretation of the award or to an additional award.

Chapter VII
Recourse Against Award

Article 34 — Application for Setting Aside as Exclusive Recourse Against Arbitral Award

(1) Recourse to a court against an arbitral award may be made only by an application for setting aside in accordance with paragraphs (2) and (3) of this article.

(2) An arbitral award may be set aside by the court specified in article 6 only if:

(a) the party making the application furnishes proof that:

(i) a party to the arbitration agreement referred to in article 7 was under some incapacity; or the said agreement is not valid under the law to which the parties have subjected it or, failing any indication thereon, under the law of this State; or

(ii) the party making the application was not given proper notice of the appointment of an arbitrator or of the arbitral proceedings or was otherwise unable to present his case; or

(iii) the award deals with a dispute not contemplated by or not falling within the terms of the submission to arbitration, or contains decisions on matters beyond the scope of the submission to arbitration, provided that, if the decisions on matters submitted to arbitration can be separated from those not so submitted, only that part of the award which contains decisions on matters not submitted to arbitration may be set aside; or
(iv) the composition of the arbitral tribunal or the arbitral procedure was not in accordance with the agreement of the parties, unless such agreement was in conflict with a provision of this Law from which the parties cannot derogate, or, failing such agreement, was not in accordance with this Law; or
(b) the court finds that:
(i) the subject-matter of the dispute is not capable of settlement by arbitration under the law of this State; or
(ii) the award is in conflict with the public policy of this State.
(3) An application for setting aside may not be made after three months have elapsed from the date on which the party making that application had received the award or, if a request had been made under article 33, from the date on which that request had been disposed of by the arbitral tribunal.
(4) The court, when asked to set aside an award, may, where appropriate and so requested by a party, suspend the setting aside proceedings for a period of time determined by it in order to give the arbitral tribunal an opportunity to resume the arbitral proceedings or to take such other action as in the arbitral tribunal's opinion will eliminate the grounds for setting aside.

Chapter VIII
Recognition and Enforcement of Awards

Article 35 — Recognition and Enforcement

(1) An arbitral award, irrespective of the country in which it was made, shall be recognised as binding and, upon application in writing to the competent court, shall be enforced subject to the provisions of this article and of article 36.
(2) The party relying on an award or applying for its enforcement shall supply the original award or a copy thereof. If the award is not made in an official language of this State, the court may request the party to supply a translation thereof into such language.[4]
(Article 35(2) has been amended by the Commission at its thirty-ninth session, in 2006)

[4] The conditions set forth in this paragraph are intended to set maximum standards. It would, thus, not be contrary to the harmonization to be achieved by the model law if a State retained even less onerous conditions.

Article 36 — Grounds for Refusing Recognition or Enforcement

(1) Recognition or enforcement of an arbitral award, irrespective of the country in which it was made, may be refused only:

(a) at the request of the party against whom it is invoked, if that party furnishes to the competent court where recognition or enforcement is sought proof that:

(i) a party to the arbitration agreement referred to in article 7 was under some incapacity; or the said agreement is not valid under the law to which the parties have subjected it or, failing any indication thereon, under the law of the country where the award was made; or

(ii) the party against whom the award is invoked was not given proper notice of the appointment of an arbitrator or of the arbitral proceedings or was otherwise unable to present his case; or

(iii) the award deals with a dispute not contemplated by or not falling within the terms of the submission to arbitration, or it contains decisions on matters beyond the scope of the submission to arbitration, provided that, if the decisions on matters submitted to arbitration can be separated from those not so submitted, that part of the award which contains decisions on matters submitted to arbitration may be recognised and enforced; or

(iv) the composition of the arbitral tribunal or the arbitral procedure was not in accordance with the agreement of the parties or, failing such agreement, was not in accordance with the law of the country where the arbitration took place; or

(v) the award has not yet become binding on the parties or has been set aside or suspended by a court of the country in which, or under the law of which, that award was made; or

(b) if the court finds that:

(i) the subject-matter of the dispute is not capable of settlement by arbitration under the law of this State; or

(ii) the recognition or enforcement of the award would be contrary to the public policy of this State.

(2) If an application for setting aside or suspension of an award has been made to a court referred to in paragraph (1)(a)(v) of this article, the court where recognition or enforcement is sought may, if it considers it proper, adjourn its decision and may also, on the application of the party claiming recognition or enforcement of the award, order the other party to provide appropriate security.

UNCITRAL NOTES ON ORGANIZING ARBITRAL PROCEEDINGS *

Introduction

Purpose of the Notes

1. The purpose of the Notes is to assist arbitration practitioners by listing and briefly describing questions on which appropriately timed decisions on organizing arbitral proceedings may be useful. The text, prepared with a particular view to international arbitrations, may be used whether or not the arbitration is administered by an arbitral institution.

Non-binding character of the Notes

2. No legal requirement binding on the arbitrators or the parties is imposed by the Notes. The arbitral tribunal remains free to use the Notes as it sees fit and is not required to give reasons for disregarding them.

3. The Notes are not suitable to be used as arbitration rules, since they do not establish any obligation of the arbitral tribunal or the parties to act in a particular way. Accordingly, the use of the Notes cannot imply any modification of the arbitration rules that the parties may have agreed upon.

Discretion in conduct of proceedings and usefulness of timely decisions on organizing proceedings

4. Laws governing the arbitral procedure and arbitration rules that parties may agree upon typically allow the arbitral tribunal broad discretion and flexibility in the conduct of arbitral proceedings.[1] This is useful in that it enables the arbitral tribunal to take decisions on the organization of proceedings that take into account the circumstances of the case, the expectations of the parties and of the members of the arbitral tribunal, and the need for a just and cost-efficient resolution of the dispute.

5. Such discretion may make it desirable for the arbitral tribunal to give the parties a timely indication as to the organization of the proceedings and the manner in which the tribunal intends to proceed. This is particularly desirable in international arbitrations, where the participants may be accustomed to differing styles of conducting arbitrations. Without such guidance, a party may find aspects of the proceedings unpredictable and difficult to prepare for. That may lead to misunderstandings, delays and increased costs.

Multi-party arbitration

6. These Notes are intended for use not only in arbitrations with two parties but also in arbitrations with three or more parties. Use of the Notes in multi-party arbitration is referred to below in paragraphs 86-88 (item 18).

Process of making decisions on organizing arbitral proceedings

7. Decisions by the arbitral tribunal on organizing arbitral proceedings may be taken with or without previous consultations with the parties. The

---

* For a commentary on the UNCITRAL Notes on Organizing Arbitral Proceedings, see Thomas J. Stipanowich, 'Soft Law in the Organization and General Conduct of Commercial Arbitration Proceedings' in Lawrence W. Newman and Michael J. Radine (eds), *Soft Law in International*

method chosen depends on whether, in view of the type of the question to be decided, the arbitral tribunal considers that consultations are not necessary or that hearing the views of the parties would be beneficial for increasing the predictability of the proceedings or improving the procedural atmosphere.

8. The consultations, whether they involve only the arbitrators or also the parties, can be held in one or more meetings, or can be carried out by correspondence or telecommunications such as telefax or conference telephone calls or other electronic means. Meetings may be held at the venue of arbitration or at some other appropriate location.

9. In some arbitrations a special meeting may be devoted exclusively to such procedural consultations; alternatively, the consultations may be held in conjunction with a hearing on the substance of the dispute. Practices differ as to whether such special meetings should be held and how they should be organized. Special procedural meetings of the arbitrators and the parties separate from hearings are in practice referred to by expressions such as "preliminary meeting", "pre-hearing conference", "preparatory conference", "pre-hearing review", or terms of similar meaning. The terms used partly depend on the stage of the proceedings at which the meeting is taking place.

List of matters for possible consideration in organizing arbitral proceedings

10. The Notes provide a list, followed by annotations, of matters on which the arbitral tribunal may wish to formulate decisions on organizing arbitral proceedings.

11. Given that procedural styles and practices in arbitration vary widely, that the purpose of the Notes is not to promote any practice as best practice, and that the Notes are designed for universal use, it is not attempted in the Notes to describe in detail different arbitral practices or express a preference for any of them.

12. The list, while not exhaustive, covers a broad range of situations that may arise in an arbitration. In many arbitrations, however, only a limited number of the matters mentioned in the list need to be considered. It also depends on the circumstances of the case at which stage or stages of the proceedings it would be useful to consider matters concerning the organization of the proceedings. Generally, in order not to create opportunities for unnecessary discussions and delay, it is advisable not to raise a matter prematurely, i.e. before it is clear that a decision is needed.

13. When the Notes are used, it should be borne in mind that the discretion

---

Arbitration (Juris, 2014).

[1] A prominent example of such rules are the UNCITRAL Arbitration Rules, which provide in article 15(1): "Subject to these Rules, the arbitral tribunal may conduct the arbitration in such manner as it

of the arbitral tribunal in organizing the proceedings may be limited by arbitration rules, by other provisions agreed to by the parties and by the law applicable to the arbitral procedure. When an arbitration is administered by an arbitral institution, various matters discussed in the Notes may be covered by the rules and practices of that institution.

Annotations

1. Set of arbitration rules

If the parties have not agreed on a set of arbitration rules, would they wish to do so

14. Sometimes parties who have not included in their arbitration agreement a stipulation that a set of arbitration rules will govern their arbitral proceedings might wish to do so after the arbitration has begun. If that occurs, the UNCITRAL Arbitration Rules may be used either without modification or with such modifications as the parties might wish to agree upon. In the alternative, the parties might wish to adopt the rules of an arbitral institution; in that case, it may be necessary to secure the agreement of that institution and to stipulate the terms under which the arbitration could be carried out in accordance with the rules of that institution.

15. However, caution is advised as consideration of a set of arbitration rules might delay the proceedings or give rise to unnecessary controversy.

16. It should be noted that agreement on arbitration rules is not a necessity and that, if the parties do not agree on a set of arbitration rules, the arbitral tribunal has the power to continue the proceedings and determine how the case will be conducted.

2. Language of proceedings

17. Many rules and laws on arbitral procedure empower the arbitral tribunal to determine the language or languages to be used in the proceedings, if the parties have not reached an agreement thereon.

(a) Possible need for translation of documents, in full or in part

18. Some documents annexed to the statements of claim and defence or submitted later may not be in the language of the proceedings. Bearing in mind the needs of the proceedings and economy, it may be considered whether the arbitral tribunal should order that any of those documents or parts thereof should be accompanied by a translation into the language of the proceedings.

(b) Possible need for interpretation of oral presentations

19 If interpretation will be necessary during oral hearings, it is advisable to consider whether the interpretation will be simultaneous or consecutive and whether the arrangements should be the responsibility of a party or the

---

considers appropriate, provided that the parties are treated with equality and that at any stage of the proceedings each party is given a full opportunity of presenting his case."

arbitral tribunal. In an arbitration administered by an institution, interpretation as well as translation services are often arranged by the arbitral institution.

(c) Cost of translation and interpretation

20. In taking decisions about translation or interpretation, it is advisable to decide whether any or all of the costs are to be paid directly by a party or whether they will be paid out of the deposits and apportioned between the parties along with the other arbitration costs.

3. Place of arbitration

(a) Determination of the place of arbitration, if not already agreed upon by the parties

21. Arbitration rules usually allow the parties to agree on the place of arbitration, subject to the requirement of some arbitral institutions that arbitrations under their rules be conducted at a particular place, usually the location of the institution. If the place has not been so agreed upon, the rules governing the arbitration typically provide that it is in the power of the arbitral tribunal or the institution administering the arbitration to determine the place. If the arbitral tribunal is to make that determination, it may wish to hear the views of the parties before doing so.

22. Various factual and legal factors influence the choice of the place of arbitration, and their relative importance varies from case to case. Among the more prominent factors are: (a) suitability of the law on arbitral procedure of the place of arbitration; (b) whether there is a multilateral or bilateral treaty on enforcement of arbitral awards between the State where the arbitration takes place and the State or States where the award may have to be enforced; (c) convenience of the parties and the arbitrators, including the travel distances; (d) availability and cost of support services needed; and (e) location of the subject-matter in dispute and proximity of evidence.

(b) Possibility of meetings outside the place of arbitration

23. Many sets of arbitration rules and laws on arbitral procedure expressly allow the arbitral tribunal to hold meetings elsewhere than at the place of arbitration. For example, under the UNCITRAL Model Law on International Commercial Arbitration "the arbitral tribunal may, unless otherwise agreed by the parties, meet at any place it considers appropriate for consultation among its members, for hearing witnesses, experts or the parties, or for inspection of goods, other property or documents" (article 20 (2)). The purpose of this discretion is to permit arbitral proceedings to be carried out in a manner that is most efficient and economical.

4. Administrative services that may be needed for the arbitral tribunal to carry out its functions

24. Various administrative services (e.g. hearing rooms or secretarial services) may need to be procured for the arbitral tribunal to be able to carry out its functions. When the arbitration is administered by an arbitral institution, the institution will usually provide all or a good part of the required administrative support to the arbitral tribunal. When an arbitration administered by an arbitral institution takes place away from the seat of the institution, the institution may be able to arrange for administrative services to be obtained from another source, often an arbitral institution; some arbitral institutions have entered into cooperation agreements with a view to providing mutual assistance in servicing arbitral proceedings.

25. When the case is not administered by an institution, or the involvement of the institution does not include providing administrative support, usually the administrative arrangements for the proceedings will be made by the arbitral tribunal or the presiding arbitrator; it may also be acceptable to leave some of the arrangements to the parties, or to one of the parties subject to agreement of the other party or parties. Even in such cases, a convenient source of administrative support might be found in arbitral institutions, which often offer their facilities to arbitrations not governed by the rules of the institution. Otherwise, some services could be procured from entities such as chambers of commerce, hotels or specialized firms providing secretarial or other support services.

26. Administrative services might be secured by engaging a secretary of the arbitral tribunal (also referred to as registrar, clerk, administrator or rapporteur), who carries out the tasks under the direction of the arbitral tribunal. Some arbitral institutions routinely assign such persons to the cases administered by them. In arbitrations not administered by an institution or where the arbitral institution does not appoint a secretary, some arbitrators frequently engage such persons, at least in certain types of cases, whereas many others normally conduct the proceedings without them.

27. To the extent the tasks of the secretary are purely organizational (e.g. obtaining meeting rooms and providing or coordinating secretarial services), this is usually not controversial. Differences in views, however, may arise if the tasks include legal research and other professional assistance to the arbitral tribunal (e.g. collecting case law or published commentaries on legal issues defined by the arbitral tribunal, preparing summaries from case law and publications, and sometimes also preparing drafts of procedural decisions or drafts of certain parts of the award, in

particular those concerning the facts of the case). Views or expectations may differ especially where a task of the secretary is similar to professional functions of the arbitrators. Such a role of the secretary is in the view of some commentators inappropriate or is appropriate only under certain conditions, such as that the parties agree thereto. However, it is typically recognized that it is important to ensure that the secretary does not perform any decision-making function of the arbitral tribunal.

5. Deposits in respect of costs

(a) Amount to be deposited

28. In an arbitration administered by an institution, the institution often sets, on the basis of an estimate of the costs of the proceedings, the amount to be deposited as an advance for the costs of the arbitration. In other cases it is customary for the arbitral tribunal to make such an estimate and request a deposit. The estimate typically includes travel and other expenses by the arbitrators, expenditures for administrative assistance required by the arbitral tribunal, costs of any expert advice required by the arbitral tribunal, and the fees for the arbitrators. Many arbitration rules have provisions on this matter, including on whether the deposit should be made by the two parties (or all parties in a multi-party case) or only by the claimant.

(b) Management of deposits

29. When the arbitration is administered by an institution, the institution's services may include managing and accounting for the deposited money. Where that is not the case, it might be useful to clarify matters such as the type and location of the account in which the money will be kept and how the deposits will be managed.

(c) Supplementary deposits

30. If during the course of proceedings it emerges that the costs will be higher than anticipated, supplementary deposits may be required (e.g. because the arbitral tribunal decides pursuant to the arbitration rules to appoint an expert).

6. Confidentiality of information relating to the arbitration; possible agreement thereon

31. It is widely viewed that confidentiality is one of the advantageous and helpful features of arbitration. Nevertheless, there is no uniform answer in national laws as to the extent to which the participants in an arbitration are under the duty to observe the confidentiality of information relating to the case. Moreover, parties that have agreed on arbitration rules or other provisions that do not expressly address the issue of confidentiality cannot assume that all jurisdictions would recognize an implied commitment to

confidentiality. Furthermore, the participants in an arbitration might not have the same understanding as regards the extent of confidentiality that is expected. Therefore, the arbitral tribunal might wish to discuss that with the parties and, if considered appropriate, record any agreed principles on the duty of confidentiality.

32. An agreement on confidentiality might cover, for example, one or more of the following matters: the material or information that is to be kept confidential (e.g. pieces of evidence, written and oral arguments, the fact that the arbitration is taking place, identity of the arbitrators, content of the award); measures for maintaining confidentiality of such information and hearings; whether any special procedures should be employed for maintaining the confidentiality of information transmitted by electronic means (e.g. because communication equipment is shared by several users, or because electronic mail over public networks is considered not sufficiently protected against unauthorized access); circumstances in which confidential information may be disclosed in part or in whole (e.g. in the context of disclosures of information in the public domain, or if required by law or a regulatory body).

7. Routing of written communications among the parties and the arbitrators

33. To the extent the question how documents and other written communications should be routed among the parties and the arbitrators is not settled by the agreed rules, or, if an institution administers the case, by the practices of the institution, it is useful for the arbitral tribunal to clarify the question suitably early so as to avoid misunderstandings and delays.

34. Among various possible patterns of routing, one example is that a party transmits the appropriate number of copies to the arbitral tribunal, or to the arbitral institution, if one is involved, which then forwards them as appropriate. Another example is that a party is to send copies simultaneously to the arbitrators and the other party or parties. Documents and other written communications directed by the arbitral tribunal or the presiding arbitrator to one or more parties may also follow a determined pattern, such as through the arbitral institution or by direct transmission. For some communications, in particular those on organizational matters (e.g. dates for hearings), more direct routes of communication may be agreed, even if, for example, the arbitral institution acts as an intermediary for documents such as the statements of claim and defence, evidence or written arguments.

8. Telefax and other electronic means of sending documents

(a) Telefax

35. Telefax, which offers many advantages over traditional means of communication, is widely used in arbitral proceedings. Nevertheless, should it be thought that, because of the characteristics of the equipment used, it would be preferable not to rely only on a telefacsimile of a document, special arrangements may be considered, such as that a particular piece of written evidence should be mailed or otherwise physically delivered, or that certain telefax messages should be confirmed by mailing or otherwise delivering documents whose facsimile were transmitted by electronic means. When a document should not be sent by telefax, it may, however, be appropriate, in order to avoid an unnecessarily rigid procedure, for the arbitral tribunal to retain discretion to accept an advance copy of a document by telefax for the purposes of meeting a deadline, provided that the document itself is received within a reasonable time thereafter.

(b) Other electronic means (e.g. electronic mail and magnetic or optical disk)

36. It might be agreed that documents, or some of them, will be exchanged not only in paper-based form, but in addition also in an electronic form other than telefax (e.g. as electronic mail, or on a magnetic or optical disk), or only in electronic form. Since the use of electronic means depends on the aptitude of the persons involved and the availability of equipment and computer programs, agreement is necessary for such means to be used. If both paper-based and electronic means are to be used, it is advisable to decide which one is controlling and, if there is a time-limit for submitting a document, which act constitutes submission.

37. When the exchange of documents in electronic form is planned, it is useful, in order to avoid technical difficulties, to agree on matters such as: data carriers (e.g. electronic mail or computer disks) and their technical characteristics; computer programs to be used in preparing the electronic records; instructions for transforming the electronic records into human-readable form; keeping of logs and back-up records of communications sent and received; information in human-readable form that should accompany the disks (e.g. the names of the originator and recipient, computer program, titles of the electronic files and the back-up methods used); procedures when a message is lost or the communication system otherwise fails; and identification of persons who can be contacted if a problem occurs.

9. Arrangements for the exchange of written submissions

38. After the parties have initially stated their claims and defences, they

may wish, or the arbitral tribunal might request them, to present further written submissions so as to prepare for the hearings or to provide the basis for a decision without hearings. In such submissions, the parties, for example, present or comment on allegations and evidence, cite or explain law, or make or react to proposals. In practice such submissions are referred to variously as, for example, statement, memorial, counter-memorial, brief, counter-brief, reply, réplique, duplique, rebuttal or rejoinder; the terminology is a matter of linguistic usage and the scope or sequence of the submission.

(a) Scheduling of written submissions

39. It is advisable that the arbitral tribunal set time-limits for written submissions. In enforcing the time-limits, the arbitral tribunal may wish, on the one hand, to make sure that the case is not unduly protracted and, on the other hand, to reserve a degree of discretion and allow late submissions if appropriate under the circumstances. In some cases the arbitral tribunal might prefer not to plan the written submissions in advance, thus leaving such matters, including time-limits, to be decided in light of the developments in the proceedings. In other cases, the arbitral tribunal may wish to determine, when scheduling the first written submissions, the number of subsequent submissions.

40. Practices differ as to whether, after the hearings have been held, written submissions are still acceptable. While some arbitral tribunals consider post -hearing submissions unacceptable, others might request or allow them on a particular issue. Some arbitral tribunals follow the procedure according to which the parties are not requested to present written evidence and legal arguments to the arbitral tribunal before the hearings; in such a case, the arbitral tribunal may regard it as appropriate that written submissions be made after the hearings.

(b) Consecutive or simultaneous submissions

41. Written submissions on an issue may be made consecutively, i.e. the party who receives a submission is given a period of time to react with its counter submission. Another possibility is to request each party to make the submission within the same time period to the arbitral tribunal or the institution administering the case; the received submissions are then forwarded simultaneously to the respective other party or parties. The approach used may depend on the type of issues to be commented upon and the time in which the views should be clarified. With consecutive submissions, it may take longer than with simultaneous ones to obtain views of the parties on a given issue. Consecutive submissions, however,

allow the reacting party to comment on all points raised by the other party or parties, which simultaneous submissions do not; thus, simultaneous submissions might possibly necessitate further submissions.

10. Practical details concerning written submissions and evidence (e.g. method of submission, copies, numbering, references)

42. Depending on the volume and kind of documents to be handled, it might be considered whether practical arrangements on details such as the following would be helpful:

-Whether the submissions will be made as paper documents or by electronic means, or both (see paragraphs 35-37);

- The number of copies in which each document is to be submitted;
- A system for numbering documents and items of evidence, and a method for marking them, including by tabs;
- The form of references to documents (e.g. by the heading and the number assigned to the document or its date);
- Paragraph numbering in written submissions, in order to facilitate precise references to parts of a text;
- When translations are to be submitted as paper documents, whether the translations are to be contained in the same volume as the original texts or included in separate volumes.

11. Defining points at issue; order of deciding issues; defining relief or remedy sought

(a) Should a list of points at issue be prepared

43. In considering the parties' allegations and arguments, the arbitral tribunal may come to the conclusion that it would be useful for it or for the parties to prepare, for analytical purposes and for ease of discussion, a list of the points at issue, as opposed to those that are undisputed. If the arbitral tribunal determines that the advantages of working on the basis of such a list outweigh the disadvantages, it chooses the appropriate stage of the proceedings for preparing a list, bearing in mind also that subsequent developments in the proceedings may require a revision of the points at issue. Such an identification of points at issue might help to concentrate on the essential matters, to reduce the number of points at issue by agreement of the parties, and to select the best and most economical process for resolving the dispute. However, possible disadvantages of preparing such a list include delay, adverse effect on the flexibility of the proceedings, or unnecessary disagreements about whether the arbitral tribunal has decided all issues submitted to it or whether the award contains decisions on matters beyond the scope of the submission to arbitration. The terms of reference

required under some arbitration rules, or in agreements of parties, may serve the same purpose as the above-described list of points at issue.

(b) In which order should the points at issue be decided

44. While it is often appropriate to deal with all the points at issue collectively, the arbitral tribunal might decide to take them up during the proceedings in a particular order. The order may be due to a point being preliminary relative to another (e.g. a decision on the jurisdiction of the arbitral tribunal is preliminary to consideration of substantive issues, or the issue of responsibility for a breach of contract is preliminary to the issue of the resulting damages). A particular order may be decided also when the breach of various contracts is in dispute or when damages arising from various events are claimed.

45. If the arbitral tribunal has adopted a particular order of deciding points at issue, it might consider it appropriate to issue a decision on one of the points earlier than on the other ones. This might be done, for example, when a discrete part of a claim is ready for decision while the other parts still require extensive consideration, or when it is expected that after deciding certain issues the parties might be more inclined to settle the remaining ones. Such earlier decisions are referred to by expressions such as "partial", "interlocutory" or "interim" awards or decisions, depending on the type of issue dealt with and on whether the decision is final with respect to the issue it resolves. Questions that might be the subject of such decisions are, for example, jurisdiction of the arbitral tribunal, interim measures of protection, or the liability of a party.

(c) Is there a need to define more precisely the relief or remedy sought

46. If the arbitral tribunal considers that the relief or remedy sought is insufficiently definite, it may wish to explain to the parties the degree of definiteness with which their claims should be formulated. Such an explanation may be useful since criteria are not uniform as to how specific the claimant must be in formulating a relief or remedy.

12. Possible settlement negotiations and their effect on scheduling proceedings

47. Attitudes differ as to whether it is appropriate for the arbitral tribunal to bring up the possibility of settlement. Given the divergence of practices in this regard, the arbitral tribunal should only suggest settlement negotiations with caution. However, it may be opportune for the arbitral tribunal to schedule the proceedings in a way that might facilitate the continuation or initiation of settlement negotiations.

13. Documentary evidence

(a) Time-limits for submission of documentary evidence intended to be submitted by the parties; consequences of late submission

48. Often the written submissions of the parties contain sufficient information for the arbitral tribunal to fix the time-limit for submitting evidence. Otherwise, in order to set realistic time periods, the arbitral tribunal may wish to consult with the parties about the time that they would reasonably need.

49. The arbitral tribunal may wish to clarify that evidence submitted late will as a rule not be accepted. It may wish not to preclude itself from accepting a late submission of evidence if the party shows sufficient cause for the delay.

(b) Whether the arbitral tribunal intends to require a party to produce documentary evidence

50. Procedures and practices differ widely as to the conditions under which the arbitral tribunal may require a party to produce documents. Therefore, the arbitral tribunal might consider it useful, when the agreed arbitration rules do not provide specific conditions, to clarify to the parties the manner in which it intends to proceed.

51. The arbitral tribunal may wish to establish time-limits for the production of documents. The parties might be reminded that, if the requested party duly invited to produce documentary evidence fails to do so within the established period of time, without showing sufficient cause for such failure, the arbitral tribunal is free to draw its conclusions from the failure and may make the award on the evidence before it.

(c) Should assertions about the origin and receipt of documents and about the correctness of photocopies be assumed as accurate

52. It may be helpful for the arbitral tribunal to inform the parties that it intends to conduct the proceedings on the basis that, unless a party raises an objection to any of the following conclusions within a specified period of time: (a) a document is accepted as having originated from the source indicated in the document; (b) a copy of a dispatched communication (e.g. letter, telex, telefax or other electronic message) is accepted without further proof as having been received by the addressee; and (c) a copy is accepted as correct. A statement by the arbitral tribunal to that effect can simplify the introduction of documentary evidence and discourage unfounded and dilatory objections, at a late stage of the proceedings, to the probative value of documents. It is advisable to provide that the time-limit for objections will not be enforced if the arbitral tribunal considers the delay justified.

(d) Are the parties willing to submit jointly a single set of documentary evidence

53. The parties may consider submitting jointly a single set of documentary evidence whose authenticity is not disputed. The purpose would be to avoid duplicate submissions and unnecessary discussions concerning the authenticity of documents, without prejudicing the position of the parties concerning the content of the documents. Additional documents may be inserted later if the parties agree. When a single set of documents would be too voluminous to be easily manageable, it might be practical to select a number of frequently used documents and establish a set of "working" documents. A convenient arrangement of documents in the set may be according to chronological order or subject-matter. It is useful to keep a table of contents of the documents, for example, by their short headings and dates, and to provide that the parties will refer to documents by those headings and dates.

(e) Should voluminous and complicated documentary evidence be presented through summaries, tabulations, charts, extracts or samples

54. When documentary evidence is voluminous and complicated, it may save time and costs if such evidence is presented by a report of a person competent in the relevant field (e.g. public accountant or consulting engineer). The report may present the information in the form of summaries, tabulations, charts, extracts or samples. Such presentation of evidence should be combined with arrangements that give the interested party the opportunity to review the underlying data and the methodology of preparing the report.

14. Physical evidence other than documents

55. In some arbitrations the arbitral tribunal is called upon to assess physical evidence other than documents, for example, by inspecting samples of goods, viewing a video recording or observing the functioning of a machine.

(a) What arrangements should be made if physical evidence will be submitted

56. If physical evidence will be submitted, the arbitral tribunal may wish to fix the time schedule for presenting the evidence, make arrangements for the other party or parties to have a suitable opportunity to prepare itself for the presentation of the evidence, and possibly take measures for safekeeping the items of evidence.

(b) What arrangements should be made if an on-site inspection is necessary

57. If an on-site inspection of property or goods will take place, the arbitral tribunal may consider matters such as timing, meeting places, other arrangements to provide the opportunity for all parties to be present, and the need to avoid communications between arbitrators and a party about points at issue without the presence of the other party or parties.

58. The site to be inspected is often under the control of one of the parties, which typically means that employees or representatives of that party will be present to give guidance and explanations. It should be borne in mind that statements of those representatives or employees made during an on-site inspection, as contrasted with statements those persons might make as witnesses in a hearing, should not be treated as evidence in the proceedings.

15. Witnesses

59. While laws and rules on arbitral procedure typically leave broad freedom concerning the manner of taking evidence of witnesses, practices on procedural points are varied. In order to facilitate the preparations of the parties for the hearings, the arbitral tribunal may consider it appropriate to clarify, in advance of the hearings, some or all of the following issues.

(a) Advance notice about a witness whom a party intends to present; written witnesses' statements

60. To the extent the applicable arbitration rules do not deal with the matter, the arbitral tribunal may wish to require that each party give advance notice to the arbitral tribunal and the other party or parties of any witness it intends to present. As to the content of the notice, the following is an example of what might be required, in addition to the names and addresses of the witnesses: (a) the subject upon which the witnesses will testify; (b) the language in which the witnesses will testify; and (c) the nature of the relationship with any of the parties, qualification and experience of the witnesses if and to the extent these are relevant to the dispute or the testimony, and how the witnesses learned about the facts on which they will testify. However, it may not be necessary to require such a notice, in particular if the thrust of the testimony can be clearly ascertained from the party's allegations.

61. Some practitioners favour the procedure according to which the party presenting witness evidence submits a signed witness's statement containing testimony itself. It should be noted, however, that such practice, which implies interviewing the witness by the party presenting the testimony, is not known in all parts of the world and, moreover, that some

practitioners disapprove of it on the ground that such contacts between the party and the witness may compromise the credibility of the testimony and are therefore improper (see paragraph 67). Notwithstanding these reservations, signed witness's testimony has advantages in that it may expedite the proceedings by making it easier for the other party or parties to prepare for the hearings or for the parties to identify uncontested matters. However, those advantages might be outweighed by the time and expense involved in obtaining the written testimony.

62. If a signed witness's statement should be made under oath or similar affirmation of truthfulness, it may be necessary to clarify by whom the oath or affirmation should be administered and whether any formal authentication will be required by the arbitral tribunal.

(b) Manner of taking oral evidence of witnesses

(i) Order in which questions will be asked and the manner in which the hearing of witnesses will be conducted

63. To the extent that the applicable rules do not provide an answer, it may be useful for the arbitral tribunal to clarify how witnesses will be heard. One of the various possibilities is that a witness is first questioned by the arbitral tribunal, whereupon questions are asked by the parties, first by the party who called the witness. Another possibility is for the witness to be questioned by the party presenting the witness and then by the other party or parties, while the arbitral tribunal might pose questions during the questioning or after the parties on points that in the tribunal's view have not been sufficiently clarified. Differences exist also as to the degree of control the arbitral tribunal exercises over the hearing of witnesses. For example, some arbitrators prefer to permit the parties to pose questions freely and directly to the witness, but may disallow a question if a party objects; other arbitrators tend to exercise more control and may disallow a question on their initiative or even require that questions from the parties be asked through the arbitral tribunal.

(ii) Whether oral testimony will be given under oath or affirmation and, if so, in what form an oath or affirmation should be made

64. Practices and laws differ as to whether or not oral testimony is to be given under oath or affirmation. In some legal systems, the arbitrators are empowered to put witnesses on oath, but it is usually in their discretion whether they want to do so. In other systems, oral testimony under oath is either unknown or may even be considered improper as only an official such as a judge or notary may have the authority to administer oaths.

(iii) May witnesses be in the hearing room when they are not testifying

65. Some arbitrators favour the procedure that, except if the circumstances suggest otherwise, the presence of a witness in the hearing room is limited to the time the witness is testifying; the purpose is to prevent the witness from being influenced by what is said in the hearing room, or to prevent that the presence of the witness would influence another witness. Other arbitrators consider that the presence of a witness during the testimony of other witnesses may be beneficial in that possible contradictions may be readily clarified or that their presence may act as a deterrent against untrue statements. Other possible approaches may be that witnesses are not present in the hearing room before their testimony, but stay in the room after they have testified, or that the arbitral tribunal decides the question for each witness individually depending on what the arbitral tribunal considers most appropriate. The arbitral tribunal may leave the procedure to be decided during the hearings, or may give guidance on the question in advance of the hearings.

(c) The order in which the witnesses will be called

66. When several witnesses are to be heard and longer testimony is expected, it is likely to reduce costs if the order in which they will be called is known in advance and their presence can be order in which it intends to present the witnesses, while it would be up to the arbitral tribunal to approve the scheduling and to make departures from it.

(d) Interviewing witnesses prior to their appearance at a hearing

67. In some legal systems, parties or their representatives are permitted to interview witnesses, prior to their appearance at the hearing, as to such matters as their recollection of the relevant events, their experience, qualifications or relation with a participant in the proceedings. In those legal systems such contacts are usually not permitted once the witness's oral testimony has begun. In other systems such contacts with witnesses are considered improper. In order to avoid misunderstandings, the arbitral tribunal may consider it useful to clarify what kind of contacts a party is permitted to have with a witness in the preparations for the hearings.

(e) Hearing representatives of a party

68. According to some legal systems, certain persons affiliated with a party may only be heard as representatives of the party but not as witnesses. In such a case, it may be necessary to consider ground rules for determining which persons may not testify as witnesses (e.g. certain executives, employees or agents) and for hearing statements of those persons and for questioning them.

16. Experts and expert witnesses

69. Many arbitration rules and laws on arbitral procedure address the participation of experts in arbitral proceedings. A frequent solution is that the arbitral tribunal has the power to appoint an expert to report on issues determined by the tribunal; in addition, the parties may be permitted to present expert witnesses on points at issue. In other cases, it is for the parties to present expert testimony, and it is not expected that the arbitral tribunal will appoint an expert.

(a) Expert appointed by the arbitral tribunal

70. If the arbitral tribunal is empowered to appoint an expert, one possible approach is for the tribunal to proceed directly to as to who should be the expert; this may be done, for example, without mentioning a candidate, by presenting to the parties a list of candidates, soliciting proposals from the parties, or by discussing with the parties the "profile" of the expert the arbitral tribunal intends to appoint, i.e. the qualifications, experience and abilities of the expert.

(i) The expert's terms of reference

71. The purpose of the expert's terms of reference is to indicate the questions on which the expert is to provide clarification, to avoid opinions on points that are not for the expert to assess and to commit the expert to a time schedule. While the discretion to appoint an expert normally includes the determination of the expert's terms of reference, the arbitral tribunal may decide to consult the parties before finalizing the terms. It might also be useful to determine details about how the expert will receive from the parties any relevant information or have access to any relevant documents, goods or other property, so as to enable the expert to prepare the report. In order to facilitate the evaluation of the expert's report, it is advisable to require the expert to include in the report information on the method used in arriving at the conclusions and the evidence and information used in preparing the report.

(ii) The opportunity of the parties to comment on the expert's report, including by presenting expert testimony

72. Arbitration rules that contain provisions on experts usually also have provisions on the right of a party to comment on the report of the expert appointed by the arbitral tribunal. If no such provisions apply or more specific procedures than those prescribed are deemed necessary, the arbitral tribunal may, in light of those provisions, consider it opportune to determine, for example, the time period for presenting written comments of the parties, or, if hearings are to be held for the purpose of hearing the

expert, the procedures for interrogating the expert by the parties or for the participation of any expert witnesses presented by the parties.

(b) Expert opinion presented by a party (expert witness)

73. If a party presents an expert opinion, the arbitral tribunal might consider requiring, for example, that the opinion be in writing, that the expert should be available to answer questions at hearings, and that, if a party will present an expert witness at a hearing, advance notice must be given or that the written opinion must be presented in advance, as in the case of other witnesses (see paragraphs 60-62).

17. Hearings

(a) Decision whether to hold hearings

74. Laws on arbitral procedure and arbitration rules often have provisions as to the cases in which oral hearings must be held and as to when the arbitral tribunal has discretion to decide whether to hold hearings.

75. If it is up to the arbitral tribunal to decide whether to hold hearings, the decision is likely to be influenced by factors such as, on the one hand, that it is usually quicker and easier to clarify points at issue pursuant to a direct confrontation of arguments than on the basis of correspondence and, on the other hand, the travel and other cost of holding hearings, and that the need of finding acceptable dates for the hearings might delay the proceedings. The arbitral tribunal may wish to consult the parties on this matter.

(b) Whether one period of hearings should be held or separate periods of hearings

76. Attitudes vary as to whether hearings should be held in a single period of hearings or in separate periods, especially when more than a few days are needed to complete the hearings. According to some arbitrators, the entire hearings should normally be held in a single period, even if the hearings are to last for more than a week. Other arbitrators in such cases tend to schedule separate periods of hearings. In some cases issues to be decided are separated, and separate hearings set for those issues, with the aim that oral presentation on those issues will be completed within the allotted time. Among the advantages of one period of hearings are that it involves less travel costs, memory will not fade, and it is unlikely that people representing a party will change. On the other hand, the longer the hearings, the more difficult it may be to find early dates acceptable to all participants. Furthermore, separate periods of hearings may be easier to schedule, the subsequent hearings may be tailored to the development of the case, and the period between the hearings leaves time for analysing the records and negotiations between the parties aimed at narrowing the points at issue by

agreement.

(c) Setting dates for hearings

77. Typically, firm dates will be fixed for hearings. Exceptionally, the arbitral tribunal may initially wish to set only "target dates" as opposed to definitive dates. This may be done at a stage of the proceedings when not all information necessary to schedule hearings is yet available, with the understanding that the target dates will either be confirmed or rescheduled within a reasonably short period. Such provisional planning can be useful to participants who are generally not available on short notice.

(d) Whether there should be a limit on the aggregate amount of time each party will have for oral arguments and questioning witnesses

78. Some arbitrators consider it useful to limit the aggregate amount of time each party has for any of the following: (a) making oral statements; (b) questioning its witnesses; and (c) questioning the witnesses of the other party or parties. In general, the same aggregate amount of time is considered appropriate for each party, unless the arbitral tribunal considers that a different allocation is justified. Before deciding, the arbitral tribunal may wish to consult the parties as to how much time they think they will need.

79. Such planning of time, provided it is realistic, fair and subject to judiciously firm control by the arbitral tribunal, will make it easier for the parties to plan the presentation of the various items of evidence and arguments, reduce the likelihood of running out of time towards the end of the hearings and avoid that one party would unfairly use up a disproportionate amount of time.

(e) The order in which the parties will present their arguments and evidence

80. Arbitration rules typically give broad latitude to the arbitral tribunal to determine the order of presentations at the hearings. Within that latitude, practices differ, for example, as to whether opening or closing statements are heard and their level of detail; the sequence in which the claimant and the respondent present their opening statements, arguments, witnesses and other evidence; and whether the respondent or the claimant has the last word. In view of such differences, or when no arbitration rules apply, it may foster efficiency of the proceedings if the arbitral tribunal clarifies to the parties, in advance of the hearings, the manner in which it will conduct the hearings, at least in broad lines.

(f) Length of hearings

81. The length of a hearing primarily depends on the complexity of the issues to be argued and the amount of witness evidence to be presented. The

length also depends on the procedural style used in the arbitration. Some practitioners prefer to have written evidence and written arguments presented before the hearings, which thus can focus on the issues that have not been sufficiently clarified. Those practitioners generally tend to plan shorter hearings than those practitioners who prefer that most if not all evidence and arguments are presented to the arbitral tribunal orally and in full detail. In order to facilitate the parties' preparations and avoid misunderstandings, the arbitral tribunal may wish to clarify to the parties, in advance of the hearings, the intended use of time and style of work at the hearings.

(g) Arrangements for a record of the hearings

82. The arbitral tribunal should decide, possibly after consulting with the parties, on the method of preparing a record of oral statements and testimony during hearings. Among different possibilities, one method is that the members of the arbitral tribunal take personal notes. Another is that the presiding arbitrator during the hearing dictates to a typist a summary of oral statements and testimony. A further method, possible when a secretary of the arbitral tribunal has been appointed, may be to leave to that person the preparation of a summary record. A useful, though costly, method is for professional stenographers to prepare verbatim transcripts, often within the next day or a similarly short time period. A written record may be combined with tape-recording, so as to enable reference to the tape in case of a disagreement over the written record.

83. If transcripts are to be produced, it may be considered how the persons who made the statements will be given an opportunity to check the transcripts. For example, it may be determined that the changes to the record would be approved by the parties or, failing their agreement, would be referred for decision to the arbitral tribunal.

(h) Whether and when the parties are permitted to submit notes summarizing their oral arguments

84. Some legal counsel are accustomed to giving notes summarizing their oral arguments to the arbitral tribunal and to the other party or parties. If such notes are presented, this is usually done during the hearings or shortly thereafter; in some cases, the notes are sent before the hearing. In order to avoid surprise, foster equal treatment of the parties and facilitate preparations for the hearings, advance clarification is advisable as to whether submitting such notes is acceptable and the time for doing so.

85. In closing the hearings, the arbitral tribunal will normally assume that no further proof is to be offered or submission to be made. Therefore, if

notes are to be presented to be read after the closure of the hearings, the arbitral tribunal may find it worthwhile to stress that the notes should be limited to summarizing what was said orally and in particular should not refer to new evidence or new argument.

18. Multi-party arbitration

86. When a single arbitration involves more than two parties (multi-party arbitration), considerations regarding the need to organize arbitral proceedings, and matters that may be considered in that connection, are generally not different from two-party arbitrations. A possible difference may be that, because of the need to deal with more than two parties, multi-party proceedings can be more complicated to manage than bilateral proceedings. The Notes, notwithstanding a possible greater complexity of multi-party arbitration, can be used in multi-party as well as in two-party proceedings.

87. The areas of possibly increased complexity in multi-party arbitration are, for example, the flow of communications among the parties and the arbitral tribunal (see paragraphs 33, 34 and 38-41); if points at issue are to be decided at different points in time, the order of deciding them (paragraphs 44-45); the manner in which the parties will participate in hearing witnesses (paragraph 63); the appointment of experts and the participation of the parties in considering their reports (paragraphs 70-72); the scheduling of hearings (paragraph 76); the order in which the parties will present their arguments and evidence at hearings (paragraph 80).

88. The Notes, which are limited to pointing out matters that may be considered in organizing arbitral proceedings in general, do not cover the drafting of the arbitration agreement or the constitution of the arbitral tribunal, both issues that give rise to special questions in multi-party arbitration as compared to two-party arbitration.

19. Possible requirements concerning filing or delivering the award

89. Some national laws require that arbitral awards be filed or registered with a court or similar authority, or that they be delivered in a particular manner or through a particular authority. Those laws differ with respect to, for example, the type of award to which the requirement applies (e.g. to all awards or only to awards not rendered under the auspices of an arbitral institution); time periods for filing, registering or delivering the award (in some cases those time periods may be rather short); or consequences for failing to comply with the requirement (which might be, for example, invalidity of the award or inability to enforce it in a particular manner).

Who should take steps to fulfil any requirement

90. If such a requirement exists, it is useful, some time before the award is to be issued, to plan who should take the necessary steps to meet the requirement and how the costs are to be borne.

WIPO ARBITRATION RULES *

I. General Provisions

Abbreviated Expressions

Article 1

In these Rules:

Arbitration Agreement	means an agreement by the parties to submit to arbitration all or certain disputes which have arisen or which may arise between them; an Arbitration Agreement may be in the form of an arbitration clause in a contract or in the form of a separate contract;
Claimant	means the party initiating an arbitration;
Respondent	means the party against which the arbitration is initiated, as named in the Request for Arbitration;
Tribunal	includes a sole arbitrator or all the arbitrators where more than one is appointed;
WIPO	means the World Intellectual Property Organization;
Center	means the WIPO Arbitration and Mediation Center, a unit of the International Bureau of WIPO.

Words used in the singular include the plural and vice versa, as the context may require.

Scope of Application of Rules

Article 2

Where an Arbitration Agreement provides for arbitration under the WIPO Arbitration Rules, these Rules shall be deemed to form part of that Arbitration Agreement and the dispute shall be settled in accordance with these Rules, as in effect on the date of the commencement of the arbitration, unless the parties have agreed otherwise.

Article 3

(a) These Rules shall govern the arbitration, except that, where any of these Rules is in conflict with a provision of the law applicable to the arbitration from which the parties cannot derogate, that provision shall prevail.

(b) The law applicable to the arbitration shall be determined in accordance with Article 61(b).

---

* See generally, WIPO Arbitration and Mediation Center, *Guide to WIPO Arbitration* (Pub. No. 919) available at: <http://www.wipo.int/amc/en/publications/>.

Notices and Periods of Time
Article 4

(a) Any notice or other communication that may or is required to be given under these Rules shall be in writing and shall be delivered by expedited postal or courier service, or transmitted by telefax, e-mail or other means of telecommunication that provide a record thereof.

(b) A party's last known residence or place of business shall be a valid address for the purpose of any notice or other communication in the absence of any notification of a change by that party. Communications may in any event be addressed to a party in the manner stipulated or, failing such a stipulation, according to the practice followed in the course of the dealings between the parties.

(c) For the purpose of determining the date of commencement of a time limit, a notice or other communication shall be deemed to have been received on the day it is delivered in accordance with paragraphs (a) and (b) of this Article.

(d) For the purpose of determining compliance with a time limit, a notice or other communication shall be deemed to have been sent, made or transmitted if it is dispatched, in accordance with paragraphs (a) and (b) of this Article, prior to or on the day of the expiration of the time limit.

(e) For the purpose of calculating a period of time under these Rules, such period shall begin to run on the day following the day when a notice or other communication is received. If the last day of such period is an official holiday or a non-business day at the residence or place of business of the addressee, the period is extended until the first business day which follows. Official holidays or non-business days occurring during the running of the period of time are included in calculating the period.

(f) The parties may agree to reduce or extend the periods of time referred to in Articles 11, 15(b), 16(b), 17(b), 17(c), 18(b), 19(b)(iii), 41(a) and 42(a).

(g) The Center may, at the request of a party or on its own motion, extend the periods of time referred to in Articles 11, 15(b), 16(b), 17(b), 17(c), 18 (b), 19(b)(iii), 69(d), 70(e) and 72(e).

Documents Required to be Submitted to the Center
Article 5

(a) Until the notification by the Center of the establishment of the Tribunal, any written statement, notice or other communication required or allowed under these rules shall be submitted by a party to the Center and a copy thereof shall at the same time be transmitted by that party to the other party.

(b) Any written statement, notice or other communication so sent to the

Center shall be sent in a number of copies equal to the number required to provide one copy for each envisaged arbitrator and one for the Center.
(c) After the notification by the Center of the establishment of the Tribunal, any written statements, notices or other communications shall be submitted by a party directly to the Tribunal and a copy thereof shall at the same time be supplied by that party to the other party.
(d) The Tribunal shall send to the Center a copy of each order or other decision that it makes.

II. Commencement of the Arbitration

Request for Arbitration

Article 6

The Claimant shall transmit the Request for Arbitration to the Center and to the Respondent.

Article 7

The date of commencement of the arbitration shall be the date on which the Request for Arbitration is received by the Center.

Article 8

The Center shall inform the Claimant and the Respondent of the receipt by it of the Request for Arbitration and of the date of the commencement of the arbitration.

Article 9

The Request for Arbitration shall contain:
(i) a demand that the dispute be referred to arbitration under the WIPO Arbitration Rules;
(ii) the names, addresses and telephone, telefax, email or other communication references of the parties and of the representative of the Claimant;
(iii) a copy of the Arbitration Agreement and, if applicable, any separate choice-of-law clause;
(iv) a brief description of the nature and circumstances of the dispute, including an indication of the rights and property involved and the nature of any technology involved;
(v) a statement of the relief sought and an indication, to the extent possible, of any amount claimed; and
(vi) any appointment that is required by, or observations that the Claimant considers useful in connection with, Articles 14 to 20.

Article 10

The Request for Arbitration may also be accompanied by the Statement of Claim referred to in Article 41.

Answer to the Request

Article 11

Within 30 days from the date on which the Respondent receives the Request for Arbitration from the Claimant, the Respondent shall address to the Center and to the Claimant an Answer to the Request which shall contain comments on any of the elements in the Request for Arbitration and may include indications of any counter-claim or set-off.

Article 12

If the Claimant has filed a Statement of Claim with the Request for Arbitration pursuant to Article 10, the Answer to the Request may also be accompanied by the Statement of Defense referred to in Article 42.

Representation

Article 13

(a) The parties may be represented by persons of their choice, irrespective of, in particular, nationality or professional qualification. The names, addresses and telephone, telefax, e-mail or other communication references of representatives shall be communicated to the Center, the other party and, after its establishment, the Tribunal.

(b) Each party shall ensure that its representatives have sufficient time available to enable the arbitration to proceed expeditiously.

(c) The parties may also be assisted by persons of their choice.

III. Composition and Establishment of the Tribunal

Number and Appointment of Arbitrators

Article 14

(a) The Tribunal shall consist of such number of arbitrators as has been agreed by the parties.

(b) Where the parties have not agreed on the number of arbitrators, the Tribunal shall consist of a sole arbitrator, except where the Center in its discretion determines that, in view of all the circumstances of the case, a Tribunal composed of three members is appropriate.

(c) Any nomination of an arbitrator made by the parties pursuant to Articles 16, 17 and 18 shall be confirmed by the Center provided that the requirements of Articles 22 and 23 have been met. The appointment shall be effective upon the Center's notification to the parties.

Appointment Pursuant to Procedure Agreed Upon by the Parties

Article 15

(a) If the parties have agreed on a procedure for the appointment of the arbitrator or arbitrators, that procedure shall be followed.

(b) If the Tribunal has not been established pursuant to such procedure within the period of time agreed upon by the parties or, in the absence of such an agreed period of time, within 45 days after the commencement of the arbitration, the Tribunal shall be established or completed, as the case may be, in accordance with Article 19.

Appointment of a Sole Arbitrator

Article 16

(a) Where a sole arbitrator is to be appointed and the parties have not agreed on an appointment procedure, the sole arbitrator shall be appointed jointly by the parties.

(b) If the appointment of the sole arbitrator is not made within the period of time agreed upon by the parties or, in the absence of such an agreed period of time, within 30 days after the commencement of the arbitration, the sole arbitrator shall be appointed in accordance with Article 19.

Appointment of Three Arbitrators

Article 17

(a) Where three arbitrators are to be appointed and the parties have not agreed upon an appointment procedure, the arbitrators shall be appointed in accordance with this Article.

(b) The Claimant shall nominate an arbitrator in its Request for Arbitration. The Respondent shall appoint an arbitrator within 30 days from the date on which it receives the Request for Arbitration. The two arbitrators thus appointed shall, within 20 days after the appointment of the second arbitrator, appoint a third arbitrator, who shall be the presiding arbitrator.

(c) Notwithstanding paragraph (b), where three arbitrators are to be appointed as a result of the exercise of the discretion of the Center under Article 14(b), the Claimant shall, by notice to the Center and to the Respondent, appoint an arbitrator within 15 days after the receipt by it of notification by the Center that the Tribunal is to be composed of three arbitrators. The Respondent shall nominate an arbitrator within 30 days after the receipt by it of the said notification. The two arbitrators thus appointed shall, within 20 days after the appointment of the second arbitrator, nominate a third arbitrator, who shall be the presiding arbitrator.

(d) If the nomination of any arbitrator is not made within the applicable period of time referred to in the preceding paragraphs, that arbitrator shall be appointed in accordance with Article 19.

Appointment of Three Arbitrators in Case of Multiple Claimants or Respondents

Article 18

Where:

(i) there are multiple Claimants and/or multiple Respondents; and

(ii) three arbitrators are to be appointed;

the multiple Claimants, jointly, in the Request for Arbitration, shall nominate an arbitrator, and/or the multiple Respondents, jointly, within 30 days after receiving the Request for Arbitration, shall nominate an arbitrator, as the case may be. If a joint nomination is not made within the applicable period of time, the Center shall appoint one or both arbitrators. The two arbitrators shall, within 20 days after the appointment of the second arbitrator, nominate a third arbitrator, who shall be the presiding arbitrator.

Default Appointment

Article 19

(a) If a party has failed to nominate an arbitrator as required under Articles 15, 17 or 18, the Center shall forthwith make the appointment.

(b) If the sole or presiding arbitrator has not been appointed as required under Articles 15, 16, 17 or 18, the appointment shall take place in accordance with the following procedure:

(i) The Center shall send to each party an identical list of candidates. The list shall comprise the names of at least three candidates in alphabetical order. The list shall include or be accompanied by a brief statement of each candidate's qualifications. If the parties have agreed on any particular qualifications, the list shall contain only the names of candidates that satisfy those qualifications.

(ii) Each party shall have the right to delete the name of any candidate or candidates to whose appointment it objects and shall number any remaining candidates in order of preference.

(iii) Each party shall return the marked list to the Center within 20 days after the date on which the list is received by it. Any party failing to return a marked list within that period of time shall be deemed to have assented to all candidates appearing on the list.

(iv) As soon as possible after receipt by it of the lists from the parties, or failing this, after the expiration of the period of time specified in the previous subparagraph, the Center shall, taking into account the preferences and objections expressed by the parties, invite a person from the list to be the sole or presiding arbitrator.

(v) If the lists which have been returned do not show a person who is acceptable as arbitrator to both parties, the Center shall be authorized to appoint the sole or presiding arbitrator. The Center shall similarly be authorized to do so if a person is not able or does not wish to accept the Center's invitation to be the sole or presiding arbitrator, or if there appear to be other reasons precluding that person from being the sole or presiding arbitrator, and there does not remain on the lists a person who is acceptable as arbitrator to both parties.

(c) Notwithstanding the provisions of paragraph (b), the Center shall be authorized to appoint the sole or presiding arbitrator if it determines in its discretion that the procedure described in that paragraph is not appropriate for the case.

Nationality of Arbitrators

Article 20

(a) An agreement of the parties concerning the nationality of arbitrators shall be respected.

(b) If the parties have not agreed on the nationality of the sole or presiding arbitrator, such arbitrator shall, in the absence of special circumstances such as the need to appoint a person having particular qualifications, be a national of a country other than the countries of the parties.

Communication Between Parties and Candidates for Appointment as Arbitrator

Article 21

No party or anyone acting on its behalf shall have any *ex parte* communication with any candidate for appointment as arbitrator except to discuss the candidate's qualifications, availability or independence in relation to the parties.

Impartiality and Independence

Article 22

(a) Each arbitrator shall be impartial and independent.

(b) Each prospective arbitrator shall, before accepting appointment, disclose to the parties, the Center and any other arbitrator who has already been appointed any circumstances that might give rise to justifiable doubt as to the arbitrator's impartiality or independence, or confirm in writing that no such circumstances exist.

(c) If, at any stage during the arbitration, new circumstances arise that might give rise to justifiable doubt as to any arbitrator's impartiality or independence, the arbitrator shall promptly disclose such circumstances to the parties, the Center and the other arbitrators.

Availability, Acceptance and Notification

Article 23

(a) Each arbitrator shall, by accepting appointment, be deemed to have undertaken to make available sufficient time to enable the arbitration to be conducted and completed expeditiously.

(b) Each prospective arbitrator shall accept appointment in writing and shall communicate such acceptance to the Center.

(c) The Center shall notify the parties of the appointment of each member of the Tribunal and of the establishment of the Tribunal.

Challenge of Arbitrators

Article 24

(a) Any arbitrator may be challenged by a party if circumstances exist that give rise to justifiable doubt as to the arbitrator's impartiality or independence.

(b) A party may challenge an arbitrator whom it has appointed or in whose appointment it concurred, only for reasons of which it becomes aware after the nomination has been made.

Article 25

A party challenging an arbitrator shall send notice to the Center, the Tribunal and the other party, stating the reasons for the challenge, within 15 days after being notified of that arbitrator's appointment or after becoming aware of the circumstances that it considers give rise to justifiable doubt as to that arbitrator's impartiality or independence.

Article 26

When an arbitrator has been challenged by a party, the other party shall have the right to respond to the challenge and shall, if it exercises this right, send, within 15 days after receipt of the notice referred to in Article 25, a copy of its response to the Center, the party making the challenge and any appointed arbitrator.

Article 27

The Tribunal may, in its discretion, suspend or continue the arbitral proceedings during the pendency of the challenge.

Article 28

The other party may agree to the challenge or the arbitrator may voluntarily withdraw. In either case, the arbitrator shall be replaced without any implication that the grounds for the challenge are valid.

Article 29

If the other party does not agree to the challenge and the challenged arbitrator does not withdraw, the decision on the challenge shall be made by the Center in accordance with its internal procedures. Such a decision is of an administrative nature and shall be final. The Center shall not be required to state reasons for its decision.

Release from Appointment

Article 30

At the arbitrator's own request, an arbitrator may be released from appointment as arbitrator either with the consent of the parties or by the Center.

Article 31

Irrespective of any request by the arbitrator, the parties may jointly release the arbitrator from appointment as arbitrator. The parties shall promptly notify the Center of such release.

Article 32

At the request of a party or on its own motion, the Center may release an arbitrator from appointment as arbitrator if the arbitrator has become *de jure* or *de facto* unable to fulfill, or fails to fulfill, the duties of an arbitrator. In such a case, the parties shall be offered the opportunity to express their views thereon and the provisions of Articles 26 to 29 shall apply *mutatis mutandis*.

Replacement of an Arbitrator

Article 33

(a) Whenever necessary, a substitute arbitrator shall be appointed pursuant to the procedure provided for in Articles 15 to 19 that was applicable to the appointment of the arbitrator being replaced.

(b) In the event that an arbitrator appointed by a party has either been successfully challenged on grounds which were known or should have been known to that party at the time of appointment, or has been released from appointment as arbitrator in accordance with Article 32, the Center shall have the discretion not to permit that party to make a new nomination. If it chooses to exercise this discretion, the Center shall make the substitute appointment.

(c) Pending the replacement, the arbitral proceedings shall be suspended, unless otherwise agreed by the parties.

Article 34

Whenever a substitute arbitrator is appointed, the Tribunal shall, having regard to any observations of the parties, determine in its sole discretion whether all or part of any prior hearings are to be repeated.

Truncated Tribunal
Article 35

(a) If an arbitrator on a three-person Tribunal, though duly notified and without good cause, fails to participate in the work of the Tribunal, the two other arbitrators shall, unless a party has made an application under Article 32, have the power in their sole discretion to continue the arbitration and to make any award, order or other decision, notwithstanding the failure of the third arbitrator to participate. In determining whether to continue the arbitration or to render any award, order or other decision without the participation of an arbitrator, the two other arbitrators shall take into account the stage of the arbitration, the reason, if any, expressed by the third arbitrator for such non participation, and such other matters as they consider appropriate in the circumstances of the case.

(b) In the event that the two other arbitrators determine not to continue the arbitration without the participation of a third arbitrator, the Center shall, on proof satisfactory to it of the failure of the arbitrator to participate in the work of the Tribunal, declare the office vacant, and a substitute arbitrator shall be appointed by the Center in the exercise of the discretion defined in Article 33, unless the parties agree otherwise.

Pleas as to the Jurisdiction of the Tribunal
Article 36

(a) The Tribunal shall have the power to hear and determine objections to its own jurisdiction, including any objections with respect to form, existence, validity or scope of the Arbitration Agreement examined pursuant to Article 61(c).

(b) The Tribunal shall have the power to determine the existence or validity of any contract of which the Arbitration Agreement forms part or to which it relates.

(c) A plea that the Tribunal does not have jurisdiction shall be raised not later than in the Statement of Defense or, with respect to a counter-claim or a setoff, the Statement of Defense thereto, failing which any such plea shall be barred in the subsequent arbitral proceedings or before any court. A plea that the Tribunal is exceeding the scope of its authority shall be raised as soon as the matter alleged to be beyond the scope of its authority is raised during the arbitral proceedings. The Tribunal may, in either case, admit a later plea if it considers the delay justified.

(d) The Tribunal may rule on a plea referred to in paragraph (c) as a preliminary question or, in its sole discretion, decide on such a plea in the final award.

(e) A plea that the Tribunal lacks jurisdiction shall not preclude the Center from administering the arbitration.

IV. Conduct of the Arbitration

General Powers of the Tribunal

Article 37

(a) Subject to Article 3, the Tribunal may conduct the arbitration in such manner as it considers appropriate.

(b) In all cases, the Tribunal shall ensure that the parties are treated with equality and that each party is given a fair opportunity to present its case.

(c) The Tribunal shall ensure that the arbitral procedure takes place with due expedition. It may, at the request of a party or on its own motion, extend in exceptional cases a period of time fixed by these Rules, by itself or agreed to by the parties. In urgent cases, such an extension may be granted by the presiding arbitrator alone.

Place of Arbitration

Article 38

(a) Unless otherwise agreed by the parties, the place of arbitration shall be decided by the Center, taking into consideration any observations of the parties and the circumstances of the arbitration.

(b) The Tribunal may, after consultation with the parties, conduct hearings at any place that it considers appropriate. It may deliberate wherever it deems appropriate.

(c) The award shall be deemed to have been made at the place of arbitration.

Language of Arbitration

Article 39

(a) Unless otherwise agreed by the parties, the language of the arbitration shall be the language of the Arbitration Agreement, subject to the power of the Tribunal to determine otherwise, having regard to any observations of the parties and the circumstances of the arbitration.

(b) The Tribunal may order that any documents submitted in languages other than the language of arbitration be accompanied by a translation in whole or in part into the language of arbitration.

Preparatory Conference

Article 40

The Tribunal shall, in general within 30 days after its establishment, conduct a preparatory conference with the parties in any suitable format for the purpose of organizing and scheduling the subsequent proceedings in a time and cost efficient manner.

Statement of Claim

Article 41

(a) Unless the Statement of Claim accompanied the Request for Arbitration, the Claimant shall, within 30 days after receipt of notification from the Center of the establishment of the Tribunal, communicate its Statement of Claim to the Respondent and to the Tribunal.

(b) The Statement of Claim shall contain a comprehensive statement of the facts and legal arguments supporting the claim, including a statement of the relief sought.

(c) The Statement of Claim shall, to as large an extent as possible, be accompanied by the documentary evidence upon which the Claimant relies, together with a schedule of such documents. Where the documentary evidence is especially voluminous, the Claimant may add a reference to further documents it is prepared to submit.

Statement of Defense

Article 42

(a) The Respondent shall, within 30 days after receipt of the Statement of Claim or within 30 days after receipt of notification from the Center of the establishment of the Tribunal, whichever occurs later, communicate its Statement of Defense to the Claimant and to the Tribunal.

(b) The Statement of Defense shall reply to the particulars of the Statement of Claim required pursuant to Article 41(b). The Statement of Defense shall be accompanied by the corresponding documentary evidence described in Article 41(c).

(c) Any counter-claim or set-off by the Respondent shall be made or asserted in the Statement of Defense or, in exceptional circumstances, at a later stage in the arbitral proceedings if so determined by the Tribunal. Any such counter-claim or set-off shall contain the same particulars as those specified in Article 41(b) and (c).

Further Written Statements

Article 43

(a) In the event that a counter-claim or set-off has been made or asserted, the Claimant shall reply to the particulars thereof. Article 42(a) and (b) shall apply *mutatis mutandis* to such reply.

(b) The Tribunal may, in its discretion, allow or require further written statements.

Amendments to Claims or Defense

Article 44

Subject to any contrary agreement by the parties, a party may amend or supplement its claim, counter-claim, defense or set-off during the course of the arbitral proceedings, unless the Tribunal considers it inappropriate to allow such amendment having regard to its nature or the delay in making it and to the provisions of Article 37(b) and (c).

Communication Between Parties and Tribunal

Article 45

Except as otherwise provided in these Rules or permitted by the Tribunal, no party or anyone acting on its behalf may have any *ex parte* communication with any arbitrator with respect to any matter of substance relating to the arbitration, it being understood that nothing in this paragraph shall prohibit *ex parte* communications which concern matters of a purely organizational nature, such as the physical facilities, place, date or time of the hearings.

Joinder

Article 46

At the request of a party, the Tribunal may order the joinder of an additional party to the arbitration provided all parties, including the additional party, agree. Any such order shall take account of all relevant circumstances, including the stage reached in the arbitration. The request shall be addressed together with the Request for Arbitration or the Answer to the Request, as the case may be, or, if a party becomes aware at a later stage of circumstances that it considers relevant for a joinder, within 15 days after acquiring that knowledge.

Consolidation

Article 47

Where an arbitration is commenced that concerns a subject matter substantially related to that in dispute in other arbitral proceedings pending under these Rules or involving the same parties, the Center may order, after consulting with all concerned parties and any Tribunal appointed in the pending proceedings, to consolidate the new arbitration with the pending proceedings, provided all parties and any appointed Tribunal agree. Such consolidation shall take into account all relevant circumstances, including the stage reached in the pending proceedings.

Interim Measures of Protection and Security for Claims and Costs

Article 48

(a) At the request of a party, the Tribunal may issue any provisional orders or take other interim measures it deems necessary, including injunctions and measures for the conservation of goods which form part of the subject matter in dispute, such as an order for their deposit with a third person or for the sale of perishable goods. The Tribunal may make the granting of such measures subject to appropriate security being furnished by the requesting party.

(b) At the request of a party, the Tribunal may order the other party to provide security, in a form to be determined by the Tribunal, for the claim or counter-claim, as well as for costs referred to in Article 74.

(c) Measures and orders contemplated under this Article may take the form of an interim award.

(d) A request addressed by a party to a judicial authority for interim measures or for security for the claim or counter-claim, or for the implementation of any such measures or orders granted by the Tribunal, shall not be deemed incompatible with the Arbitration Agreement, or deemed to be a waiver of that Agreement.

Emergency Relief Proceedings

Article 49

(a) Unless otherwise agreed by the parties, the provisions of this Article shall apply to arbitrations conducted under Arbitration Agreements entered on or after June 1, 2014.

(b) A party seeking urgent interim relief prior to the establishment of the Tribunal may submit a request for such emergency relief to the Center. The request for emergency relief shall include the particulars set out in Article 9 (ii) to (iv), as well as a statement of the interim measures sought and the reasons why such relief is needed on an emergency basis. The Center shall inform the other party of the receipt of the request for emergency relief.

(c) The date of commencement of the emergency relief proceedings shall be the date on which the request referred to in paragraph (b) is received by the Center.

(d) The request for emergency relief shall be subject to proof of payment of the administration fee and of the initial deposit of the emergency arbitrator's fees in accordance with the Schedule of Fees applicable on the date of commencement of the emergency relief proceedings.

(e) Upon receipt of the request for emergency relief, the Center shall promptly, normally within two days, appoint a sole emergency arbitrator. Articles 22 to 29 shall apply *mutatis mutandis* whereby the periods of time referred to in Articles 25 and 26 shall be three days.

(f) The emergency arbitrator shall have the powers vested in the Tribunal under Article 36 (a) and (b), including the authority to determine its own jurisdiction. Article 36 (e) shall apply *mutatis mutandis*.

(g) The emergency arbitrator may conduct the proceedings in such manner as it considers appropriate, taking due account of the urgency of the request. The emergency arbitrator shall ensure that each party is given a fair opportunity to present its case. The emergency arbitrator may provide for proceedings by telephone conference or on written submissions as alternatives to a hearing.

(h) If the parties have agreed upon the place of arbitration, that place shall be the place of the emergency relief proceedings. In the absence of such agreement, the place of the emergency relief proceedings shall be decided by the Center, taking into consideration any observations made by the parties and the circumstances of the emergency relief proceeding.

(i) The emergency arbitrator may order any interim measure it deems necessary. The emergency arbitrator may make the granting of such orders subject to appropriate security being furnished by the requesting party. Article 48 (c) and (d) shall apply *mutatis mutandis*. Upon request, the emergency arbitrator may modify or terminate the order.

(j) The emergency arbitrator shall terminate emergency relief proceedings if arbitration is not commenced within 30 days from the date of commencement of the emergency relief proceedings.

(k) The costs of the emergency relief proceedings shall be initially fixed and apportioned by the emergency arbitrator in consultation with the Center, in accordance with the Schedule of Fees applicable on the date of commencement of the emergency relief proceedings, subject to the Tribunal's power to make a final determination of the apportionment of such costs under Article 73(c).

(l) Unless otherwise agreed by the parties, the emergency arbitrator may not act as an arbitrator in any arbitration relating to the dispute.

(m) The emergency arbitrator shall have no further powers to act once the Tribunal is established. Upon request by a party, the Tribunal may modify or terminate any measure ordered by the emergency arbitrator.

Evidence

Article 50

(a) The Tribunal shall determine the admissibility, relevance, materiality and weight of evidence.

(b) At any time during the arbitration, the Tribunal may, at the request of a party or on its own motion, order a party to produce such documents or other evidence as it considers necessary or appropriate and may order a party to make available to the Tribunal or to an expert appointed by it or to the other party any property in its possession or control for inspection or testing.

Experiments
Article 51

(a) A party may give notice to the Tribunal and to the other party at any reasonable time before a hearing that specified experiments have been conducted on which it intends to rely. The notice shall specify the purpose of the experiment, a summary of the experiment, the method employed, the results and the conclusion. The other party may by notice to the Tribunal request that any or all such experiments be repeated in its presence. If the Tribunal considers such request justified, it shall determine the timetable for the repetition of the experiments.

(b) For the purposes of this Article, "experiments" shall include tests or other processes of verification.

Site Visits
Article 52

The Tribunal may, at the request of a party or on its own motion, inspect or require the inspection of any site, property, machinery, facility, production line, model, film, material, product or process as it deems appropriate. A party may request such an inspection at any reasonable time prior to any hearing, and the Tribunal, if it grants such a request, shall determine the timing and arrangements for the inspection.

Agreed Primers and Models
Article 53

The Tribunal may, where the parties so agree, determine that they shall jointly provide:

(i) a technical primer setting out the background of the scientific, technical or other specialized information necessary to fully understand the matters in issue; and

(ii) models, drawings or other materials that the Tribunal or the parties require for reference purposes at any hearing.

Disclosure of Trade Secrets and Other Confidential Information
Article 54

(a) For the purposes of this Article, confidential information shall mean any information, regardless of the medium in which it is expressed, which is:

(i) in the possession of a party;

(ii) not accessible to the public;

(iii) of commercial, financial or industrial significance; and

(iv) treated as confidential by the party possessing it.

(b) A party invoking the confidentiality of any information it wishes or is required to submit in the arbitration, including to an expert appointed by the

Tribunal, shall make an application to have the information classified as confidential by notice to the Tribunal, with a copy to the other party. Without disclosing the substance of the information, the party shall give in the notice the reasons for which it considers the information confidential.
(c) The Tribunal shall determine whether the information is to be classified as confidential and of such a nature that the absence of special measures of protection in the proceedings would be likely to cause serious harm to the party invoking its confidentiality. If the Tribunal so determines, it shall decide under which conditions and to whom the confidential information may in part or in whole be disclosed and shall require any person to whom the confidential information is to be disclosed to sign an appropriate confidentiality undertaking.
(d) In exceptional circumstances, in lieu of itself determining whether the information is to be classified as confidential and of such nature that the absence of special measures of protection in the proceedings would be likely to cause serious harm to the party invoking its confidentiality, the Tribunal may, at the request of a party or on its own motion and after consultation with the parties, designate a confidentiality advisor who will determine whether the information is to be so classified, and, if so, decide under which conditions and to whom it may in part or in whole be disclosed. Any such confidentiality advisor shall be required to sign an appropriate confidentiality undertaking.
(e) The Tribunal may also, at the request of a party or on its own motion, appoint the confidentiality advisor as an expert in accordance with Article 57 in order to report to it, on the basis of the confidential information, on specific issues designated by the Tribunal without disclosing the confidential information either to the party from whom the confidential information does not originate or to the Tribunal.

Hearings

Article 55

(a) If either party so requests, the Tribunal shall hold a hearing for the presentation of evidence by witnesses, including expert witnesses, or for oral argument or for both. In the absence of a request, the Tribunal shall decide whether to hold such a hearing or hearings. If no hearings are held, the proceedings shall be conducted on the basis of documents and other materials alone.
(b) In the event of a hearing, the Tribunal shall give the parties adequate advance notice of the date, time and place thereof.
(c) Unless the parties agree otherwise, all hearings shall be in private.

(d) The Tribunal shall determine whether and, if so, in what form a record shall be made of any hearing.

Witnesses

Article 56

(a) Before any hearing, the Tribunal may require either party to give notice of the identity of witnesses it wishes to call, whether witness of fact or expert witness, as well as of the subject matter of their testimony and its relevance to the issues.

(b) The Tribunal has discretion, on the grounds of redundance and irrelevance, to limit or refuse the appearance of any witness.

(c) Any witness who gives oral evidence may be questioned, under the control of the Tribunal, by each of the parties. The Tribunal may put questions at any stage of the examination of the witnesses.

(d) The testimony of witnesses may, either at the choice of a party or as directed by the Tribunal, be submitted in written form, whether by way of signed statements, sworn affidavits or otherwise, in which case the Tribunal may make the admissibility of the testimony conditional upon the witnesses being made available for oral testimony.

(e) A party shall be responsible for the practical arrangements, cost and availability of any witness it calls.

(f) The Tribunal shall determine whether any witness shall retire during any part of the proceedings, particularly during the testimony of other witnesses.

Experts Appointed by the Tribunal

Article 57

(a) The Tribunal may, at the preparatory conference or at a later stage, and after consultation with the parties, appoint one or more independent experts to report to it on specific issues designated by the Tribunal. A copy of the expert's terms of reference, established by the Tribunal, having regard to any observations of the parties, shall be communicated to the parties. Any such expert shall be required to sign an appropriate confidentiality undertaking.

(b) Subject to Article 54, upon receipt of the expert's report, the Tribunal shall communicate a copy of the report to the parties, which shall be given the opportunity to express, in writing, their opinion on the report. A party may, subject to Article 54, examine any document on which the expert has relied in such a report.

(c) At the request of a party, the parties shall be given the opportunity to question the expert at a hearing. At this hearing, the parties may present expert witnesses to testify on the points at issue.

(d) The opinion of any expert on the issue or issues submitted to the expert shall be subject to the Tribunal's power of assessment of those issues in the context of all the circumstances of the case, unless the parties have agreed that the expert's determination shall be conclusive in respect of any specific issue.

Dafault

Article 58

(a) If the Claimant, without showing good cause, fails to submit its Statement of Claim in accordance with Article 41, the Tribunal shall terminate the proceedings.

(b) If the Respondent, without showing good cause, fails to submit its Statement of Defense in accordance with Article 42, the Tribunal may nevertheless proceed with the arbitration and make the award.

(c) The Tribunal may also proceed with the arbitration and make the award if a party, without showing good cause, fails to avail itself of the opportunity to present its case within the period of time determined by the Tribunal.

(d) If a party, without showing good cause, fails to comply with any provision of, or requirement under, these Rules or any direction given by the Tribunal, the Tribunal may draw the inferences therefrom that it considers appropriate.

Closure of Proceedings

Article 59

(a) The Tribunal shall declare the proceedings closed when it is satisfied that the parties have had adequate opportunity to present submissions and evidence.

(b) The Tribunal may, if it considers it necessary owing to exceptional circumstances, decide, on its own motion or upon application of a party, to re-open the proceedings it declared to be closed at any time before the award is made.

Waiver

Article 60

A party which knows that any provision of, these Rules, any requirement under the Arbitration Agreement, or any direction given by the Tribunal, has not been complied with, and yet proceeds with the arbitration without promptly recording an objection to such non-compliance, shall be deemed to have waived its right to object.

V. Awards and Other Decisions

Laws Applicable to the Substance of the Dispute, the Arbitration and the Arbitration Agreement

Article 61

(a) The Tribunal shall decide the substance of the dispute in accordance with the law or rules of law chosen by the parties. Any designation of the law of a given State shall be construed, unless otherwise expressed, as directly referring to the substantive law of that State and not to its conflict of laws rules. Failing a choice by the parties, the Tribunal shall apply the law or rules of law that it determines to be appropriate. In all cases, the Tribunal shall decide having due regard to the terms of any relevant contract and taking into account applicable trade usages. The Tribunal may decide as *amiable compositeur* or *ex aequo et bono* only if the parties have expressly authorized it to do so.

(b) The law applicable to the arbitration shall be the arbitration law of the place of arbitration, unless the parties have expressly agreed on the application of another arbitration law and such agreement is permitted by the law of the place of arbitration.

(c) An Arbitration Agreement shall be regarded as effective if it conforms to the requirements concerning form, existence, validity and scope of either the law or rules of law applicable in accordance with paragraph (a), or the law applicable in accordance with paragraph (b).

Currency and Interest

Article 62

(a) Monetary amounts in the award may be expressed in any currency.

(b) The Tribunal may award simple or compound interest to be paid by a party on any sum awarded against that party. It shall be free to determine the interest at such rates as it considers to be appropriate, without being bound by legal rates of interest, and shall be free to determine the period for which the interest shall be paid.

Decision-Making

Article 63

Unless the parties have agreed otherwise, where there is more than one arbitrator, any award, order or other decision of the Tribunal shall be made by a majority. In the absence of a majority, the presiding arbitrator shall make the award, order or other decision as if acting as sole arbitrator.

Form and Notification of Awards

Article 64

(a) The Tribunal may make separate awards on different issues at different times.

(b) The award shall be in writing and shall state the date on which it was made, as well as the place of arbitration in accordance with Article 38(a).

(c) The award shall state the reasons on which it is based, unless the parties have agreed that no reasons should be stated and the law applicable to the arbitration does not require the statement of such reasons.

(d) The award shall be signed by the arbitrator or arbitrators. The signature of the award by a majority of the arbitrators, or, in the case of Article 63, second sentence, by the presiding arbitrator, shall be sufficient. Where an arbitrator fails to sign, the award shall state the reason for the absence of the signature.

(e) The Tribunal may consult the Center with regard to matters of form, particularly to ensure the enforceability of the award.

(f) The award shall be communicated by the Tribunal to the Center in a number of originals sufficient to provide one for each party, the arbitrator or arbitrators and the Center. The Center shall formally communicate an original of the award to each party and the arbitrator or arbitrators.

(g) At the request of a party, the Center shall provide it, at cost, with a copy of the award certified by the Center. A copy so certified shall be deemed to comply with the requirements of Article IV(1)(a) of the Convention on the Recognition and Enforcement of Foreign Arbitral Awards, New York, June 10, 1958.

Time Period for Delivery of the Final Award

Article 65

(a) The arbitration should, wherever reasonably possible, be heard and the proceedings declared closed within not more than nine months after either the delivery of the Statement of Defense or the establishment of the Tribunal, whichever event occurs later. The final award should, wherever reasonably possible, be made within three months thereafter.

(b) If the proceedings are not declared closed within the period of time specified in paragraph (a), the Tribunal shall send the Center a status report on the arbitration, with a copy to each party. It shall send a further status report to the Center, and a copy to each party, at the end of each ensuing period of three months during which the proceedings have not been declared closed.

(c) If the final award is not made within three months after the closure of the proceedings, the Tribunal shall send the Center a written explanation for the delay, with a copy to each party. It shall send a further explanation, and a copy to each party, at the end of each ensuing period of one month until the final award is made.

Effect of Award

Article 66

(a) By agreeing to arbitration under these Rules, the parties undertake to carry out the award without delay, and waive their right to any form of appeal or recourse to a court of law or other judicial authority, insofar as such waiver may validly be made under the applicable law.

(b) The award shall be effective and binding on the parties as from the date it is communicated by the Center pursuant to Article 64(f), second sentence.

Settlement or Other Grounds for Termination

Article 67

(a) The Tribunal may suggest that the parties explore settlement at such times as the Tribunal may deem appropriate.

(b) If, before the award is made, the parties agree on a settlement of the dispute, the Tribunal shall terminate the arbitration and, if requested jointly by the parties, record the settlement in the form of a consent award. The Tribunal shall not be obliged to give reasons for such an award.

(c) If, before the award is made, the continuation of the arbitration becomes unnecessary or impossible for any reason not mentioned in paragraph (b), the Tribunal shall inform the parties of its intention to terminate the arbitration. The Tribunal shall have the power to issue such an order terminating the arbitration, unless a party raises justifiable grounds for objection within a period of time to be determined by the Tribunal.

(d) The consent award or the order for termination of the arbitration shall be signed by the arbitrator or arbitrators in accordance with Article 64(d) and shall be communicated by the Tribunal to the Center in a number of originals sufficient to provide one for each party, the arbitrator or arbitrators and the Center. The Center shall formally communicate an original of the consent award or the order for termination to each party and the arbitrator or arbitrators.

Correction of the Award and Additional Award

Article 68

(a) Within 30 days after receipt of the award, a party may, by notice to the Tribunal, with a copy to the Center and the other party, request the Tribunal to correct in the award any clerical, typographical or computational errors. If the Tribunal considers the request to be justified, it shall make the correction within 30 days after receipt of the request. Any correction, which shall take the form of a separate memorandum, signed by the Tribunal in accordance with Article 64(d), shall become part of the award.

(b) The Tribunal may correct any error of the type referred to in paragraph (a) on its own initiative within 30 days after the date of the award.
(c) A party may, within 30 days after receipt of the award, by notice to the Tribunal, with a copy to the Center and the other party, request the Tribunal to make an additional award as to claims presented in the arbitral proceedings but not dealt with in the award. Before deciding on the request, the Tribunal shall give the parties an opportunity to be heard. If the Tribunal considers the request to be justified, it shall, wherever reasonably possible, make the additional award within 60 days of receipt of the request.

VI. Fees and Costs

Fees of the Center

Article 69

(a) The Request for Arbitration shall be subject to the payment to the Center of a non-refundable registration fee. The amount of the registration fee shall be fixed in the Schedule of Fees applicable on the date on which the Request for Arbitration is received by the Center.
(b) Any counter-claim by a Respondent shall be subject to the payment to the Center of a non-refundable registration fee. The amount of the registration fee shall be fixed in the Schedule of Fees applicable on the date on which the Request for Arbitration is received by the Center.
(c) No action shall be taken by the Center on a Request for Arbitration or counter-claim until the registration fee has been paid.
(d) If a Claimant or Respondent fails, within 15 days after a reminder in writing from the Center, to pay the registration fee, it shall be deemed to have withdrawn its Request for Arbitration or counter-claim, as the case may be.

Article 70

(a) An administration fee shall be payable by the Claimant to the Center within 30 days after the Claimant has received notification from the Center of the amount to be paid.
(b) In the case of a counter-claim, an administration fee shall also be payable by the Respondent to the Center within 30 days after the Respondent has received notification from the Center of the amount to be paid.
(c) The amount of the administration fee shall be calculated in accordance with the Schedule of Fees applicable on the date of commencement of the arbitration.
(d) Where a claim or counter-claim is increased, the amount of the administration fee may be increased in accordance with the Schedule of

Fees applicable under paragraph (c), and the increased amount shall be payable by the Claimant or the Respondent, as the case may be.

(e) If a party fails, within 15 days after a reminder in writing from the Center, to pay any administration fee due, it shall be deemed to have withdrawn its claim or counter-claim, or its increase in claim or counter-claim, as the case may be.

(f) The Tribunal shall, in a timely manner, inform the Center of the amount of the claim and any counter-claim, as well as any increase thereof.

Fees of the Arbitrators

Article 71

The amount and currency of the fees of the arbitrators and the modalities and timing of their payment shall be fixed by the Center, after consultation with the arbitrators and the parties, in accordance with the Schedule of Fees applicable on the date on which the Request for Arbitration is received by the Center.

Deposits

Article 72

(a) Upon receipt of notification from the Center of the establishment of the Tribunal, the Claimant and the Respondent shall each deposit an equal amount as an advance for the costs of arbitration referred to in Article 73. The amount of the deposit shall be determined by the Center.

(b) In the course of the arbitration, the Center may require that the parties make supplementary deposits.

(c) If the required deposits are not paid in full within 30 days after receipt of the corresponding notification, the Center shall so inform the parties in order that one or other of them may make the required payment.

(d) Where the amount of the counter-claim greatly exceeds the amount of the claim or involves the examination of significantly different matters, or where it otherwise appears appropriate in the circumstances, the Center in its discretion may establish two separate deposits on account of claim and counter-claim. If separate deposits are established, the totality of the deposit on account of claim shall be paid by the Claimant and the totality of the deposit on account of counter-claim shall be paid by the Respondent.

(e) If a party fails, within 15 days after a reminder in writing from the Center, to pay the required deposit, it shall be deemed to have withdrawn the relevant claim or counter-claim.

(f) After the award has been made, the Center shall, in accordance with the award, render an accounting to the parties of the deposits received and return any unexpended balance to the parties or require the payment of any amount owing from the parties.

Award of Costs of Arbitration

Article 73

(a) In its award, the Tribunal shall fix the costs of arbitration, which shall consist of:

(i) the arbitrators' fees;

(ii) the properly incurred travel, communication and other expenses of the arbitrators;

(iii) the costs of expert advice and such other assistance required by the Tribunal pursuant to these Rules; and

(iv) such other expenses as are necessary for the conduct of the arbitration proceedings, such as the cost of meeting and hearing facilities.

(b) The aforementioned costs shall, as far as possible, be debited from the deposits required under Article 70.

(c) The Tribunal shall, subject to any agreement of the parties, apportion the costs of arbitration and the registration and administration fees of the Center between the parties in the light of all the circumstances and the outcome of the arbitration.

Award of Costs Incurred by a Party

Article 74

In its award, the Tribunal may, subject to any contrary agreement by the parties and in the light of all the circumstances and the outcome of the arbitration, order a party to pay the whole or part of reasonable expenses incurred by the other party in presenting its case, including those incurred for legal representatives and witnesses.

VII. Confidentiality

Confidentiality of the Existence of the Arbitration

Article 75

(a) Except to the extent necessary in connection with a court challenge to the arbitration or an action for enforcement of an award, no information concerning the existence of an arbitration may be unilaterally disclosed by a party to any third party unless it is required to do so by law or by a competent regulatory body, and then only:

(i) by disclosing no more than what is legally required; and

(ii) by furnishing to the Tribunal and to the other party, if the disclosure takes place during the arbitration, or to the other party alone, if the disclosure takes place after the termination of the arbitration, details of the disclosure and an explanation of the reason for it.

(b) Notwithstanding paragraph (a), a party may disclose to a third party the names of the parties to the arbitration and the relief requested for the purpose of satisfying any obligation of good faith or candor owed to that third party.

Confidentiality of Disclosures Made During the Arbitration

Article 76

(a) In addition to any specific measures that may be available under Article 54, any documentary or other evidence given by a party or a witness in the arbitration shall be treated as confidential and, to the extent that such evidence describes information that is not in the public domain, shall not be used or disclosed to any third party by a party whose access to that information arises exclusively as a result of its participation in the arbitration for any purpose without the consent of the parties or order of a court having jurisdiction.

(b) For the purposes of this Article, a witness called by a party shall not be considered to be a third party. To the extent that a witness is given access to evidence or other information obtained in the arbitration in order to prepare the witness's testimony, the party calling such witness shall be responsible for the maintenance by the witness of the same degree of confidentiality as that required of the party.

Confidentiality of the Award

Article 77

The award shall be treated as confidential by the parties and may only be disclosed to a third party if and to the extent that:

(i) the parties consent; or

(ii) it falls into the public domain as a result of an action before a national court or other competent authority; or

(iii) it must be disclosed in order to comply with a legal requirement imposed on a party or in order to establish or protect a party's legal rights against a third party.

Maintenance of Confidentiality by the Center and Arbitrator

Article 78

(a) Unless the parties agree otherwise, the Center and the arbitrator shall maintain the confidentiality of the arbitration, the award and, to the extent that they describe information that is not in the public domain, any documentary or other evidence disclosed during the arbitration, except to the extent necessary in connection with a court action relating to the award, or as otherwise required by law.

(b) Notwithstanding paragraph (a), the Center may include information concerning the arbitration in any aggregate statistical data that it publishes concerning its activities, provided that such information does not enable the parties or the particular circumstances of the dispute to be identified.

VIII. Miscellaneous

Exclusion of Liability

Article 79

Except in respect of deliberate wrongdoing, the arbitrator or arbitrators, WIPO and the Center shall not be liable to a party for any act or omission in connection with the arbitration.

Waiver of Defamation

Article 80

The parties and, by acceptance of appointment, the arbitrator agree that any statements or comments, whether written or oral, made or used by them or their representatives in preparation for or in the course of the arbitration shall not be relied upon to found or maintain any action for defamation, libel, slander or any related complaint, and this Article may be pleaded as a bar to any such action.

LIST OF REFERENCES

Ashford P, *The IBA Rules on the Taking of Evidence in International Arbitration: A Guide* (Cambridge University Press, 2014).

Caron D and Caplan LM (eds), *The UNCITRAL Arbitration Rules: A Commentary* (2nd edn, Oxford University Press, 2013).

Chew LKH, *Singapore Arbitration Handbook* (LexisNexis, 2003).

Croft C, Kee C and Waincymer J (eds), *A Guide to the UNCITRAL Arbitration Rules* (Cambridge University Press, 2013).

Davidson F, Dundas H and Bartos D, *Arbitration (Scotland) Act 2010* (2nd edn, W. Green, 2014).

Derains Y and Schwartz EA, *A Guide to the ICC Rules of Arbitration* (3rd ed, Kluwer Law International, July 2015) (forthcoming).

Dundas H, 'Chapter 27: Arbitration in Scotland' in Lew JDM and others (eds), *Arbitration in England, with Chapters on Scotland and Ireland* (Kluwer Law International, 2013), pp. 595-626.

Explanatory Memorandum to the Arbitration Act 2010, available at: <http://www.irishstatutebook.ie/pdf/2010/en.act.2010.0001.pdf>.

Explanatory Note by the UNCITRAL secretariat on the 1985 Model Law on International Commercial Arbitration as amended in 2006.

Friedland P and Nyer D, 'Drafting Arbitration Clauses Before and After a Dispute' in Lawrence W. Newman and Michael J. Radine (eds), *Soft Law in International Arbitration* (Juris, 2014).

Fry J, Simon Greenberg S and Mazza F, *The Secretariat's Guide to ICC Arbitration* (ICC Publication No. 729E, 2012).

Gouiffès L and Kozyreff L, 'Commentary on the New French International Arbitration Law: Towards Quicker and More Efficient Arbitration Proceedings' (2012) 18 Columbia Journal of European Law 45.

Grierson J and Hooft A, *Arbitrating under the 2012 ICC Rules: An Introductory User's Guide* (Kluwer Law International, 2012).

Gusy MF, Hosking JM and Schwarz FT, *A Guide to the ICDR International Arbitration Rules* (2nd ed., Oxford University Press, June 2015) (forthcoming).

Harris B, Planterose R and Tecks J, *Arbitration Act 1996: Commentary* (5th edn, Wiley Blackwell, 2014).

Hibbert P, *Civil Evidence for Practitioners* (4th edn, Sweet & Maxwell, 2014).

IBA Working Party, 'Commentary on the revised text of the 2010 IBA Rules on the Taking of Evidence in International Arbitration'.

Karrer P, 'Swiss Rules of International Arbitration of the Swiss Chambers' Arbitration Institution in Institutional Arbitration – Commentary' in Schütze RA (ed), *Institutional Arbitration* (Beck/Hart, 2013).

Kay M and others (eds), *Blackstone's Civil Practice 2013: The Commentary* (Oxford University Press, 2012).

Kronke H and others (eds), *Recognition and Enforcement of Foreign Arbitral Awards: A Global Commentary on the New York Convention* (Kluwer Law International, 2010).

Ma G and Brock D (eds), *Arbitration in Hong Kong: A Practical Guide* (3rd ed, Sweet & Maxwell, 2014).

Mansfield B, *Arbitration Act 2010 and Model Law: A Commentary* (Clarus Press, 2012).

Merkin R and Flannery L, *Arbitration Act 1996* (5th edn, Informa, 2014).

Merkin R and Hjalmarsson J, *Singapore Arbitration Legislation: Annotated* (Informa, 2009).

Moser MJ and Bao C, *Guide to the HKIAC Arbitration Rules* (Oxford University Press, 2015) (forthcoming).

Newman LW, 'Disclosure of Documents and Presentation of Evidence in International Arbitration: ICDR Guidelines for Arbitrators Concerning Exchange of Information' in Newman LW and Radine MJ (eds), *Soft Law in International Arbitration* (Juris, 2014).

Online platform on the New York Convention <http://www.newyorkconvention1958.org/>.

Ragnwaldh J and Andersson F, *A Guide to the SCC Arbitration Rules* (Kluwer Law International, August 2015) (forthcoming).

Reed L, Mangan M and Choong J, *A Guide to the SIAC Arbitration Rules* (Oxford University Press, 2014).

Reed L, Paulsson J, Blackaby N, *A Guide to ICSID Arbitration* (2nd edn, Kluwer Law International, 2010).

Savage J, *The SIAC and International Arbitration in Singapore* (Kluwer Law International, October 2015) (forthcoming).

SIAC, *Singapore Arbitral Awards* (LexisNexis, 2012).

Stipanowich T, 'Soft Law in the Organization and General Conduct of Commercial Arbitration Proceedings' in Newman LW and Radine MJ (eds), *Soft Law in International Arbitration* (Juris, 2014).

Sussman E, 'Ethics in International Arbitration, Soft Law Guidance for Arbitrators and Party Representatives' in Lawrence W. Newman and Michael J. Radine (eds), *Soft Law in International Arbitration* (Juris, 2014).

UNCITRAL 2012 Digest of Case Law on the Model Law on International Commercial Arbitration (1985, with amendments as adopted in 2006).

Wade S, Clifford P and Clanchy J, *A Commentary on the LCIA Rules* (Sweet & Maxwell, forthcoming).

Webster TH, *Handbook of Investment Arbitration: Commentary, Precedents and Models for ICSID Arbitration* (Sweet & Maxwell, 2012).

WIPO Arbitration and Mediation Center, Guide to WIPO Arbitration (Pub. No. 919) available at: <http://www.wipo.int/amc/en/publications/>.

Wolff R (ed), *The New York Convention: Commentary* (Beck/Hart, 2012).

Yu J, Cao L and Moser M, *A Guide to the CIETAC Arbitration Rules* (Oxford University Press, 2015) (forthcoming).

Zuberbühler T, Hofmann D, Oetiker C and Sellier TR, *IBA Rules of Evidence: Commentary on the IBA Rules on the Taking of Evidence in International Arbitration* (European Law Publishers, 2012).

Zuberbühler T, Müller C and Habegger P (eds), *Swiss Rules of International Arbitration: Commentary* (2nd edn, Schulthess Verlag, 2013).

FURTHER READING

BOOKS

Blackaby N and others (eds), *Redfern & Hunter on International Arbitration* (6th ed, Oxford University Press, January 2015) (forthcoming).

Karrer P, *Introduction to International Arbitration Practice* (Kluwer Law International, 2014).

Lew JDM, Mistelis L and Kröll SM, *Comparative International Commercial Arbitration* (Kluwer Law International, 2003).

Mcilwrath M and Savage J, *International Arbitration and Mediation: A Practical Guide* (Kluwer Law International, 2010).

Moses MI, *The Principles and Practice of International Commercial Arbitration* (2nd ed, Cambridge University Press, 2012).

Rubino-Sammartano M, *International Arbitration Law and Practice* (3rd ed, Jusris, 2014).

Tackaberry J and Marriott A, *Bernstein's Handbook of Arbitration and Disputes Resolution*, vol. 2 (Sweet & Maxwell, 2003).

Waincymer J, *Procedure and Evidence in International Arbitration* (Kluwer Law International, 2012).

ARBITRAL AWARDS AND COURT DECISIONS

CLOUT: Case Law on UNCITRAL texts, available at: <http://www.uncitral.org/uncitral/en/case_law.html>

Collection of ICC Arbitral Awards/ Recueil des Sentences Arbitrales de la CCI 1974-2013

International Centre for Settlement of International Disputes Online Decisions and Cases, available at: <https: icsid.worldbank.org/ICSID>

Yearbook Commercial Arbitration, available at: <http://www.kluwerarbitration.com/>

ACKNOWLEDGEMENTS

The Chartered Institute of Arbitrators would like to thank the following institutions and copyright holders for permission to reproduce the material contained within this publication. Every effort has been made to trace and contact all the relevant copyright holders. In the unlikely event of an inadvertent oversight, we apologise to those concerned and undertake to include suitable acknowledgements in all future editions upon request.

American Arbitration Association
1633 Broadway #2C1
New York
NY 10019
United States
Tel:+1212-484-3266
Website: https://adr.org

Attorney-General's Chambers
1 Upper Pickering Street,
Singapore 058288
Tel: +65 6908 9000
Website: https://app.agc.gov.sg/

China International Economic and Trade Arbitration Commission
6/F, CCOIC Building
No.2 Huapichang Hutong
Xicheng District
Beijing 100035
P.R. China
Tel: +86 10 64646688
Website: http://www.cietac.org

Department of Justice
23rd Floor, High Block
Queensway Government Offices
66 Queensway
Hong Kong
Tel: +(852) 2867 2198
Website: http://www.doj.gov.hk/eng

Emmanuel Gaillard
Shearman & Sterling LLP
114, avenue des Champs-Elysées
75008 Paris
France
Tel: +33 1 53 89 71 40
Website: http://www.shearman.com/en

Hong Kong International Arbitration Centre
38th Floor Two Exchange Square
8 Connaught Place
Hong Kong S.A.R.
China
Tel: +(852) 2525-2381
Website: www.hkiac.org

Houses of the Oireachtas
Kildare Street
Dublin 2
Ireland
Tel: +353 1 618 3000
Website: http://www.oireachtas.ie/parliament/

ICSID Secretariat
1818 H Street, N.W.
MSN J2-200
Washington, D.C. 20433
USA
Tel: +(202) 458-1534
Website: https://icsid.worldbank.org

International Bar Association
4th Floor, 10 St Bride Street
London, EC4A 4AD
United Kingdom
Tel: +44 (0)20 7842 0090
Website: www.ibanet.org

International Chamber of Commerce
33-43 avenue du Président Wilson
75116 Paris
France
Tel: +33 (0) 1 49 53 28 28
Website: www.iccwbo.org

London Court of International Arbitration
70 Fleet Street
London EC4Y 1EU
United Kingdom
Tel: +44 (0) 20 7936 6200
Website: www.lcia.org

The Arbitration Institute of the Stockholm Chamber of Commerce
Brunnsgatan 2
SE-111 38 Stockholm
Sweden
Tel: +46 8 555 100 50
Website: www.sccinstitute.com

The National Archives
Legislation Service Team
Kew
Richmond
Surrey
TW9 4DU
Tel: +44 (0) 20 8876 3444
Website: http://www.nationalarchives.gov.uk/

Singapore International Arbitration Centre
32 Maxwell Road
#02-01, Maxwell Chambers
Singapore 069115
Tel: +65 6221 8833
Website: www.siac.org.sg

UNCITRAL Secretariat
Vienna International Centre
P.O. Box 500
A-1400 Vienna
Austria
Tel:+ 43-(1) 26060-4060
Website: www.uncitral.org

World Intellectual Property Organization
34, Chemin des Colombettes
CH-1211 Geneva 20
Switzerland
Tel: +41 22 338 9111
Website: www.wipo.int/portal/en/

Printed in Great Britain
by Amazon

79872311R00417